Poets through their letters

From the Tudors to Coleridge

Poets through their letters

From the Tudors to Coleridge

Martin Seymour-Smith

v.1

Holt, Rinehart and Winston
New York   Chicago   San Francisco

To Andrew and
Christine Mylett

Contents

This is neither a history of letter-writing in England nor an exhaustive survey of every letter written by every poet. It is a series of studies of poets made through their personal letters. Only in one isolated case, that of Swift's *Letter of Advice to a Young Poet*, have I discussed at any length an 'open' letter, intended for publication. Some poets, such as Shakespeare, left no letters; they have not been discussed. Others, such as Jonson, left few, and have been dealt with comparatively briefly. The letters of yet others—Burns, for example— though numerous, are not as revealing as one could wish; these have also been accorded shorter treatment.

This volume is devoted to British poets from Wyatt to Coleridge (born 1772); a succeeding one will deal with British and American poets from Byron to Frost.

The letters of poets have been highly prized at least since Pope collected, improved and printed his. Before that, they tended to be preserved not because the writer was a poet but because he was distinguished in some other field. In this century every scrap of paper written on by poets—and by what Swift called poetito's—is carefully sought after. The collection of poets' correspondence by universities and private individuals has become a cult—as will emerge in the successor to this volume.

I have considered my material less as correspondence than as a means of elucidating the poetry of those who wrote it. If we are interested in poetry, then we study the personalities of poets not in order to appreciate their epistolary skill but in order to understand their poems more fully. If I had wanted to admire them as letter-writers, then more space in this book would have been devoted to Cowper, less to Coleridge; Cowper was a more accomplished letter-writer. As it is, however, priority has been given to important poets —not to important letter-writers.

The source of quotations from letters has invariably been indicated. Sometimes I have silently omitted editorial details: conjectural emendations, which would seem obvious to everybody, slips of the pen, etc. Most contractions, including initials, have been silently expanded; but, as far as possible, original spelling and punctuation have been retained. The long s has been changed to its modern form; v becomes u, where appropriate, and *vice versa*.

Andrew Mylett suggested the theme of this book to me, and my profound gratitude for his continued encouragement and enormous help is expressed in my dedication. I am also grateful to my wife, my daughter Charlotte, my parents, David Rees, C. H. Sisson, James Reeves and Keith Brace for their aid, which ranged from the obtaining of difficult books through typing and retyping to valuable discussion and advice. As always, my heartfelt thanks to the Bexhill-on-Sea branch of the East Sussex County Library—and to the London Library, the efficiency and unfailing courtesy of which so lightens the lives of writers such as myself.

Martin Seymour-Smith
Bexhill-on-Sea
November 1968

I

Educated letters in the sixteenth and seventeenth centuries, although supposed to be distinguished by 'friendly feeling', were never what would now be termed informal. They were modelled on the classical epistle, the study of which formed a vital part of every boy's education, and they more often resembled essays than letters in the modern sense. Any educated writer would be continuously conscious of rules he had been taught at school. Milton's frigid letters are an extreme example of this; Donne's are certainly in the same formal tradition, though his mind is continually seeking to circumvent it in order to achieve greater freedom of expression.

By the time of Dryden there had been a relaxation of the rules: a more purely personal, less self-consciously rhetorical note crept in, which paved the way for the eighteenth-century letter-writers such as Lady Mary Wortley Montagu, Chesterfield, Walpole and, finally, Cowper, whose completely relaxed style might be said to represent both the culmination of eighteenth-century epistolary art and the stepping-stone to the spontaneity and confessionalism of such romantic poets as Coleridge and Keats.

For side by side with the teaching of the classical epistle in the schools, interest in letter-writing developed amongst the rising mercantile classes. The first printed English letter-writer, *The Enimie of Idlenesse* (1568), was translated from the French, but Nicholas Breton's popular, amusing and successful formulary, *Poste with a Packet of Madde Letters* (1602), was largely his own work. The theory behind such formularies, both manuscript and printed, was classical; at first they tended to follow the Latin collections, with their divisions into such categories as Demonstrative, Deliberative, Judicial, Gratulatory and so on. But while the outline of the theory remained the same, it soon became simplified; the vernacular began to take over. There is nothing classical in spirit, for example, about this opening of Breton's: 'Master Wyldgoose, it is not your huftie tuftie can make me afraid of your bigge lookes. . . .'

Samuel Richardson's *Letters Written to and for Particular*

Friends (1741) draws on previous formularies, but is 'the work of a moralist': his interests 'were not rhetorical but ethical'.[1] The emphasis has shifted from style to morals; within the next seventy or eighty years it shifted from morals to self-expression.

It is not surprising, then, that in the period 1500–1750 substantially interesting collections of poets' letters are exceptional. No poet, not even Pope, discusses poetry at length and habitually. Gray was the first English poet to do so. Nevertheless, a great deal can be learned about Sidney, Spenser, Donne, Marvell, Swift, Pope, and, to a somewhat smaller extent, Dryden, from their letters, and I have devoted a separate chapter to each of these poets. The rest of this chapter is devoted to a briefer survey of the period. Poets such as Shakespeare, who left no letters, or Fulke Greville or George Herbert who left few and those not of any particular literary or psychological interest, have not been discussed.

Sir Thomas Wyatt (1503-42)

2

Sir Thomas Wyatt was the earliest English poet to leave a substantial body of letters behind him. One of them is included in a formulary. They were not preserved because he was a poet but because he was a diplomat of some importance in the service of Henry VIII and, more particularly, of Henry's chief minister, Thomas Cromwell.[2] Although a pioneer and an experimentalist in form, translation and satire, Wyatt—unlike Skelton—was essentially an occasional poet. There is nothing in his letters about poetry or his practice of it. They are valuable to the student of his poetry only inasmuch as they reveal what kind of man he was, what his attitude was towards his exacting tasks as a diplomat, and the kind of vicissitudes he had to endure.

If Wyatt ever made remarks on literature in his letters, this would have been to his friend, fellow-poet and courtier, Sir Francis Bryan, or to the younger Earl of Surrey, who was certainly his poetic disciple and possibly his personal friend. But no such correspondence, if it existed, survives. The letters give a picture of a reluctant, witty, nervous but conscientious and resourceful servant of the King; most are detailed diplomatic reports, addressed to Henry or to Cromwell, whose importance is solely historical.

Wyatt led an eventful, dangerous and short life. His father, Henry, had been tortured for his adherence to the Tudor cause during the reign of Richard III, and was rewarded for his fortitude by Henry VII and by his son. Thomas, born at Allington Castle in Kent in 1503, first turned up at Court as a Sewer (i.e. Cupbearer) Extraordinary in 1516, presumably while he was still at St. John's

College, Cambridge, which he had entered in the previous year. He married Lord Cobham's daughter, Elizabeth, in 1520 or before, and their son, also Thomas—he was to be executed in Mary's reign for leading the rebellion that bears his name—was born in 1521. He separated from his wife (who seems to have been the offending party) and lived with Elizabeth Darrell, when in England, from about 1538 until the time of his last arrest in 1540. In 1524 Wyatt became Clerk of the King's Jewels. By then he must have been celebrated as one of the most accomplished poets of the Court. He went on his first diplomatic mission in 1526, to France, and on another to Italy in the following year. In Ferrara he was arrested by the Spaniards and held to ransom for 3000 ducats, but soon managed to escape. No letters survivè from this early and perhaps least taxing period of Wyatt's life, but it is clear that he used his time in France and Italy to his own literary advantage, and that his translations from and imitations of such poets as Marot, Ariosto, Serafino and Petrarch were written after these visits.

He was a prisoner in the Tower on three occasions. The first was in May 1534, when he was involved in an affray in which a serjeant of London was killed. He was soon out. His second and third imprisonments were more serious. In 1536, when Anne Boleyn was charged with adultery, he was imprisoned on suspicion of having been one of her lovers. Kenneth Muir, his biographer, believes that he had been to bed with her, but before the King married her. One not unlikely story tells of how he actually warned the King that Anne was not a suitable Queen, and of how Henry commended Wyatt, but ordered him to say nothing. At all events, he was expected by some to suffer with the rest of those who were beheaded with the Queen, and was fortunate to be released. His letters tell us nothing of this.

The third time Wyatt suffered imprisonment was perhaps, for him, the most serious of all. He had long been associated with Bishop Edward Bonner, a hypocrite and careerist, on diplomatic missions to Francis I of France and the Holy Roman Emperor, and had offended him, probably by his general superiority of character and his habit of blunt speech. Bonner had long tried to discredit Wyatt, but Cromwell suppressed his complaints. On the fall of Cromwell, Wyatt's position became much more difficult. The suppressed complaints were found amongst Cromwell's papers, and appear to have formed the basis of the accusations against Wyatt. 'Wittie he is,' Bonner had written,

> and plesant amongs companye, contented to make and kepe chere, but that he will eyther forget his emprisonement [of 1536], or moore regarde thaffairs of the king then his own glorie, yea or soo to consider the affaires that he wooll

ernestlie displease themperour or Grandevele, the great
papiste [under Mary, Bonner himself was to condemn a
number of protestants to burning], hitherto have I nothing
seen to make me beleve it, and harde I ween it will be to
bring suche appearance that of reason I ought to beleve it.[3]

Wyatt was ordered to write in answer to the charges, and did so in
a letter to the Privy Council.[4] This, like his carefully prepared speech
of defence, shows that he was a man of dignity, adroitness and wit.
Eventually, he seems to have pleaded guilty to the charges in
exchange for his freedom (a not unusual procedure: it saved the face
of the prosecution), which was granted to him on condition that he
returned to his wife. He did this, but remembered Elizabeth Darrell
and their illegitimate son in his will. He was back in the King's
favour by the end of the year. In September 1542 Henry sent him to
welcome the Spanish envoy at Falmouth and escort him to London.
On the way he became ill, and died at Sherborne.

   Non-literary as they are, some parts of Wyatt's letters are
worth quoting for the light they cast upon his character. For example,
writing to his young son just after his wedding, in April 1537, he no
doubt remembered the failure of his own marriage when he advised
him:

Love wel and agre with your wife, for where is noyse and
debate in the hous, ther is unquiet dwelling. And mitch
more wher it is in one bed. Frame wel your self to love, and
rule wel and honestly your wife as your felow, and she shal
love and reverens you as her hed. Such as you are unto her
such shal she be unto you. . . . And the blissing of god for
good agrement between the wife and husband is fruyt of
many children, which I for the like thinge doe lack, and the
faulte is both in your mother and me, but chieflie in her.[5]

In another letter written to his son in the same year, Wyatt's remarks
about honesty and truth to oneself, although stiffly homiletic, in the
epistolary manner of the time, cannot be taken as wholly conventional:

. . . I meane not that honestye that the comen sort callith
an honist man: Trust me that honist man is as comen a
name as the name of a good fellow. . . . Seke not, I pray
the, my son, that honesty which aperith and is not in
dead. . . .
   The coming to this pointe that I wold so fayne have
you have is to consider a mans awne self, what he is and
wherfor he is. And herin let him think verilye that so goodly
a work as man is, for whom all other things wer wroght,
was not wroght but for goodly things.[6]

There is more than an echo of this in an apparently original (i.e. not, as many of Wyatt's, translated or imitated) poem from the Devonshire MS.:

> I am as I am and so wil I be,
> But how that I am none knoith trulie,
> Be yt evill, be yt well, be I bonde, be I fre,
> I am as I am and so will I be.

> I lede my lif indifferentelye,
> I meane no thing but honestelie,
> And thoughe folkis judge full dyverslye,
> I am as I am and so will I dye.

> I do not reioyse nor yet complaine,
> Bothe mirthe and sadnes I doo refraine,
> Ande use the meane sins folkes woll fayne,
> Yet I am as I am be it pleasure or payne,

> Dyvers do judge as theye doo troo,
> Some of plesure and some of woo,
> Yet for all that no thing theye knoo,
> But I am as I am where so ever I goo.

> But sins judgers do thus dekaye,
> Let everye man his judgement say;
> I will yt take yn sporte and playe,
> For I am as I am who so ever saye naye.

> Who judgith well, well god him sende;
> Who judgith evill, god theim emende;
> To judge the best therefore intende,
> For I am as I am and so will I ende.

> Yet some there be that take delight
> To judge folkes thought for envye and spight,
> But whyther theye judge me wrong or right,
> I am as I am and so do I wright.

> Prayeng you all that this doo rede
> To truste yt as you doo your crede,
> And not to think I change my wede,
> For I am as I am howe ever I spede.

> But how that is I leve to you;
> Judge as ye list false or true;
> Ye kno no more than afore ye knewe;
> Yet I am as I am whatever ensue.

> And from this minde I will not flee;
> But to you all that misjuge me
> I do proteste as ye maye see
> That I am as I am and so will I bee.

The lack of literary references in Wyatt's letters aptly demonstrates the position of poetry in the Tudor age. Wyatt was one of the most important of early English poets, and even in his lifetime was renowned more for his skill at making songs than for his abilities as a diplomat; but no theories about the proper social status of the poet, or even about the relationship between poetry and experience, occupied his mind. He was the most casual of all major innovators, doubtless largely because of his age and the pressure put upon him by the circumstances of his aristocratic birth; if we had every letter he wrote, we should find little or nothing to relate to his poetic practice.

Thomas Kyd (1558–94)

3

Thomas Kyd was one of the most unfortunate as well as most influential of earlier Elizabethan dramatists. Two letters he wrote to the Keeper of the Great Seal of England, Sir John Puckering, preserved in his own hand, give poignant testimony to his misfortune, and tell us something of his past life; they are also important documents in the life of Marlowe, and cast lurid light on the difficult and dangerous conditions in which early Elizabethan dramatists, even ones as timid as Kyd, worked.[7]

The atmosphere in London in the spring of 1593 was tense. Demoralized by the Plague, the common people began to inveigh against the foreigners—mostly Flemings and Huguenots—in their midst. The Privy Council, naturally enough, associated the xenophobic manifestations that were seriously troubling its exercise of power with 'atheism'. Ralegh, though still unhappily in disgrace with the Queen, even spoke against the aliens in the House of Commons—though he was the only M.P. to do so.

Whitgift, Archbishop of Canterbury, and therefore a member of the Privy Council, took advantage of this uneasy situation to organize a witch-hunt for Puritans and all other manner of heretics. Anti-alien posters, some of them skilfully written, were going up in the streets, and on 11 May 1593 the Privy Council announced that 'some extraordinarie paines and care' must immediately be taken to examine suspected persons; torture was to be used.

By 12 May Kyd was in prison. Evidently someone had suggested that libellous verses on foreigners such as had been appearing in the streets might be discovered in his room. They were not; but among papers Kyd later claimed to have handed over voluntarily was a document that the officials in charge of the investigation held to be 'vile hereticall Conceipts denying the deity of

Jhesus Christ our Saviour'. Kyd must immediately have testified that these papers were the property of his erstwhile room-mate, Christopher Marlowe, and that they had accidentally become mixed up with his own.

Meanwhile, Marlowe himself was the guest of Sir Thomas Walsingham at his estate of Scadbury in Kent, where he was writing *Hero and Leander*. Almost certainly because of Kyd's revelation he was sent for by the Privy Council, to which he reported on 20 May. They ordered him to 'give his daily attendance' on them 'until he shall be licensed to the contrary'. Within ten days he was dead, stabbed in the eye; whether merely because of his furious temperament or because he knew too much it is unlikely that anyone will ever know.

Kyd's first letter to Sir John Puckering, who was then virtual leader of the Privy Council, was written after Marlowe's death and after his own release from prison. But, as it makes evident, he did not escape without penalty:

> for more assurance that I was not of that vile opinion, Lett it but please your Lordship to enquire of such as he conversd with all, that is (as I am geven to understand) with *Harriot*, *Warner*, *Royden* and some stationers in Paules churchyard, whom I in no sort can accuse nor will excuse by reson of his companie, of whose consent if I had been, no question but I also shold have been of their consort, for *ex minimo vestigo artifex agnoscit artificem*.
>
> Of my religion & life I have alredie geven some instance to the late commissimen & of my reverend meaning to the state, although perhaps my paines and— undeserved tortures felt by some, wold have ingendred more impatience when lesse by farr hath dryven so manye *imo extre caulas* which it shall—never do with me.
>
> But whatsoever I have felt R. ho: this is my request not for reward but in regard of my trewe innocence that it wold please your Lordship so to [. . . . . .] the same & me, as I maie still reteyne the favors of my Lord, whom I have servd almost theis vi yeres nowe, in credit untill nowe, & nowe am utterlie undon without herein be somewhat donn for my recoverie, ffor I do knowe his Lordship holdes your honor & the state in that dewe reverence, as he wold no waie move the leste suspicion of his loves and cares both towards hir sacred Majestie yo Lordships and the lawes whereof when tyme shall serve I shall geve greater instance which I have observed.
>
> As for the libel laide unto my chardg I am resolved with receyving of the sacrement to satisfie your Lordship &

the world that I was neither agent nor consenting therunto Howbeit it some outcast *Ismael* for want or of his owne dispose to lewdnes, have with pretext of duetie or religion, or to reduce himself to that he was not borne unto by enie waie incensd your Lordships to suspect me, I shall beseech in all humillitie & in the feare of god that it will please your Lordships but to censure me as I shall prove my self, and to repute them as they ar in deed *Cum totius iniustitiae nulla capitalior sit quam coru, qui tum cum maxime fallunt id agunt vt viri boni esse videant ffor* doubtles even then your Lordships shal be be sure to breake [. . . .] their lewde designes and see into the truthe, when but their lyves that herein have accused me shalbe examined & typped up effectually, soe maie I chaunce with *paul* to liue & shake the vyper of my hand into the fier for with the ignorant suspect me guiltie of the former shipwrack. And thus (for nowe I feare me I growe teadious) assuring your good Lordships that if I knewe eny whom I cold justlie accuse of that damnable offence to the awefull Majesty of god or of that other mutinous sedition towrd the state I wold as willinglie reveale them as I wold request your Lordships better thoughtes of me that never have offended you.

At my last being with your Lordship to entreate some speaches from you in my favor to my Lorde, whoe (though I thinke, he rest not doubtfull of myne inocence) hath yet in his discreeter judgment feared to offende in his reteyning me, without your honours former pryvitie; So is it nowe R. ho: that the denyall of that favour (to my thought reasonable) hath mov'de me to conjecture some suspicion, that your Lordship holds me in, concerning *Atheisme*, a deadlie thing which I was undeserved chargd withall, & therefore have I thought it requisite, aswell in duetie to your Lordship, & the lawes, as also in the feare of god, & freedom of my conscience, therein to satisfie the world and you:

The first and most (thoughe insufficient) surmize that euer was therein mightest be raisde of me, grewe thus. When I was first suspected for that libell that concern'd the state, amongst those waste and idle papers (which I carde not for) & which unaskt I did deliver up, were founde some fragments of a disputation, toching that opinion, affirmd by Marlowe to be his, and shuffled with some of myne (unknown to me) by some occasion of our wrytinge in one chamber twoe yeares synce.

My first acquaintance with this Marlowe, rose vpon his bearing name to serve my Lo: although his Lordship never knewe his service, but in writing for his plaiers. ffor never cold my L. endure his name, or sight, when he had heard of his conditions, nor wold indeed the forme of devyne praiers used duelie in his Lordships house, have quadred with such reprobates.

That I shold love or be famyler frend, with one so irreligious, were verie rare, when *Tullie* saith *Digni sunt amicitia quibe in ipsis inest causa cur diligantur* which neither was in him, for person, quallities, or honestie, besides he was intemperate & of a cruel hart, the verie contraries to which, my greatest enemies will saic by me.

It is not to be nombred amongst the best conditions of men, to taxe or to opbraide the deade *Quia mortui non mordent*, But thus muche have I (with your Lordships favour) dared in the greatest cause, which is to cleere my self of being thought an *Atheist*, which some will sweare he was.

Kyd, tortured on the rack—'my paines and—undeserved tortures'—was now a broken man, to die within sixteen months, doubtless as a result of his sufferings. In dedicating his translation of Garnier's *Cornelie*, his last work, to the Countess of Sussex, he spoke of 'those so bitter times and privie broken passions that I endured in the writing it'.

This is one of the most pathetic stories in English literature: a timid and gentle man, whose dramatic genius has not even yet been fully acknowledged, was made the innocent victim of the merciless agents of the Privy Council and of their illiterate but, we may be sure, cruelly sophisticated torturers. Kyd did not even realize that the 'vile hereticall' papers had been copied by someone from a book of 1549, *The Fall of the Late Arrian*, by John Proctor, whose purpose had actually been to refute their anti-Trinitarian (not atheistic) contents; Proctor had quoted them only to refute them. Had Kyd known this, he would surely have quickly said so: it would have been a strong point in his defence.

He has been accused of informing on Marlowe, and it is clear from his letter that he did at least protest that the papers had been in Marlowe's possession, and never in his. But his ignorance of their source demonstrates that this was nothing less than the truth. Doubtless he felt, and with justice, that the redoubtable Marlowe could himself deal easily enough with the charge. It is likely he could have done. Furthermore, by the time he came to write the letter Marlowe was dead, and he desperately needed Puckering's authority to clear himself with the 'my Lorde' who had been his patron for six years but who had now nervously disowned him.[8] That meant starvation. Since Marlowe was now beyond anything the Privy Council could do to him he might as well be made into the scapegoat.

In 1921 another, probably fragmentary, letter by Kyd to Puckering was discovered. It almost certainly followed the longer letter, and represented a further plea for grace. Like the other letter, it would have been written during 'those so bitter times' that Kyd endured between leaving prison and his death in the following year. Its chief interest is the bearing it has on Marlowe:

> Pleaseth it yor hono^{r}able l^p toching marlowes monstruous opinions as I cannot but wth an agreved conscience think on him or them so can I but paticulariz fewe in the respect of them that kept him greater company, Howbeit in discharg of dutie both towrds god yor l^{ps} & the world thus much haue I thoug*ht* good breiflie to discover in all humblenes ffirst it was his custom when I knewe him first & as I heare saie he contynewd it in table talk or otherwise to iest at the devine scriptures gybe at praie^{r}s, & stryve in argum^t to frustrate & confute what hath byn spoke or wrytt by prophets & such holie men/
> 1 He wold report St John to be o^r savio^r Christes Alexis I cover it wth reverence and trembling that is that Christ did loue him wth an extraordinary loue/
> 2 That for me to wryte a poem of S^t paules conversion as I was determined he said wold be as if I shold go wryte a book of fast & loose, esteming Paul a Jugler.
> 3 That the prodigall Childs portion was but fower nobles, he held his purse so neere the bottom in all pictures, and that it either was a iest or els fowr nobles then was thought a great patrimony not thinking it a pable.
> 4 That things esteemed to be donn by devine powe^r might haue a aswell been don by observation of man all wch he wold so sodenlie take slight occasion to slyp out as I & many others in regard of his other rashnes in attempting soden pryvie iniuries to men did ouerslypp though often reprehend him for it & for which god is my witnes as well by my lords comaundm^t as in hatred of his life & thoughts I left & did refraine his companie/
> He wold pswade wth men of quallitie to goe vnto the k of Scotts whether I heare Royden is gon and where if he had livd he told me when I sawe him last he meant to be/

This catalogue of Marlowe's 'monstruous opinions' accords with a 'note Containing the opinion of one Christopher Marly Concerning his Damnable Judgement of Religion . . .' which Richard Baines, a spy, confidence-man and informer who was probably hanged in December 1594, handed in to the Privy Council at about the same time as Marlowe was murdered. According to Baines, Marlowe had said that Moses, instead of Paul, was 'but a Jugler', that 'Christ was a bastard and his mother dishonest', that Protestants 'are Hypocriticall asses', that John used Christ 'as the sinners of *Sodoma*', that Christ used whores, and so on (now views all respectable enough to be noised, from time to time, from the best pulpits).

Since there could not have been collusion between Kyd and Baines, the general agreement of their two accounts of him does tend to establish that Marlowe was not only intelligent but also unwisely outspoken. His so-called 'blasphemies', while they express more of defiance and scorn of authority than considered opinion, show him to have been well ahead of his time in his appraisal of the nature of official religion.

The two documents, the one composed by a despairing fellow-poet who knew the subject was dead, the other by a spy and informer, give us a very rare glimpse of how, in that violent time, a poet might express himself in private, and of his view of authority. Marlow, whose technical loyalty was not in doubt, and who could probably easily have discredited Baines's testimony, was young, violent and exceptionally forthright. But was his enlightenment about the nature of society and its religious organization (compare the shrewdness and wisdom of his 'blasphemies' with the actual cruelties of Whitgift) quite so exceptional? Personal loyalty to the Queen and private faith apart, we need not imagine that the majority of Marlowe's fellow-poets—even such as Kyd, who was as meek as his name—held opinions too far removed from his. But they were more cautious or more cunning. It is possible that Marlowe lost his life because of ill-temper and a penchant for consorting with dangerous men; it is likely that he lost it because he could not keep his mouth shut. But he was an 'atheist' and dangerous only in the eyes of such men as Whitgift and Baines, than whose ideas his own were markedly more Christian.

Sir Walter Ralegh (*c.* 1552–1618)

4

Many of the letters of Walter Ralegh have been preserved;[9] most relate to his activities as a man of affairs. Ralegh's influence at Elizabeth's Court, to which he was introduced in 1581—probably by the Earl of Sussex—after impressive service in Ireland, has been exaggerated by literary critics. Sir John Neale's assessment of his actual political importance is that 'Elizabeth never had . . . belief in his abilities as a statesman'.[10]

But for more than ten years he was her chief favourite, highly influential in all save major affairs of state, and it was well worth the while of such ultimately weightier figures as Burleigh to ask for his assistance in small matters. As a 'new man', attacked for his plebeian origins and envied for the very real intimacy he had managed in spite of them to achieve with the Queen, he felt that the arrival of the young Essex at Court was a threat to him, and Essex in turn disliked him; but as Sir John Neale points out, he was never a serious rival to Essex in his quest for real power in the land.

However, right though Sir John may be in his estimate of Ralegh's historical importance, there can be little doubt about his literary eminence. A man to whom poetry was apparently only one of the many necessary accomplishments that went together to make up an Elizabethan man of 'wit', Ralegh's lyrics and the long fragment of the *11th Book of the Ocean* [i.e. Sir 'Water'] *to Scinthia* make up a corpus that few even of those critics who obsess themselves with questions of poetic majority and minority could unhesitatingly label as 'minor'. The *Scinthia* fragment, which survives in what is undoubtedly Ralegh's own hand at Hatfield House, is incomplete and not fully corrected; some passages are so difficult that Ralegh's editor, justifiably, calls them 'very dark', and 'cannot claim' that she is 'more enlightened than another'. Yet it is, and is universally allowed to be, a poem of great beauty and great sadness, whose ostensible theme is the poet's sorrow at his loss of the Queen's favour. It was, we can now be certain, written in 1592 when Ralegh was imprisoned in the Tower because he had been unwise enough to marry Elizabeth Throgmorton, one of the Queen's maids of honour, without her permission. Sir John Neale writes:

> Raleigh did his best by exuberant specimens of the Court's pleasant conceit of love to make his peace with the irate Belphoebe . . . hearing that the Queen was on the Thames, Raleigh had begged to be let row himself in disguise near enough to see her. On being refused he had become dangerously mad.[11]

Sir John then quotes from a letter that Ralegh wrote to Cecil—a letter meant for the Queen's eyes—and comments: 'This characteristic effusion—as artificial in conceit as any shepherd and shepherdess of contemporary poetry—must not, on peril of showing an egregious lack of humour, be taken seriously'.[12]

Now this letter, as Walter Oakeshott rightly remarks in his careful and revealing study of Ralegh's relationships with the Queen, while 'theatrical', is particularly interesting because of 'its relationship to the longest of Raleigh's existing poetical works, the draft of the 11th and the opening books of the *Ocean to Cynthia*'.[13] He goes on to assert that any critic who denies real feeling to the *11th Book* 'is himself devoid of perception'. In contrast to Sir John, he sees the letter to Cecil itself as 'in some degree' intense.

Since the poem is certainly deeply felt, and seems to arise from feelings expressed in the letter, Sir John appears to be wrong in dismissing it as unserious and wholly 'conceited'. He can be right, surely, only if the poem's subject is no more than ostensibly the loss of Cynthia's favour, if Ralegh was playing a subtle and complex double-game: trying to regain his influence with the Queen, for power's sake, by pretending to be broken-hearted in both prose and verse, and being patently insincere in the wholly purposive prose of the letter, but sincere in the poetry because the false theme hid a real one, perhaps unconscious, which it could accommodate. But the poem does not stand up to such an interpretation.

Ralegh was enigmatic even by the standards of an age that itself seems largely enigmatic to us. What was the nature of his 'love' for Cynthia? Was it altogether ambitious, part of a pleasing and accomplished game that also led to highly profitable results for the brilliant courtier? What is the *11th Book* 'about'? Could the exquisite quality of its sadness, whatever its wider implications, have arisen from emotions as utterly artificial and as timeserving as Sir John discerns in the letter to Cecil?

The letter itself helps us to answer these questions; the crucial point is not what it purports to say, but the degree of its sincerity. Is Ralegh merely a disappointed man playing the Courtly love-game, or are his feelings really hurt?

> I pray be a mean to her Majesty for the signing of the bills for the Gards' coats, which are to be made now for the Prograsse, and which the Cleark of the Cheeck hath importunde me to write for.
>
> My heart was never broken till this day, that I hear the Queen goes away so far of,—whom I have followed so many years with so great love and desire, in so many journeys, and am now left behind her, in a dark prison all alone. While she was yet nire at hand, that I might hear of her once in two or three dayes, my sorrows were the less: but even now my heart is cast into the depth of all misery. I that was wont to behold her riding like *Alexander*, hunting like *Diana*, walking like *Venus*, the gentle wind blowing her fair hair about her pure cheeks, like a nymph; sometime siting in the shade like a Goddess; sometime singing like an angell; sometime playing like *Orpheus*. Behold the sorrow of this world! Once amiss, hath bereaved me of all. O Glory, that only shineth in misfortune, what is becum of thy assurance? All wounds have skares, but that of fantasie; all affections their relenting, but that of womankind. Who is the judge of friendship, but adversity? or when is grace witnessed, but in offences? There were no

divinety, but by reason of compassion; for revenges are brutish and mortall. All those times past,—the loves, the sythes, the sorrows, the desires, can they not way down one frail misfortune? Cannot one dropp of gall be hidden in so great heaps of sweetness? I may then conclude, *Spes et fortuna, valete.* She is gone, in whom I trusted, and of me hath not one thought of mercy, nor any respect of that that was. Do with me now, therefore, what you list. I am more weary of life then they are desirous I should perish; which if it had been for her, as it is by her, I had been too happily born.

Your's, not worthy any name or title. . . .[14]

Leaving aside for the moment the question of the meaning of the poem, I think that we can conclude from the letter that Ralegh was more than merely suffering from pique, frustrated ambition or jealousy of Essex. The key to his state of mind may perhaps be found in Sir John Neale's statement: 'Elizabeth never had . . . belief in his abilities as a statesman'. In a letter to Cecil of approximately the same time, about the rebellion in Ireland, he complains:

I wrote in a letter of Mr. Killegreew's, ten days past, a prophesye of this rebellion, which when the Queen read, she made a scorn at my conceat; but yow shall find it but a shoure of a farther tempest. If yow please to sent me word of what yow hear, I will be laught at again in my opinion touching the same. . . .[15]

And to the Lord Admiral, Howard of Effingham, he says, paranoically, at the end of a letter about naval affairs:

. . . I must humblie thank your Lordship for your most honorable care of me in this unfortunat accident. But I see ther is a determinacion to disgrace mee and ruin mee. And therefore I beseich your Lordship not to offend Her Majestye any farther by sewing for me.

And he concludes by requesting, melodramatically, that he may 'be stayd no on [one] houre from all the extremetye' of the law: 'if that might be to litle, would God . . . that I might feed the lions . . . to save labor'.[16]

The passage in the first letter about the 'beauty' of the Queen was certainly just part of the 'game'—the courtly game Ralegh had been playing with consummate mastery for more than ten years. But his bitterness about the Queen's treatment of him, significantly emerging in the form of a complaint against her refusal to listen to his political advice, was entirely unfeigned. He remained out of favour for four years, and there are many similar expressions of bitterness

in letters of this period, of which the following is only one example:
'Law and Conscience is not sufficient in thes days to upholde me
. . . hatreds are the cinders of affection, and therefore to make me a
sacrifize shall be thanksworthye. . . .'[17] Was he recalling a line from
the *11th Book*:

> From these so lost what may th' affections bee,
> What heat in Cynders of extinguisht fiers?

Perhaps too much has been made of Ralegh as a divided man: cruel,
intriguing, ambitious and arrogant on the one hand, gently poetic
and unworldly on the other. He was never 'in love' with the Queen,
but was obliged to behave as if he were: it was her choice as much
as his; it was also the recognized method of approach to her. As a
'new man' he inevitably met with the often dangerous hostility of
the aristocratic element: this alone is enough to explain that arrogance of which his enemies made so much. Was he, however, as
'divided' as we have always tended to imagine?

For an allegedly self-seeking man, he was curiously ineffectual:
he formed no party, which he might easily have done; and he frequently arranged things badly for himself. He was perfectly capable
of taking a line displeasing to the Privy Council. The circumstances
under which he courted and married his wife are unknown. The
allegation that he got her with child and was forced to marry her by
the Queen—accepted by Sir John Neale—is probably untrue, although we do know from a letter of 10 March 1591/2 to Cecil that
he untruthfully protested 'before God, ther is none, on the face
of the yearth, that I would be fastned unto'.[18]

Ralegh was a man of action: he relieved his considerable
mental tensions in action whenever the Queen would allow him,
which was not as often as he would have liked. But he was more
of an idealist than he has been given credit for. We willingly allow
Sidney his idealism; why not Ralegh his? His relationship with the
Queen was courtly in form, but from his point of view it was much
more than merely opportunist. He was idealistically patriotic, and
saw the Queen as someone who was, or who should have been, the
embodiment of the nation's will. He had served her not with a
merely clever, self-seeking, superficial gallantry, but with deep and
devoted seriousness. The real subject of the *11th Book* is the nature
of Ralegh's devotion to the Queen; and though it is probable that he
had previously written some (now lost) fragments that he might
have fitted into it, I think he planned to write an epic, in the traditional
twelve books, while in the Tower, but began it at the bitter end.

It has been argued that in the *11th Book* Ralegh betrayed his
wife: that he wrote it in order to regain the Queen's favour, and
pretended in it to flatter her with a pretence of sexual love. Thus,
he could say in it

> my error never was for thought
> Or ever could proceed from sence of Lovinge.

And thus, the argument continues, in a letter to Cecil of 8 February
1593/4, in which she thanked him for a gift of 'tablets' and begged
him to help her divert her husband from his plans to go to the East
Indies or Guinea, Lady Ralegh could write, in her inimitable spelling
(it seems to anticipate the forger William Henry Ireland):

> I reseved your tabells of no less rare device than the sentans
> within [refers to an anagram or puzzle inscribing the
> tablets] was cumforttabell. If faith wear broken with mee I
> was yet farr away, but that I feare, if all hartes weare opene
> and all desiars knowne, might without so gret curiosetye of
> desciphering reed her owne desteni in a playne alphabett,
> but wee ar both great belevars, and therein we flatter our
> seulevs and nurishe our owne mindes with what wee
> would.[19]

The statement that might seem to support the view of Ralegh as a
fundamentally insincere man is 'If faith wear broken with mee I
was yet farr away . . .'; but it is, as Oakeshott remarks, 'a pretty
long shot'.

　　However, there is no evidence that the *11th Book* was written
to please the Queen, or that she ever saw it. The MS. must have
come into Cecil's possession when Ralegh left it behind in the
Tower on his release; but it seems to be a fair copy, and presumbly
Ralegh retained his first draft or drafts. Nor does he, in the *11th
Book*, appear to mean by the word 'Love' erotic love—whether
Lady Ralegh thought he did or not.

　　But the meaning of the passage from her 1593/4 letter to
Cecil is irrecoverable. We do not know the motto that inscribed the
'tablets'. My own conjecture, however, is that it implies the exact
opposite of the sense in which it is most usually taken. Cecil may,
as has been suggested, have drawn her attention to the apparently
offensive lines in the *11th Book*; but I think Lady Ralegh's 'If faith
wear broken with mee I was yet farr away' means 'if my husband
was ever unfaithful to me in any sense to which I might object
then it was before he knew me'. The enigmatic remainder of the
sentence means, perhaps: 'if only the Queen my mistress understood the nature of my husband's love for her—if only her vanity
would allow him not to pretend to love her sexually so that he
could tell her truly what she means to him; then she would see
what Essex, of whom she believes what she wants to believe, really
has in store for her'. If I am right, and Ralegh had convinced his
wife of the truth of his feelings and of his forebodings about Essex,
then Essex was to prove him right within a few years.[20] In any case,

the nobility of the poem itself demonstrates that in 1592 Ralegh's grief was neither as affected nor as subjective as has usually been supposed; if he suffered despair, it was from much higher motives than is generally allowed.

Ben Jonson (1572–1637)

5

Ben Jonson, although at various times bricklayer's apprentice, actor, court-satellite and government agent, was the first substantial professional man of letters in Britain. In contrast to his more casual and more gifted friend Shakespeare, he called for higher literary standards than anyone before him; he would certainly have welcomed the opportunity to make a living from poetry alone.

Unfortunately only nineteen of his letters have survived.[21] They tell us less about Jonson's personality than about some of the difficulties in which he became involved—and consequently about the general predicament of poets and dramatists in the early years of the seventeenth century.

Seven refer to Jonson's imprisonment in 1605 for the unauthorized publication of *Eastward Ho*, a collaboration between himself, Chapman and Marston.[22] Drummond recorded in 1619 that Jonson told him that

> he was delated by Sir James Murray to the King for writting some thing against the Scots in a play Eastward hoe & voluntarily Imprissonned himself with Chapman and Marston, who had written it amongst them. the report was that they should then have their ears cutt & noses. after their delivery he banqueted all his friends, there was Camden Selden and others. at the midst of the Feast his old Mother Dranke to him & shew him a paper which she had (if the Sentence had taken execution) to have mixed in the Prison among his drinke, which was full of Lustie strong poison & that she was no churle she told she minded first to have Drunk of it herself.[23]

This is true in substance, although some of the details are suspect. Probably Sir James Murray did 'delate' *Eastward Ho*, since he or someone like him was mocked in it; but Marston does not seem to have been imprisoned, which casts slight doubt on Jonson's boast that he joined both his fellow playwrights 'voluntarily'. Doubtless he anticipated the inevitable. James I objected to the gibes at the Scots (in one cancelled passage Virginia is described as peopled 'only by a few industrious Scots, perhaps, who indeed are dispersed over the face of the whole earth'; they are notable friends to England 'when they are out on't') and the fact of publication.

Jonson worked hard to gain his release, in letters written to Salisbury, the Countess of Bedford, Pembroke and others. In her book on Jonson and the intentions of his play *Cataline His Conspiracy*,[24] Barbara de Luna suggests that Jonson may have had his studied obsequiousness to Salisbury—

> Your Lordship will be the most honor'd Cause of our Liberty, where freing us from one prison, you shall remove us to another, which is aeternally to bind us and our Muses, to the thankfull honoring of you and yours to Posterity; as your owne vertues have by many descents of Ancestors ennobled you to time[25]

—in mind when he condemned himself in the epigram *To My Muse* for having committed 'most fierce idolatory' to 'a worthless lord'.

This is likely: the ruthless and sly Salisbury did prove 'worthless', as Jonson implied to Drummond in 1619.

Apparently the letters succeeded in their purpose, for he was soon out of prison. Occasionally the rhetoric in them is worthy of the poet, as when he writes, 'The Anger of the Kinge is death (saith the wise man) and in truth it is little less with mee and my friend, for it hath buried us quick'.[26]

A letter of 20 December 1631, addressed to his patron the Earl of Newcastle, is exceptional in that it gives us a touching and charming picture of Jonson in his last years. The Sir Thomas Badger referred to at the beginning was not only Master of the King's Harriers but also a keen amateur actor. Jonson's postcript was true: the appropriate part of the Reportary of Court of Aldermen reads 'it is ordered . . . that Mr. Chamberlain shall forbeare to pay any more fee or wages unto Benjamin Jonson the Citties Cronologer untill he shall have presented . . . some fruits of his labours in that his place'; in 1634 he got the salary back, with arrears, through the intervention of his friend the Earl of Dorset.

> My Noble and most honor'd Lord.
> I my selfe beeing no substance, am faine to trouble You with shaddowes; or (what is less) an Apologue, or Fable in a dreame. I being strucken with the Palsey in the Yeare 1628. had by Sir Thomas Badger some few monthes synce, a Foxe sent mee for a present; which Creature, by handling, I endeavored to make time, aswell for the abateing of my disease, as the delight I tooke in speculation of his Nature. It happen'd this present year 1631, and this verie weeke, being the weeke Ushering Christmas, and this Tues-

day morneing in a dreame, (and morneing dreames are truest) to have one of my servants come up to my Bed-side, and tell mee, Master, Master the Foxe speakes. Whereat, (mee thought) I started, and troubled, went downe into the Yard, to witnes the wonder; There I found my Reynard, in his Tenement the Tubb, I had hyr'd for him, cynically expressing his owne lott, to be condemn'd to the house of a Poett, where nothing was to bee seene but the bare walls, and not any thing heard but the noise of a Sawe, dividing billatts all the weeke long, more to keepe the family in exercise, then to comfort any person there with fire, save the Paralytick master; and went on in this way as the Foxe seem'd the better Fabler, of the two. I, his Master, began to give him good words, and stroake him: but Reynard barking, told mee; those would not doe, I must give him meate; I angry, call'd him stinking Vermine. Hee reply'd, looke into your Cellar, which is your Larder too, You'le find a worse vermin there. When presently called for a light, mee thought, I went downe, & found all the floore turn'd up, as if a Colony of Moles had beene there, or an army of Salt-Peter men; Whereupon I sent presently into Tuttle-street, for the Kings most Excellent Mole-chatcher to relieve mee, & hunt them: But hee when hee came and veiw'd the Place; and had well marked the Earth turn'd up, tooke a handfull, smelt to it, And said, Master it is not in my power to distroy this vermine; the K: or some good Man of a Noble Nature must helpe you. This kind of Mole is call'd a *Want*,[27] which will distroy you, and your family, if you prevent not the workeing of it in tyme, And therefore god keepe you and send you health.

The interpretation both of the Fable, and Dreame is, that I wakeing doe find Want the worst, and most workeing Vermine in a house. and therefore my Noble lord, and next the King, my best Patron: I am necessitated to tell it you. I am not so impudent to borrow any sume of your Lordship, for I have no faculty to pay: but my needs are such, and so urging, as I doe beg, what your bounty can give mee, in the name of good Letters, and the bond of an ever-gratefull and acknowledging servant

To your honour

B. Ionson

Yesterday the barbarous Court of Aldermen
have withdrawne their Chander-ly Pension,
for Verjuice, & Mustard.   33^{li}–6^s–8^d.[28]

But Jonson's most intriguing and revealing letter is to Donne. It was first printed in *A Collection of Letters made by Sir Tobie Mathews*, which, edited by the younger Donne, printed many of Donne's own letters for the first time; here it was headed 'A letter from Ben. Johnson to Doctor Donne, in clearing himself upon a former accusation'. In spite of the 'Doctor', the letter must belong to 1609 or 1610, probably the latter.

> You cannot but believe, how dear and reverend your friend-ship is to me, (though all testimony on my part, hath been too short to expresse me) and therefore would I meet it with all obedience. My mind is not yet so deafned by injuiries, but it hath an ear for counsell. Yet, in this point, that you presently disswade, I wonder how I am mis-understood; or that you should call that an imaginarie right, which is the proper justice, that every clear man owes to his innocency. Exasperations I intend none, for Truth cannot be sharp but to ill natures, or such weak ones, whom the ill spirit's suspition or credulity still possesse. My Lady may believe whisperings, receive tales, suspect and condemn my honestie; and I may not answer, on the pain of losing her; as if she, who had this prejudice of me, were not already lost. O no, she will do me no hurt, she will think and speak well of any [my?] faculties. She cannot there judge me; or if she could, I would exchange all glory, (if I had all mens abilities) which could come that way for honest simplicitie. But, there is a greater penaltie threatned, the losse of you my true friend; for others I reckon not, who were never had, you have so subscribed your self. Alas, how easie is a man accused, that is forsaken of defence! Well, my modesty shall sit down, and (let the world call it guilt, or what it will) I will yet thank you, that counsell me to a silence in these oppresures, when confidence in my right, and friends may abandon me. And, lest your self may undergo some hazard, for my questioned reputation, and draw jealousies or hatred upon you, I desire to be left to mine own inno-cence which shall acquit me, or Heaven shall be guilty.
>
> Your ever true Lover.[29]

The background of this letter is complex and far-ranging, and for all the details and a full and acute discussion I must once more refer readers to Dr. de Luna's book, *Jonson's Romish Plot*. Jonson's editors, Herford and Simpson, seem to have believed that it alluded to some kind of bedchamber scandal in which Jonson had been involved, and to little more. Actually, although 'My Lady' probably does refer, as they maintained, to Jonson's and Donne's common patroness, the Countess of Bedford, the letter, as Dr. de Luna has shown, is about something far less trivial than a bedchamber scandal.

As she suggests, Jonson's language would not have been so serious if he had been dealing with a mere sexual escapade: he was no prude or sex-moralist, and never felt the need to affect self-righteousness when writing about such matters.

Briefly, the background is this. In 1596 Jonson went to prison for a time for his part in the lost play *The Ile of Dogs*. Two years later he killed a fellow-actor, Gabriel Spencer, in a duel. Either in 1597, or while awaiting his trial on the charge of killing Spencer, he was converted to Catholicism by a visiting priest. He remained of the faith until, according to his own account, 1610. Yet his Catholicism in no way hindered his career.

At about the same time as he feasted his mother and friends in celebration of his release from prison over the *Eastward Ho* affair, he attended an exclusively Catholic supper party, given by Robert Catesby, the instigator of the Gunpowder Plot. Perhaps the Plot itself was not alluded to on this occasion; but it certainly was at subsequent supper parties. These were not attended by Jonson himself, but by his very close friend Sir John Roe. A letter written by Jonson to Cecil, now Lord Salisbury, in November 1605,[30] clearly indicates that he was acting as a secret agent in the matter. It has now become evident that he played a more important role in the Gunpowder Plot than has hitherto been supposed. Salisbury certainly knew of the existence of the Plot before he received the famous warning letter: it seems possible that the man who first informed him was Jonson himself, and that he in turn gathered his information from Sir John Roe.

But Jonson, as Dr. de Luna has so ably demonstrated, got no credit for this from his contemporaries. Instead, he was regarded with increasing resentment, both as a traitor to his fellow-recusants and a creature of Salisbury. The resentment continued for many years, eventually stirring him to write *Cataline* in his own defence.

The 'former accusation' ('let the world call it guilt, or what it will') of which Jonson was clearing himself in the letter to Donne, then, was not a trivial one: it was nothing less than that of being a traitor to his own kind. This explains 'And, lest your self may undergo some hazard, for my questioned reputation, and draw jealousies or hatred upon you . . .': Donne himself was an ex-Catholic who had engaged in official anti-Catholic propaganda; he was now in the precarious position of badly needing favours from those in high places.

But it was not pro-Catholic feeling that incensed Jonson's enemies: understandably angered by his arrogant attitude to them, frustrated by his undoubted genius, they objected to his having obtained preferment by what they thought of as a low trick. Jonson felt, passionately, that this was unfair; but, for obvious reasons, he

could not speak out. 'Alas, how easie is a man accused, that is fore-
saken of defence!' he protested to Donne.

Were his enemies justified in their accusations, or was he
indeed—as he protested so vehemently—innocent?

This question can never be answered with certainty: the
evidence is too thin. But it seems likely that Jonson's indignation
was justified: that his motives throughout the affair of the Gunpowder
Plot were not only patriotic but also intelligent. For although
James I was as inept a King as he was a contemptible man, the
Gunpowder Plot was a lunatic affair. No responsible contemporary
could have wished it to succeed. Nor has any historian worthy of
the name had much sympathy to spare for the conspirators: there
are better men over whom to shed tears. The message of *Cataline*,
Jonson's considered defence of his behaviour, is, in Dr. de Luna's
phrase: 'Country' before 'Religion'. Politically, Catholicism was a
bad cause in early seventeenth-century England—as bad a cause as
racism is now. And just as anyone who today helped to bring down
a racist government, whether it cost the lives of a number of racists
or not, might be justly proud, so Jonson felt about his part in the
foiling of the Gunpowder Plot. The parallel is a just one.

But was Jonson ever really a Catholic? My conjecture is that
he was not; like Dr. de Luna, I am suspicious of the 'conversion'
he underwent in jail in 1597 or 1598. He continued to enjoy the
patronage, as Dr. de Luna observes, of such 'arch-Protestants' as
the Queen and Robert Cecil, second son of Lord Burleigh (created
Earl of Salisbury 1605); he remained hostile to Essex, whom
Catholics generally tended to regard as their white hope for toleration. It is at least possible that Robert Cecil saw a useful man in
Jonson early on, and conscripted him (under pressure) as a fake
Catholic who might one day pick up something important.

While Jonson was in prison he was certainly visited by a
Catholic priest. This is probably why spies, 'two damn'd Villans',
were 'placed' 'to catch advantage of him'—one of these may have
been the Robert Poley who was present at Marlowe's death;[31] but,
Drummond says he told him, 'he was advertised by his Keeper.
. . .'[32] Jonson had a low opinion of such men: of these two he later
wrote, in his *Epigrammes* (LIX):

> Spies, you are lights in state, but of base stuffe,
> Who, when you have burnt yourselves down to the snuffe,
> Stinke, and are throwne away. End faire enough.

But he was in serious trouble, and it may well be that he listened, or
was forced to listen, to a proposition, put to him by these 'spies' on
behalf of Cecil, that he should pose as a newly converted Catholic.
Jonson's complex character, in which a wilfully coarse-grained
directness jostled with a sophisticated, subtle, subversive cunning,

has seldom been properly understood. Such a role, since it was in an excellent cause, might well have appealed to his sense of the dramatic. It also saved him from an unpleasant scrape.

It was not in Jonson's character to take any official religion seriously enough to be prepared to risk his career for it. He escaped from a number of quite serious scrapes, including ones over *Poetaster* and *Sejanus* as well as *Eastward Ho*, in a manner that suggests that some very highly placed person might, at any rate sporadically, have been protecting his interests. Was the 'fox' in Jonson simultaneously serving a good cause and grinningly using Cecil's protection to go as far as possible in satire on 'great' men?

Would he, even though engaged in secret work for the government, have told Salisbury in the letter of November 1605 about the Plot that

> to tell your Lordship playnly my heart, I thinke they are All enwear'd in it, as it will make 500 Gentlemen lesse of the Religion within this weeke, if they carry theyre understanding about them[33]

if he had been a true Catholic? It seems incredible, for the information is quite gratuitous, the kind of opinion that a genuine Catholic, even one who tried to be loyal to his country, would have kept to himself.

It may be objected that in the next year, 1606, Jonson and his wife were hauled in front of the Consistory Court for refusing to take Communion. But, once again, there are some odd features of this case, which suggest that it may have been a put-up job. For Jonson promised 'to conforme him selfe according as' certain learned men 'shall advise him & perswade him'. Just as it would have amused Brainworm or Volpone to say they were Catholics when they were not, so it might have amused the sardonic Jonson, who, as he said to Drummond in 1619, was 'for any religion as being versed in both'.[34] As Dr. de Luna says,

> There is something altogether too showy about the choice off the Dean of St. Paul's, the Archbishop of Canterbury's chaplain, and others. . . . Surely these busy men had better things to do . . . unless of course the King or Cecil had commanded the sessions, as serving a useful propaganda purpose.[35]

All this is speculation; but the hypothesis of Jonson as an anti-Catholic government agent, playing his own poetic game, is attractive in that it argues for a vein in him which critics of the plays have noted well enough, but which all his biographers have missed.

6

A number of letters by and to William Drummond of Hawthornden (1585–1649), eccentric inventor and Laird as well as poet, are included in the 1711 folio edition of his *Works*.[36] While some are valuable for the information with which they provide scholars on matters of the dating of various poets' works, they reveal little of Drummond himself, except that he was of a retiring and generous disposition.

Thus, in a letter of 1618 to Michael Drayton he speaks of *Polyolbion* as having 'ravished' him and put him 'into a new trance'.[37] His *Apologetical Letter* of 2 March 1635, addressed to Sir Robert Kerr (Earl of Ancrum), is much less studied, and is probably his most impressive letter. In this he protested, with some courage, against the arrest and trial of Lord Balmerino for having been in possession of an 'infamous libel' against the King. Since the so-called libel was Presbyterian in origin, and Drummond was anti-Presbyterian, his plea for the right of free speech is notable. But few of Drummond's views of contemporary poetry and poets (chiefly Ben Jonson) are preserved in the form of letters. Of somewhat more interest is a letter written to him by his close friend Sir William Alexander in the spring of 1620. Alexander (*c.* 1567–1640), the Scots poet and playwright who became Earl of Stirling, was at James I's court helping the King in a translation of the Psalms. He tried to enlist Drummond's aid in this unenviable task, and the letter he sent to him on 18 April 1620 in reply to a version of a psalm that Drummond had sent him aptly characterizes James I in his capacity as literary man—here, clearly, he is hindering literature, as one would expect:

> I received your last letter, with the Psalm you sent; which I think very well done. I had done the same long before it came, but he [the King] prefers his own to all else, though perchance, when you see it, you will think it the worst of the three. No man must meddle with that subject, and therefore I advise you to take no more pains therein; but I, as I have ever wished you, would have you to make choice of some new subject, worthy of your pains, which I should be glad to see. I love the Muses as well as ever I did, but can seldom have the occasion to frequent them. All my works are written over in one book, ready for the press; but I want leisure to print them.[38]

Of a later generation, the letters of Sir John Suckling (1609–42) were preserved as *Letters to Several Eminent Persons*.[39] Despite Tucker Brooke's remark that there are 'few better personal letters than his',[40] they are sadly disappointing, consisting for the most part of such conceits as this, in a letter to an unnamed lady:

Here lies Don Alonzo
Slain by a Wound receiv'd under
His left pap
The Orifice of which was so
Small, no Chirugeon cou'd
Discover it.
Reader,
If thou would'st avoid so strange
a death
Look not upon Lucinda's *eyes.*[41]

It is a pity that even his one surviving letter to his fellow-poet, Carew,[42] characterized like himself as 'dissolute', should exemplify all Suckling's artifice but none of the delicacy and subtlety that give his best poems such distinction: we should welcome further information about the enigmatic poet who sometimes seems more to resemble the Restoration wits than his Caroline contemporaries, and yet who differs sharply from either group. A few letters written at a time of political crisis, particularly one to Henry German [i.e. Jermyn] 'in the Beginning of Parliament, 1640',[43] are more cogent and less flippant in tone; but beyond exhibiting the views of a moderate though committed Royalist, they tell us little about Suckling—except to confirm his already known capacity for seriousness.

John Milton (1608–74)

7

The forty-one known letters of John Milton, all but ten of which appeared in his lifetime in a badly edited publication of 1674, are the most unrewarding of any major poet.[44] Only the student of rhetoric could be expected to gain any satisfaction from them. Insufferably tedious, they tell us scarcely anything about him and nothing about his poetry. As a basis for judgement or explanation of him, they are almost valueless. Most are in Latin, and are painstakingly modelled on the Latin Epistle as practised in the Renaissance. Milton learned to write in this style at school, and even his late letters are never very far from it.

Thus, writing in Latin on 21 September 1656 to the sixteen-year-old Richard Jones, his ex-pupil who afterwards became Viscount Ranelagh, he says:

You are right in feeling assured of my affection for you;

and I would have that assurance grow daily firmer, in proportion to the increase in your goodness of disposition and virtue of which you give me proof.[45]

If empty of feeling or meaning, this is harmless; but it is of little interest.

The least formal of his Latin letters are two to Charles Diodati, his closest friend. Diodati, son of an Italian domiciled in England and his English wife, was born at about the same time as Milton, went to St. Paul's with him, became a physician, and died in 1638. Both Milton's letters to him date from September 1637. One passage in the later letter, of 23 September, Milton might have written as an apology for himself as a stiff and formal correspondent:

... I would not have true friendship tried by the test of letters and good wishes, which may all be feigned; but its roots and the source of its strength should go deep into the mind, and it should spring from a pure origin. ... the written word is less essential than a lively recollection of virtues on both sides. ...

He goes on to describe his secret thoughts:

You make many eager enquiries, even asking about my thoughts. I will tell you, Diodati, but let me whisper it in your ear, to spare my blushes, and allow me for a moment to speak to you in a boastful strain. What am I thinking about? you ask. So help me God, of immortality. What am I doing? Growing wings and learning to fly; but my Pegasus can only rise on tender pinions as yet, so let my new wisdom be humble.[46]

But the most revealing letter Milton ever wrote, which even so is not very revealing, was not included in the 1674 collection: it was addressed, in English, to an unknown friend, probably in 1633 when he was twenty-five. It has been conjectured that the addressee was Thomas Young, an Anglican clergyman who was Milton's tutor from his tenth until his fourteenth year. Young ultimately became a Presbyterian; he was learned, but was always a Puritan by inclination. In 1633 he may well have been urging Milton to enter the ministry. But Milton was bursting with ambition, and hoped that he could become famous by the exercise of his poetic talent. He had great difficulty in writing this letter, as the two much corrected drafts of it preserved in the Trinity College Manuscript show: he was undergoing a private crisis. As W. A. and A. T. Turner comment, 'In this letter his confidence is uncertain but his convictions are clear'.

Sir, besides that in sundry other respects I must acknowledge

me to proffit by you when ever wee meet, you are often to
me, & were yesterday especially, as a good watch man to
admonish that the howres of the night passe on (for so I
call my life as yet obscure, & unserviceable to mankind) &
that the day with me is at hand wherein Christ comands all
to Labour while there is light. Which because I am persuaded you doe to no other purpose then out of a true
desire that god should be honourd in every one; I therfore
thinke my selfe bound though unask't, to give you account,
as oft as occasion is, of this my tardie moving; according to
the præcept of my conscience, which I firmely trust is not
without god. Yet now I will not streine for any set apologie,
but only referre my selfe to what my mynd shall have at
any tyme to declare her selfe at her best ease. But if you
thinke, as you said, that too much love of Learning is in
fault, & that I have given up my selfe to dreame away my
Yeares in the armes of studious retirement like Endymion
with the Moone as the tale of Latmus goes, yet consider
that if it were no more but the meere love of Learning,
whether it proceed from a principle bad, good, or naturall
it could not have held out thus Long against so strong
opposition on the other side of every kind, for if it be bad
why should not all the fond hopes that forward Youth &
Vanitie are fledge with together with Gaine, pride, & ambition call me forward more powerfully, then a poore regard-
lesse & unprofitable sin of curiosity should be able to with
hold me, whereby a man cutts himselfe off from all action
& becomes the most helplesse, pusilanimous & unweapon'd
creature in the world, the most unfit & unable to doe that
which all mortals most aspire to, either to defend & be
usefull to his freinds, or to offend his enimies. Or if it be
to be thought an naturall pronenesse there is against that
a much more potent inclination inbred which about this
tyme of a mans life sollicits most, the desire of house &
family of his owne to which nothing is esteemed more
helpefull then the early entring into credible employment,
& nothing more hindering then this affected solitarinesse
and though this were anough yet there is to this another
act if not of pure, yet of refined nature no lesse available
to dissuade prolonged obscurity, a desire of honour &
repute, & immortall fame seated in the brest of every true
scholar which all make hast to by the readiest ways of
publishing & divulging conceived merits as well those that
shall as those that never shall obtaine it, nature therefore
would præsently worke the more prævalent way if there
were nothing but this inferiour bent of her selfe to restraine

her. Lastly this Love of Learning as it is the pursuit of somthing good, it would sooner follow the more excellent & supreme good knowne & præsented and so be quickly diverted from the emptie & fantastick chase of shadows & notions to the solid good flowing from due & tymely obedience to that comand in the gospell set out by the terrible seasing of him that hid the talent. it is more probable therfore that not the endlesse delight of speculation but this very consideration of the great comandment does not presse forward as soone as may be to undergo but keeps off with a sacred reverence & religious advisement how best to undergoe, not taking thought of beeing late so it give advantage to be more fit, for those that were latest lost nothing when the maister of the vinyard came to give each one his hire. & heere I am come to a streame head copious enough to disburden it selfe like Nilus at seven mouthes into an ocean, but then I should also run into a reciprocall contradiction of ebbing & flowing at once & doe that which I excuse myselfe for not doing, preach & not preach. Yet that you may see that I am something suspicious of my selfe, & doe take notice of a certaine belatednesse in me I am the bolder to send you some of my nightward thoughts some while since (because they com in not altogether unfitly) made up in a Petrarchian stanza. which I told you of
. . . .
by this I beleeve you may well repent of having made mention at all of this matter, for if I have not all this while won you to this, I have certainly wearied you to it. this therfore alone may be a sufficient reason for me to keepe me as I am least having thus tired you singly, I should deale worse with a whole congregation, & spoyle all the patience of a parish, for I my selfe doe not only see my owne tediousnesse but now grow offended with it that has hinderd me thus long from coming to the last and best period of my letter, & that which must now cheifely work my pardon that I am. . . .[47]

8

Until Swift and Pope, and then Gray, such letters of poets as have survived provide little interest or amusement. Some of the most entertaining are found in John Wilmot, Earl of Rochester's two volumes of *Familiar Letters* (1697),[48] but—as in the case of Suckling —there is not much here to help in the explanation of the enigmatic character who lived the life of a Hobbesian materialist, and yet who satirized his times with an indignation markedly non-materialistic in origin, and who died a repentant Christian.

The diplomat Matthew Prior (1664–1721) has the distinction of having been the most accomplished poet between the death of Dryden in 1700 and the rise of Pope. A large number of his letters survive in manuscript, and some of these were collected in a volume of the Historical Manuscripts Commission. Others are quoted in biographies and by his editors, Messrs. Wright and Spears, in their notes to the poems.[49] Most are on diplomatic subjects and are of little interest except to the historian; others are important in establishing the dates of his poems.

Part of a letter Prior wrote to an unidentified person— Wright and Spears conjecture a patron or the son of a patron—some years after he had published the part-prose, part-verse burlesque *The Hind and the Panther Transvers'd* (1687), of which he was co-author with Charles Montagu, conveys a lucid impression of the odium Dryden incurred by the publication of his pro-Catholic allegory, *The Hind and the Panther* (1687). 'The D: of B:' is the Duke of Buckingham, author of *The Rehearsal*, the play Marvell 'transpros'd'.

> Mr: Dryden turning R: C: wrote a Poem which he called the H. and the P. By the H. he means the Church of R: and the C. of E: by the P. The Argument of the whole Work is that the P: walking abroad one Evening was met by the H. and invited to her Cell, and there entertained with aboundance of Civility. They talk together of the Plot and the Test, real presence in the Sacrament, Infalibility in matters of Faith. Tell one another two long Stories in which they allude to the State each C: has of late been under, and is in at present, and so bid each other good Night.
>
> When People expected a great deal from so famous a Man on so fine a subject, Out comes this Poem applauded by the Pa: and at first a little dreaded by the Protestants: but the noise it made (like that of the Log in Æsop's Fable) was only terrible at first, like the Log to[o] the Poem was found lumpish and rediculous, & so soon trampled and insulted on by every One. The main Objection against it was that the matter of it was false and invidious, and the way of its writing ungentile & rayling; but Billingsgate Manners in better Language, and Far below even the dignity of Satyr, for which the Author has formerly been beaten. For it affirms that the Reformation took its Original from the Lust of K. H. VIII, and the luxury and incontinence of Martin Luther, that the C. of E. sides with the

Phanatics against the K. that her Doctrines continue or change just as the State pleases with many other indignities as malicious as any Jesuit could invent, & yet so very absurd as hardly as Irishman would repeat 'em.

The second Objection was that this piece contradicted the known rules of Poetry and even common Sense, for the whole being a Fable, the Beasts who speak should have references to the Characters of the Persons they represent; thus by a Lion, a Wolf or a Fox, we mean a fierce, a rapacious, or a designing Man because the Nature of these Creatures and the Inclinations of such Men bear something of resemblance and proportion. Now, by his two Beasts how can we Understand the Two Churches? The C: of R: is no more like a Hind than 'tis like an Elephant, & the Rhinoceros is as good a representation of the C. of E. as the Panther.

Then the Beasts should keep such Company as tis likely they may love, as tis probable they should know, or else 'tis not a Fable. A Hind, who is so quiet and innocent a beast would not in all probability be much delighted in the Conversation of so fierce & Cruel a Creature as a Panther, or if She was, they would discourse rather of Woods and Shades and Streams than of St Paul to the Corinthians and the Council of Trent. The Hind, I fancy would not run over the Fathers, or repeat the Canon Law and the Code, and if She did the Panther would scarse be able to tell her where she quoted false or when She argued foul.

Amongst Authors who have written a Fable, Correct and well Horace has told the common Tale of the City M: and the C: M: in Latin, and Mr: Cowley has Translated it into English. This Fable we have rediculed and told in the same way Mr Dryden does his H: and P: it being really as probable and Natural that two Mice should take a Coach, go to the Tavern, get drunk, break windows and be taken by the Constable, as that a Hind and a Panther should sit up all Night together a talking; One proving Oates and Bedlow were Villains, and desiring the Penal Laws may be Repealed, and t'other defending the Doctrines of Non resistance and Passive Obedience.

To make the thing yet more rediculous we took the same humour the D: of B: had some years since in his play, the Rehearsal; that is we Bring in B: by whom we mean D: defending (as his way is) the foolishest things in his Poem, and Smith & Johnson by whom we mean any two Gentlemen of Tolerable Sense and judgment finding those faults which are most Obvious, and urging B. to be rediculous.[50]

Another letter, addressed on 4 February 1707 to Lord Halifax (the Charles Montagu with whom he had collaborated in 1687) voices a frequent complaint of early eighteenth-century poets: Prior was seeking a job, and Edmund Curll had just published his poems without his permission:

> Some rogue of a bookseller has made a very Improper Collection of what He calls my writings . . . multilated . . . in such a Manner as may do Me harm. . . . I mention this, my Lord, desiring your Lordship to believe this book was printed without my knowledge or consent. . . .[51]

Rather more interesting in their own right than Prior's letters —though we have yet to see these as a whole—are those of John Gay (1685–1732).[52] Gay rose from linen-draper's apprentice to favourite of the great, notably the Duke and Duchess of Queensberry. Of an easy-going disposition, he was insecure, a place-hunter and something of a snob—though in a quite inoffensive manner. Yet, although life treated him kindly (the reverses he experienced were never very serious), and gave him the true friendship of such men as Swift, Arbuthnot and Pope, there is an obstinate, though half-concealed, streak of bitterness running through his work. The muted, good-humoured quality of this bitterness may best be seen in *The Hare*, the last poem of the first series of 'excellent unregarded' (as Swift referred to them) *Fables* he wrote for Prince William. Delightful companion though he was, he despised himself for his own meekness, and even for his too happy disposition. As C. F. Burgess writes in his introduction to the letters, Gay 'the would-be satirist' is 'notably indecisive', for he 'was evidently never able to despise the world as Swift professed to do'. Yet he saw a kind of poetic strength in thus 'despising the world', and one side of him genuinely yearned to do this. But he did not have the necessary toughness.

Nevertheless, he sometimes voices his dissatisfaction in his letters, as when he says to the diplomat Francis Colman, on 23 August 1721,

> I cannot be now and then without some thoughts that give me uneasiness, who have not the least prospect of ever being independent; my Friends [here he refers not to his literary but to his aristocratic friends] do a great deal for me, but I think I could do more for them.

A little later he adds, as if in expression of his own mood,

> Dear Colman be as cheerfull as you can, never sink under

a disappointment, I give you the advice which I have always endeavourd to follow. . . .[53]

That his 'uneasiness' was not the result of a passing mood may be inferred from a letter to Swift of 22 December 1722, sixteen months later. He had not written to Swift for eight years, and that he did so now indicates that the source of his unhappiness lay less in mere material disappointment than in a conviction that his weakness or laziness or courtly ambitions, or all three, constituted a serious barrier to his poetic aspirations.

> After every post-day for these 8 or 9 years I have been troubled with an uneasiness of Spirit, and at last I have resolv'd to get rid of it and write to you; I dont deserve that you should think so well of me as I really deserve, for I have not profest to you that I love you as much as ever I did, but you are the only person of my acquaintance almost that does not know it. Whoever I see that comes from Ireland, the first Question I ask is after your health, of which I had the pleasure to hear very lately from Mr Berkeley. I think of you very often, no body wishes you better, or longs more to see you. Duke Disney who knows more news than any man alive, told me I should certainly meet you at the Bath the last Season, but I had one comfort in being dissappointed that you did not want it for your health; I was there for near eleven weeks for a Cholick that I have been troubled with of late, but have not found all the benefit I expected. I lodge at present in Burlington house, and have received many Civilitys from many great men but very few real benefits. They wonder at each other for not providing for me, and I wonder at 'em all. Experience has given me some knowledge of them, so that I can say that tis not in their power to dissappoint me. You find I talk to you of myself, I wish you would reply in the same manner. I hope though you have not heard from me so long I have not lost my Credit with you, but that you will think of me in the same manner as when you espous'd my cause so warmly which my gratitude never can forget.[54]

Granted that he was very easily cast down ('Every Post gives me fresh mortification, for I am forgot by every body' he exclaims petulantly to Mrs. Howard in a letter of September 1724), Gay was a poet of considerable talent, whose satirical impulse, muted though it was by his love of comfort, resembled Swift's. There is no reason to doubt that Swift's suggestion of a Newgate pastoral set him actually to write *The Beggar's Opera*. And although his attempt to castigate 'the young Machivillains of his Country', in a letter of 16 August 1714 to Swift, is, as Burgess states, tedious, laboured and self-consciously what he conceived the recipient might desire, there is no reason to doubt the sentiments or the irony of his letter of August 1723 to Mrs. Howard. Mrs. Howard, unlike Swift, was a person of the Court. As Burgess notes, this letter contains an 'early suggestion of the format of *The Beggar's Opera*'.

> I have long wish'd to be able to put in practice that valuable worldly qualification of being insincere, one of my chief reasons is that I hate to be particular, and I think if a man cannot conform to the customs of the world, he is not fit to be encourag'd or to live in it. I know that if one would be agreeable to men of dignity one must study to imitate them, and I know which way they get Money and places. I cannot indeed wonder that the Talents requisite for a great Statesman are so scarce in the world since so many of those who possess them are every month cut off in the prime of their Age at the Old-Baily. How envious are Statesmen! and how jealous are they of rivals! A Highway-man never picks up an honest man for a companion, but if such a one accidentally falls in his way; if he cannot turn his heart He like a wise Statesman discards him. Another observation I have made upon Courtiers, is, that if you have any friendship with any particular one you must be entirely govern'd by his friendships and resentments not your own, you are not only to flatter him but those that he flatters, and if he chances to take a fancy to [a] man whom you know that he knows to have the Talents of a Statesman you are immediately to think both of them men of the most exact Honour. in short, you must think nothing dishonest or dishonourable that is requir'd of you, because if you know the world you must know that no Statesman has or ever will require any thing of you that is dishonest or dishonourable. Then you must suppose that all Statesmen, and your friend in particular, (for Statesmen's friends have always seem'd to think so) have been, are, and always will be guided by strict justice, and are quite void of partiality and resentment. You are to believe that he never did or can propose any wrong thing, for whoever has it in his power to dissent from a Statesman in any one particular, is not capable of his friendship. this last word friendship I have been forc'd to make use of several times though I know that I speak improperly for it has never been allow'd a Court term. This is some part of a Court Creed, though it is impossible to fix all the Articles. for as men of Dignity believe one thing one day, and another the next, so you must daily change your faith and

opinion. therefore the method to please these wonderfull and mighty men, is never to declare in the morning what you believe 'till your friend has declar'd what he believes, for one mistake this way is utter destruction. I hope these few reflections will convince you that I know something of the Art of pleasing great men. I have strictly examin'd most favourites that I have known, and think I judge right, that almost all of them have practic'd most of these rules in their way to performent. I cannot wonder that great men required all this from their Creatures, since most of them have practic'd it themselves, or else they had never arriv'd to their dignitys. . . .[55]

Swift admired *The Beggar's Opera*, which Gay completed in January or February 1727/8, because it aptly expressed and was certainly influenced by his own view of criminals as small-time prototypes of great and influential men. In writing to Swift in the midst of its success at the Playhouse in Lincoln's Inn Fields, where it broke all records by running for sixty-two nights, he was able to say, 'I know this account will give you pleasure, as I have push'd through this precarious Affair without servility or flattery'.[56] And he added, in tribute to Swift's understanding of the theme, 'As to any favours from Great men I am in the same state you left me; but I am a great deal happier as I have no expectations'.[57] And on 16 May he is glad to inform Swift that a sermon had been preached against the opera, 'which I look upon as no small addition to my fame'.[58] The sermon had been preached by a future Archbishop of Canterbury, then Chaplain to the King, Thomas Herring; it seems to have been what today would be regarded as a reactionary onslaught, myopically condemning Gay for presenting crime in a favourable light.

It is interesting that Gay, although he was a loyal partisan of Pope, does not in his letters to him treat him as a mentor: it was Swift whom he regarded in this light. Thus, on 9 November 1729, he assures Swift that although he has often

> twitted me in the teeth with hankering after the Court, in that you mistook me, for I know by experience that there is no dependance that can be sure but a dependance upon ones-self. . . .[59]

The twitting had not been wholly mistaken; but when Gay discovered his true self, it was to Swift that he turned most of all. And Swift regarded him highly, continuing to 'twit' him with laziness, a charge he took seriously, for he continually denied it: for the two final sentences of his last letter (16 November 1732), which is to Swift, read:

> I have not been idle while I was in the Country, and I

know your wishes in general & in particular that industry may always find it's account. Believe me, as I am, unchangeable in the regard, Love & esteem I have for you.[60]

9

Edward Young (1683–1765) lived for so long that he properly belongs to two ages. Although *Night Thoughts* (1742–4) was immensely popular, it is markedly inferior to his seven earlier satires, collected under the title of *Love of Fame*, or *The Universal Passion* (1725–8), which influenced Pope. His most important work, the critical *Conjectures on Original Composition* (1759), cast in the form of a letter to his friend Samuel Richardson, is the most remarkable essay on poetry in the hundred years before Wordsworth's Preface to *Lyrical Ballads*, but has been consistently neglected.[61] It was a surprising essay to come from a man whose most famous work, *Night Thoughts*, was more popular than in any serious sense original. For it attacked the principles of 'imitation' and asserted, wonderfully for its time, 'there is something in poetry beyond prose reason, there are mysteries not to be explained'.

Unfortunately Young's personal letters, which, in the latter part of his life, he often composed on horseback, never reach this level; as a whole, they more resemble those of a pleasant, eccentric, poetizing parson (he was Vicar of Welwyn from 1730 until his death) than of a poet or a shrewd critic. His letters to Richardson, a group of which were printed in the *Monthly Magazine* at the beginning of the last century, are extremely tedious, and hardly repay reading. The first of his letters to be preserved is addressed to his friend Thomas Tickell, whose translation of the first book of the *Iliad* was just being unfavourably compared with Pope's.[62] It is both honest and reassuring: clearly Young, while wishing to raise his friend's spirits, thought Pope's version was better English poetry though less faithful to Homer:

> Be assured I want no new inducement to behave myself like your friend. To be very plain, the University almost in general gives the preference to Pope's translation; they say his is written with more spirit, ornament and freedom, and has more the air of an original. I inclined some . . . to compare the translation with the original; which was done, and it made some small alterations in their opinions, but still Pope was their man. The bottom of the case is this, they were strongly prepossessed in Pope's favour, from a wrong notion of your design before the poem came down; and the sight of yours has not force

enough upon them to make them willing to contradict
themselves, and own they were in the wrong; but they go
far for prejudiced persons, and own yours is an excellent
translation, nor do I hear any violently affirm it to be worse
than Pope's, but those who look on Pope as a miracle . . .
even these zealots allow that you have outdone Pope in
some particulars.

    Upon the whole I affirm the performance has gained
you much reputation, and when they compare you with
what they should compare you, with Homer only, you are
much admired. It has given I know many of the best judges
a desire to see the *Odyssey* by the same hand, which they
talk of with pleasure, and I seriously believe your first piece
of that will quite break their partiality for Pope, which your
Iliad has weakened, and secure your success. Nor think my
opinion groundlessly swayed by my wishes, for I observe,
as prejudice cools, you grow in favour, and you are a better
poet now than when your Homer first came down. I am
persuaded fully that your design cannot but succeed here,
and it shall be my hearty desire and endeavour that it may.[63]

Young was a true eccentric—perhaps the quaintness of *Night
Thoughts* is its most attractive and original characteristic—who
vainly awaited preferment in the Church for thirty-five years. Many
of his letters were written to the Duchess of Portland; one of 3 May
1742, on the subject of their friend Dr. Alured Clarke's imminent
death, is typical:

The doctor retains his spirits, and is cheerful under circumstances that fright the bystander. Now this would be
impossible, was there not an indulgent Being who frights
us with the appearance of remote evils, in order to give
entrance to His fear into our hearts, and when those evils
come supports us under them beyond our expectation, and
more still beyond our deserts. Dr. Clarke's behaviour
brings to my memory some lines which I have formerly
read, whether it be in Fletcher perhaps your Grace can
tell. After the author has represented a good man, whose
name is Philander, on his death-bed behaving to the surprise of all about him, he adds—
'As some tall tower, or lofty mountain's brow
Detains the sun, illustrious from its height,
When rising vapours, and descending shades,
In damps and darkness drown the spacious vale,
Philander thus augustly reared his head
Undamped by doubt, undarknened by despair;
At that black hour, which general horror sheds

On the low level of inglorious minds,
Sweet peace, and heavenly hope, and humble joy,
Divinely beamed on his exalted soul.
With incommunicable lustre bright.'
I hope in God, Madam, we may see our Philander again,
before these verses are applicable to him in their full
extent. . . .[64]

The quotation was not from Fletcher, but from Young's own *Night Thoughts*, the first part of which appeared in the following month. Here (in the letter) a not uninteresting notion is wrapped up in an unconfident piety, which is just the weakness of Young's poetry. He overcame his timidity in prose, in the *Conjectures on Original Composition* and in *The Centaur not Fabulous* (1754), which dealt boldly with aristocratic immorality; but his letters, although 'merry' and often quaint, are usually too contrived to be of great interest.

Such letters as survive of the not unimportant poet Mark Akenside (1721–70),[65] whom Smollett introduced into *Peregrine Pickle* as 'the ode writing doctor', provide sparse material for the study of his unfashionable if unobtrusive eclecticism. The Rev. R. A. Willmott, 'incumbent of Bear Wood', who edited Dyer's and Akenside's works well by mid-nineteenth-century standards, speaks of Akenside's friend and patron 'Jeremiah Dyson, as a name never to be mentioned by any lover of genius, or noble deeds, without affection and reverence', and quotes from Akenside's earliest known letter to him, of 18 August 1742: 'If you will excuse me for being thus selfish, I sincerely and heartily offer you my friendship'.[66] Such effusions are unlikely to interest the modern reader, although Willmott's description of Akenside himself is more appealing:

> His appearance was not prepossessing, the complexion being
> pale and sickly . . . a powdered wig in a stiff curl, together
> with an artificial heel, heightened the grotesque seriousness
> of his general aspect. . . . His temper was irritable, and
> sometimes brutal, if a patient . . . showed any hesitation
> or difficulty in swallowing the medicines which he pres-
> cribed. Of his harsh behaviour to women, a curious
> explanation has been discovered in the bitter remembrance
> of an early disappointment. . . . He had no wit, and seldom
> took a jest complacently. . . .[67]

Despite his unattractive personality (the worst charge against him is one of brutality, in a brutal age, to his charity patients at Christ's Hospital), Akenside's *The Pleasures of the Imagination* (1744), although pompous, is an interesting effort to express the pre-occupations of a temperament that was not characteristic of its times. Where a poet's impulse was original in this age, which was

not interested in originality, he often ended up in quaintness or
eccentricity—as we have seen in the case of Young. Akenside does not
escape from this, as his ambitious 'Inquiry into ridicule' in Book III
of *The Pleasures of Imagination* shows; but Willmott's quotation from
a letter he wrote about this passage demonstrates his seriousness:

> As for the poem, I am only just respiring from a pretty bold
> undertaking, not only in poetry, let me tell you, but even in
> philosophy,—namely, to develope and describe the general
> species and laws of ridicule in the characters of men, and
> give an universal idea of it in every other subject. I have
> been grievously put to it in the descriptive part. The general
> idea of the poem is rather bashfully candid—excuse the
> phrase—and ill admits any appearance of satire, though this
> inquiry was absolutely necessary to the plan, as relating to
> the materials and ground of comedy.[68]

Akenside spent some time in Leyden as a medical student, and
expressed his dislike of it in an *Ode: On Leaving Holland* that begins:

> Farewell to Leyden's lonely bound,
> The Belgian Muse's sober seat;
> Where dealing frugal gifts around
> To all the favourites at her feet,
> She trains the body's bulky frame
> For passive, persevering toils;
> And lest, from any prouder aim,
> The daring mind should scorn her homely spoils,
> She breathes maternal fogs to damp its restless frame.

A passage from a letter to Dyson of 7 April 1744 anticipates the poem:

> I will not spend time in giving you my sentiments of Holland
> or Leyden. One thing struck me very strongly, the absurd
> inconsistence between their ceremonious foppishness (mis-
> called politeness), and their gross insensibility to the true
> decorum in numberless instances. Such is their architecture,
> their painting, their music; such their dress, the furniture
> of their houses, the air of their chariots, and the countenance
> of their polity, that when I think of England, I cannot help
> paying it the same veneration and applause, which at
> London I thought due only to Athens, to Corinth, or to
> Syracuse.[69]

John Dyer (*c.* 1700–57), whose *The Country Walk* is a much better
poem than the more famous *Grongar Hill*, was temperamentally the
opposite of his friend Akenside. His letters show him as having
been 'gentle, unaffected and devout'.

William Shenstone (1714–63) was once highly thought of as
a letter-writer, but his artificial and cumbersome style has less

appeal now than it did in the eighteenth century.[70] His letters are
of most concern to the student of late Augustan architecture and
landscape; his famous garden at Leasowes was ultimately of much
greater significance in this field than were any of his poems in
the field of literature.

The letters of James Thomson (1700–48) have not been
collected, but are attractive.[71] It is amusing to find the future author
of *The Castle of Indolence* (1748) saying to his friend Dr. Cranston,
in 1720, 'If nature had thrown me in a more soft and indolent
mould. . . .'[72] It is also amusing to find him writing to the same
correspondent fifteen years later of how Pope's

> letters were piratically printed by the infamous Curll.
> Though Mr. Pope be much concerned at their being
> printed, yet they are full of wit, humour, good sense, and
> what is best of all, a good heart.[73]

What would he have thought if he had known who had really been
responsible for the publication of Pope's letters?

Through Thomson's letters we see him travelling on the
Continent as tutor, in need of money, in love (with a Miss Young,
whom he did not marry) and tactfully refusing his patron and
fellow-poet Lyttleton's recommendation of a suitable wife:

> I should have answered your kind, and truly friendly letter
> some time ago. . . . I have considered it in all lights and
> in all humours, by night, by day, and even during these
> long evenings. But the result of my consideration is not
> such as you would wish. My judgment agrees with you,
> and you know I first impressed yours in her favour. She
> deserves a better than me. . . .[74]

But his charm as a letter-writer comes out most fully in his letters
to his fellow-Scot David Mallett, of which this one of 2 August
1726 is a good specimen:

> After a tedious silence I had yours. Far from defending
> these two lines in my translation, I damn them to the lowest
> depth of the poetical Tophet, prepared of old for Mitchell,
> Morrice, Rook, Cooke, Beckingham, and a long &c.
> Wherever I have evidence, or think I have evidence, which is
> the same thing, I'll be as obstinate as all the mules in Persia.
>
> I have racked my brain about the common blessing
> of the sun you say is forgot, as much as ever s[avage] did
> his, in that elaborate description of the tooth ache Dr.
> Young disconcerted, without being able to hit on it. Your
> hint of the sapphire, emerald, ruby, strike my imagination
> with a pleasing taste, and shall not be neglected; but I am
> resolved not to correct till I have first rough-writ the whole.

In the enclosed sheets of "Summer," I raise the sun to nine or ten o'clock; touch lightly on his withering of flowers; give a group of rural images; make an excursion into the insect kingdom; and conclude with some suitable reflections. I have written a good deal more; you will be notoriously guilty of poetical injustice, if you make me not a proper return.

My idea of your Poem is a description of the grand works of Nature raised and animated by moral and sublime reflections; therefore before you quit this earth you ought to leave no great scene unvisited. Eruptions, earthquakes, the sea wrought into a horrible tempest, the abyss amidst whose amazing prospects, how pleasing must that be of a deep valley covered with all the tender profusion of the Spring. Here if you could insert a sketch of the deluge, what more affecting and noble? Sublimity must be the characteristic of your piece.

Millan is to buy Woodward's History this day for himself, and will transmit to you immediately.

I have not seen these reflections on the Dr.'s "Installment," but hear they are as wretched as their subject. The Dr.'s very buckram has run short on this occasion; his affected sublimity even fails him, and down he comes with no small velocity.

A star to us, a comet to the foe.

So sings the Knight with the woeful countenance speaking of the King.

Shall drive the bloody Jesuits from Thorn,
A thorn to them, to us a rose he'll prove,
A thorn to them, to us a rose of love.

You triumph over us translators for excelling your original, which is as if a tailor should reckon himself an hero for killing a ——. How dare you immerse yourself in his utter darkness? Death! to sing after a cuckoo; and abet the murderer of the classics—lies cold in earth—shut out from life and light.

Wit, friendship, mirth, compos'd his gentle mind.

The muses blush that these and several others, should be called in imitation of the Latin jargon; which rather than imitated should be eschewed, as Job did evil. In earnest, it was a weakness in you to stoop to his importunity. It is not that I am displeased at the English verses; but that you should (detestable!) be said to imitate the Latin.

You complain of your dullness, I only of your haste.[75]

I

Although Sidney wrote

> In truth, I sweare I wish not there should be
> Graved in my epitaph a Poet's name

and called poetry[76] his 'unelected vocation', he was highly articulate on the subject in *An Apologie for Poetrie*. There would, however, be little excuse for treating him here at great length, since although a fair number of his letters have survived, they are disappointing in literary and even in psychological terms. One would hardly expect them, of course, to be otherwise. Sidney was a professional courtier: he thought of literature as an ornament to a virtuous life, not as an end in itself. He preferred action whenever he could achieve it, and did most of his writing in periods of enforced idleness. His most important work, *An Apologie for Poetrie*, for example, was almost certainly written during 1580, when he left Court after offending the Queen. He published nothing, and would have considered it beneath him to do otherwise.

Born in 1554, the year after his maternal grandfather, the Duke of Northumberland, died on the scaffold, Sidney was cut out by his family circumstances to become a public servant. His uncle was the Earl of Leicester, to whose Protestant faction he remained attached throughout his life; his father was a diplomat, and became Lord-Deputy of Ireland. He entered Shrewsbury School in 1564, where he first met his life-long friend Fulke Greville, the most unaccountably neglected poet of Sidney's generation. Here he studied Latin and possibly some Greek. He was at Christ Church in 1568, with the future martyr, Edmund Campion, William Camden (who perhaps later instilled a love of Sidney into his pupil, Ben Jonson), Richard Hooker, and the eccentric Catholic poet, Richard Stanihurst, who made many experiments with quantitative metre, most of them grotesque. Here he learnt the art of disputation, which was later to serve him well in the composition of *An Apologie for Poetrie*; he left, without taking a degree, in 1571, to become a courtier.

In 1572 Sidney went to France in the train of the Earl of Lincoln; the Massacre of St. Bartholomew affected him deeply, and threw him into deep sympathy with the philosophies of a number of Huguenots, of whom the most important were Hubert Languet and Philippe du Plessis-Mornay, whose *La Verité de la Religion Chrestienne* he began to translate twelve years later. His Latin correspondence with Languet, who had more influence upon him than perhaps any other individual, is justly celebrated.

After three years of travelling in Germany, Austria, Hungary, Italy and the Low Countries, Sidney returned home. His sojourn abroad confirmed him in his Protestantism, and for the rest of his life all his political aims were directed towards the cause of the creation of a European Protestant League. This was Languet's dream. The Queen's flirtations—as Sidney regarded them—with the Catholic powers irritated him, and like his uncle he had some sympathies with Puritanism.

Between 1575 and his death he spent some time—first at Leicester House and then at Wilton, the seat of his sister, Mary, who married the Earl of Pembroke in 1577—in the company of poets, such as his friend Greville, Sir Edward Dyer and Spenser. As Geoffrey Shepherd writes,[77] he became 'the centre of a learned literary group, an unconstituted academy which was investigating the resources of the English language for high literary purposes'.

In 1579 Sidney challenged the Earl of Oxford to a duel; the Queen forbade it. By the standards of his time Sidney seems to have been largely in the wrong in the matter of this famous quarrel over a game of tennis,[78] but he may have seen in his adversary the personification of what Shepherd calls an 'aesthetic and irresponsible affection of valour and culture' which he regarded as unpatriotic, dangerous and unwholesome. Even at this distance of time, it is easy to sympathize with Sidney: Oxford was not as serious a man. Certainly, too, the Earl was an advocate of the Queen's marriage with Anjou, which Sidney bitterly opposed.

In 1580, true to his beliefs, he wrote a long and bold letter to the Queen in which he tried to dissuade her from marrying Anjou; soon afterwards he found it politic to leave Court. He was back by 1581. He married Frances, the fifteen-year-old daughter of Sir Francis Walsingham, in 1583. It was probably in 1582 that he wrote *Astrophil and Stella*, the first English sonnet-sequence. It is a pity that he never referred, in his letters or his criticism, to Wyatt or to Surrey, from whom he learned the English version of the form.

By 1585 Queen Elizabeth realized that her policy of conciliation with Spain had failed. Sidney's cause was therefore beginning to come into its own. He tried to join Drake's expedition against the Spaniards, but was recalled by the Queen and sent, with his uncle, to the Netherlands. In November he became Governor of

Flushing. In 1586, in a minor skirmish, he was wounded in the thigh (having characteristically thrown aside his thigh-pieces on seeing that the Lord-Marshal was without his); he died twenty-two days later.

2

Sidney was practical, serious, lively, intelligent: the perfect English embodiment of Castiglione's courtier. His ideas were not original, but his arrangement and presentation of them were. He consciously tried to be 'peerless' in his behaviour—and often succeeded. Both before and after his death he was regarded as the flower of Europe, and of England in particular. About his poetry critics cannot quite agree. Was he a Petrarchan to the core—'the English Petrarch', as his contemporaries called him? Or did he, as Professor David Kalstone (much more convincingly) asserts,[79] display a subtly ironic hostility to the Petrarchan tradition, thus anticipating Donne in more than just a few direct-sounding phrases? Was his passion for Penelope Rich, the Stella of the sonnet-sequence, totally artificial? His letters throw no light on these important questions, which cannot therefore be discussed here; but they do help to round out our picture of him; and they do confirm the usual view of him as a gentleman *par excellence*, with an intensely practical programme. They reveal him to have been an unselfish man who willingly did favours for others and even refused to make profit from the misfortunes of those he regarded as his enemies. A letter to his friend Sir Christopher Hatton begs him to help a Master Dennye, who is 'a good honest fellow . . . butt beeinge a basterd', cannot sue for some land he wants.[80] He tried to help recusants, and wrote to Lady Kytson explaining that there was 'a present intention of a general mitigation, to be used in respect of recusants'.[81] When he was desperately in debt he was offered a share of the recusant forfeitures, but wrote to Leicester, 'Truly I lyke not their persons and much worse their religions, but I think my fortune very hard that my reward must be built uppon other mens punishements'.[82] There is no record of his having accepted the offer. The gesture that led to his death may seem to us quixotic to the point of foolishness; but it has to be understood in the context of his times.

The correspondence with Languet[83] is important in the history of ideas; but Languet was not so much a literary man as a political theorist and an advocate of Protestantism. Languet did write verses—but most men of learning were expected to be able to do so as a matter of course. He had high hopes for Sidney; but these certainly did not include hopes for his poetry or for his distinction in literature. He loved Sidney dearly—was even sentimental, perhaps homosexually so, about him—and kept nothing from him. Writing to him from Vienna in December 1574, when Sidney had just entered his nineteenth year, he said:

> I beg you will not show anyone the foolish letters I send to you. I write without selection all that my mind in its changing moods suggests to me, and it is enough for me if I succeed in making you believe that you are very dear to me.[84]

These changing moods never suggested poetry as a vital subject.

There is some doubt as to how much Sidney knew about music, in spite of the fact that he set himself the task of fitting poems to it. But that he loved song is indisputable. He says so in *An Apologie for Poetrie*, and in a letter to his uncle the Earl of Sussex of 16 December 1577 he writes:

> I was bolde of late to move your Lordeshippe in the cace of the poore stranger musicien. He hathe alreddy so furr tasted of yowr Lordeshippes goodnes as I am rather in his behalfe humbly to thanke yowr Lordeshippe yet his cace is suche as I am muche contrained, to continew still a suiter to yowr Lordeshippe for him.[85]

In the letter to his brother, of 18 October 1580, the whole of which is quoted below, he tells him to 'keepe and increase your musick, yow will not beleive what a want I finde of it in my meloncholie times'. Does this mean that he does not know as much about it as he wishes, or merely that he takes solace in it? That he knew at least the rudiments is suggested not only by the fact that in his family home at Penshurst there was a collection of instruments (for use, not decoration) but also by a remark in a letter to Languet on 19 December 1573 from Venice, in which he says he is 'learning the sphere, and a little music'.[86]

He again alluded to his melancholy, and to the manner in which he avoided it, in a letter to Languet from Padua of 4 February 1574:

> Of Greek literature I wish to learn only so much as shall suffice for the perfect understanding of Aristotle. For though translations are made almost daily, still I suspect they do not declare the meaning of the author plainly or aptly enough; and besides, I am utterly ashamed to be following the stream, as Cicero says, and not go to the fountain head. Of the works of Aristotle, I consider the politics to be the most worth reading; and I mention this in reference to your advice that I should apply myself to moral philosophy. Of the German language, my dear Hubert, I absolutely despair. It has a sort of harshness, you know very well

what I mean, so that at my age I have no hope that I shall ever master it, even so as to understand it. . . . I readily allow that I am often more serious than either my age or my pursuits demand; yet this I have learned by experience, that I am never less a prey to melacholy than when I am earnestly applying the feeble powers of my mind to some high and difficult object. But enough of this.[87]

That he says he only 'suspected' that contemporary translations of Aristotle were inadequate suggests that his Greek was rudimentary. However this may be, by 1578 he was telling his brother to read not the *Politics* but the *Ethics*—a possibly significant shift of view, since although the two treatises are linked, the former deals with how men are made good, while the latter deals simply with the good man. That the distinction meant something very real to the Elizabethans is shown by Spenser's original plan for *The Faerie Queen*: the first twelve books were to deal with 'private' virtues, the second twelve with public ones.

On 24 July in the same year Languet wrote a letter to Sidney from Vienna that gives us some idea of what the young man meant, in terms of promise and personality, not only to Languet but also to other of the best minds in Europe:

> If you had been in good health, I should have been amused at your complaints of the ungracious behaviour of your friends who went away without bidding you farewell. You imagine, perhaps, my dearest Sidney, that all men have the same obliging character as yourself. Unless you alter your opinion, you will be always meeting with persons who will excite your wrath and give you cause for complaining. I consider that in these days men do a great deal, if they do not actually betray their friends; any additional good feeling must be set down as clear gain, as something over and above the conditions of ordinary friendship. I see, however, by your last letter that you have digested your wrath, and suffered yourself to be talked over, and so you set right in words what is past mending in deeds. You will have to adopt this plan many times before you reach my age, unless you wish to pass your whole life in quarrelling.[88]

Sidney usually studied towards an end; often this end was the 'art of war'; his introspection and his 'melancholy' were no doubt closely connected with moods of frustration and enforced inactivity. On 10 March 1578 he wrote to Languet of how he could see his Protestant cause withering at Court (as at that time it seemed to be), and of how he was meditating 'some Indian project'. Doubtless it was this frustrated mood which, nine days earlier, has caused him to write to Languet in an unusually cynical and self-interrogatory frame of mind:

> The use of the pen, as you may perceive, has plainly fallen from me; and my mind itself, if it was ever active in anything, is now beginning, by reason of my indolent ease, imperceptibly to lose its strength, and to relax without any reluctance. For to what purpose should our thoughts be directed to various kinds of knowledge, unless room be afforded for putting it into practice, so that public advantage may be the result, which in a corrupt age we cannot hope for? Who would learn music except for the sake of giving pleasure, or architecture except with a view to building? But the mind itself, you will say, that particle of the Divine Mind, is cultivated in this manner. This indeed, if we allow it to be the case, is a very great advantage: but let us see whether we are not giving a beautiful but false appearance to our splendid errors. For while the mind is thus, as it were, drawn out of itself, it cannot turn its powers inward for thorough self-examination; to which employment no labour that men can undertake is in any way to be compared. Do you not see that I am cleverly playing the stoic? Yea, and I shall be a cynic too, unless you reclaim me. . . .[89]

Languet himself, it is clear enough from his letters to Sidney, wanted him to give up his interest in the art of war (although he shared Sidney's anti-Spanish feelings) and come to Germany. But Sidney's desire to come to personal grips with Spain overrode not only his interest in literature but also his affection and respect for Languet. As readers of his poetry and criticism, however, we owe most to the periods when his political ambitions were frustrated.

Sidney was by no means as self-contradictory and enigmatic as Sir Walter Ralegh; but, like all the Elizabethans, he was to some extent a divided man. The states of mind that produced his ambition seem divorced from those that produced his poetry. Answering Languet's fears that Italy might become prey to the Turks from Venice on 15 April 1574 he wrote of 'these baneful Italians', and of Italy as 'the rotten member . . . which has now so long infected the Christian body';[90] yet it was Italian humanism and culture that influenced him most as a writer and as a thinker. He seems never to have been aware of either this contradiction or of any of the contradictions in himself. The good nature and fairmindedness that Languet and so many others praised in Sidney emerge in this same letter, when he describes the Pope—his spiritual enemy *par excellence* —as 'quite what men call "a good fellow" '.

3

But of course Sidney was not perfect. In May 1578 he wrote this totally unjustified letter to his father's secretary, Edward Molyneux, the dignity and maturity of whose reply put Sidney effectively in his place:

> Mr Mollineax
>   Few woordes are beste. My lettres to my Father have come to the eys of some. Neither can I condemne any but yow for it. If it be so yow have plaide the very knave with me; and so I will make yow know if I have good proofe of it. But that for so muche as is past. For that is to come, I assure yow before God, that if ever I know yow do so muche as reede any lettre I wryte to my Father, without his commandement, or my consente, I will thruste my Dagger into yow. And truste to it, for I speake it in earnest. In the meane time farwell. . . .[91]

Sidney's two surviving letters to his attractive but somewhat wayward younger brother, Robert, are important as indicating some of his beliefs and attitudes: letter-writers of this century were anxious, as we have seen in the case of Wyatt, to define their moral positions when addressing younger relatives. The first letter, the exact date of which cannot be determined, but which probably belongs to 1578, is the less interesting and the more homiletic. He tells Robert to travel in order to improve himself, rather than to claim that he has travelled:

> I thinke you have read Aristotles Ethicks if you have, you knowe it is the begyning, and foundacion of all his workes, the good ende which everie man doth & ought to bend his greatest actions, I am sure you have imprinted in your minde, the scope, and marke, you meane by your paines to shoote att, for if you should travayle but to travaile or to saie you have travailed, certainelie you shall prove a Pilgrim to noe Saint. But I presume soe well of you, that though a greate nomber of us never thought in our selves whie wee went, but onlie of a certaine tickling humour to doe as an other man hath done, your purpose is being a Gentleman borne, to furnish your selfe with the knowledge of such thinges, as maie be serviceable to your Countriee, and fitt for your calling which certainelie standes not in the chaunge of ayre, for the warmest sonne makes not a wise man, noe more in learning languages, (although they bee of good serviceable use,) for wordes are but wordes, in what language soever they bee, and much lesse in that all of us

come home full of disguisementes, not onlie of our apparrell, but of our countenaunces, as though the creditt of a travayler stood all uppon his outside.[92]

He goes on to discuss the virtues and shortcomings and political importance of various countries—'France above all other most needefull for us to marke . . . next in Spaine & the Lowe Countries then Germany. . . .' And once again he expresses his low opinion of Italy:

As for Italy I knowe not what wee have, or can have to doe with them, but to buye their scilkes and wynes, and for other provinces (excepting Venice) whose good lawes, & customes wee can hardly proporcion to our selves, because they are quite of a contrarie goverment, there is little there but tyranous oppression, & servile yeilding to them, that have little or noe rule over them. And for the men you shall have there, although some in deede be excellentlie lerned, yett are they all given to soe counterfeit lerning, as a man shall learne of them more false groundes of thinges, then in anie place ells that I doe knowe for from a tapster upwardes they are all discoursers. In fine certaine quallities, as Horsmanshipp, Weapons, Vauting, and such like, are better there then in those other countries, for others more sounde they doe little excell neerer places.[93]

The second letter to Robert, of 18 October 1580, is worth quoting in full, particularly for its reference to the poet. In *An Apologie* Sidney is defending the poet against, in particular, the then academically familiar charge of being a liar; it is noteworthy that he here uses the phrase 'are gallantly to be marked'. This seems to confirm that he was already thinking about the arguments of *An Apologie* by 1580, and that Stephen Gosson's *The School of Abuse* may have served to prompt it. As a whole this letter gives a pleasant and informal glimpse of Sidney, the affectionate and this time not too moralizing elder brother. The 'toyfull booke' which he hopes to send by February is *Arcadia*.

My deere brother, for the mony yow have receaved, assure your selfe (for it is true) there is nothing I spend so pleaseth me as that which is for yow. If ever I have abilitie yow will finde it, if not, yet shall not any brother living be better beloved then yow of me. I cannot write now to H. White, doe yow excuse me. For his nephew, they are but passions in my father, which wee must beare with reverence, but I am sory he should returne till he had the fruite of his travell, for yow shall never have such a servant as he would prove, use your owne discretion therin.[94] For your countenance I would for no cause have it diminished in Germany; in Italy your greatest expence must be upon worthi men, and not upon housholding. Looke to your diet (sweete Robin) and hould upp your hart in courage and vertue truly greate part of my comfort is in yow. I know not my selfe what I ment by braverie in yow, so greatly yow may see I condemne yow, be carefull of your selfe and I shall never have cares. I have written to Mr Savell, I wish yow kept still togeather, he is an excellent man; and there may if yow list passe good exercises betwixt yow and Mr Nevell there is greate expectation of yow both. For the method of writing Historie, Boden hath written at large, yow may reade him and gather out of many wordes some matter. This I thinke in haste a story is either to be considered as a storie, or as a treatise which besides that addeth many thinges for profite and ornament; as a story, he is nothing but a narration of thinges done, with the beginings, cawses, and appendences therof, in that kinde your method must be to have *seriem temporum* very exactlie, which the Chronologies of Melanchton, Tarchagnora, Languet, and such other will helpe yow to. Then to consider by that [the following words are illegible] as yow not your selfe, Zenophon to follow Thucidides, so doth Thucidides follow Herodotus, and Diodorus Siculus follow Zenophon. So generally doe the Roman stories follow the Greeke, and the perticuler stories of present Monarchies follow the Roman. In that kinde yow have principally to note the examples of vertue or vice, with their good or evell successes, the establishments or ruines of greate Estates, with the cawses, the tyme and circumstances of the lawes they write of, the entrings, and endings of warrs, and therin the stratagems against the enimy, and the discipline upon the soldiour, and thus much as a very Historiographer. Besides this the Historian makes himselfe a discourser for profite and an Orator, yea a Poet sometimes for ornament. An Orator in making excellent orations *e re nata* which are to be marked, but marked with the note of rhetoricall remembrances; a Poet in painting forth the effects,[95] the motions, the whisperings of the people, which though in disputation one might say were true, yet who will marke them well shall finde them taste of a poeticall vaine, and in that kinde are gallantly to be marked, for though perchance they were not so, yet it is enough they might be so. The last poynt which tendes to teach profite is of a Discourser, which name I give to who soever speakes *non simpliciter de facto, sed de qualitatibus et circumstantiis facti*; and that is it which makes me and many others rather note much with our penn then with out minde, because wee leave all thes discourses to the confused trust of our memory because they being not tyed to the tenor of a question as Philosophers use sometimes plaies the Divine in telling his opinion and reasons in religion, sometimes the Lawyer in shewing the cawses, and benefites of lawes, sometimes a Naturall Philosopher in setting downe the cawses of any strange thing which the story bindes him to speake of, but most commonly a Morall Philosopher, either in the ethick part when he setts forth vertues or vices and the natures of Passions, or in the Politick when he doth (as often he doth) meddle senten-tiouslie with matters of Estate. Againe, sometimes he gives precept of warr both offensive, and defensive, and so lastlie not professing any art, as his matter leades him he deales with all arts which because it carrieth the life of a lively exemple, it is wonderfull what light it gives to the arts themselves, so as the greate Civillians helpe themselves with the discourses of the Historians, so doe Soldiours, and even Philosophers, & Astronomers, but that I wish herein, is this, that when yow reade any such thing, yow straite bring it to his heade, not only of what art, but by your logicall subdivisions, to the next member and parcell of the art. And so as in a table be it wittie word of which Tacitus is full, sentences, of which Livy, or similitudes wherof Plutarch, straite to lay it upp in the right place of his store-house, as either militarie, or more spetiallie defensive militarie, or more perticulerlie, defensive by fortification and so lay it upp. So likewise in politick matters, and such a little table yow may easelie make, wherwith I would have yow ever joyne the historicall part, which is only the example of some stratageme, or good cownsaile, or such like. This write I to yow in greate hast, of method, without method, but with more leysure & studie (if I doe not finde some booke that satisfies) I will venter to write more largely of it unto yow. Mr Savell will with ease helpe yow to sett downe such a Table of Remembrance to your selfe, and for your sake I perceive he will doe much, and if ever I be able I will deserve it of him, one onely thing as it comes unto my minde lett me remember yow of, that yow con-sider wherin the Historian excelleth, and that to note, as Dion Nicœus in the searching the seacrets of Government; Tacitus, in the pithy opening the venome of wickednes, & so of the rest. My time exceedingly short will suffer me to write no more leisurely. Stephen can tell yow who stands with me while I am writing. Now (deere Brother) take

delight likewise in the mathematicalls, Mr Savell is excellent
in them. I thinke yow understand the sphere, if yow doe, I
care little for any more astronomie in yow. Arithmatick, and
geometry, I would wish yow well seene in, so as both in
matter of nomber and measure yow might have a feeling,
and active judgment I would yow did beare the mechanicall
instruments wherein the Dutch [the following words are
illegible]. I write this to yow as one, that for my selfe have
given over the delight in the world but wish to yow as
much if not more then to my selfe. So yow can speake and
write Latine not barbarously I never require great study in
Ciceronianisme the cheife abuse of Oxford, *Qui dum verba
sectantur, res ipsas negligunt*. My toyfull booke I will send
with Gods helpe by February, at which time yow shall
have your mony. And for .200^{li}. a yeare, assure your selfe
if the Estate of England remaine yow shall not faile of it,
use it to your best profite. My Lord of Leister sendes yow
forty pownds as I understand by Stephen, and promiseth
he will continue that stipend yearly at the least, then that
is above commons, in any case write largely and diligently
unto him, for in troth I have good proofe that he meanes
to be every way good unto yow. The odd .30^{li}. shall come
with the hundred or els my father and I will jarle. Now
sweete brother take a delight to keepe and increase your
musick, yow will not believe what a want I finde of it in
my melancholie times. At horsemanshipp when yow exercise
it reade Grison Claudio, and a booke that is called La gloria
delcavallo, withall, that yow may joyne the through contem-
plation of it with the exercise, and so shall yow profite
more in a moneth then others in a yeare, and marke the
bitting, sadling, and curing of horses. I would by the way
your worship would learne a better hand, yow write worse
than I, and I write evell enough; once againe have care of
your dyet, and consequently of your complexion, remember,
gratior est veniens in pulchro corpore virtus. Now Sir for
newes I referr my selfe to this bearer, he can tell yow how
idlie wee looke on our Naighbours fyres, and nothing is
happened notable at home, save only Drakes returne, of
which yet I know not the seacreat poyntes, but about the
world he hath bene, and rich he is returned. Portugall wee
say is lost, and to conclude my eies are almost closed upp,
overwatched with tedeous busines. God bless yow (sweete
boy) and accomplish the joyfull hope I conceive of yow,
once againe commend me to Mr Nevell, Mr Savell, &
honest Harry White, and bid him be merry. When yow
play at weapons I would have yow gett thick capps & brasers,

and play out your play lustilie, for indeed tickes, & daliances
are nothing in earnest for the time of the one & the other
greatlie differs, and use aswell the blow, as the thrust, it is
good in it selfe, & besides exerciseth your breath and strength,
and will make yow a strong man at the Tournei and Barriers.
First in any case practize the single sword, & then with the
dagger, lett no day passe without an hower or two such
exercise the rest studie, or conferr diligentlie, & so shall
yow come home to my comfort and creditt. Lord how I
have babled, once againe farewell deerest brother.[96]

That Sidney could be intemperate may be seen from his angry and
unjustified letter to his father's secretary; he seems also to have
acted over-impetuously in his quarrel with Oxford. Languet, then
at Cologne, probably misunderstood the whole affair; but Sir
Christopher Hatton at Court obviously did understand it: a letter
of Sidney's to him, of 28 August 1579, makes it clear that he had
made a personal appeal to Sidney before the matter of the
duel came before the Council. Sidney was adamant in his refusal
to give way:

As for the matter dependinge betwene the Earle of Oxford
and me, certaynly, Sir, howe soever I mighte have forgeven
hym, I should never have forgeven my self, yf I had layne
under so proude an injurye, as he would have laide uppon
me, neither can any thinge under the sunne make me
repente yt, not any miserye make me goo one half worde
back frome yt: lett him therefore, as hee will, digest itt: for
my parte I thincke, tyinge upp, makes some thinges seeme
fercer, then they would bee.[97]

Sidney is popularly supposed to have been banished from Court for
writing a long letter to Queen Elizabeth setting forth his reasons
for opposing the projected French marriage. But a letter to Leicester,
of 2 August 1580, reveals this was not so. He may have withdrawn
from Court as a matter of policy; but the reason he gives Leicester—
that he was too poor to stay there—is likely to be the true one. His
letter to the Queen had been circulated and one copy had fallen into
Anjou's own hands; his friends at Court, Leicester, Hatton, and
others, sensing the prevailing wind, were by now encouraging the
Queen to make the marriage. Sidney was probably unwilling to be
present at Court and thus to embarrass his friends by not recanting:

Righte honorable and singular good Lord. I have now
brought home my sister, who is well amended bothe of
her paine and disease. For my selfe I assure yowr Lordeshippe uppon my trothe, so full of the colde as one can not
heere me speake: whiche is the cawse keepes me yet frome

the cowrte since my only service is speeche and that is stopped. As soone as I have gottne any voice I will waite on yowr Lordeshippe if so it please yow. Althoughe it bee contrary to that I have signified to her Majestie of my wante, I dowt not her Majestie will vouchesafe to aske for me, but so longe as she sees a silk dublett uppon me her Highnes will thinke me in good cace. At my departur I desyred Mr Vichamberlaine he woolde tell her Majestie necessity did even banishe me frome the place. And allwaies submitting myselfe to yowr judgement and commandement, I thinke my best, either constantly to waite, or constantly to holde the course of my poverty, for comming and going neither breedes deserte, nor wittnesseth necessity. Yet if so it please yowr Lordeshippe I hope within 3 or 4 daies this colde will bee paste, for now truly I weare a very un-pleasante company keeper. My Lorde and my sister do humbly salute yow, and I remaine to do yowr commande-ment as fur as my lyfe shall enhable me.[98]

During this period, from 1579 until his appointment in the Nether-lands, Sidney did not enjoy the Queen's favour. Whatever she may have thought about him privately, she did not find it politic to indulge him. Her neglect of him, perhaps to be explained by Burleigh's dislike of his family, puzzled many foreign observers, particularly William of Orange. It is more than a pity that his literary correspondence of this time has not survived; for the evidence of his literary activities—apart from what he actually wrote—comes entirely from other sources, including, as we shall see, Spenser. Mr. John Buxton, in his *Sir Philip Sidney and the English Renaissance*, accepts the traditional view that Sidney 'told' Spenser to write *The Faerie Queen*.[99] However this may have been, it seems unlikely that Spenser wrote the poem Sidney wanted him to write; we should give much to possess even one letter from Sidney on the subject of Spenser's projected epic. But more is to be discovered about Sidney's influence on Spenser from letters written by the latter.

I

Apart from official dispatches from Ireland, with which we need not here be concerned, and a few dedicatory epistles preceding poems (including one dedicating *Colin Clouts Come Home Againe* to Ralegh), no more than three of Spenser's letters survive.[100] All were published in his lifetime: two (presumably) without his active consent, and one, the longish one to Ralegh prefacing *The Faerie Queen*, by his own wish. Spenser's exchange of letters with Gabriel Harvey is interesting in that it reveals certain of Spenser's pre-occupations about prosody as a young man, and tells us something about his relations with Sidney and his faction; the letter to Ralegh is important in that, although a 'public' letter in the sense that it is really addressed to all his readers of the present and the future, it is his sole surviving comment on his intentions in *The Faerie Queen*.

The events of Spenser's life were not sensational. He was born in 1552, and educated at Merchant Taylors' School under Richard Mulcaster, who had a profound influence on him. Some of his prentice work appeared in a volume called *The Theatre of Voluptuous Worldlings* (1569). After taking his Cambridge M.A. (Pembroke Hall) in 1576, he entered the service of the Bishop of Rochester. In 1579 he was at Leicester House, and acquainted with Sidney and Sir Edward Dyer; *The Shepherds' Calendar*, dedicated to Sidney, was entered in the Stationers' Register in 1579, in which year he also married Machabyas Childe, who was about twenty years old.

In 1580, having already begun some part of *The Faerie Queen*, Spenser accompanied Arthur, Lord Grey de Wilton, the new governor, to Ireland as his secretary. In 1581 he obtained the post of Clerk of the Chancery for Faculties, almost a sinecure, since the work (which consisted of issuing and recording dispensations granted by the Archbishop of Dublin) was done by a deputy. He held this post for seven years. In 1582 Grey was recalled. Spenser held a number of posts in Ireland until his death, the most important of which was deputy to Lodowick Bryskett, Clerk of the Council of

Munster. He lived near Dublin until late in the 'eighties, when he moved to the large estate of Kilcolman, near which Ralegh owned a large tract of land; this was his home until almost the end of his life.

The Faerie Queen Books I, II and III, dedicated to the Queen, appeared in 1590, but parts, at least, must have been circulating in England in the preceding years. Spenser visited England in 1589, and probably read some of his poem to the Queen at Court. She granted him a pension of £50 per year for life in 1591. By 1593 he was back in Ireland, both quarrelling with his neighbour Lord Roche about the boundaries between their estates and getting married to Elizabeth Boyle. His first wife, who had died, bore him a girl and a boy; by Elizabeth he had one son. He visited England again in 1595 and 1596, when Books IV, V, and VI of *The Faerie Queen* were published. Perhaps because of James VI of Scotland's complaint about the treatment of his mother as Duessa in Book V, he apparently received no reward for this.

In the autumn of 1598 Irish rebels sacked his estate, and Spenser arrived in London at Christmas with dispatches from the governor of Munster. He died less than a month later, at the age of forty-six.

Two Cantos of Mutabilitie was not published until the 1609 edition of *The Faerie Queene;* but many other poems had appeared in the 'nineties, among them *Amoretti* and *Epithalamion* (1594), *Colin Clouts Come Home Againe* (1595), and the *Fowre Hymnes* (1595).

Spencer's exchange of letters with Gabriel Harvey took place in 1579/80; they were published in 1580. The later letter appeared first, in *Three Proper and wittie familiar letters: lately passed betweene two University men: touching the Earth-quake in Aprill last, and our English refourmed versifying* . . .; the earlier letter is in *Two other very commendable Letters of the same mens writing: both touching the foresaid Artificiall Versifying.* . . . It is not known whether Harvey himself, or another, had them printed; Spenser certainly had nothing to do with the matter. According to Nashe, Harvey 'publiquely divulged these letters', but Nashe was Harvey's enemy. They are certainly, as C. S. Lewis remarked, 'dull, laboured things'; but they remain important because of what they tell us about Spenser's life and intentions at the time he wrote them, and (primarily) because they show him making experiments in the so-called 'English' versification, which he later abandoned.

Spenser begins by telling Harvey how much he values his friendship and advice; apparently Harvey has told him to go ahead and publish what must have been *The Shepherds' Calendar*; he reiterates his doubts about it, and refers to the 'she' in whose honour he says it was written. This is 'Rosalind' (to whom Harvey refers in one of his answers), which the mysterious 'E. K.', in his

Epistle to Harvey printed in the first edition of *The Shepherds'*
Calendar, says is an anagram. Beyond this brief mention, Spenser's
letters give no further clue as to the identity of 'Rosalind', a question as vexed as it is of small account. Two references in this letter,
which is dated 5 October 1579, to a Mistress Kirke, with whom
Spenser seems to have been lodging, do, however, strengthen the
view that 'E. K.', the often ridiculous glossator of *The Shepherds'*
Calendar, was an Edward Kirke—and not Spenser himself, or
Fulke Greville, as some scholars have thought.

> Good Master G. I perceive by your most curteous and
> friendly Letters your good will to be no lesse in deed, than
> I alwayes esteemed. In recompence wherof, think I beseech
> you, that I wil spare neither speech, nor wryting, nor aught
> else, whensoever, and wheresoever occasion shal be offred
> me: yea, I will not stay, till it be offred, but will seeke it,
> in al that possibly I may. And that you may perceive how
> much your Counsel in al things prevaileth with me, and
> how altogither I am ruled and over-ruled thereby: I am now
> determined to alter mine owne former purpose, and to
> subscribe to your advizement: being notwithstanding re-
> solved still to abide your farther resolution. My principal
> doubts are these. First, I was minded for a while to have
> intermitted the uttering of my writings: leaste by over-
> much cloying their noble eares, I should gather a contempt
> of myself, or else seeme rather for gaine and commoditie to
> doe it, for some sweetnesse that I have already tasted. Then
> also, meseemeth, the work too base for his excellent Lord-
> ship, being made in Honour of a private Personage un-
> knowne, which of some yl-willers might be upbraided, not
> to be so worthie, as you knowe she is: or the matter not so
> weightie, that it should be offred to so weightie a Personage:
> or the like. The selfe former Title stil liketh me well ynough,
> and your fine Addition no lesse. If these, and the like doubtes,
> maye be of importaunce in your seeming, to frustrate any
> parte of your advice, I beseeche you without the least selfe
> love of your own purpose, councell me for the beste: and
> the rather doe it faithfullye, and carefully, for that, in all
> things I attribute so muche to your judgement, that I am
> evermore content to annihilate mine owne determinations,
> in respecte thereof. And indeede for your selfe to, it sitteth
> with you now to call your wits and senses togither (which
> are always at call) when occasion is so fairely offered
> Estimation and Preferment. For, whiles the yron is hote, it
> is good striking, and minds of Nobles varie, as their Estates.
> *Verum ne quid durius.*

I pray you bethinke you well hereof, good Maister G. and forthwith write me those two or three special points and caveats for the nonce, *De quibus in superioribus illis mellitissimis longissimisque Litteris tuis.* Your desire to heare of my late beeing with hir Majestie, muste dye in it selfe. As for the twoo worthy Gentlemen, Master *Sidney* and Master *Dyer*, they have me I thanke them, in some use of familiarity: of whom, and to whome, what speache passeth for youre credite and estimation, I leave your selfe to conceive, having alwayes so well conceived of my unfained affection and zeale towardes you. And nowe they have proclaimed in their ἀρειωπάμῶ a generall surceasing and silence of balde Rymers, and also of the verie beste to: in steade whereof, they have, by authoritie of their whole Senate, prescribed certaine Lawes and rules of Quantities of English sillables for English Verse: having had thereof already great practise, and drawen mee to their faction. Newe Bookes I heare of none, but only of one, that writing a certaine Booke, called *The Schoole of Abuse*, and dedicating it to Maister *Sidney*, was for hys labor scorned: if at leaste it be in the goodnesse of that nature to scorne. Suche follie is it, not to regarde aforehande the inclination and qualitie of him to whome wee dedicate oure Bookes. Suche mighte I happily incurre entituling *My Slomber* and the other Pamphlets unto his honor. I meant them rather to Maister *Dyer*. But I am, of late, more in love wyth my Englishe Versifying than with Ryming: whyche I should haue done long since, if I would then haue followed your councell.[101]

The reference to Sidney's and Sir Edward Dyer's having had him 'in some use of familiarity' has been taken by some to mean close friendship. Taking this in conjunction with 'W. L.'s' poem of commendation printed at the beginning of the first fragment of *The Faerie Queen*—

So Spenser was by Sidney's speaches wonne
To blaze her fame. . . .

. . . .

What though his taske exceed a humaine witt,
He is excus'd, sith Sidney thought it fitt.

—some critics, John Buxton among them, have decided that Spenser wrote his epic at Sidney's behest. But there is little evidence for this fancy. Spenser discussed versification with Sidney, Dyer and (presumably) Greville because he was thrown into their company at Leicester House; this does not mean that he became a close friend. And Spenser continued to employ the archaisms of *The*

Shepherds' Calendar, although Sidney stated his strong dislike of them in *An Apologie*. *The Faerie Queene*, although its constituent parts were influenced by divers poetic styles and systems, was an originally conceived work.

The background to the remarks about 'English' versification needs to be understood. Harvey's position in the controversy is a somewhat ambiguous one, and has not been fully understood or explained by all the critics who deal with it. This may be due, at least in part, to Harvey's tendency to discuss the subject in a flippant and laboured manner. As William Webbe wrote in *A Discourse of English Poetrie* (1586),

> if hee had chosen some graver matter, and handled but with halfe that skyll which I knowe he could have doone, and not powred it fourth at a venture, as a thinge betweene jest and earnest, it had taken greater effect then it did.[102]

The discussion of English prosody has always been bedevilled by a confusion between *accent* (which is relatively determined, by stress, pitch and other factors) and *quantity* (which is determined only by duration). The two are related: a short syllable often coincides with a lightly stressed one, a long with a heavily stressed one—but the relationship is tenuous, and no rules can be made to determine it. Greek, Latin, French and Italian verse are 'scanned' by a quantitative system; English verse is most naturally and easily understood to consist of a series of accentual patterns—but no one has devised a satisfactory and universal method of 'scanning' it. The subject is beset with difficulties, which have not been altogether alleviated by the introduction of machines able to measure various factors in oral performances of poetry.

At the end of the sixteenth century there was little agreement among scholars and poets, and little understanding of the essential differences between English and Latin verse. It was thought, at least by such scholars as Roger Ascham, that rhyme was 'barbarous', merely a means of making prose look like poetry. Ascham called rhyme 'folie', and a 'fault'; even when he praised Surrey's translation of Virgil for not rhyming, he attacked it for being

> not distinct by trew quantitie of sillabes . . . our English versifing without quantitie . . . be sure signes that the verse is either borne deformed, unnaturall, and lame, and so verie unseemlie to looke upon, except to men that be gogle eyed them selves.[103]

This means that Ascham, seduced by the 'correctness' of foreign scansion, simply could not understand Surrey's English blank verse. The poet George Gascoigne's *Certain Notes of Instruction Concerning the Making of Verse or Ryme in English* (1575) is sensible by contrast. Allowing rhyme as a matter of course, he wrote:

> And in your verses remember to place every worde in his natural *Emphasis* or sound, that is to say, in such wise, and with such length or shortnesse, elevation or depression of sillables, as it is commonly pronounced or used.[104]

This is the most sensible, if simple, statement on prosody of the sixteenth century, but it must have gone largely unheeded by theorists (if not by poets such as Spenser in their practice). At some time in the 'sixties or 'seventies Thomas Drant (died *c.* 1578), Archdeacon of Lewes, translator of Horace and author of *A Medicinable Morall* (1566), formulated 'rules' for the making of English verse. These were never printed, and have not survived; but we can be fairly sure that they consisted of a grotesque and unusable system by which the spelling of words governed the 'quantities' of their syllables. For Drant and his contemporaries thought (wrongly) that the quantities of Latin words were determined by their spelling. We can feel that it is exceedingly fortunate that these rules and the kind of thinking that produced them were not taken seriously for more than a few years. Certainly Sidney and his circle—as we learn from this letter—took them to heart for a time. There are eight experiments in classical metres in *Arcadia*, most of which fail; but no sign of anything like this in *Astrophel and Stella* or in Greville's *Caelica*. It has been suggested that quantitative scansion appealed to Sidney only because he was interested in the problem of setting words to music; but there is an element of special pleading in this. It was not his only reason.

That Sidney and his circle had 'in their ἀρειῳπάῃῳ' proclaimed 'a generall surceasing and silence of balde Rhymers' need not be taken too seriously. However earnestly Sidney applied himself to Drant's rules, he soon gave them up. As for the *areopagus*: this was no more than a joke, as Spenser himself makes clear in his facetious remarks (quoted below) about 'their whole Senate'. But the term has been taken seriously; and there has been some misunderstanding of Harvey's exact position in the controversy. At worst, the student finds himself confronted with such statements as this:

> Harvey was an ardent advocate of . . . Latin prosody . . . and he tried his best . . . to force Spenser's genius into accordance with his theories. He very nearly killed off *The Faerie Queene* before its birth, but Spenser evaded the commands of Harvey's [*sic*] 'Areopagus' (formed to spread his views).[105]

At best, he may find writers identifying Sidney's views, which were based on Drant, with Harvey's, which, as we shall see, were not. In his valuable study of Spenser's poetry,[106] Professor William Nelson writes '. . . the example of Sidney and his circle, rather than Harvey's advice, drew him to his short-lived interest in experimenting with classical metres'. This, although true, tends to suggest that Harvey's views were not at variance with Sidney's; and it contradicts by implication John Buxton's characteristically too forthright assertion that 'Harvey by his ridicule put an end to the experiments in quantitative scansion that for a few months had beguiled Sidney and Spenser'. In fact we do not know what permanent influence, if any, either Sidney or Harvey had upon Spenser; but we can read what the two latter wrote to each other on the subject. Spenser's letter of 5 October 1579 continues, after conveying 'E. K.'s' commendation to Harvey, and acknowledging the receipt of a letter:

> Truste me, your Verses I like passingly well, and envye your hidden paines in this kinde, or rather maligne, and grudge at your selfe, that woulde not once imparte so muche to me. But once, or twice you make a breache in Maister *Drants* Rules: *quod tamen condonabimus tanto Poetæ tuæque ipsius maximae in his rebus autoritati.* You shall see when we meete in London (whiche, when it shall be, certifye us) howe fast I have followed after you in that Course: beware, leaste in time I overtake you. *Veruntamen te solum sequar, (ut sæpenumero, sum professus,) nunquam sanè assequar dum vivam.*
>
> And nowe requite I you with the like, not with the verye best, but with the verye shortest, namely with a few Iambickes: I dare warrant they be precisely perfect for the feete (as you can easily judge), and varie not one inch from the Rule. I will imparte yours to Maister *Sidney* and Maister *Dyer* at my nexte going to the Courte. I praye you, keepe mine close to yourselfe, or your verie entire friendes, Maister *Preston*, Maister *Still*, and the reste.

Iambicum Trimetrum.

Unhappie Verse, the witnesse of my unhappie state,
   Make thy selfe fluttring wings of thy fast flying
   Thought, and fly forth unto my Love whersoever she be:

Whether lying reastlesse in heavy bedde, or else
   Sitting so cheerelesse at the cheerfull boorde, or else
   Playing alone carlesse on hir heavenlie Virginals.

If in Bed, tell hir, that my eyes can take no reste:
   If at Boorde, tell hir, that my mouth can eate no meate:
   If at hir Virginals, tell hir, I can heare no mirth.

Asked why? say: Waking Love suffereth no sleepe:
  Say, that raging Love dothe appall the weake stomacke:
  Say, that lamenting Love marreth the Musicall.

Tell hir, that hir pleasures were wonte to lull me asleepe:
  Tell hir, that hir beautie was wonte to feede mine eyes:
  Tell hir, that hir sweete Tongue was wonte to make me
    mirth.

Nowe doe I nightly waste, wanting my kindely reste:
  Nowe doe I dayly starve, wanting my lively foode:
  Nowe doe I alwayes dye, wanting thy timely mirth.

And if I waste, who will bewaile my heavy chaunce?
  And if I starve, who will record my cursed end?
  And if I dye, who will saye: *this was Immerito*?

I thought once agayne here to have made an ende, with a heartie *Vale* of the best fashion: but loe, an ylfavoured myschance. My last farewell, whereof I made great accompt, and muche marvelled you shoulde make no mention thereof, I am nowe tolde (in the Divels name) was thorough one mans negligence quite forgotten, but shoulde nowe undoubtedly have beene sent, whether I hadde come, or no. Seeing it can now be no otherwise, I pray you take all togither, wyth all their faultes: and nowe I hope, you will vouchsafe mee an answeare of the largest size, or else I tell you true, you shall bee verye deepe in my debte: notwythstandying, thys other sweete, but shorte letter, and fine, but fewe Verses. But I woulde rather I might yet see youre owne good selfe, and receive a Reciprocall farewell from your owne sweete mouth.
[Here follow 114 lines of Latin verse.]
I was minded also to have sent you some English verses: or Rymes, for a farewell, but by my Troth I have no spare time in the world, to thinke on such Toyes, that you know will demaund a freer head, than mine is presently. I beseeche you by all your Curtesies and Graces let me be answered ere I goe: which will be, (I hope, I feare, I think) the next weeke, if I can be dispatched of my Lorde. I goe thither, as sent by him, and maintained most what of him: and there am to employ my time, my body, my minde, to his Honours service. Thus with many superhartie Commendations and Recommendations to your selfe, and all my friendes with you, I ende my last Farewell, not thinking any more to write unto you, before I goe: and withall committing to your faithfull Credence the eternal

Memorie of our everlasting friendship, the inviolable
Memorie of our unspotted friendshippe, the sacred Memorie
of our vowed friendship: which I beseech you Continue
with usuall writings, as you may, and of all things let me
heare some Newes from you. As gentle M. *Sidney*, I thanke
his good Worship, hath required of me, and so promised
to doe againe. *Qui monet, ut facias, quod jam facis;* you
knowe the rest. You may always send them most safely to
me by *Mistresse Kerke*, and by none other. So once againe,
and yet once more, Farewell most hartily, mine owne good
Master H. and love me, as I love you, and thinke upon
poore *Immerito*, as he thinketh uppon you.[107]

This demonstrates that Harvey's position was not the same as
Drant's, and it is therefore hard to see why some writers have
supposed that it was. Certainly, if Spenser's curious poem does not
vary 'one inch' from Drant's 'Rule', then this could have had
nothing to do with the way in which English was then spoken. But
how does Harvey reply? After a facetious beginning, acknowledging
Spenser's 'large, lavish, Luxurious, Laxative letter', and some idle
talk on what he has been doing, he goes on:

Your Englishe *Trimetra* I like better than perhappes you
will easily beleeue, and am to requite them wyth better, or
worse, at more conuenient leysure. Marry, you must pardon
me, I finde not your warrant so sufficiently good and
substauntiall in Lawe that it can persuade me they are all
so precisely perfect for the seete, as your selfe ouer-partially
weene and ouer-confidently avouche: especiallye the thirde,
whyche hathe a foote more than a Lowce (a wonderous
deformitie in a righte and pure SENARIE), and the sixte,
whiche is also in the same Predicament, vnlesse happly one
of the feete be sawed off wyth a payre of SYNCOPES: and
then shoulde the Orthographie haue testified so muche:
and, in steade of *Hēauēnlĭ Virgĭnāls*, you should haue
written *Heaūnlĭ Virgnāls*, and *Virgnāls* againe in the ninth,
and should haue made a Curtoll of *Immērĭto* in the laste:
being all notwithstandyng vsuall, and tollerable ynoughe,
in a mixte and licentious IAMBICKE: and of two euilles
better (no doubte) the fyrste than the laste, a thyrde superfluous sillable than a dull SPONDEE. Then me thinketh you
haue in my fancie somwhat too many SPONDEES beside:
and whereas TROCHEE sometyme presumeth in the firste
place, as namely in the second Verse, *Make thy*, whyche
thy by youre Maistershippes owne authoritie muste needes
be shorte. ... Nowe, Syr, what thinke you I began to
thinke with my selfe, when I began to reade your warrant

first, so boldly and venterously set downe in so formall and
autentique wordes as these, PRECISELY PERFIT, AND NOT AN
INCH FROM THE RULE: Ah Syrrha, and Iesu Lord, thought
I, haue we at the last gotten one, of whom his olde friendes
and Companions may iustly glory *In eo solum peccat, quod
nihil peccat*, and that is yet more exacte and precise in his
English Comicall Iambickes than euer M. WATSON himselfe
was in his Latin Tragicall Iambickes, of whom M. *Ascham*
reporteth that he would neuer to this day suffer his famous
Absolon to come abrode, onely because *Anapaestus in locis
paribus* is twice or thrice vsed in steade of *Iambus*? A small
fault, ywisse, and such a one, in M. ASCHAMS owne opinion,
as perchaunce would neuer haue beene espyed, no neither
in *Italy* nor in *Fraunce*. But when I came to the curious
scanning and fingering of euery foote and syllable: So here,
quoth I, M. WATSONS *Anapaestus* for all the worlde: A
good horse, that trippeth not once in a iourney: and M.
IMMERITO doth but as M. WATSON, and in a manner all
other *Iambici* haue done before him: marry, he might haue
spared his preface, or, at the least, that same restrictiue
and streightlaced terme PRECISELY, and all had been well
enough: and I assure you, of my selfe, I beleeue, no peece
of a fault marked at all. But this is the Effect of warrantes,
and perhappes the Errour may rather proceede of his
Master N. DRANTES Rule than of himselfe. . . . to saye
trueth, partly too to requite your gentle courtesie in beginning to me, and noting I knowe not what breache in your
gorbellyed Maisters Rules: which Rules go for good, I
perceiue, and keepe a Rule, where there be no better in
presence.[108]

Harvey's answer is extremely tedious, but it is clear enough that,
even if in spite of his tendencies towards facetiousness, he understood (what Spenser at this time apparently thought he did not)
that the scansion of English verse must have some relationship with
the way English is spoken. In view of Spenser's exquisite ear we
cannot, of course, take all this very seriously. Does it mean that he
did not take Harvey seriously? This can hardly be the case, for, of
all his contemporaries, Spenser was the one who remained loyal to
Harvey, as the sonnet, written in July 1586, which calls him 'happy
above happiest men', who never fawns for 'the favour of the great',
'like a great lord of peerelesse liberty', unequivocally shows. It
seems more likely that Mr. Buxton is right, and that Harvey may,
if accidentally, have caused Spenser to drop his interest in quantitative scansion. On the other hand, we cannot be quite sure how
fundamentally interested he ever was in the subject.

Spenser wrote another letter to Harvey in April 1580, in which he maintained the discussion:

I like your late Englishe Hexameters to exceedingly well, that I also enure my Penne sometime in that kinde: whyche I fynd indeede, as I have heard you often defende in worde, neither so harde, nor so harshe, that it will easily and fairely yeelde it selfe to our Moother tongue. For the onely, or chiefest hardnesse, whych seemeth, is in the Accente: whyche sometimes gapeth, and as it were yawneth il-favouredly, comming shorte of that it should, and some-time exceeding the measure of the Number, as in *Carpenter*, the middle sillable being used shorte in speache, when it shall be read long in verse, seemeth like a *lame Gosling that draweth one legge after hir*: and *Heaven* being used shorte as one sillable, when it is in verse stretched out with a *Diastole*, is like *a lame Dogge that holdes up one legge*. But it is to be wonne with Custome, and rough words must be subdued with Use. For, why a Gods name may not we, as else the Greekes, have the kingdome of oure owne Language, and measure our Accentes by the sounde, reserving that Quantitie to the Verse? . . .

I would hartily wish, you would either fend me the Rules and Precepts of Arte, which you observe in Quantities, or else followe mine, that M. Philip Sidney gave me, being the very same which M. Drant devised, but enlarged with M. Sidneys own judgements, and augmented with my Observations, that we might both accorde and agree in one: leaste we overthrowe one an other, and be overthrown of the rest. Truste me, you will hardly beleeve what greate good liking and estimation Maister *Dyer* had of your *Satyricall Verses*, and I, since the viewe thereof, having before of my selfe had speciall liking of *English Versifying*, am even nowe aboute to give you some token, what, and howe well therein I am able to doe: for, to tell you trueth, I minde shortely at convenient leysure, to sette forth a Booke in this kinde, whiche I entitle *Epithalamion Thamsis*, whyche Booke, I dare undertake wil be very profitable for the knowledge, and rare for the Invention and manner of handling. For in setting forth the marriage of the Thames: I shewe his first beginning, and offspring, and all the Countrey, that he passeth thorough, and also describe all the Rivers through-out Englande, whyche came to this Wedding, and their righte names, and right passage, &c. A worke, beleeve me, of much labour, wherein notwithstanding Master *Holinshed* hath muche furthered and advantaged me, who therein

hath bestowed singular paines, in searching oute their firste
heades and sourses: and also in tracing and dogging outer
all their Course, til they fall into the Sea.

> O Tite, siquid, ego,
> Ecquid erit pretij?

But of that more hereafter. Nowe, my *Dreames* and *Dying
Pellicane*, being fully finished (as I partelye signified in my
laste Letters) and presentlye to bee imprinted, I wil in
hande forthwith with my *Faery Queene*, whyche I praye
you hartily send me with al expedition: and your frendly
Letters, and long expected Judgement wythal, whyche let
not be shorte, but in all pointes suche, as you ordinarilye
use, and I extraordinarily desire. . . .

> *Postscripte.*
>
> I take best my *Dreames* shoulde come forth alone, being
> growen by meanes of the Glosse (running continually in
> maner of a Paraphrase) full as great as my *Calendar*. Therin
> be some things excellently, and many things wittily dis-
> coursed of E. K. and the pictures so singularly set forth,
> and purtrayed, as if *Michael Angelo* were there, he could (I
> think) nor amende the beste, nor reprehende the worst. I
> know you woulde lyke them passing wel. Of my *Stemmata
> Dudleiana*, and especially of the sundry Apostrophes therein,
> addressed you knowe to whome, must more advisement be
> had, than so lightly to sende them abroade: howbeit, trust
> me (though I doe never very well) yet in my owne fancie,
> I never dyd better. *Veruntamen te sequor solum: nunquam
> vero assequar.*[109]

Spenser's position at this time is clear: he allows for one way of
speaking words in ordinary speech and another of speaking them
in verse. Harvey, in the most important part of his long reply, is in
no doubts about this:

> But hoe I pray you, gentle sirra, a word with you more. In
> good sooth, and by the faith I beare to the Muses, you shal
> never have my subscription or consent (though you should
> charge me wyth the authoritie of five hundreth Maister
> DRANTS) to make your *Carpenter*, our *Carpenter*, an inche
> longer or bigger than God and his Englishe people have
> made him. Is there no other Pollicie to pull downe Ryming
> and set uppe Versifying but you must needes correcte
> *Magnificat*: and againste all order of Lawe, and in despite
> of Custome, forcibly usurpe and tyrannize uppon a quiet
> companye of wordes that so farre beyonde the memorie of

man have so peaceably enjoyed their several Priviledges
and Liberties, without any disturbance or the leaste con-
trolement? . . . Else never heard I any that durst presume
so much over the Englishe (excepting a fewe suche stam-
merers as have not the masterie of their owne Tongues) as
to alter the Quantitie of any one sillable, otherwise than
oure common speache and generall receyued Custome
woulde beare them oute.[110]

From what follows it seems that Harvey, while he understood the
impossibility of any such system as Drant's being successfully
applied to English verse, was nevertheless set upon some kind of
compromise. Highly critical of Ascham and Drant, he remains
determined to capitalize on the academic movement to exchange, as
he puts it, 'Barbarous and Balductum Rymes with Artificial Verses'.
As C. S. Lewis suggests, he is 'sailing to a possible, though . . .
undesirable, destination: the accentual hexameters of Longfellow'.[111]
However, this was sensible compared to Drant's system; it is a pity
that Harvey never realized himself, for he was no fool. But his odd
limitations are well illustrated by the fact that he became Nashe's
most fruitful butt—Nashe may have lacked charity (as polemicists
have to do when at work) and he may have exaggerated (as when he
claims that Harvey, told once by Queen Elizabeth that he looked
like an Italian, immediately affected an Italian accent), but he faithfully expresses the ridiculous side of the man's character.

Spencer's preoccupation with quantitative scansion is not very
important in terms of his own poetry, since, outside letters to Harvey,
he never practised what he preached—except perhaps in lost works.
But his position in this sterile controversy is instructive, in that it
shows how abstract theory can beguile even the most accomplished
practitioners into irrelevant absurdity—after all, Spenser's ear for
English rhythms has only been equalled by other poets (always
excepting Shakespeare); it has not been surpassed.

The other interesting aspect of these two letters is the first
mention of *The Faerie Queen* and of other of his works, some of
which are lost (or were never completed), such as the *Dying
Pellicane* and the *Epithalamion Thamesis* (written, he tells Harvey,
in quantitative verse), which is not to be confused with the *Epithalamion* published in 1594. We do not know, of course, what part of
The Faerie Queen Spenser sent Harvey, or, indeed, whether it is
represented in the published version. Harvey apparently thought
little of it at that time, for he wrote in reply:

I have nowe sent hir [The Faerie Queene] home at the
laste, neither in better nor worse case than I founde hir.
And must you of necessitie have my Judgement of hir in
deede: To be plaine, I am voyde of all judgement, if your

NINE COMŒDIES . . . come not neerer ARIOSTŒS COMOEDIES, eyther for the finenesse of plausible Elocution or the rarenesse of Poetical Invention, than that the ELVISH QUEENE doth to his ORLANDO FURIOSO, which, notwithstanding, you will needes seeme to emulate, and hope to overgo, as you flatly professed your self in one of your last Letters. . . . If so be the FAERYE QUEENE be fairer in your eie than the NINE MUSES. . . . Marke what I saye, and I will not say that I thought; but there an end for this once, and fare you well, till God or some Aungell putte you in a better minde.[112]

2

Spenser's letter to Ralegh, printed in front of the first instalment of *The Faerie Queen*, is (at any rate ostensibly) a declaration of intent, for it is headed

A LETTER OF THE AUTHORS, expounding his whole intention in the course of this worke: which, for that it giveth great light to the reader, for the better understanding is hereunto annexed. . . .

However, few modern critics accept it at its face value: it is, they assert, a conventional 'apology', having little relationship to the meaning or 'intentions' of the poem as a whole.

Earlier critics regarded Spenser as a delightful poet whose greatest work, *The Faerie Queen*, was a patchwork of stories without serious organization. More recent critics assume that all his poetry, but especially *The Faerie Queen*, is masterfully and subtly constructed according to definite principles. But they differ widely in their view of which principles. . . . A good example of critical self-confidence (or over-confidence) in this respect is Professor Kathleen Williams's book *Spenser's Faerie Queen*,[113] which treats an admittedly unfinished poem as a 'unified whole': the pattern of the meaning of the poem, she maintains, is established by the end of each book; the unwritten books would simply have extended, not added to, this meaning.

Spenser has been a gift to modern critics, because an inescapable corollary of their argument is that he cannot be properly appreciated without the help of their critical exegeses: the principles upon which he constructed his poetry are discoverable by critics— and only by critics. Whether a poetry that needs to be related to various systems of thought and belief before it can be properly (as opposed to more fully) understood is as rewarding as a poetry that speaks for itself is not a question that can be discussed in this context. The question here is what relationship the letter to Ralegh bears to *The Faerie Queen*. Can we take it at its face value? It reads as though we can:

Sir, knowing how doubtfully all Allegories may be construed, and this booke of mine, which I have entituled the Faery Queene, being a continued Allegory, or darke conceit, I haue thought good, aswell for avoyding of gealous opinions and misconstructions, as also for your better light in reading therof, (being so by you commanded,) to discover unto you the general intention and meaning, which in the whole course thereof I have fashioned, without expressing of any particular purposes, or by accidents, therein occasioned. The generall end therefore of all the booke is to fashion a gentleman or noble person in vertuous and gentle discipline: Which for that I conceived shoulde be most plausible and pleasing, being coloured with an historicall fiction, the which the most part of men delight to read, rather for variety of matter then for profite of the ensample, I chose the historye of King Arthure, as most fitte for the excellency of his person, being made famous by many mens former workes, and also furthest from the daunger of envy, and suspition of present time. In which I have followed all the antique Poets historicall; first Homere, who in the Persons of of Agamemnon and Ulysses hath ensampled a good governour and a vertuous man, the one in his Ilias, the other in his Odysseis: then Virgil, whose like intention was to doe in the person of Aeneas: after him Ariosto comprised them both in his Orlando; and lately Tasso dissevered them again, and formed both parts in two persons, namely that part which they in Philosophy call Ethice, or vertues of a private man, coloured in his Rinaldo; the other named Politice in his Godfredo. By ensample of which excellente Poets, I labour to pourtraiet in Arthure, before he was king, the image of a brave knight, perfected in the twelve private morall vertues, as Aristotle hath devised; the which is the purpose of these first twelve bookes: which if I finde to be well accepted, I may be perhaps encoraged to frame the other part of polliticke vertues in his person, after that hee came to be king.

To some, I know, this Methode will seeme displeasaunt, which had rather have good discipline delivered plainly in way of precepts, or sermoned at large, as they use, then thus clowdily enwrapped in Allegoricall devises. But such, me seeme, should be satisfide with the use of these dayes, seeing all things accounted by their showes, and nothing esteemed of, that is not delightfull and pleasing to commune sence. For this cause is Xenophon preferred before Plato, for that the one, in the exquisite depth of his judgement, formed a Commune welth, such as it should be;

but the other, in the person of Cyrus, and the Persians, fashioned a governement, such as might best be: so much more profitable and gratious is doctrine by ensample, then by rule. So have I laboured to doe in the person of Arthure: whome I conceive, after his long education by Timon, to whom he was by Merlin delivered to be brought up, so soone as he was borne of the Lady Igrayne, to have seene in a dream or vision the Faery Queen, with whose excellent beauty ravished, he awaking resolved to seeke her out; and so being by Merlin armed, and by Timon throughly instructed, he went to seeke her forth in Faerye land. In that Faery Queene I meane glory in my generall intention, but in my particular I conceive the most excellent and glorious person of our soveraine the Queene, and her kingdome in Faery land. And yet, in some places els, I doe otherwise shadow her. For considering she beareth two persons, the one of a most royall Queene or Empresse, the other of a most vertuous and beautifull Lady, this latter part in some places I doe expresse in Belphœbe, fashioning her name according to your owne excellent conceipt of Cynthia: (Phœbe and Cynthia being both names of Diana.) So in the person of Prince Arthure I sette forth magnificence in particular; which vertue, for that (according to Aristotle and the rest) it is the perfection of all the rest, and conteineth in it them all, therefore in the whole course I mention the deedes of Arthure applyable to that vertue, which I write of in that booke. But of the xii, other vertues, I make xii. other knights the patrones, for the more variety of the history: Of which these three bookes contayn three.

The first of the knight of the Redcrosse, in whome I express Holynes: The seconde of Sir Guyon, in whome I sette forth Temperaunce: The third of Britomartis, a Lady Knight, in whome I picture Chastity. But, because the beginning of the whole worke seemeth abrupte, and as depending upon other antecedents, it needs that ye know the occasion of these three knights severall adventures. For the Methode of a Poet historical is not such, as of an Historiographer. For an Historiographer discourseth of affayres orderly as they were donne, accounting as well the times as the actions; but a Poet thrusteth into the middest, even where it most concerneth him, and there recoursing to the thinges forepaste, and divining of thinges to come, maketh a pleasing Analysis of all.

The beginning therefore of my history, if it were to be told by an Historiographer should be the twelfth booke, which is the last; where I devise that the Faery Queene

kept her Annuall feaste xii. dayes; uppon which xii. severall
dayes, the occasions of the xii. severall adventures hapned,
which, being undertaken by xii. severall knights, are in
in these xii. books severally handled and discoursed. The
first was this. In the beginning of the feast, there presented
him selfe a tall clownishe younge man, who falling before
the Queene of Faries desired a boone (as the manner then
was) which during that feast she might not refuse; which
was that hee might have the atchievement of any adventure,
which during that feaste should happen: that being graunted,
he rested him on the floore, unfitte through his rusticity for
a better place. Soone after entred a faire Ladye in morning
weedes, riding on a white Asse, with a dwarfe behind her
leading a warlike steed, that bore the Armes of a knight,
and his speare in the dwarfes hand. Shee, falling before the
Queene of Faeries, complayned that her father and mother,
an ancient King and Queene, had bene by an huge dragon
many years shut up in a brasen Castle, who thence suffred
them not to yssew; and therefore besought the Faery
Queene to assygne her some one of her knights to take on
him that exployt. Presently that clownish person, upstarting,
desired that adventure: whereat the Queene much wonder-
ing, and the Lady much gainesaying, yet he earnestly
importuned his desire. In the end the Lady told him, that
unlesse that armour which she brought would serve him
(that is, the armour of a Christian man specified by Saint
Paul v. Ephes.) that he could not succeed in that enterprise; which being forthwith put upon him, with dewe
furnitures thereunto, he seemed the goodliest man in al
that company, and was well liked of the Lady. And efte-
soones taking on him knighthood, and mounting on that
straunge Courser, he went forth with her on that adventure:
where beginneth the first booke, vz.

A gentle knight was pricking on the playne, &c.
The second day there came in a Palmer, bearing an

Infant with bloody hands, whose Parents he complained to
have bene slayn by an Enchaunteresse called Acrasia; and
therfore craved of the Faery Queene, to appoint him some
knight to performe that adventure; which being assigned to
Sir Guyon, he presently went forth with that same Palmer:
which is the beginning of the second booke, and the whole
subject thereof. The third day there came in a Groome,
who complained before the Faery Queene, that a vile
Enchaunter, called Busirane, had in hand a most faire Lady,
called Amoretta, whom he kept in most grievious torment,

because she would not yield him the pleasure of her body. Whereupon Sir Scudamour, the lover of that Lady, presently tooke on him that adventure. But being vnable to performe it by reason of the hard Enchauntments, after long sorrow, in the end met with Britomartis, who succoured him, and reskewed his love.

But by occasion hereof many other adventures are intermedled; but rather as Accidents then intendments: As the love of Britomart, the overthrow of Marinell, the misery of Florimell, the vertuousnes of Belphœbe, the lasciviousness of Hellenora, and many the like.

Thus much, Sir, I have briefly overronne to direct your understanding to the wel-head of the History; that from thence gathering the whole intention of the conceit, ye may as in a handfull gripe al the discourse, which otherwise may happily seeme tedious and confused. So, humbly craving the continuance of your honorable favour towards me, and th' eternall establishment of your happiness, I humbly take leave.[114]

C. S. Lewis says, to some extent reflecting the views of Josephine W. Bennett,[115] that this letter 'gives us, no doubt, the design that was uppermost in Spenser's mind when he wrote the letter. It had not, in its entirety, been in his mind at all stages during the composition of that fragment [the first three books]. It had been in some degree abandoned when he wrote [the *Mutabilitie* cantos].'

It is unwise to quarrel with this point of view. But of course, the letter does tell us more than just that the poem is an allegory. The use of the form 'Ingrayne' (for Geoffrey of Monmouth's *Ingern*) tells us that Spenser had read Malory—if only ultimately to repudiate his Arthur as too Catholic and too medieval for his own Elizabethan, nation-building purposes. Indeed, perhaps the fact that the poem as it existed at his death does not exactly reflect the letter misleads us as to how much the letter does tell us.

It is true that it is conventional inasmuch as it parallels sixteenth-century critical doctrine. The purpose of the poem is said to be 'to fashion [here meaning 'to portray', not 'to train'] a gentleman or noble person in vertuous and gentle discipline'. The first book ought to be the twelfth (he says); but his method is that of a poet, not that of a historiographer. Like Virgil, he 'thrusteth into the middest'. His view of what 'poetry' can do that 'history' cannot accords well with Sidney's in *An Apologie*; neither view is original, since both go back to Plato and Aristotle.

The argument that Spenser's letter to Ralegh represented his plan for the poem only at the time he wrote it (presumably in 1589/90, for publication as a preface to Books I, II and III) is the natural outcome of the modern view that what was originally intended as a narrative romance became transformed into a moral allegory at a comparatively late stage. It is said that the poem is not, as Spenser claimed, 'a continued allegory': allegory is sustained only throughout the first two books, and the poem then degenerates into a series of isolated tales in the next four. This may be so, although not all critics (Professor Kathleen Williams is one) would agree. But Spenser actually admits something like it in the letter, both at the beginning and the end, where he speaks, perhaps nervously, of 'accidents'. It may be more accurate, then, to formulate the view in another way: Spenser did not superimpose a moral intention upon an originally merely romantic one; rather, he came to see that what he may originally have considered to be a romantic narrative amounted to something more than this. The poem occupied many years of his life. There is a difference, if only a subtle one. The letter represents, in my own view, what Spenser had come to see in the first three books of his poem—quite as much as his 'intentions for the rest of it'. And, *pace* some modern critics of Spenser, there are bound to be 'accidents' in even the most super-subtle of schemes.

A less disputable aspect of the letter is Spenser's statement about Queen Elizabeth's role in the poem. Professor Nelson[116] has shown that Spenser's language indicates his familiarity with the legal notion of the sovereign as 'body natural' (the real person, subject to human frailties), and 'body politic', which is free of all error. Thus she is both a 'royall Queene' and a 'beautifull Lady'.

Spenser said here as much as he wanted to say, perhaps could say, about his first three books; he gives us many valuable clues. He does not give us a key—the key to the poem is the poem itself—but nothing in it is actually untrue (unless we take the contradiction between the description of Guyon's quest in the letter and in the poem itself as an indication that Spenser wrote the letter before he had completed the poem); without it we should know less about the poem than we do.

Spenser was an ambitious and disappointed man, who reasonably hoped for much more substantial rewards from his poetry than he ever received. One may suspect that he put up with Ireland with such a good grace in the happy expectation that something much better was to follow. When he published the first three books he must have hoped for rather more than the £50 a year he received. The letter (perhaps Ralegh, wiser in the ways of the Court than he, advised him for his own advantage to write it—Spenser acknowledges that he 'commanded' it) was perhaps more strategic than critical in intention. It is careful to follow Renaissance critical precept, to admit Classical and continental models—rather than medieval, or the partly pseudo-Chaucer to whom, above all other poets, Spenser felt himself to be the natural heir. It aims of course to please the

Queen, to make crystal clear to Her Majesty just how profoundly and importantly she was being complimented; and to displease no one else. But at the same time, behind its admittedly conventional mask, it explains as best it can what Spenser had now come to see this work in progress as representing, if only in abstract terms. And when dealing in abstractions Spenser was not happy or effective, as we may infer from his remarks to Harvey about versification. The unity of *The Faerie Queen* comes not from any system that Spenser may have discerned arising from it as he wrote it—that was a rough and ready thing, necessary to carry the writing itself forward—but from the consistency of the poet's own vision as he applied himself to his narrative materials. The poem is most happily read not in terms of the ideas that can be imagined in (or actually inferred from) it, but in terms of the quality of this vision.

I

Donne was the first English poet whose letters have survived in significant bulk: more than two hundred are extant. This is largely because his son printed a collection of 129 in 1651.[117] The verdict of his most recent biographer, Professor Edward Le Comte, is that they are 'disappointing'. Most, he writes, are 'ornate exercises in etiquette', 'sometimes . . . nothing else'. 'Literary, the letters are not concerned with literature. . . . Rarely does Donne make even a passing allusion to his own literary productions.'[118]

It is true that Donne's letters seldom refer specifically to his poetry—although when they do they are exceptionally interesting—and that they contain few startling biographical revelations. But the extent to which biographers, including Professor Le Comte, rely on them, and quote them, suggests that the best are more necessary to an understanding of Donne than the word 'disappointing' allows. They throw light, however obliquely, on this most difficult of English poets at each of the vital stages of his life. A truer estimate of their worth, therefore, is that of Miss Helen Gardner and Father Timothy Healy: 'Donne's letters are in the old formal style of letter-writing, modelled on the classical epistle, and having something of the quality of an essay. Even so, they tell us much of Donne's mind and are an invaluable commentary on his life and poetry'.[119]

It is risky to take all the sentiments expressed in letters of this period at face value. Letters were artificial in at least the sense that the writer was supposed to be on his best behaviour, to be observing decorum. Correspondents were seldom relaxed, and Donne himself hardly ever. But the evidence provided by his letters on such subjects as his attitude to his 'irregular' youth and, particularly, to the poems he wrote during it, his marriage, and his decision to take orders is always as valuable as that provided by other sources—particularly Walton, whose pious and sometimes inaccurate celebration of the saintly and repentant Dean at the too obvious expense of the young rake represents not so much an exaggeration (because Donne himself made much of his early 'sins') as an over-simplification. Interpreted with care, and with due allowance made for the formal letter-writing practices of the time and for Donne's own materially weak position in the period of his life before he took orders, these letters provide, as Miss Helen Gardner and Father Healy have implied, an indispensable picture of their author, which cannot be found elsewhere.

2

Donne was probably born in the early part of 1572, but certainly between 1571 and 1573. His parents were both Roman Catholics. His father, a wealthy ironmonger who may have had a reputation for sharp practice, died in 1576. His mother, who remarried twice, remained a Roman Catholic throughout her long life. Her father, John Heywood (grand-nephew of Sir Thomas More) the epi-grammatist and playwright, had spent his last years in Flanders on account of his religion. In June 1574 John Heywood's brother, Thomas, a Roman Catholic priest, was executed for saying a mass in a house only two streets from Bread Street, where Donne lived. In 1593 Donne's brother Henry died of fever in Newgate, whither he had been sent for harbouring a priest. He thus early knew of the inconveniences incurred by those who chose to follow the old religion.

Donne studied at Hart Hall, Oxford—notorious at the time as a crypto-Catholic institution—where he made friends with Henry Wotton, poet and future ambassador. He was unable to take his degree because he was unable to subscribe to the Thirty-Nine Articles and to the Oath of Supremacy. He probably went on to Cambridge afterwards for a time, but was of course unable to take a degree there either.[120]

Donne's first extant letter (if it is his), to an unknown recipient, perhaps his friend Christopher Brooke, dates from August 1597. He had accompanied Essex on his successful foray to Cadiz in the previous year, and was again with him on the ill-fated Islands voyage (to the Azores). This letter describes the situation in Plymouth after the fleet, which set out in July, had been driven back by a series of storms. Donne's verse letter, *The Storme*, addressed to Christopher Brooke, was written in the same month. The prose letter attacks the burghers of Plymouth ('quasi ply-mouth') for their meanness ('I think when we came in the burghers tooke us for the Spanish fleet for they have either hid or convayd all there mony'), and ends in a riot of puns: 'In one bad bare word the want is so generall that the lord generall wants, and till this day wee wanted the lord generall'.[121]

No other letter survives from the period of Donne's youth: from when he left Trinity College, Cambridge, until he became Sir Thomas Egerton's secretary in 1598. This is unfortunate, for it was probably during these years that he wrote the *Elegies*, the *Satires*, some of the *Songs and Sonets* and the prose *Paradoxes*. All we know about his activities is that he was at Thavies Inn in 1591, and that he studied law at Lincoln's Inn from 1592 until November 1594; he was fined for not serving as Steward of Christmas at Lincoln's Inn. Probably he travelled on the Continent between 1594 and 1595, financing himself with £750 he had received upon coming of age. Walton says that he went to Italy and Spain, which seems almost certain. His interest in Spanish literature was lifelong. By July 1595 he was acting as tutor to Thomas Danby, a fifteen-year-old boy. According to a satire upon him, itself an imitation of his own style, by Everard Guilpin,[122] who had once been a friend, he became 'a reveller ridiculous', and got through his fortune quickly (£750 was worth, very roughly, £15,000 or $45,000 of our money). Gosse, in his *Life and Letters of John Donne* (1899), deduces from the earliest poems that Donne had an adulterous affair. Little attention need now be paid to the actual details of his absurdly over-literal biographical interpretation, but there is more reason to suppose that Donne did have such an affair (or affairs) than that he did not.

In 1598 he was still doing well: he obtained the post of secretary to the Lord Keeper of the Great Seal, Sir Thomas Egerton, the most distinguished lawyer of his generation, through the good offices of his eldest son, Thomas Egerton, and his stepson Francis Wooley, whom he met on the Azores voyage. The young rebel and author of the *Elegies* and the five *Satyres*, which had probably circulated widely and would certainly have outraged official circles, was becoming more serious about his career; or perhaps it was simply that he had got through his money, as Guilpin implies. At all events, things went auspiciously for him. His employer said, when he regretfully dismissed him, that he was fitter to serve a king than a subject. Then, at the end of 1601, after serving as M.P. for Brackley in the short-lived Parliament of that year, he secretly married Ann More, the eighteen-year-old daughter of another M.P., and a very influential man, Sir George More of Loseley in Surrey. This brought disaster upon him.

Donne and the fifteen-year-old Ann fell in love some time after 1598. Ann was the niece of Egerton's second wife, Elizabeth, and she frequently stayed, sometimes for long periods, in Egerton's official residence, York House in the Strand, where Donne also lived. After her aunt died in 1600 she was for some months the only woman in the house. Walton says that Donne's friends tried to put him off, but in vain. The courtship lasted at least eighteen months, more probably nearly three years. None of the correspondence which must have passed between Losely and York House has survived.

Not many of the other letters that Donne wrote at the time of his courtship are extant. One of autumn 1599, probably to Sir Henry Wotton in Ireland, is exceedingly formal, speaking of its writer as 'one who had rather bee honest than fortunate'.[123] Another, to the same, written during the following year, although equally formal in that it too fashionably renounces the courtier's life of 'vice' and cynically condemns woman, may reflect an anxiety that was much troubling Donne at this time. He writes:

> I am no Courtier, for without having lived there desirously I cannot have sin'd enough to have deserv'd that reprobate name. I may sometimes come thither and bee no courtier as well as they may sometymes go to chapell and yet are no Christians.

The comparison Donne chooses to employ to show how he can attend Court and yet not be 'of it' is revealing. The Court is evil (he uses the word a few lines on: 'I am there now where, because I must do some evill I envy your being in the country . . .') and yet he is there; perhaps he still has unconscious feelings that 'chapel', too, is 'evil'. And the comparison reveals, too, that Donne is perfectly aware that one may go to Rome and do as the Romans do (for one of his temperament, there was never a sensible alternative), and not be of Rome at all.

At some time Donne, we know, must have made up his mind to renounce Catholicism and to take up the Established Religion. It is quite impossible that without assurances to Egerton that he was not still a Roman Catholic he could have become his secretary: the Lord Keeper could not have appointed a known papist. As Donne was known to come from a strict Catholic family, he may even have been called upon for some kind of official renunciation. Walton says that he threw off Romanism at twenty, but Donne himself contradicts him in a passage in *Pseudo-Martyr* (1610), where he is at subtle pains to point out that his conversion was slow, sturdily non-opportunist and thorough.[124] The letter to Wotton of 1600 suggests that Donne may still have felt some guilt and uneasiness about it. Perhaps he still felt impelled to ask himself the question, 'Am I a true Christian?' Basically it confirms the truthfulness of his account (which gives no hints about dates) in *Pseudo-Martyr*.

The last paragraph of the same letter shows that Donne was not less immune than others of his age to the fascinations of the Earl of Essex, or to dissatisfaction with the behaviour of the ageing Queen. He had excellent opportunities to know Essex, who was a prisoner in York House between October 1599 and March 1600. Donne here writes of him that he and his train are no more missed

from Court than 'the Aungells which were cast downe from heaven'.
He shows his profound and subtle understanding of hysterical illness by saying of Essex's illness: 'the worst accidents of his sicknes
are that he conspires with it & that it is not here beleeved'. He
concludes by suggesting, with characteristic, ironic shrewdness, that
Essex 'understood not his age: for it is a naturall weaknes of
innocency'.[125] Grierson and others have suggested that Donne's
strange poetic fragment, *The Progress of the Soule* (dated August
1601, by Donne himself), is an attack on Queen Elizabeth, prompted
by the fate of Essex: the soul of the apple Eve ate, the soul of heresy,
was to end up, it is alleged, in the body of the Queen. There is some
evidence for this view in the poem itself, but Miss Helen Gardner
seems to challenge it in a footnote in her edition of the *Songs and
Sonets*.[126] Certainly the letter to Wotton shows that he was sympathetic towards Essex, but it proves nothing about the intentions
of the poem, which are highly complicated and which themselves
seem to have undergone metamorphosis in the author's mind as he
wrote the first 520 lines of it—all that he did write.

Two letters written some time in the following year to
Wotton are more interesting. The first accompanies a MS. of his
Paradoxes. Twenty-one of these *Paradoxes and Problemes* appeared
in *Juvenilia* (1633), but they were first printed in a complete form,
together with a reprint of *Ignatius his Conclave* and other prose
writings, by Donne's son in 1652. They match, in prose, Donne's
earliest poems: they are deliberately cynical, 'outrageous', superior,
ingenious and witty. They have such titles as *A Defence of Womens
Inconstancy, That Women Ought to Paint, That it is Possible to
Finde Some Vertue in Some Women* and so on. What Donne thought
of these eye-catching prose pieces at the age of twenty-eight, when
he could hardly have wished them to circulate beyond a circle of
intimate friends, is certainly instructive on the subject of what he
thought at this time about his poems of the same period, most
particularly the *Elegies* and *Satyres*, with which he associates them:

> Only in obedience I send you some of my paradoxes: I love
> you and myself and them too well to send them willingly
> for they carry with them a confession of their lightnes, and
> your trouble and my shame. But indeed they were made
> rather to deceave tyme than her daughter truth: although
> they have beene written in an age when any thing is strong
> enough to overthrow her. If they make you to find better
> reasons against them they do their office: for they are but
> swaggerers: quiet enough if you resist them. If perchaunce
> they be pretly guilt, that is their best for they are not
> hatcht: they are rather alarums to truth to arme her than
> enemies: and they have only this advantadg to scape from

being caled ill things that they are nothings. Therefore take
heed of allowing any of them least you make another. Yet
Sir though I know their low price, except I receive by your
next letter an assurance upon the religion of your friendship
that no coppy shalbee taken for any respect of these or any
other my compositions sent to you, I shall sinn against my
conscience if I send you any more. I speake that in playnes
which becomes (methinks) our honestyes; and therfore call
not this a distrustfull but a free spirit: I meane to acquaint
you with all myne: and to my satyrs there belongs some
feare and to some elegies, and these perhaps, shame. Against
both which affections although I be tough enough, yet I
have a ridling disposition to bee ashamed of feare and afrayd
of shame. Therefore I am desirous to hyde them with out
any over reconing of them or their maker. But they are not
worth thus much words in theyre disprayse.[127]

Beneath the polite, clever banter, Donne is seriously and intelli-
gently appraising the *Paradoxes*. He is nervous about the *Elegies*
and *Satyres*, but not prepared to jettison them: they are to be
passed only to friends, but not widely circulated. He is 'desirous
to hyde them', but not to destroy them. He is 'ashamed of feare and
afrayd of shame'.

This letter is as eloquent of Donne's regard (even if it is a
limited regard) for his early poetry as it is of his very understandable
apprehensions about its possible effect on those in high places,
upon whom he now depended for his living. Had he been the simple
opportunist that some have made him out to be (though this is now
a largely discredited view) he need not have bothered with poetry at
all; certainly he would have done all he could to suppress those early
poems, rather than send them out to friends.

The next letter, which may or may not be to Wotton, is
quoted in full. It contains the only known reference Donne made to
a play by Shakespeare:

I am no great voyager in other mens works: no swallower
nor devowrer of volumes nor pursuant of authors. Perchaunce it is because I find borne in my self knowledg or
apprehension enough, (for without forfeiture or impeach-
ment of modesty I think I am bond to God thankfully to
acknowledg it) to consyder him and my self: as when I
have at home a convenient garden I covet not to walk in
others broad medows or woods, especially because it falls
not within that short reach which my foresight embraceth,
to see how I should employ that which I already know; to
travayle for inquiry of more were to labor to gett a stomach
and then find no meat at home. To know how to live by

the booke is a pedantery, and to do it is a bondage. For
both hearers and players are more delighted with voluntary
than with sett musike. And he that will live by precept
shalbe long without the habite of honesty: as he that would
every day gather one or two feathers might become brawne
with hard lying before he make a feather bed of his gettings.
That Erle of Arundell that last dyed (that tennis ball whome
fortune after tossing and banding brikwald into the hazard)
in his imprisonment used more than much reading, and to
him that asked him why he did so he answered he read so
much lest he should remember something. I am as far from
following his counsell as hee was from Petruccios: but I
find it true that after long reading I can only tell you how
many leaves I have read.[128] I do therfore more willingly
blow and keep awake that smale coale which God hath
pleased to kindle in mee than farr off to gather a faggott of
greene sticks which consume without flame or heat in a
black smoother: yet I read something. But indeed not so
much to avoyd as to enjoy idlenes. Even when I begun to
write these I flung away Dant the Italian, a man pert
enough to bee beloved and too much to bee beeleeved:[129]
it angred me that Celestine a pope [so] far from the manners
of other popes, that he left even their seat, should be the
court of Dants witt bee attached and by him throwne into
his purgatory. And it angred me as much, that in the life of
a pope he should spy no greater fault, than that in the
affectation of a cowardly securyty he slipt from the great
burthen layd upon him. Alas! what would Dant have him
do? Thus wee find the story related: he that thought himself next in succession, by a trunke thorough a wall whispered
in Celestines eare counsell to remove the papacy: why
should not Dant be content to thinke that Celestine tooke
this for as imediate a salutacion and discourse of the holy
ghost as Abrahim did the commandment of killing his
sonn? If he will needs punish retyrednes thus, what hell
can his witt devise for ambition?[130] And if white integryty
merit this, what shall *Male* or *Malum* which Seneca con-
dems most, deserve? But as the chancellor Hatton being
told after a decree made, that his predecessor was of another
opinion, he answered hee had his genius and I had myne:
So say I of authors that they thinke and I thinke both
reasonably yet posibly both erroniously; that is manly: for
I am so far from perswading yea conselling you to beleeve
others that I care not that you beleeve not mee when I say
that others are not to bee beleeved: only beleeve that I love
you and I have enough.

I have studied philosophy, therefore marvayle not if I make such accompt of arguments *que trabuntur ab effectibus*. [131] [132]

This is a curious letter, for it was undoubtedly at about this time that Donne began to read in depth. As Miss Helen Gardner has pointed out, the author of *The Progresse of the Soule* must already have been reading more curious works than the Latin verse, mostly by Ovid, Horace and Martial, that is the main influence on the *Satyres* and the *Elegies*. Yet here he says he reads to enjoy rather than to avoid idleness, and launches a general attack on the idea of living by precept. One should not, perhaps, try to make more of it than that however widely poets may read, they still value their independence and originality; and that self-conscious poets (and who was more self-conscious than Donne?) are articulate on this point. The opening phrase echoes the *Epistle* to the reader preceding *The Progresse of the Soule*: 'I have no purpose to come into any mans debt'. Donne is here speaking as a writer (he can mean nothing but this by 'that small coale which God has pleased to kindle in mee'), and his conviction is surely plain: literature should be based at least as much on personal experience as on reading. He does, as he points out, read; but not in order to get copy. This does not mean that he was not influenced by other writers (we know that he was), or that he did not read (we know that he did, and especially so in the first decade of the century); it does suggest that he regarded experience as primary so far as his own poetry was concerned. But this, of course, does not mean that all his poems are exact autobiographical records, as Gosse thought; it means no more than that he had experienced what he wrote about. We always need to bear in mind when reading him that, as Eliot pointed out, thought was for him experience.

The section about Celestine is tortuous and difficult, beginning with a typically ingenious punning remark about Dante, who had evidently irritated him—although Donne was to be indebted to him when he wrote *Ignatius his Conclave*. Once again Donne's uneasiness about his abandonment of Roman Catholicism, which he is nervously unable to suppress, crops up. There is a cheap and casuistic gibe at the Papacy; but, more significantly, an attack on Dante for his intolerant placing of Celestine in Purgatory (in fact Dante placed him very near to the entrance to hell),[133] and a plea for tolerance itself. His mind seems to move quickly from the matter of Roman Catholicism to the matter of tolerance, to relieve the pressure upon his emotions from both directions. The passage is yet another example of the astonishingly 'modern' temper of his thinking: 'let them think one way and I another,' he seems to say— 'and we may both be wrong.'

3

The results of Donne's secret marriage soon gave him plenty to think about. It used to be suggested that he made this marriage in order to get hold of a fortune (Sir George More was rich) and to tie himself more securely to the Egerton family. But nothing could have prejudiced his career more than the action he took, and he was clearly aware of the dangers. In secretly marrying Ann More he broke both civil and canon law; he must, too, have been aware of the irascible personality and irremediable stupidity of his father-in-law. He had been avidly pursuing his career, seeing to it that no copies were made of writings that might have told against him (although sending them to those he felt might appreciate them). It is evident from his letters that he did not equate official success with unofficial, poetic merit, or policy with honesty. He loved Ann, and defied everything to unite himself with her. He may have hoped, against hope, to reap advantage from his action; but the letter he sent to his father-in-law through the 'Wizard Earl', Henry Percy, ninth Earl of Northumberland, makes it clear enough that he knew exactly what kind of position he had got himself into. Percy, as Gosse observed, was the kind of man who might well have attracted Donne: a friend of Essex, he was an alleged crypto-Catholic who loved intrigue for its own sake. He was to pay the price for his predilections by spending fifteen years in the Tower on a (mis-founded) charge of being involved in the Gunpowder Plot. One can see in Donne's choice of him as go-between, as in his fascination with Essex, the subversive side of his nature; he would have been better advised to have chosen a duller man. One can imagine the pleasure Percy took from this melodramatic situation, and from his own officiously correct part in it.

Donne married Ann More on about 5 December 1601, but did not write to her father until 2 February 1602. The parliament of which both he and his father-in-law were members did not break up until 19 December, when Ann (presumably) went back to Losely. This must have been a tense fortnight for Donne: surreptitious visits to his wife's bedroom in York House at night, and meetings by day with Sir George, perhaps at the House of Commons and certainly at York House itself. It was the kind of atmosphere upon which the poet in Donne thrived; he had written about it, almost prophetically, in *The Perfume*:

> Once, and but once found in thy company,
> All thy suppos'd escapes are laid on mee;
> And as a thiefe at barre, is question'd there
> By all the men, that have beene rob'd that yeare,
> So am I, (by this traiterous meanes surpriz'd)
> By thy Hydroptique[134] father catechiz'd.

Walton says that Sir George had 'some intimation' of the relationship.

> If *The Undertaking*, which begins
> I have done one braver[135] thing
> Then all the *Worthies* did,
> Yet a braver thence doth spring,
> Which is, to keepe that hid. . . .

a poem whose theme is self-consciously Neoplatonic—love being seen as an esoteric mystery to be hidden from the eyes of the vulgar —dates from this time, or arises from his experiences of it, it possesses an unexpectedly and perhaps characteristically ironic note in the light of his circumstances: the Platonic ideal is triumphantly contrasted with the tensions produced by the act of keeping love 'hid'.

Donne's first letter to Sir George, when it came, was obsequious and fawning. Having made the necessary rebellious gesture, he was no more willing to suffer for it—reasonably, we may feel—than he had been for his family's religion. He did his best to exculpate his friends the Brooke brothers (vainly in the event, since both went to prison for a time) for their part in the affair—Christopher had given the bride away and Samuel had performed the ceremony— and for the rest, attempts to appease Sir George's wrath in as conventional a manner as possible: 'I know this letter shall find you full of passion. . . . I humbly beseeche you so to deal . . . as the persuasions of Nature, Reason, Wisdome, and Christianity shall inform you. . . .'[136] However, Sir George being a man of influence, he soon found himself in the Fleet prison, and dismissed—if unwillingly—from his position.

His next letter, written from the Fleet (from which he was released within a few days to confinement in his own chambers, probably owing to Egerton's efforts) on 11 February is in the same tone.[137] His subsequent letter of 13 February 1601/2 to Sir George, written just after his release, is biographically important for a number of reasons:

> From you, to whom next to God I shall owe my health, by enjoying by your mediation this mild change of imprisonment, I desire to derive all my good fortune and content in this world; and therefore, with my most unfeigned thanks, present to you my humble petition that you would be pleased to hope that, as that fault which was laid to me of having deceived some gentlewomen before, and that of loving a corrupt religion, are vanished and smoked away (as I assure myself, out of their weakness they are), and that as the devil in the article of our death takes the advantage of our weakness and fear, to aggravate our sins to our conscience, so

some uncharitable malice hath presented my debts double
at least.

How many of the imputations laid upon me would
fall off, if I might shake and purge myself in your presence!
But if that were done, of this offence committed to you I
cannot acquit myself, of which yet I hope that God (to
whom for that I heartily direct many prayers) will inform
you to make that use, that as of evil manners good laws
grow, so out of disobedience and boldness you will take
occasion to show mercy and tenderness. And when it shall
please God to soften your heart so much towards us as to
pardon us, I beseech you also to undertake that charitable
office of being my mediator to my Lord, wh m as upon
your just complaint you found full of justice, I doubt not
but you shall also find full of mercy, for so is the Almighty
pattern of Justice and Mercy equally full of both.

My conscience, and such affection as in my conscience becomes an honest man, emboldeneth me to make
one request more, which is, that by some kind and comfortable message you would be pleased to give some ease of
the afflictions which I know your daughter in her mind
suffers, and that (if it be not against your other purposes) I
may with your leave write to her, for without your leave I
will never attempt anything concerning her. God so have
mercy upon me, as I am unchangeably resolved to bend all
my courses to make me fit for her, which if God and my
Lord and you be pleased to strengthen, I hope neither my
debts which I can easily order, nor anything else shall interrupt. Almighty God keep you in His favour, and restore me
to His and yours.[138]

While we can be quite sure that Donne's real feelings towards his
father-in-law were more in tune with those he had displayed towards
his imaginary (or real) mistress's father in *The Perfume*, this letter
shows he intended to keep that side of his nature well in check. He
needed to do so if only for his wife's sake. He makes an unequivocal
avowal of Protestantism, and cannot deny that he has been sexually
promiscuous. It is surely significant that the poet who had previously
so wittily cursed women for their inconstancy should now be begging
pardon for having deceived them: it suggests that the attacks on
women in the earlier *Songs and Sonets* have an ironic sub-function
as guilty rationalizations of his own infidelities.

But in spite of his obsequious and perhaps almost unavoid-
able insincerity in this impossible position, his humanity asserts
itself: he asks to be allowed to communicate with his wife. By playing
on the sympathy of the Countess of Derby, Sir Thomas Egerton's

new wife, and her daughters, and never ceasing to apply pressure on Sir George by letters and personal entreaties, Donne gradually weathered the storm. Sir George even tried to get Egerton to re-appoint him as secretary, which of course could not be done without too much loss of official face. His spirits rose, however, and he felt able to write in a jaunty vein to his friend Henry Goodyer (one of his favourite correspondents, a courtier and eventually the pro-prietor of a great Warwickshire estate, Polesworth) on 23 February, maintaining that officialdom, by imprisoning him and the Brookes, had 'implicitly justified' the marriage.[139] His optimism was justified: on April 27 the Commissioners of Canterbury pronounced the marriage valid, and Ann was allowed to join him. Sir George relented —but only to the point of not withholding his approval. He did withhold cash, and was no doubt delighted to have the excuse to do so.

From 1602 until 1605 Donne and his wife lived by the charity of Sir Francis Wooley (stepson of Egerton by his second marriage) on his estate at Pyrford on the River Wey in Surrey. Two children were born there, and Donne must have written many of the *Songs and Sonets* there. From now until his ordination in 1615 Donne was materially at his lowest level—poor, and refused advance-ment of any sort; but perhaps spiritually at his highest—defiantly in love, and married to the woman he loved.

Few letters survive from this period. A suspiciously formal one to Sir George More is mostly on the subject of letters: 'No other kind of conveyance is better for knowledge, or love'; 'The Evangels and Acts teach us what to believe, but the Epistles of the Apostles what to do'. Evidently he had sent him a MS. of the *Paradoxes and Problemes*, for he asks him not to pass them on, at least not until he has 'reviewed' them, and to let him know who has copies. . . .[140] Here he perhaps displayed a weakness and over-confidence common to most writers, if only intermittently: he would like to be appreciated by those incapable of understanding him.

4

Donne is supposed to have suffered from melancholy while at Pyrford. There are letters addressed to him (probably from Christo-pher Brooke) complaining that he does not come up to London often enough, and urging him to cheer up. In these Sir George More is referred to in a derogatory way, as if to show that Donne spoke to his personal friends about his father-in-law in a rather different and more contemptuous manner than he used in his letters to him. Possibly Donne put two faces towards the world: a cheerful one towards his wife, a melancholy one towards his friends. Certainly his natural ambitions were frustrated, but he was no stranger to the fashionable affection of melancholy, as the newly discovered and widely reproduced Lothian portrait confirms. Thus, he casually signs a letter to Goodyer, written to condole with him on the loss of his wife, *'your honest unprofitable friend'*.[141] But it is unlikely that only melancholy kept him out of London: he was content to be with his wife. The happiness of his private life would not have prevented his complaining to his friends about his situation, which was still fraught with anxiety. The period of his most serious, wholly unaffected, melancholy seems to date from about 1606.

In 1605 Donne and his wife moved to Camberwell, to the house of Sir Thomas Grymes, where a son was born. In February 1605 he received permission to go abroad. If he took advantage of this, he was back by 1606, because in that year he and Ann moved into their own house, in Mitcham. Donne now rented an apartment for his own use in the Strand, and apparently spent about half his time there.

He was now employed. At Pyrford he had spent much of his time studying Civil and Canon Laws; the knowledge he had acquired, together with the fact that he was himself an ex-Catholic, gave him excellent qualifications to act as research-assistant (as Professor Le Comte aptly calls it) to Thomas Morton. Morton, a parson who later became Bishop of Durham (he died, 'with perfect intellectuals and a cheerful heart', in 1659 at the age of ninety-five), had been chosen by James I to direct a propaganda campaign that had the admirable aim of demolishing Roman Catholicism by argument. Morton was respected as a theological opponent even by the Jesuits. He in turn could hardly have chosen a fitter assistant than Donne, for although James I's attitude towards the Catholics inevitably became tougher after Gunpowder Plot, his original intention, and Morton's job, was to convert people to Anglicanism by essentially peaceful means—and Donne was, above all, a tolerant man. In his religious controversy he always preferred a reasonable tone. 'I do (I thank God) naturally and heartily abhor all schism in religion . . .' he wrote to Goodyer from Paris on 9 April 1612;[142] and to Sir Tobie Matthew from Cologne in September 1619,

> . . . forms of Religion destroy not moralitie, nor civil offices. . . . I have been sometimes glad to hear, that some of my friends have differed from me in Religion. It is some degree of an union to be united in a serious meditation of God, and to make any Religion the rule of our actions. . . .'[143]

His task apart, Donne's main and real interest in the problem of Roman Catholicism was psychological: *Pseudo-Martyr* (published in 1610) was as psychological—rather than theological—an attack on the Catholic martyrs as a mere exercise in controversy could be.[144] But there can be little doubt that Donne approved of the peaceful objects of the work he was engaged upon—which involved helping (perhaps ghosting for) Morton in the productions of such works as the Latin *Apologia Catholica*. He drew on the knowledge he acquired during these years when he came to write *Pseudo-Martyr* and the satirical *Ignatius his Conclave* (1611).

When Morton became Dean of Gloucester in June 1607 Donne was once again out of a job. According to Walton, Morton tried to persuade him to enter the Church, but Donne refused. Walton suggests that his reasons were over-modesty and fear of being unworthy; but his reluctance was more complexly motivated: there was the emotional factor of his Roman Catholic heritage (to write against Rome is not quite the same thing as actually to become an Anglican priest), and there were his hopes of secular preferment. In autumn 1608 he applied for a post in Ireland, and in the following spring for an appointment in Virginia. He obtained neither. Before that, just at the time Walton tells us that Morton was trying to make a priest of him, he was writing to Goodyer from his lodgings in the Strand, on 13 June 1607, asking him to use his good offices to obtain him a post in the Queen's household.[145] He suffered greatly from frustration, as Swift was to do after him, at his consistent failure to obtain the kind of secular preferment which his abilities deserved. Only when he finally entered the Church did he effectively sublimate his bitterness.

During 1608/9 Donne wrote his treatise in defence of suicide, *Biathanatos*,[146] one of his strangest works, which he did not publish; from this time on he seems to have been writing when he was not studying or travelling. There is no need to doubt Walton's assertion that during these years before his ordination he was on intimate terms with the nobility, and that the King himself enjoyed his company, especially at mealtimes. It would be interesting to know what Donne really thought of that occasionally well-intentioned, but always ridiculous, ignoble and ineffective monarch; for it seems to have been he, above all others, who forced Donne into the Church by deliberately refusing him secular preferment.

5

The years spent in the house at Mitcham, when Ann was producing children at the rate of roughly one a year, were the most depressed and depressing of his life; things did not really improve until he became the tenant of the Drurys in Drury Lane in 1610. It is certainly one of the most psychologically interesting and revealing periods of his life, and a number of letters survive from it, many of them to Goodyer. One of the earliest of these may refer to the birth of Francis Donne, who was born on 8 January 1607, and died in infancy. It describes

> the saddest lucubration and nights passage that ever I had. For it exercised those hours, which, with extreme danger of her, whom I should hardly have abstained from recompensing for her company in this world, with accompanying her out of it; encreased my poor family with a son,'[147]

Is the mood of dejection expressed in this and other letters he wrote to Goodyer at this time a fashionable 'mask'? Were his 'crises' always 'intellectual ones', as Gosse asserts?

On the contrary, it seems that he was now gripped by a morbid melancholy—a melancholy that led him to write a whole treatise on suicide. . . . But surely J. B. Leishman, in disagreeing with Gosse, over-simplifies when he writes, 'He loved his wife, but he could not conceal from himself the fact that she had undone him, and that he, perhaps had undone her'.[148] He was as likely to feel guilt about his wife's poor health as any other sensitive man; but for Donne to feel that the burdens and responsibilities of his marriage were heavy was not necessarily the same thing as to regard his wife as having, herself, 'undone' him (the reference is of course to Walton's report that a now lost letter to Ann from Donne just after his dismissal by Egerton concluded 'John Donne, Anne Donne, Un-done'). There seems to be no evidence of any bitterness directed personally at Ann.

His morbid state may more credibly be attributed to an acute anxiety about his position, partly financial and partly ambitious, reinforced by a less materialistic form of anxiety: the propriety of taking up, as a sceptic, a 'position', particularly the position of a priest in a Church with whose point of view he sympathized but perhaps did not, at this time, wholeheartedly share. There was always in his mind the regret that history is cruel to truth; that, above all, is what his later remark about being glad that some of his friends had differed from him in religion implies:[148] he knew that different temperaments have different ways of approach to the same truths, and that in so knowing he was out of temper with the official practices of his time. In another letter to Goodyer, which most probably alludes to *Biathanatos* (of which he was, he says, having copies made), he says:

> Since my imprisonment in my bed,[149] I have made a meditation in verse, which I call a Litany;[150] the word you know imports no other than supplication, but all Churches have one forme of supplication, by that name. . . . That by which it will deserve best acceptation, is, That neither the

Roman Church need call it defective . . . nor the Reformed
can discreetly accuse it. . . .[151]

The tone here is suggestive on the matter of why Donne could not
bring himself to enter the Church at this time.

A man who possesses as much psychological insight into
himself as Donne is likely to suffer, especially when his own security
seems to be threatened. People, as Max Eastman once said in conversation to Freud, tend to stop thinking when their thoughts might
lead them to conclusions that they cannot face. Donne had not
stopped thinking, was incapable of doing so; but he did not find the
opposition between the desires of his free, unattached, enquiring
mind and the harsh facts of his life, for the betterment of which he
was required to commit himself, any easier to face. Doubtless he
blamed his own passion for truth as much, and in as ironic a spirit,
as his marriage (surely a product of his capacity to love, rather than
an 'ambitious' step) for the poverty and uncertainty of his circumstances.

Writing poetry was a means, if not a materially helpful one,
of resolving this tension. Towards the end of the letter to Goodyer
quoted above there is a tantalizing reference to his poetry—
tantalizing because there is a blank space, in the 1651 text, at just
the point where Donne may have been about to name, or in some
way identify, a poem he has sent to Goodyer. The *lacuna* is followed
by these words:

> . . . opinion of the song, not that I make such trifles for
> praise; but because as long as you speak comparatively of
> it with mine own, and not absolutely, so long am I of your
> opinion even at this time; when I humbly thank God, I
> ask & have, his comfort of sadder meditations; I doe not
> condemn in my self, that I have given my wit such evapora-
> tions, as those, if they be free from prophaneness, or obscene
> provocations.

The letters he wrote to Goodyer at this period are on the whole
more interesting than the ones to Magdalen Herbert (mother of Sir
Edward Herbert—later Lord Herbert of Cherbury—and George
Herbert), who became one of his most powerful patronesses in 1607.
The latter are very much of their time, full of niceties about what is
flattery and what is not, of condemnations of 'vanity and vice', and
of gallantries which, while extravagant and witty, tell us little about
the writer. They are chiefly valuable as a guide to the framework
in which the much subtler poems to her were written.

A letter to Goodyer dated 15 August 1607 is what Gosse
aptly calls 'a sort of essay in epistolary friendship'. Although it
reads stiltedly, it is more direct than the letters to Magdalen Herbert;

Donne must have regarded supplicatory letters, or letters to patrons and patronesses, as falling into altogether a different category. 'Letters,' he tells Goodyer, 'have truly the same office as oaths.' Oaths 'amongst light and empty men' are mere interjections, but with 'the weightier they are sad attestations'. He goes on to protest sincerity and deprecates his worth as a correspondent, but in a more formal manner.[152] In another letter, written at about the same time, he calls friendship his 'second religion', and sends 'another ragge of verses' with it (those *To Sir Henry Goodyere* beginning 'Who makes the Past' in *Letters to Severall Personages*),[153] which are a good example of how charmingly and convincingly Donne could moralize without the least trace of offensiveness or smugness.

Letter-writing occupied much of Donne's attention during these years. He seems to have written to Goodyer every Tuesday, and began a letter of 9 October 1607 to Sir Thomas Lucy:

> I make account that the writing of letters, when it is with any seriousness, is a kind of ecstasy, and a departure and secession and suspension of the soul, which doth then communicate itself to two bodies: and as I would every day provide for my soul's last convoy, though I know not when I shall die, and perchance I shall never die; so for these ectasies in letters, I oftentimes deliver my self over in writing when I know not when those letters shall be sent to you, and many times they never are, for I have a little satisfaction in seeing a letter written to you upon my table, though I meet no opportunity of sending it.[154]

This is characteristically formal; but it also shows what letter-writing meant to Donne.

The long spell of dejection that produced *Biathanatos* is, in fact, strongly evident in the letters Donne wrote during 1608:

> . . . we ask you how you do, and tell how we are, which I cannot of myself. If I knew that I were ill, I were well. . . .
>
> But, in the diseases of the mind there is no criterion, no canon, no rule, for our own taste and apprehension and interpretation should be the judge, and that is the disease itself. Therefore sometimes when I find myself transported with jollity and love of company, I hang leads at my heels, and reduce to my thoughts my fortunes, my years, the duties of a man, of a friend, of a husband, of a father, and all the incumbencies of a family; when sadness dejects me, either I countermine it with another sadness, of I kindle squibs about me again, and fly into sportsfulness and company: and I find ever after all, that I am like an exorcist, which had long laboured about one, which at last appears to have the mother,[155] that I still mistake my disease.[156]

The pleasantnesse of the season displeases me. Every
thing refreshes, and I wither, and I grow older and not
better, my strength diminishes, and my load growes, and
being to passe more and more stormes, I finde that I have
not only cast out my ballast which nature and time gives,
Reason and discretion, and so am as empty and light as
Vanity can make me; but I have over fraught my self with
Vice, and so am ridd[l]ingly subject to two contrary wrackes,
Sinking and Oversetting, and under the iniquity of such a
disease as inforces the patient when he is almost starved,
not only to fast, but to purge. . . .

In this same letter he goes on to relate his own mental sickness, in
the most revealing way, to the notion of corruption of the body:

. . . Certainly as the earth and water, one sad, one fluid,
make but one bodie: so to aire and vanity, there is but one
Centrum morbi. And that which later Physicians say of our
bodies, is fitter for our mindes: for that which they call
Destruction, which is a corruption and want of those funda-
mentall parts whereof we consist, is Vice: and that *Collectio
stercorum*, which is but the excrement of that corruption, is
our Vanity and indiscretion: both these have but one root
in me, and must be pulled out at once, or never.[157]

Here we have a morbid and yet singularly self-penetrating introspection, feeding itself upon intellectual speculations about bodily
corruption. The physiological aspect of death, considered in minute
detail, was a subject that Donne returned to again and again throughout his life, especially in his Sermons. A man of exquisite sensibility
and compulsive self-consciousness, he was unable to avoid this kind
of speculation. As a preacher he was able to avoid some of the self-
torment that it involved, by harnessing it to a purpose; in his thirties
he could not commit himself to any purpose.

6

What was the nature of his sickness—for sickness it was, by his own
admission—during the years at Mitcham? By one of those astonishing
intuitive leaps so anticipatory of the scientific thought of the future,
Donne was able to refer to his own condition as hysterical. He even
compares himself to an hysteric ('to have the mother'). On the face
of it the reference can only be to what was and often still is vulgarly
understood as 'the hysterics'; but the context of the letter itself
(and of other letters written from Mitcham) makes it clear that
Donne was thinking of something much more akin to modern

psychiatric definitions of hysteria—particularly anxiety-hysteria. It would not be helpful or even relevant to attempt to prove that Donne, whom we cannot really know in the sense that we should need to know him to diagnose him (if we were psychiatrists as well as literary critics, an unhappily rare combination), was an 'anxiety-hysteric'. It is, however, important to recognize his extraordinarily 'modern' insights into his own condition.

Donne's obsession with death was intimately connected with sexual guilt. Attitudes to death, experience of sex (a word that Donne was the first to use in its modern sense) in its erotic aspect, and experience of love are intimately connected, and nowhere more explicitly so than in Donne's own poetry. In Donne's surviving letters he is not explicit (and it is unlikely that he was so in any of his letters) about the exact nature of his feelings for his wife. We know that she bore him an almost endless stream of children (and that he was opposed to birth-control in any form[158]), and we know that he was made unhappy by her sufferings as well as his own. But he did not always confine himself to self-pity, or shut himself away from his household. In a letter of 1608, headed in the 1651 *Letters A V Merced* ('to Your Honour'), certainly to Goodyer, he wrote:

> I write not to you out of my poor Library, where to cast mine eye upon good Authors kindles or refreshes sometimes meditations not unfit to communicate to near friends; nor from the high way, where I am contracted, and inverted into my self; which are my two ordinary forges of Letters to you. But I write from the fire side in my Parler, and in the noise of three gamesome children; and by the side of her, whom because I have transplanted into a wretched fortune, I must labour to disguise that from her by all such honest devices, as giving her my company, and discourse, therefore I steal from her, all the time which I give this Letter. . . .

Within a few words he goes on:

> As I have much quenched my senses, and disused my body from pleasure, and so tried how I can indure to be mine owne grave, so I try now how I can suffer a prison. And since it is to build but one wall more about our soul, she is still in her own center, how many circumferences soever fortune or our own perverseness cast about her. I would I could as well intreat her to go out, as she knows whither to go. But if I melt into a melancholy whilest I write, I shall be taken in the manner: and I sit by one too tender towards these impressions, and it is so much our duty, to

avoid all occasions of giving them sad apprehensions, as
S. Hierome accuses *Adam* of no other fault in eating the
Apple, but that he did it *Ne contristaretur delicias suas.* . . .[159]

It is clear that this apparently abrupt transition from talk of his wife
to more abstractly metaphysical talk of the soul is not a transition
from one subject to another at all; he reveals this by coming back
to the subject of his wife, and in one breath. The letter gives us a
particularly invaluable picture of Donne, the author of so many
poems about love, and about the object of his love being his very
soul, sitting in his 'parler' with the woman to whom so many of
his poems must primarily refer. It shows us that, widely and deeply
read as he was, his poems are not abstract and merely intellectual
exercises, as has sometimes been claimed. True, they transcend
their occasion, and body it forth in a subtle, exotic and sometimes
obscure way—but they undoubtedly arise from it. It gives us a clue
to the too-often neglected psychological subject-matter of the poems,
which have suffered from a deluge of ideological, even theological
interpretation that has sometimes obscured their human content and
therefore the quality of feeling that they convey. They are profound
comments upon the nature of, possibilities inherent in, and frustrations
of sexual love.

In a letter of September 1608, to Goodyer, Donne has spoken
of 'Monkes' who were 'excusable in their retirings' because they had
consumed none of the world's 'sweetness, nor begot others to burden
her'. He goes on:

> But for me, if I were able to husband all my time so thriftily,
> as not onely not to wound my soul in any minute by actuall
> sinne, but not to rob and cousen her by giving any part to
> pleasure or businesse, but bestow it all upon her in medita-
> tion, yet even in that I should wound her more, and contract
> guiltinesse: As the Eagle were very unnaturall if because she
> is able to do it, she should pearch a whole day upon a tree,
> staring in contemplation of the majestie and glory of the
> Sun, and let her young Eglets starve in the next. Two of
> the most precious things which God hath afforded us here,
> for the agony and exercise of our sense and spirit, which
> are a thirst and inhiation after the next life, and a frequency
> of prayer and meditation in this, are often envenomed, and
> putrefied, and stray into a corrupt disease: for as God doth
> thus occasion, and positively concurre to evill, that when a
> man is purposed to do a great sin, God infuses some good
> thoughts which make him choose a lesse sin, or leave out
> some circumstance which aggravated that; so the devill
> doth not only suffer but provoke us to some things naturally
> good, upon condition that we shall omit some other more

necessary and more obligatory. And this is his greatest subtilty; because herein we have the deceitfull comfort of having done well, and can very hardly spie our errour because it is but an insensible omission, and no accusing act. With the first of these I have often suspected my self to be overtaken; which is, with a desire of the next life: which though I know it is not meerly out of a wearinesse of this, because I had the same desires when I went with the tyde, and enjoyed fairer hopes than now: yet I doubt worldly encombrances have encreased it. I would not that death should take me asleep. I would not have him meerly seise me, and onely declare me to be dead, but win me, and overcome me. When I must shipwrack, I would do it in a Sea, where mine impotencie might have some excuse; not in a sullen weedy lake, where I could not have so much as exercise for my swimming. Therefore I would fain do something; but that I cannot tell what, is no wonder. For to chuse, is to do: but to be no part of any body, is to be nothing. At most, the greatest persons, are but great wens, and excrescences; men of wit and delightful conversation, but as moales for ornament, except they be so incorporated into the body of the world, that they contribute something to the sustentation of the whole. This I made account that I begun early, when I understood the study of our laws: but was diverted by the worst voluptuousness, which is an Hydroptique immoderate desire of humane learning and languages beautifull ornaments to great fortunes; but mine needed an occupation, and a course which I thought I entrred well into, when I submitted my self to such a service, as I thought might imploy those poor advantages, which I had. And there I stumbled too, yet I would try again: for to this hour I am nothing, or so little, that I am scarce subject and argument good enough for one of mine own letters: yet I fear, that doth not ever proceed from a good root, that I am so well content to be lesse, that is dead. . . . [160]

The two preceding letters from which I have quoted suggest that Donne's difficulties at this time arose not only from philosophical and theological considerations, but also from emotional and domestic ones. The former arose from the latter, rather than vice versa. He does not for the time being regard himself as going 'with the tide' at all. Nor is it at all likely that what he calls his 'voluptuousness', his 'disuse' of his body 'from pleasure', is a reference to his early days. He seems to feel guilt because he cannot restrain himself from sexual activity, and thus burdens his wife and the world. This complex brooding could be called neurotic; but Donne was continually searching to find the right intellectual answer, to do the right emotional thing. For him the two things had to come together. His sexual compulsions fascinated but finally repelled him. Semen he later called an 'excremental jelly'; it is obvious from this and from other writings that he was tormented by the masturbatory, self-satisfying, purely relief-giving aspects of his sexual contact with his wife.

This is not to make an understanding of his poems conditional upon his biography; it is, however, to increase our awareness of a theme in his poetry that has not had the attention it merits. The interpretation that I now offer of certain aspects of his poems is based on a study of their text, as any valid interpretation must be; but since it is contentious, I support it by reference to certain letters, from some of which I have already quoted.

7

Few of the poems in the collection known as *Songs and Sonets* can be dated with anything approaching certainty. The fullest discussion of the problems is to be found in Miss Helen Gardner's edition, in which she divides the poems into groups. The three poems I propose to discuss are all included by Miss Gardner in her second group, which she argues were written after 1600: *Twicknam Garden, The Ecstasie* and, especially, *Love's Alchemie*. None of these particular poems can be dated with certainty, although the general consensus is that they were written between 1605 and 1613.

Grierson connected certain of Donne's poems (including *The Relique* and *The Funerall*) with Mrs. Herbert, and others (including *Twicknam Garden*) with Lady Bedford. Whether he was right or wrong is irrelevant to an interpretation of their meanings. Donne certainly wrote poems 'for his lady patrons', and he probably politely exchanged poems with Lady Bedford. But it is presumptuous, without any evidence, to suppose that he was involved with them in any sexual sense. All the evidence we have outside the poetry—references in letters and a regular stream of children—suggests that Donne's sexual activity was restricted to his wife; there is nothing to suggest that he was in love with anyone else. The content of the poems I have mentioned relates rather to Donne's sexual situation in regard to one woman—his wife—than to his intellectual speculations or to his polite flirtations with married patronesses. Their meaning for us is not affected by this; but it is important that they should not be made to seem either literary exercises or clever variations on Petrarchan or other themes. They are impelled by deep feeling. That they may, formally, be addressed to Mrs. Herbert or Lady Bedford and even contain references to them or to their environments, does not mean that they are 'about' those ladies: the situations of their ostensible recipients acted as 'objective correlatives'. Both Lady Bedford and Mrs. Herbert were intellectuals, perfectly capable of understanding difficult poems; Ann Donne, almost certainly, was not. Again, this does not mean that Donne was not writing out of his experience of marriage. These are not love poems in the sense that some of the earlier *Songs and Sonets* are—such poems as *The Canonization*, probably written in early marriage. Their tone is different: more tortured, dense, mature, reflective, serious—and while they contain flashes of the earlier cleverness, wit and disdain, they are generally less reckless, affectedly cynical and expostulatory.

I hope to show, for example, that J. B. Leishmann's view of *Love's Alchemie*,[161] the most ostensibly cynical poem of the group, as 'deliberately outrageous', does not go far enough. Leishmann in his stimulating and useful book, *The Monarch of Wit*, is in general (as his title suggests) attempting to prove that Donne was more 'clever', if magnificently so, than serious. *Love's Alchemy* strikes me as being, on the contrary, both clever (Donne's inability not to be has blinded many critics to his seriousness) and serious. Miss Gardner is more cautious than Leishmann, but, like other commentators, accepts the conclusion of the poem as being uncompromisingly 'insulting' to women.[162] In her commentary she quotes a passage from a letter of 14 March 1608 to Goodyer: 'The later Physitians say, that when our naturall inborn preservative is corrupted or wasted, and must be restored by a like extracted from other bodies; the chief care is that the Mummy have in it no excelling quality, but an equally digested temper'. (The theory was that dead bodies, preserved in bitumen, acted as a restorative.) But this sentence is immediately preceded by a disquisition on virtue, which Miss Gardner does not quote:

> He is not virtuous, out of whose actions you can pick an excellent one. Vice and her fruits may be seen, because they are thick bodies, but not virtue, which is all light; and vices have swellings and fits, and noise, because being extremes, they dwell far asunder, and they maintain both a foreign war against virtue, and a civil against one another, and affect sovereignty, as virtue doth society.[163]

There is an interesting partial parallel to this in a verse-letter to Rowland Woodward:

> There is no Vertue, but Religion:
> Wise, valiant, sober, just, are names, which none
> Want, which want not Vice-covering discretion.

Seeke we then our selves in our selves; for as
Men force the Sunne with much more force to passe,
By gathering his beames with a christall glass;

So wee, If wee into our selves will turne,
Blowing our sparkes of vertue, may outburne
The straw, which doth about our hearts sojourne.

You know, Physitians, when they would infuse
Into any' oyle, the Soules of Simples, use
Places, where they may lie still warme, to chuse.

Here we have the same concern with the nature of virtue linked
with a medical metaphor. In the verse-letter the reference is to the
purification of metals; the 'oyle' is presumably metal in its liquid
state.[164] In the letter to Goodyer the reference is, as we have seen,
to the belief that certain extracts from preserved dead bodies could
be used to revitalize their exhausted—or, note Donne's own alternative word, 'corrupted'—counterparts in living bodies.

There is a further medical (or rather, alchemical) reference
in *Love' Alchemie*, at the end of the first stanza.

Some that have deeper digg'd loves Myne then I,
Say, where his centrique happinesse doth lie:
   I have lov'd, and got, and told,
But should I love, get, tell, till I were old,
I should not finde that hidden mysterie;   5
     Oh, 'tis imposture all:
And as no chymique yet th' Elixar got,
   But glorifies his pregnant pot,
   If by the way to him befall
Some odoriferous thing, or medicinall,   10
So, lovers dreame a rich and long delight,
But get a winter-seeming summers night.

Our ease, our thrift, our honor, and our day,
Shall we, for this vaine Bubles shadow pay?
   Ends love in this, that my man,   15
Can be as happy'as I can; If he can
Endure the short scorne of a Bridgroomes play?
     That loving wretch that sweares,
'Tis not the bodies marry, but the mindes,
   Which he in her Angelique findes,   20
   Would sweare as justly, that he heares,
In that dayes rude hoarse minstralsey, the spheares.
Hope not for minde in women; at their best
Sweetness and wit, they' are but *Mummy*, possest.

The 'Elixar' is one of the quintessences, often identified with the Philosopher's Stone, which are perfectly pure and can therefore cure all diseases. It has, then, an obvious connection with the notion of the Mummy as curative; but while the Mummy's function is medical, the Elixir's is both medical and virtuous.

The framework of this poem is a mood of frustrated bitterness; perhaps Donne did become incidentally impatient with his wife's lack of 'minde'. It is not entirely successful because although the subject-matter is entirely serious, the poet allows himself to revert to an earlier flippancy of tone: the inexorably savage self-criticism of the poem is oddly obscured by its cynical tone. I use the word 'obscured' because although Donne reveals himself in this poem he does not achieve—cannot achieve—the tone he seeks: his earnestness of meaning is reflected not in a gravity of manner but in the more purely intellectual aspects of the poem—the strict sense gleams palely beneath the misleading, if uneasy, casualness. The use of the first person is less personal than it is in many of the *Songs and Sonets*.

Lines 1–6 are simple enough to understand on the face of it (the use of 'got', meaning 'gathered as a crop', 'cornered', and 'procreated', is an indication of the person of whom Donne was thinking as he wrote the poem), although the tone tends to distract critical attention from the meaning of the words. Donne does, admittedly, expostulate that 'centrique happiness' in love is an 'imposture'; but the rhythmical emphasis on 'Say' cuts across the expostulatory tone, making it clear that he means by it 'reveal', 'tell me': we know that he believed in the existence of a 'hidden mysterie', and that he was perfectly aware of the Platonic tradition of *not* revealing the esoteric mystery of love to the 'profanum vulgas' (indeed, as Miss Gardner writes, it 'is characteristic' of the poems she groups together as having been written later[165]). So in one sense, a sense that contrasts sharply with his mood and with the corresponding tone of the poem, he is satirically identifying himself with the 'profanum vulgus'. This suggestion is reinforced by lines 15–16, where he is reduced, as a lover, to the level of his servant. 'Deeper digg'd' and 'centrique' are of course sexual references; what is ostensibly a reference to Platonic love becomes a despairing mockery of it by means of *double ententes*.

In lines 7–12 he goes on to compare the lovers' reality of a short, cold (i.e. unnatural) summer's night contrasted with their dream of 'rich and long delight', with the way in which the alchemist is distracted from his task of discovering 'th' Elixar'—the perfectly pure substance, virtue, truth—by his discoveries, which he vaunts ('glorifies'), of sweet-smelling or medically beneficial 'things'. Once again this figure is echoed in a letter to Goodyer, 19 August 1614, which Grierson cites: '. . . I am now, like an alchemist, delighted with discoveries by the way, though I attain not mine end.'[166] There are implications here that cannot be ignored. At least the reality of the lovers' 'dreams' is acknowledged; is the possibility of their realization, as opposed to a cynical definition of what they are likely to get instead, actually denied? The subtle comparison with the alchemist's procedures suggests that it is not. The existence of 'th' Elixar' itself is not, after all, denied; we may infer, rather, that alchemists fail to discover it because they allow themselves to become distracted by the materially pleasant or merely utilitarian by-products of their task. That the 'dream' is not in itself a vain one is perhaps implied even by the fact that a cold night in summer is unnatural: it is not what lovers get that is natural, but what they don't get. At the same time, of course, Donne must be alluding to the familiar theme of the brevity of the sexual act (anticipating 'our day' in line 13), the desire for which, however, is one of the reasons for a lover's 'dreame' of 'rich and long delight'. What actually distracts the lovers from the discovery of their elixir Donne does not directly tell us; but he implies an answer in lines 8–10. After all, what, except the physical aspects of sex, can parallel, in the lovers' experience, the objects that distract the alchemist's attention from his real task? (The alchemist boasts about his discovery of these objects, just as Donne in earlier poems had to some extent adopted a boastful tone about his sexual conquests and his 'masculinity'.)

However, we can here narrow down the idea of mutual erotic enjoyment to specifically male erotic enjoyment: the poem is by a man, about women. Donne's use of the phrase 'glorifies his pregnant pot'[167] reinforces the suggestion that physical sex experienced in a certain (predominantly masculine) way is profoundly distracting.

Lines 13–14 form a rhetorical question. Only in terms of superficial tone is the ironic answer 'of course not'. The question frames itself as: 'Shall we give up our material ease, position in the world, wealth and brief sexual pleasures[168] for the sake of "a rich and long delight", the "centrique happinesse" of love?' The real answer, and we should not allow ourselves to ignore Donne's awareness of this, is, of course, 'yes'. Bubbles may easily be burst; they are delicate; but they do exist. 'Vain' is cruelly ironic. Lines 15–18 make this clear, for the answer to the question they ask is clearly supposed to be 'it cannot do so'. We can agree with Miss Gardner's explanation of line 18: 'endure the soon-past indignity of the role of a Bridegroom'; but what does 'a Bridegroomes play' involve as well as the act he had to put on at his raucous wedding festivities (which Donne evidently disdained)? Clearly, his role as a physical lover: another act that is undignified if, performed *as* a role, it goes against his real nature. Furthermore, the sexual act as thus performed is 'short' and denotes scorn for the beloved, in that she is treated as an object.

Leishmann is not altogether wrong when he says that this 'outrageous' poem is basically a protest against the too superficially canvassed platonic idea that only the minds marry, and not the bodies. Donne was impatient with any kind of superficiality, or with vulgarizations of profound ideas. But Leishmann ignores the seriousness of the sense. Lines 18–22 ironically contrast the sexy vulgarity of wedding feasts with the music of the spheres: they mean that one cannot be conventionally erotic and serious in love at the same time. They also (since no one can discern the music of the spheres through 'rude hoarse minstralsey') mean that he who denies the body is a 'wretch' (a fool, but also an unfortunate fellow)— even if a 'loving' one; he is 'loving' because he is at least aware of the existence of the dream of 'rich and long delight', although he only pretends to discern it in conventional eroticism. What Donne is really attacking here is not seriousness in love, but sexual vulgarity —and, at a deeper level, lust in himself: his inability to sublimate lust into love.

The crucial last two lines are not, I think, 'insulting' to women, but rather savagely self-critical—or, one might more precisely say, since Donne is not very explicit here about himself, critical of conventional 'masculinity'. Because his outbursts against women (mostly, but not all, early) are so well-known, the nature of his attitude towards men has been neglected. That he did, if in a fashionable way, vituperate against women I do not seek to deny (though it seldom comes out in his letters); nor have I ignored the admittedly 'anti-woman' surface of this particular poem. But I fail to see how these lines, interpreted carefully, insult women. 'Hope not for minde in women' is a statement that is made somewhat abruptly, for there is absolutely no hint of criticism of women in the lines preceding it (the implied criticism is of 'sex'); if it is supposed to be the reason for man's failure to achieve 'rich and long delight', then it certainly has no relation to what precedes it: it is led up to in no way at all, however the poem be interpreted. It is quite possible that Donne, when he was writing the poem, did, at a conscious level, intend to insult womanhood. But there is a great deal of difference (in a poem) between wanting to express a mood and expressing what one truly feels. Donne was too good a poet to falsify his feelings altogether.

At this point (up to 'spheares') the words have accumulated the following sense, 'You can't treat women as sexual objects and then hope for them to have masculine-type minds, in order for you to play at vulgar Platonism. The idea that only the minds marry is typical of such wishful thinking—it's just as familiar as men's lies, to women when they want to treat them as sexual objects, to the effect that their minds as well as their bodies are beautiful.' This interpretation is borne out by a study of the complex meaning of the next one-and-a-half lines. We can paraphrase them simply as follows: 'At their best women are sweet and witty; when you're married to them or when you've sexually possessed them they're no more than dead bodies (they become your mother).' The key word is 'possest'. This crude but instinctive conception of male sexual performance goes with the 'rude hoarse minstralsey' of wedding festivities. Furthermore, there is a contradiction between 'Hope not for minde in women' and the statement that they are 'sweetnesse and wit' at their best; for 'wit' in seventeenth century parlance itself means 'mind', 'intelligence', 'genius'. Miss Gardner says that it 'seems' here to be used in its modern sense of 'superficial cleverness'; but there is little warrant for her suggestion besides her preconception about the general meaning of the poem. If 'wit' is used in the sense in which Donne would normally have used it, then the lines must bear the meaning: 'Women are *not* at their best when they're "possest".' The inescapable implication, of course, is that if you love them (truly) then they can be something different. This does not cut 'sex' out, but it does cut out the profound vulgarity of 'possession'.

Again, the description of 'possest' women as mummies does not carry with it merely the attribution of 'dead, good for nothing'. It means (1) that they have been reduced to sexual objects by the exercise upon them of pure lust, and (2) that they are used by men merely to relieve themselves sexually, in a wholly unserious, 'medical' (therapeutic) manner: they are 'preserved' by men for this very purpose.[169]

This interpretation fits more meaningfully into the context of both Donne's poetry and his life as he reveals it in his letters than does the more superficial treatment of it as a clever squib. In spite of the presence in the poem of bitterness and impatience, it can be related directly to his feelings as he wrote to Goodyer by the fire in his parlour at Mitcham, in the letter already quoted. It is a poem of despair; but the cynical framework that Donne chose for it is, in the circumstances, a tactless and unsuitable one. In other poems on this and allied themes he was more successful. However, I have chosen to protract my discussion of this particular poem because it typified Donne's complex mental state in his middle years. Professor Arnold Stein, in a stimulating book about Donne, describes the poem only in general terms; but these somewhat resemble my own, although he evidently finds it a better poem than I do.[170] He says that it 'is a lyric satire that purges the mind by making two extremes destroy each other'. This is a brilliant comment, as is Professor Stein's whole passage on the poem. I dissent from his praise of the poem as 'a stunning piece of satire' only because I feel that it is (as Professor Stein himself writes) 'not conclusive', and because in it Donne so obviously wants to get away from satire; certainly, however, it is crucial, and it functions stunningly indeed in the context of Donne's development. Nevertheless, it lacks the gravity and beauty of other poems in the same group. Sourly magnificent, it fails as a lyric, but yearns too lyrically for a status beyond that of satire. The extremes do not, in effect, 'destroy each other' in a finally poetic sense; they merely appear to do so. (We could, of course, as C. S. Lewis said of Eliot's irritable pronouncement that *Hamlet* was an 'artistic failure', do with more such failures; but, as we can easily infer from his state of mind as we know it to have been, and from the tortuousness of *Love's Alchemie* itself, Donne could not.)

8

Twicknam Garden is a much more integrated poem, the opening of which Grierson rightly relates to the passage in the letter to Sir Henry Goodyer already quoted ('. . . The pleasantnesse of the season displeases me. . . .').[171] Miss Gardner points out that 'Manna was a type or figure of the Host. Love performs the Eucharistic miracle in reverse. . . .'[172] But the poem should not be read as an 'attack' on women or even on physical love. It bitterly relates physical love to the notion of the Fall, and identifies the 'Serpent' of Paradise with the penis (line 9). The last two lines of the poem,

> O perverse sexe, where none is true but shee,
> Who's there fore true, because her truth kills me.

are usually interpreted as meaning that the woman to whom the poem is addressed is similar to other women in not being what she seems, for her faithfulness ('truth') to another is only cruelty to him. But is this a conventional love poem in so directly personal a sense? The last two lines represent a paradox, which in general terms may be expressed thus: 'Only women are true. Although they ought to be loved truly, they prevent men from doing this by making their truthfulness sexually seductive.' In the sexual act the man 'dies' (is 'killed' by woman's truth): that is, he has an orgasm of a selfish type, which causes his loving nature to die. This may seem over-subtle, but is really only another way of expressing a perennial problem: how to love physically without selfishness, how to achieve perfect fulfilment in 'sex', as Donne was the first to call it, without feelings of guilt. And over this consideration must always hang at least the notion that abstinence may be the only solution.

The Ecstasie deals with precisely the same problem, but from the different, less sexually tense viewpoint of the lover who is, for the time being, spiritually united with his mistress. Beginning by describing this state, in which the only 'babies' they get are in each other's eyes (such images were called babies), the poem moves bravely on into a consideration of the part the body should play in love. The conventional interpretation has been that the poem is a plea for physical sex, provided spiritual love is present. Miss Gardner challenges this view, and maintains that the lovers' return to their bodies is only in accordance with the doctrine of 'the circle of love'; the lovers have a 'duty to reveal love to men'; 'Prince and Kingdom need each other and are indeed inconceivable without each other': there is, she asserts, no plea here for 'sex'.[173] Her interpretation has met with respect, but does not seem to have persuaded many critics.

Miss Gardner bases her interpretation of the poem on the collocation of doctrines about love to be found in Leone Ebreo's *Dialoghi d'Amore*, which Donne is likely to have read. She admits that the first twelve lines of the poem are fraught with sexual meanings, but asserts that this is only because Donne wants to suggest that his lovers are young and ardent. There is no 'disappointment' in the witticism about 'looking babies', because 'desire for physical propagation is not a feature of Donne's love-poetry'. Here, perhaps, Miss Gardner begins to be somewhat perverse and over-scholastic in her interpretation. Certainly Donne's love poems are seldom cast in the form of 'pleas for propagation' (as is Marvell's *To His Coy Mistress*); but they leave the reader in no doubt that their writer is subject to a desire for it. If Miss Gardner can call upon Ebreo's *Dialoghi d'Amore* in support of her view, then we are entitled to call upon the evidence of Donne's life to the effect that not only did he continually long to procreate his kind, but also that he did so. And even the little that there is in his letters about his relations with his wife makes it clear enough that his poems were written out of his own experience. This makes no difference to the meaning of the poems; but it does show that poems arise from psychological reality rather than from philosophical abstractions, however these may have influenced their composition. Miss Gardner's view of *The Ecstasie* is, however, valuable inasmuch as it draws attention to the crudity of the conventional interpretation: for the poem reveals a 'physical' solution very different in psychological kind from the one envisaged by the conventional interpretation. One of the most important features of the conclusion of the poem is its tentative delicacy: the fact that the lovers reanimate their bodies implies that they will love with their bodies. But such a type of physical love cannot but be left undefined. For the poem clings resolutely to the truth of the matter: it is only a plea for a morally valid return to physical love. It does not claim to have made such a return. Therefore the proper experience of physical love, from this platonic viewpoint, is, strictly speaking, unknown. What we can say is that, set against the guilt-ridden experience of physical love as outlined in other poems, this kind of love would be very different. *The Ecstasie* cites a possibility; it does not describe an achieved reality; both Miss Gardner and her critics are right, but Miss Gardner has done the more valuable service by pointing out that the poem is no conventional advocation of 'sex'. In another letter to Goodyer, written in 1608/9, Donne said: 'But truly wheresoever we are, if we can but tell our selves truly what and where we would be, we may make any state and place such. . . .'[174] It is this faith in possibilities, this defence of idealism, that sustains *The Ecstasie*, which is a description of and justification of aspirations, not a plea for sex or for abstinence from it.

9

In 1610 and 1611 Donne allowed the publication of his *Anniversaries*, written to mourn the death of Sir Robert Drury's young daughter Elizabeth, whom he had never met or even seen.[175] In 1612 Donne accompanied Sir Robert and Lady Drury on a ten-month continental tour, leaving his wife in the care of her sister on the Isle of Wight. From Paris on 14 April 1612 he wrote to his close friend George Gerrard about the publication of the *Anniversaries*. This letter casts important light upon the attitude to publication of both Donne and his literary contemporaries of similar social background; and upon Donne's ideas about the subject-matter of poetry. (But three years later he was, as we shall see, again considering publication.)

> Of my Anniversaries, the fault that I acknowledge in my self, is to have descended to print any thing in verse, which though it have excuse even in our times, by men who professe, and practise much gravitie; yet I confesse I wonder how I declined to it, and do not pardon my self: But for the other part of the imputation of having said too much, my defence is, that my purpose was to say as well as I could: for since I never saw the Gentlewoman, I cannot be understood to have bound my self to have spoken just truths, but I would not be thought to have gone about to praise her, or any other in rime; except I took such a person, as might be capable of all that I could say. If any of those Ladies think that Mistris *Drewry* was not so, let that Lady make her self fit for all those praises in the book, and they shall be hers.[176]

This supports the suggestion that Donne had been jealously criticized by his own patronesses, as well as by others, for having been too extravagant in praise of a girl he had never seen. He is saying here, quite clearly, that while he politely and sincerely believes Elizabeth Drury to have been an apt symbol for 'all that I could say', he had been writing about something else. His sincerity can be in question here only for those who, like his patronesses, were jealous, or those who have over-literal minds: a patron had called upon him to write an elegy, and he had seen—and felt—in the request an opportunity to write poetry that had already been pressing at him. That it had been pressing on him is evident from the quality of the poems. Sir Robert Drury offered him the occasion, and no doubt provided him with the 'objective correlative' that he needed. The original request probably came to Donne through his sister Anne, whose idea it may have been. He was attached to the Drurys, and grateful to them; we need not feel that the grief and sense of loss—of a beautiful, talented and beloved young girl—that they transmitted to him did not have its own impact on his sensibility. Nevertheless, Elizabeth Drury herself is of course merely incidental to the meaning of the *Anniversaries*.

On the subject of publication Donne is specific: he does not condemn the practice in others (perhaps he was thinking of his friend Ben Jonson), but he feels that he has 'descended' and 'declined' to it. This was still the standard 'aristocratic' view, though it was not to last for many more years.

Donne took holy orders on 23 January 1615. But until that day or very shortly before it he remained adamantly secular—which was perfectly logical of him, as well as characteristic. We have already seen how, in Professor Le Comte's words, he stood 'on the sidelines of dispute' in matters of religion when he told Goodyer that he detested all schism. Writing to Sir Tony Mathew, a Catholic, from Paris in 1611/12 he says,

> That we differ in our wayes, I hope we pardon one another. Men go to *China*, both by the Straights, and by the *Cape*. I never mis-interpreted your way; nor suffered it to be so, wheresoever I found it in discourse. For I was sure, you took not up your Religion upon trust, but payed ready money for it, and at a high Rate. And this taste of mine towards you, makes me hope for, and claime the same disposition in you towards me.[177]

Donne's dislike of schism is not concrete evidence of reluctance to enter the ministry. But there is no doubt whatever that he would have preferred a secular position, until he at last realized that the King was determined to have him in the Church, and to offer him no other kind of opportunity. Professor Le Comte is highly critical of Donne at what he calls 'this fawning time', but surprisingly fails to make allowances for his absolute need to rely upon the set epistolary formulae for sueing for favour.

Donne was being pressed to become a priest; eventually, and not without struggle, he gave in. If he wished to rise at all he had no alternative but to rise in the Church. When in 1613 he asked Lord Hay to pass on his decision to the King's favourite, Sir Robert Ker[178] (the accepted way of doing things), he said that 'one good fruit' of his decision, 'to make my profession Divinity', would be that his 'prayers for your Lordship's happiness shall be, in that station, more effectual with God';[179] Professor Le Comte solemnly calls this 'base' because it is not 'a Gospel certainty'! Actually it means nothing at all: it is simply an elegantly clever remark in the epistolary manner of the time. But Professor Le Comte's comments on Donne's subsequent letter to Ker himself are even more severe. Donne, he says in an ill-advised metaphor, is being a catamite. Actually the letter[180] is, once again, written to a set formula: the writing of it in such a manner, with its humble beseechings, was an inevitable corollary of Donne's decision 'to make my profession Divinity'. That a student of seventeenth-century England should be unable to recognize this is startling. Official letters in official forms are no better guides to seventeenth-century people's motives or feelings than our circumspect politeness to tax-collectors is a guide to our feelings about them as individuals.

When Donne was not writing to persons in high places his tone was very different, as a letter of 28 July 1614 to his brother-in-law, Robert More, from 'his poor hospital', demonstrates. He is frankly annoyed with a party of Danes for coming to Court just at a time when he has 'near hopes'; he speaks of statesmen 'who can find matter of state in any wrinkle in the King's socks'. There is no respect for the Court or for important personages here.[181]

Certainly, however, these years immediately preceding his entrance into the Church were difficult and unhappy ones for Donne. He had indicated his willingness to become a priest, but did not give up hoping for a secular position. It is unlikely that he felt anything but private mortification at his absolute need to depend upon patronage. One feels less inclined to defend than to explain his conduct. Professor Le Comte's melodramatic charge that he was guilty of fawning insincerity is as gross an over-simplification as is his later characterization of Donne the priest as 'sincere' and 'reformed'. If Donne did deplore the falseness of protocol in his time there was nothing he could do about it. He was ambitious; he was also insecure. Therefore when his patron Robert Ker, now Earl of Somerset, married Frances Howard, he was expected to produce an *Epithalamion*, which he did. The tone of Professor Le Comte's comment is revealing: 'He missed the sight of that evil woman going to the altar with her hair down on her shoulders as a virgin'. Frances Howard had got her marriage to the third Earl of Essex annulled on the grounds that it had not been consummated. One can be sure that in private Donne was vastly amused by the whole scandal (though not, perhaps, by the later revelation of Frances Howard's part in the murder of Overbury). We can certainly criticize his obsequious adherence to protocol—but in doing so we must criticize a whole age. There are no exceptions. Lying did not come easily or naturally to him: he indulged in it not for its own sake, not to obtain political power, but to achieve a position commensurate with his talents.

Professor Le Comte's bias against him at this time of his life is so pronounced that he even wilfully misinterprets him: writing to Sir Robert Ker in May 1614, having just recovered from a dangerous illness, Donne said,

> Yet I have scaped no better cheap than that I have paid death one of my children for my ransom. Because I loved it well, I make account that I dignify the memory of it by mentioning of it to you, else I should not be so homely. Impute this brevity of writing to you upon no subject to my sickness. . . .[182]

Professor Le Comte says that this letter, 'in its abject apology for mentioning "no subject", the death of a child, is no more agreeable than the others of this period'. But 'no subject' refers to the writer's personal grief and misfortunes, not to the child; we may even catch a gleam of irony in the phrasing of the 'abject apology'.

In December 1614 Donne was awaiting ordination. He needed to pay his debts, and apparently he wished to, or was being pressed to, publish his poems. It was a curious time for one who had hitherto disdained publishing to make such a decision, but in a letter of 20 December 1614 he told Goodyer:

> . . . One thing more I must tell you; but so softly, that if that good Lady were in the room,[183] with you and this Letter, she might not hear. It is, that I am brought to the necessity of printing my Poems, and addressing them to my L. Chamberlain.[184] This I mean to do forthwith; not for much publique view, but at mine own cost, a few Copies. I apprehend some incongruities in the resolution; and I know what I shall suffer from many interpretations: but I am at an end, of much considering that; and, if I were as startling in that kinde, as ever I was, yet in this particular, I am under an unescapable necessity, as I shall let you perceive, when I see you. By this occasion I am made a Rhapsoder of mine own rags, and that cost me more diligence, to seek them, than it did to make them. This made me aske to borrow that old book of you, which it will be too late to see, for that use, when I see you: for I must do this, as a valediction to the world, before I take Orders. But this is it, I am to ask you; whether you made any such use of the letter in verse, *A nostre Comtesse chez vous*, as

that I may not put it in, amongst the rest to persons of that rank; for I desire very very much, that something should bear her name in the book, and I would be just to my written words to my *L. Harrington*, to write nothing after that.[185] I pray tell me as soon as you can, if I be at liberty to insert that: for if you have by any occasion applied any pieces of it, I see not, that it will be discerned, when it appears in the whole piece. Though this be a little matter, I would be sorry not to have an account of it, within as little after New Years tide, as you could.[186]

What does he mean by this? He is 'brought to the necessity' of printing a few copies of a book of poems; he will tell Goodyer precisely why when he sees him. But he nevertheless goes on to explain further: publication is 'a valediction to the world' before he enters the Church. Such a thought must have been in his mind when he ended the elegy for Harrington with the announcement that he was giving up poetry. It suggests that 'the necessity' of printing the poems was an internal rather than an external one, that for the time being he felt all poetry was incompatible with the profession of divinity. It has been suggested that the Lord Chamberlain himself was putting pressure on Donne to dedicate a volume of poems to him. This seems unlikely: the publication of even Donne's most innocuous poems—say, the outrageously witty but not very 'religious' holy poems he had been writing since 1609— would hardly have pleased the foolish, testy and tasteless monarch from whom the Lord Chamberlain probably hoped eventually to gain religious preferment for Donne.

Which of his poems was Donne thinking of collecting together? Certainly not the notorious *Elegies* or *Satires* of his youth. But how many of the *Songs and Sonets* (so called by the 1635 editor of his poems) would he have included? These had not circulated widely—but they had circulated. It seems at least possible that he would have liked, defiantly, to include any of his poems, of whatever type, that he felt to be poetically successful. Of course, he could not have considered actually doing this; had the publication taken place at all, it would have been a compromise. It seems most likely that Donne convinced himself into thinking, or pretending to think, that he positively needed to strengthen his position with Somerset in this way—but that his real motive was a last-minute desire to print his poems and to stake a claim as a literary man. We have seen that his attitude to the publication of his *Anniversaries*, as expressed to a fellow gentleman, George Gerrard, was the one to be expected from a man of his position; but how sorry had he really been, despite the apparent disdain? He did not despise Ben Jonson—a professional literary man who published nearly everything he wrote—and we may feel that at this point of time, trapped by the necessity of being circumspect, Donne wanted to make at least a final gesture.

His reluctance to enter the Church is not in dispute. No doubt he did have feelings of unworthiness; but his feelings of unwillingness to abandon his freedom to be speculative, sceptical and, when he wanted to be, syncretic, were more powerful. The main medium in which he expressed this most important side of himself was, of course, poetry. It is not to impugn the Anglican ministry or his eventual decision to enter it to point out that during 1610–14 he saw the poetic, imaginative, free side of himself as essentially in conflict with the 'divine' side. His announcement in the Harrington obsequies that his muse would henceforth be silent, and his statement to Goodyer that he 'must' publish his poetry as 'a valediction to the world' make this clear. And it is to Donne himself that we owe the famous distinction between 'Jack Donne' and 'Dr. Donne'. In a letter to Sir Robert Ker (who had now become Earl of Ancrum) he said of *Biathanatos*, a copy of which he was sending him, that when after finishing it he had sent it to 'some particular friends in both Universities' they had pointed out that it had 'a false thread in it, but not easily found' (they were bound to do so, since it defended, under certain circumstances, the act of suicide). He went on:

> Keep it, I pray, with the Same jealousie; let any that your discretion admits to the sight of it, know the date of it; and that it is a book written by *Jack Donne*, and not by Dr. *Donne* . . . if I die . . . publish it not, but yet burn it not. . . .[187]

Of course, he was never able to relinquish *Jack Donne*, and as Miss Gardner wisely points out, there is a sense in which everything he wrote was by Jack rather than the Doctor. Even in 1619, when he settled into his position as a divine, he is still ambiguous: 'publish it not, but yet burn it not'. He always knew that his poetry would survive as well as his 'divinity'. But his remarkable sincerity, a quality that almost all his critics accord him, demanded of him that if he should become a divine, then he should behave as one—rejecting his past 'worldliness'. It was a relief to do so. We know the date of his ordination, 23 January 1614/5, from the short letter he wrote to Sir Edward Herbert (George Herbert's brother, later Lord Herbert of Cherbury) on that day; in it he mentioned that he had now, 'by the orders of our Churche, receyved a new character'.[188] He could not give up poetry, but henceforth his love affair was to be not with women and the world, but with death.

10

Donne did not, as Walton implied, become a saint after he entered
the Church. But he did play the part of a divine with dramatic
gusto, becoming the foremost preacher of his time. We do not, and
perhaps this has some significance, need to be Christians to respond
to the rhetoric and wisdom of his sermons which, while framed in
restrained and conventional (if often absurd) theological terms, are as
ingenious and individual as any that have survived in literature. He
found any kind of ecclesiastical rigidity—such as that of Laud—
extremely distasteful, and he disliked any form of intolerance. Wholly
loyal to the Church, he was not particularly devoted to its ceremonies.
His attitude, once again, was modern and forward-looking. He was
the only churchman amongst his contemporaries who could conceiv-
ably have been at home in the Church of today.

    The events of Donne's life after his ordination may be briefly
told. In the autumn of 1616 he became Reader in Divinity to the
Benchers of Lincoln's Inn, which involved preaching over fifty
sermons a year. In the next year, worn out with bearing children,
his wife died at the age of thirty-three. In 1619 he went to Germany
as a member of an embassy sent out by James I with the vain
intention of promoting peace among the German princes. A year
after returning, in 1621, Donne was made Dean of St. Paul's. Then
began his real fame as a preacher; his sermons began to attract
increasingly large crowds. He was a generous benefactor to all kinds
of people and causes. He had some disputes with the old actor
Edward Alleyn, whom his daughter Constance had married; Alleyn
seems to have been the offending party. Laud had decided by 1630
that Donne was safe enough to be entrusted with a bishopric, but
these plans were dropped because of his serious illness. He died in
1631.

    After 1616 Donne's letters became self-consciously those of
a priest: he usually writes as a priest is expected to write. It is not
known for certain exactly when he wrote a letter to his mother, Mrs.
Elizabeth Rainsford, consoling her on the death of a daughter; but
it is likely that it was written after he had taken orders, during 1616.
It has a consciously priest-like tone, which we do not find in earlier
letters:

> When I consider so much of your life, as can fall within my
> memorie and observation, I find it to have been a Sea,
> under a continuall Tempest, where one wave hath ever
> overtaken another. Our most wise and blessed Saviour
> chuseth which way it pleaseth him, to conduct those which
> he loves, to his Haven, and eternall Rest.[189]

This is a son consoling his mother in the terms of his profession.

And for the time being this profession did inhibit other activities. In 1615 Goodyer suggested that he write a poem to the Countess of Huntingdon, and Donne replied:

> . . . I have these two reasons to decline it. That that knowledge which she hath of me, was in the beginning of a graver course, than of a Poet, into which (that I may also keep my dignity) I would not seem to relapse. The Spanish proverb informes me, that he is a fool which cannot make one Sonnet, and he is mad which makes two.[190]

The letters of these last fifteen years of Donne's life, although as deliberately formal and sometimes as ingenious as ever, are less subtle in their descriptions of his moods and aspirations. He frequently discusses his illnesses (he seems to have suffered from a conjunction of malign tertiary malaria and a recurrent throat infection), but has lost his confusion and gained purpose.

He makes few references to poetry. In a letter written to the King's favourite, Buckingham, in 1623 he spoke of it as having been 'the Mistresse of my youth'; Divinity was 'the wyfe of mine age'.[191] Another reference to poetry, in a letter of March 1625 to Sir Robert Ker, has been widely misinterpreted through inattention to its context. Ker had applied to him for an elegy on the Marquess of Hamilton, whom Donne had almost certainly known. He replied:

> I presume you rather try what you can do in me, than what I can do in verse: you know my uttermost when it was best, and even then I did best when I had least truth for my subjects. In this present case there is so much truth as it defeats all poetry.[192]

This does not mean quite what it has sometimes gleefully been taken to mean, that Donne's love poetry was never based on experience. He is speaking in the context of elegaic poetry, and is almost certainly thinking of the *Anniversaries*, on the death of Elizabeth Drury, whom he had never met. It is unlikely that he even liked to think of the *Songs and Sonets*, at any rate in his capacity as Dean of St. Paul's; but the *Anniversaries* had been published, and he had explained this in the letter of 1614 (already quoted) to George Gerrard.

Donne, although his view of life was compulsively poetic, never officially acknowledged poetry as his main activity. He is nearer to Sidney in this than to his admired friend Ben Jonson, who spoke in his own voice when he wrote in *The Poetaster*:

> And if this age can hope no other grace—
> Leave me! There's something come into my thought
> That must and shall be sung high and aloof,
> Safe from the wolf's black jaw, and the dull ass's hoof.

Donne, an even more rewarding poet than Jonson, could never have written like this. The first professional literary men, all of them dramatists as well as poets, were either wild in temperament, like Marlowe and Robert Greene, or solidly middle class in origin, like Middleton and Jonson. Donne, whose intellect was one of the most violently active of all poets, was eventually emotionally cautious, even fearful. After his first 'outrageous' poems, his rakish behaviour, his impulsive marriage, he increasingly preferred to write and behave within permitted frameworks. He was circumspect; afraid—as we have seen from some of his letters—of the effect that some of his work might have on more timid or formal minds than his own, and yet he was never prepared to jettison it altogether. It is easy enough to see the origin of his circumspection in the experiences of his childhood, during which he saw the kind of things that happened to people who were not prepared to go with the prevailing wind. We need not think—in view of his writings it is impossible to think—that Donne ever threw himself wholeheartedly into support of the powers-that-be. His was not a completely divided personality, like Bacon's: half sly, treacherous, ambitious politician and half sweet, wise, philosophical essayist and altruistic scientific investigator. One of the keys to his immensely complex character is his use of ironic contrast: his violently subversive exploitation of highly conventionalized frameworks. His respect for the forms and conventions in which he wrote is more than ingenious; it is, finally, ironic. The ultimate irony of Jack Donne's complete 'sincerity' as the Doctor did not escape him, either; it was, and remains, a triumph. Christians can rejoice in the totality of his conversion; non-Christians can accept the metaphorical framework within which he operated henceforth.

I

Marvell's personality, despite efforts to explain it in terms of various sorts of ideologies, remains an enigma. Those intricacies of neo-Platonic thought that have, not erroneously, been traced in his poetry do not suffice to explain his transition from Royalist to 'Cromwell's poet', from delicate and subtle lyrical poet to rough, sometimes doggerel, satirist and prose pamphleteer. Just over four hundred of his letters survive (including a few recently discovered); these offer perhaps fewer clues to the real nature of the man, to his beliefs and his motives, than his poems. But, considering the difficulties presented by the latter, they cannot be ignored. For in order to understand more fully the scarcely more than two thousand lines that make up the corpus of Marvell's non-satirical poetry, we need to understand the man who wrote them. As a poet Marvell has suffered from interpreters' inclination to bog him down in abstractions: he is too seldom discussed in psychological terms, too often in those of ideas. Thus in Harold E. Toliver's interesting analysis[193] *To His Coy Mistress* becomes no more than a dry Platonic treatise—which it patently is not.

Marvell was a learned and travelled man, whose poetry reflected multitudinous influences, including those of Latin and French poetry; his work incorporates much of the thought that was current in his time—including, of course, neo-Platonism; but his poems have meanings outside the limitations of philosophical and theological discussion. The *Horatian Ode* may appear to be a complex of borrowings of various kinds of contemporary attitudes;[194] it is much more important that it expresses, with an exquisite subtlety, the intellectual and emotional position of a poet, of a man dedicated to justice and to truth, at a time of political upheaval. If in analysing a poem we reduce its author to a merely mechanical and heartless reproducer of various shades of opinion, we rob the poem of its poetic value. We then lose the value of its originality as a statement, together with the potency of its serenity, which is the wisdom it derives from its concentration upon the truth rather than upon points of view or systems of thought.

Marvell was an ironist of skill and effectiveness; the satirical techniques he employed in prose influenced Swift—which, since he was famously no enemy of religious dissent, is remarkable. But while his ironic skill has been recognized by critics at least from Augustine Birrell onwards, they have seldom accorded to Marvell the dignity of having preserved, behind the apparent vagaries of his political behaviour and writings, a consistent point of view. If the poet Marvell has been described too often as a philosophical theologian, then the satirist has been too easily dismissed as an inconsistent opportunist, or a 'Machiavellian'. This approach assumes that a political life (as it has actually to be lived) is in no sense inferior to a poetic—an independent—life (if it can be managed). I doubt if Marvell shared this view, and I consequently often read him as a cynical, disappointed, but witty and amused ironist where others do not.

Marvell does not in his letters refer to his own or to anyone else's poetry; but, besides being historically interesting and self-revealing, if chiefly in the subtle deliberation of their reticence, they do support my view of him, which is, briefly, that he was an eventually frustrated poet, who found an honourable outlet, but not a wholly satisfying one, in politically subversive activity.

2

Marvell was born in 1621, the son of a parson who, had he not been drowned before the Civil War began, would probably have sided with Parliament; Anthony à Wood described him as 'calvinistic'. Marvell's biographer, Pierre Legouis, says that 'resistance to oppression ran in the family'. Marvell spent his childhood in Hull, went to Hull Grammar School, and was at Trinity College, Cambridge, from 1633 until 1640. In 1639 he seems for a short time to have run away to London and become converted to Roman Catholicism; but his father, catching up with him in a bookshop, persuaded him to go back to college. He may have left Cambridge under some kind of cloud; Legouis remarks that he 'was not, at any rate in his last years at Trinity, a model student'.

Marvell fought for neither side in the Civil War, although his early sympathies were Royalist. It is likely that he travelled to Spain, Italy, Holland and France—a letter of Milton's of 1652/3 says he had done so 'to very good purpose . . . and the gaining of these four languages'.[195] He may have financed his Grand Tour by acting as a tutor; otherwise his means of livelihood between 1640 and 1650 is obscure. However, between 1650 and 1657 he was certainly for most of the time earning his living as a private tutor, first to Mary Fairfax, the twelve-year-old daughter of the parliamentary General Fairfax, who had resigned, and then to Cromwell's unofficial (but later official) ward, William Dutton.

In June 1650 Marvell wrote his best known poem, the *Horatian Ode*, which was not published until after his death. Later that year he wrote two more poems. One was decidedly pro-Royalist and anti-Parliamentarian; but the other, in Latin, was a tribute to Oliver St. John, the new Ambassador to the United Provinces and a hated enemy of all Royalists. By February 1652/3 Marvell had left the Fairfaxes and was making application, through his friend Milton, for a post under the new régime. The 'enigmas', as M. Legouis calls them, of his refusal to fight on either side, and of his apparent conversion from Royalism to Republicanism, will be discussed below. He had almost certainly written the best of his lyrical poems, those upon which his reputation rests, before he left the Fairfaxes.

Marvell served Cromwell in various ways until his death in 1658. He wrote a long celebration of the first anniversary of his election in December 1654, took his ward Dutton to France in 1656, and was made Latin Secretary in September 1657. He was one of the M.P.s for Hull in Richard Cromwell's only Parliament, but was supplanted by Sir Harry Vane when the Rump was recalled. Re-elected as junior member for Hull in the Convention Parliament, and then again for the so-called Pensionary Parliament (1661–79) he remained an M.P. for the rest of his life.

As member for Hull, Marvell was in opposition, though never quite so obviously as to get himself into trouble. He is said to have enjoyed the friendship of the King. His savage verse satires were invariably printed anonymously; one of his friends, John Ayloffe, whose own satires were hardly stronger than Marvell's, was executed. Marvell, however, never expressed Republican sentiments. He fought unceasingly for the cause of toleration for the Dissenters, and continued his friendship with Milton. When, after the Restoration, Milton was arrested, on a void warrant, he effected his release by drawing attention to the matter in Parliament.

Marvell's chief prose work is the ironic *The Rehearsal Transpros'd* (1672–3), in two parts, which was a popular success. This was an answer to certain writings by a worthless but not untalented turncoat called Samuel Parker, who was eventually made a Bishop by James II. Marvell died, unmarried (Mary Palmer, who passed herself off as his widow in the note 'To the Reader' in the first, 1681, edition of his poems, probably did so only in order to regain £500 for two bankrupts Marvell had befriended), in 1578, of malaria or of the medical treatment, of bleeding, that was then prescribed for it. Nothing supports the legend of his having been poisoned for political reasons.

3

All but about a dozen of Marvell's letters are printed in H.M.
Margoliouth's edition of the *Poems and Letters*.[196] 294 of these are
semi-official dispatches to the Hull Corporation from the House of
Commons, and a further 69 (addressed to Hull Trinity House) deal
with the matter of the erection of a lighthouse in the mouth of the
Humber, a cause Marvell took up for the Corporation at the House
of Commons. By far the most interesting letters are those of a more
personal nature to his nephew William Popple, his friend Sir Henry
Thompson, and to various others—including ones to Milton and
Cromwell. Doubtless more letters would have survived had not
'one William Skinner' destroyed them by handing them to his maid
'to put under pie-bottoms'.

The letters to the Hull Corporation are neither completely
without flattery nor devoid of irony. But beyond laconically reporting what has gone on in the House of Commons, they tell us little
or nothing about Marvell; they very rarely even tell the Corporation
which way Marvell himself voted. They must be of value to historians, but they tell his literary biographer little more than that
Marvell was a highly conscientious M.P., and that he was capable
of poker-faced reporting. The most famous example of this occurs
in his letter of 4 December 1660, where he writes:

> To day our house was upon the Bill of Attaindor of those
> that have been executed, those that are fled, & of Cromwell
> Bradshaw Ireton & Pride And tis orderd that the Carkasses
> & coffins of the foure last named shall be drawn, with what
> expedition possible, upon an hurdle to Tyburn, there be
> hangd up for a while & then buryed under the gallows.[197]

This apparently unnecessary callousness, even in communicating to
the hard-headed men who had returned him, has puzzled commentators. For had not Marvell written, two years before, of how
'we, since thou [i.e. Cromwell] art gone . . .

> Wander like ghosts about thy loved tombe;
> And lost in tears, have neither sight nor mind,
> To guide us upward through this region blinde.'

And even if 'Carkasse' could mean 'body' without rudeness (as M.
Legouis reminds us), the choice of word hardly seems appropriate.
Augustine Birrell comments, simply, 'Nerves were tough in those
days'; and M. Legouis, possibly a little more perturbed, for the
Marvell of his imagination is a Puritan and Cromwell-lover until
the end of his days, writes '. . . it would be unfair to blame Marvell
for the tone of this correspondence . . . his electors . . . expected
from their representative facts, not ideas. . . .'[198]

   Neither of these comments is adequate. The nerveless reportage of the fate of Cromwell's body is only one of the most extreme examples of the flatness of Marvell's semi-official prose-style as it is displayed in these letters to his constituents (from whom he earned 6s 8d per day when Parliament was sitting). M. Legouis himself, writing of the *Horatian Ode*, mentions what he calls Marvell's 'almost inhuman aloofness'. What has gone unnoticed is that the deliberately non-committal style of his parliamentary letters, especially when they deal with subjects (such as religious tolerance) which we know he felt strongly about, reflects the ability for impartiality that he had already shown, not only in the *Ode*, but also in the 'enigmatic' neutrality he preserved during the Civil War itself. The non-emotiveness that is a feature of the parliamentary letters is more significant and individual than either Birrell or M. Legouis suggest. His letters are so strictly functional as to be ironically so. They do only the job they are meant to do, and suggest that Marvell privately regarded not only them, but also what they reported, with a poetically resigned and cynical eye. It must be remembered that what a man thinks of his work need not affect the conscientiousness with which he does it.

   However, the penchant for impartiality that has been noted in Marvell is something that appears in more than only his letters and in the *Ode*: when it manifests itself—as it so often does in the letters to Hull—as a concentration upon bare fact, as opposed to any kind of comment upon it, it parallels a certain aspect of his practice in his satires. M. Legouis writes 'Just as in his letters he shows himself a gazette-writer in prose, here in his satire he reveals himself a political journalist in verse'. This is an aspect of the technique employed in his best satires, such as *The Last Instructions to a Painter* (published 1669, but written earlier), rather than their chief feature. But this kind of presentation of bare facts, or non-emotive recording of events, does operate in Marvell, right from the time of the *Ode*, as a particular, perhaps unique, kind of irony: an irony he chose to exercise when, as a man, he was placed in the position of being unable to influence events. 'Men', says M. Legouis, 'for Marvell, direct events, or if they allow themselves to be driven by events, that is indolence or cowardice on their part'.[199] Marvell's position as satirist is: 'I cannot direct events, but I will not be driven by them'. This is obvious from the anonymous poems he wrote when he assumed the mask of anti-Court party political satirist. But in the earlier Marvell, the lyric poet, there existed an acute tension between the quietist, the contemplator of the pastoral, the 'retired' poet—and the activist. It is seen in the *Ode*, a very early poem, which is an attempt to resolve it. These two forces are most plainly seen, respectively, in the lyrics and in the satires.

   Did Marvell stop writing lyrical poetry because the gift left

him? Or did he find that the times in which he lived made the
writing of his kind of poetry impossible? And if so, did he form an
attitude to this fact, from which he created a *persona*—an attitude
that, however unobtrusively, however passively, underlay his whole
output in his later years? For the poet in Marvell never quite died.
In his best satire—and it is one that is universally acknowledged as
being from his pen—*The Last Instructions to a Painter* there are at
least two passages in which he quite deliberately departs from his
basically satirical purpose. In the first passage, describing the Dutch
Admiral de Ruyter's progress up the Thames, he dwells upon the
purely pastoral aspect of what was the prelude to a serious defeat
for the English:

> *Ruyter* the while, that had our Ocean curb'd,
> Sail'd now among our Rivers undisturb'd:
> Survey'd their Crystal Streams, and Banks so green,
> And Beauties e're this never naked seen.
> Through the vain sedge the bashful *Nymphs* he ey'd;
> Bosomes, and all which from themselves they hide.
> The Sun much brighter, and the Skies more clear,
> He finds the Air, and all things, sweeter here.
> The sudden change, and such a tempting sight,
> Swells his old Veins with fresh Blood, fresh Delight.
> Like am'rous Victors he begins to shave,
> And his new Face looks in the *English* Wave.
> His sporting Navy all about him swim,
> And witness their complaisence in their trim.
> Their streaming Silks play through the weather fair,
> And with inveigling Colours Court the Air.
> While the red Flags breath on their Top-masts high
> Terrour and War, but want an Enemy.
> Among the Shrowds the Seamen sit and sing,
> And wanton Boys on every Rope do cling.
> Old *Neptune* springs the Tydes, and Water lent:
> (The Gods themselves do help the provident.)
> And, where the deep Keel on the shallow cleaves,
> With *Trident's* Leaver, and great Shoulder heaves.
> *Æolus* their Sails inspires with *Eastern* Wind,
> Puffs them along, and breathes upon them kind.
> With Pearly Shell the *Tritons* all the while
> Sound the Sea-march, and guide to *Sheppy Isle*.
>   So have I seen in *April's* bud, arise
> A Fleet of Clouds, sailing along the Skies:
> The liquid Region with their Squadrons fill'd,
> The airy Sterns the Sun behind does guild;
> And gentle Gales them steer, and Heaven drives,

When, all on sudden, their calm bosome rives
With Thunder and Lightning from each armed Cloud;
Shepherds themselves in vain in bushes shrowd.
Such up the stream the *Belgick* Navy glides,
And at *Sheerness* unloads its stormy sides.

The other passage, where, as Professor G. F. de Lord has pointed out,[200] Marvell echoes not only Spenser and Shakespeare, but also his old metaphysical self, occurs (with slight variations) in *The Loyal Scot* as well as in *The Last Instructions*:

Not so brave *Douglas*; on whose lovely chin
The early Down but newly did begin;
And modest Beauty yet his Sex did Veil,
While envious Virgins hope he is a Male.
His yellow Locks curl back themselves to seek,
Nor other Courtship knew but to his Cheek.
Oft has he in chill *Eske* or *Seine*, by night,
Harden'd and cool'd his Limbs, so soft, so white,
Among the Reeds, to be espy'd by him,
The *Nymphs* would rustle; he would forward swim.
They sigh'd and said, Fond Boy, why so untame,
That fly'st Love Fires, reserv'd for other Flame?
Fixt on his Ship, he fac'd that horrid Day,
And wondred much at those that run away:
Nor other fear himself could comprehend,
Then, lest Heav'n fall, e're thither he ascend.
But entertains, the while, his time too short
With birding at the *Dutch*, as if in sport:
Or Waves his Sword, and could he them conjure
Within its circle, knows himself secure.
The fatal Bark him boards with grappling fire,
And safely through its Port the *Dutch* retire:
That precious life he yet disdains to save,
Or with known Art to try the gentle Wave.
Much him the Honours of his ancient Race
Inspire, nor would he his own deeds deface.
And secret Joy, in his calm Soul does rise,
That *Monk* looks on to see how *Douglas* dies.
Like a glad Lover, the fierce Flames he meets,
And tries his first embraces in their Sheets.
His shape exact, which the bright flames infold,
Like the Sun's Statue stands of burnish'd Gold.
Round the transparent Fire about him glows,
As the clear Amber on the Bee does close:
And, as on Angels Heads their Glories shine,
His burning Locks adorn his Face Divine.

9—PTTL

But, when in his immortal Mind he felt
His alt'ring Form, and soder'd Limbs to melt;
Down on the Deck he laid himself, and dy'd,
With his dear Sword reposing by his Side.
And, on the flaming Plank, so rests his Head,
As one that's warm'd himself and gone to Bed.
His Ship burns down, and with his Relicks sinks,
And the sad Stream beneath his Ashes drinks.
Fortunate Boy! if either Pencil's Fame,
Or it my Verse can propagate thy Name;
When *Œta* and *Alcides* are forgot,
Our *English* youth shall sing the Valiant *Scot.*

Marvell made enemies in the latter part of his life, and therefore collected a number of the usual calumnies. One of these was to the effect that he had tried to make a living out of poetry and had failed. There is no evidence for this—only against it. But smears often contain a modicum of truth—not of the kind that would benefit the smearer's malevolence, but that is sometimes interesting to biographers. For Marvell was as well equipped as Dryden to make a living out of literature, both by writing plays and by getting himself the kind of patronage that, in the Seventeenth Century, was an essential part of a writer's income. He could certainly have written plays, and his encomiastic verse (what there is of it) is as effective as Dryden's. In fact, if M. Legouis is justified in called Marvell's physical neutrality during the Civil War an 'enigma', then is it not equally justified to call his failure to become a literary man an enigma, too?

But is Marvell's neutrality so enigmatic? We may doubt it. When the Civil War broke out he was only twenty-one. To adhere to either side was equally honourable—equally, one might now say, 'intelligent'. The choice was as desperate a one as has ever been presented to people in English history. Who would not prefer to travel on the continent? And especially if one were young, and concerned more with the writing of poetry than with politics. For whenever Marvell's lyrical poems were written, it was certainly between 1640 and 1565 (but it is much more likely to have been during 1653-4). There are irresistible chronological reasons for supposing that Marvell's decision to become an employee of the Republicans (first in a personal capacity as a tutor, though he had made application for a political post; then as Latin Secretary) coincided with his ceasing to write lyrical poetry.

The *Ode* was written in June 1650, and perhaps marks the initial stage of this deliberate transition from poet to, not politician, but poet-reluctantly-turned-politician. It probably comes before the real poems have been written. Whether Marvell had met Fairfax or not by June 1650, and whether Fairfax's position is or is not reflected in the *Ode*, there is no doubt that Marvell's taking up of a private appointment with a Parliamentary General who had retired for conscientious reasons was an appropriate step for the author of so uncommitted a poem. Marvell himself is the 'forward Youth', who wishes to 'appear' (as a poet), and the first eight lines of the Ode have an ironic force too simple to have struck many critics. For poets do not like forsaking their '*Muses* dear' or donning armour— and their reasons are as moral as personal. Not that Marvell blames Cromwell too much here: the point of what is said about Cromwell is not at all that he is 'great' (obviously, in historical terms, he is 'great'—but this sort of thing is far too imprecise for Marvell), or that he is liked or disliked, but that he is not a poet, and does not think like one. Critics have on the whole failed to discern the object- ivity of this poem: the irony it generates, which has been called 'inhuman', operates as an overwhelming sense of poetic despair. The *Ode* presents a historical version of an *angst* that is as old as tragedy, as old as mankind: the difference between man as he is and man as he ought to be; between conscientious, poetic man (man as poet) and man in criminal history (man in action, as he behaves); between the poet, the 'forward Youth', as he ought to be—and the poet doomed by his own ambition first prompted by his need to exist, which is how he *does* 'appear'.

We cannot, of course, take the *Ode* as marking the end of Marvell's poetic activities. What it does show, however, is Marvell's consciousness of the position he felt himself to be in: historically, Cromwell was the coming man, the ruler. Moreover, Cromwell was now (the King being dead) necessary to survival, both national and personal. Characteristically, he accepts this—although he is still con- stitutional monarchist enough to assume, along with so many of Cromwell's enemies, that he deliberately frightened Charles into flying from Hampton Court, thus setting in motion the events that led to his execution. (However, while we now know that Cromwell did not actually 'plan' Charles's escape, we can hardly deny that it played into his hands—so that Marvell's *Ode* is still poetically truthful, if not historically accurate.) But the acceptance of Cromwell (of power), means that there will be no more poetry. As I remarked above, the *Ode* is an attempt to resolve the tension between the quietist and the activist. But the attempt fails. Such a resolution cannot be made, we are ironically informed. It is like trying to resolve a conflict between a desire to starve and the need to eat. The final lines ('The same *Arts* that did *gain*/A Pow're must it maintain'), with their savagely ironic and yet wistful use of the word '*Arts*', make it clear that the poet knows what the future is going to be like. And if he himself subsequently goes off to Fairfax's house, in which the books are so patently dusted (Fairfax having resigned),

and the languishing numbers so beautifully sung in the shadows, to
write his best poems, then this is a final gesture; he is already aware
of the martial situation. And so, at any rate from when he takes up
employment as a servant of Cromwell's government, all of Marvell's
verse is politically directed; he no longer deals in gardens or in
love. But the poet of gardens and love continues to exist, bitterly,
cleverly, painfully, beneath the impassive mask of the man of affairs.

4

Marvell's two earliest surviving letters are to Cromwell and Milton
respectively. On 28 July 1653, soon after Marvell had taken over
his duties with Cromwell's future ward William Dutton, he wrote
to the Protector from the Eton home of John Oxenbridge, where
the boy had been placed:

> May it please your Excellence,
>   It might perhaps seem fit for me to seek out words
> to giue your Excellence thanks for my selfe. But indeed the
> onely Ciuility which it is proper for me to practise with so
> eminent a Person is to obey you, and to performe honestly
> the worke that you haue set me about. Therefore I shall
> use the time that your Lordship is pleas'd to allow me for
> writing, onely to that purpose for which you haue giuen me
> it: That is to render you some account of Mr Dutton. I
> haue taken care to examine him seuerall times in the presence
> of Mr Oxenbridge, as those who weigh and tell ouer mony
> before some witnesse ere they take charge of it. For I thought
> that there might possibly be some lightnesse in the Coyn,
> or errour in the telling, which hereafter I should be bound
> to make good. Therefore Mr Oxenbridge is the best to
> make your Excellence an impartiall relation thereof. I shall
> onely say that I shall striue according to my best under-
> standing (that is according to those Rules your Lordship
> hath giuen me) to increase whatsoeuer Talent he may haue
> already. Truly he is of a gentle and waxen disposition: and,
> God be praisd, I can not say that he hath brought with him
> any euill Impression, and I shall hope to set nothing upon
> his Spirit but what may be of a good Sculpture. He hath
> in him two things which make Youth most easy to be
> managed, Modesty which is the bridle to Vice, and Emula-
> tion which is the Spurr to Virtue. And the Care which your
> Excellence is pleas'd to take of him is no small incourage-
> ment and shall be so represented to him. But aboue all I
> shall labour to make him sensible of his Duty to God. For

then we begin to serue faithfully, when we consider that
he is our Master. And in this both he and I ow infinitely
to your Lordship, for hauing placed us in so godly a family
as that of Mr Oxenbridge whose Doctrine and Example are
like a Book and a Map, not onely instructing the Eare but
demonstrating to the Ey which way we ought to trauell.
And Mrs Oxenbridge hath a great tendernesse ouer him
also in all other things. She has looked so well to him that
he hath already much mended his Complexion: And now
she is busy in ordring his Chamber, that he may delight
to be in it as often as his Studyes require. For the rest, most
of his time hitherto hath been spent in acquainting our
selves with him: and truly he is very chearfull and I hope
thinks us to be good company. I shall upon occasion hence-
forward informe your Excellence of any particularityes in
our litle affairs. For so I esteem it to be my Duty. I have
no more at present but to give thanks to God for your
Lordship, and to beg grace of him, that I may approve
my selfe.[201]

At the beginning of this letter Marvell employs the familiar formal
style, but for elaborately ironic purposes that Cromwell was quite
incapable of understanding. We have to remember that Marvell
regarded himself as a poet and therefore as independent; he regarded
both the necessity of employment and the disturbing effects of
political upheaval with as much resentment as most other poets;
this grave, wholly private and not personally hostile irony is typical
of him. 'But indeed the onely civility which it is proper for me
to practise with so eminent a Person is to obey you. . . . I shall
use the time that your lordship is pleas'd to allow me for writing,
onely to that purpose for which you have given me it'—the forward
youth is certainly letting his books gather dust now. It may be
objected that I am reading irony or personal emotion into what is
more epistolary form; but the chief feature of much formal letter-
writing is its total lack of sincerity; Marvell was never given to
insincerity, and to avoid it he made a conscious use of irony. Thus
the deadpan flatness of his descriptions of the doings of a Parliament
we know he despised is itself a sort of desperate irony, eloquently
saying, 'Let me only *describe* this dishonest farce'. If we are going
to be subtle about Marvell's poems—and no one can deny either
that they are almost as subtle as any poems in the language or that
modern criticism has been subtle in dealing with them—then we
are entitled to be subtle about his letters; to expect at least a degree
of the irony and subtlety that exist in his poetry to be present in the
letters. It needs to be emphasized, however, that Marvell's irony is
not, in this letter, about Cromwell personally, more than any other

man of power. Cromwell, appropriately, is to be quite unaware of it. The irony is about the situation. We get here, as we get so often in the later Marvell, a private state of mind, an unobtrusive assertion of independence, within an unexceptionable 'public', or formal, framework. The letter is superficially just what it purports to be; but the man Marvell impresses himself upon it with such delicacy that the effect is sarcastically critical, dryly resigned. He mockingly exploits epistolary propriety and humility. Thus Marvell's 'best understanding' is now composed only of 'Rules your Lordship hath given me'. It is the tone of the whole, the plainness, that shows the humility to be mock, that gives the last phrase—'that I may approve myselfe'—an ironic sting that in a more obsequious letter it would lack. Marvell's age made poetry impossible; but he took his revenge upon it, quietly, in the best way he could.

The letter to Milton, written from Eton on 2 June 1654, is an amusing account, couched in terms calculated to be soothing to Milton, of Marvell's difficulties when acting as intermediary between two very touchy men. For the 'my Lord' referred to is almost certainly Bradshaw, the Regicide who was admired by Milton and to whom he had written earlier in the year recommending Marvell's appointment to a government position. Masson in his *Life of Milton* stated that Bradshaw was staying in or near Eton at this time, but unfortunately adduced no evidence. However, since Milton's *Defensio Secunda* had been published a few days earlier, it seems certain that it is the 'your Book' of this letter. Marvell was one of Milton's closest friends, and seems to have owed a good deal to him; but this did not prevent him from being a touch satirical (although not overtly so, Milton's sense of humour being suspect) about his position of mediator between two great personages.

The letters alluded to are lost. Colonel Overton, a friend of Milton's, was Governor of Hull, and was now being interrogated about his alleged incitement of the Northern troops to rebellion; he was close to Cromwell, but apparently entertained scruples, for he was a prisoner in the Tower from 1655 until after Cromwell's death.

Honoured Sir,
I did not satisfie my self in the Account I gave you, of presenting your Book to my Lord, although it seemed to me that I writ to you all which the Messengers speedy Returne the same night from Eaton would permit me. and I perceive that by Reason of that Hast I did not give you satisfaction neither concerning the Delivery of your Letter at the same Time. Be pleased therefore to pardon me, and know, that I tenderd them both together. But my Lord read not the Letter while I was with him, which I attributed

to our Despatch, and some other Businesse tending thereto, which I therefore wished ill to so farr as it hindred an affaire much better and of greater Importance; I mean that of reading your Letter. And to tell you truly mine own Imagination, I thought that He would not open it while I was there, because He might suspect that I delivering it just upon my Departure might have brought in it some second Proposition like to that which you had before made to him by your Letter to my Advantage. However I assure my self that He has since read it, and you, that He did then witnesse all Respect to your person, and as much satisfaction concerning your work as could be expected from so cursory a Review and so sudden an Account as He could then have of it from me. Mr Oxenbridge at his Returne from London will I know give you thanks for his Book, as I do with all Acknowledgement and Humility for that you have sent me. I shall now studie it even to the getting of it by Heart: esteeming it according to my poor Judgement (which yet I wish it were so right in all Things else) as the most compendious Scale, for so much, to the Height of the Roman eloquence. When I consider how equally it turnes and rises with so many figures, it seems to me a Trajans columne in whose winding ascent we see imboss'd the severall Monuments of your learned victoryes. And Salmatius and Morus make up as great a Triumph as That of Decebalus, whom too for ought I know you shall have forced as Trajan the other, to make themselves away out of a just Desperation. I have an affectionate Curiosity to know what becomes of Colonell Overtons businesse. And am exceeding glad to thinke that Mr Skyner is got near you, the Happinesse which I at the same Time congratulate to him and envie. There being none who doth if I may so say more zealously honour you then.[202]

Several other of the letters, mostly personal, which Margoliouth collects under the label 'miscellaneous', have points of interest. When Marvell is writing to his close friend William Popple (the son of his brother-in-law, Edmund Popple, who had risen to an influential position among the Hull merchants) on 14 April 1670 about the King's sudden appearance in the House of Lords, claiming 'from his Ancestors' the right 'to be present at their deliberations', he comments, 'It is true that this has been done long ago, but it is now so old, that it is new, and so disused that at any other, but so bewitched a Time, as this, it would have been looked on as an high Usurpation, and Breach of Privilege'. And of the Lords' preposterous attempt to restore the King 'to all civil or ecclesiasical

Prerogatives which his Ancestors had enjoyed at any Time since the Conquest', he says 'There was never so compendious a Piece of absolute universal Tyranny'. And of the Commons: 'We are all venal Cowards, except some few'.[203]

Reporting the same events officially to Mayor Tripp (16 March 1670), Marvell notes only:

> That which is most extraordinary since my last to you is that his Majesty hath for this whole week come every day in person to the House of Lords & sate there during their debates & resolutions. And yesterday the Lords went in a body to Whitehall to give him thanks for the honour he did them therein.

Of the Lords' attempt to restore the King to his former privileges he says nothing, beyond a passing allusion to the fact that if the Conventicles Bill (to which anti-nonconformist piece of legislation Marvell was bitterly opposed) were passed, yet the King might be able to dispense with it wholly, because of the 'reserving clause' 'for his Majestyes ancient prerogative in all Ecclesiastical things'.[204]

But although Marvell makes no attempt to disguise his opinions on affairs when writing to his personal friends, he is still laconic, relying on his style of unfolding events to express his views about them. The following letter to William Popple (28 November 1670) speaks for itself:

> *Dear Will,*
> I need not tell you I am always thinking of you. All that has happened, which is remarkable, since I wrote, is as follows. The Lieutenancy of *London*, chiefly *Sterlin*, the Mayor, and *Sir J. Robinson* alarmed the King continually with the Conventicles there. So the King sent them strict and large Powers. The *Duke of York* every Sunday would come over thence to look to the Peace. To say Truth they met in numerous open Assemblys, without any Dread of Government. But the Train Bands in the City, and Soldiery in *Southwark* and Suburbs, harrassed and abused them continually; they wounded many, and killed some Quakers, especially while they took all patiently. Hence arose two Things of great Remark. The Lieutenancy, having got Orders to their Mind, pick out *Hays* and *Jekill*, the innocentest of the whole Party, to shew their Power on. They offer them illegal Bonds of five thousand Pounds a Man, which if they would not enter into, they must go to Prison. So they were commited, and at last (but it is a very long Story,) got free. Some Friends engaged for them. The other was the Tryal of *Pen* and *Mead*, Quakers, at the old Baily. The Jury not finding them guilty, as the Recorder

and Mayor would have had them, they were kept without Meat or Drink some three Days, till almost starved, but would not alter their Verdict; so fined and imprisoned. There is a Book out which relates all the Passages which were very pertinent, of the Prisoners, but prodigiously barbarous by the Mayor and Recorder. The Recorder, among the rest, commended the *Spanish* Inquisition, saying it would never be well till we had something like it. The King had Occasion for sixty thousand Pounds. Sent to borrow it of the City. *Sterlin, Robinson*, and all the rest of that Faction, were at it many a Week, and could not get above ten thousand. The Fanatics, under Persecution, served his Majesty. The other Party, both in Court and City, would have prevented it. But the King protested Mony would be acceptable. So the City patched up, out of the Chamber, and other Ways, twenty thousand Pounds. The Fanatics, of all Sorts, forty thousand. The King, though against many of his Council, would have the Parliament sit this twenty fourth of October. He, and the Keeper, spoke of Nothing but to have Mony. Some one Million three hundred thousand Pounds, to pay off the Debts at Interest; and eight hundred thousand Pounds, for a brave Navy next Spring. Both Speeches forbid to be printed, for the King said very little, and the Keeper, it was thought, too much in his politic simple Discourse of foreign Affairs. The House was thin and obsequious. They voted at first they would supply Him, according to his Occasions, *Nemine*, as it was remarked, *contradicente*; but few Affirmatives, rather a Silence as of Men ashamed and unwilling. *Sir R. Howard, Seymour, Temple, Car*, and *Hollis*, openly took Leave of their former Party, and fell to head the King's Busyness. There is like to be a terrible Act of Conventicles. The *Prince of Orange* here is much made of. The King owes Him a great Deal of Mony. The Paper is full.[205]

This shows, as clearly as any letter he wrote, what Marvell thought about oppression and injustice, and how he expressed his thoughts to his close friends. One sentence, 'The Fanatics, under Persecution, served his Majesty', is typically Marvellian in its compression and far-reaching irony.

It is seldom that Marvell, beyond referring to the things he did not like with single derogatory adjectives (thus, the Conventicle Bill is 'terrible'), departs from his technique of simply describing events in order to deprecate them. But in a letter of late April 1671 to Popple his feelings get the better of him:

I think it will be my lot to go on an Honest Fair Employment into *Ireland*. Some have smelt the Court of *Rome* at that Distance. There I hope I shall be out of the Smell of our.[206]

Such outspokenness is exceptional.

In a letter of 9 August 1671 to an unknown friend in Persia, Marvell alludes to an incident that he commemorated in verse:

> One *Blud*, outlawed for a Plot to take *Dublin* castle . . . a most bold, and yet sober, Fellow, some Months ago seized the Crown and Sceptre in the Tower, took them away, and, if he had killed the Keeper, might have carryed them clear off. He, being taken, astonished the King and Court, with the Generosity, and Wisdom, of his Answers. He and all his Accomplices, for his Sake, are discharged by the King, to the Wonder of all.[207]

Marveill's Latin lines on this incident exist separately; a delightful English version occurs in *The Loyal Scot*:

> When daring Blood to have his rents regain'd
> Upon the English Diadem distrain'd,
> Hee Chose the Cassock Circingle and Gown
> The fittest Mask for one that Robs a Crown.
> But his Lay pitty underneath prevailed
> And while hee spared the keepers life hee fail'd.
> With the preists vestments had hee but put on
> A Bishops Cruelty, the Crown had gone.

Blood's choice of disguise gave Marvell an opportunity to express his opinion of Bishops (as persons, not as functionaries); to the end of his life he blamed Laud for the Civil War. His undoubted antipathy to Bishops and his sympathy for the Dissenters have caused many critics, including M. Legouis, to assume that he was himself a Puritan; but dislike for one thing does not, in a man like Marvell, imply attachment to what is generally opposed to it. Marvell's poetry is too lush simply to be labelled 'Calvinistic'; his well-known liking for wine and the occasional scatology of his prose are not features of a Puritan. He probably respected the Cromwellian administration for its freedom from corruption and for its efficiency; he certainly respected his friend Milton; but his own levity, sense of humour, lack of solemnity (as in the poem on Blood quoted above), do not suggest a very conventional kind of Puritan. Burnet called him 'the livliest droll of the age'. He may even have been, so far as orthodox religion is concerned, a sceptic. M. Legouis himself admits that the 1650 *Ode* is thoroughly 'pagan'—though he does not point out that its paganism, while in one sense accepted by its author, is a part of its ultimate irony, inasmuch as Christianity is supposed to lead to peace. Attempts to Christianize Marvell's poems have not been convincing. The theological framework of many of them does not necessarily argue for a theological content—let alone for an orthodox one. The question of Marvell's beliefs remains as much a mystery as that of Shakespeare's; there is less warrant for M. Legouis's assertion of Marvell's Puritanism than there is for his poetry and his patriotism (he entitles his book *Andrew Marvell: Poet, Puritan, Patriot*).

Marvell was an opposition M.P., but this is not an argument for his disbelief in constitutional monarchy. Nor is his dislike of bishops necessarily more than a dislike of certain persons (clergy are most hated by other clergy, not by atheists): perhaps it reflects a characteristic questioning of the relevance of orthodoxies and establishments. Marvell, we know, was a most courageous man. It is odd, then, if he was a convinced Puritan, that there should be no evidence of it in his private letters or in his anonymous pamphlets. With reference to the latter, he might just as well have been hung for a sheep as for a lamb. His reticence on the subject seems to have been neither politic nor strategic, but fundamental. My own conviction is that he was a religious sceptic, with allegiances divided between Anglican flexibility and Puritan seriousness.

M. Legouis seems to think that Marvell remained a convinced Cromwellian in politics and religion for the rest of his life. But is it as simple as that? His last two prose works *Mr. Smirke . . .* (printed together with an *Essay Concerning Councils . . .*) and *An Account of the Growth of Popery . . .* (1677), if they could have been proved to be his, would have rendered him liable to at least imprisonment. Why should he have limited himself in these works only to undermining the logic of Anglican intolerance, as distinct from Anglicanism itself (this is the theme of the *Essay Concerning Councils . . .* , which was the really offensive part of the publication), and to an attack on 'popish conspirators' and on French designs?

Suppose we grant what is unlikely: that he was cautious in these. There is still a private letter, of 1 July 1676, to his friend Sir Edward Harley, concerning *Mr. Smirke*. Now this letter is itself cautious both in that it is deliberately unsigned, and in that Marvell nowhere actually admits that he is the author of *Mr. Smirke*. I quote the latter half:

> Here are diverse books come out lately. The Catholick Naked Truth, by a Papist. A modest Survey of a discourse intitled the Naked Truth (the poore mans book) by Burnet. The Conference before the Lady Tirwhit by Burnet and Stillingfleet. Dr Stillingfleets answer to Godwin, where in his prefatory Epistle to the Bishop of London dated May the 30th he seems to have read the sheet so seditious and defamatory to Christian Religion. the book said to be Marvels makes what shift it can in the world but the Author

walks negligently up & down as unconcerned. The Divines of our Church say it is not in the merry part so good as the Rehearsall Transpros'd, that it runns dreggs: the Essay they confesse is writ well enough to the purpose he intended it but that was a very ill purpose. The Bishop of Londons Chaplain said it had not answered expectation. Dr Turner first met it at Broom's went into a Chamber & though he were to have dined which he seldome omits nor approves of Fasting yet would not come down but read it all over in consequence. The Bishop of London has carryed it in his hand at Council severall days, showing his friends the passages he has noted but none takes notice of them. No man in the Town appears more curiously & studiously concerned against it then Dr Bates (most upon the score of the Nicene Councill) But why? It dos not against his Corporation Oath teach that it is lawfull to take arms against persons Commissionated by his Majestys authority. But some years agoe I heard that he said Marvell was an Intelligencer to the King of France. Twas about the same time that the Doctor was in pension to another Monarch. I know not what to say: Marvell, if it be he, has much staggerd me in the busnesse of the Nicene & all Councills, but had better have taken a rich Presbyterians mony that before the book came out would have bought the whole Impression to burne it. Who would write? What saith the poor man.[208]

The question is, would Marvell have gone out of his way to remark to a close friend, who knew perfectly well that he had written *Mr. Smirke* (Ponder, its printer, had been committed in the previous May for issuing it without a license), that 'It dos not against his Corporation Oath teach that it is lawfull to take arms against persons Commissionated by his Majestyes authority', unless he meant it? It is true that the end of this letter is, as Margoliouth writes in a note, 'a dodge', in case it is intercepted by the authorities, to prevent *formal* proof of his authorship; but the preceding statement, about his attitude to rebellion, rings true. Furthermore, as Marvell hints (and it is a fact), the Presbyterians were nearly as annoyed with him over *Mr. Smirke* as were the Anglican Establishment—no doubt because of his levity. The picture is of an independent, sceptical thinker, advocating toleration and resistance of Roman Catholic authoritarianism, rather than of a single-minded Cromwellian Puritan. Marvell's dislike of Roman Catholicism was as political as religious (though he used religious arguments to attack it, as any good satirist would): it was justified by historical events; few then had good reason to advocate toleration for Popery: their subjection to it was, after all, being planned. M. Legouis's final remarks on Marvell's religious position are undecided: he is Cromwellian; he anticipates the Deists; 'all sense of the supernatural had not died out in him by 1672. . . .' To say simply that he was 'Cromwellian' is clearly an over-simplification. Cromwell was a Puritan, even if he did get caught up in the familiar tangle between the need for tolerance and the desire for comprehension. Marvell, who had not to bear the burden of maintaining the power he had gained, could afford to be more speculative; was a poet, not a soldier and dictator.

There is an important passage in a letter to Popple of 15 July 1676. He has been writing about the reception of the contents of *Mr. Smirke*, and he goes on:

> indeed I ment all very well but tis not evry ones good fortune to light into those hands where he may escape for a man of good intentions lesse then this I could not say in due & humble acknowledgement of your favourable interpretation of mee, for the rest I most heartily rejoyce to understand it the same god whoe hath chosen you out to beare soe eminent a testimony to his truth, hath given you alsoe that christian magnanimity to hold up without any depression of spirit against its & your opposers, what they intend further I know not neither am I curious my soul shall not enter into their secrets, but as long as God shall lend you life & health I reckon our church is indefectible, he therefore long preserve you to his honour & further service which shall be the constant prayer of my Lord your Ldships must humble & most faythfull servant.[209]

The phrase 'our church is indefectible' undoubtedly indicates his acceptance of the Anglican compromise. After all, he cannot be paying ironic lip-service in public; he is writing to a private person, one of his closest friends. The position, so far as we can understand it, is not far from Donne's. Later (1687) Popple himself was to publish *A rational Catechism*, in which, M. Legois tells us, he calls the Gospel 'a plain rule for living well', and says that revelation would have been unnecessary but for 'the Vulgar sort of People'.[210]

'Did Marvell think so meanly?' M. Legouis asks, unhappily. There is no evidence at all that he did not. But such 'thinking' is not in any way 'mean'; nor does it inform us of much about Marvell's personality. A man who thought like this in Marvell's time would have been a Moderate (not a High) Anglican; he might have sympathized with the Puritans' insistence upon freedom of individual conscience, but would not have shared their fanaticism and would have diverged from them on some constitutional grounds. He would have been an independent, as Marvell clearly was: not inconsistent, or a 'Machiavellian', yet committed to no single political or religious doctrine, and therefore difficult to describe in conventional terms.

Marvell's quarrel was never with the Church, but with venal politicians and with an abominable set of Bishops.

As for the matter of 'Revelation': if there is not much about it to be found in Marvell's works, then this is perhaps because he disliked 'public' revelation, and thought it the opposite of 'mean' to be reticent. Had he been a Puritan he would certainly have been positively in favour of it. His poems are in themselves, after all, 'revelations' of a much more notable sort. He may have written them mainly for his own satisfaction (he published none of his lyrics); they certainly show how his private mind worked. The fact that so little of his important poetry was published, in an age when publication was hardly any longer thought of as a vulgarity, may in itself be added evidence of Marvell's natural reticence.

In the original 1681 edition of the poems there are two Latin elegies for the sons of Marvell's friend John Trott. Mary 'Marvell' (i.e. Mary Palmer), or whoever arranged the book for her, included a covering letter to Trott himself, which must have been written in the summer of 1667. Marvell himself could never have supposed that this letter would be published—the version we have is certainly a draft, found amongst his papers after his death. It is a characteristically careful and conscientious letter of condolence, and in it we may suppose that Marvell revealed some hint of the complexion of his religion. Is it wholly conventional? Puritan? Orthodox? Or is it, so far as its subject decently allows it to be, individual, not in the 'enthusiastic' Puritan sense, but in the broad Anglican sense?

> I have not that vanity to believe, if you weigh your late Loss by the common ballance, that any thing I can write to you should lighten your resentments: nor if you measure things by the rule of Christianity, do I think it needful to comfort you in your own duty and your Sons happiness. Only having a great esteem and affection for you, and the grateful memory of him that is departed being still green and fresh upon my Spirit, I cannot forbear to unquire how you have stood the second shock[211] at your sad meeting of Friends in the Country. I know that the very sight of those who have been witnesses of our better Fortune, doth but serve to reinforce a Calamity. I know the contagion of grief, and infection of Tears, and especially when it runs in a blood. And I my self could sooner imitate then blame those innocent relentings of Nature, so that they spring from tenderness only and humanity, not from an implacable sorrow. The Tears of a family may flow together like those little drops that compact the Rainbow, and if they be plac'd with the same advantage towards Heaven as those are to the Sun, they too have their splendor: and like that bow while they

unbend into seasonable showers, yet they promise that there
shall not be a second flood. But the dissoluteness of grief,
the prodigality of sorrow is neither to be indulg'd in a
mans self, nor comply'd with in others. If that were allow-
able in these cases, *Eli's* was the readiest way and highest
complement of mourning, who fell back from his seat and
broke his neck. But neither does that precedent hold. For
though he had been Chancellor, and in effect King of *Israel*,
for so many years; and such men value as themselves so
their losses at an higher rate then others; yet when he heard
that *Israel* was overcome, that his two Sons *Hophni* and
Phineas were slain in one day, and saw himself so without
hope of Issue, and which imbittered it further without
succession to the Government, yet he fell not till the News
that the Ark of God was taken. I pray God that we may
never have the same paralel perfected in our publick con-
cernments. Then we shall need all the strength of Grace
and Nature to support us. But upon a private loss, and
sweetned with so many circumstances as yours, to be
impatient, to be uncomfortable, would be to dispute with
God and beg the question. Though in respect of an only
gourd an only Son be inestimable, yet in comparison to
God man bears a thousand times less proportion: so that it
is like *Jonah's* sin to be angry at God for the withering of
his Shadow. *Zipporah*, though the delay had almost cost her
husband his life, yet when he did but circumcise her Son,
in a womanish pevishness reproacht *Moses* as a bloody
husband. But if God take the Son himself, but spare the
Father, shall we say that he is a bloody God. He that gave
his own Son, may he not take ours? 'Tis pride that makes a
Rebel. And nothing but the over-weening of our selves and
our own things that raises us against divine Providence.
Whereas *Abraham's* obedience was better then Sacrifice.
And if God please to accept both, it is indeed a farther
Tryal, but a greater honour. I could say over upon this
beaten occasion most of those lessons of morality and
religion that have been so often repeated and are as soon
forgotten. We abound with precept, but we want examples.
You, Sir, that have all these things in your memory, and
the clearness of whose Judgment is not to be obscured by
any greater interposition, it remains that you be exemplary
to others in your own practice. 'Tis true, it is an hard task
to learn and teach at the same time. And, where your selfe
are the experiment, it is as if a man should dissect his own
body and read the Anatomy Lecture. But I will not heighten
the difficulty while I advise the attempt. Only, as in difficult

things, you will do well to make use of all that may strengthen and assist you. The word of God: The society of good men: and the books of the Ancients. There is one way more, which is by diversion, business, and activity; which are also necessary to be used in their season. But I my self, who live to so little purpose, can have little authority or ability to advise you in it, who are a Person that are and may be much more so generally useful. All that I have been able to do since, hath been to write this sorry Elogie of your Son, which if it be as good as I could wish, it is as yet no undecent imployment. However I know you will take any thing kindly from your very affectionate friend and most humble Servant.[212]

Some of this, such as the Biblical precepts, is commonplace. But the letter is redeemed from cliché by its manner. The first part, until the name of Eli is brought in, harks back, in its highly 'metaphysical' style, to Marvell's poems of fifteen years earlier. The metaphor of the rainbow formed by the tears of the mourning family recalls the poems he wrote about tears and mourning: *Eyes and Tears* and the sardonic *Mourning*. Incidentally, the letter is far from conventionally Puritan in tone, both in the careful and intelligent balance it achieves between personal grief and the providential fact of death, and, most particularly, in its refusal to treat God's destroying will with Old Testament relish. It is possible to deduce from it, I think, that Marvell was not an atheist; but not much more. However, as M. Legouis remarks in his only comment on it, when Marvell wrote the sentence, 'And where your self are the experiment, it is as if a man should dissect his own body and read the Anatomy Lecture', the 'lurid metaphysical light still shone' in him. One might infer more: that this, the most characteristic sentence of all, reveals Marvell's real interest—in the psychology, rather than the theory, of grief. What he means here is: 'Find out what the grief means.' The poet was still at work in him.

And so Marvell's letters are more rewarding than they might have seemed at first sight. They teach us to dig well beneath the blandness of their surface, and therefore the surface of his poems; they provide us, in their flat way, with a poet's view of Restoration politics; they show that, despite his capacity for aloofness, Marvell was a warm friend; they are evidence of the means by which he retained his intellectual and emotional integrity. It may seem a pity that the letters he wrote while acting as tutor at Fairfax's, when he was in all probability writing his best poems, are lost. Perhaps, although it is unlikely, they provided pie-bottoms. But we may guess that they said little about the poetry. For Marvell had high standards: the poems speak for themselves. One can hardly imagine his spoiling their qualities of subtlety and delicacy by commenting upon them.

Marvell is shrewdly non-confessional: his poems are themselves too acutely personal. The careful covering-up process displayed in the letters becomes, in the poems, a technique. M. Legouis thinks that Swift's praise of *The Rehearsal Transpros'd* in *A Tale of a Tub* is 'almost excessive'; but Swift understood Marvell. Both men sought to suppress the passion in their own natures, for fear of the consequences. Swift's letters, too, are full of devices—although much more elaborate and numerous—for allowing the reader to infer the brutal truth, rather than stating it to him. Both saw the two faces of the truth as brutal: the criminality of history (facts, events) and the impotence of the observer passionately sensitive to such criminality, to alter it. And both, in spite of this fear of self-revelation, were gifted with the capacity to make close friends. Both hated oppression.

Marvell remains mysterious. In his life-time he resisted vulgar speculation about himself, and now his poems resist the ultimately vulgar attempts of critics to marry them to religious or philosophical systems.

I

Only sixty-two of Dryden's letters have survived; many of these were written in the last ten years of his life, when he was not in favour with the Court. As his biographer, Charles E. Ward, writes in his edition of the letters, he 'lived before the days when poets and playwrights wrote letters with one eye on posterity, and indeed before the commercial value of such private correspondence was widely recognized'.[213]

Whatever view is taken of Dryden's merits as a poet, he is a figure of the utmost importance. In him more than in any other single writer we may note the transition from 'barbarism' to 'correctness': he ushers in the Augustan age.

Dryden cannot be called a bad or unpleasant man, in the sense that Pope can and sometimes is. As a satirist, he was motivated more by instincts of self-defence than by envy and aggressiveness or spite. Even his roughest satire has a core of good humour; when it rises to its best (as in the famous passage on Shaftsbury in *Absalom and Achitophel*) it turns into, at the least, acute psychological appraisal. Even *Mac Flecknoe*, which cannot be said to spare Shadwell, has quite as much good, intelligent fun about it as malice. Dryden is the least malevolent of major satirists.

He was born into a good but poor Northamptonshire family in 1631. Educated at Westminster School, in 1650 he became a scholar of Trinity College, Cambridge. Both sides of his family inclined towards Parliament during the Civil War. He appears to have stayed at Cambridge until 1657, when he took up a government appointment. Throughout his life he was obliged to support himself by his pen, at first mainly by the writing of plays, later by becoming Charles II's official satirist, and later still by translation. He married Lady Elizabeth Howard in 1663, and although they did not always live together, and Dryden probably kept a mistress, they remained on good terms; his affection for and loyalty to all three of his sons was never in doubt, as plainly appears from his letters. He married above himself, but his wife brought him no financial relief.

His heroic plays were highly successful during the 'sixties, but he became unpopular, was attacked in satires and even beaten up in the street (though not at the behest of Rochester, as was once believed). He ably served Charles II with his satires on Monmouth and Shaftesbury, and in 1668 became the first official Poet Laureate.

The poet of *Religio Laici* (1682) is certainly a Protestant; but soon after the accession of James II Dryden became a Roman Catholic. There is no reason to suppose that this was not a wholly sincere conversion, since although it happened to coincide with the arrival of a Catholic monarch, Dryden steadfastly refused to swear allegiance to William and Mary after the 1688 Revolution. Despite his religion and consequent unpopularity at the Court of William and Mary, Dryden was towards the end of his life widely regarded as the greatest writer of his age; but he had never posed as such. Although he was honoured by almost all his younger literary contemporaries at Will's Coffee House, and although his chief fame is as a satirist, he was a reticent, uneccentric man who disliked quarrels. He died in 1770 and was buried in Westminster Abbey.

After small but technically elegant beginnings, celebrating both Cromwell and then Charles II, Dryden published *Annus Mirabilis* in 1667; his first really important poem, the satire *Absalom and Achitophel*, was published in 1681; the second part appeared in 1682. Then followed, in quick succession, *The Medall* (1682), *Mac Flecknoe* (1682) and *Religio Laici*. All these, from *Absalom and Achitophel* onwards, were written in the service of Charles II; they are convincing because Dryden revered constituted authority, and was most happy when he felt he could defend it with complete sincerity.

Between *Annus Mirabilis* and the first of his satires he had been writing plays, including an adaptation of *The Tempest*, *The Conquest of Granada*, *Aurang-Zebe* and *All For Love*.

The three-part fable *The Hind and the Panther* (1687) is essentially a defence of his religious and political position, although commentators cannot entirely agree about its intentions. In the last ten years of his life he made many translations, including *The Aeniad*, and returned to writing plays. His critical prose is mostly scattered amongst his Dedications and Prefaces, although *Dramatick Poesie* (1668) is a separate essay.

2

Whether Dryden 'founded' Augustanism by accident or design, whether or not he was a good influence on English poetry, his letters tell us relatively little about him. While they are never self-consciously 'literary' or formal, they display all his considerable reticence. He emerges (so far as he emerges at all), in some ways unexpectedly, as an attractive and modest man, who had a better developed sense of decency than the mass of his contemporaries. The renowned monarch of Will's Coffee House makes no appearance. There is no reason to suppose that this picture would be substantially changed by the discovery of more letters.

In a letter written to the poet Rochester, with whom Dryden was then on good terms, in about April/May of 1673, there is an interesting anticipation of his portrait of the Duke of Buckingham as Zimri in *Absalom and Achitophel*, written eight years later.

> . . . I hope your Lordship will not omitt the occasion of laughing at the Great Duke of B—— who is so oneasy to [him] self by pursueing the honour of Lieutenant Generall which flyes him, that he can enjoy nothing he possesses. Though at the same time, he is so unfit to command an Army, that he is the onely Man in the three Nations who does not know it. Yet he still picques him self, like his father, to find another Isle of Rhe in Zealand . . . and will not be satisfyed but with his own ruine and with ours. Tis a strange quality in a man to love idlenesse so well as to destroy his Estate by it; and yet at the same time to pursue so violently the most toilesome, and most unpleasant part of businesse.

Dryden continues:

> These observations would easily run into lampoon, if I had not forsworn that dangerous part of wit, not so much out of good nature, But at least from the inborn vanity of poets.

This shrewd candour is often evident in the letters, as when he says (again to Rochester, in an earlier passage in the same letter), '. . . thinking it selfe, is a kind of paine to a witty man; he finds so much more in it to disquiet, than to please him'.[214]

A letter of July 1677 to Lord Latimer mentions that the King himself had a hand in at least the plot of one of Dryden's unsuccessful comedies, *Mr. Limberham* or *The Kind Keeper*:

> . . . the Kings Comedy lyes in the Sudds . . . it will be almost such another piece of businesse as the fond Husband, for such the King will have it, who is parcell poet with me in the plott; one of the designes being a story he was pleasd formerly to tell me; and therefore I hope he will keep the jeast in countenance by laughing at it.[215]

Evidently the King did not do so, for *Mr. Limberham* was banned from performance after playing for only three nights at Dorset

Garden—by Royal command.[216] Probably the King's share in it amounted to no more than the furnishing of an anecdote, upon the strength of which Dryden was only too delighted to be able to claim him as 'parcell poet'.

The essential Dryden was too tolerant and intelligent a critic wholly to approve of Thomas Rymer.[217] Nevertheless, his letters, among other of his writings, show that his respect—despite reservations—for this rule-bound advocate of the classical went deep. Dryden was not one of those critics whose views transcend those of his time: his one reference to Marvell compares him to Martin Marprelate, and he was thoroughly in tune with his age in stating that Edmund Waller was 'the father of our English numbers . . . unless he had written, none of us could write'. In a letter to the Earl of Dorset written in mid-1677 he says of Rymer's *Tragedies of the Last Age*,

> 'tis certainly very learned, & the best piece of Criticism in the English tongue. . . . If I am not altogether of his opinion, I am so, in most of what he sayes: and thinke my selfe happy that he has not fallen upon me, as severely and as wittily as he has upon Shakespeare, and Fletcher. for he is the only man I know capable of finding out a poets blind sides. . . .[218]

In the same year he had second thoughts, and produced *Heads of an Answer* (to Rymer's *Tragedies of the Last Age*); but he still wrote of it with respect.

In a letter of about March 1693 to the critic John Dennis (later to quarrel famously with Pope), Dryden expresses his most balanced view of Rymer's criticism:

> Shakespear had a Genius for it [tragedy]; and we know, in spite of Mr. R— that Genius alone is a greater Virtue (if I may so call it) than all other Qualifications put together. You see what success this Learned Critick has found in the World, after his blaspheming Shakespear. Almost all the Faults which he has discover'd are truly there; yet who will read Mr. Rym— or not read Shakespear? For my own part I reverence Mr. Rym—s Learning, but I detest his Ill Nature and his Arrogance. I indeed, and such as I, have reason to be afraid of him, but Shakespear has not.[219]

In May 1693, writing to William Walsh, Dryden says that he will be 'proud' to enter 'into the lists' on behalf of the 'Moderns' as against the 'Ancients'. This mostly superficial controversy, about dramatic principles, had been raging for some years, with Rymer the unswerving champion of the cause of the Ancients, and with Dryden (most sensibly of all) the defender of the modern drama against both factions—'though not', as he explained, 'against Rymer' him-self. This was because Dryden was at that time engaged in his own critique of Rymer (and others), in the Dedication (to Lord Radcliff) of his third Miscellany of Poems, *Examen Poeticum*.

In August 1693, in a letter to his publisher Tonson, Dryden speaks more disparagingly of Rymer: he had heard that the Queen has commanded him, as her Historiographer (a post Dryden himself had held under Charles II and James II, and of which he had been deprived in 1688), 'to fall upon my Playes'. 'I doubt not his malice,' he says, 'from a former hint you gave me: & if he be employd, I am confident tis of his own seeking; who you know has spoken slightly of me in his last Critique: & that gave me occasion to snarl againe'.[220] Actually the Royal command was not obeyed.

All in all, Dryden seems to have felt reluctance about attacking Rymer: he does not refer to him by name in the Dedication to Radcliff, although he attacks him; and he called him a 'great critic' as late as 1700, in his Preface to the *Fables*. Nevertheless, the attack in the Dedication to Radcliff is sharp and just, and confirms the view that Dryden was at his very best when he had been prompted to write in defence of himself or of his position. 'Ill writers are usually the sharpest censors' and '. . . the corruption of a poet is the generation of a critic' must have been written with Rymer in mind: this unfortunate man, a conscientious and important historian despite his lack of literary judgement, had written a rhymed, 'classical', immaculately meritless tragedy called *Edgar*.

3

Such letters as we have concerning Dryden's personal affairs show him in a good light, neither too fawning nor too arrogant. He exercises the same fairness and temperateness that distinguish him as a critic.

In 1682 his son Charles was temporarily suspended from Westminster School by Dr. Busby, who had been Dryden's own headmaster. His letter to Busby on this occasion is a model of what such a letter should be, and is worth quoting in full for the light it casts on Dryden's sensibility.

> Sir
>
> If I could have found in my selfe a fitting temper, to have waited on you, I had done it, the day you dismissed my sonn from the College: for he did the message; and, by what I find from Mr Meredith, as it was deliverd by you to him: namely that you desird to see me; and had somewhat to say to me concerning him. I observ'd likewise somewhat of kindnesse in it, that you sent him away, that you might

not have occasion to correct him. I examin'd the business;
and found it concernd his haveing been Custos[221] foure or
five dayes together. But if he admonishd, and was not
believd because other boyes combind to discredit him with
false witnesseing, and to save them selves, perhaps his crime
was not so great. Another fault it seemes he made which
was goeing into one Hawkes his house with some others;
which you hapning to see, sent your servant to know who
they were; and he onely returnd you my sonns name: so
the rest escapd: I have no fault to find with my sonns
punishment; for that is and ought to be reserv'd to any
Master, much more to you who have been his fathers. But
your man was certainly to blame to name him onely; and tis
onely my respect to you, that I do not take notice of it to
him. My first rash resolutions were to have brought things
past any composure, by immediately sending for my sonns
things out of the College: but upon recollection I find I
have a double tye upon me not to do it. one my obligations
to you for my Education: another my great tendernesse of
doeing anything offensive to my Lord Bishop of Rochester,
as cheife Governour of the College. It does not consist
with the honour I beare him and you, to go so precipitately
to worke: no not so much as to have any difference with
you, if it can possibly be avoyded. Yet As my sonn stands
now, I cannot see with what credit he can be elected: for
being but sixth, and (as you are pleasd to judge,) not
deserving that neither, I know not whether he may not go
immediately to Cambridge, as well as one of his own
Election went to Oxford this yeare by your consent. I will
say nothing of my second sonn, but that after you had been
pleasd to advise me to waite on my Lord Bishop for his
favour, I found he might have had the first place, if you
had not opposd it: and I likewise found at the Election,
that by the paines you had taken with him, he in some sort
deservd it: I hope, Sir, when you have given your selfe the
trouble to read thus farr, you, who are a prudent man, will
consider, that none complaine, but they desire to be re-
concild at the same time: there is no mild Expostulation at
least, which does not intimate a kindnesse and respect in
him who makes it. Be pleasd if there be no merit on my
side. to make it your own act of grace to be what you were
formerly to my sonn. I have done something, so farr to
conquer my own Spirit as to ask it: and, indeed, I know not
with what face to go to my Lord Bishop, and to tell him I
am takeing away both my sonns: for though I shall tell him
no occasion; it will looke like a disrespect to my old Master;

of which I will not be guilty if it be possible. I shall add no more, but hope I shall be so satisfyed with a favourable answer from you, which I promise to my selfe from your goodnesse and moderation, that I shall still have occasion to continue.[222]

Dryden's five extant letters to the young William Walsh, of whom he appears to have thought highly, are valuable as showing his kindliness, modesty and soundness as a mentor, as well as some aspects of his practice as a poet. The best example, which demonstrates Dryden's careful and considered approach to writing, belongs to late 1691, when Walsh was twenty-eight. Walsh had sent Dryden three poems: an *Elegy to his False Mistress* (an imitation of Ovid), a *Dialogue Concerning Women*, and an epigram, *Gripe and Shifter*. When the epigram appeared in 1792 Walsh had amended the lines exactly as Dryden suggested; as Ward observes, these letters to Walsh provide 'the sole example of the poet's definite corrections of a particular poem for another poet', although it has always been known that Dryden was constructively helpful to younger writers. The finished version of Walsh's epigram reads as follows:

> Rich Gripe does all his Thoughts and Cunning bend,
> T' encrease that Wealth he wants the Soul to spend.
> Poor Shifter does his whole Contrivance set
> To spend the Wealth, he wants the Sense to get.
> How happy wou'd appear to each his Fate,
> Had Gripe his Humour, or he Gripe's Estate!
> King Fate and Fortune, blend 'em if you can,
> And of two Wretches, make one happy Man.

This, alas, represents the dilettante Walsh's highest efforts in verse; but he is important in that, as a protégé of Dryden's, he early instilled into Pope the idea of poetry as a species of 'correctness'. By astute flattery of both Dryden and Pope he was able to get his own imitative verses vastly overpraised by both. Nevertheless, it is to Dryden's credit that he took so much trouble over him—as this letter shows:

> You command me Deare Sir, to make a kind of critique on your Essay: 'tis an hard province; but if I were able to undertake it, possibly, a greater proofe of friendship is scarcely to be found; where to be truly a friend, a man must seeme to exercise a little malice. As it happens, I am now incumberd with some necessary business, relating to one of my Sonns; which when it is over, I shall have more leysure to obey you, in case there appeare any farther need. There is not the least occasion of reflecting on your disposition of the piece, nor the thoughts. I see nothing to

censure in either of them. Besides this the style is easy and
naturall; as fit for Dialogue, as if you had set Tully before
you; and as gallant as Fontenelle in his plurality of Worlds.
In the correctness of the English there is not much for me
to animadvert. Be pleasd therefore, to avoid the words,
don't, can't, shan't, and the like abbreviations of syllables;
which seem to me to savour of a little rusticity. As for
Pedantry you are not to be taxd with it. I remember I
hinted somewhat of concluding your Sentences with pre-
positions or conjunctions sometimes, which is not elegant,
as in your first sentence—(See the consequences of). I find
likewise, that you make not a due distinction betwixt that,
and who; a man *that* is not proper; the relative *who* is
proper. *That*, ought alwayes to signify a thing; *who*, a
person. An acquainttance *that* wou'd have *undertook* the
business; true English is, an acquaintanance who wou'd
have *undertaken* the business. I am confident I need not
proceed with these little criticisms, which are rather cavil-
lings, Philareque, or the Critique on Balzac, observes it as
a fault in his style, that he has in many places written
twenty words together (en suitte) which were all Mono-
syllables. I observe this in some lines of your Noble Epigramm: and am often guilty of it myselfe through hastinesse.
Mr. Waller counted this a vertue of the English tongue, that
it cou'd bring so many words of the Teutonique together,
and yet the smoothness of the Verse not vitiated. Now I am
speaking of your Epigramm, I am sure you will not be
offended with me for saying, there is some imperfection in
the two last lines.

Blend 'em together, Fate, ease both theire paine;
And of two wretches make one happy man. The word blend
includes the sense of *together*; ease both their paine: paine
is Singular, both is Plurall. But indeed *paine* may have a
collective and plurall signification. Then the Rhyme is not
full of pain and Man. An half rhyme is not always a fault;
but in the close of any paper of verses, tis to be avoyded.
And after all, tell me truly, if those words, ease both their
paine; were not superfluous in the sence, and onily put, for
the sake of the rhyme, and filling up the verse. It came into
my head to alter them, and I am affrayd for the worse.

Kind Fate, or Fortune, blend them, if you can: And,
of two wretches, make one happy man. Kind fate looks a
little harsh: fate without an epithet, is always taken in the
ill sence. *Kind* added, changes that signification. (Fati valet
hora benigni.) The words (if you can) have almost the
same fault I tax'd in your ending of the line: but being

better considerd, that is, whether fortune or fate, can alter
a Man's temper, who is already so temperd: and leaving it
doubtfull, I thinke does not prejudice the thought, in the
last line. Now I begin, to be in for Cakes and Ale; and why
should I not put a quere on those other lines? Poor Shift,
does all his whole contrivance set, To spend that wealth he
wants the Sence to get. All his whole Contrivance, is but
all his Contrivance, or his whole Contrivance; thus, one of
those words, lookes a little like tautology. Then an ill
natur'd man might ask, how he cou'd spend wealth, not
having the sence to get it? But this is trifling, in me. For
your sence is very intelligible; which is enough to secure it.
And, by your favour, so is Martial's: Viribus hic non est,
hic non est utilis annis: and yet in exactness of Criticism,
your censure stands good upon him.—I am call'd to dinner,
and have only time to add a great truth; that I am from
the bottome of my Soul, Deare Sir, Your most humble
Servant and true lover

> John Dryden.
Your apostrophe's to your Mistresse, where you
break off the thrid of your discourse, and address youre-
self to her, are, in my opinion, as fine turnes of gallantry,
as I have mett with anywhere.[223]

Dryden's letters contain little about his religious and political
position; what there is tends to vindicate him from the familiar
although now not much canvassed charge of having been an insincere timeserver. Macaulay, in his Whig zeal, grossly misrepre-
sented Dryden in a continually reprinted article in the *Encyclopaedia
Britannica*; it was not until the twentieth century that this unfair
view of him as a bribe-taker and thoroughly dishonest man was
corrected by unbiassed research.

Dryden was no rebel. He believed, though not uncritically,
in the *status quo*—whatever the *status quo* happened to be. (So, of
course, although in a very different way indeed, did Donne.) As a
young man he wrote stanzas in praise of Oliver Cromwell, which
were soon followed by ones in praise of Charles II—with whom he
was more naturally in sympathy. Shortly after James II ascended to
the throne he became converted to Roman Catholicism. For many
years this was seen as a deliberately cynical act. Such a view, however, does not accord with what we know of Dryden or with what
little he said about the matter in his letters. In the letter to Dennis of
March 1693 in which he had appraised Rymer, he also wrote:

> For my Principles of Religion. I will not justifie them to
> you. I know yours are far different. For the same Reason I
> shall say nothing of my Principles of State. I believe you

in yours followed the Dictates of your Reason, as I in mine
do those of my Conscience. If I thought my self in an
Error, I would retract it; I am sure that I suffer for them;
and Milton makes even the Devil say, That no Creature is
in love with Pain. For my Morals, betwixt Man and Man,
I am not to be my own Judge. I appeal to the World if I
have Deceiv'd or Defrauded any Man: And for my private
Conversation, they who see me every day can be the best
Witnesses, whether or no it be Blameless and Inoffensive.
Hitherto I have no reason to complain that Men of either
Party shun my Company. I have never been an Impudent
Beggar at the Doors of Noblemen: My Visits have indeed
been too rare to be unacceptable; and but just enough to
testifie my Gratitude for their Bounty, which I have fre-
quently received, but always unask's, as themselves will
Witness. I have written more than I needed to you on this
Subject: For I dare say you justifie me to your self.[224]

There can be no doubt that Dryden really did suffer pain and
distress for his beliefs after 1688. He lost his positions as Poet
Laureate and Historiographer, and, of course, his salary.[225] Nor did
his conversion bring him any special rewards from the Court of
James II. In a letter of February 1686/7 to an old friend, the poet
and playwright Sir George Etherege, he wrote:

I cannot help hearing, that white Sticks[226] change their
Masters, & that officers of the Army are not immortall in
their places because the King finds they will not vote for
him in the next Sessions. Oh that our Monarch wou'd
encourage noble idleness by his own example, as he of
blessed memory did before him for my minde misgives me,
that he will not much advance his affairs by Stirring.[227]

This passage is of particular interest in its bearing on Dryden's real
position. Professor Louis Bredvold believes that he was a moderate
Catholic, who disapproved of James's disastrous policies; he cites
the fable of the Swallows in *The Hind and the Panther* as an
expression of this disapproval.[228] Certainly Dryden approved more
positively of Charles II's policy of letting well alone, of not 'stirring';
there is little evidence that he admired James II's attempts to restore
Roman Catholicism as the Established Religion. The worst that
might be said of him is that he acquiesced, if only in various negative
ways, in James II's illegal actions. He can hardly be criticized for
remaining loyal to James himself. As late as February 1696/7, in a
letter to the Earl of Chesterfield, he wrote:

I have hinder'd it[229] thus long in hopes of his [James II's]
return, for whom, and for my Conscience I have sufferd,

that I might have laid my Authour at his feet: But now finding that Gods time for ending our miseries is not yet. . . .[230]

And writing to his cousin Mrs. Steward on November 1699, not long before he died, he says:

> If they [the Court of William and Mary] will consider me as a Man, who have done my best to improve the Language, and Especially the Poetry, & will be content with my acquiescence under the present Government, & forbearing satire on it, that I can promise, because I can perform it: but I can neither take the Oaths, nor forsake my Religion, because I know not what Church to go to, if I leave the Catholique; they are all so divided amongst them selves in matters of faith, necessary to Salvation: & yet all assumeing the name of Protestants. May God be pleasd to open your Eyes, as he has opend mine: Truth is but one; & they who have once heard of it, can plead no Excuse, if they do not embrace it.[231]

There can be no question of the complete sincerity of this. Perhaps the key to Dryden's Jacobite Catholicism is to be found in his need for certitude at all costs: as he became older this need transferred itself from the realm of the material to that of the spiritual. His was not an adventurous or an explorative, but rather a consolidating mind. His belief in astrology (that it persisted after his conversion is conclusively proved by a letter to his sons of 1697[232]) is not at first sight characteristic; but it may be attributed to his strong need for security, to his anxiety to establish that 'everything will be all right'. However, we do not possess enough information about his character to be certain about any such relatively intimate psychological details.

His non-satirical poetry is all surface elegance, grand eloquence, magnificence, or versified argument (as in *The Hind and the Panther*); he gives little away about himself. His satire springs more directly from the pressures that life exerted upon him, but his lyrical poetry is not personal: it delights in and finely celebrates classical form, honest propriety and the pomp of constitutionally established authority. It seldom examines any of the realities that lie behind them, preferring grace to passion, honest decency to truth.

But Dryden was never a frivolous or an untruthful man, as his letters show; indeed, that he became the father of 'correctness' in English poetry was to a large extent owing to the accidents of his cautious temperament and the effect he had on the shallow young sycophant, Walsh. What is most admirable about him, even when he is wrongly censuring his Elizabethan and Jacobean predecessors, is his seriousness, honesty and lucidity.

I

Jonathan Swift was born on 30 November 1667, in Dublin. His putative father, also Jonathan, had died, perhaps in the preceding March. Swift was probably his son, although it has been plausibly suggested that he was the son of Sir John Temple, father of Sir William, and Master of the Rolls in Dublin.[233] Swift's early life is wrapped in mystery: there is his own extraordinary, perhaps hysterical, story of how he was kidnapped by his nurse and taken off to Whitehaven for three years, where he was taught to spell and read the Bible. Certainly he saw little, perhaps nothing, of his mother during his childhood: soon after he went to Kilkenny Grammar School in 1673 she had moved, with his elder sister Jane, to Leicester.

In 1682 he entered Trinity College, Dublin, where he did not distinguish himself academically; he took a poor degree in February 1685/6. He was often fined, not only for routine offences such as missing chapel, but also for starting 'tumults' in college and insulting officials. It has been suggested that he did badly at college because of subconscious resentment at the way his uncle and (nominal) guardian, Godwin Swift, had treated him; it is more likely that, besides being of a rebellious disposition, he found the curriculum and the teachers boring: much of the abstract thinking that he satirized in later years was well in evidence at Trinity.

In 1688 Swift, now twenty, settled for a time with his mother at Leicester. In 1689 he entered the household of Sir William Temple at Moor Park in Surrey, where he was to remain, on and off, until Temple's death. He returned to Ireland in 1690, but was soon back with Temple. It was at about this time that he first began to suffer from the disease that troubled him increasingly throughout his life, 'Ménière's Syndrome', as it became known in 1861, an affliction of the middle ear sometimes known as 'labyrinthine vertigo'. The symptoms, as described by sufferers, are acutely unpleasant and alarming, and can reduce the patient to a state of extreme panic. At Moor Park Swift met and acted as tutor to Hester Johnson,

'Stella' (1680/1–1727/8), daughter of the housekeeper to Lady Giffard, Temple's widowed sister. He remained on enigmatically close terms of friendship with her for the rest of her life.

Temple's influence upon Swift can hardly be overestimated, in spite of the resentment Swift felt, and was always to feel, about certain aspects of his treatment of him. He left Moor Park in 1694 for Ireland, was ordained (he became a Doctor of Divinity in 1700) and obtained the living of Kilroot, where he settled for over a year. However, in May 1696, disappointed by his failure to obtain further preferment, he returned to Temple, who had missed him. In the years immediately following he wrote *A Tale of A Tub* and *The Battle of the Books*. On Temple's death in 1699 he found himself, at the age of thirty-one, in a difficult position: 'mature but unprovided for', as Bonamy Dobrée aptly puts it.[234] The history of the next fifteen years is one of continual voyages between England and Ireland, of hopes and fears. *A Tale of A Tub* caused a sensation on its publication in 1704, and Swift also gained some reputation as Temple's literary executor. Before 1710 he was a nominal supporter of the Whigs and a friend of Addison and Steele; in 1710 he began to write for the Tory *Examiner*, supporting Harley and St. John. The next three years saw him at the height of his influence, both as an advisor to great men and as the chief Tory pamphleteer. He never enjoyed the personal favour of the Queen, but was highly esteemed both by Harley, a moderate Tory, and St. John (Bolingbroke), a vicious but brilliant politician whose zeal against the Dissenters happened to appeal to Swift, and to whom he remained loyal. It was in about 1707 that Swift met Esther Vanhomrigh, 'Vanessa' (1687/8–1723), perhaps the one real love (in a sexual sense) of his life. His letters to her contain many references to drinking coffee: these may allude to specifically sexual contacts.

In 1713 Swift was 'rewarded' for his services with the Deanery of St. Patrick's, Dublin. He had expected better: the position represented, for him, nothing less than exile. His political hopes were shattered by the death of Queen Anne and the fall of the Tories; but by 1713 he was a leading literary celebrity, associated with Parnell, Gay, Pope and the genial amateur, Dr. Arbuthnot. However, he accepted his exile (he pointed out, significantly, that he would rather be a king amongst slaves than a slave amongst kings), and by the early Twenties his famous last period, as the 'Irish patriot', had begun, with *The Drapier's Letters*. After this he visited England only twice: in 1726 and once again in 1727, in his sixtieth year. *Gulliver's Travels*, written between 1720 and 1725, was published in 1726. His health did not finally break down until he was over seventy. The notion that he was 'mad' in his last years is erroneous, but he became senile, and Guardians in Chancery were appointed some three years before his death in 1745. The first collected edition of his works had appeared in Dublin in 1734, in four volumes, published by George Faulkner.

2

A knowledge of Swift's letters is essential to an understanding of the man and his work, not least because, as their most recent editor, the late Sir Harold Williams, has written, he exhibited no particular desire to see them in print.[235] They often have more art in them than their writer liked to admit, but they are—in contrast to Pope's letters—essentially private communications. They must be one of the main bases of any study of him, and few of them are without some kind of significance.

They exhibit all Swift's powers, all the facets of his many-sided personality. He can be direct, fiercely discreet, ironic, sardonic, 'terrible', playful, loving and merely formal and polite. We should be careful not to try to make a too consistent figure out of all these aspects of his character, by applying ideas divorced from psychological reality. Much labour has been expended upon interpreting the man and his works, and some of this is invaluable; but it is as well to bear in mind what he himself wrote:

> If a Man would register all his Opinions upon Love, Politicks, Religion &c. beginning from his Youth, and so go on to Old Age, what a Bundle of Inconsistencies and Contradictions would appear at last.[236]

Furthermore, Swift was an ironist, the most convoluted and subtle ironist of all time: we cannot always be absolutely confident, at a remove of more than two centuries, that we catch his exact shade of meaning. No writer throve more from the exercise of an iron control; in few writers has the conflict between intellect and passion, reason and emotion, been so intense.

Sometimes, as in *The Battle of the Books*, Swift's parody of what he hated became in itself a passionate exercise: he triumphed because, while satirizing, while fascinatedly parodying the procedures of his enemies, he informed these procedures with the creative energy they lacked—thus exposing, by implication, yet another aspect of their pedantic paucity. His success as a satirist partially depends, indeed, on his energy. As has been well said, Swift differed from must other satirists of his time because he cared: it was this, as well as his imaginative vigour, that gave him energy.

One of the psychological factors that go towards the making of a satirist, especially a satirist of Swift's type, who uses a variety of masks (the linen draper, the 'reasonable' narrator of *A Modest Proposal*, the foolish fellow of *A Letter of Advice to a Young Poet*, and so on), is a fear of facing the world as a single integrated personality. Such a fear certainly haunted Swift. The only period in his life when he came near to 'opening out' socially was that of his success during the years of Oxford's political ascendancy. Even then he played the bully, demanding proper 'advances' from anyone who wanted to know him. Such aggressiveness betokens, of course, basic social insecurity. His well-known attachment to the practice of making compliments by seeming to dispraise,

> His [Voiture's] Genius first found out the Rule
> For an obliging Ridicule
> He flatters with peculiar Air
> The Brave, the Witty and the Fair;
> And Fools would fancy he intends
> A Satyr where he most commends [*To Mr. Delany*]

is defensive, whatever precedents he may have claimed for it from the work of Voiture[237]: he was afraid of the power of his own emotions, and thus found emotional (and sexual) gestures difficult, sometimes impossible, to make. The practice of censure in order to praise also represents a rationalization of the malevolent element in his satire: everything, if possible, had to be disguised by 'raillery'. Thus, a good deal of the poetry he wrote, after his preliminary excursion as a 'Pindaric' poet, in the sixteen-nineties, when it is not directly satirical, is deliberate raillery. But the man who claimed that his motto was 'Vive la bagatelle' also wrote to his friend, the Tory squire Knightley Chetwode, his neighbour in Ireland, 'I am sometimes concerned for persons, because they are my friends, but for things never, because they are desperate'.[238]

The greatest disappointment of Swift's career was the failure of his hopes and ambitions when Oxford and Bolingbroke failed to make up their differences and to act together. He recalled it all vividly, at a time when his faculties were just beginning to dim through old age, in a letter to the second Earl of Oxford, written twenty-three years later:

> . . . Your father and my Lord Bolingbroke, had a misunderstanding with each other. . . . I laboured to reconcile them as much as I was able. . . . I expostulated with them both. . . . They grew more estranged every day. . . . I spoke very freely to them both; and told them, I would retire, for I found all was gone. . . .[239]

But in spite of this, and of the fact that they had failed to save him from exile to Ireland, Swift remained loyal—some would say fanatically loyal—to both Oxford and Bolingbroke. And in writing to Bolingbroke, by whose character Swift was perhaps deceived—for if any statesman in English history has had an unequivocally 'bad character', then it was Bolingbroke—he never reproaches him for the past. And when Oxford was put in the Tower, Swift offered to give up everything to serve him. Undoubtedly he meant it. This disinterested, even romantic loyalty to the statesmen who might well be said to have served his career badly, to have failed to appreciate his genius, is an important element in Swift's character. He may have hated 'enthusiasm', especially where it stank of dissent; he had the enthusiasm of ten men in his personal loyalties.

But something had happened to Swift much earlier than this; something more fundamental to his emotions than even the fall of his Tory friends. This is often ignored or misinterpreted. It has to do with the collapse of his hopes of achieving a poetry of a very different order from the poetry with which we are familiar— *Cadenus and Vanessa*, the verses on his own death, and the scatological poems. It is aptly reflected, as we shall see, in his change of attitude towards the woman, Jane Waring ('Varina'), to whom he proposed marriage, between 1696 (when he proposed and she turned him down) and 1700 (when she changed her mind and announced herself willing to be his wife).

3

Nowhere does Swift talk so much about his poetry as he does at the very beginning of his life. That he launched himself not as a prose writer, but as a poet—his first publication was the turgid *Ode to the Athenian Society*—is sometimes forgotten. Six of his early poems, totally different in style from what followed, survive—seven if we include *A Description of Mother Ludwell's Cave*, ascribed to him, with some justice, by Middleton Murry but derisively rejected by Harold Williams.[240]

Poets' juvenilia are, of course, nearly always different from the work of their maturity; but Swift was well over twenty when these poems were written, and the contrast in his case is sharper than usual. The poems are, as a whole, florid and tedious; but they are important in the study of Swift's work. We see him here as we never see him again. He is, in a word, starry-eyed. The disappearance of this element from his public personality after 1698 or thereabouts is so absolute as to be suspicious. Did Swift really change his views on poetry, or merely his poetic practice? The evidence is to be found in the poems themselves, in his letters—and in *A Letter of Advice to a Young Poet* (Dublin, 1721), which will be dealt with later.

Apart from isolated lines and, in a few cases, passages, the early poems are failures. There can be no argument about this, and the intense interest they hold for us should not be allowed to obscure it. In his life of Swift Dr. Johnson claims he was told that when

Dryden (to whom Swift was distantly related through his mother) was shown these early pieces he said, 'Cousin Swift, you will never be a poet'. It is almost certain, however, that what Dryden really said was, 'Cousin Swift, turn your thoughts another way, for nature has never formed you for a Pindaric poet'[241]: this sounds much more like Dryden—just as the terseness of his remark in Johnson's report sounds more like Johnson himself. However, Johnson is assuredly correct in ascribing Swift's 'perpetual malevolence' towards Dryden to this remark or to one like it. Not only did he use him as a butt in his two earliest satires, but also he pursued his reputation, on and off, for the rest of his life. In a letter to Thomas Beach of 1735, which will later be quoted, he speaks of him as 'one I have often blamed as well as pitied'.

However, his antipathy towards Dryden is not the only evidence that Swift was inordinately sensitive about his Muse (of whose presence the early poems are as inordinately full). In 1718, long after he had renounced 'Pindaric' poetry, he made friends with Patrick Delany, then a Junior Fellow of Trinity College, Dublin, and with Thomas Sheridan (grandfather of the dramatist). Sheridan was a facetious jester, schoolmaster and parson, of whom, in Swift's own words—'The two devils of inadvertency and Forgetfulness' had 'got fast hold'. Sheridan, with no more tact than he later evinced by preaching a sermon for the anniversary of George I's accession on the text 'Sufficient unto the day the evil thereof', had written a (now lost) squib in which Swift's muse was represented to be dead 'and making a funeral solemnity with asses, owls, &c.'; he 'gave the copy among all his acquaintance'. This description (1729) is by Swift himself, who still remembered it vividly eleven years later. At the time he sent to Delany, whom he had probably known a little longer, this letter, together with his poem *To Dr. Delany* (the autograph of both letter and poem can still be seen at the Forster Library in South Kensington):

> I allow in all justice you ought to be ten times more a friend to Mr Sheridan than to me; and yet I can demand of you to keep a secret of a lesser Friend from a greater. Therefore I expect you will not tell Mr Sheridan one word of the inclosed, nor shew it him thô in Confidence. But you are to know that I have long thought severall of his Papers, and particularly that of the Funerall, to be out of all the Rules of Raillery, I ever understood, and if you think the same you ought to tell him so in the manner you like best, without bringing me into the Question, else I may be thought a Man who will not take a Jest; to avoid which Censure with you, I have sent you my thoughts on that Subject in Rime; but why in Rime, I know not, unless because it gives

me an Opportunity of expressing my Esteem for you—which
is greater than I care to tell you whatever I may do to
others.[242]

There is some typically expressed bitterness in the poem, too:

> To you the Muse this verse bestows,
> Which might as well have been in Prose;
> No Thought, no Fancy, no Sublime,
> But simple Topicks told in Rime.

This is not absolutely unequivocal, a mere expression of Swift's
famous—perhaps too famous—dislike of enthusiasm. The circumstances in which it was written tell us that 'no Sublime' is not simply
a reiteration of Swift's anti-romantic principles: there is a note of
regret. Sheridan had unwittingly opened an old wound. It is one of
the relatively few occasions when Swift gave full expression to his
offence with a private friend.[243] To understand why he took such
offence it is necessary to look more closely into what survives of his
early poetry, and into his attitude to it.

4

The worst of the early poems is *The Ode to the Athenian Society*.
Swift's prefatory letter, which was published in *The Athenian
Gazette* along with it, is of little interest. It contains such phrases as
'I submit it wholly to the Correction of your Pens', and the doubtless sincere remark that 'nothing at present can more highly oblige
me' than 'two or three lines . . . of your Pleasure upon it'.[244] The
Ode itself is, as Sir Herbert Read remarks in his fine essay on Swift's
poetry, 'long and desperately wearisome',[245] except that occasionally,
in the general welter of self-abasement and praise of the wisdom of
the great men of the Athenian Society (which was, incidentally, as
ridiculous as any ode ever addressed to it), Swift produces a more
characteristic thought.

> But Censure's to be understood
> Th' *Authentick mark* of the Elect

for example, has a touch of real indignation about it, and anticipates
a famous aphorism of later years, 'When a true Genius appears . . .
you may know him by this Sign, that the Dunces are all in Con-
federacy against him'.[246] Chiefly, however, Swift tries to drown his
own worldly ambition in a tide of adulation, ending

> . . . *Men, who liv'd and dy'd without a Name,*
> *Are the chief Heroes in the sacred List of Fame.*

The subject, however, inasmuch as there is a real subject, is clearly
the young Swift's desire for fame. But even in this, the most bathetic
piece of verse Swift ever wrote, the extravagance of feeling, so uncharacteristic of the later poetry and prose, is genuine: it is not
assumed simply for the sake of producing verse that will be acceptable. Swift is bubbling over with enthusiasm and innocent hopefulness.

On 3 May 1692 he wrote a letter to his cousin Thomas Swift
(who also wrote poetry) which contains a long passage about his
poetic activities:

> It makes me mad to hear you talk of making a Copy of verses
> next morning, which tho indeed they are not so correct as
> your others are what I could not do under 2 or 3 days, nor
> does it enter into my head to make any thing of a sudden but
> what I find to be exceeding silly stuff except by great chance,
> I esteem the time of studying Poetry to be 2 hours in a
> morning, and that only when the humor sits, which I esteem
> for the flower of the whole Day, and truly I make bold to
> employ them that way and yet I seldom write above 2
> Stanzas in a week I mean such as are to any Pindarick Ode,
> and yet I have known my self in so good a humor as to
> make 2 in a day, but it may be no more in a week after, and
> when all's done, I alter them a hundred times, and yet I do
> not believe my self to be a laborious dry writer, because if
> the fitt comes not immediatly I never heed it but think of
> something else, and besides, the Poem I writt to the Athen.
> Society was all ruff drawn in a week, and finishd in 2 days
> after, and yet it consists of 12 stanza and some of them
> above thirty lines, all above 20, and yet it is so well thought
> of that the unknown Gentlemen printed it before one of
> their Books, and the Bookseller writes me word that another
> Gentleman has in a book calld the History of the Athen
> Society, quoted my Poem very Honorably (as the fellow
> calld it) so that perhaps I was in a good humor all the week,
> or at least Sir William Temples speaking to me so much in
> their Praise made me zealous for their cause, for really I
> take that to be a part of the Honesty of Poets that they can
> not write well except they think the subject deserves it. But
> that it self will not allways hold, for I have had an ode in
> hand these 5 months inscribed to my late Lord of Canterbury
> Dr Sancroft, a gentleman I admire at a degree more than I
> can express, putt into me partly by some experience of him,
> but more by an unhappy reverend Gentleman my Lord the
> Bishop of Ely with whom I usd to converse about 2 or 3
> years ago, and very often upon that Subject, but I say, I

cannot finish it for my life, and I have done nine stanzas and do not like half of them, nor am nigh finished, but there it lyes and I sometimes add to it, and would wish it were done to my desire, I would send it to my Bookseller and make him print it with my name and all, to show my respect and Gratitude to that excellent person, and to perform half a Promise I made His Lordship of Ely upon it—I am not mistaken in my critick, for it is written To thee all conq— &c in that Poem, nor do I like your mending it any better, therefore give it another wipe, and then it will be one of my Favorits.—I have a sort of vanity, or Foibless, I do not know what to call it, and which I would fain know if you partake of it, it is (not to be circumstantiall) that I am over-fond of my own writings, I would not have the world think so for a million, but it is so, and I find when I writt what pleases me I am Cowley to my self and can read it a hundred times over, I know 'tis a desperate weakness and has nothing to defend it but it's secrecy, and I know farther, that I am wholly in the wrong, but have the same pretence the Baboon had to praise her Children, and indeed I think the love in both is much alike, and their being our own ofspring is what makes me such a blockhead, I am just the same way to yours, and thô I resolve to be a severe critick, yet I can not but think I see a thousand beautyes, and no faults in what you take any pains about, for as to the rest I can easily distinguish when either of us have been idle. I am just so to all my acquaintance I mean in proportion to my love of them, and Particularly to Sir William Temple. I never read his writings but I prefer him to all others at present in England, Which I suppose is all but a piece of selflove, and the likeness of humors makes one fond of them as if they were ones own— I do not at all like your ordering yr fortune, On my Conscience you'll be a beggar and I was just going to ask you the old musty question what to you Propose &c? I confess a persons happiness is a thing not to be slighted so much as the world thinks, I mean with being too anxious for the future, but I deny yours to be a present happiness, and I was going to call you a poor ignorant contented Fellow for thinking [it is] but that if you do, your very thoughts make it so, And I will not take the Pains to lug you out only to give you demonstration that you are under water, All that I can say is that I wish to God you were well provided for thô it were with a good living in the Church—This Virgil sticks plaguily on my hands, I did about 200 lines and gave it to Lady Giffard for a Sample, and she and Sir William Temple like it as I would have them. I like yr stile to the Girl, but

you make no Conscience because 'tis to a Woman, and
therefore borrow from rich Mr Cowly, well 'tis cleanlyly
absurd and if she has any sense your entertainment is very
agreeable, but igad I can not write anything easy to be
understood thô it were but in praise of an old Shooo and
sometime or other I will send you something I writt to a
young lady in Ireland which I call the Ramble,[247] and it
will show what I say is true. . . .[248]

The passage beginning 'I have a sort of vanity. . . .' shows that
Swift, if not yet mature, already had that involuntary compulsion
to self-analysis that was to distinguish him from all the other
Augustans. We never find Pope so casually owning to such thoughts.
The letter tells us more, though. It evinces Swift's passionate desire
to succeed as a poet, and, more importantly, whom he considered to
be his chief master at this time: Abraham Cowley, who died in
1667, generally esteemed above all other poets, including Milton.
It was Cowley who influenced Swift to write in 'Pindarick' form;
the fashion never entirely died out, even among the Augustans. He
quoted from Cowley sixteen years later, with approval; the abandonment of him as an influence apparently did not involve any revulsion
for his poetry. *Clad all in Brown* (1728), a scatological parody of the
tenth poem of Cowley's *Mistress*, indicates familiarity with the
poem, but not contempt.

But the key statement in the letter is: 'really I take that to
be a part of the Honesty of Poets that they can not write well except
they think the subject deserves it'. Swift, because Temple had
praised it, had managed to persuade himself that he cared about
the Athenian Society. The remark makes it clear, as the early poems
do, that Swift then regarded the sort of poetry he wished to write
as distinct from satire. Thus, in the *Ode to Sancroft* he wrote, of 'the
angry slighted Muse':

> No province now is left her but to rail,
> And Poetry has lost the art to praise. . . .

One of the assumptions of all four of the 'Pindaric' pieces is that, in
Murry's words, 'the Muse, by nature and inclination, is eager to
celebrate virtue and innocence'—in a word, 'to praise'. Contrary to
general belief, Swift never changed this fundamental assumption;
but he did change his own way of writing verse.

The best of the early poems are the two latest: *To Mr.
Congreve* and *Occasioned by Sir William Temple's Late Illness and
Recovery*, composed, respectively, in the November and December
of 1693. Swift mentioned the Congreve poem in a letter of 6
December 1693 to his cousin Thomas, where he says that it was
designed as a prologue for any of his plays: 'They are almost 250

lines, not Pindarick. . . .'[249] It is difficult, owing both to Swift's mixed feelings about his old school- and college-mate's success and to his changing attitude to the Muse. But there are impressive passages, as well as the prophetic lines:

> *My hate, whose lash just heaven has long decreed*
> *Shall on a day make sin and folly bleed.*

At the end of the poem to Temple, Swift finally settles his quarrel with the Muse:

> Madness like this no fancy ever seiz'd,
> Still to be cheated, never to be pleas'd;
> Since one false beam of joy in sickly minds
> Is all the poor content delusion finds.—
> There thy enchantment broke, and from this hour
> I here renounce thy visionary pow'r;
> And since thy essence on my breath depends,
> Thus with a puff the whole delusion ends.

The poem, as Professor Ehrenpreis points out, takes as its point of departure an idea from Temple's essay *On Poetry*: '. . . true poetry being dead, an Apparition of it walked about'.[250] But he has overlooked two echoes of the same phrase in earlier poems:

> For Learning's mighty Treasure's look
>   In that deep Grave a Book,
> Think she there does all her Treasures hide
> And that her troubled Ghost still haunts there since she
>   dy'd . . .

and:

> Say, Muse, for thou, if any know'st
> Since the bright essence fled, where haunts the reverend
>   ghost?

Clearly Temple's statement made a deep impression upon him. Its context in the essay, *On Poetry*, is that poetry has declined and decayed since ancient times:

> The first Change of Poetry was made by translating it into Prose. . . . 'Tis probable, the old Spirit of Poetry [in Rome] being lost or frighted away by those long and bloody Wars with such barbarous Enemies, this new Ghost began to appear in its Room. . . .

Most of Swift's critics rightly equate the 'Muse' of his early poems with his idealistic view of Temple, with whom—in the manner of all idealizing young men—he soon became disillusioned: it is true that one easily discernible strand running through these early poems is a wholly personal one, of hero-worship of Temple declining into disillusion. But Temple is not all that Swift meant by the Muse. Although he rejected Temple as hero-figure, Swift never rejected his own, original views, of the Muse as an inspirer to 'Praise', and of poetry as 'Exalted'. His own Muse, it is true, groped 'her uncouth way', and quit, '*the narrow path of Sense*/For a dear Ramble thro' Impertinence'; but this was because he found his times and his own temperament incompatible with the kind of poetry he believed in. His chagrin when he found he could not write it was intense. But it is a serious mistake to assume that he ever rejected a standard that he found neither himself nor his age could reach.

5

For Swift 'things' were always 'desperate'. This attitude was by no means just a reflection of an unhappy, neurotic temperament and a blasted career. Swift firmly believed that England had been in decline since the execution of Charles I. The golden age, for him, lay between the Reformation (though, realist that he was, he deprecated Henry VIII himself, believing that Henry had effected the English Reformation by an accident) and the Civil War. Behind all the negative features of his personality and writings lay a deeply emotional regard for a past that he saw as both more stable and less factious. In 1729 he called a couplet from one of Congreve's poems,

> Believe it, Men have ever been the same,
> And all the Golden Age, is but a Dream,

'a vile and false moral'.[251] He has frequently been accused of insincerity as a priest and of 'lack of interest' in God; but he disliked abstract speculation about God not because he was not interested in God but because he regarded it as foolish, as well as factious and blasphemous. We can sympathize: working priests, and Swift was a conscientious one, ought to dislike theologians, just as working poets ought to distrust prescriptive critical theorists. Swift's positive emotions were in any case so strong that he dared not indulge himself in them. He was a man of great feeling—so great, that he hid it beneath 'raillery' (to his male friends), baby-talk (to Stella) and cruel irony (to his enemies and opponents). This feeling lies behind even the most savage of his poems; he had more regard for feeling, for 'sublimity', in poetry than had any of his contemporaries. But he could not express it. His satire arose not from a warped nature but from a frustrated one.

The psychological pattern of his attitude towards the present and the past, towards the unpleasant and the pleasant, is perfectly and charmingly illustrated in a letter he wrote to his friend Charles Ford on 12 November 1708:

I have observed from my self and others (and I think it the wisest Observation I ever made in my Life) that Men are never more mistaken, than when they reflect upon past things, and from what they retain in their Memory, compare them with the Present. Because, when we reflect on what is past, our Memoryes lead us onely to the pleasant side, but in present things our Minds are chiefly taken up with reflecting on what we dislike in our Condition. So I formerly used to envy my own Happiness when I was a Schoolboy, the delicious Holidays, the Saterday afternoon, and the charming Custards in a blind Alley; I never considered the Confinement ten hours a day, to nouns and Verbs, the Terror of the Rod, the bloddy Noses, and broken Shins.[252]

He said exactly the same thing in a more famous passage in a letter to Bolingbroke and Pope of 5 April 1729:

I remember when I was a little boy, I felt a great fish at the end of my line which I drew up almost on the ground, but it dropt in, and the disappointment vexeth me to this very day, and I believe it was the type of all my future disappointments. I should be ashamed to say this to you, if you had not a spirit fitter to bear your own misfortunes, than I have to think of them.[253]

What he could not bear, emotionally, was his nostalgia for a state of innocence, enthusiasm and virtue, which he projected into the history of an era earlier than his own. He even did all he could to suppress his feelings, to the point of dwelling upon those physical things that struck him (doubtless for 'Freudian' reasons) as the most unpleasant. It is too easy to forget that such a work as *A Modest Proposal* is essentially a profoundly humanitarian document, dealing with the subjects of mercy, justice and kindness.

6

Swift's outwardly bitter reaction from his early idealism is aptly reflected in his affair with Jane Waring, 'Varina', of which all our knowledge is derived from his two letters to her. None of hers to him has survived. She was the daughter of the late Archdeacon of Dromore, and the effect she had upon Swift has been grossly underrated by every biographer except Murry.

In February 1695/6 Swift was appointed to the prebendary of Kilroot. Soon afterwards Temple wrote asking him to come back (cousin Thomas had not filled his place competently). Swift was glad to go, but he was, or believed himself to be, in love. On 29 April 1696 he wrote this letter (I have omitted one irrelevant passage) to Varina.

Madam,
Impatience is the most inseparable quality of a lover, and indeed of every person who is in pursuit of a design whereon he conceives his greatest happiness or misery to depend. It is the same thing in war, in courts, and in common business. Every one who hunts after pleasure, or fame, or fortune, is still restless and uneasy till he has hunted down his game: and all this is not only very natural, but something reasonable too; for a violent desire is little better than a distemper, and therefore men are not to blame in looking after a cure. I find myself hugely infected with this malady, and am easily vain enough to believe it has some very good reasons to excuse it. For indeed, in my case, there are some circumstances which will admit pardon for more than ordinary disquiets. That dearest object upon which all my prospect of happiness entirely depends, is in perpetual danger to be removed for ever from my sight. Varina's life is daily wasting, and though one just and honourable action would furnish health to her, and unspeakable happiness to us both, yet some power that repines at human felicity has that influence to hold her continually doating upon her cruelty, and me upon the cause of it. This fully convinces me of what we are told, that the miseries of man's life are all beaten out on his own anvil. Why was I so foolish to put my hopes and fears into the power or management of another? Liberty is doubtless the most valuable blessing of life; yet we are fond to fling it away on those who have been these 5000 years using us ill. Philosophy advises to keep our desires and prospects of happiness as much as we can in our own breasts, and independent of anything without. He that sends them abroad is likely to have as little quiet as a merchant whose stock depends upon winds, and waves, and pirates, or upon the words and faith of creditors, every whit as dangerous and inconstant as the other.
I am a villain if I have not been poring this half hour over the paper merely for want of something to say to you:— or is it rather that I have so much to say to you, that I know not where to begin, though at last 'tis all very likely to be arrant repetition? . . .
'You have now had time enough to consider my last letter, and to form your own resolutions upon it. I wait your answer with a world of impatience, and if you think fit I

should attend you before my journey, I am ready to do it. My Lady Donegall tells me that 'tis feared my Lord Deputy will not live many days; and if that be so, 'tis possible I may take shipping from hence; otherwise I shall set out on Monday fortnight for Dublin, and, after one visit of leave to his Excellency, hasten to England: and how far you will stretch the point of your unreasonable scruples to keep me here, will depend upon the strength of the love you pretend for me.' In short, Madam, I am once more offered the advantage to have the same acquaintance with greatness that I formerly enjoyed, and with better prospect of interest. I here solemnly offer to frego it all for your sake. I desire nothing of your fortune; you shall live where and with whom you please till my affairs are settled to your desire: and in the mean time I will push my advancement with all the eagerness and courage imaginable, and do not doubt to succeed.

Study seven years for objections against all this, and by Heaven they will at last be no more than trifles and put-offs. 'Tis true you have known sickness longer than you have me, and therefore perhaps you are more loath to part with it as an older acquaintance: But listen to what I here solemnly protest, by all that can be witness to an oath, that if I leave this kingdom before you are mine, I will endure the utmost indignities of fortune rather than ever return again, though the king would send me back his deputy. And if it must be so, preserve yourself, in God's name, for the next lover who has those qualities you love so much beyond any of mine, and who will highly admire you for those advantages which shall never share any esteem from me. Would to Heaven you were but a while sensible of the thoughts into which my present distractions plunge me: they hale me a thousand ways, and I not able to bear them. 'Tis so, by Heaven: The love of Varina is of more tragical consequence than her cruelty. Would to God you had treated and scorned me from the beginning. It was your pity opened the first way to my misfortune; and now your love is finishing my ruin: and it is so then. In one fortnight I must take eternal farewell of Varina; and (I wonder) will she weep at parting a little to justify her poor pretences of some affection to me? and will my friends still continue reproaching me for the want of gallantry, and neglecting a close siege? How comes it that they all wish us married together, they knowing my circumstances and yours extremely well, and I am sure love you too much, if it be only for my sake, to wish you any thing that might cross your interest or your happiness?

Surely, Varina, you have but a very mean opinion of the joys that accompany a true, honourable, unlimited love; yet either nature and our ancestors have hugely deceived us, or else all other sublunary things are dross in comparison. Is it possible you cannot be yet insensible to the prospect of a rapture and delight so innocent and so exalted? Trust me, Varina, Heaven has given us nothing else worth the loss of a thought. Ambition, high appearance, friends, and fortune, are all tasteless and insipid when they come in competition; yet millions of such glorious minutes are we perpetually losing, for ever losing, irrecoverably losing, to gratify empty forms and wrong notions, and affected coldnesses and peevish humour. These are the unhappy incumbrances which we who are distinguished from the vulgar do fondly create to torment ourselves. The only felicity permitted to human life we clog with tedious circumstances and barbarous formality. By Heaven, Varina, you are more experienced, and have less virgin innocence than I. Would not your conduct make one think you were hugely skilled in all the little politic methods of intrigue? Love, with the gall of too much discretion, is a thousand times worse than with none at all. 'Tis a peculiar part of nature which art debauches, but cannot improve. We have all of us the seeds of it implanted in ourselves, and they require no help from courts or fortune to cultivate and improve them. To resist the violence of our inclinations in the beginning, is a strain of self-denial that may have some pretences to set up for a virtue: but when they are grounded at first upon reason, when they have taken firm root and grown up to a height, 'tis folly—folly as well as injustice, to withstand their dictates; for this passion has a property peculiar to itself, to be most commendable in its extremes, and 'tis as possible to err in the excess of piety as of love.

These are the rules I have long followed with you, Varina, and had you pleased to imitate them, we should both have been infinitely happy. The little disguises, and affected contradictions of your sex, were all (to say the truth) infinitely beneath persons of your pride and mine; paltry maxims that they are, calculated for the rabble of humanity. Oh, Varina, how imagination leads me beyond myself and all my sorrows! 'Tis sunk, and a thousand graves lie open!—No, Madam, I will give you no more of my unhappy temper, though I derive it all from you.

Farewell, Madam, and may love make you a while forget your temper to do me justice. Only remember, that if you still refuse to be mine, you will quickly lose, for ever lose, him that is resolved to die as he has lived, All your, Jon. Swift.

I have here sent your Mr. Fletcher's letter, wherein I hope I do not injure generosity or break trust, since the contents are purely my own concern. If you will pardon the ill hand and spelling, the reason and sense of it you will find very well and proper.[254]

Professor Ehrenpreis suggests that Swift was 'looking for a negative' here[255]; but if he was, he was taking a remarkable risk. And why did he—as we shall see—put Varina to such humiliation four years later, if he had not meant this proposal seriously? Professor Ehrenpreis considers the letter totally rhetorical; Murry, on the other hand, considered it to be 'manly', to contain 'fervid love-idealism' and to belong to 'the heyday of the blood'.[256] Regardless of the language employed, who is right?

The equivocation Professor Ehrenpreis detects by 'poking about among the rhetoric' does exist, as the rhetoric most certainly and ponderously does; but it is not as crucial as he thinks it is (one suspects that it fits in with a Freudian theory of Swift's sexual incapacity that he is going to propound at a later stage of his as yet unfinished biography). And even if it is rhetorical, can Professor Ehrenpreis find any love-letters of that age that are free from rhetoric? All young men (Swift was twenty-nine) have subconscious reservations about marriage; this does not prevent them from going through with it. Murry is assuredly correct, both in his supposition that Swift consciously wanted Varina to consent to marry him, and in characterizing his letter as idealistic rather than merely rhetorical.

It is true that there is a certain frigidity and emotional awkwardness about the letter: Swift does not describe (for his beloved's pleasure) the qualities in her that make him love her. But we cannot read too much into this: we do not know what had passed between them personally, or in earlier letters, or what Varina was like; nor do we know to what extent Swift was personally inhibited by shyness. Even if the awkwardness does have a more sinister psychological meaning, then we are still not entitled to assume that Swift did not *think* that he meant what he said, that he was consciously 'looking for a negative'. Unconscious motives are vitally important, but their existence should not blind us to the fact that people often carry out conscious intentions in spite of them. Even if Swift really was looking for rejection from Varina—because, perhaps, he felt that his own mother had similarly rejected him— this does not change the positive nature of his invitation. The fact of rejection would not, in any case, be made less hurtful because it had been subconsciously desired.

There were more letters from Swift to Varina after he reached Moor Park, but they are lost. Professor Ehrenpreis suggests that the letter following the one of 19 April may have been 'less molten' in its diction; it may equally well have been even more so, and contained pleas. We do not know. But in 1700, when Swift was back in Dublin, Varina evidently decided that he was now a better prospect: she wished to re-open negotiations. On 4 May 1700 Swift sent her this reply:

Madam, I am extremely concerned at the account you give of your health; for my uncle told me he found you in appearance better than you had been in some years, and I was in hopes you had still continued so. God forbid I should ever be the occasion of creating more troubles to you, as you seem to intimate! The letter you desired me to answer I have frequently read, and thought I had replied to every part of it that required [it]; however, since you are pleased to repeat those particulars wherein you desire satisfaction, I shall endeavour to give it you as well as I am able. You would know what gave my temper that sudden turn, as to alter the style of my letters since I last came over. If there has been that alteration you observe, I have told you the cause abundance of times. I had used a thousand endeavours and arguments, to get you from the company and place you are in; both on the account of your health and humour, which I thought were like to suffer very much in such an air, and before such examples. All I had in answer from you, was nothing but a great deal of arguing, and sometimes in a style so very imperious as I thought might have been spared, when I reflected how much you had been in the wrong. The other thing you would know is, whether this change of style be owing to the thoughts of a new mistress. I declare, upon the word of a Christian and a gentleman, it is not; neither had I ever thoughts of being married to any other person but yourself. I had ever an opinion that you had a great sweetness of nature and humour, and whatever appeared to the contrary, I looked upon it only as a thing put on as necessary before a lover: but I have since observed in abundance of your letters such marks of a severe indifference, that I began to think it was hardly possible for one of my few good qualities to please you. I never knew any so hard to be worked upon, even in matters where the interest and concern are entirely your own; all which, I say, passed easily while we were in the state of formalities and ceremony; but, since that, there is no other way of accounting for this untractable behaviour in you, but by imputing it to a want of common esteem and friendship for me.

When I desired an account of your fortune, I had no such design as you pretend to imagine. I have told you many a time, that in *England* it was in the power of any young fellow of common sense to get a larger fortune than ever you pretended to. I asked, in order to consider whether it were sufficient, with the help of my poor income, to make one of your humour easy in a married state. I think it comes to almost a hundred pounds a year; and I think at the same time that no young woman in the world of the same income would dwindle away her health and life in such a sink, and among such family conversation: neither have all your letters been once able to persuade that you have the least value for me, because you so little regarded what I so often said upon that matter. The dismal account you say I have given you of my livings I can assure you to be a true one; and, since it is a dismal one even in your own opinion, you can best draw consequences from it. The place where Dr. *Bolton* lived is upon a living which he keeps with the deanery; but the place of residence for that they have given me is within a mile of a town called *Trim*, twenty miles from hence; and there is no other way but to hire a house at *Trim*, or build one on the spot: the first is hardly to be done, and the other I am too poor to perform at present. For coming down to *Belfast*, it is what I cannot yet think of, my attendance is so close, and so much required of me; but our Government sits very loose, and I believe will change in a few months; whether *our part* will partake in the change, I know not, though I am very apt to believe it; and then I shall be at leisure for a short journey. But I hope your other friends, more powerful than I, will before that time persuade you from the place where you are. I desire my service to your mother, in return for he remembrance: but for any other dealings that way, I entreat your pardon: and I think I have more cause to resent your desires of me in that case, than you have to be angry at my refusals. If you like such company and conduct, much good do you with them! My education has been otherwise. My uncle *Adam* asked me one day in private, as by direction, what my designs were in relation to you, because it might be a hindrance to you if I did not proceed. The answer I gave him (which I suppose he has sent you) was to this effect: 'That I hoped I was no hindrance to you; because the reason you urged against a union with me was drawn from your indisposition, which still continued; that you also thought my fortune not sufficient, which is neither at present in a condition to offer you: That if your health and my fortune were as they ought, I would prefer you above all your sex; but that, in the present condition of both, I thought it was against your opinion, and would certainly make you unhappy: That, had you any other offers which your friends or yourself thought more to your advantage, I should think I were very unjust to be an obstacle in your way.' Now for what concerns my fortune, you have answered it. I desire, therefore, you will let me know if your health be otherwise than it was when you told me the doctors advised you against marriage, as what would certainly hazard your life. Are they or you grown of another opinion in this particular? Are you in a condition to manage domestic affairs, with an income of less (perhaps) than three hundred pounds a year? Have you such an inclination to my person and humour, as to comply with my desires and way of living, and endeavour to make us both as happy as you can? Will you be ready to engage in those methods I shall direct for the improvement of your mind, so as to make us entertaining company for each other, without being miserable when we are neither visiting nor visited? Can you bend your love and esteem and indifference to others the same way as I do mine? Shall I have so much power in your heart, or you so much government of your passions, as to grow in good humour upon my approach, though provoked by a ——? Have you so much good-nature as to endeavour by soft words to smooth any rugged humour occasioned by the cross accidents of life? Shall the place wherever your husband is thrown be more welcome than courts or cities without him? In short, these are some of the necessary methods to please men, who, like me, are deep-read in the world; and to a person thus made, I should be proud in giving all due returns towards making her happy. These are the questions I have always resolved to propose to her with whom I meant to pass my life; and whenever you can heartily answer them in the affirmative, I shall be blessed to have you in my arms, without regarding whether your person be beautiful, or your fortune large. Cleanliness in the first, competency in the other, is all I look for. I desire, indeed, a plentiful revenue, but would rather it should be of my own; though I should bear from a wife to be reproached for the greatest.

I have said all I can possibly say in answer to any part of your letter, and in telling you my clear opinion as to matters between us. I singled you out at first from the rest of women; and I expect not to be used like a common lover. When you think fit to send me an answer to this without ——, I shall then approve myself, by all means you shall command, Madam, | Your most faithful humble servant.[257]

This letter is—there is no doubt about it whatever—one of revenge for her slight of him in 1696: consider only 'without regarding whether your person shall be beautiful'. The 1696 letter may have contained hard conditions for marriage. But the conditions now advanced are absurd, particularly in the way they are actually stated: 'Will you be ready to engage in those methods I shall direct for the improvement of your mind . . . ?' Certainly the writer was 'looking for a negative' here; and no doubt Varina (who died unmarried some twenty years later) did not trouble to reply. Swift knows perfectly well that his letter is emotionally preposterous and cruel. And yet this was how he continued, so far as women were concerned. What is here savage and hurting later became tempered by a sort of self-protective humour; but the ladies had to accept it or be dismissed. If they flirted with him—and many did—then it was on his terms and not on theirs. The unpardonable thing with Swift was to humiliate him in any way; the humiliation Varina inflicted upon him, which was basically sexual, caused him never to expose his feelings to a woman again (except, probably, to Vanessa in the strictest privacy). But this must not be taken to mean that he never again secretly entertained such feelings.

The whole affair repeats the pattern of Swift's relations with the Muse of his early poems, the last of which (the one ostensibly occasioned by Temple's recovery from illness) was written in 1694. In that case he had discovered (perhaps cousin Dryden had helped, to his posthumous cost) that he could not write 'sublime' poetry (such poetry as Marvell had written, and which Cowley tried to write, and might have seemed to the youthful Swift actually to have written). In this case he discovered that the kind of love-feelings he expressed (however clumsily) in the letter of April 1696 to Varina did not fall on fertile soil. If his reactions were unusually violent— he dismissed the Muse with a puff, and Varina with a more than spiteful letter—he was nevertheless right in his diagnosis of his own situation.

The language of the poems did not match up to the extravagance of the feelings they tried to express, and the result was bathetic; Miss Waring did not respond vehemently to his vehemence in April 1696. But it was not language or Miss Waring that was basically 'wrong'—it was Swift's feelings. They were immoderate, and they led him into humiliation. He hated them. This lies at the heart of his lifelong distrust of enthusiasm as such, and of his unique insistence—as a poet as well as a prose-writer—upon physical reality. Only a man always tempted to regard beauty idealistically and extravagantly, who was capable of worshipping it, could have written the scatologcal poems, could have made the observation that 'Cela, Celia, Celia shits'. Otherwise there is no object in such an observation: to a less sublime-minded person it is obvious enough. The point of drawing attention to this is to emphasize that Swift was never free from such enthusiastic temptations. Had he become so, he would not have needed to remind himself so brutally and so continuously of the converse. He was brutal to Varina when the opportunity presented itself; but he learned his lesson from her.

His age was a brutal and paradoxical one, of delicate euphemisms and filthy physical conditions; it was difficult, perhaps impossible, to express feeling in a direct manner. Poetry, in contrast to what it had been before Dryden, became, at best, a kind of versified critical prose, at worst, a vehicle for self-glorification. Swift is one of the few true poets of that prose-age, although he achieved it by adopting the role of an anti-poet: he scraped up the age's anti-lyrical resources, as no one else did, to tell the truth about it and himself. He prophesied correctly when he ended his *Ode to Temple* with the lines:

> Whate'er I plant (like Corn on barren Earth)
>   By an equivocal Birth
> Seeds and runs up to Poetry.

Had Swift pursued the positive side of his vision, and pursued it successfully, he would have been a Blake, isolated, alone and eccentric. He compromised by accepting the friendship of his younger literary contemporaries. But could even a Blake have arisen, let alone functioned, in that age?

7

Swift never wrote about Shakespeare or any other poet of the Elizabethan or Jacobean ages in his letters. He admired and was influenced by Marvell's prose satire, but never mentioned his poetry. He mentioned Milton once or twice, calling himself an 'admirer'. The extent of his knowledge of these writers is not certainly known. He quoted, or misquoted, from Shakespeare on several occasions, with the unmistakable air of one who knows him well. In a mock 'bill' which he presented to Oxford in 1711 (for a joke) he includes 'A Shakespear the Folio Edition' among the other items. Shakespeare is praised in *A Letter to a Young Poet*; his acquaintance with his work is not in question.

Swift's failure to mention any of the poets of the previous

age is no evidence that he disliked, disapproved of, or was bored by
them. It may even, in this case, be evidence to the contrary. As we
have seen, he disliked dwelling upon whatever had pleased or excited
him in the past. He said nothing at all about the portrait of Charles I
('drawn by Van Dyke') that was given to him by his friend James
Stopford in 1725; but it had a place of honour in his house. We
find nothing in Swift (as, of course, we do in Pope) about Shakespeare,
or any poet before Dryden, being 'incorrect'.

In any case, he wrote little about poetry at all (past or present)
in his letters. When he mentioned his own poems, it was usually
merely to say that they had been written, or pirated, or published.
When he was sent poems by other people he was almost always as
brief and non-committal about them as decency and kindness would
allow. William Diaper is told to stop translating—Swift is 'a little
angry when those who have a genius lay it out in translations' (he
disapproved of Pope's activities as a translator)—but the copy of
his verses is 'very agreeable' and 'were highly approved by all' 'our
great men'[258] to whom he had shown them. He had previously
told Stella that Diaper's poem, *The Dryades*, was 'a very good
one',[259] and he did much to help its author—but his praise to his
face was not fulsome. Even when Pope sent him poems Swift was
as terse as he could possibly be. He never filled a whole letter with,
or even devoted much more than a paragraph, to his comments.
He was proud, as anyone might be, to acknowledge himself as having
originally suggested *The Dunciad*, and was warm about the poem
to Pope; but it is curious that he should have wanted Pope to give
the names of his victims in full. In a letter of 16 June 1728 he told
Pope:

> I have often run over the *Dunciad* in an Irish edition (I
> suppose full of faults) which a gentleman sent me. The Notes
> I could wish to be very large, in what relates to the persons
> concerned; for I have long observed that twenty miles from
> London no body understands hints, initial letters, or town-
> facts and passages; and in a few years not even those who
> live in London. I would have the names of those scriblers
> printed indexically at the beginning or end of the Poem,
> with an account of their works, for the reader to refer to. I
> would have all the Parodies (as they are called) referred to
> the authors they imitate—When I began this long paper, I
> thought I should have filled it with setting down the several
> passages I had marked in the edition I had, but I find it
> unnecessary, so many of them falling under the same rule.
> After twenty times reading the whole, I never in my opinion
> saw so much good satire, or more good sense, in so many
> lines. How it passes in Dublin I know not yet; but I am
> sure it will be a great disadvantage to the poem, that the

persons and facts will not be understood, till an explanation comes out, and a very full one. I imagine it is not be published till towards winter, when folks begin to gather in town. Again I insist, you must have your Asterisks filled up with some real names of real Dunces.[260]

This is odd from the author of the line (written in 1731)

He lash'd the Vice but spar'd the Name

(which he nearly always made a point of doing), unless we grant that Swift fully realized what kind of writer Pope was: that, even as satirist, he was different from himself. Since he made such a point of 'sparing the name', his special urging of Pope not to do so must have meant something important—if only to himself. The whole passage is of great interest:

> "Perhaps I may allow, the Dean
> "Had too much Satyr in his Vein;
> "And seem'd determin'd not to starve it,
> "Because no Age could more deserve it.
> "Yet, Malice never was his Aim;
> "He lash'd the Vice but spar'd the Name.
> "No Individual could resent,
> "Where Thousands equally were meant.
> "His Satyr points at no Defect,
> "But what all Mortals may correct;
> "For he abhorr'd that senseless Tribe,
> "Who call it Humour when they jibe:
> "He spar'd a Hump or crooked Nose,
> "Whose Owners set not up for Beaux.
> "True genuine Dulness mov'd his Pity,
> "Unless it offer'd to be witty.
> "Those, who their Ignorance confess'd,
> "He ne'er offended with a Jest;
> "But laugh'd to hear an Idiot quote,
> "A Verse from *Horace*, learn'd by Rote.

The mention of a 'Hump' suggests that Pope was not far from his mind as he wrote these lines.

The Dunciad had then been out for three years; it had caused Swift (who admired its vitriolic skill) to think deeply about satire, and to examine his own satirical motives. *Verses on the Death of Dr. Swift* is the result of this thought. He worked very hard indeed at the poem: an earlier draft (which Swift pretended was not his), *The Life and Genuine Character of Dr. Swift*, has been entirely recast and expanded in the revised version. That he was at this time thinking about the subject of satire in general, and of himself as satirist, is also shown by the theme of the longish *A Panegyric on the Reverend Dean Swift* . . . (1730) and by *A Dialogue between an Eminent Lawyer and Dr. Swift* . . . (1730), which begins:

> Since there are persons who complain
> There's too much satire in my vein. . . .

Not long afterwards, in a letter to Charles Ford, he wrote:

> I envy Mr. Pope for his being railed at. I think all men of wit should employ it in Satyr, if it will onely serve to vex Rogues, though it will not amend them. If my Talent that way were equal to the sourness of my temper I would write nothing else.[261]

Swift in his satire did seek, often successfully, to 'amend' rather than to 'vex' rogues: he was not boasting when he claimed that

> The Dean did by his pen defeat
> An infamous destructive Cheat.

There is a sardonic quality in the last sentence of the passage from the letter to Ford quoted above: it reveals guilt at and honest acknowledgement of his own 'sourness', but at the same time records a determnation not to use satire merely 'to vex'. It is important to note, in this connection, that Swift's low opinion of the Irish by no means inhibited him in fighting for their rights. Pope attacked literary and social pretensions; Swift used satire as a humanitarian tool. But he did not condemn Pope for three reasons: he was flattered by the younger man's careful deference, he liked, or at the very least was deeply touched by, him personally—and he admitted, with a candour of which Pope was totally incapable, 'sourness' of temper, envy and rancour, in himself.

Swift made few allusions in his letters to *Verses on the Death of Dr. Swift*. But he regarded them as important: writing to John Gay and the Duchess of Queensbury (Gay's patroness) on 1 December 1731, he mentioned:

> I have been severall months writing near five hundred lines on a pleasant Subject, only to tell what my friends and enemyes will say on me after I am dead. I shall finish it soon, for I add two lines every week, and blott out four, and alter eight, I have brought in you and my other friends, as well as enemyes and Detractors.[262]

In 1739 he entrusted the full text to William King, for publication in London. Acting under the directions of Pope, King caused a mutilated text of the poem to be printed: he cut out hundreds of lines, and often substituted altered ones from the quite different earlier draft, which had been printed (probably with the connivance of Pope himself) in 1733. Swift was furious, and immediately had his Dublin publisher, Faulkner, put out an authorized edition.

King wrote to Mrs. Whiteway (who now increasingly dealt with Swift's affairs, and whom he trusted implicitly) on 6 March 1738/9 explaining why 'he' had made certain alterations. But Pope was at his elbow as he wrote:

> They [i.e. 'the Doctor's friends'] were of opinion that these lines,
>
> > He lash'd the vice, but spared the name,
> > No individual could resent
> > Where thousands equally were meant—
>
> might be liable to some objection, and were not, strictly speaking, a just part of his character; because several persons had been lashed by name, a *Bettesworth*, and in this poem, *Charteris* and *Whitshed*, and for my part, I do not think, or ever shall think, that it is an imputation on a Satirist to lash an infamous fellow by name.

This (and we can confidently take it as Pope's, because he said exactly the same thing in a letter of his own, of 25 September 1738, to the Earl of Orrery) indicates that Pope was fully aware both of what these lines suggested about himself, and, possibly, of Swift's implied intellectual contempt in telling him to fill in the names in his own satires. The examples of the 'objection' to which the lines might be 'liable' are patently absurd; the added rejoinder shows that Pope had winced. He even, in the person of King, attempted to criticize it, at the same time demonstrating that he completely failed to understand the poem. The paragraph preceding that quoted above reads:

> . . . the latter part of the poem might be thought by the public a little vain, if so much were said by himself of himself. They [i.e. Swift's friends] were unwilling that any imputation of ths kind should lie . . . considering there is not the least tincture of vanity appearing in any of his former writings. . . .[263]

Posterity has endorsed Swift in perceiving that the lines are not 'vain'. But perhaps Pope was still smarting from Swift's letter to him of 1 May 1733, in which he had said:

> All things in verse good or bad that London produces, are printed here, among the rest, the Essay on Man. . . . No body names you for it here (we are better judges, and I do not rally) It is too Philosophical for me. . . .[264]

Swift knew perfectly well that the *Essay on Man* was Pope's—

Bolingbroke had quoted a line from it in a letter to him not long previously. But whatever the causes of Pope's malice, he had a specific interest in creating a picture of an increasingly vain Dean, as will become evident when we come to deal with his machinations at the time of this letter.[265]

8

Swift's view of the nature of poetry, as he expressed it in his writings, is a negative one. Pope and his circle, all men younger than himself, and leading lights in that English literary world from which he felt cut off, were his friends and admirers; pointedly, he does not criticize their work. Indeed, he praises it; but with the subtle reserve already exemplified. He fully realized that his age was not conducive to the writing of the kind of poetry he himself had begun by trying to write. We can hardly therefore assert, however, that his was the kind of sensibility that wanted to be in tune with its age.

His letter of 12 April 1735 to the poetical wine-merchant of Wrexham, Thomas Beach (who cut his throat in 1737, being 'afflicted with a terrible disorder in his head') is instructive. Beach had sent Swift his poem *Eugenio*.

> After the fate of all poets, you are no favourite of fortune; for your letter of March 31st did not come to my hands till two days after Sir William Fownes's death, who, having been long afflicted with the stone and other disorders, besides great old age, died about nine days ago. If he had recovered, I should certainly have waited on him with your poem, and recommended it and the author very heartily to his favour. I have seen fewer good panegyrics than any other sort of writing, especially in verse, and therefore I much approve the method you have taken; I mean, that of describing a person who possesseth every virtue, and rather waiving that Sir William Fownes was in your thoughts, than that your picture was like in every part. He had indeed a very good natural understanding, nor wanted a talent for poetry; but his education denied him learning, for he knew no other language except his own; yet he was a man of taste and humour, as well as a wise and useful citizen, as appeared by some little treatises for regulating the government of this city; and I often wished his advice had been taken.
>
> I read your poem several times, and showed it to three or four judicious friends, who all approved of it, but agreed with me, that it wanted some corrections; upon which

I took the number of lines, which are in all two hundred and ninety-nine, the odd number being occasioned by what they call a triplet, which was a vicious way of rhyming, wherewith Dryden abounded, and was imitated by all the bad versifiers in Charles the Second's reign. Dryden, though my near relation, is one I have often blamed as well as pitied. He was poor, and in great haste to finish his plays, because by them he chiefly supported his family, and this made him so very uncorrect; he likewise brought in the Alexandrine verse at the end of the triplets. I was so angry at these corruptions, that above twenty-four years ago I banished them all by one triplet, with the Alexandrine, upon a very ridiculous subject. I absolutely did prevail with Mr. Pope, and Gay, and Dr. Young, and one or two more, to reject them. Mr. Pope never used them till he translated Homer, which was too long a work to be so very exact in; and I think in one or two of his last poems he hath, out of laziness, done the same thing, though very seldom. . . .

He begins by alluding to his oft-reiterated belief that poetry arises from ill-fortune, another way of saying that it arises from despair. This is the theme of his poem, *The Progress of Poetry* (1720). He is pleased with Beach's poem because it is a 'panegyric': is positive, rather than satirical. He is, as usual, not fulsome in his praise (doubtless the poem, which has never been reprinted, is poor); and he is characteristically honest in gently pointing out that Fownes (the subject) was not quite the embodiment of all virtue that Beach made him out to be. There follows a reference to Dryden, and a paragraph (I have not quoted it) of suggested corrections—every one of which Beach is said to have adopted.

Swift's own dislike for the triplet was a quirk occasioned by his hatred of Dryden. One can hardly legitimately 'blame' and 'pity' a man for using triplets ending in an Alexandrine; nor, by Swift's own standards, was Dryden ever 'very uncorrect'. But his determination to ridicule the triplet had had happy results twenty-six years before. He calls the subject of *A Description of a City Shower* (1710) 'very ridiculous' in the letter to Beach, and refers to its concluding lines,

> Sweepings from Butchers Stalls, Dung, Guts and Blood,
> Drown'd Puppies, stinking Sprats, all drench'd in Mud,
> Dead Cats and Turnip-Tops come tumbling down the Flood.

which form the most effective triplet in the whole of English poetry. Few things in his life pleased Swift so much as the success of this poem when it was first published in the *Tatler*. He repeatedly mentioned, in his letters to Stella at the time, with obvious pleasure,

how well it was being received. There is nothing quite like it in
English poetry, either before or after. Swift had recently been
much influenced by Addison: he had already allowed him to revise
and alter (considerably for the worse) two of his poems. *A Description
of a City Shower* reflects both this influence, which is in the direction
of 'correctness', and Swift's reaction from it; but it does so in a most
unusual and poetic manner, the complexities of which are highly
instructive.

'The whole poem', as Harold Williams observes, 'is built on
scenes and incidents observed', and he quotes Swift to Stella (8
November 1710):

> I will give ten shillings a week for my lodging; for I am
> almost st—k out of this with the sink and it helps me to
> verses in my Shower.

This is reflected in the couplet:

> Returning Home at Night you'll find the Sink
> Strike your offended Sense with double Stink.

What Swift was aiming at was absolute realism, but, sardonically,
within the limits of 'correctness'. He had already written *A Description of the Morning* (he wrote to Stella that he much preferred the
later poem), which is more straightforwardly descriptive. There are
one or two well brought off, realistic jokes in *Morning*, such as
Betty stealing from her master's bed to discompose her own, and
the duns collecting at his Lordship's door. But *A City Shower* is
more ambitious. It delicately parodies (though without personal
malice) the Addisonian notion of the 'poetical', and then pricks the
bubble with grotesque metaphors:

> Mean while the South rising with dabbled Wings,
> A Sable Cloud a-thwart the Welkin rings,
> That swill'd more Liquor than it could contain,
> And like a Drunkard gives it up again.

The 1727 Miscellanies adds to the title the words '*In Imitation of*
VIRGIL'S Georg.', obviously with Swift's authority. Addison had
translated Book IV of the *Georgics*, the description of bees; he was
also a devoted admirer of Dryden; his own verse contains many
triplets (although usually without the final Alexandrine). The complex pattern of Swift's total intentions begins to emerge.

It is clear that he was deliberately both imitating and at the
same time technically improving upon the Addisonian style—which
was no more than Dryden's bequest, although in poetically undistinguished hands. As used by Addison it is pointlessly ornate. Its
'correctness' operates in a void. The writer concentrates upon style
and descriptive elegance to such an extent that he eschews reality.

Swift takes up, perfects and employs this elegance to achieve a true description. The description of the shower is, as Murray writes, 'unforgettable'. It has the freshness of a shower itself. Swift was genuinely diffident about his poetry, as well as fairly naive (when younger) about public reaction to it; and yet no parodic exploitation of contemporary literary practice has been so unobtrusive and at the same time sardonic. Swift's acceptance of Augustan correctness, as seen in his own poetry, was sardonic as well as modestly timid. To call it merely ironic would be too extreme: this omits the element of his own diffidence and lack of poetic self-confidence. In one of the very earliest of his 'non-sublime' poems, *Mrs Harris's Petition* (1701) Swift had skilfully adapted the habits of everyday speech, as no one else yet had, to verse. In *A City Shower* he adapted the current poetic style—to realistic description. The poem's conclusion does not laugh at Dryden; rather, it deflates the high-flying Addisonian imitation of Dryden's style, reducing the subject-matter to its appropriate level—and incidentally it creates an effective poem. Swift saw that the contemporary style was not poetically suitable for 'moralizing', but only for description or satire. He paid some lip-service to the practice of moralizing, because it reminded him of poetic seriousness; his own verse remained incapable of it.

However, as I have pointed out, his satire differed from Pope's: when he urged him to fill in the names of the victims in *The Dunciad*, he did so because he felt that the poem could not otherwise survive. He said as much in an important letter to Charles Wogan, begun in July and ended on 2 August 1732.

The provenance of this letter is interesting. Wogan (who had known the young Pope) was a Jacobite exile, and was therefore a potentially fascinating figure to Swift. He had escaped from Newgate after taking part in the Jacobite Rebellion of 1715 and had had a romantic history (once made the subject of a deplorable Hollywood film): he had daringly rescued Clementina Sobieski from Innsbruck so that she might wed the Old Pretender. He sent to Swift, in 'a green Velvet Bag', a prose account of this exploit, together with some 'Miltonick verse' paraphrasing the psalms. He also enclosed a letter, asking Swift to 'correct' the poems, and saying that he believed 'the People of England and Ireland had quite lost all Remains of Elegance and Taste, since their top Entertainments were composed of Scenes of Highwaymen, and Prostitutes. . . .' This was a direct indictment of the *Beggars' Opera*, the subject of which, 'a Newgate pastoral', Swift had himself suggested to Gay in a letter.

Swift might well have ignored Wogan's letter, or made a curt acknowledgement. After all, he had attacked Gay, and he was an exile and a rebel. Instead he took the trouble to write a long reply, showing in it not only his personal loyalty to Pope but also his

equivocal attitude towards satire. Though Wogan's 'grave and sublime' poem is unlikely to have been very good, Swift's attention to it,
and his general uneasiness of tone when aligning himself with Pope,
Gay and Arbuthnot, show that he was still obsessed with the possibilities of—if not involved in trying to write—a non-satirical
poetry.[267]

He had read Thomson's *The Seasons* (which appeared in
1730 in collected form), and in his nervousness brought Milton
into the argument (which he seldom did). The difficulties Swift had
in answering Wogan are made manifest by his admission that he had
had the 'packet' by him for at least two months, and by his actual
delay in finishing the letter. It is significant that Young, 'the gravest
among us', comes at the head of the recommended list of reading:
Young's remarkable *Satires* are more generalized than those of Pope,
and notable for the lack of personal spite. Swift said (ironically?) that
he felt Young was not 'merry' enough; but this merely emphasizes
the extent to which one aspect of his extreme gravity disturbed
Swift—it was something he had long ago abandoned.

Sir,

I received your Packet at least two Months ago, and
took all this Time not only to consider it maturely myself,
but to show it to the few judicious Friends I have in this
Kingdom. We all agreed that the Writer was a Scholar, a
Man of Genius and of Honour. We guessed him to have
been born in this Country from some Passages, but not
from the Style, which we were surprized to find so correct
in an Exile, a Soldier, and a Native of *Ireland*. The History
of yourself, although part of it be employed in your Praise
and Importance, we did not dislike, because your Intention
was to be wholly unknown, which Circumstance exempts
you from any Charge of Vanity. However, altho' I am
utterly ignorant of present Persons and Things, I have made
a Shift, by talking in general with some Persons, to find out
your Name, your Employments, and some of your Actions,
with the Addition of such a Character as would give full
Credit to more than you have said (I mean of yourself) in
the dedicatory Epistle.

You will pardon a natural Curiosity on this Occasion,
especially when I began with so little that I did not so much
as untie the Strings of the Bag for five Days after I received
it, concluding it must come from some *Irish* Fryar in *Spain*,
filled with monastick Speculations, of which I have seen
some in my Life, little expecting a History, a Dedication, a
poetical Translation of the Penitential Psalms, Latin Poems,
and the like, and all from a Soldier. In these Kingdoms you

would be a most unfashionable military Man, among Troops
where the least Pretension to Learning, or Piety, or common
Morals, would endanger the Owner to be cashiered. Al-
though I have no great Regard for your Trade, from the
Judgment I make of those who profess it in these Kingdoms,
yet I cannot but highly esteem those Gentlemen of *Ireland*,
who, with all the Disadvantages of being Exiles and Strangers,
have been able to distinguish themselves by their Valour and
Conduct in so many Parts of *Europe*. I think above all other
Nations, which ought to make the *English* ashamed of the
Reproaches they cast on the Ignorance, the Dulness, and the
Want of Courage, in the *Irish* Natives; those Defects,
wherever they happen, arising only from the Poverty and
Slavery they suffer from their inhuman Neighbours, and the
base corrupt Spirits of too many of the chief Gentry, &c.
By such Events as these, the very *Grecians* are grown slavish,
ignorant, and superstitious. I do assert that from several
Experiments in travelling over both Kingdoms, I have
found the poor Cottagers here, who could speak our Language, to have much better natural Taste for good Sense,
Humour, and Raillery, than ever I observed among People
of the like Sort in *England*. But the Millions of Oppressions
they lye under, the Tyranny of their Landlords, the ridiculous
Zeal of their Priests, and the general Misery of the whole
Nation, have been enough to damp the best Spirits under
the Sun.

I return to your Packet. Two or three poetical Friends
of mine have read your Poems with very good Approbation,
yet we all agree some Corrections may be wanting, and at
the same Time we are at a Loss how to venture on such a
Work. One Gentleman of your own Country, Name, and
Family, who could do it best, is a little too lazy; but, however, something shall be done, and submitted to you. I have
been only a Man of Rhimes, and that upon Trifles, never
having written serious Couplets in my Life; yet never any
without a moral View. However, as an Admirer of *Milton*,
I will read yours as a Critick, and make Objections where I
find any Thing that should be changed. Your Directions about
publishing the Epistle and the Poetry will be a Point of some
Difficulty. They cannot be printed here with the least Profit
to the Author's Friends in Distress. *Dublin* Booksellers
have not the least Notion of paying for a Copy. Sometimes
Things are printed here by Subscription, but they go on so
heavily, that few or none make it turn to Account. In
London it is otherwise, but even there the Authors must be
in Vogue, or, if not known, be discovered by the Style; or

the Work must be something that hits the Taste of the Publick, or what is recommended by the presiding Men of Genius.

When *Milton* first published his famous Poem, the first Edition was very long going off; few either read, liked, or understood it, and it gained Ground merely by its Merit. Nothing but an uncertain State of my Health, caused by a Disposition to Giddiness (which, although less violent, is more constant) could have prevented my passing this Summer into *England* to see my Friends, who hourly have expected me: In that Case I could have managed this Affair myself, and would have readily consented that my Name should have stood at Length before your Epistle, and by the Caprice of the World, that Circumstance might have been of Use to make the Thing known, and consequently better answer the charitable Part of your Design by inciting People's Curiosity. And in such a Case, I would have writ a short Acknowledgment of your Letter, and published it in the next Page after your Epistle; but giving you no Name, nor confessing my Conjecture of it. This Scheme I am still upon, as soon as my Health permits me to return to *England*.

As I am conjectured to have generally dealt in Raillery and Satyr, both in Prose and Verse, if that Conjecture be right, although such an Opinion hath been an absolute Bar to my Rising in the World, yet that very World must suppose that I followed what I thought to be my Talent, and charitable People will suppose I had a Design to laugh the Follies of Mankind out of Countenance, and as often to lash the Vices out of Practice. And then it will be natural to conclude, that I have some Partiality for such Kind of Writing, and favour it in others. I think you acknowledge, that in some Time of your Life, you turned to the rallying Part, but I find at present your Genius runs wholly into the grave and sublime, and therefore I find you less indulgent to my Way by your Dislike of the *Beggar's Opera*, in the Persons particularly of *Polly Peachum* and *Macheath*; whereas we think it a very severe satyr upon the most pernicious Villainies of Mankind. And so you are in Danger of quarrelling with the Sentiments of Mr. *Pope*, Mr. *Gay* the Author, Dr. *Arbuthnot*, myself, Dr. *Young*, and all the Brethren whom we own. Dr. *Young* is the gravest among us, and yet his Satyrs have many Mixtures of sharp Raillery. At the same Time you judge very truly, that the Taste of *England* is infamously corrupted by *Sholes* of Wretches who write for their Bread; and therefore I had reason to put Mr. *Pope* on writing the Poem, called the

Dunciad, and to hale those Scoundrels out of their Obscurity
by telling their Names at length, their Works, their Adventures, sometimes their Lodgings, and their Lineage; not
with *A—'s and B—'s* according to the old Way, which
would be unknown in a few Years.

As to your Blank-verse, it hath too often fallen into
the same vile Hands of late. One *Thomson*, a *Scots*-Man,
has succeeded the best in that Way, in four Poems he has
writ on the four Seasons. yet I am not over-fond of them,
because they are all Description, and nothing is doing,
whereas *Milton* engages me in Actions of the highest
Importance, *modo me Romae, modo ponit Athenis*. And
yours on the seven Psalms, *&c.* have some Advantages that
Way.

You see *Pope, Gay*, and I, use all our Endeavours to
make folks Merry and wise, and profess to have no Enemies,
except Knaves and Fools. I confess myself to be exempted
from them in one Article, which was engaging with a
Ministry to prevent if possible, the Evils that have over-run
the Nation, and my foolish Zeal in endeavouring to save
this wretched Island. Wherein though I succeeded absolutely in one important Article, yet even there I lost all
Hope of Favour from those in Power here, and disobliged
the Court of *England*, and have in twenty years drawn
above one thousand scurrilous Libels on myself, without
any other Recompence than the Love of the *Irish* Vulgar,
and two or three Dozen Sign-Posts of the *Drapier* in this
City, beside those that are scattered in Country Towns,
and even these are half worn out. So that, whatever little
Genius God hath given me, I may justly pretend to have
been the worst Manager of it to my own Advantage of any
Man upon Earth.

Aug. 2] What I have above written hath long lain by
me, that I might consider further: But I have been partly
out of Order, and partly plagued by a Lawsuit of ten Years
standing, and I doubt very ill closed up, although it concerns
two Thirds of my little Fortune. Think whether such
Periods of Life are proper to encourage poetical and philosophical Speculations. I shall not therefore tire you any
longer, but, with great Acknowledgment for the Distinction
you please to shew me, desire to be always thought, with
great Truth and a most particular Esteem, Sir, | Your most
obedient | and obliged Servant, | J. Swift.

We have sometimes Editions printed here of Books
from *England*, which I know not whether you are in a
Way of getting. I will name some below, and if you approve

of any, I shall willingly increase your Library; they are small, consequently more portable in your Marches, and, which is more important, the Present will be cheaper for me.

Dr. YOUNG's Satyrs	Art of Politicks
Mr. GAY's Works	[By James Branston]
Mr. POPE's Works	and some other Trifles
POPE's DUNCIAD	in Verse, *&c.*[268]
GAY's Fables	

9

After the Queen's death Swift felt abandoned and exiled. He grumbled about his isolation, but made little attempt to break out of it. He visited England in 1726 and 1727 chiefly in order to escape the emotional consequences of Stella's imminently expected death: his letters from England to Sheridan, Delany and Stopford make this clear. But the admiration of Pope and Pope's friends meant a great deal to him; without them he would have felt lonelier as a writer. However, Delany and even Sheridan were closer friends (he confided his emotions about Stella's illness to them, but not to Pope, who had to guess); but they were wholly amateur writers. No one who feels a persecuted exile—and Swift's sense of persecution was intense—is going to abandon the adulation of his most brilliant younger contemporaries if he can help it. Thus Swift never openly reproached Pope— as he might well have done, considering the anger he felt over the *Miscellanies* and over Pope–King's issue of the garbled and cut version of the *Verses on the Death of Dr. Swift*. He was content to be reticent when he disagreed, to explain away all evidences of Pope's treachery as misunderstandings; he was even prepared to 'submit' his poems to Pope, for his approbation. Doubtless his pretended reluctance about Faulkner's project to issue his collected works in Dublin in the mid-Thirties (for he carefully supervised most of the edition) was in order to appease Pope. But he did not trust him— and with good reason. But Pope cast an extraordinary spell over most of his friends; Swift was not more immune to it than others. There is even something a little pathetic in the spectacle of the Dean, just twenty-one years Pope's senior, pretending that while he is not at all anxious that Faulkner should print his works, he cannot prevent him—when really all he wanted to do was to rescue them from the kind of distortion some of them had already undergone in Pope's hands. Ford told Swift in a letter of 6 November 1733 that 'that jumble with Pope, &c. in three volumes' (i.e. the *Miscellanies*) put him in a rage whenever he met it.[269] He was not reproved for this remark.

Swift's reluctance to reveal his feelings, loves and positive beliefs has its roots in his own psychology; but his reticence on the specific subject of poetry owes at least something to his fear of offending Pope. Perhaps this helps to explain why he never acknowledged *Letter of Advice to a Young Poet* (published in Dublin in 1721), why it is in places a confused performance—and why certain critics have even refused to attribute it to him. It is likely, however, to be Swift's: it contains a number of characteristic touches, and is exactly reflected, equivocations and all, in *On Poetry, A Rapsody* (1733). *A Letter* has brilliant passages, but does not amount— beneath its several layers of irony—to an absolutely coherent or complete statement on poetry. It is unlikely that Swift, in the position he found himself, was capable of making such a statement. But in writing about the subject he could not help attacking its practice in his own day, by acknowledging, however intricately, the necessity of elements that were missing from it. We must not imagine that he thought Pope 'worse' than himself as a poet (in the verses on his own death he admits, without any irony, I think, that he envied him), even if he had misgivings about his satirical motives; it was simply that he felt poetry in his time was dead. But many factors inhibited him from directly expressing, or even fully consciously holding, this opinion: Pope's reverence for Dryden (who had 'founded', or at least established Augustanism), his own fear of direct emotion, a desire not to appear obscurantist, and the psychologically defensive regard for correctness that he had himself developed.

The perhaps faintly rueful mask Swift adopts in *A Letter of Advice*[270] is that of one who has 'never made one *Verse*' since he was at school, 'where I suffered too much for my Blunders in *Poetry* to have any love to it ever since'. This nicely matches his frequent semi-ironic disclaimer that he was a poet ('have been only a Man of Rhimes, and that upon *Trifles*'—in the letter to Wogan of July/August 1732, already quoted): and it refers to his early, serious failures. And by saying 'I am not able from any Experience of my own, to give you those instructions you desire, neither will I Declare (for I love to conceal my Passions) how much I lament my neglect of *Poetry* . . .' he is able to set a properly ironic tone: this writer is in no position to say anything true about poetry! If he does say anything right, then it will be for the wrong reason. But Swift was at the same time telling the bitter truth: he *does* love to conceal his passions; he *does* lament his neglect of poetry. . . .

Essentially, the letter affirms that poetry is a lofty and serious art, on a level with religion. The first paragraph, which speaks of 'the great use of *Poetry* to Mankind and Society', has usually been taken to express his opposition to an extravagantly enthusiastic view of poetry; but the point of the irony is that although poetry *should* be valuable to mankind, it is not. Swift says that he would not despair to disprove that 'it is impossible to be a good *Soldier, Divine,* or *Lawyer* without some taste of *Poetry*', and that Sidney in his *Defence* 'argues there as if he really believed himself'. Swift is not here attacking Sidney, but is being bitterly sarcastic about the earlier poet's idealism, by comparing the modern state of affairs with that of Sidney's time. Swift certainly does not mean that soldiers or lawyers or clergymen should not have 'some taste of *Poetry*'; but he knows very well that they do not. Read carefully, the *Letter* is not an attack on enthusiasm but a sour affirmation of Sidney's position—except that there is now no real poetry, nor are there the conditions to make it possible. Thus he goes on:

> . . . I am not yet convinc'd, that it is at all necessary for a modern Poet, to *believe in God*, or have any serious sense of Religion . . . that smallest quantity of Religion . . . will muddy and discompose the brightest Poetical Genius.

In one of his most savage poems, *The Author on Himself* (1714). Swift had written of the 'dull Divines' who

> . . . pausing o'er a Pipe, with doubtful Nod,
> Give hints that Poets ne'er believe in God.

Gulliver's description of the ideal Reason of the Houyhnhnms is that, because it is not 'mingled, obscured, or discoloured by passion or interest', it '*strikes you with immediate conviction*'. It may therefore be described as lyrical, intuitive, innocent, inspired. It is this kind of intuitive and poetic recognition of experience that Swift equates both with 'Religion' and with 'Poetry', and which he is therefore careful ironically to belittle here:

> Religion presupposes Heaven and Hell . . . and twenty other Circumstances, which taken seriously, are a wonderful check to Wit and Humour, and such as a true Poet cannot possible give in to with a saving to his Poetical License. . . .

It does not really much matter whether we share Swift's own 'immediate conviction' of the truth of Christianity: what is important is his implied equation of true poetry (although not of himself as poet) with what he takes to be the best and most selfless elements in mankind.

Swift goes on to advise the young poet to read the Scriptures, for 'Our modern Poets' 'have read them Historically, Critically, Musically, Comically, Poetically, and every other way except *Religiously*. . . . For the Scriptures are undoubtedly a Fund of Wit, and a Subject *for* Wit'. In fact, he adds, if the Sacred Books were shut up, 'our Wit would run down like an Alarm'.

The Scriptures here stand for truth, and what Swift means is that while modern poets merely utilize and batten on the energy of truth (as they must in order to be successful), they are not devoted to it: they plunder it for their own ends. After ironically stating that poets need not be learned, he suddenly interpolates a non-ironic remark that is nevertheless not out of the character of the narrator: 'Many are too *Wise* to be Poets, and others too much Poets to be *Wise*'. This refers first to his present, then to his 'Pindaric' beginnings: at the same time, it indicts his age, when 'things' are 'desperate'.

He speaks as himself (but again, not out of the character of his narrator) when he says that 'the great Shakespear' was no scholar, but was 'an excellent poet', and when he agrees with the statement that had Shakespeare been a better scholar he would have been a worse poet. In a sense the confusion is justified: Swift is here writing as a critic, although under the mask of a fashionable fool, and the true critic of poetry should obviously be learned—whereas, of course, the true poet, such as Shakespeare, need not be a critic. What we have to note here is the absence of any of the qualifications (usual in Swift's day) about Shakespeare's unfortunate and 'barbaric' failure to observe the rules. The next passage, which is difficult, must be quoted in full:

> For to speak my private Opinion, I am for every Man's working upon his own Materials, and producing only what he can find within himself, which is commonly a better Stock than the owner knows it to be. I think Flowers of Wit ought to spring, as those in a Garden do, from their own Root and Stem, without Foreign Assistance. I would have a Man's Wit rather like a Fountain that feeds it self invisibly, than a River that is supply'd by several Streams from abroad.
>
> Or if it be necessary, as the Case is with some barren Wits, to take in the Thoughts of others, in order to draw forth their own, as dry Pumps will not play till Water is thrown into them; in that Necessity, I would recommend some of the approv'd Standard-Authors of Antiquity for your Perusal, as a Poet and a Wit; because *Maggots* being what you look for, as *Monkeys* do for *Vermin* in their Keepers Heads, you will find they abound in good old Authors, as in rich old Cheese, not in the new; and for that Reason you must have the Classicks, especially the most *Wormeaten* of them, often in your Hands.
>
> But with this Caution, that you are not to use those Ancients as unlucky Lads do their old Fathers, and make no Conscience of picking their Pockets and pillaging them. Your Business is not to steal *from* them, but to improve *upon* them, and make their Sentiments your own; which is

an effect of great Judgment, and tho' difficult, yet very possible, without the Scurvy Imputation of Filching: For I humbly conceive, tho' I light my Candle at my Neighbour's Fire, that does not alter the Property, or make the Wyck, the Wax, or the Flame, or the whole Candle, less my own.

Possibly you may think it a very severe Task, to arrive at a competent Knowledge of so many of the Ancients, as excel in their Way; and indeed it would be really so, but for the short and easie Method, lately found out, of Abstracts, Abridgments, and Summaries, &c. which are admirable Expedients for being very learned with little or no *Reading*, and have the same Use with Burning-Glasses, to collect the diffus'd Rays of Wit and Learning in Authors, and make them point with Warmth and Quickness upon the Reader's Imagination. And to this is nearly related that other modern Device of consulting Indexes, which is to read Books *Hebraically*, and begin where others usually end; and this is a compendious Way of coming to an Acquaintance with Authors: For Authors are to be us'd like *Lobsters*, you must look for the best Meat in the *Tails*, and lay the *Bodies* back again in the Dish. Your cunningest *Thieves* (and what else are *Readers*, who only read to *borrow*, i.e. to *steal*) use to cut off the Portmanteau from behind, without staying to dive into the Pockets of the Owner. Lastly, you are taught thus much in the very Elements of Philosophy, for one of the first Rules of Logick is *Finis est primus in intentione*.

The first paragraph, which recalls the scene between the spider and the bee in *The Battle of the Books*, is not an attack on originality, but on modern 'mechanical', artificial subjectivism. Swift makes this clear when he goes on to satirize the contemporary poets' superficial use of the classics. The point he is making, as John M. Bullitt notes, is that modern poetry has 'lost its contact with humane learning and moral values'.[271] The modern poet—Pope is typical—merely steals from the classics, 'improves' them in order to make an impression: the meat in the tails of the classical authors is of course what can be used in them—the bodies, the important part of them, can be ignored. Seventeen years earlier, in *Vanbrug's House* (1703), Swift had written:

> So, Modern Rhymers strive to blast
> The Poetry of Ages past,
> Which having wisely overthrown
> They from it's Ruins build their own.

It is odd that Swift does not absolve Pope or even Gay from these general charges; he could easily have done so by speaking of them disapprovingly here, or by employing the technique of positing a correct conclusion for the wrong reasons (as he did in the case of Shakespeare a page or two before). Did he, in his heart, consider Pope exempt? When ten years later he 'eulogized' Pope in *A Libel on Dr. Delany*, Pope took the opportunity of protesting by pretending, although with tact, that the poem was not by Swift: 'We have here some verses in your name, which I am angry at. Sure you wou'd not use me so ill as to flatter me? I therefore think it is some other weak Irishman'. It is obvious that Pope was annoyed: did he see through the superficial eulogy to the sarcasm? The lines of 'eulogy' are curiously ambiguous:

> Hail! Happy *Pope*, whose gen'rous Mind,
> Detesting all the statesmen kind,
> Contemning *Courts*, at *Courts* unseen,
> Refus'd the Visits of a Queen;
> A soul with ev'ry Virtue fraught
> By *Sages*, *Priests* or *Poets* taught;
> Whose filial piety excels
> Whatever *Grecian* story tells:
> A Genius for all Stations fit,
> Whose *meanest Talent* is his Wit:
> His Heart too great, though Fortune little,
> To lick a *Rascal Statesman's* Spittle.
> Appealing to the Nation's Taste,
> Above the Reach of Want is plac't:
> By Homer dead was taught to thrive,
> Which Homer never cou'd alive.
> And, sits aloft on *Pindus* Head,
> Despising *Slaves* that *cringe* for Bread.

The story that Pope had fled from Twickenham to escape a visit from the Queen was a false one—this may have been one of the things that annoyed him. Did he appreciate the delicate irony of Swift's portrayal of him as a man above party faction? Moreover, the couplet

> No Wonder you [the Dean himself] should think it *little*
> To *lick a Rascal Statesman's Spittle*

had recently appeared in Swift's clandestine *A Panegyric on Dean Swift* (1730); Pope may well have felt puzzled. But he could hardly have been pleased by the six concluding lines: he well knew what Swift thought of the ' Nation's Taste'. Swift, more than anyone else, had helped Pope with subscriptions for his Homer out of friendship; but he disapproved of translation.

> By Homer dead was taught to thrive,
> Which Homer never cou'd alive

is certainly not complimentary. Even *'meanest Talent'* may be
critical, depending on attaching the sense of 'spiteful' as well as
'small' to 'mean': it is, after all, obvious enough that Pope's greatest
talent was his wit. Then there is the odd contradiction between
'Fortune little' and 'thrive', which reinforces the notion that Swift
could not always contain his real feelings about Pope's career, and
about Pope as poet (if not about Pope) as he drew to the close of his
'tribute'. Put the couplet about Homer into a satirical context and it
would belong there quite naturally. In the passage from *A Letter of
Advice* already quoted (on page 194) above Swift is sarcastic about
those who 'improve' the classics; doubtless he disliked translations
for this reason.

As to the question of true originality (as opposed to the
subjectivism Swift deplores), we must momentarily digress from
the subject of *A Letter* to consider Swift's attitude to it. Early on he
had defined 'genius' (in *Proposals for Correcting the English Tongue*)
as the capacity 'to open new scenes and to discover a vein of true
and noble thinking'. He was exceedingly sensitive to the charge of
unoriginality. Lord Bathurst, in a shrewd and rallying letter of
9 September 1730, wrote:

> I'll take your Works to Peices & show you that it is all
> borrow'd or stoln, have not you borrow'd the sweetness of
> your Numbers from Dryden and Waller, have not you
> borrow'd thoughts from Virgil and Horace. . . .[272]

This teasing, which extended to saying the prose works were merely
echoes of Cervantes and Rabelais, is evidence that Bathurst had
heard Swift talk, and fully understood his susceptibilities.

Swift's reply, a substantial part of which is given below, was
unusually thoughtful. He admired Bathurst's letter (recognizing its
shrewdness), and we see that it immediately put him in mind of
Temple's essay in which the Ancients are preferred to the Moderns.
What he applauds is Bathurst's use of his own technique (which he
had discovered in Voiture) of praising by censure: he feels complimented precisely because Bathurst regards his works as *not* being
'all borrow'd or stoln'. In the verses on his own death he wrote

> To steal a Hint was never known,
> But what he writ was all his own.

And in the *Advertisement* to the 1735 *Poems* Swift (for he is almost
certain to have been the writer)

> . . . we cannot conceal . . . that the Author never was
> known either in Verse or Prose to borrow any Thought,
> Simile, Epithet, or particular Manner of Style; but what-
> ever he writ . . . is an original in itself.

The scrub . . . verses' referred to in Swift's reply are *A Panegyric
on the Reverend Dean Swift*. . . . The 'one fault of which I am
really guilty' is (as Sir Harold Williams observes in a footnote) a
deficiency of wit:

> You never had commenc'd a *Dean*,
> Unless you other Ways had trod
> Than those of *Wit*, or Trust in God.

Indeed, all of Swift's many usages of the word 'wit' are highly
equivocal, since he did not think it an adequate endowment for a
human being.

> Your Lordship hath done me an unspeakable injury. I
> happened to let fall in one of my letters that I showed you
> to all comers as a boast of my corresponding with you;
> And y^r Lordship in the highest degree of malice hath
> written to me in such a manner that I cannot communicate
> the particulars to my nearest friends.
>
> When Sr Wm Temple writ an Essay preferring the
> Ancient Learning to the Modern, it was said that what he
> writ showed he was mistaken; because he discovered more
> learning in that Essay than the ancients could pretend to:
> But it is none to tell you that I would give the best thing I
> was ever supposed to publish in exchange to be author of
> your letters.
>
> I pretend to have been an improver of Irony on the
> subject of Satyr and praise: but I will surrender up my
> title to your Lordship. Your injustice extends further. You
> accuse me of endeavouring to break off all Correspondence
> with you, & at this same time demonstrate that the accusation
> is against yourself. You threatened to pester me with letters
> if I will not write. If I were sure that my silence would force
> you to one letter in a quarter of a year, I would be wise
> enough never to write to you as long as I live.
>
> I swear your Lordship is the first person alive that
> ever made me lean upon my Elbow when I was writing to
> him, and by Consequence this will be the worst letter I
> ever writ. I have never been so severely attacked, nor in so
> tender a point, nor by weapons against which I am so ill
> able to defend myself, nor by a person from whom I so
> little deserved so cruel a treatment, and who in his own
> Conscience is so well convinced of my innocence upon every
> article. I have endorsed y^r name & date, and shall leave it
> to my Executors to be published at the head of all the libells
> that have been writ against me, to be printed in five Volumes

in folio after my death. And among the rest a very scrub
one in verses lately written by myself.

For, having some months ago much & often offended
the ruling party, and often worried by libellers I am at the
pains of writing one in their style & manner, & sent it by
an unknown hand to a Whig printer who very faithfully
published it. I took special care to accuse myself but of one
fault of which I am really guilty, and so shall continue as I
have done these 16 years till I see cause to reform—but
with the rest of the Satyr I chose to abuse myself with the
direct reverse of my character or at least in direct opposition
to one part of what you are pleased to give me.[273]

Considering that Swift prided himself on not 'leaning on his Elbow'
(i.e. taking thought) when he wrote (although he did so much more
often than he admitted), and said so to Pope, we can judge how
much Bathurst's letter—both in what it said, and as a performance—
affected him.

The next part of *A Letter of Advice* concerns the respective
merits of rhyme and blank verse; its purpose is to show how absurd
the controversy actually is. Thus, he is 'overjoy'd to hear, that a
very ingenious Youth of this town' is now putting *Paradise Lost*
into rhyme, 'which will make your Poem, in that only defective,
more Heroick and Sonorous than it has hitherto been'. Was Swift
recalling Dryden, who, not very creditably to his critical faculties,
changed his view about this aspect of the poem several times?

The writer of the pamphlet recommends various games and
'diminutive Sports' as useful to the would-be poet; here the target
is the artificiality, the manufactured, uninspired nature, of modern
poetry. Thus, poets are very like shoemakers—although the writer
remarks of this comparison that he may seem 'to trifle in so serious
a matter'. In this way Swift pours even more scorn upon the poetry
of his time. He continues:

A *Common-place-book*, is what a provident Poet cannot
subsist without, for this proverbial Reason, that *great Wits
have short Memories*; and whereas, on the other hand, *Poets*
being *LYARS* by Profession, ought to have good Memories;
to reconcile these, a Book of this sort is in the nature of a
Supplimental Memory; or a Record of what occurs remarkable in every Days Reading or Conversation: There you
enter not only your own original Thoughts, (which a
hundred to one, are *few* and *insignificant*) but such of other
Men as you think fit to make your own by entring them
there. For take this for a Rule, when an Author is in your
Books, you have the same demand upon him for his *Wit*,
as a Merchant has for your *Money*, when you are in his.

By these few and easy Prescriptions (with the help of a good *Genius*) 'tis possible you may in a short time arrive at the Accomplishments of a *Poet*, and shine in that Character.

The ironically approving equation of modern poets with '*LYARS*' clarifies the drift of his real thought: poetry should deal with truth. He re-emphasizes this equation at the end of a paragraph that occurs a little further on:

> As for your choice of *Subjects*, I have only to give you this Caution; That as a handsome way of Praising is certainly the most difficult point in Writing or Speaking, I wou'd by no means advise any young Man to make his first Essay in *PANEGYRICK*, besides the danger of it; for a particular Encomium is ever attended with more ill Will, than any general Invective, for which I need give no Reasons; wherefore, my Counsel is, that you use the *Point* of your *Pen*, not the *Feather*. Let your first Attempt be a *Coup d'Eclat* in the way of *Libel*, *Lampoon* or *Satyr*. Knock down half a score Reputations, and you will infallibly raise your Own, and so it be with *Wit*, no matter with how little Justice; for Fiction is your Trade.

There is some bitterness here: Swift's own first 'Essays' had been in '*PANEGYRICK*', and they had been failures in two senses. The attack on satire that follows this passage is an attack on the habits of an age, and on Swift himself as much as on anyone else. 'The *Sublime*, indeed,' he writes, 'is not so common with us, but ample amends is made for that want in the great abundance of the *Admirable* and *Amazing*, which appears in all our Compositions.'

The end of the *Letter* consists of 'some poor Thoughts of mine for the Encouragement of *Poetry* in this Kingdom' (i.e. Ireland). He wants a Grub Street in Dublin, and for 'our Poetical *Vapours*' to be carried off in 'a common Drain'. The intent of this last section is to satirize the disrepute into which poetry has fallen: people should retain not only fools and chaplains in their service, but also 'poets'. There is no 'Masterly Poet' in the Kingdom, but 'a Multitude of *Poetmasters*, *Poetito's*, *Parcel-Poets*, *Poet-Apes* and *Philo-Poets*'.

A Letter of Advice is certainly not an attack—at any rate, not an overt one—on Pope or on any other of Swift's friends. Nor does it amount to a positive statement of Swift's views on poetry: we can only deduce these from what he condemns. The question is: does it exempt any modern poetry from its implied strictures? No doubt some critics would say that it did. My view is that it expresses, however obliquely, a belief that all modern poetry (including Swift's own) is unworthy. The first twenty-four lines of *On Poetry: A Rapsody* express the same feeling, equally obliquely; and they reiterate Swift's preoccupation with the question of where his talent lies, his ambivalent attitude towards his genius for satire: on one hand he actually uses satire both as a vehicle for praise and to defend the interests of the wretched Irish; on the other he says he would have written 'nothing else' but satire like the *Dunciad*, had his talent been equal to the sourness of his temper. But in his courageous genius for self-appraisal he was a true poet, and less in tune with his age than any of his contemporaries.

I O

The differences between Swift and Pope, both satirists of magnitude, are instructive. This is why I have emphasized them. Their friendship was not based on a true affinity of mind or heart. Swift is formally affectionate to Pope in his letters, but not relaxed and easy as he is with Stopford ('Jim') or Delany or even Sheridan—whose fecklessness, we know, irritated him considerably. It is quite likely that he got as much real pleasure from Delany's occasional verses as he did from Pope's; towards Pope, when it came to the moment of truth, he was respectful but reticent. His letters to him became increasingly intellectual in content, the salutations more and more exquisitely elaborate and formal. He was careful either to write what Pope wanted to hear (in his edition of Temple's letters Swift praised Temple for adapting his style to the needs of his correspondents), or to make semi-programmatic, railling statements that he knew would amuse and gain wide currency. One of his most famous pronouncements occurs in a letter to Pope of 29 September 1725:

> I have ever hated all Nations professions and Communityes and all my love is towards individualls for instance I hate the tribe of Lawyers, but I love Councellor such a one . . . but principally I hate and detest that animal called man, although I hartily love John, Peter, Thomas and so forth. . . . I have got Materials towards a Treatis [*Gulliver's Travels*] proving the falsity of that Definition *animale rationale*; and to show it should be only *rationis capax*. Upon this great foundation of Misanthropy (though not Timons manner) The whole building of my Travells is erected: And I never will have peace of mind till all honest men are of my Opinion: by Consequence you are to embrace it immediatly and procure that all who deserve my Esteem may do so too.[274]

At the end of the passage Swift is joking; but beneath the raillery it is evident that he knews Pope is not of his opinion. Pope's reply is cautious and clever, but not, I think, fully understanding (as has often been claimed). At all events, Swift did not think so, for in his reply of 26 November 1725 he says '. . . I tell you after all that I do not hate Mankind, it is vous autres who hate them because you would have them reasonable Animals, and are Angry for being disappointed'. He is good-humoured, but perfectly serious—and deep and shrewd—in what he charges. He alone of his age saw that there was much more in mankind than was dreamt of in Pope's philosophy.

Pope, in his reply to the letter of 29 September 1725, told Swift that he had the idea of 'writing a Set of Maximes in opposition to all Rochefoucaults Principles'; Swift, in his letter of 26 November 1725, was quick to respond:

> . . . you are so hardy as to tell me of your Intentions to write Maxims in Opposition to Rochefoucault who is my Favorite because I found my whole character in him, however I will read him again because it is possible I may have since undergone some alterations—Take care the bad poets do not outwit you, as they have served the good ones in every Age, whom they have provoked to transmit their Names to posterity. Maevius is as well known as Virgil, and Gildon will be as well known as you if his name gets into your Verses; and as to the difference between good and bad Fame is a perfect Trifle. . . .[275]

Swift's verses on his own death were occasioned by La Rochefoucault's maxim 'Dans l'adversité de nos meilleurs amis nous trouvons quelque chose, qui ne nous deplaist pas'; it has often been claimed by critics that his remark that he 'found his whole character' in La Rochefoucault was a bad piece of self-characterization. This does not go far enough. He had been interested in La Rochefoucault for many years, and had introduced him to Esther Vanhomrigh. In a letter to him written on 6 June 1713 she had said:

> . . . I have been studying of Rochfoucaut to see if he describes as much self love as I found in my self a Sunday and I find he falls very short of it.[276]

Swift in his solitude, dwelt much on the problems of self-love and self-interest: dwelt on them directly and emotionally, rather than in terms of the theological or philosophical or literary orthodoxies of his time. His observation, for example, that Milton's 'book of divorces' was only an 'occasional treatise' because 'he had a shrew for his wife' was an unusual one in its time. Beneath Swift's raillery about La Rochefoucault's cynicism lay a serious concern with the element of self-love that he recognized in himself and knew operated in all human beings. It represented a profound criticism of the lack of self-knowledge that he saw in the people around him. One of the weaknesses of Augustan poetry, as poetry, is that it strives to impress rather than to illuminate. Swift knew his poetry could not illuminate in the way he felt poetry should—in the *Epistle to a Lady* (1733), for Lady Acheson (his best 'pupil' after Stella's death), he wrote

> Thus, Shou'd I attempt to climb,
> Treat you in a Stile sublime,
> Such a Rocket is my Muse,
> Shou'd I lofty Numbers chuse,
> E'er I reach'd *Parnassus* Top
> I shou'd burst, and bursting drop.
> All my *Fire* would fall in Scraps. . . .

He knew, from bitter experience, that any attempt of his at '*Fire*' would 'fall in Scraps', and kept his style plain. But he did his best, deliberately stripping his poems of all pretentiousness. His style is less ornate than that of any of his contemporaries, his rhythms infinitely more varied and original. The little he does owe technically is owed to Butler rather than to Dryden, whom the rest of his age followed.

Criticism of the scatological poems has shown as much neurosis in critics as in Swift. The poet in Swift exploited what was, evidently, a 'Freudian' situation in himself in order to make profound symbolic statements about human beings and about the nature of physical love. But critics have been put off by what they regard, sometimes rather pathetically, as 'unfortunate' subject-matter; or, like Murry, they have felt that Swift was misogynistic and 'humanly wrong'. They miss the point when they say that Swift was like a dirty little boy, or a sick man, in these poems.

But this embarrassment in critics and readers in itself justifies the brutality of the poems. For our social indulgence in coy euphemisms about bodily functions is, fundamentally, at least as disgusting and reprehensible as Swift's obsessiveness. There are moral as well as neurotic reasons for his over-emphasis. The exploitation of the theme of the painted-up old hag was not a new one; but Swift developed it into something quite different. Parnell's *An Elegy to an Old Beauty*, which antedates Swift's *The Lady's Dressing Room* (1730) by many years, moralizes, lecturing the old Beauty to be herself; Swift merely describes. Prior's few poems on this theme are exercises. There can be no doubt about who has the most truly moral effect.

Except perhaps towards Esther Vanhomrigh and Stella, and then only intermittently and secretly, Swift found it impossible to behave warmly, unequivocally lovingly or naturally. He dammed and diverted the impulses of his heart into several different streams:

raillery, irony, nonsense, severity, the duties of what he called his 'trade'. All his undoubted tenderness towards Stella was expressed in front of a third party, for he never once saw her, as an adult, alone. Yet, for all his savagery and bearishness, he possessed more simple warmth of heart than most of the men of his age. This appears in certain of his letters, as it does in some of the birthday poems to Stella. This is an aspect of Swift that can be ignored only at the cost of completely misunderstanding him. It is not in question that he wrote none of his letters with an eye to publication. This alone, of course, makes them more reliable guides to his personality than, Pope's, say, are to his. His letter of 2 September 1727 to Sheridan, written from England when he daily expected to hear that Stella had died (she did not in fact die until the following January), is as clear an indication as any other of the simplicity and wholesomeness of heart that underlay the labyrinthine complexities of his nature, and which give his astonishingly subtle expression of them such dignity and poetic importance:

> If I had any tolerable Health, I would go this Moment to *Ireland*; yet I think I would not, considering the News I daily expect to hear from you. I have just received yours of *August* 24; I kept it an Hour in my Pocket, with all the Suspense of a Man who expected to hear the worst News that Fortune could give him; and at the same Time was not able to hold up my Head. These are the Perquisites of living long: The last Act of Life is always a Tragedy at best; but it is a bitter Aggravation to have one's best Friend go before one. I desired in my last, that you would not enlarge upon that Event; but tell me the bare Fact. I long knew that our dear Friend had not the *Stamina Vitae*; but my Friendship could not arm me against this Accident altho' I foresaw it. I have said enough in my last Letter, which now I suppose is with you. I know not whether it be an Addition to my Grief or no, that I am now extreamly ill; for it would have been a Reproach to me to be in perfect Health, when such a Friend is desperate. I do profess, upon my Salvation, that the distressed and desperate Condition of our Friend, makes Life so indifferent to me, who by Course of Nature have so little left, that I do not think it worth the Time to struggle; yet I should think, according to what hath been formerly, that I may happen to overcome this present Disorder; and to what Advantage? Why, to see the Loss of that Person for whose sake Life was only worth preserving. I brought both those Friends over, that we might be happy together as long as God should please; the Knot is broken, and the remaining Person, you know,

has ill answered the End; and the other who is now to be lost, was all that is Valuable. You agreed with me, or you are a great Hypocrite. What have I to do in the World? I was never in such Agonies as when I received your Letter, and had it in my Pocket.—I am able to hold up my sorry Head no longer.[277]

I

This account of the letters of Alexander Pope concentrates, chiefly, upon their author's unique machinations concerning their publication. Those he published in his own lifetime that comment on literature may, for some, attain the status of critical essays, or even of polished and re-polished accounts of his own 'virtue'; they have no value as private communications. They were not private. Pope never wrote a natural or spontaneous letter. His sole interest, from the beginning of his career, was in creating a desired effect or attaining a desired result. From quite early he wrote his letters with publication in mind. When at various times in his life (1735; 1736; 1737; 1741; 1742) he published collections of them, he edited, 'improved' and cut them. He also pretended that letters originally addressed to obscure individuals, such as his friend Caryll, had been addressed to famous (but safely dead) ones such as Joseph Addison and William Wycherley.

His behaviour is widely said to have been typical of that of his age. But students should know that no one of his major contemporaries did in fact behave as he did: if they like Pope, and there is no reason why they should not, then they should like him for what he was, and not for what modern critics have made him.

Swift's letters were published only at Pope's insistence. Although she is now celebrated as an eighteenth century letter-writer, the letters of Lady Mary Wortley Montagu (b. 1689) were not published until a year after her death, and then without authority. Nor were those of Lord Chesterfield (b. 1694) published within his lifetime. True, famous writers and eminent men did often think of their letters as eventually becoming available to the public; but not during their own lives. In such brutal matters as the revenge on Edmund Curll Pope was the moving spirit. Despite his exquisite sense of what was distinguished and tasteful in art, architecture and literature, Pope's actual procedures—that they were clandestine is not morally relevant—resembled those of the literary jungle, of Curll and his hacks, of Pope's avowed enemies, not of Swift, Gay, Arbuthnot, Bathurst, who were his friends. A few poets and critics (John Dennis was one of them) older than Pope had published an odd letter by or to themselves; no poet before Pope lavished even one-thousandth of the elaborate care and attention upon a comprehensive collection of his own letters to be published either during or even after his own lifetime. Yet in his Home University Library volume on *Eighteenth Century English Literature* Professor R. P. McCutcheon writes:

> That Mr. Pope recalled some of his letters and edited them considerably before publication, even in some instances changing dates and names of recipients, has seemed almost reprehensible. Yet Pope was simply following a practice *regarded in his day as sound*, and thought it no more deceitful to revise one of his own letters than one of his own poems [my italics].

This is grossly misleading. In its context (a chapter called *The Letter Writers*) it suggests that Lady Mary and the others were all given, like Pope, to making efforts to publish their own letters, to faking dates and recipients. It must be emphasized that they were not. Further, as we shall see, Pope himself undoubtedly regarded the publication of one's own letters as a bad practice: he had to create an excuse in order to achieve it in his own case.

The only people who could have regarded Pope's secret practices of revision and conflation of letters as in any sense 'sound' were the denizens of Grub Street, whose lack of standards he shared. No wonder he poured scorn on Grub Street: he lived by its principles. Professor McCutcheon should inform his readers what serious writer practised Pope's tricks—let alone on his gigantic scale.

And yet, having survived the attacks of the Romantics and Victorians, Pope has now been totally rehabilitated. Once too crudely and sanctimoniously regarded as a vituperative hunchback, he is now seen as a subtle moralist; the 'classic of our prose' (Matthew Arnold's words) is now a classic of our poetry, the movement of whose verse is reminiscent of Mozart, and whose beauties are 'Keatsian'; he was, it is said, much 'loved and loving'.

Extreme moral defensiveness, special pleading and fondness for abstractions characterize most modern criticism of Pope. His admirers assume that the romantic dislike of his poetry and the Victorian prejudice against his character are still rampant. Actually no book remotely hostile to him has appeared since 1909;[278] it is the justice inherent in the original charges, for all their over-simplicity, that puts Pope's admirers on the defensive and causes them to invent the figure of the moralist.

The view here taken of Pope's poetry and letters is not fashionable. Of modern critics only Sir Herbert Read has expressed

distaste for him.[279] However, lack of sympathy with Pope does not
necessarily derive from a morally adverse judgement of the man,
nor even from dislike of his work. He is, in some respects, lovable;
the poetry—taking it for what it is—is enjoyable for its brilliance
and wit. But Pope is not a poet at all in the sense that Marvell or
even Swift or Gay or Gray were poets: in him poetic desire for
truth for its own sake is quite lost in the need for self-glorification.
By all means let us admire Pope's skill, cleverness and elegance;
let us salute his courage and charm. Let those who love him do so—
but not for what he never was.

In 1928 T. S. Eliot wrote: 'indeed it might be said that the
man who cannot enjoy Pope as poetry probably understands no
poetry'.[280] This bullying and portentous remark, perhaps made with
a giggle behind the hand, was never developed by its originator, and
is as irresponsible as many of his other 'casual' remarks. Eliot may
have made it as a private joke: he was contemptuous of those who
took him too seriously.

However this may be, the opinionatedness of Eliot's pronouncement is typical of the general evasiveness of Pope's modern
admirers. Alan Tate seems to fall into this error in his introduction
to Sir Herbert Read's *Selected Writings*. Writing about Sir Herbert's
essay *Poetic Diction* (not included in *Selected Writings*, but to be
found in *Collected Essays in Literary Criticism*)[281] he says:

> In 'Poetic Diction' [Sir Herbert] revives Arnold's rejection
> of Dryden and Pope . . . he dismisses them with Dryden's
> own phrase 'wit-writing'. . . . I do not see how Shakespeare's
> lines [quoted by Sir Herbert from *Macbeth* to illustrate what
> he describes as their 'organic' superiority over the 'wit-
> writing' of the final lines of *The Dunciad*] imply a standard
> of organic form which allows us to reject the lines of Pope:
> I would retain both, with some awareness of their differ-
> ences.[282]

This is very interesting. No tolerant reader can possibly complain.
But it is curious that we find nothing in Mr. Tate's own valuable
critical works that tells us how, in fact, and on what grounds, he
would propose to 'retain both' and justify the view that both are
manifestations of a single thing he describes as poetry. One does
not have to be hostile to the kind of effect Pope can achieve to
recognize that it is inferior to the effects Shakespeare, Marvell or
Swift (in his negative way) can achieve. Pope's achievements simply
do not arise from the same inner processes or preoccupations. To
describe them as 'moral' because they are clever or delightful or
impressive is as perverse and uncritical as to describe detective
stories as superior to Dostoevsky because you enjoy them more at
bed-time.

2

Apart from his literary activities and one or two escapades and physical accidents, Pope's life was mostly uneventful. It could hardly have been otherwise, for he was singularly unfortunate in his physique: four-and-a-half feet in height when fully grown, Pott's disease, a tubercular infection, gave him so pronounced a curvature of the spine as to make him a hunchback. He was not as physically unattractive, particularly facially, as his Grub Street enemies made him out to be; but certainly even his closest friends regarded him—physically—as frail, a hunchback and a cripple. He was prey to bad headaches throughout his life, and his understandable attempts to eat and drink as hard as his contemporaries, in an age of hard eating and drinking, caused him endless suffering, about which he complained remarkably little.

He was born in London, of Catholic parents, in 1688—a bad year for Catholics. Pope himself remained a Roman Catholic all his life, but his religion played no part in his poetry. In 1700 his family moved to Binfield, in Windsor Forest, possibly to comply with anti-Catholic legislation. In 1705 he began to infiltrate London literary society. His *Pastorals* were published in 1709; *An Essay on Criticism* followed in 1711. By 1712, although still associated with Addison, Steele and the Whigs, he was also becoming known to Swift, Gay, Parnell and Arbuthnot; with them he formed the Scriblerus Club. The first version of *The Rape of The Lock* appeared in 1712, followed by the expanded version in 1714. From 1713 until 1720 he was occupied with his translation of the *Iliad*, published by subscription. By this means he established himself financially. No English author had made as much money out of a single project before. It was largely because the 'Little Senate' of Addison and his Whig set had (without Pope's knowledge) encouraged another poet, Thomas Tickell, to try his hand at a translation of the *Iliad* that Pope quarrelled with them. His version is not much read now, but is skilfully done according to the principles of its age. Pope got as much help as he could from better scholars than himself, notably Congreve and Rowe. Owing to his religion he had had little schooling, and was largely self-educated. He cannot be described as a scholar, but he well knew where and how to gather information.

In 1716 Pope and his family moved from Binfield to Chiswick; in the next year his father died, and in 1718 he and his mother moved to Twickenham, where he was to stay for the rest of his life. During these years he began to make enemies as well as friends. Besides his quarrel with the Addison set, he incurred the censure of the veteran critic John Dennis on account of his didactic poem *An Essay on Criticism*, and of Colley Cibber because of a comedy he wrote in collaboration with Gay and Arbuthnot, *Three Hours After Marriage*

(1717). But although his famous 'war with the dunces' had its origins in this decade, the first version of *The Dunciad*—preceded by the prose *Peri Bathous* in the third volume of the Swift–Pope *Miscellanies* (1727)—was not published until 1728.

Pope was busy from 1720 until 1726 with his edition of Shakespeare and his version of the *Odyssey*, in which he was substantially aided by Fenton and Broom; both projects further secured his financial independence. The *Odyssey* made him enemies in Grub Street; the edition of Shakespeare brought upon him the censure of a better informed scholar than himself, Lewis Theobald (pronounced 'Tibbald'), who published his *Shakespeare Restored: or a Specimen of the Many Errors . . . Committed . . . by Mr. Pope* in 1726. Although Theobald's attacks on Pope's Shakespeare were for the most part justified—and have been accepted as such by Shakespearian scholarship—Pope never forgave him, and made him the hero of the first *Dunciad*.

In 1723 he published an edition of John Sheffield, Duke of Buckingham's works; this brought him into danger, for the Government suppressed the books on the grounds that it contained Jacobite sentiments. In the same year his friend Atterbury, Bishop of Rochester, was tried by the Lords and subsequently exiled as a Jacobite; Pope courageously appeared as a witness for him.

After the first *Dunciad* he gave up translation and editing for original work. *An Essay on Man* appeared, in parts, in 1733 and 1734, and in 1735 Pope published the second volume of his *Works*; the first had appeared in 1717. Meanwhile he continued his friendships with Swift, Gay, Arbuthnot and Bolingbroke—who had been allowed to return from exile in 1725, when he settled down at Uxbridge in Middlesex with his new French wife. However, Gay died in 1732, Arbuthnot in 1735, and Pope never saw Swift after his last visit to England in 1727.

During the years at Twickenham he spent much time perfecting his garden and the famous grotto. His life was quiet except for his visits to various friends, who included Whig magnates as well as such politically impotent Tories as Bolingbroke.

In 1742 he published a new, fourth part of *The Dunciad*; in 1743 the whole revised and altered four books appeared, with Colley Cibber (in place of Theobald) as hero. At the end of May 1744, a few days after entering his fifty-seventh year, he died.

3

The history of Pope's manipulations and literary enmities is vastly complex; some details can never be known. His attitude towards his correspondence was unique, and reveals not only what kind of man but also what kind of poet he was. This is why I deal here in some detail with the devious and complex processes by which he collected, edited and published his letters, and with the methods he employed to publish his correspondence with Swift towards the end of his life.

On 19 November 1712 the twenty-four-year-old Pope, in a letter to his friend John Caryll, a fellow-Catholic, wrote:

> You see my letters are scribbled with all the carelessness and inattention imaginable: my style, like my soul, appears in its natural undress before my friend.

And in the postscript to the same letter he added, as if casually:

> I have an odd request to you that if you ever thought any of of my epistles worth preserving, you will favour me with the whole cargoe, which shall be faithfully returned to you ... there are several thoughts which I throw out that way in the freedom of my soul, that my be of use to me in a design I am lately engaged in, which will require so constant a flux of thought and invention, that I can never supply it without some assistance and 'tis not impossible but so many notions, written at different times, may save me a good deal of trouble. Pray forgive this, and keep my secret which is of consequence.[283]

The 'design' Pope was then engaged in was probably the writing of pieces for the *Guardian*; but he never used anything from his letters to Caryll in what he wrote for that paper. What he did do, although much later, was to pretend that this very letter to Caryll (not including, of course, its postscript), pieced together with others to him, had been written to Addison. As his biographer and editor, George Sherburn, sympathetically explains, the public would naturally have expected letters to the eminent Addison to appear in an edition of his letters. And what Pope's public would expect, he in due time would labour at all costs to supply.

In the years succeeding 1712 he did not, however, save all the letters he received: the MS. of his *Iliad* is written on the backs and in the margins of old letters, including a flattering one of 1706 from the bookseller and publisher Jacob Tonson, asking Pope to allow him to print his poems; the *Iliad* MS. is indeed the sole source of this and other letters to Pope not published by him. In 1712 he was probably no more than anxious that nothing creditable to himself that he might have written to Caryll should be wasted. Doubtless any notion of a future collection of his own correspondence was vague. At any rate, the letters to Caryll were to be extremely useful to him in the future, if only as material to construct ones to eminent persons that he had not sent at all.

In 1726 (dated 1727) the 'unspeakable' Edmund Curll, who would publish anything 'hot' that would sell, and who may be said to be one of the earliest true ancestors of the editors of modern popular Sunday sex- and gossip-sheets (though Curll was more literate and less self-deceiving), published *Familiar Letters to Henry Cromwell Esq; by Mr. Pope.* . . . Cromwell, who posed as a 'Restoration wit', was an untalented rhymster whom Pope had first met in Will's Coffee House. Pope had posed, too, in his many letters to Cromwell, as a fashionable man-about-town, a hard-drinking fellow with mistresses. One can sympathize. He was young, and he did, in the second decade of the century, try, as far as his poor constitution would allow him, to live up to the part of a rake. Thus, in one of his letters he wished Cromwell 'Health and Happiness. . . . A hearty stomach, and a sound Lady'; and in an early poem he made a Restoration-type joke about the 'well-worn', 'large and wide' 'Paths' of the Drury Lane whores, in such a way as to suggest that he was familiar with them. There is nothing reprehensible about the letters as written by a tiny, still immature, tragically deformed, brilliant young man who, possibly, could not even quite manage to have a prostitute. (He spoke of himself in a letter of 25 January 1711 to Caryll as 'the little Alexander that women laugh at'; and there may be a basis of truth in Colley Cibber's grotesque tale of how he rescued the nearly incompetent Pope from a diseased whore in a brothel by pulling him off her as he floundered on top of her.) But they are wholly artificial.

However, if Pope had no real mistresses, Henry Cromwell did: it was by purchasing them from a discarded one of his, Elizabeth Thomas, that Curll got hold of the Pope–Cromwell letters he put out in 1726. Sherburn says that this 'so upset Pope that he attempted, with only partial success, to persuade friends to return all letters not yet destroyed'.[285]

But was he so 'upset'? Writing to Aaron Hill, in about September 1726, he said:

> Nor am I ashamed of those Weaknesses of mine, which they have exposed in Print (the greatest of which was my thinking too candidly of them, to whom I wrote my Letters with so much unguarded Friendliness, and Freedom), since you have found a Way to turn those Weaknesses into Virtue, by your partial Regard of them. . . . I agree with you, that there is a Pleasure in seeing the Nature and Temper of Men in the plainest Undress; but few Men are of Consequence enough to deserve, or reward, that Curiosity.[286]

In view of the subsequent history of Pope's letters, the phrase about 'the plainest Undress' is not without hypocritical significance. The publication of the Pope–Cromwell letters probably delighted him: it was good publicity, and it provided him with an excuse to ask for all his old letters back from everyone.

In his preface to the 1735 edition of his letters he quotes a letter from Elizabeth Thomas to Cromwell, in which she denies that she sold any letters to Curll, but admits that she lent them to an 'ingenious person', because she thought them 'of the first rank'. The only authority for the text of this letter is Pope's own, both Cromwell and Elizabeth Thomas having conveniently died before 1735. The invention of it, with the incidental praise of himself, would have been characteristic of Pope: 'she' thought the letters 'too good to be lost in oblivion'; the 'early pregnancy' of Pope's genius was no 'dishonour to his character. . . .' Furthermore, he reprinted some of the offending letters to Cromwell in his own 1735 edition, only ostensibly seeking to discredit Curll's 1726 text. A glaring omission from Pope's own edition, however, was the slightly smutty letter of 25 April 1708, a few words from which I have quoted.[287] Curll had the autograph of this. All Pope could do about it was to invent a letter of 27 April 1708 which appeared to discredit it; Sherburn writes that one 'can only surmise its origin'.

Sherburn is more explicit about Pope's motives in the index to his massive edition of the *Correspondence* than he is in the introduction, for there he writes: '*ostensibly* to prevent publication P. in 1726 and thereafter asks for the return of his letters' (my italics).[288] He did: from his friends Hugh Bethel, Mrs. Edward Blount, Lord Digby, Swift and others. He began a letter of 17 June 1728 to Hugh Bethel:

> After the publishing of my Boyish Letters to Mr. Cromwell, you will not wonder if I should forswear writing a letter again while I live; since I do not correspond with a friend upon the terms of any other free subject of this kingdom. But to you I can never be silent, or reserved; and I am sure my opinion of your heart is such, that I could open mine to you in no manner which I could fear the whole world should know. I could publish my own heart too, I will venture to say, for any mischief or malice there's in it; but a little too much folly or weakness might (I fear) appear, to make such a spectacle either instructive or agreeable to others.
>
> I am reduced to beg of all my acquaintance to secure me from the like usage for the future, by returning me any letters of mine which they may have preserved; that I may not be hurt after my death by that which was the happiness of my life, their partiality and affection for me.[289]

He published this letter, which concludes in highly moralistic style —'I have . . . no vanity in writing . . . the greatest pleasure is to give and receive mutual Trust. . . . for many years I have . . . chosen my companions for . . . sincerity'—in 1737. Clearly, by 1728, the plan to issue a volume of his letters was hardening in his mind. We can hardly conclude otherwise (in view of what happened), for on 5 December 1726, nearly two years before the letter to Bethel, he had again written to Caryll requesting the return of his letters, this time 'to help me to put out of Curl's power any trifling remains of mine'.[290] We shall discover who eventually put into 'Curl's power' Pope's 'remains'; assuredly it was not Caryll.

4

Lewis Theobald, the most knowledgeable Shakespeare scholar of his time—although his work was soon to be superseded—had in 1726 criticized Pope's edition of Shakespeare. Two years later, Theobald further enraged Pope by editing a volume entitled *Posthumous Works of William Wycherley*. Wycherley had been one of the most amusing of the Restoration dramatists, but in later life had become a has-been and a bore. Pope, when very young, formed a friendship with him, from which a highly artificial correspondence resulted (if, indeed, it is wholly genuine); this was much influenced by the letter-writing precepts of Voiture (apparently only Swift was able to get anything unusual or lively out of Voiture). Wycherley, impressed by the young Pope's brilliance, had submitted his poems to him for 'correction'. Although the old man at first resented Pope's suggested alterations, he probably eventually agreed not to publish the poems at all. Now he was dead; but Pope regarded his works as his exclusive property. Theobald, acting in good faith at the behest of the new husband of Wycherley's widow, did print Wycherley's poems, some of them incorporating alterations that Pope knew he himself had made. Pope therefore prepared a second volume of *The Posthumous Works of William Wycherley*, printing both better texts of the poems and his correspondence with Wycherley 'proving' that Theobald's Volume I had constituted an 'injury' to the dead playwright's reputation. But although wholly responsible for it, Pope pretended to have nothing whatever to do with the intended publication, so that the prefatory address (written by himself) would not seem immodest when it read:

> . . . we can thus far consult the Fame of Two Eminent Writers, remarkable for so long a Friendship at so great an Inequality of Years, for it appears to have commenc'd when the one was above *Seventy*, the other not *Seventeen*: And that in this we publish an *Example* (very rarely to be found among any Authors, and never but among the Best) of so

much Temper, Sense of his own Deficiencies, and Deference to the Judgment of a Friend, in the One; and of so much Sincerity, Candor and zeal for the Reputation of a Friend, in the other.[291]

This anonymously 'sincere' 'Zeal' for the 'Reputation of a Friend', with its commendation of Wycherley's 'sense of his own Deficiencies', is an excellent example of damning the old one with faint praise, while more or less canonizing the young one. When writing anonymously, Pope could rise to ecstatic heights of self-praise.

However, this volume was never put on sale: either Wycherley's heirs successfully objected to it, or it ran into insoluble copyright difficulties.[292] Pope made the best of it, retaining the sheets on which the correspondence had been printed for future use.

It will have been noted that Pope acknowledged no connection with the Wycherley publication. 'He felt strongly,' wrote Sherburn, than whom there can be no better authority, 'that to be known to publish one's own letters laid one open to charges of reprehensible conceit. . . . It led to chicanery: for he would publish'.[293] Pope certainly did feel this strongly, because in his ironical condemnation of Dennis in one of his notes to *The Dunciad Variorum* he wrote: '[Dennis] . . . obtained some correspondence with Mr. *Wycherley* and Mr. *Congreve* he immediately obliged the publick with their Letters'. Pope's own methods were different and less direct. Joseph Spence jotted down a note, dated 9 August 1735, showing that Pope talked about the 'modesty or prudery of not publishing one's own letters'.[294] The subject obsessed him as it had obsessed no man before him.

5

By the late Twenties Pope, although feeling it was reprehensible and conceited, was determined to get his letters into print. The second Lord Oxford (the ex-Lord Treasurer, his father, had died in 1724, after founding the Harleian Library) was proud of his friendship with Pope, who was thus able to deposit his correspondence in the Harleian Library, get it transcribed free of charge—and have it made respectably available there. Pope initiated the process by writing, on 6 October 1729 (before the planned publication of the eventually suppressed second volume of Wycherley's works) to Oxford, to ask for his permission to deposit the Wycherley letters. Within three days Oxford replied, saying, 'I shall be very much honoured by the deposite you propose . . .', adding, 'what ever mention you make of that Library I shall be pleased with'.[295] Pope was thus able to write, in the Preface to the suppressed Wycherley volume, that 'the Originals', in 'the Authors' own Hand-Writing', might be viewed in the Harley Library. Curiously, they have now disappeared.

Curll, to whose merry unscrupulousness literary historians incidentally owe a great deal, was most active as a printer of scandalous 'biography'. Arbuthnot said that he added 'a new terror to death'. As well as having pirated the Pope–Cromwell letters in 1726, he had seriously offended Pope ten years before that.[296] In revenge, Pope, under the pretext of offering him a reconciliatory drink of sack, had administered to him an emetic 'antimonially prepared' by Arbuthnot.[297]

The relationship between the two men, so similar at heart, was likely at all times to lead to fierce incidents. Curll was always ready to do Pope down; the subtler Pope was always ready to make use of him.

In 1733 Curll advertised that he was prepared to publish a 'biography' of Pope if people would supply him with 'facts' (i.e. any kind of spice, true or untrue, but preferably the sort of smoke there is none of without fire). On 11 October of that year Curll received the following letter, signed 'P.T.':

> Mr. Curll, Understanding you proposed to write the *Life* of *Mr. Pope*, this is only to inform you, I can send you divers Memoirs which may be serviceable, if your Design be really to do him neither Injustice nor shew him Favour. I was well acquainted with his Father, and with the first part of his own Life, tho' since he has treated me as a Stranger. It is certain some late Pamphlets are not fair in respect to his Father, who was of the younger Branch of a Family in good repute in *Ireland*, and related to the Lords *Downe*, formerly of the same Name. He was (as he hath told Me himself, and he was [very different from his Son] a modest and plain honest Man) a Posthumous Son, and left little provided for, his elder Brother having what small Estate there was, who afterwards Study'd and dy'd at *Oxford*. He was put to a Merchant in *Flanders*, and acquir'd a moderate Fortune by Merchandize, which he quitted at the Revolution in very good Circumstances, and retired to *Windsor* Forest, where he purchased a small Estate, and took great Delight in Husbandry and Gardens. His Mother was one of seventeen Children of *W. Turnor* Esq; formerly of *Burfit Hall* in the — Riding of Yorkshire. Two of her Brothers were killed in the Civil Wars. This is a true Account of Mr *Pope's* Family and Parentage. Of his Manners I cannot give so good an one, yet as I would not wrong any Man, both ought to be True; and if such be your Design,

I may serve you in it, not entering into any Thing in any wise Libellous. You may please to direct an Answer in the *Daily Advertiser* this Day-sennight in these Terms—*E. C. hath received a Letter, and will comply with P. T.*[298]

It has not been conclusively proved that 'P.T.' was Pope himself; but no one now in the least doubts it. Sherburn assumes it. No other person would have known or been interested in the information given about Pope's family; and it was characteristic of him to lie to Curll, thus gaining the kind of genealogical credit in which he delighted, by claiming a non-existent tie with the Earls of Downe and a fictitious Oxford education for his uncle. The letter is a masterpiece in this respect, since no one could accuse Pope himself of exaggerating about his family. Furthermore, he knew that whether Curll, whose only interest lay in satisfying the grossest tastes and thus enriching himself, suspected him of writing the letter or not, he would still make eventual use of the opportunity it provided.

   Curll was initially cautious, however, for on 15 November 1733 Pope was obliged to send him another letter, again signed 'P.T.'. Now he wished to direct Curll's suspicions away from himself: 'I intend him the like for his Conduct towards me' is supposed to be a plain indication that 'P.T.' dislikes Pope as much as Curll does.

> Sir,—I troubled you with a Line sometime since, concerning your Design of the *Life* of Mr. *Pope*, to which I desir'd your Answer in the *Daily Advertiser* of *Thursday* the 10th Instant *October*. I do not intend my self any other Profit in it, than that of doing Justice to, and on, that Person, upon whom, Sir, you have conferr'd some Care as well as Pains in the Course of your Life; and I intend him the like for his Conduct towards me. *A propos* to his Life, there have lately fall'n into my Hands a large Collection of his *Letters*, from the former Part of his Days to the Year 1727. which being more considerable than any yet seen, and opening very many Scnes new to the World, will alone make a Perfect and the most authentick *Life* and *Memoirs* of him that could be. To shew you my Sincerity and determinate Resolution of assisting you herein, I will give you an Advertisement, which you may publish forthwith if you please, and on your so doing the Letters shall be sent you. They will make a Four or Five Sheet[1] Book, yet I expect no more than what will barely pay a Transcriber, that the Originals may be preserved in mine or your Hands to vouch the Truth of them. I am of Opinion these alone will contain his whole History (if you add to them what you formerly printed of those to *Henry Cromwell*, Esq; [*Here a part of the Letter is cut off, and the*

following Words indors'd by Curl—But you must put out an Advertisement for—] otherwise I shall not be justify'd to some People who have *Influence*, and on whom I have some *Dependance*; unless it seem to the Publick Eye as no entire Act of mine; but I may be justify'd and excus'd, if, after they see such a Collection is made by you, I acknowledge I sent some Letters to contribute thereto. They who know what hath pass'd betwixt Mr. *Pope* and me formerly, may otherwise think it dishonourable I should set such a thing a-foot. Therefore print the Advertisement I sent you, and you shall instantly hear from or see me. . . .[299]

Curll remained cautious, and nothing more happened until early 1735, when—pretending honesty—he sent both the 'P.T.' letters to Pope and asked him if he would co-operate. So far he had cleverly countered Pope's chicanery by behaving in a strictly honourable manner. Pope's intention, however, was to trick Curll into publishing for him, while apparently remaining aloof. He eventually succeeded, although Curll himself did not suffer. But Pope could not, for the moment, afford to do anything but appear to snub him.

Pope now printed his letters, in octavo volumes, and had them delivered, 'in various stages of completeness' (says Sherburn), to Curll's shop by 'Mysterious agents'. One of Pope's main assistants in the affair, 'R. Smith', was James Worsdale, a painter; Pope soon publically offered a reward of twenty guineas if 'P.T.' or 'R.S.' would 'discover the Whole of this Affair', and promised to double it if one of them could prove 'he hath acted by *Direction of any other*'. As Sherburn notes, this must have 'agitated somewhat the mind of James Worsdale'.[300]

It is instructive to note that just before he started the process by which he would make his own doctored letters the literary event of the year while appearing as Curll's victim, Pope wrote to his friend Jonathan Richardson (the painter),

> . . . I resolve to go on in my quiet, calm moral course, taking no sort of notice of men's, or women's anger or scandal, with virtue on my eyes, and truth upon my tongue.[301]

There is no doubt that Pope meant this, which is a pity: it is such pronouncements, to friends, that make the story less amusing than it might be. *A Narrative of the Method by which the Private Letters of Mr. Pope have been Procur'd and Publish'd by Edmund Curll. . . .*, published about 12 June 1735, and 'inspired if not written by Pope',[302] is one of the most deliberately deceitful documents in the history of English literature. Bearing in mind the true story, it makes amusing reading; but admirers of Pope as a moralist should surely feel more distress than amusement.

But was Pope perhaps being comic: having a glorious joke at the expense of the villainous Curll and of all the friends who believed him to be an upright man? If he was, then naturally he would have shared the joke with someone. Unfortunately (and inevitably) no letters to his 'agents' in this affair survive—almost certainly he wrote none—so we cannot tell if he laughed with them about it or not. It seems unlikely, however, from his protesting letters to his friends when the 'pirated' edition was issued that he did. It is important to remember, in view of the indignation he expressed about it, that this edition was Pope's own, printed and arranged by him: one can scarcely believe that it is so, after reading his protests. Here are two typical extracts from the letters he wrote in the weeks following publication.

> ... I have learn'd of an Excellent Machine of Curl's (or rather, his Director's) to ingraft a Lye upon, to make me seem more concern'd than I was in the affair of the Letters. . . .[303]

> I am greatly obliged to your Lordships Generosity in promising to contradict malicious Reports in my regard. I embrace 'em all with transport, while they procure me such Defenders as show I cannot be What Envy reports, for They are such as never could befriend an Ill man. I am not quite at the bottom of that Business, but very near it. . . .[304]

There is much more in this vein; and indeed, Curll did fight back, giving Pope several anxious moments.

The details of these transactions are so complex that not all of them have yet been fully understood—which is exactly what Pope intended. It is a tribute to his ingenuity that it cannot actually be proved that he was 'P.T.'.

Having at some risk (since Curll would now exert himself to get hold of and print undoctored correspondence of his which he really didn't want printed), but without having incurred a charge of 'conceit', got out an edition of his letters, Pope could now 'vindicate' himself by producing an 'authorized', 'unpirated' edition (was 'forced' to do so in 'self-defence'). The issuing of his letters became one of his chief preoccupations. As Sherburn says, his letters 'were the literary event of the year' (1735). He continues:

> Pope's manipulations of his texts were well concealed by the seeming fact that the whole affair was the fraudulent work of unscrupulous persons who had respect neither for authentic texts nor for truth. No objections arose to the factual inconsistencies in the letters. Caryll, some of whose letters

had been transferred to Addison, Wycherley, and others—transferred ostensibly by Curll or the thieves of the letters—died in the spring of 1736 and Pope's (or Curll's, as it seemed) chicanery as editor lay hidden for the most part until the Victorians got to work. Curll, however, soon knew that he was the dupe of Pope himself, and he pointed out that the early editions of 1735 used Pope's sheets of the 1729 edition of Wycherley's letters without reprinting. But Curll's disrepute was such that he was unheard, and no serious study of the editorial aspects of the printings was made in Pope's day. [305]

And so Pope's 'authorized' edition was duly published, in Folio and Quarto, in 1737. But still he had not finished.

6

For some years now he had been anxious—perhaps desperate is a more accurate word—to publish his correspondence with Swift. He was open about the reason for this: he wanted to leave a memorial to their friendship. On 17 August 1736 he wrote telling Swift, flatteringly, that he would make a great figure 'hereafter', and 'I . . . will preserve all the memorials I can that I was of your [and Bolingbroke's] intimacy'.[306] His subsequent behaviour towards Swift made it abundantly clear, however, that this memorial of friendship was much more important to him than the friendship itself.

On 3 September 1735 Swift wrote to Pope from Dublin in answer to a letter (suppressed by Pope, like all the other letters making such requests) which must have raised the question of their correspondence: Pope had asked, probably delicately, for the return of his letters. When Pope came to print this letter of Swift's, in 1740, he cut out certain passages, among which are

> . . . my memory decays so fast, that every day I less & less depend upon it. . . .'

and

> He [an acquaintance] is to dine with me when I get a healthy day. . . .'

Pope wanted not only to suppress his own requests for the letters, but also any notion that he then had grounds for regarding Swift as becoming senile and forgetful. Such omissions show that he had at first been waiting, calculatedly, for his 'friend' the Dean to become so insensible to events that he would neither notice nor care what Pope did about the letters.

However, in 1735 Pope had still to lay his hands on them. His obsessive desire to do so, and his subsequent suppression of the fact that this desire had ever existed—except in order to destroy them—is revealing. What filled him with chagrin more than anything else was Swift's reluctance to publish. Hence his later attribution of his own eagerness to Swift himself.

Swift usually avoided annoying Pope. When he did do so it was almost always in error or in spite of himself (as in the matter of the *Essay on Man*). But in the letter of 3 September 1735,[307] although he is evasive, he is explicit enough about what he thinks about any publication of the Swift–Pope correspondence. He must have struck fear into Pope's heart when he announced that though he had 'never destroyed' one of his letters, his executors had 'strict orders in my Will to burn every Letter left behind me'. He went on to say, with exquisite and not unfriendly irony towards Pope, that he did not believe that 'either of us ever leaned our Head upon our left hand to study what we should write next', and neatly evaded making a direct answer to Pope's request, except to say, perhaps tauntingly, that he was 'loth' that any letters from Pope and his few friends 'should dye before me'. In any case, he soon stated what kind of 'memorial' he would prefer (the fact that he seems therefore not to have been satisfied with the dedication of *The Dunciad* may indicate his true opinion of that work):

> I have the ambition, & it is very earnest as well as in hast to have one Epistle inscribed to me while I am alive. . . . I must once more repeat Cicero's desire to a friend, *Orna me.*

Swift's wishes in the matter did not, however, in the least interest Pope, who now embarked on a course that involved deliberately deceiving him. The late Sir Harold Williams, in the short introduction to his edition of Swift's correspondence, wrote:

> A complete history of the Swift–Pope letters in Dublin and London, and of Pope's double-dealing with Swift, under colour of unimpeachable friendship, would occupy much space and detailed study.[308]

If Pope made any serious mistake in the affair, it was to judge Swift's motives by his own, by assuming that the Dean was as passionately interested as himself in the publication of the letters. In all other respects his behaviour was impeccably treacherous and hypocritical. While he took advantage of a senility that he continually thought was more pronounced than it was (for which impression his willing but not very intelligent agent, Orrery, was largely to blame), he was at the same time terrified that Swift would die, and the letters then get into the hands of his real friends, who would not allow him to print them. Hence his eagerness to blame Mrs. Whiteway (who devotedly looked after Swift) for the publication of the letters when it did occur: he had hated, envied and feared her because of her intimacy with Swift. The interest of the whole transaction lies not in any serious injury done to Swift—who was not at all obsessed with the matter, and eventually reluctantly and wearily acquiesced in the publication (though not, as some admirers of Pope have suggested, in Pope's methods)—but in Pope's natural capacity for double-dealing, his pathological need to appear to be an unimpeachable friend and a man totally indifferent to fame.

In November 1736 Curll advertised a new volume: *Letters written by Mr. Pope and Lord Bolingbroke, to Dean Swift in the year 1723*, claiming that the original manuscripts had been 'transmitted from Ireland'; later he changed this story, asserting that they had been given to him by 'a Gentleman of Essex'. 'One guesses' (as Sherburn put it)

> that Pope himself fed these letters to Curll so that he might be able to urge Swift to let him have his letters before they were further 'misused'.

However, in a letter to Orrery of 4 March 1736/7, which he did not publish, Pope had to confess that although he had asked Swift three times to return his letters, he had received no answer:

> Yet the Dean, answering *Every other Point* of my Letter with the utmost Expressions of Kindness, is silent upon this, and the *third time* silent.

It is obvious that Swift was reluctant—and Pope realized it, for a little further on in the same letter he wrote:

> I told him, as soon as I found myself obligd to publish an Edition of Letters to my great sorrow, that I wish'd to make use of some of these, nor did I think Any Part of my Correspondencies would do me greater honour. . . . I find the Dean was not quite of the same opinion, or he would not, I think, have denyd this.[309]

He continued to work himself up into such a fine lather of hypocritical fervour and self-pity about Curll's wickedness that towards the end of the same letter he could cry out: 'The Dean, old as he is, may have the task to defend me'. He had obviously forgotten who had been responsible for the publication of his letters in the first place.

Orrery sent on this letter (which contained some fulsome flattery specially composed for the occasion) to Swift. He was also, at Pope's behest, putting personal pressure on him. By 18 March 1736/7 Orrery was able to tell Pope that he had 'carried the Point

We have been so long labouring at'.[310] Before he heard this Pope was writing to Swift in the usual terms. He had, he claimed,

> Fear of a very great and experienc'd evil, that of my letters being kept by the partiality of friends, and passing into the hands, and malice of enemies, who publish them with all their Imperfections on their head; so that I write not on the common terms of honest men.[311]

He was right enough in this last assertion. The text of this letter is derived from Pope's own 1740 printing of it, and no doubt, as Sherburn suggested, he suppressed a passage 'begging again for the return of the letters'.

By 28 March Pope had heard from Orrery, and immediately replied asking him to tell Swift that he was prepared to return to him transcripts or censored originals ('blotting out those passages so as not to be read by others').[312] He also firmly indicated that he proposed to publish; the Earl, thoroughly his creature, chose to play along with him, as Pope must have felt confident he would. This involved, of course, an assumption of Pope's innocence in the matter. . . . Whatever Orrery knew—and he must have known a great deal—he kept to himself.

Swift's reply of 31 May 1736/7 reiterated his desire for a poetic rather than an epistolary memorial; but, it is often claimed, he also tacitly accepted Pope's intention to publish by saying (of the sixty letters of Pope's which he said he had by now collected together), 'I found nothing in any of them to be left out'. His next remarks are half-sarcastic—sardonically critical—but too far above Pope's head to cause him offence:

> . . . you are the clearest of all men, by your Religion, and the whole Tenour of your life; while I am raging every moment against the Corruptions in both kingdoms. . . .[313]

Curious remarks, if they were not ironic, for an Anglican Dean to make to a Roman Catholic. Swift's statement that he had found nothing in the letters to be 'left out' does indeed imply knowledge of Pope's intention to publish; it does not imply approval. It is, I think, a laconic answer to Pope's hypocritical fussiness. The sycophantic Orrery wished to please Pope, and chose to do so by exaggerating the poorness of Swift's health and memory (thus fuelling Pope's desire to have the letters); but Swift had a shrewd idea of what was going on. Orrery had repeatedly to inform Pope that not only Mrs. Whiteway and Faulkner, but also Swift himself, attributed the instigation of the affair to him. Swift's failure to answer Pope about the letters on three separate occasions is surely eloquent of his own wishes. However, in June 1737 he did finally put the letters into Orrery's hands. It is often remarked that he had previously said that he held sixty letters; now he parted with only twenty-five. Critics are perhaps slow to recognize the possibility that Swift was quietly amused by Pope's obsessive concern about these letters, and fully realized that he was frantically concerned lest he should die or his memory fail; while Pope practised Roman Catholic saintliness, the Anglican Dean wrongly raged against mere injustice! The irony is obvious. When he told Pope that from his 1737 volume of letters (which Pope had sent him)

> there might be collected . . . the best System that ever was wrote for the Conduct of human life, at least to shame all reasonable men out of their Follies and Vices[314]

we should indeed be naive to take him at face value: he was flattering Pope, deliberately pleasing him—but castigating him with irony at the same time.

7

It was at this point that Pope descended into active treachery. Still he could not confess his real intentions. He had only wanted the letters to save them, he claimed, from 'misuse'. On several occasions he said he had burned them, implying that he had done so without taking copies.

What he really did was to have them printed and sent—in May 1740—to Swift, who was supposed to believe that the volume (which had no title-page) had originated in Ireland and was the result of the treachery of his Irish friends. The book was accompanied by an anonymous letter urging Swift to publish.

Pope had used an old friend of Swift's, Samuel Gerrard, as the pawn in this final stage of his game. On 17 May 1740 he wrote to Gerrard, who was then in Bath, but about to return to Ireland, that he had 'nothing' to send.[315] He created the opportunity for himself to tell this lie by asking Gerrard, in an earlier letter, to let him know when he intended to leave—as if he might have something to send. Just before Gerrard did leave, however, a packet was left at his lodgings by an agent of Pope (who was, naturally, not himself in Bath), addressed to Swift. It contained the clandestine volume and the anonymous letter (the handwriting of which Pope later indignantly asked to examine).

Now he began the next stage: to advertise his 'innocence'. Mrs. Whiteway and her son-in-law, he suggested, were responsible for the clandestine publication! Certainly it could not have been printed from the letters Swift had returned to him: he had burnt these. And so on. And then, in a letter to Robert Nugent of 14 August 1740, he wrote:

Sir,—I cannot enough acknowledge your obliging Endeavors as to what has given me so much apprehension, the affair of the Letters: all which, I am now convinced, has been a mere Feint to amuse us both. For last week I receivd an account from Faukener the Dublin Bookseller, "That the Dean himself has given him a Collection of Letters; of his own & mine & others, to be printed; & he civilly asks my Consent: assuring me the D. declares them genuine, & that Mr Swift, Mrs Whiteway's Son in law, will correct the press, out of his great respect to the Dean & myself." He says, they were collected by some unknown persons, & the Copy sent with a Letter, importing that "it was criminal to suppress such an amiable Picture of the Dean, & his private Character appearing in those letters, & that if he would not publish them in his life time, others would after his death."

I think I can make no Reflections upon this strange Incident, but what are truly melancholy, & humble the Pride of human Nature. That the greatest of Genius's tho Prudence may have been the Companion of Wit (which is very rare) for their whole Lives past, may have nothing left them at last but their Vanity. No Decay of Body is half so miserable! I shall write, & do, all I can upon this vexatious Incident, but I despair of stopping what is already no doubt in many hands. Can it be possible the Dean has forgot, how many years, & by how many instances, I have pressd him to secure me from this Very thing? or can it be imagind Mrs W. has remonstrated against it? The moment I had your Intimation that she would return them, I wrote to her, & embraced her offer with thanks: She answerd me, lately, that she would not send them to Mr Nugent, but by a certain Mr MacAulay: I presume now, that she would have sent but a few of no consequence; for the Bookseller tells me there are several of Lord Bolingbroke's &c (which must have been in the Dean's own custody; and one of which was printed twelve years ago.) I would therfore trouble you no more in this unlucky affair. I believe they had entertained a Jealousy of You, as the same persons did before of my Lord Orrery: They then prevented the Dean from complying to any purpose with my request: they then sent a few, just to save Appearances; & possibly to serve as a sort of plea to excuse them from being taxed of this Proceeding, which is now thrown upon the Dean himself.[316]

The hypocrisy and treachery here displayed—when it was Pope's own vanity, not Swift's (Swift was ready to acknowledge his), that had been the cause of the trouble—are unparalleled outside political and ecclesiastical history. One begins to see why Sherburn, despite his promise, never completed the biography of Pope he began with his account of the early career.

Actually, when the Dean received the small octavo volume from Gerrard, he must have realized that the letters would somehow or other be published whether he liked it or not. Consequently he made certain small revisions, inserted another letter of his, of 1721, and handed the volume over to his Dublin publisher, Faulkner (for whom he had a certain grudging regard), for immediate publication. He would be safest now if he took matters into his own hands. Pope, who had already hinted to Nugent (in the letter quoted above) that Swift had been responsible, now sententiously informed his semi-accomplice Orrery that 'We shall both join in One, which is to lament the Dean's condition, & not to irritate, but pity him'.[317] Faulkner sent off the first two sheets to Pope; but he continued his pretence of chagrin, consternation and pity for the poor vain Dean (whose verses on his own death, we remember, he had already criticised for their 'vanity'). He was in a delicate position: while he needed to protest at the appalling treachery of the people who had conspired to publish the letters, he did not wish to prevent publication. On 27 December 1740 he wrote two letters to Orrery, one private, one to be read to Faulkner and Mrs. Whiteway. To Orrery himself he wrote:

> I must pity the Dean; but it's necessary to give some answer to his Bookseller, & it shall be a Final one. But I think (all Circumstances considered) it will be better done in a Letter to your Lordship than immediately to him: I send it herewith, & wish not He only but Mrs Wh. saw, but not copyd it—For I fear the Very Shadow of my Pen may be made an ill use of. What I've said of Their *Preface* is but necessary, after such a Proposal as Mr Swift actually made; and it is in this principally I would accept your Lordships obliging Offer, to use your Name, with regard to the Advertisement inclosed, and desire you to Prescribe him the very Words of it, and you'l please to let him take them for your own drawing up. I should be sorry if he or they said any thing that might lead to a Suggestion so false, as Falkener told you Mrs W. had dropt (as if I had been privy to this Affair) For in that Case I should be oblig'd to clear myself, at the Expence of the Dean, or of some about him: The first I cannot bear to think of, in his present melancholy Condition; & the other I would rather avoid, as it would still, tho more remotely, reflect upon him. What they themselves represent of him, it is by no means fit I should divulge to the publick; and what they discover of themselves might be construed as

a hardship to expose, (tho it would be my own fullest
Vindication.) But there are Particulars that could decently
be told, of their Conduct, both to Him, & to Me, and such
as would be admitted as Proofs of the Fact I believe, in
any Court of justice. Some of them I will lay together, &
send you, in the Form of a Letter; & ask your leave (if by
their future Conduct, or the Prevalence of any Mistaken
opinion in others, I should be obliged to it) to make use of:
The remaining Circumstances I will keep for your private
View, whenever I have the pleasure again to enjoy your
Return.

Of the Book itself I think just as you do, that it was
not worth printing, but cannot now be supprest. It is plain,
that where ever it was printed, the Collected was made in
Ireland, pickd up by pieces from time to time, and begun
a good while ago. For there are some Letters of an early
date, which came later to their hands, & were inserted by
Interpolated half sheets and quarter Sheets, after the
printing of the first & second Sheets; these are marked with
Asterisks to direct the Binder where to place them? 2dly I
find (to the best of my Memory) some of the Letters your
Lordship brought over, which I burn'd just after, & therfore
could not be had on this side. 3dly There is one long Letter
from the Dean which he never sent; but was taken out of a
Pamphlet he once shewd me but never printed, writ to
justify himself after the Queens death, in Ireland. 4thly
Here are some of his Letters which I returned him; & All
those to Mr Gay, which the Duke of Queensbury & I found
among Mr G.'s papers & sent him over. But Care has been
taken[318] in this Collection to Suppress the Letter I then
wrote him, and others of mine as sollicited the Return or
the Exchange of the Letters between us; which appears
however by some of the Deans answers, which I have
chanc'd to keep & will shew you.

The other letter contained the usual pious expostulations, together
with an ugly threat to Faulkner:

If any other *Person's name*, or any *other* Circumstance [other
than the declaration that Swift alone was responsible for
publication] concerning the *Book* itself be mentioned, or
hinted at, I shall look upon it as meant to lead to an In-
sinuation (which I understand has been dropt amongst them
already) as if I secretly approved, or had been some way
privy to it.[319]

On 30 December 1740 he sent a lying 'narrative' of the whole affair in the form of a letter to Orrery[320] which, however, he never published. But he did make sure that his own London edition of the correspondence—*The Works of Mr. Alexander Pope in Prose, vol. ii*—appeared just before Faulkner's Dublin edition of 1741.

The truth is that Swift—well enough to make a few defensive revisions in the letters (who can blame him?), but then deteriorating in health (he was 73)—had at last been forced to accept just the position into which Pope pretended to have himself been forced. This played into Pope's hands, for he could now legitimately complain about Swift's having initiated publication, simultaneously revenging himself upon him for having impeded his plans. All this, we must remember, had originally been conceived as a memorial 'to the world' of Pope's great 'friendships' with Swift; the kind of friendship he practised is well illustrated by his behaviour over the matter of raising memorials to it.

8

Admirers of Pope as moralist, while hotly denying that quality of character has any relationship to poetic worth, will not easily forgive the preceding account, necessarily abbreviated though it is, of his machinations: if truth must be served, then such things are better left in the form of widely dispersed footnotes. My point is simply that Pope's own attitude to the publication of his letters cannot be said to have no bearing on the nature of the letters themselves. At the end of the 'narrative' about the Swift–Pope letters, which he did not have to publish because of greater public indifference to the matter of who had instigated the volume than he had—in his guilt—anticipated, Pope wrote that whatever 'Weakness' he should be charged with, it should not be with vanity, since

> it will evidently appear, of my Letters, that they were never writ to be printed. . . .[321]

We cannot, of course, be expected to believe this. The bulk of them were 'writ' to be printed, and to create a favourable impression of himself. But Pope's own compulsive insistence upon the contrary puts those of his critics who explain him (naively taking the hint from Yeats) as a conscious adopter of 'masks' in a different position: his hypocrisy may seem to them an unnecessary refinement; it is only too apparent that it seemed necessary to him. One may therefore say of him at least this: that he possessed a more intelligent conscience than his admirers.

We should not, however, picture Pope as sitting down to write his early letters with the printing-press itself immediately in mind. Even in later letters his first thought is often to convey a favourable impression of himself: he could revise for the press in his own time. But he could never sit down to write a letter to a friend in the relaxed if seldom absolutely unselfconscious manner of Swift or Gay. He had always to invent a picture of himself. He was less capable of writing as himself than any poet of his own or perhaps any other age. In the earlier letters (to Wycherley, Walsh, Cromwell and others) we can make allowances for his youth. But his posing did not fade as he grew older. It merely became more sophisticated. His picture of himself as a model of modesty and virtue—a picture in which he clearly believed: his injured innocence about 'imputations' was pathological in its intensity—began to obsess him, perhaps to the point of extreme neurosis. Only those who are driven by vanity need to disown it as frequently as he did.

But it is true that all this reveals only one aspect of Pope's personality, albeit an important one. His modern critics are right in insisting that the shocked Victorians concentrated on it too exclusively. For Pope as a man did gain the affection and admiration of the best writers of his time—and he deliberately, and with unerring taste, attached himself to them early on in his career. The predilections of a man such as Arbuthnot cannot be dismissed as insignificant—and Arbuthnot was very well disposed towards Pope. This could hardly have been merely because Pope was clever or ingratiating; socially he possessed not only charm but dignity and taste. Taste is not a necessary quality in poets, but it is an important and comforting one in its own right; Pope's possession of it, in exquisite proportion, together with his abundant courage in the face of physical misfortune, explains much of his appeal to such men as Swift, Arbuthnot and Bolingbroke. Swift may not (as I have already suggested) privately have approved of *The Dunciad*, but he saw—as we see—that it had a certain architectural dignity, a taste for style and superior decorum, that was lacking in all contemporary satire except perhaps Young's. Swift himself did feel, too, that bad writing was a moral matter (though he was rightly prepared to ignore it in those towards whom he was not ill disposed, or who were trying to do something he thought worthwhile). Ironically, it is probable that bad writing in itself affected Pope much less than it did Swift—but, with his instinct for the thing well done, he took advantage of the notion that it is equivalent to bad morals. He was equipped to do so, for even if his limited technique has been overrated (particularly by Professor Tillotson, who compares him to Mozart and Keats and wilfully exaggerates the musical beauties of his vowel-play), his writing is seldom, if ever, inept. Creatively, he existed wholly outside himself: his motive was to appeal to an *élite*, whatever that *élite* might represent. An interesting distinction between his and Swift's satire is that whereas Pope's is effective in proportion to the ridiculousness or ineptitude of his victims, Swift's is, on the whole, effective in proportion to the outrage to which his heart was aroused. For example, Pope's victim John Dennis really was absurd (in certain aspects); Swift's victim Partridge, the almanac-maker, was ridiculous, but he also embodied a type of wickedness. And yet, even if Pope's satire is of a lesser order—capitalizing ruthlessly on such misfortunes as he himself possessed or feared he might possess—we are certainly aware when reading it that we are in the presence of a mind superior, in taste, sensibility and a certain sort of sensitivity, to that of his victim. We may not be able to praise his poetry in the way we can praise that of others; but we can admire and learn from many of his aesthetic instincts.

We could take the view, as some Victorians did, that Pope's poetry is inferior or overrated because he was 'immoral'. But this is a dangerous over-simplification. We know, or should know, that poets are not more or less 'moral' than other men; that the notion of good morals is itself misleading in criticism; that everyone is inconsistent. We are surely entitled to adduce, however, that true poetry is not insincere or hypocritical; but our primary judgement on this point must be made from the poetry itself—not from the character of the man who wrote it. And in general we find that an incidental quality of true poetry is that, however obliquely, it is self-critical—that in one way or another it contains an assumption of failure: failure to understand, to trust, to have existed well. The psychological ambience in which Shakespeare's sonnets are written provides a usefully exact example of what I mean. Where poems tend towards personal self-justification there are usually good grounds for suspecting them as poems. Even if we regard them as 'structures' independent of their authors, such suspicions will still make themselves felt—unless we wilfully divorce ourselves from reality.

That self-justification is a strong element in Pope's verse is willingly admitted by his more honest admirers; but the admission can lead to some oddly tortuous judgements. Bonamy Dobrée, for example, writes:

> Pope [in *The Temple of Fame*], one may hazard, was beginning to see where his love of fame might lead him; this was perhaps his first exercise in self-castigation, which with him when brought to the precision of poetry tended to take the form of self-justification.[322]

The Temple of Fame is not an exercise in self-castigation but an early essay in hypocrisy: Pope is already at work resisting the 'imputation' of being hungry for fame by moralizing about it. He cannot admit that he has base motives. Through what poetically worthy kind of 'precision' self-castigation can lead to self-justification remains questionable; but the defensive tortuousness of the remark, by a critic devoted to Pope, illustrates the difficulties this poet

presents. These difficulties manifest themselves also in the dis-
agreements among critics as to which of his poems is his best. For
some, *The Rape of the Lock* is supreme; for others, *The Dunciad*;
for yet others, the moral essays and the *Epistle to Dr. Arbuthnot*.
Quite such marked disagreement is unusual among the sympathetic
critics of a single writer. There are similarly wide discrepancies
amongst critics as to what Pope's virtues as a poet actually were:
enthusiasm for his virtues as a moralist increases, it seems, as experi-
ential horizons narrow towards those of pure academicism. Certain
essays on him seem to have been conceived (if that is not an improper
word) in an area of experience insulated from all reality but that of
libraries, and dusty ones at that. It is in the most strictly academic
spheres that he is most lauded. In short, Pope is most loved by
those who confine themselves to the experiences offered by reading
books. Does what he says about poetry in his letters confirm his
critics' insistence upon the virtuousness of his own?

9

Pope's view of the nature of the poet was unequivocally based on
his idea of himself. This—it was a kind of photograph of himself
that he kept in his pocket and continually re-touched—was in turn
based upon what he felt would most appeal to the 'best' people: the
noblest, most talented, people. In this he differed from those poets
whose view of poetry is based on an observation of their poetic
faculties as they operate within themselves and in the world. Doubts
never assailed him. The Augustan age was not itself, in general, one
of doubt; but its few poets—Swift among them—did not share in
its complacency and optimism. Even Gay, a genuine although minor
poet, was essentially an insecure creature, and from his shy, decent
insecurity his poetry sprang.

From the beginning Pope was ready to state that what poetry
meant to him was whatever he thought his reader might want to
hear. To Caryll, in a letter of 20 September 1713 (which he later
printed as to Edward Blount, under a false date), he said

> I really make no other use of poetry [in the spurious 1735
> version this became 'my darling Poetry'] now than horses
> do of the bells that gingle about their ears (tho' now and
> then they toss their heads as if they were proud of 'em),
> only to travel on a little more merrily.[323]

To the same correspondent on 13 July 1714, in a more sanctimonious but similar mood, he wrote

> our schemes of government, our systems of philosophy, our
> our golden words [this is prettily altered to 'worlds' in

Pope's own 1735 version] of poetry, all are but so many shadow images and airy prospects. . . .[324]

To Bolingbroke, on 9 April 1724, in a letter not reprinted in his own lifetime, he wrote

We care not to Study, or Anatomize a Poem, but only to read it for our entertainment.[325]

This would have been Bolingbroke's own view, and Pope had seen shrewdly into him to discover it. Eleven years later, in 1735, he reprinted a letter to Henry Cromwell, dated 17 December 1710 (the only text derives from Pope himself), in which he said: 'no man can be a true Poet, who writes for diversion only'. This contradicts what he said to Bolingbroke. Had Pope sincerely changed his mind on the subject by 1724 he would, in 1735, have suppressed the passage in the Cromwell letter. But this man of masks had no face of his own: even on so important a subject as the nature of poetry he is prepared to change his mind in order to create a favourable impression.

In the same letter to Cromwell Pope attacks Richard Crashaw because he 'writ like a Gentleman' and not 'to establish a reputation, so that nothing regular or just can be expected from him'; but although Crashaw was 'uncorrect', he was not 'of the worst Versificators', considering the time in which he wrote.[326] However, it was left to Warton and then to more modern critics (secure in their view that all good poetry is 'allusive'), to point out Pope's own substantial debt to Crashaw. His various borrowings from him may be called allusions or thefts, as the critic desires; Pope himself did not care to draw attention to them, except in his own note on one line, which is quoted outright in *Eloisa to Abelard*.

However, at the age of eighteen he had asked Walsh, in a letter of 2 July 1706, 'how far the liberty of *Borrowing* may extend?' His tentative view was that

it seems not so much the Perfection of Sense, to say things that have *never* been said before, as to express those *best* that have been said *oftenest*; and that Writers in the case of borrowing from others, are like Trees which of themselves wou'd produce only one sort of Fruit, but by being grafted upon others, may yield variety.[327]

Perhaps Johnson's remarks in *The Rambler* on the subject of plagiarism are more relevant than he, himself an admirer of Pope, realized:

. . . an inferior genius may, without any imputation of servility, pursue the path of the ancients, provided he declines to tread in their footsteps.[328]

Walsh, although a dilettante with no claims to our attention other than his function as a link between Dryden and Pope, exercised a decisive influence upon the young man by advising him to be the first 'correct' poet. Quick to sense what would please his mentor, Pope had said earlier in the same letter:

> I have not attempted any thing of Pastoral Comedy, because I think the Taste of the Age will not relish a Poem of that sort.

Nothing but the 'taste of the age', and how his audience (admittedly the best of the age) would take his productions, mattered to Pope, at that time or later. So his correspondence with Walsh (for which we entirely depend on his own 1735 texts) is a stilted and self-conscious one, in which the older man instructs the younger in 'correctness' and in what fields may properly lie open to him. The most interesting letter to Walsh is one of 22 October 1706, in which he carefully expresses his thoughts on correct technique. But even here (as Sherburn implies in a footnote) he seems to have been trying to please his mentor rather than to state his own beliefs, for he says that '*Monosyllable-Lines* . . . may be beautiful to express Melancholy, Slowness or Labour' (a notion to which, as Sherburn points out, he 'repeatedly subscribed'), whereas he used them more than once to express speed, too. It is interesting that in this letter Pope also objects, as Swift so often did, to '*Alexandrine* Verses' and '*Triple Rhymes*', and criticizes Dryden for having been too free with them 'especially in his latter works'.[329]

Pope never deviated from the artificial spirit of the Walsh correspondence, although he became much subtler. According to what he said to Spence in March 1743, Walsh used to tell him

> that there was one way left of excelling, for though we had had several great poets, we never had any one great poet that was correct—and he desired me to make that my study and aim.[330]

That Pope thought this worth recalling in the year before his death is eloquent testimony to the importance of the part that Walsh played in forming him as a poet. But while Walsh, who wrote insipid, conventional verse, really did within his silly limits believe in 'correctness'—in the sense of conformity to certain rules—Pope himself was primarily interested in writing, not so much 'like a Gentleman' as 'to establish a reputation'. He was prepared to use all his considerable skills to achieve this.

Who can blame him? But we can blame the critics who equate his successful enterprise with poetry of the order of Donne or Wordsworth or Coleridge. For true poets—who recognize a distinction between poetry and prose—were the exception in this age; they existed in spite of themselves, as Swift did. Pope, driven to seek success and acclaim by his physical inferiorities, realized that no one since Dryden had really distinguished himself in poetry: there had been no 'major' poet on the scene. And he knew that this gap could be filled only by someone who was prepared to transfer the virtues of prose, lock stock and barrel, to poetry. This is what he did. As a man who was willing to be typical of his age, he thought of poetry, inasmuch as he thought of it at all, as a kind of prose; his letters prove it.

Early Augustan criticism of poetry is not subtle, particularly coherent or carefully worked out; what especially distinguishes it is its heartlessness, its emphasis on appearances. Pope's *Essay on Criticism* is, though rhymed, an ambitiously slavish imitation of this criticism. It is, specifically, a mosaic, reflecting various Augustan habits of thought and attitudes of mind; it is in no sense a whole. Just as Pope invented a 'moral' image of himself to present to the world, in judiciously edited letters, so—early on—he invented a decorous image of a 'proper' critical attitude: he was concerned with a strategy of approach, and not at all with his own genuine response to the poetry of the past, which he looked upon with the same degree of interest and affection that a producer of cider looks upon apples.

After all, to what extent did he take poetry, for its own sake, seriously? We cannot of course expect him to have approached the subject with the fervour of a Keats; but we might at least expect him to have accorded it the dignity that, say, Sidney, allowed it. . . . Yet, writing to Sir William Trumbull on 16 December 1715, when twenty-seven and already a well-known poet, he was quite prepared to say that his poetry made him feel like a 'trifler' in a national crisis.[331] And in a letter to Broome, of 4 December 1724, piously announcing that to propose to the public a translation of the *Iliad* (on which Broome and Fenton has substantially aided him) as 'purely my own' would be 'dishonest' (however, he dishonestly did it), Pope said that one 'goodnatured action or charitable intention' was more important than 'all the rhyming, jingling facilities in the world'.[332] Such facilities were his vehicle, but he was not going to appear to take them too seriously in an age that fundamentally disregarded them; the fact that he thus refers to poetry offers a clue to his true idea of its worth. Unlike Swift, *he* is never a mere 'rhymer': it is *poetry* that is nothing.

Never once does he betray the least seriousness about poetry in his letters; each discussion of it is subordinated to his desire to present a favourable picture of himself. We look in vain throughout the five volumes for a hint that it meant something to him that he needed to work out; this contrasts strongly with Swift's agonized reticence. It is curious that we find a similarly slighting attitude to poetry in some of Byron's letters—for Byron was Pope's sole admirer amongst the Romantic poets. The others came to condemn Pope; and modern criticism has answered their condemnation on critical but not on poetic grounds.

Although there is little about poetry in general in Pope's letters, there are plenty of remarks about his own poems: these, when they are not incidental, are concerned not so much with the poems themselves as with how they will be received.

Of course, objections to Pope's artificiality as a poet may be written off as 'romantically biased': he is praised by such critics as Professor Tillotson for almost the same reasons that I find him lacking. For Professor Tillotson the fact that Pope's poetry is, as he says, 'as much about morals as could be managed' is a positive virtue; so is Pope's avowed intention to please his readers by sensuousness, 'the *Truth* and the *Sentiment*'—in other words, to express the pseudo-classical and anti-psychological truisms of his age as entertainingly and creditably as possible. Thus, writing to Jacob Tonson (senior) on 7 June 1732 about his portrait of the Man of Ross in *The Use of Riches*, Pope said

> . . . I was determined the ground work at least should be *Truth* . . . but it is reasonable to pay it sometimes a little over measure . . . especially when it is done for example and encouragement to others. If any man shall ever happen to endeavour to emulate the Man of Ross, 'twill be no manner of harm if I make him think he was something more charitable and more beneficent than really he was, for so much more good it would put the imitator upon doing. And further I am satisfy'd in my conscience . . . that it was in his will, and in his heart, to have done every good a poet can imagine.[333]

It is, admittedly, a commonplace, and a problem common to all creative writers of whatever type, that truth, and reality, must inevitably be manipulated, falsified, by words. The criticism that the passage from the letter to Tonson is open to, however, is that it is remarkably superficial, even rather silly. Did Pope really contrive this portrait, however exquisitely he executed it, as an 'example and encouragement to others'? From the man who deceived and then accused his so-called friends of having his own faults this is just so much pious humbug. He did not mean it. We do not find this kind of moralistic intention in Swift (or even in Gay); by announcing it Pope was abdicating from the position of creative writer, pandering instead to the spirit of his age. He was more than merely a product of it: he deliberately set out to represent it at its hypocritical-didactic worst, quite regardless of what he too self-consciously and too often described as '*Truth*'. He based his verse not at all on any kind of process of inner revelation or exploration, but entirely on his astute recognitions of the sort of 'philosophy' that the best—the most powerful—people of his age would most appreciate.

However, as a heartless practitioner of the artificial—of taste, elegance and grace—he was truly distinguished. It is in this capacity that he can be seen to the best advantage in his letters, especially when he talks about architecture and gardening. If poetry consisted of nothing more than taste, then Pope would be as important as his admirers claim. Or if perfection of style within narrow limits, without regard to content, were enough to make a poet important, then Pope would be important for himself alone. But there is no warrant in his letters for the varying types of high seriousness of content that his critics attribute to him. The letters are frigid, formal, totally artificial; true emotion would emerge only when he was writing to agents engaged in performing business—sometimes treacherous business—for him, as Orrery was in Ireland; and then the emotion is not creditable to him.

As a man Pope did inspire affection; the letters provide little evidence of why. We must imagine his personal charm, his creditable desire to be locally nice, in order to understand this. For the letters contain more lies and half-truths than perhaps any others ever published (with the exception of official diplomatic and ecclesiastical correspondence); at the same time they lack the freshness and charm that we know Pope must have possessed as a man. The poetry, with its dazzling skill, good taste and humour, is much more entertaining. The insincere moralism of the letters was designed for its age, and does not now appeal; but the insincerity is a reflection of the essential feature of his poetry.

I

As I observed at the beginning of this book, the extent of informality in correspondence increased with the passage of time; but no previous letters had been as informal or relaxed as those of William Cowper (1731–1800).[334] Cowper is a more rewarding poet than the majority of modern critics recognize; but his scope is severely limited. He delights by his honesty, by his humanitarianism and by his gentleness, but he rarely startles or astonishes. It is for his letters that he is chiefly loved; if Walpole's surpass them in interest, they surpass Walpole's in sheer pleasantness and in mild wisdom.[334] Since the bulk of these letters should be read more perhaps for pleasure than for any other reason, I shall here give only very brief examples from Cowper's tolerant and judicious, if never deeply penetrating, criticism of Pope—for it provides one of the best reflections of the shifting taste of his age—and from his pronouncements on poetry itself.

Cowper's view of Pope is instructive and instinctive. Was he the first to see through Pope as a letter-writer? Writing to William Unwin on 8 June 1780 he speaks of a 'foolish vanity' that might have quite spoiled him and

> made me as disgusting a letter-writer as Pope, who seems to have thought that unless a sentence was well turned, and every period pointed with some conceit, it was not worth the carriage. Accordingly he is to me, except in a very few instances, the most disagreeable maker of epistles that ever I met with.[335]

And although he was unable to see the virtues of Chapman's Homer, his strictures on Pope's were even harsher: he criticized him for making Homer's persons 'speak in an inflated and strutting phraseology', and regarded his version as the least 'natural'.[336] He preferred Dryden as an original poet, because 'his beauties are such . . . as Pope with all his touching and retouching could never equal'. But he did not agree with those who 'could not allow' Pope 'to be a poet at all': 'He was certainly a mechanical maker of verses', but his industry was 'indefatigable'; and 'Never . . . were such talents and such drudgery united'.[337]

Cowper was well able, in describing his motives for writing, to sum up his own achievement as a poet. If this extract from a letter of 19 October 1781 to his cousin Mrs. Cowper seems a trifle sanctimonious, it should be remembered that throughout his life Cowper was tormented by intermittent bouts of religious mania, in which he imagined himself damned—and that he always praised the satire of his notoriously 'dissolute' schoolfellow, Charles Churchill (1731–64):

> It is a bold undertaking . . . to step forth into the world in that character of a bard, especially when it is considered that luxury, idleness, and vice, have debauched the public taste, and that nothing hardly is welcome but childish fiction, or what has at least a tendency to excite a laugh. I thought, however, that I had stumbled upon some subjects, that had never before been poetically treated, and upon some others, to which I imagined it would not be difficult to give an air of novelty by the manner of treating them. My sole drift is to be useful; a point which however I knew I should in vain aim at, unless I could be likewise entertaining. I have therefore fixed these two strings upon my bow, and by the help of both have done my best to send my arrow to the mark. My readers will hardly have begun to laugh, before they will be called upon to correct that levity, and peruse me with a more serious air. As to the effect, I leave it alone in His hands, who can alone produce it: neither prose nor verse can reform the manners of a dissolute age, much less can they inspire a sense of religious obligation, unless assisted and made efficacious by the power who superintends the truth he has vouchsafed to impart. . . .[338]

Finally, in a letter of 28 May 1790, here is his relaxed and wholly unaffected reply to his cousin Lady Hesketh's offer to use her influence to get him appointed Laureate on the death of Warton:

> My dearest Coz—I thank thee for the offer of thy best services on this occasion. But Heaven guard my brows from the wreath you mention, whatever wreath beside may herafter adorn them! It would be a leaden extinguisher, clapped on all the fire of my genius, and I should never more produce a line worth reading. To speak seriously, it would make me miserable, and therefore I am sure that thou, of all my friends, would least wish me to wear it.— Adieu, ever thine—in Homer-hurry.[339]

Like Gray before him, Cowper knew that he was too distinguished to fill a position that has been occupied only by nonentities or completely written-out poets since Dryden.

2

The most seriously, one might say startlingly, underrated of all eighteenth-century poets is George Crabbe (1755–1832). Known but not yet sufficiently appreciated as a social realist, Crabbe is also a psychologist of Chaucerian stature. The most readable of all non-lyrical poets, he is also often one of the most rewarding. The notion, frequently canvassed, that he was a novelist rather than a poet is reprehensible in that it ignores his capacity to rise to heights of intensity and complexity of expression of which prose is incapable. Not merely for a joke did Jane Austen say that he was the only man she could have married. . . .

At his least inspired Crabbe was, it must be admitted, a plodder; but at his best his humanity is informed by a shrewdness and an objectivity that save him both from ordinary political indignation and from sentimentality. The apparently drab, homespun surface of his verse frequently conceals depths of adventuresome subtlety. Then his voice is a very distinct one in English poetry.

His letters have not been collected, but some are included in his son's excellent life of him, and more are in Messrs. Broadley and Jerrold's *The Romance of an Elderly Poet*, an account of Crabbe's mainly postal flirtations with various young women after his wife's death in 1813.[340]

Crabbe's youth was eventful. He was born at Aldeburgh in Suffolk in 1755, and was writing poetry by the age of thirteen. In 1768 he became apprenticed to a surgeon-apothecary. Until 1780, when he went to London with £3 in his pocket to seek a living as a writer, he practised as a surgeon.[341] Edmund Burke became his patron, and he gained some success with *The Library* (1781). *The Village* (1783) was praised by Johnson. He abandoned medicine for the priesthood, married, and was Vicar of Muston in Leicestershire from 1789 until 1814. He published no poetry between *The Newspaper* (1785), and *Poems* (1807), but he did write (1801–2) three prose novels, which he destroyed. In 1796 his wife, Sarah, began to suffer from manic-depression, or a condition closely allied to it; this increased in severity until her death in 1813. The effect of her illness upon Crabbe has not been fully appreciated: his was no 'quiet life'. From about 1790 he had been taking opium. He continued to use it, in a progressively increasing dose, for the rest of his life: he was as much of a 'drug-addict' as Coleridge, though of a quieter sort. In 1814, after a serious illness, he moved to the parish of Trowbridge in Wiltshire, where he remained until he died in 1831. Most of his best work, written under the stress of his wife's illness, is to be found in *The Borough* (1810) and *Tales* (1812).

When Crabbe went to London in 1780 he 'experienced nothing', his son wrote, 'but disappointments and repulses: absolute want stared him in the face: a goal seemed the only immediate refuge for his head'. But in 1781 he made 'one effort more': he wrote to Edmund Burke. His letter, written out of the blue, is surely an extraordinary one: he was in absolute despair, and yet his modesty forbade him to make any boast about his poetic talent beyond the enclosure of 'verses'.

> I am sensible that I need even your talents to apologise for the freedom I now take; but I have a plea which, however, simply urged, will, with a mind like yours, Sir, procure me pardon: I am one of those outcasts on the world, who are without a friend, without employment, and without bread.
>
> 'Pardon me a short preface. I had a partial father, who gave me a better education than his broken fortune would have allowed; and a better than was necessary, as he could give me that only. I was designed for the profession of physic; but not having wherewithal to complete the requisite studies, the design but served to convince me of a parent's affection, and the error it had occasioned. In April last, I came to London, with three pounds, and flattered myself this would be sufficient to supply me with the common necessaries of life, till my abilities should procure me more; of these I had the highest opinion, and a poetical vanity contributed to my delusion. I knew little of the world, and had read books only: I wrote, and fancied perfection in my compositions; when I wanted bread they promised me affluence, and soothed me with dreams of reputation, whilst my appearance subjected me to contempt.
>
> 'Time, reflection, and want, have shown me my mistake. I see my trifles in that which I think the true light; and, whilst I deem them such, have yet the opinion that holds them superior to the common run of poetical publications.
>
> 'I had some knowledge of the late Mr. Nassau, the brother of Lord Rochford; in consequence of which, I asked his Lordship's permission to inscribe my little work to him. Knowing it to be free from all political allusions and personal abuse, it was no very material point to me to whom it was dedicated. His Lordship thought it none to him, and obligingly consented to my request.
>
> 'I was told that a subscription would be the more

profitable method for me, and therefore endeavoured to circulate copies of the enclosed Proposals.

'I am afraid, Sir, I disgust you with this very dull narration, but believe me punished in the misery that occasions it. You will conclude, that, during this time, I must have been at more expense than I could afford; indeed the most parsimonious could not have avoided it. The printer deceived me, and my little business has had every delay. The people with whom I live perceive my situation, and find me to be indigent and without friends. About ten days since, I was compelled to give a note for seven pounds, to avoid an arrest for about double that sum which I owe. I wrote to every friend I had, but my friends are poor likewise; the time for payment approached, and I ventured to represent my case to Lord Rochford. I begged to be credited for this sum till I received it of my subscribers, which I believe will be within one month: but to this letter I had no reply, and I have probably offended by my importunity. Having used every honest means in vain, I yesterday confessed my inability, and obtained, with much entreaty, and as the greatest favour, a week's forbearance, when I am positively told, that I must pay the money, or prepare for a prison.

'You will guess the purpose of so long an introduction. I appeal to you, Sir, as a good, and, let me add, a great men. I have no other pretensions to your favour than that I am an unhappy one. It is not easy to support the thoughts of confinement; and I am coward enough to dread such an end to my suspense.

'Can you, Sir, in any degree, aid me with propriety?—Will you ask any demonstrations of my veracity? I have imposed upon myself, but I have been guilty of no other imposition. Let me, if possible, interest your compassion. I know those of rank and fortune are teased with frequent petitions, and are compelled to refuse the requests even of those whom they know to be in distress: it is, therefore, with a distant hope I ventured to solicit such favour; but you will forgive me, Sir, if you do not think proper to relieve. It is impossible that sentiments like yours can proceed from any but a humane and generous heart.

'I will call upon you, Sir, to-morrow, and if I have not the happiness to obtain credit with you, I must submit to my fate. My existence is a pain to myself, and every one near and dear to me are distressed in my distresses. My connections, once the source of happiness, now embitter the reverse of my fortune, and I have only to hope a speedy end to a life so unpromisingly begun: in which (though it ought not to be boasted of) I can reap some consolation from looking to the end of it. I am, Sir, with the greatest respect, your obedient and most humble servant.[342]

Fortunately for Crabbe, Burke responded; a short time after he sent him another, much more confident and self-revealing letter; this is known as the 'Bunbury Letter', because Sir Henry Bunbury first printed it in 1838. It gives, as Howard Mills remarks in the introduction to his selection from the poet's works, a 'more trenchant and bitter account' of Crabbe's early life than the first letter to Burke, which was the only one his son knew of. I give it here with only one short omission:

It is my wish that this letter may reach you at a time when you are disengaged, but if otherwise, I intreat that it may not be immediately read, as it is sufficient to try your patience without the additional circumstance of asking your attention at an improper time. I think it right to lay before you, Sir, a farther account of myself, and lest my present or future conduct should appear in a light that they ought not, I venture to inform you more particularly of the past: nor is this my sole motive; it is painful to me to be conscious that I have given you only partial information, though the part I gave was strictly true. Nor can I, with propriety, beg your advice in my present difficult situation, without relating the steps which led to it; on the other hand, I consider how much I have troubled you, and that you probably know as much of me as you desire; I am apprehensive too that I shall not rise in your opinion by what I write, and it is my constant fear that, kind and benevolent as you are, these repeated attacks upon your patience may compel you to withdraw your assistance and leave me to lament the importunity of my applications. These reasons however do not balance their opposite ones; they oblige me to fear, but not to relinquish my purpose, and this long account is the results of a painful deliberation on the propriety of writing it. . . .

I do not mean Sir to trifle with you, but it is by no means a small matter with me how I stand in your opinion, and now when I speak of my mingled follies and misfortunes, I wish to say all I can consistently with truth in vindication of the former. I rebelled in my servitude, for it became grievous. My Father was informed of his Son's idleness and disobedience; he came, and was severe in his correction of them: I knew myself then injur'd and became obstinate, and a second visit of my Father's put an end to my slavery; he took me home with him, and with me two thirds of the money he had advanced. He then placed me on very easy terms with a man of large business in a more reputable line; but I was never considered as a regular apprentice, and was principally employed in putting up prescriptions and compounding medicines. I was, notwithstanding, well treated in every respect but the principal one, for no pains were taken to give me an idea of the profession I was to live by. I read novels and poetry, and began to contribute to Magazines and Diaries. My Master occasionally prophesy'd my ruin, and my Father advised me to quit such follies; but the former would sometimes laugh at the things he condemned, and my Father was a rhymer himself. I therefore paid little attention to these instructions, but was happy to find my signature in the Lady's Magazine was known to all the Ladies round the place I liv'd in. After four years I left my master according to our agreement: he is a man much esteemed in his profession and I believe he knows something of it, but I had not the good fortune to find it communicated to me. My Father at this time was much distressed and could not send me to London for the usual improvements. I meant to serve in a shop, but an unlucky opportunity offered itself at Aldbro', the Apothecary there was become infamous by his bad conduct, and his enemies invited me to fix there immediately. My father urged it, and my pride assented: I was credited for the shatter'd furniture of an Apothecary's shop, and the drugs that stocked it. I began to assume my late master's manner, and having some conscientious scruples I began to study also: I read much, collected extracts, and translated Latin books of Physic with a view of double improvement: I studied the Materia Medica and made some progress in Botany. I dissected dogs and fancied myself an anatomist, quitting entirely poetry, novels and books of entertainment. After one year, I left my little business to the care of a neighbouring surgeon, and came to London, where I attended the lectures of Messrs. Orme and Lowder on Midwifery, and occasionally stole round the hospitals to observe those remarkable cases, which might indeed, but which probably never would, occur to me again. On my return I found my substitute had contracted a close intimacy with my rival. He cheated me and lost my business. The second woman who committed herself to my care, died before the month after her delivery was expired; and the more I became qualified for my profession, the less occasion I found for these qualifications. My business was the most trifling and lay amongst the poor. I had a sister who starved with me:

and on her account it now pains me to say we often wanted bread; we were unwilling to add to my Father's distress by letting him see ours, and we fasted with much fortitude. Every one knew me to be poor; I was dunned for the most trifling sums, and compelled to pay the rent of my hut weekly, for my landlord was Justice of the Corporation and a man of authority. My druggist, a good-natured Quaker, gave me some friendly hints. My friends and advisers who had been zealous for my fixing in this place, entirely deserted me for this reason only, that I had not been successful by following their advice. After three years spent in the misery of successless struggle, I found it necessary for me to depart, and I came to London.

That part of my conduct which I am about to relate, I am afraid will be greatly disapproved, & I shall be happy to find, Sir, you think it not more than foolish and inconsiderate. I knew the wages of a journeyman apothecary were trifling, & that nothing could be saved from them towards discharging the obligations I lay under. It became me to look for something more; I was visionary, and looked to him from whom no help cometh.

My father, some years since, attended at the House of Commons on some election business, & he was also with the minister; I recollected to have heard him speak with some pleasure of Lord North's condescension and affability; and renouncing physic, I resolved to apply for employment in any department that I should be thought qualified for; I drew up a long and labour'd account of my motives for this application, and to prove my ignorance in the proper method of managing such applications, I accompanied my petition with a volume of verses, which beg'd leave to submit to his Lordship's perusal I was admitted to Lord North on my second calling and treated with more attention than I now should expect, though with none of that affability I had been led to hope for; what I still wonder at, is the civil part of his Lordship's behavior; my request was idle and unreasonable, he might, with the greatest propriety have dismiss'd me instantly, but whether through want of thought, or with an inclination to punish me, he gave me hope, was sorry for my circumstances, enquired who could recommend me, and was satisfied with those I named: he ordered me to apply again, and fixed a day. I am even now astonished at this unnecessary and cruel civility, it has greatly added to the inconveniences I now labour under, besides the anxiety of a long attendance growing daily more hopeless; for not only on the day fixed, but on all other days, I went regularly to Downing Street, but from my first to my last interview with his Lordship were three months. I had only a variation in the mode of answer as the porter was more or less inclined to be civil, the purport of all was the same: I wrote and entreated his Lordship to accept or refuse me: I related my extreme poverty and my want of employment, but without effect. I again beg'd him to give some message to his servant, by which I might be certain that I had nothing further to hope for: this also was ineffectual. At last I had courage to offer so small a sum as half a crown, and the difficulty vanished: His Lordshop's porter was now civil, and His Lordship surly; he dismiss'd me instantly and with some severity.

I had now recourse to my rhymes, and sent a hasty production to Mr. Dodsley, who returned it, observing that he could give no consideration for it, not because it wanted merit, but the town wanted attention; he was very obliging in his reply, for I am now convinced it does want merit. Mr. Becket returned me a similar answer to an application of the same kind. I yet indulged a boyish opinion of my productions, and determined to publish; fortunately however I had hitherto concealed my name, and I continued to do so. Nichols, who had printed some remains of Dryden, and other poets, was for this reason fixed upon to usher my piece on the world; he printed 250 copies of 'An Epistle to the Authors of The Monthly Review' which I believe are now in the warehouse of Mr. Payne the bookseller, as I never heard of any sale they had. My patrons spoke of my poem rather favourably; but Messrs the Critical Reviewers trim'd me handsomely, and though I imputed this in a great measure to envy, I was very glad that I had not exposed my name on the occasion.

I now began to think more humbly of my talents: disappointment diminished my pride and increased my prudence. I solicited a subscription. Mr. Nassau, the late Member for Malden, was well known to me, and this led me to apply to his brother for a permission to prefix his name to a dedication. Lord Rochford assented, but bade me hope more from the merit of my productions than that permission. I conveyed my proposals to my friends and obtained about 150 names, chiefly at Beccles, which are since increased, and are something more than 200. I have acquainted these people with the alteration in my intention, but I am desired to send my poem in whatever manner it comes out, and this is that certainty I spoke of to Mr. Dodsley. During a long interval betwixt my disappointment at Downing Street and that necessity which compelled me to write to you, Sir, it would be painful to me, and tedious to you, to relate the distress I felt and the progress of my despair; I knew that my subscribers would not more than pay for the printing their volumes. I was contracting new debts, and unable to satisfy old demands. I lived in terror, was imposed upon, & submitted to insults and at length so threatened, that I was willing to make use of any expedient that would not involve me in guilt as well as vexation. I could accuse myself but of folly and imprudence and these lessen'd by inexperience, and I thought that if my circumstances were known, there would be found some to relieve me. I looked as well as I could into every character that offered itself to my view, & resolved to apply where I found the most shining abilities, for I had learned to distrust the humanity of weak people in all stations. You, Sir, are well acquainted with the result of my deliberation, and I have in one instance at least reason to applaud my own judgment.

It will perhaps be asked how I could live near twelve months a stranger in London and coming without money; it is not to be supposed I was immediately credited—it is not—my support arose from another source. In the very early part of my life I contracted some acquaintance, which afterwards became a serious connexion, with the niece of a Suffolk gentleman of large fortune. Her mother lives with her three daughters at Beccles; her income is but the interest of £1,500, which at her decease is to be divided betwixt her children. The brother makes her annual income about £100: he is a rigid œconomist, and though I have the pleasure of his approbation, I have not the good fortune to obtain more, nor from a prudent man could I perhaps expect so much. But from the family at Beccles, I have every mark of their attention, and every proof of their disinterested regard. They have from time to time supplied me with such sums as they could possibly spare, and that they have not done more arose from my concealing the severity of my situation, for I would not involve in my errors or misfortunes a very generous and very happy family by which I am received with unaffected sincerity, and where I am treated as a son by a mother who can have no prudential reason to rejoice that her daughter has formed such a connexion. It is this family I lately visited, & by which I am pressed to return, for they know the necessity there is for me to live with the utmost frugality, & hopeless of my succeeding in town they invite me to partake of their little fortune, and as I cannot mend my prospects, to avoid making them worse. This, Sir, is my situation: I have added, I have suppressed nothing; I am totally at a loss how to act, & what to undertake. I cannot think of living with my friends without a view of some employment or design, & I can form none, & I cannot continue in town without such, where the expense is (to me) much greater; my present undertaking can be of no material service I find, and the unlucky circumstance of printing so much of my miscellany renders it less so. I finish this tedious account by intreating your consideration on my present state and my future prospects. I cease to flatter myself, Sir; I only wish to live and to be as little a burden as possible to my friends, but my indiscretion and my ill-fortune have so far carried me away that it requires a better judgment than my own to determine what is right for me to do; I do not wish, Sir, to obtrude my affairs too much upon you, but you have assisted and advised me, and even exclusive of the advantage I reap from your directions, I judged it right to give you this account: for all that is past I most sincerely thank you; you have comforted, you have relieved, you have honoured me; what is to come is in a situation like mine particularly mysterious; but whatever comes I will be grateful, & with a remembrance of the benefits I have received I will ever cherish the highest respect for the name and virtues of my generous benefactor.

I will wait upon you, Sir, as soon as possible with a fresh copy of my poem, correct as I have power to make it. In this I shall yet presume to ask your opinion; on any other subject it will now become me to be silent; thus far I feel a satisfaction from what I have written, that it is entirely unreserved, and that it goes to one who knows how to allow for indiscretion & to pity misfortune.[343]

It is clear from this that 'mildness', in his son's words, was 'as natural' to Crabbe 'as fortitude'. Although a Church of England parson, he was more tolerant towards dissenters than most of his brethren: those who deemed differences in religion 'of much importance' he described in a letter as 'unwise and uncharitable'.[344]

Crabbe distilled almost all his quiet subtlety, eclectic curiosity and psychological wisdom into his poetry. The letters his son prints are pleasant, but they lack the concealed edge of the poems. When he returned to London society after his wife's death he appeared old-fashioned; but it did not worry him. Parodied by the Smiths in *Rejected Addresses*, and indignantly sympathized with by a friend, he replied: 'They are extraordinary men; but it is easier to imitate style, than to furnish matter'.[345] When attacked by Hazlitt in *The*

Spirit of the Age ('Mr Crabbe, it must be confessed, is a repulsive writer') he remarked to his friend Mary Leadbeater:

> I believe I felt something indignant: but my engraved seal dropped out of the socket and was lost, and I perceived this vexed me much more than the 'spirit' of Mr. Hazlitt.[346]

One suspects that Crabbe was consciously more humorously shrewd and ironic than he ever admitted, as when he used to protest to Mary Leadbeater that he was 'a great fat Rector' who visited 'that horrible London':

> One thing only is true,—I wish I had the qualification; but I am of the world, Mary. . . . I am sorry for your account of the fever among your poor. Would I could suggest any thing! I shall dine with one of our representatives to-day; but such subjects pass off: all say, 'Poor people, I am sorry,' and there it ends. . . . I return all your good wishes, think of you, and with much regard, more than, indeed, belong to *a man of the world!*[347]

Although Crabbe was not really one of the romantic poets, he was certainly romantic by disposition, especially after the death of his wife. He genuinely preferred the company of women to men, and did not trouble to hide this from anyone. 'Damme, sir!' an old purple-faced squire is supposed to have said, 'The very first time Crabbe dined at my house he made love to my sister!' 'I have', he wrote when nearly sixty-five, 'though at considerable distances, six female friends, unknown to each other, but all dear, very dear to me.'[348]

Soon after his move to Trowbridge—exactly a year after the death of his wife—Crabbe had become engaged to a twenty-six-year-old girl, Miss Charlotte Ridout, whom he met at Sidmouth. The engagement was eventually broken off, not by Miss Ridout but by Crabbe, as a result of his own qualms: he declared to the Dean of Lincoln, on 11 February 1815 that 'I have never had such Call for Self-Denial and even yet almost doubt my victory'.[349] As Broadley and Jerrold put it, he exercised a fascinating influence over 'sentimental young ladies'; many celebrated elderly men do; but Crabbe held his impulses in check: an unknown 'Fanny' who had apparently offered herself to him, and who had told him that she honoured and revered 'age', was told:

> Your note affects me. . . . You kindly overlook my age but I cannot. . . . I certainly do not think that age makes itself respectable by ill nature and I believe neither man nor woman is the worse for being agreeable but still my dear Fanny there must be many defects in the aged which no lightness of spirits can make up. Of this we will not dispute. . . .[350]

This was no doubt why he withdrew, lonely as he was, from the marriage with Charlotte Ridout (who had gone so far as to refuse a suitor on his account).

There would be little object in quoting from the many flirtatious letters Crabbe wrote during the years following his wife's death. He was relieving his loneliness and desire by playing: for his sexual impulse, which gave his curiosity much of its energy, was still active: to Miss Elizabeth Charter, another of his girl-friends, he wrote on 26 December 1815:

> What are *my* resources dear Miss Charter in such deprivations? Making Verses is an Amusement but it is temporary and soon tires: then I am weak and foolish and perhaps vain and want to be loved and that can hardly be, and more Respect or cool Esteem is not worth much.[351]

All his frustrations were expressed in an uncharacteristic poem, *The World of Dreams*, written probably between 1815 and 1817, of which the sixth stanza reads:

> That female fiend!—Why is she there?
>   Alas! I know her.—Oh, begone!
> Why is that tainted bosom bare,
>   Why fixed on me that eye of stone?
> Why have they left us thus alone?
>   I saw the deed—why then appear?
> Thou are not form'd of blood and bone!
>   Come not, dread being, come not near!

This was not Crabbe's natural idiom; and yet here he was trying to evoke what Coleridge had evoked twenty years earlier in *The Ancient Mariner*: the 'nightmare life-in-death'. He meant what he said when he sentimentally told Miss Charter on 26 March 1819 that he was

> indeed happy to know certain Beings of your Sex, who make me half ashamed of my own but very proud of their Regard and I am grateful enough to know and feel that you my dear Miss Charter would have Administered to the Comforts of a man who however negligent he may sometimes appear, still knows the Value of your Friendship and is highly gratified by feeling that he possesses it.[352]

But he also meant what he said when he told her, in the late October of the same year:

> And do dear Lady recollect that at Sixty five a Man may— for that I am very sure of—feel a lively Interest for his Friends and dearly love to hear from them, when he finds a Repugnance in himself to sit down and describe his own Sensations.[353]

Crabbe was not altogether successful when he tried to describe his 'Sensations' in lyrical poetry, as in *The World of Dreams*; but all the 'Repugnance' can be found in his tales. He did not waste his experience, and his best work is remarkably uncrippled by moral, social or pietistic inhibitions.

3

Although he was admired by Wordsworth, Coleridge, Lamb and other notables, William Blake (1757–1827) suffered general ridicule in his lifetime. All his work—lyrics, 'prophecies', long poems, jottings in notebooks, drawings and engravings and letters—needs, uniquely, to be considered together: the definitive edition, *Complete Writings*, rightly treats every scrap that he ever wrote, even marginal annotations, as a part of the canon.[354] Blake's record of any act or thought is regarded as creative. All he did was a part of a single continuous act of self-expression.

This is logical: no other poet or artist (it is important to remember that Blake was both) has been as single-minded. Blake seldom compromised. That he was able to survive at all in a world hostile to him, and to his view of existence, was due to his artistic abilities. He could have been rich and successful; he chose instead to follow the dictates of his own inspiration.

The ninety-two of his letters known today provide no exception to this. They show a man of extraordinary integrity driven in upon himself. When comparatively early in Blake's life the Rev. Dr. John Trusler, author of *How to be Rich and Respectable*, tried to interfere with some of his designs he told him

> I really am sorry that you are fall'n out with the Spiritual World, especially if I should have to answer for it. . . . You say that I want somebody to Elucidate my Ideas. . . . That which can be made Explicit to the Idiot is not worth my care.[355]

People's only defence against this kind of thing—not untrue, but deliberately tactless, offensive, and not as innocent of personal aggression as some have tried to make out—was to say that Blake was 'mad'. (It was actually written of him that only his 'personal inoffensiveness' kept him from being locked away.) But, uncompromising though he was, it would be wrong to suggest that Blake did not fight against his isolation.

His friend John Flaxman, the artist, introduced him to the popular poet and amateur painter William Hayley, a good-hearted but severely limited, vain, foolish man whose verse Byron correctly described as 'For ever feeble and for ever tame'. Hayley was incapable of understanding anything better than the merely fashionable and ephemeral; unintelligent, he owed his success to his instinct for what would please the public; he had nothing whatever of interest to say. Blake might easily have seen this; but Hayley invited him to live near him at Felpham in order to work on the plates for his projected life of Cowper, who had just died. Blake rented a cottage in August, and in September he and his wife set out for it. Just before they did so, Blake wrote a letter of gratitude to Flaxman, showing that the new arrangement had filled him with hope and joy.

My Dearest Friend,

It is to you I owe All my present Happiness. It is to you I owe perhaps the Principal Happiness of my life. I have presum'd on your friendship in staying so long away & not calling to know of your welfare, but hope now every thing is nearly completed for our removal to Felpham, that I shall see you on Sunday, as we have appointed Sunday afternoon to call on Mrs Flaxman at Hampstead. I send you a few lines, which I hope you will Excuse. And As the time is arriv'd when Men shall again converse in Heaven & walk with Angels, I know you will be pleased with the Intention, & hope you will forgive the Poetry.

To My Dearest Friend, John Flaxman, these lines:
I bless thee, O Father of Heaven & Earth, that ever I saw Flaxman's face.
Angels stand round my Spirit in Heaven, the blessed of Heaven are my friends upon Earth.
When Flaxman was taken to Italy, Fuseli was given to me for a season,
And now Flaxman hath given me Hayley his friend to be mine, such my lot upon Earth.
Now my lot in the Heavens is this, Milton lov'd me in childhood & shew'd me his face.
Ezra came with Isaiah the Prophet, but Shakespeare in riper years gave me his hand;
Paracelsus & Behmen appear'd to me, terrors appear'd in the Heavens above
And in Hell beneath, & a mighty & awful change threatened the Earth.
The American War began. All its dark horrors passed before my face
Across the Atlantic to France. Then the French Revolution commenc'd in thick clouds,
And My Angels have told me that seeing such visions I could not subsist on the Earth,

But by my conjunction with Flaxman, who knows to forgive
Nervous Fear.[356]

There must have been an element of self-deception in Blake's
delight; yet we can hardly criticize his hopefulness. After years of
isolation, he was prepared to believe that Hayley—for all the shortcomings and shallownesses which he must surely have discerned in
him when he visited him at Felpham in July—was 'Leader of My
Angels', which was how he addressed him on 16 September 1800.
In a postscript he added: 'My fingers Emit sparks of fire with
Expectation of my future labours'.[357] On 21 and 23 September 1800
he wrote to Flaxman and his good patron Thomas Butts, respectively, to inform them of his arrival. In both letters he says that
Hayley received him 'with his usual brotherly affection'. 'I am more
famed in Heaven', he tells Flaxman, 'for my works than I could
well concieve'.[358] And to Butts he announces: 'Meat is cheaper than
in London, but the sweet air & the voices of winds, trees & birds, &
the odours of the happy ground, makes it a dwelling for immortals'.[359]
This is a typical Blakeian sentence: he saw nothing anomalous in
associating the price of meat with the notion of immortality: all he
did was part of one effort.

His excitement and state of happy hopefulness over the
Felpham arrangement, followed by bitter disillusionment, stirred
Blake into writing some of his most powerful poetry, including
'My Spectre around me night & day', *The Mental Traveller*,
Auguries of Innocence and the verse-letter to Butts of 2 October
1800. This, one of Blake's most beautiful and serene poems, belongs
to the happy period of anticipation:

> Recieve from me a return of verses, such as Felpham
> produces by me, tho' not such as she produces by her
> Eldest Son;[360] however, such as they are, I cannot resist
> the temptation to send them to you.
> To my Friend Butts I write
> My first Vision of Light,
> On the yellow sands sitting.
> The Sun was Emitting
> His Glorious beams
> From Heaven's high Streams.
> Over Sea, over Land
> My Eyes did Expand
> Into regions of air
> Away from all Care,
> Into regions of fire
> Remote from Desire;
> The Light of the Morning
> Heaven's Mountains adorning:

In particles bright
The jewels of Light
Distinct shone & clear.
Amaz'd & in fear
I each particle gazed,
Astonish'd, Amazed;
For each was a Man
Human-form'd. Swift I ran,
For they beckon'd to me
Remote by the Sea,
Saying: Each grain of Sand,
Every Stone on the Land,
Each rock & each hill,
Each fountain & rill,
Each herb & each tree,
Mountain, hill, earth & sea,
Cloud, Meteor & Star,
Are Men Seen Afar.
I stood in the Streams
Of Heaven's bright beams,
And Saw Felpham sweet
Beneath my bright feet
In soft Female charms;
And in her fair arms
My Shadow I knew
And my wife's shadow too,
And My Sister & Friend.
We like Infants descend
In our Shadows on Earth,
Like a weak mortal birth.
My Eyes more & more
Like a Sea without shore
Continue Expanding,
The Heavens commanding,
Till the Jewels of Light,
Heavenly Men beaming bright,
Appear'd as One Man
Who Complacent began
My limbs to infold
In his beams of bright gold;
Like dross purg'd away
All my mire & my clay.
Soft consum'd in delight
In his bosom Sun bright
I remain'd. Soft he smil'd,
And I heard his voice Mild

Saying: This is My Fold,
O thou Ram horn'd with gold,
Who awakest from Sleep
On the Sides of the Deep.
On the Mountains around
The roarings resound
Of the lion & wolf,
The loud Sea & deep gulf.
These are guards of My Fold,
O thou Ram horn'd with gold!
And the voice faded mild.
I remain'd as a Child;
All I ever had known
Before my bright Shone.
I saw you & your wife
By the fountains of Life.
Such the Vision to me
Appear'd on the Sea.[361]

In this mood Blake is still prepared to deceive himself about the lack of quality of the verse of Felpham's 'Eldest Son'. On 10 May 1801, he tells Butts that 'Hayley acts like a Prince';[362] on 11 September 1801, to the same correspondent, he speaks of Hayley's 'matchless industry', and describes the *Life of Cowper*, now in progress, as 'a Work of Magnitude . . . a most valuable acquisition to Literature'. He could hardly have thought this; but he did add, most interestingly, that the book would 'contain Letters of Cowper to his friends, Perhaps, or rather Certainly, the very best letters that ever were published'.[363] This shows that he was by no means immune from their therapeutically homely warmth, even though he later declared that Cowper had come to him and said 'O that I were insane always'.

But by the beginning of 1802 things have changed. On 10 January 1802 he writes to Butts:

When I came down here, I was more sanguine that I am at present; but it was because I was ignorant of many things which have since occurred, & chiefly the unhealthiness of the place. Yet I do not repent of coming on a thousand accounts; & Mr H., I doubt not, will do ultimately all that both he & I wish—that is, to lift me out of difficulty; but this is no easy matter to a man who, having Spiritual Enemies of such formidable magnitude, cannot expect to want natural hidden ones. . . . if it was fit for me, I doubt not that I should be Employ'd in Greater things; & when it is proper, my Talents shall be properly exercised in Public, as I hope they are now in private; for, till then, I leave no stone unturn'd & no path unexplor'd that tends to improvement in my beloved Arts. One thing of real consequence I have accomplish'd by coming into the country, which is to me consolation enough: namely, I have recollected all my scatter'd thoughts on Art & resumed my primitive & original ways of Execution in both painting & engraving, which in the confusion of London I had very much lost & obliterated from my mind. But whatever becomes of my labours, I would rather that they should be preserv'd in your Green House (not, as you mistakenly call it, dung hill) than in the cold gallery of fashion.—The Sun may yet shine, & then they will be brought into open air.

But you have so generously & openly desired that I will divide my griefs with you, that I cannot hide what it is now become my duty to explain.—My unhappiness has arisen from a source which, if explor'd too narrowly, might hurt my pecuniary circumstances, As my dependence is on Engraving at present, & particularly on the Engravings I have in hand for Mr H.: & I find on all hands great objections to my doing any thing but the meer drudgery of business, & intimations that if I do not confine myself to this, I shall not live; this has always pursu'd me. You will understand by this the source of all my uneasiness. This from Johnson & Fuseli brought me down here, & this from Mr H. will bring me back again; for that I cannot live without doing my duty to lay up treasures in heaven is Certain & Determined, & to this I have long made up my mind, & why this should be made an objection to Me, while Drunkenness, Lewdness, Gluttony & even Idleness itself, does not hurt other men, let Satan himself Explain. The Thing I have most at Heart—more than life, or all that seems to make life comfortable without—Is the Interest of True Religion & Science, & whenever any thing appears to affect that Interest (Especially if I myself omit any duty to my Station as a Soldier of Christ), It gives me the greatest of torments. I am not ashamed, afraid, or averse to tell you what Ought to be Told: That I am under the direction of Messengers from Heaven, Daily & Nightly; but the nature of such things is not, as some suppose, without trouble or care. Temptations are on the right hand & left; behind, the sea of time & space roars & follows swiftly; he who keeps not right onward is lost, & if our footsteps slide in clay, how can we do otherwise than fear & tremble? but I should not have troubled You with this account of my spiritual state, unless it had been necessary in explaining the actual cause of my uneasiness, into which you are so kind as to

Enquire; for I never obtrude such things on others unless question'd, & then I never disguise the truth.—But if we fear to do the dictates of our Angels, & tremble at the Tasks set before us; if we refuse to do Spiritual Acts because of Natural Fears of Natural Desires! Who can describe the dismal torments of such a state!—I too well remember the Threats I heard!—If you, who are organised by Divine Providence for Spiritual communion, Refuse, & bury your Talent in the Earth, even tho' you should want Natural Bread, Sorrow & Desperation pursues you thro' life, & after death shame & confusion of face to eternity. Every one in Eternity will leave you, aghast at the Man who was crown'd with glory & honour by his brethren, & betray'd their cause to their enemies. You will be call'd the base Judas who betray'd his Friend!—Such words would make any stout man tremble, & how then could I be at ease? But I am now no longer in That State, & now go on again with my Task, Fearless, and tho' my path is difficult, I have no fear of stumbling while I keep it. . . . I hear a voice you cannot hear, that says I must not stay, I see a hand you cannot see, that beckons me away. Naked we came here, naked of Natural things, & naked we shall return; but while cloth'd with the Divine Mercy, we are richly cloth'd in Spiritual & suffer all the rest gladly.[364]

No account of the difficulties between Hayley and Blake could be clearer—or, in fact, fairer—than this. Hayley had failed him: conceitedly he tried to dominate him, to use him as an amanuensis, and generally make sure that Blake should have no time for his own work. Considering the sort of atmosphere he generated, Blake was positively magnanimous: Hayley was unwittingly trying to crush his individuality. Finally the two men agreed that Blake should return to London; on 6 July 1803 he told Butts that 'Mr. H. is quite agreeable to our return', and added

I regard fashion in Poetry as little as I do in Painting; so, if both Poets and Painters should alternately dislike . . . I am not to regard it at all, but Mr. H. approves of My Designs as little as he does of my Poems . . . I am determin'd to be no longer Pester'd with his Genteel Ignorance and Polite Disapprobation. . . .[365]

Then, in early August, Blake was accused (probably falsely) of 'Sedition' by a Private Scofield, 'a disgraced Sergeant', whom he had turned out of his garden. Hayley came, most generously, to his aid, and eventually helped to gain his acquittal at Chichester Assizes in January 1804. Blake never forgot this, and was open-hearted in his profession of gratitude.

But the incident had deeply upset him. At the end of a long account of it in a letter of 16 August 1803 to Butts, he wrote:

> ... This perhaps was suffer'd to Clear up some doubts, & to give opportunity to those whom I doubted to clear themselves of all imputation. If a Man offends me ignorantly & not designedly, surely I ought to consider him with favour & affection. Perhaps the simplicity of myself is the origin of all offences committed against me. If I have found this, I shall have learned a most valuable thing, well worth three years' perseverance. I have found it. It is certain that a too passive manner, inconsistent with my active physiognomy, had done me much mischief. I must now express to you my conviction that all is come from the spiritual World for Good, & not for Evil.
>
> Give me your advice in my perilous adventure; burn what I have peevishly written about any friend. I have been very much degraded & injuriously treated; but if it all arise from my own fault, I ought to blame myself.
>
> O why was I born with a different face?
> Why was I not born like the rest of my race?
> When I look, each one starts! when I speak, I offend;
> Then I'm silent & passive & lose every Friend.
>
> Then my verse I dishonour, My pictures despise,
> My person degrade & my temper chastise;
> And the pen is my terror, the pencil my shame;
> All my Talents I bury, and dead is my Fame.
>
> I am either too low to too highly priz'd;
> When Elate I am Envy'd, When Meek I'm despis'd.
>
> This is but too just a Picture of my Present state. pray God to keep you & all men from it, & to deliver me in his own good time.[366]

This is Blake's most moving declaration of his 'difference' from the world. It is chastening to remember that the excellent Butts, to whom he addressed it, was almost certainly incapable of understanding it. Blake had no one at all with whom he could talk on equal terms. This accounts for much of his so-called eccentricity: it would have been a waste of time to try to explain himself in any detail.

There are many friendly letters written to Hayley during 1804 and 1805, then little more of importance until a series of letters written to Blake's artistic disciple John Linnel in the last three years of his life. Many of these allude to the symptoms of the illness, gallstones and inflammation of the gall-bladder, that eventually killed him. They are tired but serene letters. To his lifelong friend

George Cumberland on 12 April 1827, three months before his death, he wrote

> I have been very near the Gates of Death & have returned very weak & an Old Man feeble and tottering, but not in Spirit & Life, not in The Real Man The Imagination which Liveth for Ever. In that I am stronger & stronger as this Foolish Body decays.[367]

Blake's letters as we know them leave wide gaps in his life unrepresented. There is nothing of any real substance until 1799, when he was already forty-two: no information, that is to say, about the period of the very early *Poetical Sketches* or of the *Songs of Innocence and Experience*. The Felpham years are well represented, but there are only seven letters between 1805 and 1825. What they show above all is that Blake was consistent in a way that no other poet, except perhaps Shelley, has ever been. Comparatively early in his life, on 19 August 1799, he told Dr. Trusler that his designing was

> a Species by itself, & in this which I send you have been compell'd by my Genius or Angel to follow where he led; if I were to act otherwise it would not fulfill the purpose for which alone I live, which is . . . to renew the lost Art of the Greeks.[368]

He might truthfully have said this at any time in his life.

4

> But hear, on this pathetic and awful subject, the poet himself, pleading for those who have transgressed!

> One point must still be greatly dark,
> The moving *why* they do it,
> And just as lamely can ye mark
> How far, perhaps, they rue it.
> *Who made* the heart, 'tis *he* alone
> Decidedly can try us;
> He knows each chord—its various tone,
> Each spring, its various bias.
> Then at the balance let's be mute,
> We never can adjust it;
> What's done we partly may compute,
> But know not what's resisted.

> How happened it that the recollection of this affecting passage did not check so amiable a man as Dr. Currie, while he was revealing to the world the infirmities of its author?

So Wordsworth, in his justly celebrated 1816 'letter to a friend of Burns', in criticism of Burns's first biographer, James Currie. Wordsworth, like most other people, was led astray by Currie's exaggerated account of Burns's 'vices'; he had also been upset by some of the letters Currie printed: 'I well remember the acute sorrow with which, by my own fire-side, I first perused . . . some of the letters, particularly of those composed in the latter part of the poet's life'. However, as Wordsworth warmed to this theme, he rose above his habitual rectitude, to produce what is still one of the ablest defences of Burns ever written

> Who, but some inpenetrable dunce or narrow-minded puritan in works of art, ever read without delight the picture which he has drawn of . . . Tam o'Shanter?

and

> It is probable that he would have proved a still greater poet if . . . he could have controlled the propensities which his sensibilities engendered; but he would have been a poet of a different class: and certain it is, had that desirable restraint been early established, many peculiar beauties which enrich his verses could never have existed. . . . Burns . . . was a man who preached from the text of his own errors . . . whose wisdom . . . was in fact a scion from the root of personal suffering.[369]

No poet, even Shakespeare, can have been the subject of quite such a nauseating and poetically ignorant cult as Burns. This has been and still is (in the form of Burns Nights, postage stamps and other kinds of vulgar adulation) so viciously overwhelming that it is some measure of Burns's quality as a poet that he has survived at all except as a travesty of what he was. There is still no satisfactory edition of his poetry, and it was not until 1959 that his bawdy poems, an integral part of his achievement, were properly collected.[370]

The popular image of Burns is so pervasive that even the most studious and least vulgar of those who approach him for the first time are likely to be affected by it: all possible means are needed to counteract it. It is unfortunate, then, that so many of his seven hundred and nine surviving letters are examples of epistolary art rather than personal communications. Burns could, on occasion, be relaxed in his correspondence, but too often he is composing rather than writing. His education lacked little except system and a classical background, but he felt this keenly, and was self-consciously afraid of being caught out in matters of grammar or style. Although his artificiality is defensive and not indulged in for the sake of creating a false image of himself, it causes the majority of his letters to be less valuable and attractive than they might otherwise be: he was too conscious of himself when writing them.[371]

Burns was born in Argyllshire in 1759 in a clay cottage that his father William had built with his own hands. The main outline of his life until August 1787 is best told by himself, in the form of his long autobiographical letter, one of the least inhibited and most revealing that he ever wrote, to Dr. John Moore. Moore, physician and novelist, gave him wrong advice by exhorting him to write in standard English, but he was genuine and well intentioned; he had become interested in him when his friend Mrs. Dunlop, who was also Burns's friend, sent him a copy of the Kilmarnock volume, *Poems Chiefly in the Scottish Dialect* (1786). This made Burns's reputation, and gave him, for the first time in his life, a measure of self-confidence; this is reflected in the letter to Moore, which meant more to him as an autobiographical statement, a summing-up, than it did as a letter: essentially, it is an autobiographical statement disguised as a letter. True, it is sometimes laboured, nervous of inviting educated rebuff, and anxious to display its author's wide reading; but it differs from most of Burns's other letters because in it he is making a determined effort to explain himself not only to Moore but also to himself. 'I will give you,' he writes at the beginning, 'an honest narrative, though I know it will be at the expence of frequently being laughed at.' Then, after admitting that in writing 'under some very twitching qualms of conscience', he may be being 'trifling and impertinent' and 'doing what he ought not to do', he continues:

> I have not the most distant pretensions to what the pye-coated guardians of escutcheons call, A Gentleman.—When at Edinburgh last winter, I got acquainted in the Herald's Office, and looking through that granary of Honors I there found almost every name in the kingdom; but for me,
> "—My ancient but ignoble blood
> Has crept thro' Scoundrels ever since the flood"—
> Gules, Purpure, Argent, &c. quite disowned me.—My Fathers rented land of the noble Kieths of Marshal, and had the honor to share their fate.—I do not use the word, Honor, with any reference to Political principles; loyal and disloyal I take to be merely relative terms in that ancient and formidable court known in this Country by the name of CLUB-LAW.—Those who dare welcome Ruin and shake hands with Infamy for what they sincerely believe to be the cause of their God or their King—"Brutus and Cassius are honorable men."—I mention this circumstance because it threw my father on the world at large; where after many years' wanderings and sojournings, he pickt up a pretty large quantity of Observation and Experience, to which I am indebted for most of my little pretensions to wisdom.—

I have met with few who understood "Men, their manners and their ways" equal to him; but stubborn, ungainly Integrity, and headlong, ungovernable Irrascibillity are disqualifying circumstances: consequently I was born a very poor man's son.—For the first six or seven years of my life, my father was gardiner to a worthy gentleman of small estate in the neighbourhood of Ayr.—Had my father continued in that situation, I must have marched off to be one of the little underlings about a farm-house; but it was his dearest wish and prayer to have it in his power to keep his children under his own eye till they could discern between good and evil; so with the assistance of his generous Master my father ventured on a small farm in his estate.—At these years I was by no means a favorite with any body.—I was a good deal noted for a retentive memory, a stubborn, sturdy something in my disposition, and an enthusiastic, idiot piety.—I say idiot piety, because I was then but a child.—Though I cost the schoolmaster some thrashings, I made an excellent English scholar; and against the years of ten or eleven, I was absolutely a Critic in substantives, verbs and particles.—In my infant and boyish days too, I owed much to an old Maid of my Mother's, remarkable for her ignorance, credulity and superstition.—She had, I suppose, the largest collection in the county of tales and songs concerning devils, ghosts, fairies, brownies, witches, warlocks, spunkies, kelpies, elf-candles, dead-lights, wraiths, apparitions, cantraips, giants, inchanted towers, dragons and other trumpery.—This cultivated the latent seeds of Poesy; but had so strong an effect on my imagination, that to this hour, in my nocturnal rambles, I sometimes keep a sharp look-out in suspicious places; and though nobody can be more sceptical in these matters than I, yet it often takes an effort of Philosophy to shake off these idle terrors.—The earliest thing of Composition that I recollect taking pleasure in was, The vision of Mirza and a hymn of Addison's. . . . I met with these pieces in Mas[s]on's English Collection, one of my school-books. The two first books I ever read in private, and which gave me more pleasure than any two books I ever read again, were, the life of Hannibal and the history of Sir William Wallace.—Hannibal gave my young ideas such a turn that I used to strut in raptures up and down after the recruiting drum and bagpipe, and wish myself tall enough to be a soldier; while the story of Wallace poured a Scotish prejudice in my veins which will boil along there till the flood-gates of life shut in eternal rest.—Polemical divinity about this time was putting the country half-mad; and I, ambitious of shining in conversation parties on Sundays between sermons, funerals, &c. used in a few years more to puzzle Calvinism with so much heat and indiscretion that I raised a hue and cry of heresy against me which has not ceased to this hour.—

My vicinity to Ayr was of great advantage to me. . . . I formed many connections with other Youngkers who possessed superiour advantages. . . . They would give me stray volumes of books; among them, even then, I could pick up some observations; and ONE . . . helped me to a little French.—Parting with these, my young friends and benefactors, as they dropped off for the east or west Indies, was often to me a sore affliction; but I was soon called to more serious evils.—My father's generous Master died; the farm proved a ruinous bargain; and, to clench the curse, we fell into the hands of a Factor who sat for the picture I have drawn of one in my Tale of two dogs.—My father was advanced in life when he married; I was the eldest of seven children; and he, worn out by early hardship, was unfit for labour.—My father's spirit was soon irritated, but not easily broken.—There was a freedom in his lease in two years more, and to weather these two years we retrenched expences. —We lived very poorly; I was a dextrous Ploughman for my years; and the next eldest to me was a brother, who could drive the plough very well and help me to thrash.—A Novel-Writer might perhaps have viewed these scenes with some satisfaction, but so did not I: my indignation yet boils at the recollection of the scoundrel tyrant's insolent, threatening epistles, which used to set us all in tears.—

This gives as accurate an account of Burns's childhood as we are likely to find anywhere. It gives a vital account of his earliest reading, and exposes the absurdity of thinking of him as a 'peasant poet' with no more than an ordinary peasant's education. He did not, however, start to write poetry because of anything he read in books, but because of his sexual feelings, as he goes on to explain:

This kind of life, the chearless gloom of a hermit with the unceasing moil of a galley-slave, brought me to my sixteenth year; a little before which period I first committed the sin of RHYME.—You know our country custom of coupling a man and woman together as Partners in the labors of Harvest.—In my fifteenth autumn, my Partner was a bewitching creature who just counted an autumn less.— My scarcity of English denies me the power of doing her justice in that language; but you know the Scotch idiom, She was a bonie, sweet, sonsie lass.—In short, she altogether unwittingly to herself, initiated me in a certain delicious Passion, which in spite of acid Disappointment, gin-horse Prudence and bookworm Philosophy, I hold to be the first of human joys, our dearest pleasure here below.—How she caught the contagion I can't say; you medical folks talk much of infection by breathing the same air, the touch, &c. but I never expressly told her that I loved her.—Indeed I did not well know myself, why I liked so much to loiter behind with her, when returning in the evening from our labors; why the tones of her voice made my heartstrings thrill like an Eolian harp; and particularly, why my pulse beat such a furious ratann when I looked and fingered over her hand, to pick out the nettle-stings and thistles.— Among her other love-inspiring qualifications, she sung sweetly; and 'twas her favorite reel to which I attempted giving an embodied vehicle in rhyme.—I was not so presumitve as to imagine that I could make verses like printed ones, composed by men who had Greek and Latin; but my girl sung a song which was said to be composed by a small country laird's son, on one of his father's maids, with whom he was in love; and I saw no reason why I might not rhyme as well as he, for excepting smearing sheep and casting peats, his father living in the moors, he had no more Scholarcraft than I had.—

Thus with me began Love and Poesy; which at times have been my only, and till within this last twelvemonth have been my highest enjoyment.

This is important, for it shows Burns at his least laboured, trying hard to analyse himself. His feelings for the girl seem to have been predominantly sexual, and his poem about her to have been inspired both by pride and by the kind of physical passion that was to characterize his later poetry.

If there is something lacking in Burns's love poetry, then it is a lack of interest in women as persons: his sympathy with them is based on the joy they can provide, for him and for themselves, as sexual objects. In this first adolescent affair, Burns was not sick with love or in despair: he was trying to celebrate a feeling of which he as yet had only a vague awareness. The phrase, 'our dearest pleasure here below' is surely one of the keys to Burns's personality and achievement. Not all that Calvinism and gentility could do could destroy this conviction.

In the letter to Moore he returned at this point to family history and to his early literary nourishment:

My father struggled on till he reached the freedom in his lease, when he entered on a larger farm about ten miles farther in the country.—The nature of the bargain was such as to throw a little ready money in his hand at the commencement, otherwise the affair would have been impractible.— For four years we lived comfortably here; but a lawsuit between him and his Landlord commencing, after three years tossing and whirling in the vortex of Litigation, my father was just saved from absorption in a jail by phthisical consumption, which after two years promises, kindly stept in and snatch'd him away—"To where the wicked cease from troubling, and where the weary be at rest."

It is during this climacterick that my little story is most eventful.—I was, at the beginning of this period, perhaps the most ungainly, aukward being in the parish.—No Solitaire was less acquainted with the ways of the world.— My knowledge of ancient story was gathered from Salmon's and Guthrie's geographical grammars; my knowledge of modern manners, and of literature and criticism, I got from the Spectator.—These, with Pope's works, some plays of Shakespear, Tull and Dickson on Agriculture, The Pantheon, Locke's Essay on the human understanding, Stackhouse's history of the bible, Justice's British Gardiner's directory, Boyle's lectures, Allan Ramsay's works, Taylor's scripture doctrine of original sin, a select Collection of English songs, and Hervey's meditations had been the extent of my reading.—The Collection of Songs was my vade mecum.— I pored over them, driving my cart or walking to labor, song by song, verse by verse; carefully noting the true tender or sublime from affection and fustian.—I am convinced I owe much to this for my critic-craft such as it is.

This shows that what he modestly called his 'critic-craft such as it is' was owed mainly to his ability to distinguish between the true and the false—that capacity to spot 'affectation and fashion' that every true poet possesses. He responded not to the merely tender, but rather to the 'true tender'; throughout his life he at least tried to avoid self-deceit, and this is evident in even the most literary of his letters.

Burns then went on to give a general description—with commendable accuracy and a disregard, unusual for him, of how he might appear to his reader—of his early sexual escapades. Once more he is making a remarkable effort at self-analysis in an atmosphere free from prejudice or cant. Doubtless his first 'dissipations' resulted as much from his need to escape from the tensions generated by his ailing father as from the constrictions of Presbyterianism.

In my seventeenth year,[372] to give my manners a brush, I went to a country dancing school.—My father had an unaccountable antipathy against these meetings; and my going was, what to this hour I repent, in absolute defiance of his commands.—My father, as I said before, was the sport of strong passions: from that instance of rebellion he took a kind of dislike to me, which, I believe was one cause of that dissipation which marked my future years.—I only say, Dissipation, comparative with the strictness and sobriety of Presbyterean country life; for though the will-o'-wisp meteors of thoughtless Whim were almost the sole lights of my path, yet early ingrained Piety and Virtue never failed to point me out the line of Innocence.—The great misfortune of my life was, never to have AN AIM.—I had felt early some stirrings of Ambition, but they were the blind gropins of Homer's Cyclops round the walls of his cave: I saw my father's situation entailed on me perpetual labor. —The only two doors by which I could enter the fields of fortune were, the most niggardly economy, or the little chicaning art of bargain-making: the first is so contracted an aperture, I never could squeeze myself into it; the last, I always hated the contamination of the threshold.—Thus, abandoned of aim or view in life; with a strong appetite for sociability, as well from native hilarity as from a pride of observation and remark; a constitutional hypochondriac taint which made me fly solitude; add to all these incentives to social life, my reputation for bookish knowledge, a certain wild, logical talent, and a strength of thought something like the rudiments of good sense, made me generally a welcome guest; so 'tis no great wonder that always "where two or three were met together, there was I in the midst of them."—But far beyond all the other impulses of my heart was, un penchant á l'adorable moitiée du genre humain.—My heart was compleatly tinder, and was eternally lighted up by some Goddess or other: and like every warfare in this world, I was sometimes crowned with success, and sometimes mortified with defeat.—At the plough, scythe or reap-hook I feared no competitor, and set Want at defiance; and as I never cared farther for my labors than while I was in actual excercise, I spent the evening in the way after my own heart.—A country lad rarely carries on an amour without an assisting confident.

I possessed a curiosity, zeal and intrepid dexterity in these matters which recommended me a proper Second in duels of that kind; and I dare say, I felt as much pleasure at being in the secret of half the amours in the parish, as ever did Premier at knowing the intrigues of half the courts of Europe.—

The very goosefeather in my hand seems instinctively to know the well-worn path of my imagination, the favorite theme of my song; and is with difficulty restrained from giving you a couple of paragraphs on the amours of my Compeers, the humble Inmates of the farm-house and cottage; but the grave sons of Science, Ambition or Avarice baptize these things by the name of Follies.—To the sons and daughters of labor and poverty they are matters of the most serious nature: to them, the ardent hope, the stolen interview, the tender farewell, are the greatest and most delicious part of their enjoyments.—

Another circumstance in my life which made very considerable alterations in my mind and manners was, I spent my seventeenth summer on a smuggling [coast] a good distance from home at a noted school, to learn Mensuration, Surveying, Dialling, &c. in which I made a pretty good progress.—But I made greater progress in the knowledge of mankind.—The contraband trade was at that time very successful; scenes of swaggering riot and roaring dissipation were as yet new to me; and I was no enemy to social life.—Here, though I learned to look unconcernedly on a large tavern-bill, and mix without fear in a drunken squabble, yet I went on with a high hand in my Geometry; till the sun entered Virgo, a month which is always a carnival in my bosom, a charming Fillette who lived next door to the school overset my Trigonomertry, and set me off in a tangent from the sphere of my studies.—I struggled on with my Sines and Co-sines for a few days more; but stepping out to the garden one charming noon, to take the sun's altitude, I met with my Angel,

———"Like Proserpine gathering flowers,
"Herself a fairer flower"—

It was vain to think of doing any more good at school.—The remaining week I staid, I did nothing but craze the faculties of my soul about her, or steal out to meet with her; and the two last nights of my stay in the country, had sleep been a mortal sin, I was innocent.—

I returned home very considerably improved.—My reading was enlarged with the very important addition of Thomson's and Shenstone's works; I had seen mankind in a new phasis; and I engaged several of my schoolfellows to keep up a literary correspondence with me.—This last helped me much on in composition.—I had met with a collection of letters by the Wits of Queen Ann's reign, and I pored over them most devoutly.—I kept copies of any of my own letters that pleased me, and a comparison between them and the composition of most of my correspondents flattered my vanity.—I carried this whim so far that though I had not three farthings worth of business in the world, yet every post brought me as many letters as if I had been a broad, plodding son of Day-book & Ledger.—

My life flowed on much in the same tenor till my twenty third year.—Vive l'amour et vive la bagatelle, were my sole principles of action.—The addition of two more Authors to my library gave me great pleasure; Sterne and M'kenzie.—Tristram Shandy and the Man of Feeling were my bosom favorites.

Poesy was still a darling walk for my mind, but 'twas only the humour of the hour.—I had usually half a dozen or more pieces on hand; I took up one or other as it suited the momentary tone of the mind, and dismissed it as it bordered on fatigue.—My Passions when once they were lighted up, raged like so many devils, till they got vent in rhyme; and then conning over my verses, like a spell, soothed all into quiet.—None of the rhymes of those days are in print, except, Winter, a dirge, the eldest of my printed pieces; The death of Poor Mailie, John Barleycorn, And songs first, second and third: song second was the ebullition of that passion which ended the forementioned school-business.—

Next comes an account of Burns's ill-fated venture into business, as a flax-dresser in Irvine: the man he joined with for the purpose of learning the business turned out to be a thief, and the shop was burnt down, leaving Burns 'like a true Poet, not worth sixpence'. He tells Moore how while in Irvine he met Richard Brown—an educated sailor and now a sea-captain—who taught him to regard 'with levity, which hitherto I had regarded with horror'. Brown was, in this way, an important influence on Burns: he freed him from his sexual inhibitions. 'Here,' Burns observes, 'his friendship did me a mischief.' At this time (he says) he had given up 'Rhyme' except for 'some religious pieces'; but then he met the Scots poems of Robert Fergusson,[373] and 'strung anew my mildly-sounding, rustic lyre with emulating vigour'.

His father died and Burns and his brother Gilbert, who was without his 'harebrained imagination', took a neighbouring farm and vainly tried to make a success of it. Then he tells Moore how his reputation as poet began to grow:

I now began to be known in the neighbourhood as a maker of rhymes.—The first of my poetic offspring that saw the light was a burlesque lamentation on a quarrel between two rev^d Calvinists, both of them dramatis person in my Holy Fair.—I had an idea myself that the piece had some merit;

but to prevent the worst, I gave a copy of it to a friend who was very fond of these things, and told him I could not guess who was the Author of it, but that I thought it pretty clever.—With a certain side of both clergy and laity it met with a roar of applause.—Holy Willie's Prayer next made its appearance, and alarmed the kirk-Session so much that they held three several meetings to look over their holy artillery, if any of it was pointed against profane Rhymers. Unluckily for me, my idle wanderings led me, on another side, point-blank within the reach of their heaviest metal.— This is the unfortunate story alluded to in my printed poem, The Lament.—'Twas a shocking affair, which I cannot yet bear to recollect; and had very nearly given [me] one or two of the principal qualifications for a place among those who have lost the chart and mistake the reckoning of Rationality.—I gave up my part of the farm to my brother, as in truth it was only nominally mine; and made what little preparation was in my power for Jamaica. Before leaving my native country for ever, I resolved to publish my Poems.—I weighed my productions as impartially as in my power; I thought they had merit; and 'twas a delicious idea that I would be called a clever fellow, even though it should never reach my ears a poor Negro-driver, or perhaps a victim to that inhospitable clime gone to the world of Spirits.—I can truly say that pauvre Inconnu as I then was, I had pretty nearly as high an idea of myself and my works as I have at this moment.—It [is] ever my opinion that the great, unhappy mistakes and blunders, both in a rational and religious point of view, of which we see thousands daily guilty, are owing to their ignorance, or mistaken notions of themselves.—To know myself had been all along my constant study.—I weighed myself alone; I balanced myself with others; I watched every means of information how much ground I occupied both as a Man and as a Poet: I studied assiduously Nature's DESIGN where she seem'd to have intended the various LIGHTS and SHADES in my character.— I was pretty sure my poems would meet with some applause; but at the worst, the roar of the Atlantic would deafen the voice of Censure, and the novelty of west-Indian scenes make be forget Neglect.—

I threw off six hundred copies, of which I had got subscriptions for about three hundred and fifty.—My vanity was highly gratified by the reception I met with from the Publick; besides pocketing, all expences deducted, near twenty pounds.—This last came very seasonable, as I was about to indent myself for want of money to pay my freight.

—So soon as I was master of nine guineas, the price of wafting me to the torrid zone, I bespoke a passage in the very first ship that was to sail, for

"Hungry wind [ruin] had me in the wind"—

I had for some time been sculking from covert to covert under all the terrors of a Jail; as some ill-advised, ungrateful people had uncoupled the merciless legal Pack at my heels.—I had taken the last farewel of my few friends; my chest was on the road to Greenock; I had composed my last song I should ever measure in Caledonia. "The gloomy night is gathering fast," when a letter from Dr Blacklock to a friend of mine overthrew all my schemes by rousing my poetic ambition.—The Doctor belonged to a set of Critics for whose applause I had not even dared to hope.—His idea that I would meet with every encouragement for a second edition fired me so much that away I posted to Edinburgh without a single acquaintance in town, or a single letter of introduction in my pocket.—The baneful Star that had so long shed its blasting influence in my Zenith, for once made a revolution to the Nadir; and the providential care of a good God placed under me the patronage of one of his noblest creatures, the Earl of Glencairn: "Oublie moi, Grand Dieu si jamais je l'oublie!"—

I need relate no farther.—At Edin^r I was in a new world: I mingled among many classes of men, but all of them new to me; and I was all attention "to catch the manners living as they rise."—[374]

The only really important incident in his life that Burns omitted from his account of it to Moore was one that had deeply hurt his pride. In 1785 he was engaged in a love affair with Jean Armour, the daughter of a respectable mason of Mauchline; in 1786 she became pregnant, and Burns made it clear that he would marry her. But her parents shocked him by repudiating him: they would rather their daughter suffered the indignity of bearing an illegitimate child than that she should marry a ne'er-do-well. Jean herself was prevailed upon to accord with her parents' wishes, and even to withdraw from or deny the 'some sort of Wedlock' that Burns told John Arnot in a letter of April 1786 he had 'made up' with her. This letter conveys a vivid expression of Burns's state of mind at the time: his hurt pride, rage at hypocrisy, and despair:

> . . . Tell it not in Gath—I have lost—a—a—a Wife!; 'no Prince, Potentate of Commander . . . ever got a more shameful or more total defeat . . .'; 'There is a pretty large portion of bedlam in the composition of a Poet at

any time; but on this occasion I was nine parts & nine tenths, out of ten, stark staring mad.[375]

To David Brice, on 12 June 1786, he wrote:

I received your message by G. Paterson, and as I am not very throng at present, I just write to let you know that there is such a worthless, rhyming reprobate, as your humble servant still in the land of the living, tho' I can scarcely say, in the place of hope.—I have no news to tell you that will give me any pleasure to mention, or you, to hear.—Poor, ill-advised, ungrateful Armour came home on friday last.—You have heard all the particulars of that affair; and a black affair it is.—What she thinks of her conduct now, I don't know; one thing I know, she has made me compleatly miserable.—Never man lov'd, or rather ador'd, a woman more than I did her: and, to confess a truth between you and me, I do still love her to distraction after all, tho' I won't tell her so, tho' I see her, which I don't want to do.—My poor, dear, unfortunate Jean! how happy have I been in her arms!—It is not the losing her that makes me so unhappy; but for *her* sake I feel most severely.—I foresee she is in the road to, I am afraid, *eternal* ruin; and those who made so much noise, and showed so much grief, at the thought of her being *my wife*, may, some day, see her connected in such a manner as may give them more real cause of vexation.—I am sure I do not wish it: may Almighty God forgive her ingratitude and perjury to me, as I from my very soul forgive her! and may His grace be with her and bless her in all her future life!—I can have no nearer idea of the place of eternal punishment than what I have felt in my own breast on her account.—I have tryed often to forget her: I have run into all kinds of dissipation and riot, Mason-meetings, drinking matches, and other mischief, to drive her out of my head, but all in vain: and now for a grand cure: the Ship is on her way home that is to take me out to Jamaica; and then, farewel dear old Scotland, and farewel dear, ungrateful Jean, for never, never will I see you more!

You will have heard that I am going to commence Poet in print; and tomorrow, my works go to the press.—I expect it will be a Volume of about two hundred pages.—It is just the last foolish action I intend to do; and then turn a wise man as fast as possible.—[376]

The affair, which involved appearing in Church three times to receive public censure for 'sin', drove him in several directions at once: he contemplated emigration to Jamaica, sent his poems to press and began soliciting subscriptions for them (he told himself that the proceeds would pay for his voyage), and embarked on a love-affair with Mary Campbell, 'Highland Mary', to whom he probably also promised marriage, and whose death in 1786 may have been caused by giving birth to his child. In 1788 Burns, after several affairs, including an artificial and wholly verbal one with Mrs. Jane M' Lehose, married Jean. He had remained attached to her all the time, and was delighted to resume relations with her in 1788, although he pretended otherwise to Mrs. M' Lehose. Possibly life in Edinburgh was beginning to tell on him when he made the decision. He told an old schoolmate, now a teacher of medicine, in a letter of late 1787/early 1788, that 'Dissipation and business engross every moment'.[367]

Burns's letters to Mrs. M' Lehose, the Clarinda to whom he signed himself Sylvander, demonstrate, as David Daiches has pointed out, 'how far he could go in writing a certain type of senti-mental English love letter', But beyond demonstrating this skill, these letters are dull.

In late 1889 Burns and his wife went to live in a farmhouse at Ellisland, near Dumfries, where he had rented a farm. When he became an exciseman in August he had to try to combine settling down with Jean and their son (all that now survived of two sets of twins), writing poetry, farming and his new and exacting duties, which he carried out most conscientiously. This put a severe strain on his constitution, which had been weakened since early youth by the rheumatic heart disorder that eventually killed him before he had reached the age of forty. He craved the security of home, because although—as he told Mrs. Dunlop in a letter of 21 February 1789— he loved 'the social pleasures' only 'in moderation', 'here' (in Edinburgh) 'I am impressed into the service of Bacchus'.[378] And in a letter of 4 March 1789, writing from Ellisland, he told her 'To any man who has a Home . . . if that Home is like mine, the scene of Domestic comfort; the bustle of Edinburgh will soon be a business of sickening disgust'.[379]

Overwork (not drink) and anxiety eventually taxed Burns's diseased heart to the point when it could no longer function: he died in July 1796. Jean Armour was a noble and tolerant wife, who even took his child by another women into her own house; but she was no intellectual companion, and this increased his misery. He was forced by his fame (the Burns cult had its beginnings in his own lifetime, and the man Burns was its first casualty) to produce inferior verse: his contacts with the Edinburgh *literati* did him no good. His sympathy with the French Revolution endangered his position as a public servant, and he was even forced to recant. A letter of 5 January 1793 to his patron Robert Graham, Laird of Fintry, indicates to what extent he found himself obliged to suppress

his natural—and not in any case seriously disaffected—sympathies.
To Graham he declares: that he is not a member of any Republican
or Reform party, that 'I never uttered any invectives against the king
. . . the sacred KEYSTONE OF OUR ROYAL ARCH CONSTITUTION', that the
British Constitution is 'the most glorious . . . on earth', that while he
was France's 'enthusiastic votary in the beginning of the business',
her old 'avidity for conquest' had changed his mind.[380] This was
perhaps not untrue, but Burns deliberately omitted to acknowledge
to Graham the kind of irrepressible libertarianism that he expressed
in 'Scots, wha hae wi' WALLACE bled', which he admitted in a letter of
about 30 August 1793 to the most conventional of all his friends,
George Thomson, had been written in 'enthusiasm on the theme of
Liberty & Independance'.[381] There was as much enthusiasm here for
liberty as for Scottish nationalism, but the letter made it seem
innocuous.

Eventually Burns cleared himself of suspicion of being a
revolutionary and a drunkard, and was promoted. But it was an
effort. He knew, as he told a correspondent in a letter of 1794, that
a person could be a 'drunken dissipated character' and 'yet be an
honest fellow'—although, as he says, he was 'honest . . . and . . .
nothing of this'.[382] But the people upon whom he depended could not
think in this way.

It is not easy to say just what Burns's real opinions about the
Revolution and the war of 1793 were. In a letter written in 1794 to
Samuel Clarke he protests that a toast he had given at a gathering
at which he admitted to having been drunk (the letter begins 'I was,
I know, drunk last night, but I am sober this morning') was not
'obnoxious', although a certain Captain Dods has taken exception
to it. But was it in fact not 'obnoxious' at least from the idiotic
viewpoint of such a 'patriotic' Scot as Captain Dods? The toast in
question was: 'May our success in the present war be equal to the
justice of our cause': this is just the kind of clear thinking that gets
people hanged in frenetic times.[383]

One of Burns's chief channels of release from the artificial
role demanded of him by his fame as a poet amongst the genteel
and by his position as government servant, was the composition of
bawdy verse. On 25 October 1793 he writes to his farmer friend
Robert Cleghorn,

> From my late hours last night, & the dripping fogs & damn'd
> east-wind of this stupid day, I have left me as little soul as
> an oyster.—'Sir John, you are so fretful, you cannot live
> long.'—'Why, there is it! Come, sing me a BAUDY-SONG to
> make me merry!!!'

The bawdy song itself would have pleased neither the Laird of
Fintry nor Burns's employers:

In Edinburgh town they've made a law,
   In Edinburgh at the Court o' Session,
That standing pricks are fautors a',
   And guilty o' a high transgression.
Decreet o' the Court o' Session,
   Act Sederunt o' the Session,
That standing pricks are fautors a',
   And guilty o' a high transgression.
And they've provided dungeons deep,
   Ilk lass has ane in her possession,
Until the fautors wail and weep,
   There shall they lie for their transgression.
Decreet o' the Court o' Session,
   Act Sederunt o' the Session.
The rogues in pouring tears shall weep,
   By Act Sederunt o' the Session.

Burns's ambivalent attitude to 'baudy' is well exemplified in his exclamation to Cleghorn in the same letter:

> There . . . must be, some truth in original sin.—My violent propensity to B—dy convinces me of it.—Lack a day! if that species of composition be the sin against 'the Holy Ghaist'. . . .[384]

By the beginning 1795 he underwent what may have been a moment of recklessness. Could George Thomson, who had insisted that there be no 'indelicacy' in the songs that Burns contributed to his *Select Collection of Original Scottish Airs*, really have been pleased by the song beginning 'When maukin bucks, at early fucks', which was sent to him in a letter in January?[385]

   Burns's poetic energy, despite the demands made upon him by his exacting work, and despite his poor health, remained unabated until the end. He was writing until a few days of his death. As immediate expressions of the moods generated by physical love, his poems are unsurpassed. He avoided sentimentality (as Daiches says) by concentrating on the concrete. He lacked a certain kind of emotional stability—although he longed for the security he knew it could confer—but he possessed true tenderness. On the whole, however, his letters show him coping with the problem of how to exist in society; they are seldom free enough from artifice to be truly revealing. Only in his best poems was he absolutely himself.

I

Gray was an important precursor and anticipator of Romanticism; as a critic he belongs in roughly the same tradition as the bolder Edward Young of *Conjectures on Original Composition* (1759) and the Wartons. Much of his criticism is scattered throughout his letters, which are important for three other reasons: for their intrinsic charm as letters; for what they tell us of Gray's struggles to achieve a poetry in accordance with his critical principles; and for the hints they give of the latent homosexuality that was so closely related to the melancholy which characterizes so much of his poetry. A man of extreme reticence, Gray flowered most naturally and easily in letters, as many of his type do. Had he achieved no fame as a poet and man of letters, 'the most learned man in Europe', he would probably still be valued as something of a pioneer naturalist.[386]

Gray's life was uneventful; it has most appropriately been described as a 'quiet' life.[387] He was born in 1716 at his father's house in Cornhill, the fifth and only survivor of twelve children. His mother had kept a successful 'milliner's business' or 'kind of India warehouse' with her sister in the City of London. On her marriage she transferred this business to the house of her husband Philip Gray, a scrivener and exchange-broker. He was an ill-tempered, unstable man, whose pathological jealousy of and meanness towards his wife made her life a constant misery. From 1725 until 1734 Gray was at Eton, where he made friends with Horace Walpole (youngest son of the Prime Minister), Richard West and Thomas Ashton. These four, who disliked games and were precocious and literary in the manner of many small groups of boys in public schools, called themselves the Quadruple Alliance; both Walpole and West played important parts in Gray's adult life.

At the end of 1734 he went up to Peterhouse, Cambridge, where he remained until 1739. He seems to have started writing poetry seriously here, but it was all in Latin; his first recorded English verses are merely facetious ones, included in a letter to Walpole of 8 December 1734.[388] Walpole and Ashton were at

Cambridge with Gray; and while there he formed another important friendship, with Thomas Wharton, who became a fellow of Pembroke Hall and later still (on his marriage) a physician. West, with whom Gray had already formed an especially close attachment, went to Oxford; like Gray, he was forced by financial necessity to study Law. Gray had been admitted to the Inner Temple in 1735, and in 1738, when West came down from Oxford, the two men, both gloomy at the prospect of a legal career, planned to share the same room there. But the arrangement was not to be fulfilled.

Gray's father kept him short of cash during his first year at Cambridge; but at the beginning of 1736 Gray's unmarried aunt Sarah died, and instead of leaving her property to him left it to her nephew. His new financial independence gave Gray a psychological fillip: few things increase self-confidence more than independent means. His biographer, E. W. Ketton-Cremer,[389] quotes a cheeky letter he wrote from London to his Peterhouse tutor, George Birkett, a few months after he had received his small inheritance:

> As I shall stay only a fortnight longer in Town, I'll beg you to give yourself the trouble of writing out my Bills, & sending 'em. . . .[390]

And writing to West in December of the same year he began:

> You must know that I do not take degrees, and, after this term, shall have nothing more of college impertinences to undergo. . . .[391]

Gray was not looking forward to his legal studies, but must have anticipated West's company with pleasure. Then, after he had returned to Cornhill in 1739, Walpole invited him to join him on a Grand Tour, promising to defray all his expenses. Gray was closer by temperament and inclination to the delicate West than to the then somewhat immature although more sophisticated Walpole; but such an opportunity could hardly be refused.

Gray and Walpole set out for Paris in March 1739.[392] They visited Rheims, Lyons, Geneva, Turin, Genoa and Florence, and spent the whole of 1740 in Italy. In May 1741, in Reggio, they quarrelled, and Walpole continued his tour by himself. There are few details about this; but in later life Walpole took most of the blame. Apparently Gray in some way criticized Walpole in a letter (which has not survived) to Ashton, who passed it back to Walpole, who took offence. A clash was almost inevitable: Gray's interests were in landscape and antiquities, Walpole's in society and gaiety. Gray, after experiencing some financial difficulties, reached London in September 1741.

2

Gray first showed his qualities as a letter-writer while on his Grand Tour, in descriptive letters written to his mother, his father and (chiefly) to West, with whom he felt most at ease as a correspondent. His letters to West are an attractive mixture of raillery, acute observation and more formal, exalted description. This can be observed in the first part of a letter to him of 20/21 May 1740, written from Tivoli:

> This day being in the palace of his Highness the Duke of Modena,[393] he laid his most serene commands upon me to write to Mr. West, and said he thought it for his glory, that I should draw up an inventory of all his most serene possessions for the said West's perusal.—Imprimis, a house, being in circumference a quarter of a mile, two feet and an inch; the said house containing the following particulars, to wit, a great room. Item, another great room; item, a bigger room; item, another room; item, a vast room; item, a sixth of the same; a seventh ditto; an eighth as before; a ninth as abovesaid; a tenth (see No. 1.); item, ten more such, besides twenty besides, which, not to be too particular, we shall pass over. The said rooms contain nine chairs, two tables, five stools, and a cricket. From whence we shall proceed to the garden, containing two millions of superfine laurel hedges, a clump of cypress trees, and half the river Teverone, that pisses into two thousand several chamberpots. Finis.—Dame Nature desired me to put in a list of her little goods and chattels, and, as they were small, to be very minute about them. She has built here three or four little montains, and laid them out in an irregular semi-circle; from certain others behind, at a greater distance, she has drawn a canal, into which she has put a little river of hers, called Anio; she has cut a huge cleft between the two innermost of her four hills, and there she has left it to its own disposal; which she has no sooner done, but, like a heedless chit, it tumbles headlong down a declivity fifty feet perpendicular, breaks itself all to shatters, and is converted into a shower of rain, where the sun forms many a bow, red, green, blue and yellow. To get out of our metaphors without any further trouble, it is the most noble sight in the world. The weight of that quantity of waters, and the force they fall with, have worn the rocks they throw themselves among into a thousand irregular craggs, and to a vast depth. In this channel it goes boiling along with a mighty noise till it comes to another steep, where you see it a second time come roaring down

(but first you must walk two miles farther) a greater height than before, but not with that quantity of waters; for by this time it has divided itself, being crossed and opposed by the rocks, into four several streams, each of which, in emulation of the great one, will tumble down too; and it does tumble down, but not from an equally elevated place; so that you have at one view all these cascades intermixed with groves of olive and little woods, the mountains rising behind them, and on the top of one (that which forms the extremity of one of the half-circle's horns) is seated the town itself. At the very extremity of that extremity, on the brink of the precipice, stands the Sybils' temple, the remains of a little rotunda, surrounded with its portico, above half of whose beautiful Corinthian pillars are still standing and entire; all this on one hand. On the other, the open Campagna of Rome, here and there a little castle on a hillock, and the city itself on the very brink of the horizon, indistinctly seen (being 18 miles off) except the dome of St. Peter's; which, if you look out of your window, wherever you are, I suppose, you can see. I did not tell you that a little below the first fall, on the side of the rock, and hanging over that torrent, are little ruins which they shew you for Horace's house, a curious situation to observe the

> Præceps Anio, & Tiburni lucus, & uda
> Mobilibus pomaria rivis.

Mæcenas did not care for such a noise, it seems, and built him a house (which they also carry one to see) so situated that it sees nothing at all of the matter, and for any thing he knew there might be no such river in the world. Horace had another house on the other side of the Teverone, opposite to Mæcenas's; and they told us there was a bridge of communication, by which 'andava il detto Signor per trastullarsi coll' istefso Orazio'. In coming hither we crofsed the Aquæ Albulæ, a vile little brook that stinks like a fury, and they say it has stunk so these thousand years. I forgot the Piscina of Quintilius Varus, where he used to keep certain little fishes. This is very entire, and there is a piece of the aqueduct that supplied it too; in the garden below is old Rome, built in little, just as it was, they say. There are seven temples in it, and no houses at all: They say there were none.[394]

The deliberate, beautifully apt change of tone, from levity to seriousness, at 'To get out of our metaphors without any further trouble . . .' is notable, as is Gray's instinctive avoidance of stereotyped diction and the stock responses of his age to 'grand landscape'.

The manner in which his eye is already on the object of description and not on any 'sublime' preconception of it is remarkable and unusual. At the end of his life, in journal-letters, he became the first eighteenth-century Englishman to write about the Lake District as it actually was, rather than as the Augustans preconceived it.

Of more purely psychological interest is his uneasy self-portrait in a letter to West from Florence (his last extant letter from Italy) written, a few days before his quarrel with Walpole, on 21 April 1741. It is evident that Gray was well aware that although he had chosen to accept Walpole's offer, he was much closer in spirit to West.

> I know not what degree of satisfaction it will give you to be told that we shall set out from hence the 24th of this month, and not stop above a fortnight at any place in our way. This I feel, that you are the principal pleasure I have to hope for in my own country. Try at least to make me imagine myself not indifferent to you; for I must own I have the vanity of desiring to be esteemed by somebody, and would choose that somebody should be one whom I esteem as much as I do you. As I am recommending myself to your love, methinks I ought to send you my picture (for I am no more what I was, some circumstances excepted, which I hope I need not particularize to you); you must add then, to your former idea, two years of age, reasonable quantity of dull-ness, a great deal of silence, and something that rather resembles, than is, thinking; a confused notion of many strange and fine things that have swum before my eyes for some time, a want of love for general society, indeed an inability to it. On the good side you may add a sensibility for what others feel, and indulgence for their faults or weaknesses, a love of truth, and detestation of every thing else. Then you are to deduct a little impertinence, a little laughter, a great deal of pride, and some spirits. These are all the alterations I know of, you perhaps may find more. Think not that I have been obliged for this reformation of manness to reason or reflection, but to a severer school-mistress, Experience. One has little merit in learning her lessons, for one cannot well help it; but they are more useful than others and imprint themselves in the very heart. . . .[395]

Clearly Gray, more of a retiring disposition than merely shy, yearned for the private and intimate company of one of his own sex, and he now began to invest his emotional hopes in West. He had by this time wearied of Walpole (in the quarrel that occurred a few days after this letter was written it seems to have been Gray who refused reconciliation); his first sentence shows that he was looking forward intensely to seeing West again.

According to William Mason, the parson and poetaster who became Gray's friend in 1748 and after his death his biographer and the well-meaning mutilator, improver, suppressor and conflator of his letters, Gray began a tragedy, *Agrippina*, in this winter of 1741. He never finished it, but it was probably his first serious attempt to write in English verse. In April 1742 he sent West a long speech from it, which West complained was too antiquated in style (Gray's answer to this is on page 289). He saw much of West during this winter, which was probably the happiest time of his life. His last letter to him contained his first real English poem, *Noontide, an Ode* (later called *Ode to the Spring*); it was returned unopened, and soon afterwards Gray learned by chance of his friend's death from a newspaper, which printed an elegy on him (it was by Ashton).

West had been writing English poems (Matthias, one of Gray's editors, showed Samuel Rogers some 'very indecent' ones by West among papers at Pembroke Hall) for some time before Gray; this and, undoubtedly, his living presence, caused Gray himself to write English poetry. Now West's tragic and unexpected death stimulated him into his most intense period of poetic activity. At first he reacted cautiously, composing an elegant Latin elegy that was supposed to be the preface to the fourth book of a long Latin poem, *De Principiis Cogitandi*, but which really stands alone. The elegiac manner of the Latin is stereotyped, though brilliantly executed; Gray soon found that he needed to express his powerful emotions in a less rigid form. In the single month of August 1742 he wrote, at Stoke Poges in Buckinghamshire where his uncle and aunt had moved and to where his mother was to retire in December, the *Ode on a Distant Prospect of Eton College*, the *Sonnet on the Death of West* and the *Hymn to Adversity*. It is most likely that he began the *Elegy*, too, during this summer, although it was not finished until 1750.

3

Philip Gray died in November 1741. Just over a year later his widow retired, with her sister Mary, to Stoke Poges; they were able to join their third sister, Mrs. Jonathan Rogers, in the same house that Gray had visited in the summer of 1742, for she became a widow in October. During this October Gray returned to Peterhouse as a fellow-commoner, a status that exempted him from undergraduate discipline. Ostensibly he was still studying Law, and in December 1743 he actually obtained his degree in Law; but he had no serious intention of practising. With the exception of various tours of

England the rest of his life was spent between Cambridge, London and Stoke Poges. In 1745 he and Walpole became reconciled, and the friendship lasted until Gray's death. The mock-heroic *Ode* on the death of one of Walpole's cats was written in 1747, and in the following year Gray began a philosophical poem on the subject of 'the Alliance of Education and Government', but seems to have written only 107 lines. In 1750 he finished the *Elegy* and sent it to Walpole, who had already arranged the publication of four of his poems in 1747/8. Walpole circulated the new poem widely, and eventually (February 1751) arranged for its publication, too (only a day earlier than its appearance in the piratical *Magazine of Magazines*). In 1750 Gray also wrote the light-hearted *A Long Story*. Two years later Walpole published this, together with the *Elegy*, the *Hymn to Adversity* and the *Spring*, *Eton* and *Adversity* odes, in a single volume with engravings by his friend Richard Bentley.

Gray punctuated his quiet life at Cambridge with visits to Walpole, Wharton (who was now married and living at Durham) and to Stoke Poges. He wrote *The Progress of Poesy* between 1752 and 1754, and *The Bard* shortly thereafter. In 1756 he migrated from Peterhouse to Pembroke, perhaps because the high spirits of the undergraduates on his staircase did not agree with him.[396] By now he was famous, but when the Poet Laureateship was offered to him in 1757 he declined it. Between 1759 and 1761 he lived mainly in London, studying in the newly opened British Museum Library. In 1768 he was appointed Regius Professor of Modern History at Cambridge, a post he had long coveted, and which carried no duties.[387]

At the end of the next year he met the young Swiss, Charles-Victor de Bonstetten, and took him to Cambridge; Bonstetten left England in March 1770. Gray wrote no poetry during or after his acquaintance with him, but the episode is important for what it tells us of the nature of the feelings he had for so many years suppressed, and which form the unacknowledged emotional background to many of his poems. He met Bonstetten through Norton Nicholls, for whom he had originally—when Nicholls was an undergraduate in 1762—entertained perhaps similar if less intense feelings. Gray died at Cambridge in 1771.

4

As an old man Bonstetten wrote in his *Souvenirs* (1831):

> *Gray, en se condemnant à vivre à Cambridge, oubliait que le génie du poète languit dans la sécheresse du coeur. . . Je*

crois que Gray n'avait jamais aimé, c'était le mot de l'enigme,
il en était résulté une misère de coeur qui faisait contraste avec
son imagination ardente et profonde qui, au lieu de faire le
bonheur de sa vie, n'en était que le tourment. Gray avait de la
gaieté dans l'esprit et de la mélancholie dans de caractère.[398]

This characteristically Gallic (or French–Swiss) view was an over-
simplification; but there are elements of truth in it, especially in the
last sentence quoted.

One of the most reliable general histories of English literature
says this of Gray:

> Various explanations have been offered of the quantitative
> limitations of Gray's output. Perhaps he felt that devotion
> of all his leisure to mere versifying would annul his position
> of genteel amateur. . . . While hardly more melancholy
> than other lovers of *Il Penseroso*, he was a true hypo-
> chondriac . . . he was a fastidious exquisite. . . .[399]

Gray is certainly a limited poet; but by this false approach we shall
certainly fail to respond to the best in him. The above appraisal,
with due respect for the fact that it was written by one of the most
learned of scholars of the eighteenth century, is itself a typical
example of critical 'exquisite fastidiousness' in the way it evades
psychological reality by unwarrantedly dismissing Gray's melancholy
as an affectation. Gray's melancholy was not affected, although he
sometimes tended to make an affectation out of it, and his 'fastidiousness' has been much over-emphasized and misunderstood. Admittedly
he spoke of having the 'hyp', which was fashionable, to his friends;
but it was in a more serious vein that he began a letter to West:

> Mine, you are to know, is a white Melancholy, or rather
> Leucocholy for the most part; which though it seldom
> laughs or dances, nor ever amounts to what one calls Joy or
> Pleasure, yet is a good easy sort of a state, and ça ne laisse
> que de s'amuser. The only fault of it is insipidity; which is
> apt now and then to give a sort of Ennui, which makes one
> form certain little wishes that signify nothing. But there is
> another sort, black indeed, which I have now and then felt,
> that has somewhat in it like Tertullian's rule of faith, Credo
> quia impossibile est; for it believes, nay, is sure of every
> thing that is unlikely, so it be but frightful; and, on the other
> hand, excludes and shuts its eyes to the most possible
> hopes, and every thing that is pleasurable; from this the
> Lord deliver us! for none but he and sunshiny weather can
> do it. . . .[400]

This is unaffected shrewd, self-analysis. Gray was a victim of bleakly
melancholy anxiety-states, and here he describes them very clearly.

He suffered from intense nervous apprehension. Once when he was talking to someone a dog walked into the room. When asked whether it was his he said (according to Samuel Rogers), 'Do you think I would keep a dog by which I might lose my life?' This rings true. His lifelong dread of fire—which apparently made him the laughing-stock of some of the younger men at Peterhouse—sprang from this anxiety. So does the black moodiness of much of his poetry, which is less 'literary' than some critics believe.

The other main reason for Gray's melancholy outlook is to be sought in his sexual temperament. He may not have been much bothered by the need for physical sex; but all men experience some kind of sexual disturbance, at some level: we may safely take Gray's disturbance to have been homosexual, probably exclusively so. Coupled with this—and much more in evidence—was his propensity to intimate intellectual friendship with men—first with West and afterwards with men younger than himself. Writing about his attitude to Bonstetten, his biographer R. W. Ketton-Cremer observes:

> . . . by now he realized that this newcomer was arousing in him emotions such as he had never experienced before, emotions obsessive and overwhelming. All his defences were swept away. . . . He was filled with disquiet, for he understood the secrets of his own nature; he knew the existence of temptations which could not for one moment be contemplated by one who had been, all his life long, a strict observer of the laws of God and the laws of man.[401]

But it seems impossible that Gray had not known some such emotions before: no one blossoms into homosexual love at the age of fifty-five as suddenly as that. He had merely repressed his feelings about West, and then about Nicholls, more rigidly and more successfully. And he had sustained a serious shock in 1757 when his friend Henry Tuthill was deprived of his fellowship for unknown 'enormities', which were however obviously of a homosexual nature. Gray's biographers all agree that his direction to his executors in his will 'to apply the sum of two hundred pounds to the use of a charity, which I have already informed them of' might well have been for the benefit of Tuthill in his exile. Mason even hints at other financial help, given during Gray's life. Further, one of his biographers, John Mitford (1847), who had the advantage of knowing people who had known Gray, speaks of 'circumstances that spread a considerable gloom over Gray's mind, and perhaps permanently affected his spirits. . . .' It is not difficult to see why Tuthill's disgrace disturbed Gray, who knew himself to be prey (as he would have regarded it) to the same 'temptations'.

All the evidence of the sort of feeling Gray entertained for Bonstetten is in letters to him and to Nicholls, who had introduced the two men. Bonstetten in his *Souvenirs* stated that when at Cambridge (December–March 1770) with Gray he was with him *'tous les soirs de cinq heures à minuit'*, and towards the end of the visit they saw each other even more often: *'je travaille dans sa chambre'* Bonstetten told his mother. But Bonstetten's parents wanted him to come home, and eventually he had to go. Gray's growing infatuation for the boy, and his agony as the time of his departure drew nearer, are reflected in letters to Nicholls. In a joint letter from both Bonstetten and Gray of 6 January 1770, written from Cambridge—Gray's part of which Bonstetten would presumably have seen—he exclaimed, 'I never saw such a boy; our breed is not made on this model'.[402] And on 20 March 1770 he wrote:

> On Wednesday next I go (for a few days) with Mons: de B: to London. his cursed Father will have him home in the autumn, & he must pass thro France to improve his talents & morals. he goes for Dover on Friday. I have seen (I own) with pleasure the efforts you have made to recommend me to him, *sed non ego credulus illis*, nor I fear, he neither. he gives me too much pleasure, & at least *an equal share* of unquietude. you do not understand him so well as I do, but I leave my meaning imperfect, till we meet. I have never met with so extraordinary a Person. God bless him! I am unable to talk to you about any thing else, I think.[403]

Gray was now tormented by an odd mixture of jealousy and moral concern: Bonstetten's journey through France would expose him to 'hazards'. The reference to this is certainly homosexually sarcastic in a familiar enough manner.

He went to Dover to see the boat off, and on his return wrote a sad letter (4 April 1770) to Nicholls:

> . . . here am I again to pass my solitary evenings, which hung much lighter on my hands, before I knew him. this is your fault! pray let the next you send me, be halt and blind, dull, unapprehensive & wrong-headed. . . . *Was never such a gracious Creature born!* & yet—but no matter! burn my letter [the letter of 20 March 1770] that I wrote you, for I an very much out of humour with myself & will not believe a word of it. you will think I have caught madness from him (for he is certainly mad) & perhaps you will be right. oh! what things are Fathers & Mothers! I thought they were to be found only in England, but you see. . . . this place Cambridge never appear'd so horrible to me, as it does now. . . .[404]

Eight days later he was expressing his jealous anxieties about

Bonstetten, as he travelled through France, in the form of a sincere but perhaps less intensely felt moral homily—for Gray's type of homosexual feeling often guiltily distorts itself into illusions that its object is especially worthy in a moral or sometimes an intellectual sense:

> The strength and spirits that now enable me to write to you, are only owing to your last letter, a temporary gleam of sunshine. Heaven knows, when it may shine again! I did not conceive till now (I own) what it was to lose you, nor felt the solitude and insipidity of my own condition, before I possess'd the happiness of your friendship.
>
> I must cite another Greek writer [Plato] to you, because it is very much to my purpose. He is describing the character of a Genius truly inclined to Philosophy. It includes (he says) qualifications rarely united in one single mind, quickness of apprehension and a retentive memory; vivacity and application, gentleness and magnanimity: to these he adds an invincible love of truth, and consequently of probity and justice. Such a soul (continues he) will be little inclined to sensual pleasures, and consequently temperate; a stranger to illiberality and avarice being accustom'd to the most extensive views of things and sublimest contemplations, it will contract an habitual greatness, will look down with a kind of disregard on human life and on death, consequently will possess the truest fortitude. Such (says he) be the Mind born to govern the rest of Mankind. But these very endowments so necessary to a soul form'd for philosophy are often the ruin of it (especially when join'd to the external advantages of wealth, nobility, strength and beauty) that is, if it light on a bad soil; and want its proper nurture, which nothing but an excellent education can bestow. In this case he is depraved by the publick example, the assemblies of the people, the courts of justice, the theatres, that inspire it with false opinions, terrify it with false infamy, or elevate it with false applause: and remember, that extraordinary vices and extraordinary virtues are alike the produce of a vigorous Mind: little souls are alike incapable of the one or the other.
>
> If you have ever met with the portrait sketch'd out by Plato, you will know it again: for my part (to my sorrow) I have had that happiness: I see the principal features, and I foresee the dangers with a trembling anxiety. But enough of this, I return to your letter: it proves at least, that in the midst of your new gaieties, I still hold some place in your memory, and (what pleases me above all) it has an air of

undissembled sincerity. Go on, my best and amiable Friend,
to shew me your heart simply and without the shadow of
disguise, and leave me to weep over it (as I now do) no
matter whether from joy or sorrow.[405]

Gray was perhaps the one pre-Romantic poet who had the requisite
poetic genius as well as inclination to break away from the 'French'
school of Pope; but he failed to do it, in spite of his critical convictions. The above passage, where he converts his real meaning of
'I love you' into a moral homily, shows why not: he was doubly
handicapped, both by his 'sinful' homosexuality and by the habits
of his age. But in such a passage—admittedly in a private letter—
he comes near, in prose, to the frankness of Shakespeare in his
sonnets, which were also supposed to be private. In this connection
it is interesting that he chose the then totally neglected sonnet form
for his English elegy on West: it is one of the few sonnets to survive
from his age, and the only well-known one. Had he recognized the
kind of feelings Shakespeare's sonnets expressed? It seems likely.

In his next letter to Bonstetten Gray's feelings, a faintly
feline mixture of affection and jealousy, became even more transparent. When he asks him if he is 'untouch'd', by Nicholls' feelings
for him he speaks of his own:

> Alas! how do I ever moment feel the truth of what I have
> somewhere read: *Ce n'est pas le voir que de s'en souvenir*, and
> yet that remembrance is the only satisfaction I have left. My
> life now is but a perpetual conversation with your shadow.—
> The known sound of your voice still rings in my ears.—There
> on the corner of the fender you are standing, or tinkling on
> the Pianoforte, or stretch'd at length on the sofa.—Do you
> reflect, my dearest Friend, that it is a week or eight days,
> before I can receive a letter from you and as much more
> before you can have my answer, that all that time (with more
> than Herculean toil) I am employ'd in pushing the tedious
> hours along, and wishing to annihilate them; the more I
> strive, the heavier they move and the longer they grow. I
> can not bear this place, where I have spent many tedious
> years within less than a month, since you left me. I am
> going for a few days to see poor Nicholls invited by a
> letter, wherein he mentions you in such terms, as add to
> my regard for him, and express my own sentiments better
> than I can do myself.[406] 'I am concern'd (says he) that I
> can not pass my life with him, I never met with any one
> that pleased and suited me so well: the miracle to me is,
> how he comes to be so little spoil'd, and the miracle of
> miracles will be, if he continues so in the midst of every
> danger and seduction, and without any advantages, but

from his own excellent nature and understanding. I own, I am very anxious for him on this account, and perhaps your inquietude may have proceeded from the same cause. I hope, I am to hear, when he has pass'd that cursed sea, or will he forget me thus *in insulam relegatum*? If he should, it is out of my power to retaliate.'

Sure you have wrote to him, my dear Bonstetten, or sure you will! he has moved me with these gentle and sensible expressions of his kindness for you. Are you untouch'd by them?

You do me the credit (and false or true, it goes to my heart) of ascribing to me your love for many virtues of the highest rank. Would to heaven it were so; but they are indeed the fruits of your own noble and generous understanding, that has hitherto struggled against the stream of custom, passion, and ill company, even when you were but a Child, and will you now give way to that stream, when your strength is increased? Shall the Jargon of French Sophists, the allurements of painted women *comme il faut*, or the vulgar caresses of prostitute beauty, the property of all, that can afford to purchase it, induce you to give up a mind and body by Nature distinguish'd from all others to folly, idleness, disease, and vain remorse? Have a care, my ever-amiable Friend, *of loving, what you do not approve*, and know me for your most faithful and must humble Despote.[407]

On 9 May 1770, as his infatuation reached its climax, he referred to a sentence Bonstetten had used in a (lost) letter written from London during an absence from Cambridge:

I am return'd, my dear B., from the little journey I had made into Suffolk [to see Nicholls] without answering the end proposed. The thought, that you might have been with me there, has embitter'd all my hours. Your letter has made me happy; as happy as so gloomy, so solitary a Being as I am is capable of being. I know and have too often felt the disadvantages I lay myself under how much I hurt the little interest I have in you, by this air of sadness so contrary to your nature and present enjoyments: but sure you will forgive, tho' you can not sympathize with me. It is impossible with me to dissemble with you. Such as I am, I expose my heart to your view, nor wish to conceal a single thought from your penetrating eyes.—All that you say to me, especially on the subject of Switzerland, is infinitely acceptable. It feels too pleasing ever to be fulfill'd, and as often as I read over your truly kind letter, written long since from London, I stop at these words: *La mort qui peut glacer nos bras avant qu'ils soient entrelacés.*[408]

We do not know the context of Bonstetten's remark, but Gray's use of it amounts to a declaration of love. It suggests that the Swiss may have allowed himself to become more emotionally involved with Gray than he wished or felt inclined to do. This would explain his reluctance to part with Gray's letters to him—he eventually allowed his friend Matthieson to print at least some of them in 1791, having refused permission to Mason. But Gray's letter of 9 May 1770 looks suspiciously like a fragment. We can certainly see in it the relationship of Gray's melancholy to his homosexuality, with its ambiguous talk of 'the disadvantages I lay myself under'. By refusing to talk to Bonstetten about his past or about his poetry—Bonstetten wrote,

> *Le Génie poétique de Gray était tellement éteint dans le sombre manoir de Cambridge, que le souvenir de ses poésies lui était odieux. Il ne se permit jamais de lui en parler. . . . Il y avait chez Gray entre le présent et le passé un abîme infranchissable*

—Gray was mutely expressing his regret at a lifetime starved of love, confessing a degree of poetic self-defeat. In his emotional enthusiasm for Bonstetten, when they read Dryden, Pope, Milton and Shakespeare together, he would not have wished to discuss his own poems, for he recognized more than ever that because of his 'disadvantages' he had not been able to speak out in them. At this time, of all times, when so much in love that he could not conceal it even from himself, he must have wished that he could write poems that breathed the spirit of this love—but he knew he could not, and so he was, as Bonstetten put it, like '*un enfant obstiné*' when Bonstetten quoted his own verse to him.

By 22 May 1770 he was beginning to recover. He told Nicholls that Bonstetten's letter was too affected in style ('*un peu trop alambiqué*'—used by Voltaire of Corneille)[409] by 3 May 1771 he could be even more critical—and more casual.[410] He was by now more easily able to see Bonstetten as he really was, a pleasant but rather affected and empty-headed young Swiss aristocrat. He was ill in this, his last summer, and wrote to Wharton 'travel I must, or cease to exist';[411] yet he did not go to Switzerland with Nicholls to see Bonstetten, a trip that had long been planned: he put the chief blame for this on 'low spirits'.[412]

5

The preceding analysis of Gray's relationship with Bonstetten is relevant to his poetry because, as I have pointed out, it throws light upon the kind of emotions that he had been suppressing all his life, and upon the real nature of his melancholy. But if Gray had this capacity for intense feeling, it was certainly inseparable from an equally strong sense of guilt. His self-analysis in the already quoted letter[413] from Florence of 21 April 1741 to West was careful to express 'an indulgence' for others' feelings, 'faults or weaknesses', in conjunction with 'a love of truth'. The Augustan sense of decorum operated in him strongly and with unusual sincerity: he was no hypocrite or adventurer in the manner of a Pope or a Bolingbroke. His outlets were private friendships (which had to be respectable), learning, natural history and poetry. He had to learn to starve himself emotionally as far as people were concerned, and because he thus limited his experience, he also limited the emotional scope of his poetry. But he was poet enough to realize this; to realize that his way, as poet, was not the way of the 'French' school—what he called in a letter to Thomas Warton the

> *School of France*, introduced after the Restoration. Waller, Dryden, Addison, & Pope, which has continued down to our own times.[414]

Gray was not openly critical of this 'French School', but he showed himself dissatisfied with it. Ironically, his classical learning and appreciation were much sounder than those of, say, Pope. This in itself is a comment on the 'classical' element in so-called neo-classicism, which some prefer to call pseudo-classicism. As critic, as naturalist, and as appreciator of landscape Gray was in advance of his times. The careful precision of his observations of birds, plants, wild flowers and the habits of the weather reflects the poetic quality of his love of truth; his energy was deflected into this channel because he did not have to be afraid of any secret that Nature might yield.

And yet as a poet he was not the innovator he might have been: the two Pindaric odes, while Pindaric in form and in that sense more truly classical than anything that had preceded them, were a dead end both for him and for the poets who followed him. If Gray could have integrated his critical principles and his tenderly precise feelings for Nature into his poetry he could have been more than merely the author of the *Eton Ode* and the *Elegy*. But before examining the extent of his success as a poet, it is necessary to look at his critical opinions.

Some of these are to be found in his few essays,[415] but most are in his letters. They are often surprisingly informal. When he tells Wharton that Aristotle is hard to deal with because 'it tasts for all the World like chop'd Hay'[416] he is, in drawing attention to this dryness, breaking new ground. The picture of Gray as the humourless recluse—the man the young and dissipated Christopher Smart (for whom Gray later did his best) said '*walked* as though he had fouled his breeches and *looked* as though he smelt it'[417]—has truth in it, but it is the public image; it is to be doubted if he was much like this when he was at his ease with people he knew well; but this more important side of him has been sadly under-emphasized.

While West was alive, most of Gray's thoughts about literature were reserved for letters to him. It is important to remember that he was as yet hardly an English poet at all (West, himself, however, had written a number of English poems), so that his remarks to West must be regarded as preconceptions. The general views on poetry he put forward in his reply to West's criticism of his *Agrippina* fragment as 'too antiquated' are surprisingly authoritative, confident and, in the context of 1742, unusual:

> You are very good in giving yourself the trouble to read and find fault with my long harangues. Your freedom (as you call it) has so little need of apologies, that I should scarce excuse your treating me any otherwise; which, whatever compliment it might be to my vanity, would be making a very ill one to my understanding. As to matter of stile, I have this to say: The language of the age is never the language of poetry; except among the French, whose verse, where the thought or image does not support it, differs in nothing from prose. Our poetry, on the contrary, has a language peculiar to itself; to which almost every one, that has written, has added something by enriching it with foreign idioms and derivatives: Nay sometimes words of their own composition or invention. Shakespear and Milton have been great creators this way; and no one more licentious than Pope or Dryden, who perpetually borrow expressions from the former. Let me give you some instances from Dryden, whom every body reckons a great master of our poetical tongue.——Full of *museful mopeings*—unlike the *trim* of love—a pleasant *beverage*—a *roundelay* of love— stood silent in his *mood*—with knots and *knares* deformed —his *ireful mood*—in proud *array*—his *boon* was granted— and *disarray* and shameful rout—*wayward* but wise—*furbished* for the field—the *foiled dodderd* oaks—*disherited*— *smouldring* flames—*retchless* of laws—*crones* old and ugly —the *beldam* at his side—the *grandam-hag*—*villanize* his Father's fame.——But they are infinite: And our language not being a settled thing (like the French) has an undoubted right to words of an hundred years old, provided antiquity have not rendered them unintelligible. In truth, Shakespear's language is one of his principal beauties; and he has no less advantage over your Addisons and Rowes in this, than in those other great excellencies you mention. Every word in him is a picture.[418]

The assumption of Shakespeare's poetic superiority, and the use of the word 'licentious' to describe Dryden's and Pope's borrowings, sound a new note—a newer note than Gray's borrowings, in his own poetry, did. It is clear from the tone of 'every body reckons a great master of our poetical tongue' that Gray had realized that Pope's and even Dryden's essentially patronizing view of Shakespeare was not a just one. He went on in the same letter to quote eight lines from *Richard III*, and to say that they appeared to him 'untranslatable; and if this be the case, our language is greatly degenerated' —'an astounding pronouncement to complacent 18th-century readers', as Professor J. W. H. Atkins has remarked.[419] West's reply is as intelligent and far-seeing as Gray's letter to him; indeed, his extant letters as a whole strongly suggest that Gray did not overrate him, that he had a wholly good influence on him, and that his early death may have been a serious loss to English literature.

It is hard to estimate the intellectual as well as the emotional force of the blow that West's death dealt Gray. He cannot have valued Mason nearly as much, but he was kind to him (as poets nearly always have been to the inferior poetry of their admirers), and his letters to him contain some of the best of his later criticism. Shrewdly picking to pieces a 'serious ode' of Mason's in 1758, he suddenly launched into a peroration that is at once brilliantly self-analytical and diagnostic of the difficulties that assailed not only the poets of his time but also the responsible ones of our own:

> extreme conciseness of expression, yet pure, perspicuous, & musical, is one of the grand beauties of lyric poetry. this I have always aimed at, & never could attain. the necessity of rhyming is one great obstacle to it: another & perhaps a stronger is that way you have chosen of casting down your first Ideas carelessly & at large, and then clipping them here & there and forming them at leisure. this method after all possible pains will leave behind it in some places a *laxity*, a diffuseness. the frame of a thought (otherwise well invented, well-turned, & well-placed) is often weaken'd by it. do I talk nonsense? or do you understand me? I am persuaded, what I say, is true *in my head*, whatever it may be in *prose*, for I do not pretend to write prose.[420]

This should be taken together with extracts from two other letters written in the same period of his life, to Wharton and to Mason respectively. Wharton had lost a child, and asked Gray to compose an epitaph; the request led Gray to comment once again on his own difficulties:

> You flatter me in thinking, that any thing, I can do, could at all alleviate the just concern your late loss has given you:

but I can not flatter myself so far, & know how little qualified I am at present to give any satisfaction to myself on this head, & in this way, much less to you. I by no means pretend to inspiration, but yet I affirm, that the faculty in question is by no means voluntary. it is the result (I suppose) of a certain disposition of mind, which does not depend on oneself, & which I have not felt this long time. you that are a witness, how seldom this spirit has moved me in my life, may easily give credit to what I say.[421]

And to Mason on 18 January 1759, generously devoting most of his space to his friend's work, he said:

the true Lyric style with all its flights of fancy, ornaments & heightening of expression, & harmony of sound, is in its nature superior to every other style. which is just the cause, why it could not be born in a work of great length, no more than the eye could bear to see all this scene, that we constantly gaze upon. . . . the Epic therefore assumed a style of graver colours, & only stuck on a diamond (borrow'd from her Sister) here & there. . . .[422]

The critical significance of these extracts is considerable. For none of the verse of his time was lyrical in the sense in which Gray used the term; nor can the poetry of the immediately previous generation be said to have been. Gray admired Pope (he met him just before he died, praised the *Dunciad*, and told Walpole that 'Greatness of Mind' ran through his private correspondence[423]—which is exactly what Pope had planned for people to think), but even his poetry is not lyrical in Gray's sense. There is little doubt that Gray, as a critic, agreed with the rhetorical but nonetheless genuinely 'pre-Romantic' prescriptions of such writers as Lowth and Warton; but as a poet he was unable to carry them out thoroughly. His sense of his own inadequacy is clear. But equally clear are his convictions.

On 9 November 1758, again discussing a piece of Mason's own verse, he wrote:

I must not have my fancy raised to that agreeable pitch of heathenism, & wild magical enthusiasm, & then have you let me drop into moral philosophy, & cold good sense. I remember you insulted me, when I saw you last, & affected to call, that which delighted my imagination, *Nonsense*: now I insist, that Sense is nothing in poetry, but according to the dress she wears, & the scene she appears in. If you should lead me into a superb Gothic building with a thousand cluster'd pillars, each of them half a mile high, the walls all cover'd with fretwork, & the windows full of red & blue Saints, that had neither head, nor tail; and I should find the

> Venus of Medici in person perk'd up in a long nich over
> the high altar, as naked as ever she was born, do you think
> it would raise, or damp my Devotions?[424]

This amounts to a plea for a poetry in which more widely varied
forms are integrated with more widely varied emotions; I think the
key words, 'Sense is nothing . . . but according to the dress she
wears . . .', are an early assertion of the 'organic' view of poetry
that has been so familiar to us since the beginning of the nineteenth
century. If Gray had meant, as J. W. H. Atkins paraphrases him to
'insist' 'that the essence of poetry consists not in its subject-matter
but in its treatment'[425] he would not have written 'but according':
he meant, as the example of the Gothic building containing the
Venus of Medici demonstrates, that the form of a poem should be
appropriate to its subject-matter; he does not, after all, criticize the
Venus of Medici (which stands, in his example, for the subject-
matter of poetry).

This is essentially a reaction from Pope and his imitators,
with their propensities for moralizing and for accommodating any
subject in heroic couplets.

But Gray was nearly speaking the truth when he told Mason
that he himself had never attained the kind of lyricism that he
advocated, and Wharton that he did not 'pretend to inspiration'.
And yet he had the faculties of a true poet: the pre-Romantic critical
spirit is more sharply and confidently defined in his letters than in
the writings of Lowth or Warton. But poetry itself came harder to
him than to most poets.

6

Mason found in Gray's pocket-diary for 1761 some lines intended
as a sketch of his own character:

> Too poor for a bribe, and too proud to importune;
> He had not the method of making a fortune:
> Could love, and could hate, so was thought somewhat odd;
> No very great Wit, he believ'd in a God.
> A post or a pension he did not desire,
> But left Church and States to Charles Townshend and
>   Squire.[426]

This, especially the last line, is not very effective. Perhaps it is
revealing that it is not: that this is as far, in a self-portrait in verse,
as Gray could get. The interesting line is the third: an ironic assertion of a capacity for strong feeling is typical neither of Gray's age
nor of his own fiercely reticent public self. It is a clue, however

small, to the importance that he attached to feeling. It is even self-romanticizing, because although Gray was thought 'somewhat odd' (by, for example, the roistering undergraduates on his staircase at Peterhouse, by the riotous young Smart, and even by Bonstetten, who said that he thought Gray had never been in love) this was certainly not because of his capacity for emotion, which he was careful not to show. Privately, then, Gray regarded real loving and hating as a distinguishing mark. But he wrote only one love poem, and this is as insipid as it is falsely heterosexual and uninspired. Since these lines[427] appear to have been written to please her, I should here mention Gray's friendship with Miss Henrietta Speed, the nature of which tells much about his sexual characteristics.

In the summer of 1750 he was at Stoke Poges. In June he sent the finished *Elegy* to Walpole, who circulated it so freely that he found himself suddenly famous. His near neighbour Lady Cobham, her relative Miss Speed, and another friend who was staying with them, Lady Schaub, wanted to know more about the author of the celebrated poem; Lady Schaub and Miss Speed accordingly called upon him. His mother and aunt were at home, but Gray, according to his facetious account of the incident in his poem *A Long Story*, which he wrote between August and October, hid from the visitors:

> On the first marching of the troops,
>   The Muses, hopeless of his pardon,
> Conveyed him underneath their hoops
>   To a small closet in the garden.

However, he was ultimately obliged to return the call, and a close friendship sprang up between him and the gay and amusing Miss Speed. Some time later Lady Cobham, who had brought her up, seems to have been anxious to make a match between Henrietta Speed and Gray; but he was not enthusiastic. On 18 December 1750 he wrote to Wharton, who had heard of his new friendship:

> . . . my Heart it is no less yours than it has long been; & the last Thing in the World, that will throw it into Tumults, is a fine Lady.[428]

Gray's friendship with an attractive, vivacious and intelligent woman meant much to him socially, and undoubtedly it increased his self-confidence—it fully brought out the fun-maker in him—but his words to Wharton are a faithful reflection of his emotional attitude. When, in 1752, Walpole made some (now lost) playful allusion to his relationship with Miss Speed, he replied peevishly:

> I know not what you mean by hours of love, and cherries, and pine-apples. I neither see nor hear anything here [Stoke Poges], and am of opinion that is the best way.[429]

The fact that he ran to the lavatory (or depicted himself as so doing, and in a public poem) to escape her call in the first place doubtless has its psychological significance.

Before Gray wrote the *Ode on the Spring* just before West's death, he had so far as we know written only in Latin (except for the *Agrippina* fragment and a few satirical lines in a letter to Walpole). The first English poem, the *Ode on the Spring*, shows the influence of the *Gradus ad Parnassum*[430]—as much as the verse of Pope and his contemporaries—with its 'rosie-bosom'd Hours', 'Cool Zephyrs' and 'panting Herds'. But it contains a hint of the formal exquisiteness that distinguishes the *Elegy*, and its melancholy is characteristic. In including it in a letter to Walpole on 20 October 1746, four years after it was written, Gray was wearily modest:

> I annex (as you desired) another Ode. all it pretends to with you is, that it is mine, & that you never saw it before, & that it is not so long as t'other [the Eton ode].[431]

The most original lines in the poem are also the most revealing, for they contain a direct statement of the curse that Gray felt himself to be under:

> Poor Moralist! & what art Thou?
> A solitary Fly!
> Thy joys no glittering Female meets[432]

We see here not only a tentative branching-out from the Popeian position of poet-as-moralist, an attempt—however frustrated—to de-artificialize the poetic situation by self-analysis, but also a statement of heterosexual incapacity. This 'Fly'—a comparison that implies self-hate reinforced by contemporary moral notions—has 'Joys' that 'no glittering Female meets'. It is in the following lines, which conclude the poem, that we first encounter the deterministic melancholy into which Gray sublimated his guilty self-awareness:

> No hive hast thou of hoarded Sweets,
> No painted Plumage to display:
> On hasty Wings thy Youth is flown;
> Thy Sun is set; thy Spring is gone:
> We frolick, while 'tis May.

This elegant pessimism is a socially acceptable version of homosexual despair. We are entitled to read it as meaning, in personal terms: 'because my joys are homosexual I am like a fly; I cannot even be a true moralist; and there can be none of the romance of youth for me'. This personal statement is transformed in the last line into a lucubrated sentiment about the passing of time; the shift from the second person singular, when Gray is apostrophizing himself as the moralist-fly, to the first person plural, in which he tries to draw a conventional moral, is clumsy but revealing. The 'rough Mischance' and 'black Misfortune' that figure so prominently in Gray's earlier poems were most potently, for him, the curse of his homosexuality. He paints a contrast, even in this first poem, between 'The Insect-Youth',

> who are on the Wing
> Eager to taste the honied Spring
> And float amid the liquid Noon:
> Some lightly o'er the Current skim,
> Some shew their gayly-gilded Trim
> Quick-glanceing to the Sun

and the fly who has 'No painted Plumage to display'. What is interesting about the poem, then, is not its commonplace theme, but the half-concealed contrast it makes between himself and other youth. He acknowledged in a letter to Walpole of January/February 1748 that the 'thought on which my . . . ode turned' was 'stole'[433] from a poem by the author of *The Spleen*, Matthew Green, part of which he quoted. But Green's lines, which compare human beings to insects, concentrate on their varied fates; Gray concentrates on those who 'show their gayly-gilded Trim', and on himself as fly.

Caution became one of Gray's firmest characteristics, as he showed in the final stanza of his mock-heroic ode on the death of Walpole's cat Selina:

> Not all, that strikes your wand'ring Eyes,
> And heedless Hearts is lawful Prize,
> Nor all, that glisters, Gold.[434]

The *Eton Ode* was probably written after West's death. In this Gray's guilt-feelings are completely rationalized into pessimism, the character of which now becomes more individual. The famous last lines supply another clue to the general nature of the censoring mechanisms of Gray's mind:

> Thought would destroy their paradise.
> No more: where ignorance is bliss,
> 'Tis folly to be wise.

It is not only the boys' paradise that might be destroyed by thought, but also the poet's own happiness, such as it is. Everything personal becomes diffused into a general melancholy; this is scrupulously faithful in its mood to its guilty origins, but it never particularizes.

In the *Hymn to Adversity*, written in the summer of 1742 and sent in a letter to Walpole of 8 September 1751[435] (for inclusion in the collection of six poems that Walpole was preparing), Gray tried to generalize his sense of horror throughout the poem, but was too melodramatic ('Despair, & fell disease, & ghastly Poverty'); in the final stanza, however, he was able to ask the Goddess, Adversity,

> Teach me to love, & to forgive,
> Exact my own Defects to scan,
> What others are, to feel, & know myself a Man.

The emotional simplicity of these lines struck a new, if faint note; read in the light of what we know about Gray's problems, however, they take on an added pathos. For how, haunted by a sense of guilt about his emotional proclivities (whether necessarily or not, I must add, is not the point), could this unfortunate poet scan his defects 'exactly'? His was an unhappy lot, for as a poet he was of the type who is highly conscious of his own processes; he had a passion for exactness—as exemplified in his observations of Nature—but at the same time he knew that sexual or amorous feeling played an important part in the creation of poetry. As he exclaimed to Mason in a letter of December 1751

> . . . you might as well say that the *perfectionment* of poetry would be the rendering it incapable of expressing the passions.[436]

He meant more by 'the passions' than any earlier eighteenth-century writer might have done, and was one of the first poets to revive respect for them.

7

The *Elegy*, although carefully depersonalized, is Gray's grandest and most moving expression of his habit of melancholy pessimism. As a poem it is super-literary in a period that Gray himself well knew needed something unfamiliarly direct, even non-literary; but he partly compensated for this by the exquisite manner in which he stated the 'divine truisms' of which the poem is composed. The *Elegy* comes nearer to liberating true poetic instinct from emotional inhibition by style alone than any other English poem. Cheated of the chance to explore his sexual consciousness, Gray compensated by exercising a non-political and therefore a genuinely poetic and humane indignation about social injustices: the feeling is poetic because it is fully human; it is never prejudiced or sectarian.

Yet Gray knew what he ought to have written about. There is no reason to doubt the sincerity of what he said to Wharton about the poem when he sent it to him on 18 December 1750:

> . . . the Stanza's, which I now enclose to you, have had the Misfortune by Mr. W:s [Walpole's] Fault to be made still more publick, for which they certainly were never meant,

but it is too late to complain. they have been so applauded, it is quite a Shame to repeat it. I mean not to be modest; but I mean, it is a Shame for those, who have said such superlative Things about them, that I can't repeat them. I should have been glad, that you & two or three more People had liked them, which would have satisfied my ambition on this Head amply.[437]

It has been said that the poem is an elegy for West (some of whose own lines are recalled in it), or for Gray himself; alternatively, it has been called an elegy for 'average man'. It would be more exact to say that it is an elegy for both West and for Gray-as-West that has become transformed into an elegy for socially oppressed, 'humble' man: an elegy for a socially oppressed kind of love that has been half-guiltily generalized into socially oppressed 'average man'.

The indignation in the poem, which is considerable, has its unconscious emotional source in Gray's homosexual resentment. The manner in which it is concealed, and yet manages to emerge (as in the rhetorical question 'Can Honour's Voice provoke the silent Dust . . .?', which amounts, among other things, to a protest about certain crass notions of honour), is not at all unlike that in which homosexuality itself is concealed by people, and yet emerges.

Read in the light of this personal history, the *Elegy* becomes more rewarding: as a poem of protest ironically couched in a style eminently acceptable to the taste of its age. The crimes of the humble are 'confined' by their 'Lot', which forbids them to be merciless,

> The struggling Pangs of conscious Truth to hide,
> To quench the Blushes of ingenuous Shame,
> Or heap the Shrines of Luxury & Pride
> With Incense, kindled at the Muse's Flame.

But here Gray reached his highest point. He could not repeat this success—for it is a success. It is easy to see why he became as silent and obstinate as a child when Bonstetten tried to get him to talk about his poetry twenty years later: his conscience remained as fastidious as the surface of the *Elegy*. But his attempts to achieve a poetry of passion and wild strength in the two Pindaric odes and the Norse and Welsh fragments were to fail. He knew what was essentially needed almost as well as Coleridge and Wordsworth did nearly fifty years later; but his constitutional inability to be emotionally direct prevented him from achieving simplicity.

The Progress of Poesy (written between 1752 and 1754) and *The Bard* (1754–5) provide the kind of subject-matter that Gray felt was needed, but they degenerate into melodrama. Gray said to Walpole of an early draft of the first poem that even 'the very best scholars' would understand 'but a little matter here and there' of this 'high Pindarick on stilts'[438]—which was exactly why its readers objected to it when it first appeared in August 1757. By this time Gray had decided to retreat into learning: he knew that the lyrical note he had attempted to strike in *The Progress of Poesy* was not a genuine one. He never really answered the question he posed in *The Progress of Poesy*, 'Say, has he [Jove] given in vain the heavenly Muse?', but retreated into the position he had taken up, by implication, in the *Elegy*: 'Beneath the Good how far—but far above the Great'. His original sexual conflict resolved itself into an attitude of learned defiance against 'the Great'; thus the subject of a never-to-be-written poem was, according to Mason's transcription from a pocket book, to have been:

> All that men of power can do for men of genius is to leave them at their liberty, compared to birds that, when confined to a cage, do but regret the loss of their freedom in melancholy strains, and lose the luscious wildness and happy luxuriance of their notes, which used to make the woods resound.[439]

Gray's own strains were melancholy; his attempts to capture the 'luscious wildness' he felt to be necessary to poetry were technical. Unlike most of his predecessors, especially Cowley (and Pope, whose ode 'of a sublime kind' Gray stigmatized in his notes to *The Progress of Poesy* as 'not worthy of so great a man'), he determined to be neo- rather than pseudo-classical, and to make the adjective 'Pindaric' mean something: 'to make it succeed', he wrote to Wharton on 9 March 1755

> I am persuaded the Stanza's must not consist of above 9 lines each at the most. Pindar has several such Odes.[440]

The succeeding poems are no less tragically artificial, despite their attempts to draw verve from unfamiliar Welsh and Scandinavian sources. On 25 February 1768 he wrote to Walpole about a new edition of his poems, and referred to *The Fatal Sisters* and *The Descent of Odin* as 'two ounces of snuff'. He went on to explain that he liked himself better when he could write, but 'if I do not write much, it is because I cannot'.[441]

He had the skill to turn out acceptable stuff (such as his ode on the Installation of the new Chancellor of Cambridge University in 1769, a turgid piece written for duty's sake), but not the disingenuousness. The thinness of his output is not hard to explain: it lies in a combination of guilty passion and poetic integrity. His one wholeheartedly emotional gesture he made, not with a pen to a piece of paper, but to a human being: the young Bonstetten,

I

Wordsworth struggled throughout his life with a violent aversion to letter-writing.[442] In the first letter he wrote to de Quincey, on 29 July 1803, he calls himself 'the most lazy and impatient Letter-writer in the world',[443] and alludes—not for the first time in his life—to his habit of beginning a letter neatly and ending it illegibly. In 1838 he told a correspondent 'I never set any value upon my Letters . . . it has ever been my wish that they should be destroyed as soon as read'.[444] He frequently pointed out that 'I do not write any letters except on business, not even to my dearest friends'.[445] This aversion has, as I shall show, a special significance.

It is fortunate that his sister Dorothy enjoyed writing letters, and that many of those she wrote were about—some might even be said to have been on behalf of—him; what she said may usually be taken to express her brother's views.

Unlike Coleridge's passionately introspective letters, Wordsworth's, even taken in conjunction with Dorothy's more spontaneous ones, give little account of his inner life—perhaps with good reason, if we assent to F. W. Bateson's assertion that 'Wordsworth's soul was not less sick than Coleridge's . . . but more sick'.[446] Nevertheless, much may be inferred from them, all of it supporting Bateson's brilliantly revealing thesis.

William Wordsworth was born in 1770 at Cockermouth in Cumberland, the second of five children. Dorothy, the only girl, was born twenty months later. His father was a lawyer employed as steward and general factotum to Sir James Lowther, a powerful and unpopular local political magnate. When Wordsworth's father died, in 1783, Lowther owed him over £4000; his heirs were unable to regain the money until nineteen years had passed. When his mother died in 1778, William was sent to live with his disagreeable maternal grandparents in Penrith, on the other side of the county. Dorothy was sent to Halifax, and he did not see her at all for nine years, and then only for short periods. He went off to Cambridge a few weeks after she returned to Penrith in the summer of 1787.

Wordsworth was unhappy with the Cooksons, his grandparents, but happy at Hawkshead School under the guidance of its poetry-loving and enlightened headmaster, William Taylor, who died young, while Wordsworth was still his pupil.

While at St. John's College, Cambridge, he visited Italy, Germany, Switzerland and France (1790); in 1791, after taking his degree, he returned to France, where he met Marie Anne (Annette) Vallon. He had a love-affair with her, and she gave birth to his daughter, Anne-Caroline, in December 1792. Before Christmas he was back in London; because of the war with France, if for no other reason, he was unable to rejoin Annette Vallon, whom he had certainly promised to marry. After 1792 and for most of the rest of this decade his political opinions were radical.

After three years of indeterminate wandering William settled down with his sister at Racedown Lodge, in Dorset, in September 1795. In this year he met Coleridge, probably at Bristol. Two years later Wordsworth and Dorothy moved to Alfoxden House, in Somerset. In 1798 they joined Coleridge and a friend on a trip to Germany; while Coleridge travelled the Wordsworths settled at Goslar, Hanover. All three were back in England by April 1799.

By the beginning of the next century the Wordsworths were settled in Dove Cottage, Grasmere, the parish of which they never left. In 1802, after a visit (in the company of Dorothy) to France to see Annette Vallon and his daughter, Wordsworth married Mary Hutchinson, with whom and with whose family he had been acquainted since early childhood. Mary had been a frequent companion of his university years, and was a close friend of Dorothy's. Mary's sister, Sara (Coleridge's 'Asra'), was not at first permanently at Dove Cottage—occasionally she was away, looking after her farming brothers—but was nevertheless considered as an integral part of the household. Until 1804 the Coleridges were near neighbours.

By this time Wordsworth had published *An Evening Walk* and *Descriptive Sketches* (1793), *Lyrical Ballads* (1798), anonymously with Coleridge, and the revised two-volume *Lyrical Ballads* (1800) with its famous Preface. He had begun the *Prelude* (completed in 1805, but never published in his lifetime), and written scraps of *The Recluse*, a long philosophical poem which he never finished. Coleridge's intimacy with the Wordsworths and Sara Hutchinson continued until he went to Malta in 1804; during his absence John Wordsworth, the much loved younger brother of William and Dorothy, was drowned when the ship of which he was captain, the *Abergavenny*, went down off the Dorsetshire coast (1805). Although Wordsworth lost two children (both in 1812), and his married daughter, Dora, died in 1847, John's death was the severest single blow of his life. John, who had lost money on two previous voyages, intended, wrote Wordsworth in a letter to his friend and patron, the painter Sir George Beaumont, to 'work for me (that was his language), for me and his sister; and I was to endeavour to do something for the world'.[447]

In 1813 Wordsworth's financial security was ensured when he was appointed Distributor of Stamps for Westmorland and part of Cumberland. The area was later extended. This post, which involved collecting Inland Revenue duties, was not the sinecure it has sometimes been called; however, it was worth more than £400 a year. Meanwhile his political opinions had shifted to the right and continued to move in this direction; the process was started by his disillusion with Napoleon. But he had never been a natural radical.

After moving from Dove Cottage to Allan Bank in 1808,[448] and then to the Old Vicarage at Grasmere after the deaths of the two children, the Wordsworths finally settled at Rydal Mount. He continued to write verse until the end of his life, and his public reputation steadily increased from about 1820. On Southey's death in 1843 he reluctantly accepted the Poet Laureateship, although on condition, in Sir Robert Peel's words, that 'nothing should be *required*' of him. Dorothy lapsed into premature senility in 1835, after repeated illnesses; Sara died in the same year. Wordsworth died in 1850, a revered public figure, at the age of eighty.

2

The question that used frequently to be asked about both Wordsworth and Coleridge was, 'What happened?': both suffered a notorious poetic decline—Coleridge after the *Dejection* letter of 1802, Wordsworth after 1806/7. It is now less fashionable to ask this. Coleridge's enormous actual achievement as critic and writer of prose, largely obscured by his own too frequently reiterated sense of failure, has been seen more clearly; moreover, he remained more consistently capable of poetry than Wordsworth. And although attempts to rehabilitate the post-1807 Wordsworth as a poet have been unconvincing[449] and have persuaded few, he is no longer regarded as a political apostate, a man who betrayed his early revolutionary principles by turning into a mindless and insincere reactionary. His loss of poetic power was once facilely explained, by radically-minded readers, as a result of his abandonment of his supposedly revolutionary principles. It is now recognized that his nature was innately conservative—that his early radicalism was out of character. What interests us now are the reasons for it.

But it is true, whatever may be said to the contrary, that Wordsworth did dramatically lose his poetic power: the poet did turn into a preacher. And in so far as we are interested in him as a poet, he provides us with an object-lesson: he exemplifies, with

unusual clarity, a case of poetic decline. How can it be explained?
By alterations in his character, his political outlook, his emotional
attitudes—or by the nature of his experience? Wordsworth's letters—
and those of his sister relating to him—are of great assistance in
framing an answer.

Wordsworth's first surviving letter, written to Dorothy from
his 1790 tour of the Continent, apologizes for 'egotism', and twice
for an illegible hand and a 'desultory style'. A stiff and dutiful
description of Switzerland and the Swiss, it was plainly written
with great effort. Immature though it is, it sets the tone for all but
a few of the letters he was ever to write.[450] He found communication
of this kind a painful duty. Writing to his fellow undergraduate,
William Mathews, son of a bookseller and a frequent correspondent
of his early years, on 3 August 1791 he found it hard to impart
advice—Mathews was at loggerheads with his parents and at a loss
as to what to do with his life—and lapsed into a friendly but im-
personal and unhelpful series of moral platitudes. Mathews did say
that they had afforded him consolation—but this can hardly have
been more than courtesy.[451] Clearly Wordsworth felt that he ought
to give advice, but was unable to do so freely. Waiting at Brighton
to embark for France on 23 November 1791 he wrote again to
Mathews; now the tone is less stiff, for he is speaking of his own
state of mind, and of uncertainties about his own future:

> I am doomed to be an idler through my whole life. I have
> read nothing this age, nor indeed did I ever. Yet with all
> this I am tolerably happy. Do you think this ought to be a
> matter of congratulation to me, or no? For my own part I
> think certainly not.

And once more he apologizes for 'outrageous egotism'.[452]

Clearly the natural habit of the young Wordsworth was to
talk—and think—exclusively about himself, an impulse which
caused him to feel excessive guilt, but which proved irresistible.
There was unusually small difference in Wordsworth—even at this
stage, when he had not realized his vocation—between the self-
expressive poet, the solitary, and the man-in-society: all extroversion
was an effort to him. His dreaminess and what he thought of as his
'idleness' were really early symptoms of the unrealized vocation. In
other words, rather than poetry being his eventual solution of the
social problems posed by his egotism, the egotism and self-absorbtion
were themselves the result of tentative poetic ambitions.

In Orleans he met Annette Vallon, who bore his child, Anne-
Caroline, in December 1792 (she was baptized, and probably born,
on the same day: 15 December). Unless Caroline was premature by
more than two months, she must have been conceived by the time
Wordsworth wrote an important letter to Mathews on 17 May 1793,

from Blois. The odds are overwhelmingly that she had been, that Wordsworth and Annette had become lovers in Orleans before leaving there for her home in Blois, which they probably did in March. But he need not have known by then about the pregnancy. If he ever discussed this affair in a letter, it has not survived. How important was it to him?

The only record that he left of it is *Vaudracour and Julia*, a story inserted into *The Prelude* as an excuse for not including the incident as a part of his own story, and later cut, altered and printed as a separate poem (1820). It was probably written in April 1804; but earlier drafts may have existed. The story itself was suggested to him not only by his own experience but also by an anecdote in a book written by the sentimental radical Helen Maria Williams, whom the youthful Wordsworth had admired. He contradicted himself in the few statements he made about the source of the poem, which, again, he never mentioned in a letter; but his general tendency seems to have been to disclaim originality (and thereby auto-biographical significance).

Most writers on Wordsworth have assumed that he was deeply distressed by his inability to marry Annette. Mrs. Mary Moorman, the author of the standard biography,[453] speaks of the 'storm of passion' Annette raised in him, and Sir Herbert Read[454] writes of the affair as the 'deepest experience' of his life. These writers assume—although they concede that the older Annette doubtless made whatever running had to be made—that Wordsworth was passionately in love with her. But the sole evidence for this is in certain wholly unconvincing lines in *Vaudracour and Julia*, describing the mutual feelings of the two lovers.

Let us now consider the only two surviving letters Wordsworth wrote from France after he had met Annette, of which the one to Mathews of 19 May 1792 is the more important. These were, after all, written on the spot and at the time of the involvement. Since his arrival in Blois from Orleans, he tells Mathews, 'day after day and week after week have stolen insensibly over my head with inconceivable rapidity'. He the commiserates with Mathews over another reversal he has experienced in his personal affairs, and goes on to suggest, with his usual stiffness, that 'resolution' may gain them both a remunerative position in 'the field of Letters'. He asks him to be 'particular' in his answer on this subject, and continues, despite his recent (and doubtless current) sexual experiences, that 'It is at present my intention to take orders, in the approaching winter or spring. Had it been in my power, I certainly should have wished to defer the moment.' He then points out that he would prefer 'a literary plan', which would yield 'a decent harvest'. What he may be implying here is that he has responsibilities which he acknowledges but does not want to fulfil.

It was in Blois that Wordsworth met the French army officer Michel Beaupuy, a supporter of the Revolution. (Annette herself later became an ardent Royalist, and even risked her life in this cause.) Beaupuy's personality made a deep impression on him, and in *The Prelude* Wordsworth claimed that he had been instrumental in changing him into an ardent radical. But he had not felt this influence by 17 May (Beaupuy, however, did not leave Blois until late July), as F. M. Todd has shown:[455] for in the letter to Mathews he refers to the English monarchy as 'a free country, where every road is open', and his discussion of what then seemed to nearly everyone to be the poor prospects of the Revolutionary armies is unconcerned. He ends:

> I shall return to England in the autumn or the beginning of winter. . . . we might then more advantageously than by letter consult upon some literary scheme . . .'.[456]

The most remarkable thing about the letter, however, is that it does not so much as hint at the existence of Annette Vallon, or even at a romantic attachment, or mere obligation, in Wordsworth's life. Now although Wordsworth may not have known that Annette was pregnant—she may not have been absolutely certain herself— we must take it for granted that he was her lover. Doubtless when he heard the news of her condition he changed his attitude to her; but a change of attitude is not the same as, and does not imply, a falling in love. Mathews was a close friend, and this letter, with its continued discussion of old literary plans and its failure to hint at any kind of emotional attachment, suggests that Wordsworth's feelings were not ardent, that Mrs. Moorman's 'storm of passion' is an unwarranted, somewhat sentimental, assumption. This view does not necessarily involve an agreement with Professor Todd's assertion that 'had he never met Annette, there is no reason to believe that his political or poetic development would have been materially different'.[457] On the contrary, his abandonment of Annette and their daughter probably had a profound effect upon him. He may have *intended* to marry her, to do the decent thing, but his legendary good luck intervened for him on 1 February 1793, when England declared war on France. Letters written by Annette to William and Dorothy in March 1793, which they did not receive, show that she expected marriage. The important question is, had he ever really wanted to marry her? There is, at any rate, nothing at all to suggest that he had.

Wordsworth's next extant letter, to his brother Richard, was written on 3 September 1792, by which time he must have known exactly how things stood. He was not on sympathetic terms with Richard, so it is hardly surprising that he did not confide in him. He tells him that he will be in London in September, perhaps for 'a few weeks', 'about my publication'.[458] This visit was cancelled, and instead he went to Orleans with Annette at some time in September, finished *Descriptive Sketches*, the poem based on his Swiss tour of 1790, and then to Paris, alone, at the end of October. As soon as he heard that Anne-Caroline had been safely born, perhaps even before this, he returned to England without revisiting Orleans. He did not see Annette again until he went to Calais, with Dorothy, in 1802.

As we have seen, Wordsworth suppressed the whole incident in *The Prelude*, substituting for it the rather absurd tale—about two lovers who have an illegitimate child—*Vaudracour and Julia*. In this the villains are Vaudracour's parents, with their inexorable opposition to his marriage to Julia. This is parallel to the opposition of Wordsworth's uncles, who almost disowned him when they learnt what had happened. But whatever Wordsworth may have said about his intentions to Annette or to anyone else, we may fairly have a suspicion (it cannot be more than that) that both the war and his relatives' attitude were balm to his secret soul. In the 1805 *Prelude* he wrote

> Reluctantly to England I returned,
> Compelled by nothing else than absolute want
> Of funds for my support. . . .

Later he changed this to

> Dragged by a chain of harsh necessity
> So seemed it—now I thankfully acknowledge
> Forced by the gracious providence of Heaven.

We are told that Wordsworth's uncles 'must' have refused him money to continue in France. But must they? In the 3 September letter to Richard he asked for £20 casually enough, and without giving his real reasons for wanting it. Furthermore, he went off to Paris in October, leaving Annette in Orleans at a time when it might be supposed that she needed his presence (she was staying with friends, in whose house she eventually had the child; there is no reason to assume that these people were so hostile to Wordsworth as to deny him access to her). Nor did he go to Orleans to see her and the child before returning to England—odd, unromantic behaviour for a man really in love. The alteration to the text of the 1805 Prelude may well represent a secretly conscientious attempt to get nearer to the truth of the matter at the same time as appeasing Mrs. Wordsworth's feelings.

3

Writing to Jane Pollard on 16 February 1793 Dorothy spoke of the (poetic) pursuits 'which have so irresistible an Influence over William', and which, she added, 'deprive him of the Power of chaining his attention to others discordant to his feelings'.[459] In this sentence may be discovered the key to one of the most important aspects of Wordsworth's personality. The simple-minded Annette, whether Dorothy was aware of it at the time or not, was essentially 'discordant to his feelings', and to the 'outrageous egotism' of his poetic vocation. He had linked her to him, doubtless at her behest, by that most tenuous of links: sex.

But whatever his state of emotions about her, by the time he got back to London at the end of 1792 he was a changed man in two ways. He was an ardent republican where before he had been a passive sympathizer; and he was equally ardent (as the September letter to Richard from Blois, which speaks of plans for coming to London to arrange for his 'publication', implies) in pursuit of his poetic vocation.

Wordsworth stayed with his brother Richard in London for seven months. He must often and confidentially have written to Dorothy (although they did not meet again until February 1794) because she quoted him in her own letters to Jane Pollard. She was then his only true friend. A letter from Annette of March 1793 shows that they already planned to share a cottage, and to send for her and Anne-Caroline. Dorothy often alludes to this 'gilded cottage' in her letters to Jane Pollard. But William did little or nothing about getting a job. Instead he associated with various radicals and republicans—people he met through Joseph Johnson, the publisher of his two volumes of poems—and made vague noises about attempting to obtain a tutorship. The idea of the Church was gladly given up: 'all professions I think are attended with great inconveniences but that of the priesthood the most',[460] he wrote to Mathews in 1794. Dorothy quotes passages from two letters he wrote to her during his stay in London:

> . . . How much do I wish that each emotion of pleasure and pain that visits your heart should excite a similar pleasure or a similar pain within me, by that sympathy which will almost identify us when we have stolen to our little cottage! I am determined to see you as soon as ever I have entered into an engagement: immediately I will write to my uncle, and tell him that I cannot think of going any where before I have been with you. Whatever answer he gives me I certainly will make a point of once more mingling my transports with yours. Alas! my dear sister how soon must this happiness expire, yet there are moments worth ages.

> With reference to our meeting, this scheme will not at all affect it as in case of my not meeting with any employment we shall probably be in North Wales about the time of your going into Yorkshire and it will be easy for me to see you at Halifax. Oh my dear, dear sister with what transport shall I again meet you, with what rapture shall I again wear out the day in your sight. I assure you so eager is my desire to see you that all obstacles vanish. I see you in a moment running or rather flying to my arms.

Already then, the celebrated bond between brother and sister was forged. Whose company was he really most looking forward to when they all got into that little cottage? Annette's or Dorothy's? There is no doubt about Dorothy's feelings for him. In the same letter, to Jane Pollard, she writes, harking back to her childhood:

> . . . Love warm as fired our [William's and her] little hearts when we built our airy castles leaning upon each others arms in some corner where we have stolen from our playfellows, and where we did not fear to hazard observations which others would have laughed at or despised as foolish and unmeaning. Oh my dear girl it was the language of the heart.[461]

There are similarly rapturous passages in other letters of this time. Williams fully reciprocated these feelings of affection. His sister loved him and believed in him. Until he met Coleridge in 1795, and intensified his ties with the Hutchinson sisters in 1799–1800, no one else did.

Probably Wordsworth's understandably guilty state of mind over the affair with Annette was at least as strong a factor in his new republicanism as the influence of Beaupuy. If his poems of the next few years—and the play, *The Borderers*—are any guide, he was haunted not by unrequited love but by a sense of having sinned, and by the idea of evil. A show of political activism provided a welcome release from this inner moral pressure. Furthermore, republicanism was 'libertarian', and this might provide the only possible justification (in Wordsworth's own mind) for his sexual behaviour; radicalism as a whole must have attracted him partly for this reason. He was probably not as soft on himself as Dorothy, who had told Jane Pollard that 'the Excuse might have been found in his natural disposition'.[462] But both his sexual imprudence of 1792 and his political position—though not his sympathy for the underprivileged—were fundamentally out of character. *A Letter to the Bishop of Llandaff on the Extraordinary Avowal of his Political Principles . . . by a Republican*,[463] written in the spring of 1793 but not published until after Wordsworth's death, is an anti-monarchical answer to a reprint of a sermon with the unpleasant title of *The Wisdom and Goodness of God in having made both Rich and Poor. A Letter*, which could have got Wordsworth into trouble if someone, probably Joseph Johnson, had not dissuaded him from publishing it, is not an original or convincing work; but it is written with overt passion. As F. M. Todd has pointed out, its arguments closely follow those of Godwin's *Political Justice*, the second volume of which had recently been issued.[464] It would be wrong, in view of its dependence on other writings, to use the *Letter* as a demonstration of Wordsworth's intellectual development; it is rather evidence of the theoretical position he convinced himself he had reached.

His hatred of the war, which he retrospectively overemphasized in *The Prelude*, for obvious reasons, did not prevent its being for him, in Professor Todd's words, 'a not unrelieved catastrophe', since it enabled him to defer his plans and hopes (if they were, even consciously, hopes) for the future with Annette.

On 17 February 1794, temporarily reunited with Dorothy at Keswick, Wordsworth told William Mathews that he still did not know what he was going to do.[465] *A Letter to the Bishop of Llandaff . . .*, the first version of *Guilt and Sorrow*—the result of experiences during a solitary walk across Salisbury Plain in the summer of 1793—the Godwinian *The Convict*, were behind him. On 23 May 1794 he replied to a proposition of Mathews's that they should start a monthly magazine. Clearly it was going to be uncompromisingly radical:

> You mention the possibility of setting on foot a monthly Miscellany from which some emolument might be drawn. I wish, I assure you most heartily, to be engaged in something of that kind; and if you could depend on the talents, and above all the industry of the young man you speak of, I think we three would be quite sufficient with our best exertions to keep alive such a publication. But, as you say, how to set it afloat!
>
> I am so poor that I could not advance anything, and I am afraid you are equally unable to contribute in that way! Perhaps however this might be got over if we could be sure of the patronage of the public. I do not see that my being in the country would have any tendency to diminish the number or deduct from the value of my communications. It would only prevent me from officiating as an editor; and, as you are I suppose both resident in Town, that circumstance would not be of much consequence. I wish much to hear further from you on this head, as I think if we could once raise a work of this kind into any reputation it would really be of consequence to us both.

But much is to be attended to before we enter the field. What class of readers ought we to aim at procuring; in what do we, each of us, suppose ourselves the most able, either to entertain or instruct?

Of each other's political sentiments we ought not to be ignorant; and here at the very threshold I solemnly affirm that in no writings of mine will I ever admit of any sentiment which can have the least tendency to induce my readers to suppose that the doctrines which are now enforced by banishment, imprisonment, &c, &c, are other than pregnant with every species of misery. You know perhaps already that I am of that odious class of men called democrats, and of that class I shall for ever continue. In a work like that of which we are speaking, it will be impossible, (and indeed it would render our publication worthless, were we to attempt it,) not to inculcate principles of government and forms of social order of one kind or another. I have therefore thought it proper to say this much in order that if your sentiments—or those of our coadjutor—are dissimilar to mine, we may drop the scheme at once. Besides essays on Morals and Politics, I think I could communicate critical remarks upon Poetry, &c, &c, upon the arts of Painting, Gardening, and other subjects of amusement. But I should principally wish our attention to be fixed upon Life and Manners, and to make our publication a vehicle of sound and exalted Morality.

He then mentions his two published poems:

. . . I am correcting and considerably adding to those poems which I published in your absence. It was with great reluctance I huddled up those two little works and sent them into the world in so imperfect a state. But as I had done nothing by which to distinguish myself at the University, I thought these little things might show that I could do something.[466]

Wordsworth had said, in *A Letter to the Bishop of Llandaff* . . . that political enquiry was 'the most fruitful field of human knowledge'; there can be no doubt that he thought he meant it. Furthermore, he was, ostensibly, politically-minded throughout his life, and in 1833 told an American visitor that he had given 'twelve hours thought to the conditions and prospects of society, for one to poetry'.

But this side of Wordsworth was never an essential one; nor, as I have suggested, was his republicanism as intimately bound up with his early poetic inspiration as critics used to make out. The letter to Mathews of 23 May 1794 shows that he felt himself to be a convinced and idealistic republican and (ironically 'odious') democrat, but not that his poetry was bound up with it. The framework of *Guilt and Sorrow* (*Salisbury Plain*) is political, and so is that of *The Convict*; but what is poetically interesting in the poems is non-political. True, Wordsworth told Francis Wrangham that *Salisbury Plain* had been written 'partly to expose the vices of the penal law and the calamities of war as they affect individuals';[467] but the real interest, and that of *The Convict*, lies in the poet's description of the behaviour of oppressed individuals. Nor is the tragedy, *The Borderers* (1795), primarily political: it deals with the problem of evil; and the problem, whether cast in an anti-Godwinian mould or not—there is controversy on the point—is Wordsworth's own.[468]

The weakness of these pre-Coleridge poems is, in fact, that the author's poetic impulse is directed into irrelevant political channels: he believes that his poetic inspiration is political, but it is not. His real subject (though he did not know it) was already the social outcast: the vagrant, the convict—the poet himself, the outrageous egotist 'doomed to be an idler'. And the value of the poems lies in their exploration of the theme of individuals being acted upon, by adverse circumstances, to produce evil.

For much of his life, however, Wordsworth did use the respectability, the social propriety, of holding 'political' views as a device to hide his less public-minded, more subversive, poetic interests. That as a poet pure and simple he had been 'Most pleased when most uneasy',[469] that his inspiration derived from kinds of uneasiness, always disturbed his consciousness. One might say that the intentions of *The Prelude*, which is, structurally, an anti-poem, are to disguise the relationship of the poetry to the uneasiness. The 'pantheistic' doctrine of *The Prelude* (1805), worked out by Wordsworth and superimposed on to the material of his experience, is artificial and unpoetic in the sense that it is a philosophical afterthought, part of the too self-conscious development of 'the philosophic mind'. There is a passage in a letter to Mathews of 7 November 1794 that flatly contradicts this famous doctrine—a doctrine that is central only in the sense that it is imposed as such. Wordsworth was nursing his friend Raisley Calvert in Keswick; he expected him to die (he did so in January 1795, leaving Wordsworth £900); he had grown more wary of the idea of starting a radical magazine (called *The Philanthropist*)—'The more nearly we approached the time fixed for action, the more strongly was I persuaded that we should decline the field.'—and he could not in any case leave the dying Calvert. Then, towards the end of this letter, he wrote:

I begin to wish much to be in Town. Cataracts and mountains are good occasional society, but they will not do for constant companions. . . . This is a country for poetry it is true; but the muse is not to be won but by the sacrifice of time, and time I have not to spare.[470]

This more than reflects a passing mood of despondency about poetry: it again suggests that Wordsworth was determined to put his energies into political activism, as an escape from the disturbing propensities of poetry. A few weeks later, however, presumably replying to a suggestion of Mathews that he should become a parliamentary reporter, he says that his 'nervous headaches . . . when exposed to a heated atmosphere' would disqualify him from this.[471]

By the time he settled down with Dorothy at Racedown Lodge in September 1795 Wordsworth had met Coleridge. Under the daily influence of Dorothy, and of Coleridge's intelligent hero-worship, he began a remarkable spate of poetic activity. His poems now became less ostensibly political. The Juvenalian satire he wrote in collaboration with his friend Francis Wrangham, some of which is included in letters to him of 20 November 1795[472] and of *c.* 25 February 1796[473] is utterly uncharacteristic, ineffective and laboured —and was never published by Wordsworth. His tone about politics in the letters to Wrangham is not intense, but mechanical and casual—nothing like as ferocious as that of his earlier letters to Mathews, when he had needed to substitute political passion for guilt in order to survive emotionally. But he was not through with emotional crises: the continuous society of Dorothy, the excitement of friendship with Coleridge, plunged him into the intense disturbance of poetic creation at its height.

4

By 5 March 1798, when Dorothy wrote to Mary Hutchinson from Alfoxden, Wordsworth was hard at work expanding *The Ruined Cottage*, which he later wove into the first book of *The Excursion* (1814). He completed the first draft, now lost, in the spring of 1797. Dorothy told Mary that he had been unwell and weak, but was now better:

> His faculties seem to expand every day—he composes with much more facility than he did, as to the *mechanism* of poetry, and his ideas flow faster than he can express them.[474]

Wordsworth, then, was in full spate. But did he enjoy writing?
The letters of 1798–1804 are full of evidence suggesting that

composition, for a reason never divulged by him, imposed an enormous, nearly intolerable strain upon his mental and physical constitution. Dorothy had already alluded to his weakness and 'langour' in her letter to Mary. Now, writing to James Tobin, brother of the dramatist John Tobin, on 6 March 1798 from Alfoxden, Wordsworth himself said, 'There is little need to advise me against publishing; it is a thing which I dread as much as death itself'. This was at a time when he was, as he said in the same letter, writing 'a poem in which I contrive to convey most of the knowledge of which I am possessed'[475] (the projected *Recluse*), and when he was, as he told Joseph Cottle, publisher of *Lyrical Ballads*, 'very rapidly adding to my stock of poetry'.[476] Was there an emotional reason, going far beyond fear of censure, that accounted for this dread of publication?

Lyrical Ballads was published anonymously in September 1798, only a few days before Wordsworth, Dorothy, Coleridge and his friend Chester left for Germany. Wordsworth's attitude was one of doubt; the spur to publication had come from Coleridge, who acted throughout on Wordsworth's behalf. If he mentioned the volume to Henry Gardiner in a letter from Germany[477] in such a way as to suggest that he did not dread publication quite as much as death, when back in England, at Sockburn, on 27 July 1799, he told Cottle in a postscript,

> My aversion from publication increases every day, so much so, that no motives whatever, nothing but pecuniary necessity, will, I think, ever prevail upon me to commit myself to the press again. . . .[478]

and shortly afterwards, enraged by Southey's enviously hostile review in the *Critical Review*, he again emphasized to Cottle that he had 'published these poems for money and money alone'.[479]

Wordsworth's dislike of any kind of adverse criticism is not alone enough to account for this; besides, at this period of his life he could tolerate a greater measure of criticism than he ever could later.

After the Wordsworths had parted (amicably) from Coleridge and his friend in Germany, they went to the 'lifeless town' of Goslar. In a letter of 14 or 21 December 1798, all in Dorothy's hand but partly dictated by Wordsworth, he spoke of being prevented from writing by

> an uneasiness at my stomach and side, with a dull pain about my heart. I have used the word pain, but uneasiness and heat are words which more accurately express my feeling—at all events it renders writing unpleasant.

The letter goes on to quote two of the best known of the 'Lucy' poems, written in Goslar, in early versions that are not as familiar as they should be.[480] These will be discussed later. It is worth noting here, however, that Wordsworth considered Coleridge's criticisms of them (which have not survived) and of the other verse Dorothy had transcribed in the letter as 'in general . . . just'.[481]

On returning to England the Wordsworths visited Mary Hutchinson at Stockburn, and then settled into Dove Cottage. William's poetic activity continued unabated. He was getting on with parts of what would become *The Prelude* as well as writing many other poems. Yet on Christmas Eve 1799 he told Coleridge 'Composition I find invariably pernicious to me, and even penmanship if continued for any length of time at one sitting'.[482] This intense and oft-repeated idea of composition as pernicious rather than laborious or difficult is revealing. He means that it made him feel ill. In a long letter of 10 September 1800 to her old friend Jane, *nee* Pollard, now Marshall, Dorothy spoke of William's bad health.

> . . . since our arrival in England . . . he writes with so much feeling and agitation that it brings on a sense of pain and internal weakness about the left side and stomach, which now often makes it impossible for him to write when he is in mind and feelings in such a state that he could do it without difficulty.[483]

In a letter of 29 April 1801 to Mary Hutchinson, enclosing a new Lucy poem ('I travell'd among unknown men'), Dorothy remarked that William was better through taking a 'stomachic medicine', but that his digestion was 'still very bad',

> he is always very ill when he tries to alter an old poem, but new composition does not hurt him so much. I hope he will soon be able to work without hurting himself.[484]

References to difficulties over both composition and the manual act of writing continue. After his marriage, during the tour of Scotland he made with Dorothy and Coleridge in August/September 1803, he suffered from melancholy and moodiness. Even Coleridge, himself sick, noticed it and recorded it.[485]

On his return Wordsworth wrote to Sir George Beaumont— an indifferent painter but a good friend and generous patron to Coleridge and, more especially, to Wordsworth—on 14 October 1803, excusing himself for not having written earlier:

> Owing to a set of painful and uneasy sensations which I have, more or less, at all times about my chest, from a disease which chiefly affects my nerves and digestive organs, and which makes my aversion from writing little less than madness, I deferred writing to you. . . . I do not know

from what cause it is, but during the last three years I
have never had a pen in my hand for five minutes, before
my whole frame becomes one bundle of uneasiness; a
perspiration starts out all over me, and my chest is oppressed
in a manner which I cannot describe. . . .

At the same time as he was enduring this ill health—it was tantamount to a condition that made writing poetry nearly impossible—
his political views were undergoing a change. England was daily
expecting a French invasion. Wordsworth tells Sir George Beaumont,
in the same letter:

They are sadly remiss at Keswick in putting themselves to
trouble in defence of the country. . . . At Grasmere we
have turned out almost to a man. We are to go to Ambleside
on Sunday to be mustered, and put on, for the first time,
our military apparel.[486]

The revolutionary, anti-Establishment young man has almost disappeared: he reacts to the Napoleonic threat in a perfectly normal,
patriotic manner.

The aversion to writing continued into 1804. On 6 March
1804 he told de Quincey of the 'unpleasant feelings which I have
connected with the act of holding a pen. . . .'[487] After this such
references, in Dorothy's and William's letters, abruptly cease,
suggesting that the condition passed. He had settled into marriage.
Yet it was during the years of feeling ill that Wordsworth wrote the
vast majority of his best poems. *Vaudracour and Julia*, a poem that
entirely fails to deal with the issues of personal guilt that lie behind
its conception, was written in the late spring of 1804—at just about
the time the newly married Wordsworth's health, at any rate from
the evidence of the letters, began to improve. And in the February
of 1804, under the influence of conversations with Coleridge, he
wrote the confused, half-despondent—but later conventionalized—
first version of *Ode to Duty*. The subject is significant. It is now
time to investigate the causes of Wordsworth's six-year period of
uneasiness and nervous illness.

5

F. W. Bateson had already supplied the main part of the answer.
His *Wordsworth: A Reinterpretation* is among the best of biographical
studies of English poets: its combination of scholarly discipline and
critical intuition is exemplary. Bateson's thesis is, briefly, that by
1798–9, when he was in Goslar, Wordsworth discovered to his
horror that, after increasing intellectual and emotional intimacy, he

physically desired his sister and that she reciprocated his feelings. The Lucy poems he interprets as a symbolic 'killing off' of Dorothy-as-sexual-guilt-object. His identification of Lucy with Dorothy is conclusive. He at no time suggests—and I follow him in this, though with some doubt—that the incestuous passion was ever consummated.

I here follow the main outlines of Bateson's thesis, and am deeply indebted to it; but I elaborate and extend it, and my own discussion of it is of course based on evidence provided by letters. The fact that subsequent writers on Wordsworth, including Mrs. Moorman, have stolidly refused to come to terms with Bateson, have failed to discuss his thesis seriously, must make the un-prejudiced reader highly suspicious. It is not enough for Mrs. Moorman to remark, without mentioning Bateson, that there is no need to read what she calls 'morbid implications' into evidence she herself quotes. We can have no hope of understanding Wordsworth's or anyone else's poetry if we are afraid to examine its so called 'morbid' elements. Perhaps a refutation does remain to be made; but it will not, and cannot validly, be couched in terms of shocked horror. Poetry is beyond this: it deals with invisible as well as visible realities, and considerations of it must preclude all varieties of neurotically genteel, pre-Freudian susceptibility as well as merely thoughtless sensationalism.

Wordsworth's lifelong condition, as Bateson suggests, was nearer to solipsism than egotism. Human contact such as that implied in writing letters was, as we have seen, an effort to him. Indeed, the value of his best poetry lies largely in its revelations about what may be called the solipsist aspect of the human condition: about man's loneliness. He was an extraordinarily lucky man; he was also, at least in ordinary terms, an abominably selfish one. A great part of his luck consisted in his ability to collect people around him, mostly women, who enjoyed servilely ministering to his needs. Their enjoyment is not wholly attractive or praiseworthy. But Bateson's thoroughgoing revelation of the formidability of the problem the poet had to solve, detailed examinations of his later Toryism such as F. M. Todd's, and Mrs. Moorman's careful investigations of the facts of his later life, have all helped to show that he was not always simply a dishonourable political apostate who lapsed into a reprehensible Toryism.

Nevertheless, after about 1810 he was not, and cannot be represented as, an altogether agreeable figure. I have more or less ignored his later letters in this study—because they have no bearing on poetry: Wordsworth's later verse, with the exception of odd tiny oases, had no bearing on poetry. It is lifeless, lacking in tension, prosy, sermonizing, smug. He reached his lowest level, perhaps, in the *Sonnets upon the Punishment of Death* (1839-40)—not because their arguments are in favour of capital punishment (although this, as a poetic theme, is surely bad enough), but because they are deplorably unpoetic, dreary and pompous. F. M. Todd has written that a great injustice has been done to Wordsworth 'by loose talk about his attitude to capital punishment', and has pointed out that there is 'no evidence that he opposed the abolition of the death sentence for any crimes but those that are still capital offences today' (he wrote in 1957). He further claims that his poems on the subject display 'consistent humanitarianism'.[488]

Now certainly Wordsworth's attitude—this issue, of capital punishment, is an instructive example—has been exaggerated. But to call the *Sonnets upon the Punishment of Death* 'consistently humanitarian' is misleading: they are, rather, consistently insensitive, because in their eagerness to maintain a rigidly Establishment view-point they ignore human considerations. The notably pessimistic Wordsworth's pious hope that a time will come when mankind will advance to a condition in which capital punishment will not be needed, but that in the meantime we ought to retain it, is a patently insincere means of obscuring his satisfaction with the then merciless *status quo*. The argument that death is not, in any case, to be 'most dreaded', besides being patronizing and hypocritical, is equally insincere. The whole performance is undistinguished, self-deluding and complacent. Furthermore, by not pleading for abolition for lesser crimes than murder Wordsworth shows himself, by implication, as a supporter of retention.

Two of his letters mention the subject. Writing to Basil Montagu on 22 October 1831, he said

> I am decidedly of opinion that, in the case of forgery, both humanity and policy require that an experiment should be made to ascertain whether it cannot be dispensed with.[489]

This may not be evidence that he opposed the abolition of capital punishment for lesser offences; it is certainly not evidence that he advocated it: he grudgingly allows the propriety of an experiment to abolish it in one case. By 3 November 1841, just after he had written the sonnets advocating hanging, his attitude had hardened into one of insensitive and unreasonable ferocity, as his letter to Henry Taylor (editor of the *Quarterly Review*, which printed them, and author of a statistical survey) shows:

> Thanks for your statistical paper; but allow me to say statistics both on this and on almost every other truly important subject are much less respected by me than they appear to be by your judgement. Here is a paper showing that Capital Punishments are much diminished, but not throwing (as how could it?) a single ray of light on the cause. May not that be mainly, not that there is less occasion

for them, but that notions of a feeble and narrow-minded humanity, and spurious Christianity, have spread so as to prevent prosecutions, or have influenced judges in their charges, for instance, Judge Maule in more cases than one, and juries in their verdicts.[490]

The last paragraph reveals an attitude by no means reasonable or humanitarian; we see that in this instance Wordsworth's conservatism concealed a passion for severity that arose not from any serious conviction, but from a neurosis, a private relish for the preservation of severity towards the unfortunate, frightening enemy: the old solitary, his incestuous self. Here, far from a 'consistent humanitarian', is an old man petulantly crying out for blood—in a manner with which readers of the correspondence columns of reactionary newspapers will be all too familiar—actually distressed because there have been too few hangings. He speaks of 'spurious Christianity', but his own Christianity, as exemplified in the depressing sonnet-sequence, *Ecclesiastical Sketches*, was wholly defensive: he loved the Church only because it was a rallying-point for the reaction that played so vitally therapeutic a part in his later life. That his lifelong hatred of injustice and poverty existed side by side with this neurotic attitude is beside the point.

But, as Bateson has suggested, when we understand what the nature of the alternative was, we can hardly fail to admire—if 'reluctantly' (it is Bateson's word)—even this disagreeable later Wordsworth. It is not a question of making judgements, but rather of recording what happened. There is a sense in which the materially luckiest of all English poets suffered, poetically, the cruellest fate.

6

Why did Wordsworth fall in love with Dorothy? One explanation (which, curiously enough, Bateson does not mention—though perhaps he felt, reasonably, that it spoke for itself) is that he did not share his adolescence with her. Such conditions—obviously—remove at least one of the natural bars, the built-in inhibitions, to incest. Then, of course, Dorothy herself was both devoted to him and completely in tune with his nature: some of her early remarks about her relationship with him have been quoted, and there are more in the same ecstatic vein. The passages written around the time of William's engagement and marriage that Bateson quotes from her *Journals* make the repressedly sexual basis of her attachment to him quite clear.

But there is more to it than this. As we have seen, Wordsworth, even the outward-facing man, was a remarkably self-absorbed creature: the external world, with its vague threat to his own existence—to what Bateson in another context calls his 'closed but completely coherent subjective world'—alarmed him. This is really what he meant when he insisted to Sir George Beaumont that 'I am naturally slow in forming new attachments and wish that those about me should be so too, thinking it always the safer side to err upon. . . .'[491] And when he spoke to James Losh of his drowned brother John (16 March 1805) as a man who 'lived all his life with all the deepest parts of his nature shut up within himself'[492] he might have been speaking of himself.

Given this peculiar temperament, then, and having once been seduced from his dream-like state into a merely animal expression of sexuality by a simple, passionate, older woman of another nationality, with financially and emotionally embarrassing results, it was hardly surprising that Wordsworth's sexual energies should become canalized in the direction of his devoted sister: one of his own blood, and in this sense a part of himself. He must have suffered a reaction against all physical sexuality after the Annette affair: his whole life is a prime example of the type of man who can never afford to lose face. So that between 1894 and 1899 his natural (and powerful) sexual impulses, bottled up, were unconsciously directing themselves towards Dorothy. Bateson quotes part of a curious fragment he wrote in early 1798 at Alfoxden, but even he does not perhaps realize its full implications. Mrs. Moorman, who quotes the whole poem, naively suggests that the lines are a 'throw-back to the "gothic" style of his earlier work'.[493] But this is an inadequate comment.

> Away, away, it is the air
>   That stirs among the withered leaves;
> Away, away, it is not there,
> Go, hunt among the harvest sheaves.
> There is a bed in shape as plain
> As from a hare or lion's lair
> It is the bed where we have lain
> In anguish and despair.
>
> Away, and take the eagle's eye,
>   The tyger's smell,
> Ears that can hear the agonies
> And murmurings of hell;
> And when you there have stood
> By that same bed of pain,
> The groans are gone, the tears remain.
> Then tell me if the thing be clear,
>   The difference betwixt a tear
> Of water and of blood.

These are, as Bateson observes, almost the only overtly 'sexual' lines Wordsworth ever wrote. (Nor, it need hardly be added, did he ever print them.) Their confusion reflects a partial recognition of his physical desire for his sister: the last three lines, with their reference to 'water' and 'blood' (which is thicker than water) make this clear. The 'bed of pain' is the bed in which Wordsworth, in fantasies (or dreams), repressed from memory as soon as he experienced them, made love to his sister. The 'groans' are orgasmic; they are followed by tears because, and only because, the lovers are brother and sister.

Poetry does not derive power from the quality of the situations that occasion it, but from the ultimate objectivity, the disinterestedness, of its author's examination of those situations. Wordsworth was an obstinate man, whose poetic conscience might have triumphed over many situations that were, conventionally speaking, morally dubious. But (again Bateson has made the point) marrying Dorothy was not even a legally possible solution. Horror of incest is more or less universal. We do not have to make an effort to understand Wordsworth's sense of horror. Yet whether incest is actually 'sick' must remain an open question. There is no evidence, outside our horror of it, that it is.

Coleridge, who could be extremely stuffy about socially unacceptable practices—for example, homosexuality—said of it, in an 1812 lecture,

> As to infants, they are told, without any reason assigned, that it [incest] could not be so; and perhaps the best security for moral rectitude arises from a supposed necessity. Ignorant persons recoil from the thought of doing anything that has not been done, and because they have always been informed that it must not be done.[494]

Did his surprisingly objective attitude to the subject arise from an earlier intuitive sympathy with Wordsworth's and Dorothy's situation?

Certainly by the time he found himself alone with her in lodgings in the icy and lonely town of Goslar in 1798–9 Wordsworth realized that he wanted Dorothy as a lover. Coleridge, writing to Sara Hutchinson on 10 August 1802 (when William and Dorothy were at Calais visiting Annette and Caroline prior to William's marriage), said

> I seem, I know not why, to be beating off all Reference to Dorothy and William, & their Letters. . . . I wish, I wish, they were back!—when I think of them in Lodgings at Calais, Goslar comes back upon me; & of Goslar I never think but with dejection.—Dear little Caroline!—Will she be a ward of Annette?—Was the subject too delicate for a Letter?—I suppose so.[495]

(The reference to Caroline and Annette has been 'heavily inked out' in the MS.) This implies a subtle, perhaps intuitive, recognition of some suffering endured at Goslar beyond mere cold and loneliness; a realization that William's 'solution', of marriage with respect and friendship, but without love, represented an agony to be endured by Dorothy and William in their lodgings at Calais that reminded him of the situation at Goslar. It has been asked why Dorothy and William remained so long at Calais, and what they did. As William married a few weeks after, it seems reasonable to suppose that they wanted to take this last opportunity to be alone together, as nearly lovers as was possible. Wordsworth, in a fragment of about 1800 addressed to Dorothy, had been as frank as he dared about the matter:

> The dear companion of my lonely walk,
> My hope, my joy, my sister, and my friend,
> Or something dearer still, if reason knows
> A dearer thought, or in the heart of love
> There be a dearer name.

If Wordsworth could be as candid as this in a poetic fragment then it is likely that the sensitive, sympathetic and understanding Coleridge had more than a hint of the real situation. Furthermore, as well as being a declaration of incestuous love (within a polite framèwork), these lines are wholly explicit about Wordsworth's intentions: 'if *reason* knows/A dearer thought . . .' he says. The 'solution' had to be based on 'reason'. We cannot but sympathize. The tension produced in Wordsworth between 'the voice of conscience' (which 'had only contradictory advice to offer', as Bateson says, in telling him to love Dorothy 'when incest is a deadly sin') and subservience to an external authority (the Establishment personified by the Church of England and Toryism) produced his best poems. He did not give up immediately or easily. But it is no wonder that while he was writing these poems, composition seemed 'pernicious' to him, and made him feel uncomfortable and ill. For in the best poems he was trying to obey the voice of a paradoxically sick conscience. I have remarked before in this book that the writing of poetry entails, among other things, an acknowledgement of shortcomings, of evil in the self (in this sense, at least, poetry is strictly non-therapeutic); hence Wordsworth's early aversion to writing—and hence his later, more intense aversion: the 'evil' he had to acknowledge now seemed to go hideously deep. He was no flamboyant Byron, no part-entertainer who needed (in the film-star manner that Byron anticipated) to flaunt his improprieties in the face of an openly shocked, but secretly thrilled bourgeois world.

7

In Devon Dorothy gave Wordsworth the emotional support he needed after the sexual shock of the Annette affair, and in his difficulties over his vocation. It was Coleridge, however, with his penetrating understanding and empathic appreciation of the scope and nature of Wordsworth's poetic powers, who gave him external encouragement and stimulus. Coleridge was 'intellectual' where Wordsworth was not, and if the Preface to the 1800 *Lyrical Ballads* was actually written by Wordsworth it was nevertheless inspired by Coleridge. Wordsworth himself told W. R. Hamilton in a letter of 4 January 1838 that

> The Preface was written at the request of Mr. Coleridge out of sheer good nature . . . he pressed the thing upon me and but for that it would never have been thought of.[496]

Coleridge later criticized sections of it (in *Biographia Literaria*); but the essential point is that although much that is critically vital in it is Wordsworth's own—in that it arises from his own poetic practice —this was formulated only through Coleridge's efforts and catalytic ability.

Wordsworth depended upon Coleridge to an extent that he usually found difficult to admit. After he had ritually killed, by marriage and official embracement of the Anglican Church, the incestuous viper in himself that produced his poetry, he naturally required to pursue his poetic vocation. But since Wordsworth could no longer rely upon Dorothy in quite the same way as he had done, he turned increasingly to Coleridge—who, however, grew increasingly critical, despite his continuing commitment to the idea of Wordsworth as the greatest poet of the age. If we grant that Coleridge had at least an intuitive notion of what was amiss in Wordsworth's emotional life, then his much-criticized persistence in urging him to write the long poem, the projected *Recluse* (to which *The Prelude*, so named by Mary Wordsworth when she published it after Wordsworth's death, was the necessary preliminary), may be seen in a rather different light. The best account of Wordsworth's intentions in this never written poem, which exactly reflect the original prescription, may be found in his Preface to the 1814 edition of *The Excursion*.[497] The *Recluse* was to have 'for its principal subject the sensations and opinions of a poet living in retirement'. One can begin to appreciate what Coleridge had in mind, and to realize that when he complained of Wordsworth's wasting his time on short poems ('. . . in my present mood I am wholly against the publication of any small poems'[498]) he was unhappily aware of the nature of the strains that the 'small poems' imposed. As Wordsworth's official attitudes hardened, as the therapeutic mask became reality, as he degenerated from poet into preacher, he became more and more desirous of completing *The Recluse*: this had Coleridge's approval (so important to him, whatever he pretended), it was 'philosophical', it was written by 'a poet living in retirement'; it might therefore be a legitimate poem. The wish to achieve it became a habit of mind, not only with Wordsworth but with Dorothy, too. Mrs. Moorman quotes some lines addressed to Coleridge from an early note-book that express Wordsworth's dependance on Coleridge for its continuation:

> . . . I seemed to need
> Thy cheering voice, or ere I could pursue
> My voyage, resting else for ever there.[499]

Letters to Coleridge on the subject of the projected poem show how his need to write it increased. When Coleridge was about to set off for Malta, Wordsworth wrote, perhaps tactlessly:

> I am very anxious to have your notes for *The Recluse*. I cannot say how much importance I attach to this; if it should please God that I survive you, I should reproach myself forever in writing the work if I had neglected to procure this help.[500]

On 29 March he wrote again, in the same terms (note the prudent '3 fourths'):

> My dearest Coleridge,
>   Your last letter but one informing us of your late attack was the severest shock to me, I think, I have ever received. I walked over for the letter myself to Rydale and had a most affecting return home, in thinking of you and your narrow escape. I will not speak of other thoughts that passed through me, but I cannot help saying that I would gladly have given 3 fourths of my possessions for your letter on *The Recluse* at that time. I cannot say what a load it would be to me, should I survive you and you die without this memorial left behind. Do, for heaven's sake, put this out of the reach of accident immediately. We are most happy that you have gotten the Poems, and that they have already given you so much pleasure. Heaven bless you for ever and ever. No words can express what I feel at this moment. Farewell, farewell, farewell.[501]

One may even justly suspect that the undeviatingly self-regarding Wordsworth was keener to have the notes than his friend's continuing life. At all events, he made no secret of his need for him, and in January 1805 was telling Sir Walter Scott that when Coleridge returned and settled in a part of the country 'better suited to his state of health, we shall remove and settle near him'.[502] In October of the same year, after the shock of John's death by drowning, 'The expectation of Coleridge not a little unhinges me'.[503]

On 18 September 1806 he wrote to Coleridge offering to come to London to meet him, and admonishing him for not at least giving Mrs. Coleridge a reason for his failure to come north (she was the reason he did not). There is an amusing phrase in this letter, revealing how the Wordsworth household revolved around the poet: '*we* shall have no ease till *I* have seen you' (my italics).[504] When Coleridge did return and after some delays parted from his wife and came to live (December 1806/February 1807) with the Wordsworths and Sara at Sir George Beaumont's Coleorton farm-house, in Leicestershire, the personal and domestic situation proved incapable of carrying the weight of Wordsworth's poetic need. Coleridge was ill and in love with Sara Hutchinson; he was jealous and pathologically suspicious of her regard for Wordsworth, and (more reasonably) of her contribution to the general spirit of self-sacrifice and devotion to William that pervaded the household; he had had morbid sexual fantasies about William and Sara even before he set off to Malta, such as that Mary would die and William marry her; now he fancied—though privately—that he had discovered them in bed together; he was tiresome and demanding in the house. There can be no doubt that he was a serious nuisance.

But the Wordsworths may have been complacent towards Coleridge during this time of supreme crisis. Dorothy hoped, in a letter of 3 January 1808 to Lady Beaumont, referring to *The Friend*, that Coleridge's 'exertions for the cause of human nature (such I may call them) will be animated by his strong sentiments of friendship and veneration for my brother'.[505]

Eventually, in 1810, Wordsworth broke the friendship, not deliberately, but casually: he warned Basil Montagu of Coleridge's tiresomeness as a house-guest. Montagu and his wife passed this on, perhaps with added tittle-tattle, to Coleridge. There was justification for what Wordsworth felt, and some excuse for his indiscretion. The only people who behaved with undoubted stupidity and officiousness were Montagu and his foolish wife, and later Catherine Clarkson—wife of the humanitarian, Thomas Clarkson, a neighbour of the Wordsworths, and an intimate of Coleridge's—with her 'meddlesome talebearing'. But unfortunately Wordsworth, when faced with the fact of Coleridge's deeply wounded feelings, retreated into condescending pomposity and a mood of unyielding rectitude. With no one in his sycophantic household to criticize him for his unfriendly hardness (the lively and independent-minded Sara, more intelligent than her sister, had by now been tamed), his sterile intransigence was allowed to go unchecked.[506] Dorothy's righteous letters[507] on the subject to Catherine Clarkson do her and

her household little more credit than their attitude to their neighbour, de Quincey, when in 1815 he purposed to marry a lady of a
lower social order than himself, by whom he had had a child: the
father of Caroline was 'reserved' on this matter. As it grew older
the household became more and more self-righteous, self-satisfied,
complacent and conformist.

Wordsworth himself wrote little about the affair, the exception
being a letter to Catherine Clarkson of 6 May, 1812, of which only
this part is extant:

> ... I came to Town with a *determination* to confront
> Coleridge and Montagu upon this vile business. But
> Coleridge is most averse to it; and from the difficulty of
> procuring a fit person to act as referee in such a case, and
> from the hostility which M. and C. feel towards each
> other, I have yielded to C.'s wish, being persuaded that
> much more harm than good would accrue from the inter-
> view. I have not seen C., nor written to him. Lamb has
> been the medium of communication between us. C. intimated
> to me by a letter addressed to Lamb that he would transmit
> to me a statement, begun some time ago, in order to be sent
> to Miss Hutchinson, but discontinued on account of his
> having heard that she had 'already *decided* against him.' A
> very delicate proposal! Upon this I told Lamb that I should
> feel somewhat degraded by consenting to read a paper,
> begun with such an intention and discontinued upon such
> a consideration. Why talk about '*deciding*' in the case?
> Why, if in this decision she had judged amiss, not send the
> paper to rectify her error? or why draw out a paper at all
> whose object it was to win from the sister of my wife an
> opinion in his favour, and therefore to my prejudice, upon
> a charge of *injuries*, grievous injuries, done by me to him:
> before he had openly preferred his complaint to myself,
> the supposed author of these injuries? All this is unmanly,
> to say the least of it.
>
> Upon coming home yesterday I found, however, a
> letter from him, a long one, written apparently and sent
> before he could learn my mind from Lamb upon his pro-
> posal. The letter I have not opened; but I have just written
> to Lamb that if Coleridge will assure me that this letter
> contains nothing but a naked statement of what he believes
> Montagu said to him, I will read it and transmit it to
> Montagu, to see how their reports accord. And I will then
> give my own, stating what I believe myself to have said,
> under what circumstances I spoke, with what motive, and
> in what spirit. And there, I believe, the matter must end;

only I shall admonish Coleridge to be more careful how he makes written and public mention of injuries done by me to him.

There is some dreadful foul play, and there are most atrocious falsehoods, in this business; the bottom of which, I believe, I shall never find, nor do I much care about it. All I want is to bring the parties for once to a naked and deliberate statement upon the subject, in order that documents may exist to be referred to as the best authority which the case will admit. . . .[508]

Mrs. Moorman finds this sort of thing admirably objective, and agrees with Crabb Roginson's comment of the time, that 'Healthful coolness is preferable to the heat of disease': the matter, she thinks, had been 'scarred by emotion'. But the good Robinson, who was eventually instrumental in bringing about the official reconciliation, was one of the original Wordsworthians; he had no notion of the kind of intimacy that had once existed between the two men—or of what Wordsworth owed to Coleridge's genius, or of what Coleridge had suffered through ill health, over-deference to Wordsworth, and ill luck, as well as through his own shortcomings. Lamb, on the other hand, thought ill of Wordsworth for his coldness.

One's own attitude to the affair must eventually be determined by whether one thinks intimate friendship, with its manifold disadvantages, is worth while; or whether one prefers polite social intercouse, with its obvious conveniences. The truth is that Wordsworth was by 1810 afraid of Coleridge's natural feeling as well as repelled by his morbid emotionalism; he could not bring himself to make a gesture of friendship. He could not, as we have seen, even bring himself to open Coleridge's letter unless it contained only 'a naked statement'. . . . Coleridge, reasonably, interpreted this gesture—in conversation with Robinson—as *'insulting'* or unfriendly'. Possibly he recognized that Wordsworth's chief motive in coming to London to settle the business was to clear his own name rather than to renew the friendship, for rumours had got about. He had 'begged' that if Coleridge refused to go through with the humiliating ordeal of 'appearing before' himself and Montagu, he would 'no longer continue to talk about the matter'.

Not long after *The Excursion* was published in 1814 Coleridge wrote about it, on 3 April 1815, to Lady Beaumont. He did not think it equal to *The Prelude*, and

I have sometimes fancied, that having by the conjoint operations of his own experiences, feelings, and reason *himself* convinced *himself* of Truths, which the generality of persons have either taken for granted from their Infancy, or at least adopted in early life, he has attached all their own depth and weight to doctrines and words, which come almost as Truisms or Common-place to others.[509]

Wordsworth's reaction to this—Lady Beaumont revealed the letter to him—which called forth a reasonable, soothing and expertly critical letter from Coleridge,[510] should be given in full. The poem Wordsworth spitefully refers to at the beginning of his letter is the admiring *Lines to William Wordsworth* . . . (1807), which had been sent to Lady Beaumont (who did not return it, despite requests); Coleridge printed a depersonalized version of it (*To a Gentleman*) in *Sybilline Leaves* in 1817.

> My dear Coleridge,
>   Let me beg out of kindness to me that you would relinquish the intention of publishing the Poem addressed to me after hearing *mine* to you. The commendation would be injurious to us both, and my work when it appears, would labour under a great disadvantage in consequence of such a precursorship of Praise.
>   I shall be thankful for your remarks on the Poems, and also upon the Excursions, only begging that whenever it is possible reference may be made to some passages which have given rise to the opinion whether favourable or otherwise; in consequence of this not having been done (when indeed it would have been out of Place) in your Letter to Lady B— I have rather been perplexed than enlightened by your *comparative* censure. One of my principal aims in the Ex[n]: has been to put the commonplace truths, of the human affections especially, in an interesting point of view; and rather to remind men of their knowledge, as it lurks inoperative and unvalued in their own minds, than to attempt to convey recondite or refined truths. Pray point out to me the most striking instances where I have failed, in producing poetic effect by an overfondness for this practice, or through inability to realize my wishes.
>   I am happy to hear that you are going to press.
>   And believe me my dear Coleridge in spite of your silence
>   Most affectionately yours
>   W. Wordsworth
>
> I hope to send you the White Doe in a few days. Some prefatory lines have found their way into the Courier, much to my regret, and printed with vile incorrectness. I remain in Town nearly three weeks longer.[511]

After this came *Biographia Literaria* (1917),[512] in which Coleridge, as he told R. H. Brabant in a letter of 29 July 1815, gave a full account (*raisonné*) of the Controversy concerning Wordsworth Poems and Theory, in which my name has been so constantly included—I have no doubt, that Wordsworth will be displeased—but I have done my Duty . . . in . . . compleatly subverting the Theory & in proving that the Poet himself has never acted on it except in particular Stanzas which are the Blots of his Composition.[513]

Wordsworth told R. P. Gillies, on 19 June 1817, with a no doubt affected casualness of tone, that he had

not read Mr. Coleridge's 'Biographia' having contented myself with skimming parts of it; so that you will not be surprized when I tell you that I shall never read a syllable of Mr. Jefferson [sic: Jeffrey's] Critique. Indeed I am heartily sick of even the best criticism, of course cannot humor an inclination to turn to the worst.[514]

He was indeed 'sick of even the best criticism': for Coleridge had dared to criticize as well as praise him. As Mrs. Moorman says, with unconscious humour, 'at no time would Wordsworth have allowed people to pick and choose among his poetry'. Spitefully, egotistically blind to the service Coleridge had once done to his genius, he protested to Crabb Robinson that the book had given him no pleasure: Coleridge professed to write about himself but wrote merely about Southey and Wordsworth; 'the praise is extravagant and the censure inconsiderate'. Even Robinson, in his account of this conversation, felt bound to add: 'I recollected hearing Hazlitt say that Wordsworth would not forgive a single censure mingled with however great a mass of eulogy'.[515]

On 27 December 1817 Wordsworth and Coleridge met, in company, for the first time since 1812. Wordsworth sulked, and Robinson wrote,

I was for the first time in my life not pleased with Wordsworth. . . . The manner of Coleridge towards Wordsworth was most respectful, but Wordsworth towards Coleridge was cold and scornful.[516]

They met again on 30 December, and Wordsworth avoided Coleridge; at one point, says Robinson, 'I heard . . . Coleridge quoting Wordsworth's verses, and Wordsworth quoting—*not* Coleridge's but his own'.[517] That, unhappily, is one of the chief aspects of the relationships between the two men. After 1817 they kept up their acquainceship, and even went to the continent together, with Wordsworth's daughter Dora, in 1828. But the real friendship was gone.

Ultimately Wordsworth made handsome, if posthumous

amends. In 1835, hearing of the death of James Hogg (whom he had not much liked), he was impelled to write the *Extempore Effusion on the Death of James Hogg*, which is an elegy for six rather mixed poets (Hogg, Scott, Lamb, Coleridge, Crabbe, Felicia Hemans), but perhaps mostly for Coleridge. The misery and death of poets was a theme that had always moved him when he was at his most emotional. Of Coleridge he then wrote:

> Nor has the rolling year twice measured,
> From sign to sign, its steadfast course,
> Since every mortal power of Coleridge
> Was frozen at its marvellous source;

> The rapt one, of the godlike forehead,
> The heaven-eyed creature sleeps in earth. . . .

And it should be recalled that, even while Coleridge lived, he tenderly looked after his helpless, hapless, lovable and poetically and critically gifted son, Hartley.

8

It remains to trace the course of Wordsworth's unexpectedly dramatic losing battle with his daemon, from his discovery of the state of his sexual feelings at Goslar in 1798 until the death of his brother and his almost simultaneous final realization that he could not rely on Coleridge to keep him alive poetically, which he expressed in *A Complaint* ('There is a change—and I am poor'), written in December 1806 or January 1807. Bateson marks the real beginning of Wordsworth's poetic decline as the summer of 1806 (rather than 1807, the date posited by Matthew Arnold). This coincides not only with the exact date of the *Elegaic Stanzas suggested by a picture of Peele Castle . . .* (July 1806)—which, as I shall later suggest, is really an announcement of the poetic end—but also with the dawning of Wordsworth's realization that Coleridge could be of no more use to him.

A Complaint was written shortly after Coleridge's arrival at Coleorton. He came back from Malta a different man: white-haired, swollen with dropsy, agonized by his necessary decision to part from his wife and by his thwarted love for Asra; he was too helplessly distracted by his own affairs to act any longer as Wordsworth's consistent admirer and poetic catalyst. Dorothy's increasing disillusionment with Coleridge, expressed in many letters written between 1806 and 1810 (the year of the breach), may perhaps be attributed as much to her disappointment at his decreasing value as a chattel to her brother's genius as to her undoubtedly genuine grief at his unhappiness.

Wordsworth's temperament, unlike Coleridge's, could never afford to question its own properties. Wordsworth was always 'right'. At Bateson remarks, and it is worth repeating, he was 'sicker' than Coleridge: he could not afford to be 'wrong'. It is one of the supreme ironies that he became, for so many early Victorians, a paradigm of virtue; and yet this is logical enough, if only in Victorian terms. Furthermore, although we, as Wordsworth's present readers, cannot possibly endorse the increasing dreariness of the post-1806 poems, we can and should admire the 'resolution and independence' of the best poems of 1799–1806. We can now see them as superbly courageous, as well as being profoundly meaningful on the subject of the innocence of childhood and its loss in adult life. It should be emphasized that the incest *motif* postulated by Bateson does not detract from, or in any way challenge, the various general interpretations of Wordsworth's poems that have been put forward; it merely enriches our reading of them by increasing our knowledge of the poet. And after all, there are few left who believe that 'Incest is so nasty!' is an adequate response.

Wordsworth sent *She Dwelt Among the Untrodden Ways* and what became *Strange Fits of Passion have I Known* (both written at Goslar) to Coleridge, but in unfamiliar early versions that are worth quoting in full. This is the relevant passage from the letter:

> In the last stanza of this little poem you will consider the words 'Long time' as put in merely to fill up the measue but as injurious to the sense—

1

My hope was one, from cities far
    Nursed on a lonesome heath:
Her lips were red as roses are,
    Her hair a woodbine wreath.

2

She lived among the untrodden ways
    Besides the springs of Dove,
A maid whom there were none to praise,
    And very few to love;

3

A violet by a mossy stone
    Half-hidden from the eye!
Fair as a star when only one
    Is shining in the sky!

4

And she was graceful as the broom
    That flowers by Carron's side;

But slow distemper checked her bloom,
And on the Heath she died.

5

Long time before her head lay low
    Dead to the world was she:
But now she's in her grave, and Oh!
    The difference to me!

The next poem is a favorite of mine—i.e. of me, Dorothy.

I

One, when my love was strong and gay,
    And like a rose in June,
I to her cottage bent my way,
    Beneath the evening Moon.

2

Upon the moon I fixed my eye
    All over the wide lea;
My horse trudg'd on, and we drew nigh
    Those paths so dear [to] me.

3

And now I've reached the orchard-plot,
    And as we climbed the hill,
Towards the roof of Lucy's cot
    The moon descended still.

4

In one of those sweet dreams I slept,
    Kind nature's gentlest boon,
And all the while my eyes I kept
    On the descending moon.

5

My horse moved on; hoof after hoof
    He raised and never stopped,
When down behind the cottage roof
    At once the planet dropped.

6

Strange are the fancies that will slide
    Into a lover's head,
'O mercy' to myself I cried
    'If Lucy should be dead!'

7

> I told her this; her laughter light
>   Is ringing in my ears;
> And when I think upon that night
>   My ears are dim with tears.[518]

Bateson has drawn attention to many perplexing features of the published (1800) version of the former poem,[519] resolving them as a scrupulous defiance and exclusion of 'phenomenal reality' (e.g. how can *ways* be *untrodden*?), a method that combines 'positive and negative ideas so that they cancel each other out', by which the reader finds himself 'according a momentary credibility to a non-rational reality'. Bateson's analysis of the finished poem is eminently satisfactory in general terms; examination of some aspects of the first version tends to strengthen his conclusions. If Wordsworth became fully conscious of physical desire for his sister at Goslar, as Bateson suggests, then it must have been extremely shocking to him. His answer was ritually to kill Dorothy off (as Lucy) in these two poems and in '*Three Years she grew . . .*', also written at Goslar. But because of his guilt she must not, in a sense, be allowed to exist at all, but must be represented as a de-sexualized wraith, a ghost, a folk-spirit, *dwelling* among *untrodden* ways.

The final alterations all tend to strengthen this impression. The first stanza is cancelled: its language is too concrete: Lucy is the poet's 'hope', who is unequivocally beautiful (lines 3–4). The other cancelled stanza, the fourth, is similarly concrete, and employs the phrase 'slow distemper'. In the last stanza Wordsworth admits in his letter that 'Long time' is 'injurous to the sense'; but the final version is equally ambiguous, covering up by vagueness the original meaning, which is: 'Lucy–Dorothy, the incest-object, had to be "dead to the world" before I actually killed her off with this poem, because I acknowledge that this incest-situation existed before I realized it: therefore *that* Lucy–Dorothy was dead even then, in the logical interests of the act of total repression of the incident that I am now engineering'.

The other poem is more obviously improved in its final version, but the draft contains revealing details, such as 'strong and gay', i.e. not made ill and depressed by 'unhealthy', distempering revelations. The cancelled final stanza points the biographical moral (Wordsworth rightly judged that the poem did not need it): '*she* thinks that she still is alive, and laughs at my story; but *I* am fearful, because I know I've had to kill off the aspect of her that is the most guiltily potent of all to me; once I was worried that she was dead, and was relieved because I then found she wasn't; now I know she is'. (It is curious that so many readers of the poem should have missed the significance of one aspect of the opening stanza that

Wordsworth substituted for the cancelled final one: why should the fits of passion be *strange*, and why should he think at all of having to *dare* to tell them? It is so 'Wordsworthian' that we tend not to question it.) Implicit in these two poems, and in the version of *Nutting* that is quoted in the same letter, is an anxiety that the necessary ritual death of the beloved moon-inspiress will cut off poetic inspiration. *Nutting* most clearly reflects this anxiety. The 'maiden' of this version must be Dorothy, because in a recently discovered fragment of the poem[520] she is addressed as Lucy, and it is she and not the poet who makes that curiously (in its over- and undertones) sexual assault on the hazels, with a 'keen look/Half cruel in its eagerness', making her seem like 'A houseless being in a human shape'—which is exactly what, as Lucy, she became: a ghost, 'a houseless being', because intolerable in human, incestuous shape. In the published version of the poem, as in the one quoted in the letter, it is William himself who commits the 'merciless ravage'. As Bateson implies, the childhood experience was a shared one: the poet could write about Dorothy or William interchangeably, because they were so close. The violent assault on nature could well represent the unnaturalness of incest, which has been 'committed' by both. This is the version of Nutting (not very different from the received one) quoted in the 1799 Goslar letter:

> Among the autumnal woods, a figure quaint,
> Equipped with wallet and with crooked stick
> They led me, and I followed in their steps,
> Tricked out in proud disguise of beggar's weeds
> Put on for the occasion, by advice
> And exhortation of my frugal dame.
> Motley accoutrement! of power to smile
> At thorns, and brakes, and brambles, and in truth
> More ragged than need was. They led me far,
> Those guardian spirits, into some dear nook
> Unvisited, where not a broken bough
> Drooped with its withered leaves, ungracious sign
> Of devastation; but the hazels towered
> Tall and erect, with milk-white clusters hung,
> A virgin scene!—A little while I stood,
> Breathing with such suppression of the heart
> As joy delights in; and with wise restraint
> Voluptuous, fearless of a rival, eyed
> The banquet;—or beneath the trees I sate
> Among the flowers, and with the flowers I played;
> A temper known to those who, after long
> And fruitless expectation, have been blest
> With sudden happiness beyond all hope.

—Perhaps it was a bower beneath whose leaves
The violets of five seasons re-appear
And fade, unseen by any human eye;
Where fairy water-breaks do murmur on
For ever, and I saw the sparkling foam,
And with my cheek upon the mossy stones,
That like a flock of sheep were fleeced with moss,
I heard the murmur and the murmuring sound
In that sweet mood when pleasure loves to pay
Tribute to ease; and, of its joy secure,
The heart luxuriates with indifferent things,
Wasting its kindliness on stocks and stones,
And on the vacant air. Then up I rose,
And dragged to earth both branch and bough, with crash
And merciless ravage: and the shady nook
Of hazels, and the green and mossy bower,
Deformed and sullied, patiently gave up
Their quiet spirit: and unless I now
Confound my present being with the past,
Even then, when from the bower I turned away,
Exulting, rich beyond the wealth of kinds,
I felt a sense of pain when I beheld
The silent trees, and the intruding sky.—
Then, dearest Maiden! move along these shades
In gentleness of heart; with gentle hand
Touch, for there is a spirit in the woods.[521]

These lines were, said Wordsworth to Coleridge, 'The conclusion of a poem of which the beginning is not written'; but the beginning never was written. The imagery of the poem is highly sexual: his 'guardian spirits' lead Wordsworth into a 'dear nook/Unvisited', an unsullied part of nature. The scene there is 'virgin'. But temptations exist, as the androgynous imagery suggests: the hazels are 'tall and erect', though 'virgin' like a woman. The dual nature of the imagery supports Bateson's view that this was a shared experience, in which Wordsworth and Dorothy were interchangeable. But the final version is written in his own persona, so that Wordsworth calmly enjoys the 'unseen' violets (reminiscent of Lucy herself, who was a violet 'half-hidden' by a 'mossy stone', upon which, here, the poet leans his cheek). Until the startling 'Then up I rose . . .' and 'sweet mood' is preserved, a note of menace being sounded only in the sexually ambiguous nature—the sense that the 'tall and erect' hazels actually suggest a threat to the 'virginity' of the scene— of the description of the 'dear nook'. Some tension inherent in the idyllic situation causes the poet to rise and 'mercilessly' desecrate the natural scene, 'deforming' and 'sullying' it. The act is sexual, rape-like: it is carried out to relieve sexual tension, with feelings of exultation, ecstasy and yet pain. There is relief that it is only a 'nook' that is being 'sullied', but pain at the loss of innocence involved. Wordsworth is fumblingly anticipating the theme, of loss of visionary power, of the 1802/3 *Intimations* ode. Dorothy, the 'dearest Maiden', is exhorted to be 'gentle', to remain in communion with the spirit of the woods, which he has now lost. The place he had 'deformed and sullied' was the 'mossy bower' (the notion of a mossy bower is not very far, but far enough, from that of a love-nest, or, of course, of a vagina) where the 'unseen' violets appeared: one can discern, through the strange ambiguity and psychological incongruity of the whole, that Wordsworth early connected the threat of loss of 'the visionary gleam' with guilty sexual impulses. The place where he makes an essentially innocent communion with Nature, a communion that itself owes so much to Dorothy, is destroyed by a sexual impulse so horrifying that the very existence of sex itself has to be overtly denied (only to emerge in the unmistakable 'underthought', as Hopkins would have called it).

The suppressed eroticism of *Nutting* is truly sinister, and gives a clue to the state of the poet's mind when he wrote it. Eventually he could claim 'I only have relinquished one delight'[522] in order to enjoy Nature again; but by then he was turning himself into official optimist, whose official joy came from iron resolve rather than from inner conviction.

9

Whenever in the period 1795–1806 Wordsworth was being overtly 'political' in a doctrinaire sense, as he was retrospectively in much of *The Prelude*, he was inventing defence mechanisms, preparing acceptable versions of his early life, pretending that sex had not entered into it. But such shorter poems as *Michael* and *The Brothers* (both 1800) were less political than humanitarian: they had their basis in feeling rather than in ideas. There can be no better defence of them than Wordsworth's own, in the letter he wrote to Charles James Fox on 14 January 1801, when he sent him a copy of the 1800 *Lyrical Ballads*. What he says here reiterates much of the 1800 Preface. Coleridge had suggested that letter should be sent out, with presentation copies, to several prominent people, and he himself wrote all of them except the one to Fox, which, as Mrs. Moorman says, was 'Wordsworth's alone'[523] (Coleridge disliked Fox):

> Sir,
>   It is not without much difficulty, that I have summoned the courage to request your acceptance of these

Volumes. Should I express my real feelings, I am sure that I should seem to make a parade of diffidence and humility.

Several of the poems contained in these Volumes are written upon subjects, which are the common property of of Poets, and which, at some period of your life, must have been interesting to a man of your sensibility, and perhaps may still continue to be so. It would be highly gratifying to me to suppose that even in a single instance the manner in which I have treated these general topics should afford you any pleasure; but such a hope does not influence me upon the present occasion; in truth I do not feel it. Besides, I am convinced that there must be many things in this collection, which may impress you with an unfavorable idea of my intellectual powers. I do not say this with a wish to degrade myself; but I am sensible that this must be the case, from the different circles in which we have moved, and the different objects with which we have been conversant.

Being utterly unknown to you as I am, I am well aware, that if I am justified in writing to you at all, it is necessary, my letter should be short; but I have feelings within me which I hope will so far shew themselves in this Letter as to excuse the trepass which I am afraid I shall make. In common with the whole of the English People I have observed in your public character a constant predominance of sensibility of heart. Necessitated as you have been from your public situation to have much to do with men in bodies, and in classes, and accordingly to contemplate them in that relation, it has been your praise that you have not thereby been prevented from looking upon them as individuals, and that you have habitually left your heart open to be influenced by them in that capacity. This habit cannot but have made you dear to Poets; and I am sure that, if since your first entrance into public life there has been a single true poet living in England he must have loved you.

But were I assured that I myself had a just claim to the title of a Poet, all the dignity being attached to the Word which belongs to it, I do not think that I should have ventured for that reason to offer these volumes to you: at present it is solely on account of two poems in the second volume, the one entitled '*The Brothers,*' and the other '*Michael,*' that I have been emboldened to take this liberty.

It appears to me that the most calamitous effect, which has followed the measures which have lately been pursued in this country, is a rapid decay of the domestic affections among the lower orders of society. This effect the present Rulers of this country are not conscious of, or they disregard it. For many years past, the tendency of society amongst almost all the nations of Europe has been to produce it. But recently by the spreading of manufactures through every part of the country, by the heavy taxes upon postage, by workhouses, Houses of Industry, and the invention of Soup-shops &c. &c. superadded to the encreasing disproportion between the price of labour and that of the necessaries of life, the bonds of domestic feeling among the poor, as far as the influence of these things has extended, have been weakened, and in innumerable instances entirely destroyed. The evil would be the less to be regretted, if these institutions were regarded only as palliatives to a disease; but the vanity and pride of their promoters are so subtly interwoven with them, that they are deemed great discoveries and blessings to humanity. In the mean time parents are separated from their children, and children from their parents; the wife no longer prepares with her own hands a meal for her husband, the produce of his labour; there is little doing in his house in which his affections can be interested, and but little left in it which he can love. I have two neighbours, a man and his wife, both upwards of eighty years of age; they live alone; the husband has been confined to his bed many months and has never had, nor till within these few weeks has ever needed, any body to attend to him but his wife. She has recently been seized with a lameness which has often prevented her from being able to carry him his food to his bed; the neighbours fetch water for her from the well, and do other kind offices for them both, but her infirmities encrease. She told my Servant two days ago that she was afraid they must both be boarded out among some other Poor of the parish (they have long been supported by the parish) but she said, it was hard, having kept house together so long, to come to this, and she was sure that 'it would burst her heart.' I mention this fact to shew how deeply the spirit of independence is, even yet, rooted in some parts of the country. These people could not express themselves in this way without an almost sublime conviction of the blessings of independent domestic life. If it is true, as I believe, that this spirit is rapidly disappearing, no greater curse can befal a land.

I earnestly entreat your pardon for having detained you so long. In the two poems, '*The Brothers*' and '*Michael*' I have attempted to draw a picture of the domestic affections as I know they exist amongst a class of men who are now almost confined to the North of England. They are small independent *proprietors* of land here called statesmen, men of respectable education who daily labour on their own little properties. The domestic affections will always be strong amongst men who live in a country not crowded with population, if these men are placed above poverty. But if they are proprietors of small estates, which have descended to them from their ancestors, the power which these affections will acquire amongst such men is inconceivable by those who have only had an opportunity of observing hired labourers, farmers, and the manufacturing Poor. Their little tract of land serves as a kind of permanent rallying point for their domestic feelings, as a tablet upon which they are written which makes them objects of memory in a thousand instances when they would otherwise be forgotten. It is a fountain fitted to the nature of social man from which supplies of affection, as pure as his heart was intended for, are daily drawn. This class of men is rapidly disappearing. You, Sir, have a consciousness, upon which every good man will congratulate you, that the whole of your public conduct has in one way or other been directed to the preservation of this class of men, and those who hold similar situations. You have felt that the most sacred of all property is the property of the Poor. The two Poems which I have mentioned were written with a view to shew that men who do not wear fine cloaths can feel deeply. 'Pectus enim est quod disertos facit, et vis mentis. Ideoque imperitis quoque, si modo sint aliquo affectu concitati, verba non desunt.' The poems are faithful copies from nature; and I hope, whatever effect they may have upon you, you will at least be able to perceive that they may excite profitable sympathies in many kind and good hearts, and may in some small degree enlarge our feelings of reverence for our species, and our knowledge of human nature, by shewing that our best qualities are possessed by men whom we are too apt to consider, not with reference to the points in which they resemble us, but to those in which they manifestly differ from us. I thought, at a time when these feelings are sapped in so many ways that the two poems might co-operate, however feebly, with the illustrious efforts which you have made to stem this and other evils with which the country is labouring, and it is on this account alone that I have taken the liberty of thus addressing you.

Wishing earnestly that the time may come when the country may perceive what it has lost by neglecting your

advice, and hoping that your latter days may be attented
with health and comfort.

I remain, With the highest respect and admiration,
Your most obedient and humble Servant
W Wordsworth[524]

This is a much more serious and genuine letter than the earlier one
to the Bishop of Llandaff. Here he appeals, with the detachment
and authority of a poet in his own right, to a politician. We need
not take what he says literally, that the poems were actually written
in order to show that the poor could feel deeply; but it is an absolutely
justified afterthought. The poems he commends to Fox's attention
deal with individuals; and it is the fate of the individual personality
under the new order—rather than political injustice—that worries
Wordsworth, as F. M. Todd points out.[525] The letter should be
read as a dignified appeal from a poet to a politician to recognize a
fact that politicans tend to ignore; it gives body to the over-
theoretical and sometimes strangled voice of the 1800 Preface. As
F. M. Todd writes, it demonstrates 'that he now sees the political
question as but one aspect, and possibly a minor one, of a larger
aspiration'.[526] Fox wrote a kind reply, but did not like *Michael* or
The Brothers.

In 1838 Sir Henry Bunbury reprinted the letter without
permission; Wordsworth was angry, but told Bunbury that although
he had only a vague recollection of it, he was not aware 'that any
reason exists why I should particularly regret that it has seen the
light'.[527] There was nothing in it, even then, that seemed to contradict the Toryism he had come to embrace. But by 1838 his sympathy for other people had vanished. His dislike of change had
hardened into an unreasoning fear of it. One can tell from what he
said to Bunbury that he was not proud of the letter. Yet he had
cause to be, for it is, as Bateson says, 'a sociological masterpiece'.

Another important letter, which illuminates and in some
ways improves upon both the 1800 and the 1802 Prefaces is one that
Wordsworth wrote to a seventeen-year-old admirer, an undergraduate at Glasgow, John Wilson,[528] in June 1802. Here he re-
stated, in balder terms than he had dared to allow himself in the
Preface, his theory of poetic diction and his attack on the notion of
the poet as a superior being. This, in terms of literary criticism,
really was 'liberal'.

> . . . You seem to be desirous of my opinion on the influence
> of natural objects in forming the character of Nations. This
> cannot be understood without first considering their influence
> upon men in general, first, with reference to such objects as
> are common to all countries; and, next, such as belong
> exclusively to any particular country, or in a greater degree

to it than to another. Now it is manifest that no human
being can be so besotted and debased by oppression, penury,
or any other evil which unhumanizes man, as to be utterly
insensible to the colours, forms, or smell of flowers, the
[voices] and motions of birds and beasts, the appearances
of the sky and heavenly bodies, the general warmth of a
fine day, the terror and uncomfortableness of a storm, &c.
&c. How dead soever many full-grown men may outwardly seem to these things, all are more or less affected by
them; and in childhood, in the first practice and exercise
of their senses, they must have been not the nourishers
merely, but often the fathers of their passions. There cannot be a doubt that in tracts of country where images of
danger, melancholy, grandeur, or loveliness, softness, and
ease prevail, that they will make themselves felt powerfully
in forming the characters of the people, so as to produce
an uniformity or national character, where the nation is
small and is not made up of men who, inhabiting different
soils, climates, &c., by their civil usages and relations
materially interfere with each other. It was so formerly, no
doubt, in the Highlands of Scotland; but we cannot perhaps
observe much of it in our own island at the present day,
because, even in the most sequestered places, by manufactures, traffic, religion, law, interchange of inhabitants,
&c., distinctions are done away, which would otherwise
have been strong and obvious. This complex state of society
does not, however, prevent the characters of individuals
from frequently receiving a strong bias, not merely from the
impressions of general nature, but also from local objects
and images. But it seems that to produce these effects, in
the degree in which we frequently find them to be produced,
there must be a peculiar sensibility of original organization
combining with moral accidents, as is exhibited in *The
Brothers* and in *Ruth*; I mean, to produce this in a marked
degree; not that I believe that any man was ever brought
up in the country without loving it, especially in his better
moments, or in a district of particular grandeur or beauty
without feeling some stronger attachment to it on that
account than he would otherwise have felt. I include, you
will observe, in these considerations, the influence of
climate, changes in the atmosphere and elements, and the
labours and occupations which particular districts require.

And he goes on to attack the 'aristocratic' approach in unequivocally
scornful terms:

... many fine ladies could not bear certain expressions in *The Mother* and *The Thorn*, and as in the instance of Adam Smith, who, we are told, could not endure the ballad of *Clym of the Clough*, because the author had not written like a gentleman. Then there are professional and national prejudices forevermore. Some take no interest in the description of a particular passion or quality, as love of solitariness, we will say, genial activity of fancy, love of nature, religion, and so forth, because they have [little or] nothing of it in themselves; and so on without end. I return then to [the] question, please whom? or what? I answer, human nature, as it has been [and ever] will be. But where are we to find the best measure of this? I answer, [from with]in; by stripping our own hearts naked, and by looking out of ourselves to[wards men] who lead the simplest lives, and those most according to nature; men who have never known false refinements, wayward and artificial desires, false criticisms, effeminate habits of thinking and feeling, or who, having known these things, have outgrown them. This latter class is the most to be depended upon, but it is very small in number. People in our rank in life are perpetually falling into one sad mistake, namely, that of supposing that human nature and the persons they associate with are one and the same thing. Whom do we generally associate with? Gentlemen, persons of fortune, professional men, ladies, persons who can afford to buy, or can easily procure, books of half-a-guinea price, hot-pressed, and printed upon superfine paper. These persons are, it is true, a part of human nature, but we err lamentably if we suppose them to be fair representatives of the vast mass of human existence. And yet few ever consider books but with reference to their power of pleasing these persons and men of a higher rank; few descend lower, among cottages and fields, and among children.

But parallel to this kind of thinking, the result of free and uninhibited feeling, we find Wordsworth already expounding the doctrine of the poet-as-teacher:

You have given me praise for having reflected faithfully in my Poems the feelings of human nature. I would fain hope that I have done so. But a great Poet ought to do more than this: he ought, to a certain degree, to rectify men's feelings, to give them new compositions of feeling, to render their feelings more sane, pure, and permanent, in short, more consonant to nature, that is, to eternal nature, and the great moving spirit of things. He ought to travel before men occasionally as well as at their sides. ...

He goes on to 'illustrate this' by pointing out that his 'Friend's' (characteristically he does not name Coleridge) poem in *Lyrical Ballads* will 'rectify' the 'false notions' of the nightingale that have prevailed (perhaps he was thinking of Fox, who in his reply to Wordsworth had praised Coleridge's poem for this very reason).

The holding of this doctrine was to become a major symptom of Wordsworth's poetic failure. Even his adumbrations of it here tend to contradict the spirit of his attack on gentility:

> . . . nothing is a fit subject for poetry which does not please. But here follows a question, Does not please whom? Some have little knowledge of natural imagery of any kind, and, of course, little relish for it; some are disgusted with the very mention of the words 'pastoral poetry,' 'sheep,' or 'shepherds'; some cannot tolerate a poem with a ghost or any supernatural agency in it; others would shrink from an animated description of the pleasures of love, as from a thing carnal and libidinous; some cannot bear to see delicate and refined feelings ascribed to men in low conditions of society, because their vanity and self-love tell them that these belong only to themselves and men like themselves in dress, station, and way of life; others are disgusted with the naked language of some of the most interesting passions of men, because either it is indelicate, or gross, or vulgar. . . . It is not enough for me as a Poet, to delineate merely such feelings as all men *do* sympathise with; but it is also highly desirable to add to these others, such as all men *may* sympathise with, and such as there is reason to believe they would be better and more moral beings if they did sympathise with.[529]

A poet may consider poetry to be, in the widest sense, educative; but he is wise if he writes his own poems by 'stripping his own heart naked', in his own way, rather than in the person of a teacher. A poet cannot strip his heart naked and at the same time consciously propose to rectify men's feelings; he may, however, achieve the latter (to a limited extent) by eschewing it and sticking to the former. It is one of the paradoxes of poetry. But Wordsworth's conviction that he was a moral instructor continued to harden as his poetic powers decreased.

> It is such an animating sight to see a man of genius, regardless of temporary gains, whether of money or praise, fixing his attention solely upon what is intrinsically interesting and permanent, and finding his happiness in an entire devotion of himself to such pursuits as shall most ennoble human nature,[530]

he wrote to Beaumont on 20 July 1804: the notion of writing poetry
was becoming less abreactive, less painful, more satisfyingly a duty.

It was the self-abasing Coleridge, in resentful mood, who
first diagnosed the disease of the poet Wordsworth, in a letter to
Thomas Poole of 14 October 1803:

> Indeed, I owe it to Truth & Justice as well as to myself to
> say, that the concern, which I have felt in this instance
> [Wordsworth had failed to call on him when he was ill],
> and one or two other *crying* instances, of self-involution in
> Wordsworth, has been almost wholly a Feeling of friendly
> Regret ... I saw him more & more benetted in hypo-
> chondriacal Fancies, living wholly among *Devotees*—having
> every the minutest Thing, almost his very Eating & Drinking,
> done for him by his Sister, or Wife—& I trembled, lest a
> Film should rise, and thicken over his moral Eye.

He went on to say that as Wordsworth's habit of writing a 'multitude
of small Poems' was 'hurtful' to him,

> I rejoice therefore with a deep & true Joy, that he has at
> length yielded to my urgent ... requests ... & will go
> on with the Recluse exclusively.—A Great Work, in which
> he will sail; on an open Ocean ... unfretted by short tacks,
> reefing, & hauling and disentangling the ropes ... this is
> his natural Element—the having been out of it has been his
> Disease—to return into it is the specific Remedy, both
> Remedy and Health. ... I have seen enough, positively to
> give me feelings of hostility towards the plan of several
> poems in the L. Ballads ... he found himself to be ...
> the Head & founder of a *Sect* in Poetry: & assuredly he
> has written ... poems ... with a *sectarian* spirit, & in a
> sort of Bravado.[531]

This is shrewd criticism, although Coleridge was not altogether well-
advised in his attempts to get Wordsworth to write a long philosophical poem. But he saw the dangers of the stifling attentions of
his family, and of his self-assessment as the leader of a school. It is
true that a 'film' did in the course of time 'thicken over his moral
Eye'. Furthermore, Coleridge's desire for *The Recluse* was at least
partly impelled by his desire for Wordsworth's peace of mind. His
solution, the long philosophical poem, was at least as effective as
Wordsworth's own. For, although he failed to write *The Recluse*,
he wrote few more short poems of the kind that were 'hurtful' to him.

By 1807 Wordsworth had become programmatic. He was
beginning to enjoy himself in the role of a great poet-educator, as
this passage from a letter of 21 May 1807 to Lady Beaumont shows:

It is an awful truth, that there neither is, nor can be, any genuine enjoyment of poetry among nineteen out of twenty of those persons who live, or wish to live, in the broad light of the world—among those who either are, or are striving to make themselves, people of consideration in society. This is a truth, and an awful one, because to be incapable of a feeling of poetry, in my sense of the word, is to be without love of human nature and reverence for God.

Upon this I shall insist elsewhere; at present let me confine myself to my object, which is to make you, my dear friend, as easy-hearted as myself with respect to these poems. Trouble not yourself upon their present reception; of what moment is that compared with what I trust is their destiny?—to console the afflicted; to add sunshine to day-light, by making the happy happier; to teach the young and the gracious of every age to see, to think, and feel, and, therefore, to become more actively and securely virtuous; this is their office, which I trust they will faithfully perform, long after we (that is, all that is mortal of us) are mouldered in our graves. I am well aware how far it would seem to many I overrate my own exertions, when I speak in this way, in direct connexion with the volume I have just made public.

I am not, however, afraid of such censure, insignificant as probably the majority of those poems would appear to very respectable persons. I do not mean London wits and witlings, for these have too many foul passions about them to be respectable, even if they had more intellect than the benign laws of Providence will allow to such a heartless existence as theirs is; but grave, kindly-natured, worthy persons, who would be pleased if they could. I hope that these volumes are not without some recommendations, even for readers of this class: but their imagination has slept; and the voice which is the voice of my poetry, without imagination, cannot be heard. . . .

Later in the same letter he seized avidly upon, and thus paraphrased, Coleridge's observation:

every great and original writer, in proportion as he is great or original, must himself create the taste by which he is to be relished; he must teach the art by which he is to be seen . . . my writings . . . will, in their degree, be efficacious in making men wiser, better, and happier.[532]

There is still dignity and poetic intelligence in this. But by the next year he could say: 'I wish either to be considered as a Teacher, or as nothing'.[533] It is ironic but not surprising that by the time

Wordsworth began to think of himself only as a 'great and original' teacher he was capable of no more than occasional and very widely separated flickers of real poetry.

The actual process of self-elevation into the Great Teacher had started much earlier, perhaps almost coincidentally with Wordsworth's realization of the nature of his feelings for his sister. We see the germ of it in the letter to John Wilson. Coleridge had been responsible for the publication of the 1798, anonymous, *Lyrical Ballads*; the pre-Goslar Wordsworth had been afraid of publication, if not as positively reluctant as he claimed. But by 1799 he had become so anxious for the success of the two-volume second edition, which he now regarded as essentially his own achievement, that he was even prepared to omit *The Ancient Mariner*. On 24 June 1799, writing to Cottle from Sockburn, he asks *'what number'* of the 1798 edition had been sold, and adds,

> From what I can gather it seems that the Ancyent Marinere has upon the whole been an injury to the volume, I mean that the old words and the strangeness of it have deterred readers from going on. If the volume should come to a second edition I would put in its place some little things which would be more likely to suit the common taste.[534]

He had once before announced his intention of doing this in a letter of 2 June 1799, again to Cottle.[535] Wordsworth's infamous note to *The Ancient Mariner*, when it finally did appear (relegated to the back of the book), openly and patronizingly begged the indulgence of the public for its 'great defects': 'the principle person has no distinct character'; 'he does not act, but is continually acted upon'; 'the events . . . do not produce each other'; 'the imagery is somewhat too laboriously accumulated'. But he simultaneously awarded himself the 'gratification of informing such Readers as may have been pleased with this Poem' (which he allowed did possess 'many delicate touches of passion') that they owed 'their pleasure in some sort' to him. This, besides revealing a jealousy scarcely justified by Coleridge's attitude towards him, was unpleasantly equivocal: while he did not wish to stand condemned as an opponent of the poem, should it later be accorded the praise that he knew, in his heart, it deserved, he meanwhile enviously half-hoped it would fail.

Mrs. Moorman naively points out that Wordsworth's dislike of the idea of publication stands in 'curious contrast' to his desire that the 1798 volume should be a financial success and justify a second edition.[536] This confusion is explained by the psychological changes that were occurring in Wordsworth as a result of the Goslar experience: his desire for public success and determination to ensure that Coleridge's performance should neither prejudice nor outshine his own, began only after the return from Goslar.

10

But for some time afterwards he continued to write poems that both excited him and satisfied his poetic impulse—even at the cost of his health. He was able to do this when his material was effectively, though not dishonestly, de-sexualized. As he told Wilson, he did not object, in principle, to 'animated' descriptions 'of the pleasures of love', or to the 'naked language of some of the most interesting passions of men'. It was a question of his own special needs.

Thus the sexual element is suppressed in another Lucy poem, transcribed by Dorothy and sent in a joint letter to Mary Hutchinson on 29 April 1801. This suppression makes the poem as strange as the previous four in the group. Dorothy tells Mary that the poem is 'to be read after "She dwelt among" ':

> I travell'd among unknown men,
>> In lands beyond the sea;
> Nor, England, did I know till then
>> What love I bore to thee.
>
> 'Tis past, that melancholy dream!
>> Nor will I quit thy shore
> A second time; for still I seem
>> To love thee more and more.
>
> Among thy mountains did I feel
>> The gladness of desire;
> And she I cherish'd turn'd her wheel
>> Beside an English fire.
>
> Thy mornings showed, thy nights concealed,
>> The bowers where Lucy play'd;
> And thine is too the last green field
>> Which Lucy's eyes survey'd.

This curious poem was pointedly included in a letter to the child-hood friend of Dorothy's who was to become Wordsworth's wife-of-convenience.[537] Was it meant to be some kind of apology or reassurance about Annette? If Mary understood the 'I' of the poem to be William—as she would—then she would immediately have been reminded of his early sojourn in France rather than his shorter German trip. By then she must have known about Annette. William might appear to be saying: 'Don't worry, I love England and you much better than any adventures I may once have had'.

But the poem is certainly very odd. Is the 'she I cherish'd' supposed to be the dead Lucy of the final stanza or not? (He had known Mary long before Annette.) Did Wordsworth perhaps actually convince himself, and later announce to his immediate circle, that the celebrated Lucy, subject of a group of six poems that meant so much to him that he included all but one of them in letters,[538] was Mary's sister, Margaret, whom he had known in youth and who died of consumption in 1796?[539] Or did he allow it to be assumed that this was the case? He broke his rule when he changed the 'Emma' (Dorothy) of *Among All Lovely Things My Love Had Been* (1802) to 'Lucy' in the published version (the earliest version of this was sent in a letter to Coleridge of 16 April 1802,[540] and was acknowledged to be about an incident that had taken place between brother and sister 'about seven years ago'); but this only goes to show that confusion existed in Wordsworth's mind as to whom, if anyone, he should publically acknowledge Lucy to represent. In an early version of the same poem, preserved by Sara Hutchinson, the 'Emma' is changed not to 'Lucy' but to 'Mary'. . . . Bateson asks, 'Had Wordsworth tried to allay Mary Hutchinson's jealousy by pretending that this poem at any rate was intended for her?'[541]

It seems most likely, however, that Margaret provided a useful alibi for his feelings about Dorothy. The subservient Mary herself, ready for a lifetime of service, could not have objected to any of this. All we can certainly know is that Wordsworth himself— according to de Quincey—later maintained a mysterious silence about the identity of Lucy, and that Coleridge, before he had been able to talk personally to Wordsworth about it, guessed that she was Dorothy:

> . . . whether it ['A slumber did my spirit seal . . .'] had any reality, I cannot say.—Most probably, in some gloomier moment he had fancied the moment in which his Sister might die'.[542]

But Lucy has a more than merely Dorothy-function; if she had not, then the poems would not possess vitality. Only 'I travell'd among unknown men' is a failure: Wordsworth was juggling with the truth rather than trying to express it. It is not so important to 'identify' Lucy, easy as it is to do so, as to understand what Wordsworth meant by her, for this helps us to understand her meaning for us. And for us, she is the beloved who becomes an object of sexual appetite and is therefore transformed into 'Nature'; it is a profound and poetic theme. For Wordsworth himself, the personally inspiring Dorothy became criminally desirable, threatening his innocence; she was therefore ritually absorbed by 'Nature' (combining the functions of the 'natural', as anti-incestuous, with the more conventional 'Nature'): turned into 'rocks and stones and trees' that could, hopefully, continue to inspire him as a poet. Wordsworth associated the visionary innocence of his childhood with Dorothy, and although *Lucy Gray* (1799) is not regarded as a member of the Lucy group— the title name derives from a song by Robert Anderson—this simple and pathetic ballad-story probably provided him with his starting-point for the series. The important factor, in this connection, is that a child called Lucy dies—is killed, in fact, by the weather (i.e. by 'Nature').

In 'She dwelt among the untrodden ways', probably the first of the series proper to be written, Lucy becomes the 'Maid' she really was (although the child-associations are continued in 'Three years she grew . . .', in which, in the eyes of Nature, she is both a 'Child' and a 'Girl'), but the tragic emphasis is still on the fact of her death. The sexual element of the poet's feelings for Lucy is muted—this is one of the reasons why these love poems are mysterious—but not wholly suppressed. It is most explicit in 'Strange fits of passion . . .', in which the narrator has a 'passion' which, since he will only 'dare to tell' it in a '*lover's*' ear, can presumably only be that of a lover; he 'loved' Lucy; and finally, he is himself an acknowledged lover, into whose head 'wayward thoughts', of death, slide. It is impossible to ignore the universal, ineluctable love–orgasm–death association in connection with the death of Lucy in this, and therefore in the rest of the series. But in the succeeding poems the presentation of the 'I' of the poem as a lover becomes more equivocal and altogether less overt.

However, elements of sensuality sometimes creep in. In 'Three years she grew . . .' it is 'Nature' itself who is turned into the lover, whose 'darling' Lucy is, and whose face will take on the beauty of 'murmuring sound'; with suspicious innocence, 'vital feelings of delight' will 'swell' her 'virgin bosom'. As in *Lucy Gray*, Nature is destroying Lucy, but now she is a lovely and mature creature: incest is a crime against Nature, therefore Nature must be the instrument of her death as well as of her beatification. In *Louisa* (1801), which can reasonably be related to the Lucy poems, since it is certainly about Dorothy, the poet wants to kiss the 'rains' that 'sparkle' on the cheek of a nymph-like creature who has already become the kind of nature-spirit into which, in 'Three years she grew . . .', he transformed Lucy. In the final poem of the series, based on an incident that 'took place about seven years ago between Dorothy and me', Emma–Lucy–Dorothy is 'my Love'.

By June 1802 Wordsworth had found a practical solution. The Lowther debt had been settled, he was actively planning marriage to Mary, and was soon about to go to Calais to make a final settlement with Annette. Dorothy told Sara and Mary, in a letter of 14 June 1802, that she had 'a kind of stupefaction and headache . . . a feeling of something that has been amiss'. In the same letter William, being 'exceedingly sorry' that the latter part of the *Leech-gatherer* (as they always referred to *Resolution and Independence*) had displeased Sara, tells her how he felt when he wrote it (his quotations come from a lost draft):

I describe myself as having been exalted to the highest pitch of delight by the joyousness and beauty of Nature and then as depressed, even in the midst of those beautiful objects, to the lowest dejection and despair. A young Poet in the midst of the happiness of Nature is described as over-whelmed by the thought of the miserable reverses which have befallen the happiest of all men, viz Poets—I think of this till I am so deeply impressed by it, that I consider the manner in which I was rescued from my dejection and despair almost as an interposition of Providence. 'Now whether it was by peculiar grace A leading from above'— A person reading this Poem with feelings like mine will have been awed and controuled, expecting almost some-thing spiritual or supernatural—What is brought forward? 'A lonely place, a Pond' 'by which an old man *was*, far from all house or home'—not stood, not sat, but '*was*'—the figure presented in the most naked simplicity possible. This feeling of spirituality or supernaturalness is again referred to as being strong in my mind in this passage—'*How came he here* thought I or what can he be doing?' I then describe him, whether ill or well is not for me to judge with perfect confidence, but this I can *confidently* affirm, that, though I believe God has given me a strong imagination, I cannot conceive a figure more impressive than that of an old Man like this, the survivor of a Wife and ten children, travelling alone among the mountains and all lonely places, carrying with him his own fortitude, and the necessities which an unjust state of society has entailed upon him. You say and Mary (that is you can say no more than that) the Poem is *very well* after the introduction of the old man; this is not true, if it is not more than very well it is very bad, there is no intermediate state. You speak of his speech as tedious: everything is tedious when one does not read with the feelings of the Author—'*The Thorn*' is tedious to hundreds; and so is the *Idiot Boy* to hundreds. It is in the character of the old man to tell his story in a manner which an *impatient* reader must necessarily feel as tedious. But Good God! Such a figure, in such a place, a pious self-respecting, miserably infirm, and [   ] Old Man telling such a tale!

My dear Sara, it is not a matter of indifference whether you are pleased with this figure and his employ-ment; it may be comparatively so, whether you are pleased or not with *this Poem*; but it is of the utmost importance that you should have had pleasure from contemplating the fortitude, independence, persevering spirit, and the general moral dignity of this old man's character. Your feelings upon the Mother, and the Boys with the Butterfly, were not indifferent: it was an affair of whole continents of moral sympathy.

This was an unmistakable message to the sisters that they must appreciate Wordsworth's poems as he directed (not that he did not take heed of their suggestions in due course: he evidently did). Dorothy, though sick, felt impelled to take up her pen in further admonition:

> Dear Sara
> When you happen to be displeased with what you suppose to be the tendency or moral of any poem which William writes, ask yourself whether you have hit upon the real tendency and true moral, and above all never think that he writes for no reason but merely because a thing happened—and when you feel any poem of his to be tedious, ask yourself in what spirit it was written—whether merely to tell the tale and be through with it, or to illustrate a particular character or truth etc etc.[543]

The great and fatal question, which Bateson formulates as 'What must Wordsworth do to be happy?', was in process of being answered —and Dorothy was the willing co-architect of the answer. Here she is seen instructing Sara, and therefore Mary, in their duties as first readers of William's moral works, and in how best to subdue within themselves any feelings of criticism that they might have. Their subservience was to help to kill his genius, help produce such tedious and reprehensible stuff as the *Ecclesiastical Sonnets*. . . . Meanwhile, it is hardly coincidental that the trade of the man from whom Wordsworth drew so much inspiration (he had met him, while walking with Dorothy, in 1800) was leech-gathering: leeches were used, of course, to draw off unwanted blood. We recollect that early fragment, 'Away, away, it is the air',[544] with its 'tear Of/water and of blood'. What this meant to Wordsworth is obvious (although the function of the leech-gatherer in the poem is no more than curative in a general sense).

　　While Wordsworth could continue to hope for Coleridge's support, he managed, although painfully, to stay alive; sickening thoughts of his real love remained with him, creating enough tension to produce real poetry. Then John was drowned. He could not face up to his grief, or to the knowledge that John might not have died if he had not desired to 'work for me' while he, Wordsworth, did 'something for the world'. So at the same time as he genuinely mourned the loss, he willed himself into a false acceptance of official Christianity:

A thousand times have I asked myself, as your tender

sympathy led me to do, 'why was he taken away?' and I
have answered the question as you have done. In fact, there
is no other answer which can satisfy and lay the mind at
rest. Why have we a choice and a will, and a notion of
justice and injustice, enabling us to be moral agents? Why
have we sympathies that make the best of us so afraid of
inflicting pain and sorrow, which yet we see dealt about so
lavishly by the supreme governor? Why should our notions
of right towards each other, and to all sentient beings within
our influence, differ so widely from what appears to be His
notion and rule, if everything were to end here? Would it
not be blasphemy to say that, upon the supposition of the
thinking principle being destroyed by death, however inferior
we may be to the great Cause and Ruler of things, we have
more of love in our nature than He has? The thought is
monstrous; and yet how to get rid of it, except upon the
supposition of *another* and a *better world*, I do not see.[545]

This, despite its bitterness, represented a resolve—understandable
in the circumstances—to embrace a belief for which there was no
warrant in Wordsworth's genuine response to his experience. He
now abandoned his instincts. Coleridge, upon whom he perhaps
almost mechanically counted to maintain his poetic inspiration, was
away in Malta and perhaps lost for ever; Wordsworth sincerely
believed that he might die. Therefore the dead John, the brother
of his blood no less than Dorothy was the sister, became in his
mind a kind of surrogate for Coleridge: had he not been properly
working to bring in funds so that William might serve and rectify
the world, and had he not therefore been devoted to the Great
Cause in a way that the recalcitrant Coleridge, with his irritating
personal problems and his own irrelevant genius, was not? Thus
this sentence from a letter of 16 March 1805, to James Losh:

We have lost so much hope and gladsome thought, John
who was almost perpetually in our minds was always there
as an object of pleasure, never was presented to us in any
other point of view; in this he differed from all our friends,
from Coleridge in particular, in connexion with whom we
have many melancholy, fearful and unhappy feelings, but
with John it was all comfort and expectation and pleasure,[546]

The note of resentment is unmistakable: John had died in doing
his duty; Coleridge was allowing his own troubles to distract him
from his. As Dorothy, reflecting her brother's worst fears, wrote to
Catherine Clarkson,

We look forward to Coleridge's return with fear and painful
hope—but indeed I dare not look to it—I think as little as I

can of him. Oh my dear friend my heart seems to be shut against worldly hope! Our poor John was the life of the best of all our hopes.[547]

And in the *Elegiac Stanzas* (1806) Wordsworth serenely, with a true poet's uncanny intuition of what is to come, bade a final farewell to poetry. He had hoped, in the *Intimations* Ode, to recapture the visions of his innocent childhood by entering into poetic trances. Now, paradoxically, his native pessimism and gloom re-asserted themselves. Beaumont had thoughtfully concealed from him his painting of Peele Castle in a storm, worried that it might remind him of the death of John. But Wordsworth saw the picture, and was moved to write the *Elegiac Stanzas*. He wrote to Beaumont on 1 August 1806:

> . . . your delicacy in not leading me to the picture did not escape me. . . . The picture was to me a very moving one; it exists in my mind at this moment as if it were before my eyes.[548]

He begins the poem by recollecting his own stay in the neighbourhood of Peele Castle, when the sea had been calm, and goes on:

> Ah! then, if mine had been the Painter's hand,
> To express what then I saw; and add the gleam,
> The light that never was, on sea or land,
> The consecration, and the Poet's dream;
>
> I would have planted thee, thou hoary Pile,
> Amid a world how different from this!
> Beside a sea that could not cease to smile;
> On tranquil land, beneath a sky of bliss.
>
> . . .
>
> So once it would have been—'tis so no more;
> I have submitted to a new control:
> A power is gone, which nothing can restore;
> A deep distress hath humanised my Soul.
>
> Not for a moment could I now behold
> A smiling sea, and be what I have been:
> The feeling of my loss will ne'er be old;
> This, which I know, I speak with mind serene.

At one level Wordsworth is here admitting that his own insistent question (as Bateson formulated it, 'What must Wordsworth do to be happy?'), is based on a helpless optimism, that his domestic heaven ('God keep the rest of us together! the set is now broken', he had written to his brother Richard on first hearing of the news[549]) is essentially selfish. He tacitly admits, with great and persuasive feeling, the egocentricity of this all-important scheme by use of the startling statement 'A deep distress hath *humanized* my Soul'. But at a profounder level he is acknowledging the final impossibility of again seeing 'The things which I have seen', or of gaining 'sight of that immortal sea'.

These lines are not as simple as they seem. They were occasioned by a profound shock, under the influence of which Wordsworth reverted to earlier, fundamentally distressing habits of feeling. The details of the poem are more curious than one might expect in what is generally taken to be merely 'a tremendous act of renunciation', a welcoming of the loss of his peculiar power, which might have cut him off from the world. The paradox is that, inasmuch as he wrote no more than one or two real poems afterwards we, as his readers, may well object that he did cut himself off from the world, even more effectively than heretofore: the life he lived after 1806, considered apart from the verse it produced, while more honourable, and more characterized by humanity, than is sometimes supposed, can hardly be held up as exemplary. What he is admitting in the lines quoted above, under the stress of a bereavement that has aroused guilt in him, is that his soul, when full of the power (that is now gone), is in some what 'inhuman'. Why should he feel this? It is even perverse. Is poetic power inhuman?

> . . . the look with which it braves,
> Cased in the unfeeling armour of old time,
> The lightning, the fierce winds, and trampling waves.

The key word is 'unfeeling'. For, given the kind of feeling that is needed to write poetry—feeling that in the end proved too much for Wordsworth—he could not have so serenely welcomed the coming trials, acknowledged the facts of pain, in the two final stanzas:

> Farewell, farewell the heart that lives alone,
> Housed in a dream, at distance from the Kind!
> Such happiness, wherever it be known,
> Is to be pitied; for 'tis surely blind.

> And welcome fortitude, and patient cheer,
> And frequent sights of what is to be borne!
> Such sights, or worse, as are before me here—
> Not without hope we suffer and we mourn.

The 'tremendous' renunciation, then, was really one of feeling. As Sir Herbert Read observes in his study of Wordsworth, he became 'hard': instead of living nearer 'the Kind', he more and more frequently relapsed into the mood of the '*up*, askance, pig look' that Coleridge had reluctantly and privately noted in 1803.[550] The solution of 1802—marriage—with Dorothy to instruct Mary and Sara in the Wordsworthian requirements, had not been an ignoble one: it harmed nobody, even if Mary's real function as bed-mate and child-bearer was as substitute for Dorothy. In 1802, the help of Coleridge was still in the offing. But in 1805 the shock of John's death, its inescapable reality, challenged the poetic efficacy of his solution, bringing with it intolerable generalized feelings of pain and guilt. So the old incest-guilt, the sharpest of all, vibrated once again in Wordsworth's mind; the penalty for desire for a sister had been the blood of a brother. The lonely heart whose visions had been Dorothy-inspired now seemed something only to be 'pitied'. Wordsworth paid a heavy price for having a sister for a muse: a poetic silence that lasted for nearly half a century.

Samuel Taylor Coleridge (1772–1834)

I

Strikingly confessional, emotional, often reeking of self-pity and repellently hypochondriacal, at other times brilliant, shrewd and warm in the analyses they offer of his own and other people's motives and characters, Coleridge's many letters[551] provide an indispensable key to his poetry and personality, as all his biographers[552] and critics[553] have recognized by the frequency with which they quote and refer to them.

Here I have concentrated exclusively on Coleridge the poet as opposed to Coleridge the philosopher, ever-reluctant journalist, metaphysician, theologian, encyclopaedist and mage—except inasmuch as his indulgence in these other activities throws light upon his poetry. Because Coleridge is indisputably his own best biographer, I have tried, as far as possible, to give an account of the crucial events in the early and decisive part of his life in the words of his letters. It has also been necessary to make references, though as sparingly as possible, to Coleridge's Notebooks,[554] which provide an invaluable supplement to and sometimes commentary on the letters.

Coleridge (the name, according to his own testimony, and we need not go further, is pronounced as 'a Trisyllabic Amphimacron!') had many failings of a too obvious kind; he thus used to attract the prurient attention of moralistic biographers and critics. He was, to say the least, a hypochondriac, a drug-addict, an emotionalist, a whiner and a drinker. In a word, he was 'soft'. Sir Edmund Chambers's biography of him is punctuated by sneers and, finally, puzzledly disapproving—caught between pious respect for the awesome quality of its subject's mind, the apodictic magnificence of the finest poems, and the apparently totally squalid inefficiency of the life as it was lived. Yet, despite the undeniable messiness of this life, Chambers's biography is ultimately a more reliable guide to the critical limitations of Chambers than it is to Coleridge himself. It is unfortunate that Chambers, a great Elizabethan scholar, ever chose this subject. For Coleridge, as diarist, letter-writer and conversationalist—and above all as poet—was on many occasions able to transcend his own messiness, or existential inefficiency, or whatever we may like to call it: his piercingly accurate and unashamed analyses of his own failings endow him with a supreme humanity. He possessed an astonishingly shrewd intelligence and an uncanny intuition. His sordid shortcomings, considered in the light of his courageously simple desire to be a good man, seem, by contrast with his abilities, to be almost banal. This combination of divine brilliance and mundane failure is irresistible: he is, in Wordsworth's phrase when he heard of his death, 'the most wonderful man' we know. His glittering eye still holds us, 'wonderfully', in his diverse works. Realistic comment about his character such as is notably found in Mr. Geoffrey Yarlott's excellent study of him[555] has sharply modified over-facile theorizing about the transcendental excellences of his philosophy. But implied condemnations of his 'weakness', whenever they are conceived in the moral throat, somehow turn into sour subjective revelations before they reach the page. Such is the power of this frail giant.

2

For our knowledge of Coleridge's childhood we are almost entirely dependent on five autobiographical letters he wrote in response to a request from Thomas Poole, one of his closest friends. One of the strangest and most revealing aspects of Coleridge's character is his indifference, or apparent indifference, to his mother. He was born on 21 October 1772, the youngest of ten children; his father, vicar and schoolmaster of Ottery St. Mary in Devon, died in 1781. But Ann Coleridge, his mother, did not die until November 1809, when he was thirty-seven. He was not emotionally affected by her death. While he never directly attached any blame to her, he never spoke of her with real affection or even interest. His first autobiographical letter to Poole[556] deals with his family antecedents. The second goes on at length, and affectionately, about his father—'not a first-rate Genius', but 'a first-rate Christian', 'a perfect *Parson Adams*'—and describes the fortunes of his various brothers; but of his mother he says only, and then in an aside: 'My Mother was an admirable Economist, and managed exclusively'.[557] In the third letter, 'From October 1775 to October 1778', he writes:

> My Father was very fond of me, and I was my mother's darling—in consequence, I was very miserable. For Molly, who has nursed my Brother Francis, and was immoderately fond of him, hated me because my mother took more notice of me than of Frank—and Frank hated me, because my

mother gave me now & then a bit of cake, when he had none—quite forgetting that for one bit of cake which I had & he had not, he had twenty sops in the pan & pieces of bread & butter with sugar on them from Molly, from whom I received only thumps & ill names.—So I became fretful, & timorous, & a tell-tale—& the School-boys drove me from play, & were always tormenting me—& hence I took no pleasure in boyish sports—but read incessantly. My Father's Sister kept an *every-thing* Shop at Crediton— and there I read thro' all the gilt-cover little books that could be had at that time, & likewise all the uncovered tales of Tom Hickathrift, Jack the Giant-killer, &c & &c &c &c—/—and I used to lie by the wall, and *mope*—and my spirits used to come upon me suddenly, & in a flood—& then I was accustomed to run up and down the church-yard, and act over all I had been reading on the docks, the nettles, and the rank-grass.—At six years old I remember to have read Belisarius, Robinson Crusoe, & Philip Quarle [Quarll) —and then I found the Arabian Night's entertainments— one tale of which (the tale of a man who was compelled to seek for a pure virgin) made so deep an impression on me (I had read it in the evening while my mother was mending stockings) that I was haunted by spectres, whenever I was in the dark—and I distinctly remember the anxious & fearful eagerness, with which I used to watch the window, in which the books lay—& whenever the Sun lay upon them, I would seize it, carry it by the wall, & bask, & read—. My Father found out the effect, which these books had produced—and burnt them.—So I became a *dreamer*—and acquired an indisposition to all bodily activity—and I was fretful, and inordinately passionate, and as I could not play at any thing, and was slothful, I was despised & hated by the boys; and because I could read & spell, & had, I may truly say, a memory & understanding forced into almost an unnatural ripeness, I was flattered & wondered at by all the old women—& so I became very vain, and despised most of the boys, that were at all near my own age—and before I was eight years old, I was a *character*—sensibility, imagination, vanity, sloth, & feelings of deep & bitter contempt for almost all who traversed the orbit of my understanding, were even then prominent & manifest.

From October 1778 to 1779.—That which I began to be from 8 to 6, I continued from 6 to 9.—In this year I was admitted into the grammer school, and soon out-stripped all of my age.—I had a dangerous putrid fever this year—My Brother George lay ill of the same fever in the next room.——My poor Brother Francis, I remember, stole up in spite of orders to the contrary, & sate by my bedside, & read Pope's Homer to me—Frank had a violent love of beating me—but whenever that was superseded by any humour or circumstance, he was always very fond of me— & used to regard me with a strange mixture of admiration & contempt—strange it was not—: for he hated books, and loved climbing, fighting, playing, & robbing orchards, to distraction. . . .[558]

Here we see much of the later Coleridge in embryo: the effortless intellectual brilliance and arrogance, the poetic susceptibility to the supernatural, the 'dangerous' illnesses, the way in which ordinary people—personified by his brother Frank—regarded him with a mixture of 'admiration and contempt'. Coleridge, as a 'mind', did not have to try to distinguish himself. But was he, we may wonder, hiding a deep resentment in that seemingly casual phrase, 'I was my mother's darling'?

The next autobiographical letter gives the famous account of his quarrel with Frank and subsequent flight:

From October 1779 to Oct. 1781.—I had asked my mother one evening to cut my cheese *entire*, so that I might toast it: this was no easy matter, it being a *crumbly* cheese—My mother however did it— / I went into the garden for some thing or other, and in the mean time my Brother Frank *minced* my cheese, 'to disappoint the favorite'. I returned, saw the exploit, and in an agony of passion flew at Frank— he pretended to have been seriously hurt by my blow, flung himself on the ground, and there lay with outstretched limbs—I hung over him moaning & in a great fright—he leaped up, & with a horse-laugh gave me a severe blow in the face—I seized a knife, and was running at him, when my Mother came in & took me by the arm— / I expected a flogging—& struggling from her I ran away, to a hill at the bottom of which the Otter flows—about one mile from Ottery.—There I stayed; my rage died away; but my obstinacy vanquished my fears—& taking out a little shilling book which had, at the end, morning & evening prayers, I very devoutly repeated them—thinking *at the same time* with inward & gloomy satisfaction, how miserable my Mother must be!—I distinctly remember my feelings when I saw a Mr Vaughan pass over the Bridge, at about a furlong's distance—and how I watched the Calves in the fields beyond the river. It grew dark—& I fell asleep—it was towards the latter end of October—& it proved a dreadful stormy night— [1] I felt the cold in my sleep, and dreamt that I was pulling the blanket over me, & actually pulled over me a dry thorn bush, which lay on the hill—in my sleep I had rolled from the top of the hill to within three yards of the River, which flowed by the unfenced edge of the bottom.—I awoke several times, and finding myself wet & stiff, and [1] cold, closed my eyes again that I might forget it.—In the mean time my Mother waited about half an hour, expecting my return, when the *Sulks* had evaporated— I not returning, she sent into the Church-yard, & round the town—not found!—Several men & all the boys were sent to ramble about & seek me—in vain! My Mother was almost distracted—and at ten o'clock at night I was *cry'd* by the crier in Ottery, and in two villages near it—with a reward offered for me.—No one went to bed—indeed, I believe, half the town were up all one night! To return to myself—About five in the morning or a little after, I was broad awake; and attempted to get up & walk—but I could not move—I saw the Shepherds & Workmen at a distance— & cryed but so faintly, that it was impossible to hear me 30 yards off—and there I might have lain & died—for I was now almost given over, the ponds & even the river near which I was lying, having been dragged.—But by good luck Sir Stafford Northcote, who had been out all night, resolved to make one other trial, and came so near that he heard my crying—He carried me in his arms, for near a quarter of a mile; when we met my father & Sir Stafford's Servants.—I remember, & never shall forget, my father's face as he looked upon me while I lay in the servant's arms— so calm, and the tears stealing down his face: for I was the child of his old age.—My Mother, as you may suppose, was outrageous with joy—in rushed a *young Lady*, crying out —'I hope, you'll whip him, Mrs Coleridge!'—This woman still lives at Ottery—& neither Philosophy or Religion have been able to conquer the antipathy which I *feel* towards her, whenever I see her.—I was put to bed—& recovered in a day or so—but I was certainly injured—For I was weakly, & subject to the ague for many years after—.—[559]

The implications of this childhood episode have often been pointed out. It is the earliest example of Coleridge's compulsive need to draw dramatic attention to himself whenever he felt slighted. Throughout his life, he tended to use illness as an excuse for his failings or even as an emotional weapon.

The last of the autobiographical letters tells of Coleridge's happiness at his uncle's, where he was spoiled, 'both mind and body', and often called a prodigy, and of his unhappiness at Christ's Hospital, where the food was bad. His uncle, he said, was proud of him, and used to take him from coffee-house to coffee-house, 'where I drank, & talked & disputed, as if I had been a man'.[560] Here, early on, we see the exhibitionist, indulged by everyone because of his brilliance. Coleridge resentfully felt himself to be an 'orphan' at Christ's Hospital—because there was no one there who loved him in particular. His lack of interest in his mother was surely due to what he regarded as her failure towards him. She was a prototype of his wife: the stupid woman who could not discern his brilliance. All his life Coleridge needed love; he could not be a complete man without it. In considering this, however, it is important to remember that he was capable of giving love in as good a measure as he received it. His need for affection destroyed him as a man; his capacity for it redeems him as a poet.

Coleridge went up to Jesus College, Cambridge, in October 1791. While there he certainly, in contrast to Wordsworth, indulged in the usual excesses of drinking and whoring. In a letter of 20 May 1801 to Humphry Davy he speaks of 'all the loose women I had known, from my 19th to my 22nd year, that being the period that comprizes my unchastities. ... I remembered my vices, & the times thereof, but not their objects',[561] a confession that gives the lie to the notion, once common and still not abandoned, that he was 'under-sexed'. Actually his more celebrated spiritualizing faculty arose, in part, from the troubling intensity of his carnality.

By the beginning of 1793 Coleridge's lifelong capacity for making himself unhappy had already manifested itself, although his letters at this time remain for the most part gay and facetious. Many of them are to his elder brother, the Reverend George (always his severest critic, but at this time faintly inclined to excuse his follies on account of youth), and to the Evans family. The widowed Mrs. Evans and her three daughters, one of whom, Mary, was later to become his first love, had befriended him while he was at Christ's Hospital. He seems to have regarded Mrs. Evans as a substitute mother, and even addresses her as 'Mama!' on one occasion.[562] In a letter of 13 February 1792 to Mary he enclosed some specimens of his verse; it is accomplished, idealistic and derivative, as this extract demonstrates:

> Thus thro' it's silent tenor may my Life
> Smooth it's meek stream, by sordid Wealth unclogg'd,
> Alike unconscious of forensic storms,
>   And Glory's blood stain'd palm![563]

Dorothy Wordsworth, describing Coleridge's appearance to Mary Hutchinson a few years later, alluded to his 'not very good teeth'.

One wonders whether an incident described in a letter of February 1792 to Mrs. Evans had anything to do with it:

> Yesterday a Frenchman came dancing into my room, of which he made but three steps, and presented me with a card—I had scarcely collected, by glancing my eye over it, that he was a Tooth monger, before he seized hold of my muzzle, and baring my teeth (as they do a Horse's in order to know his age) he exclaimed as if in violent agitation— Mon Dieu! Monsieur—all your teeth will fall out in a day or two, unless you permit me the honour of *scaling* them!— This ineffable piece of Assurance discovered such a Genius for Impudence, that I could not suffer it to go unrewarded —so after a hearty laugh I sat down, and let the rascal *chouse* me out of half a guinea by scraping my grinders— the more readily indeed, as I recollected the great penchant, which all your family have for delicate teeth.[564]

On 2 April 1792 Coleridge is 'cashless', and asking George for 'ten or five' pounds.[565] On 6 August he is in Exeter, 'very comfortable', except, characteristically, for 'Cloacinae templis infaustissimus'; Coleridge was never reticent about the condition of his bowels.[566] By 13 January 1793, having just failed to win the Craven Scholarship, he is in really serious trouble: debts have 'corroded my Spirits greatly for some time past'. He plans to publish, by subscription, a volume of translations from the Latin and Greek writers to pay these off.[567] On 5 February 1793 he tells Mrs. Evans that he has been very ill with a bad tooth, which has now been extracted, and that

> in point of Spirits I am but the Dregs of my former self—a decaying flame agonizing in the Snuff of a tallow Candle— a kind of hobgoblin, clouted and bagged up in the most contemptible Shreds, Rags, and Relics of threadbare Mortality. . . .

At the end of this letter he speaks, prophetically, of his 'castle-building Imagination'.[568] Two days later he writes to Mary Evans in the lowest spirits: he has been set a 'swinging Imposition for missing Chapel', his head aches, the weather is 'gloomy', both his coats have holes at the elbows; however, he is learning the violin, is able to make some poor jokès, and signs himself 'with ardour of fraternal friendship Your affectionate S. T. Coleridge'.[569]

His next extant letter, to George, at this time of his first adult crisis, in describing his feelings about his brothers, demonstrates his capacity for self-analysis. Frank had died, 'Yet his Death filled me rather with Melancholy than Anguish'. The people of Devon, when at length he did revisit his birthplace, he had found to be 'gross with openness, and cunning without refinement'. He then discusses his feelings for two surviving brothers, Edward and James, with that puzzling mixture of personal resentment, cringing sense of moral inferiority and objectively shrewd analysis that is so characteristic of him:

> But of the state of my feelings with regard to my Brothers, James and Edward, how shall I speak with Truth, yet Delicacy?—I will open my whole heart to you.—Fraternal Affection is the offspring of long Habit, and of Reflection.— But when I first went into the country, I had scarcely seen either James or Edward—they had neither been the com- panions or the guardians of my childhood.—To love them therefore was a sensation yet to be learnt—: to be learnt at an age, when my best affections had been forestalled; and when long wont to admire and esteem the few, I loved —I deemed admiration and esteem necessary parts in the constitution of affection.—I soon perceived, that Edward never thought—that all his finer feelings were the children of accident—and that even these capricious sensibilities were too often swallowed in the vanity of appearing great to little people.—In my brother James I recognized a man of reflection, and *therefore* of virtue—but as the object of that reflection was from his peculiar situation necessarily himself, I saw or thought, I saw, an interested somewhat— a too great attention to external appearances—a warmth in his own concerns, a coldness in those, that related to others, which seemed to render him unapt to be beloved.—Add to this—that both the one and the other exacted a deference, which conscious of few obligations to *them*, aware of no *real* inferiority, and laughing at the artificial claims of primo- geniture, I felt myself little inclined to pay.—However, I will write to them—I will assume the semblance of Affection perhaps, by persevering in appearing, I at last shall learn to be, a Brother.
> —I have taken your advice with regard to the mourning—when perfectly convenient to you, I shall accept your offer of the note with gratitude.[570]

Doubtless Coleridge could have been equally candid about George himself; but he still felt himself to be dependent on this senior brother. As Geoffrey Yarlott has most persuasively pointed out, because of his childhood insecurity, and for other reasons, Coleridge throughout his life sought after 'sheet-anchor' relationships with men: he tended to turn, first George, then, in turn, Southey, Poole, Wordsworth, even Morgan and finally Gillman, into father-figures, sometimes to their embarrassment and consternation. Without warmly expressed sympathy he felt emotionally starved. At this time he still vainly hoped for it from George. In the end, with Gillman, he had to turn himself into the sort of 'Christian' who might be worthy of it.

By the summer his debts amounted to £148 17s. 1¼d. (Taking everything into consideration, it is the equivalent of a modern undergraduate's debt of at least £1000.) He went to Ottery, where his brothers told him off but gave him some money. On his way back to Cambridge he frittered away so much of it (no one has said what on: Drink? Women? Gambling?) that he dared not 'insult' his tutor, to whom he was the most seriously in debt, with what he had left. He rushed off to London in despair, and seems almost immediately to have further complicated his affairs by falling in love with Mary Evans; previously he had divided his merely flirtatious attentions between her and her sisters. Possibly the romantic righteousness of a Grand Passion helped to distract him from his financial waywardness.

He bought a ticket in the Irish Lottery, but, not surprisingly, it failed to restore his fortunes. And so, on 2 December 1793, meeting a recruiting officer in Chancery Lane, he enlisted in the King's Light Dragoons, under the improbable name of Silas Tomkyn Comberbache. After a few months spent in Reading, Henley, High Wycombe, and then Reading again, during which he was well treated (as a special case: he usually managed this) by his officers, Coleridge's brothers bought him out. By 10 April 1794 he was back at Jesus, his college debts paid off for him by his long-suffering brothers. On 23 February, when he was still at Henley awaiting discharge, he was ready to admit anything to anybody, and thus gave George this abject account of how he had spent 1793:

> . . . I feel a painful blush on my cheek, while I write it— but even for the Un. Scholarship, for which I affected to have read so severely, I did not read three days uninterruptedly—for the whole six weeks, that preceded the examination, I was almost constantly intoxicated! My Brother, you shudder as you read——
>
> When the state of my affairs became known to you, and by your exertions, and my Brothers' generous Confidence a fair Road seemed open to extrication—Almighty God! What a sequel!——
>
> I loitered away more money on the road, and in town than it was possible for me to justify to my Conscience— and when I returned to Cambridge a multitude of petty Embarrassments buzzed round me, like a Nest of Hornets —Embarrassments, which in my wild carelessness I had forgotten, and many of which I had contracted almost

without knowing it—So small a sum remained, that I could
not mock my Tutor with it—My Agitations were delirium
—I formed a Party, dashed to London at eleven o'clock at
night, and for three days lived in all the tempest of Pleasure
—resolved on my return—but I will not shock your religious
feelings—I again returned to Cambridge—staid a week—
such a week! Where Vice has not annihilated Sensibility,
there is little need of a Hell! On Sunday night I packed up
a few things,—went off in the mail—staid about a week in
a strange way, still looking forwards with a kind of recklessness to the dernier resort of misery—An accident of a very
singular kind prevented me—and led me to adopt my
present situation—where what I have suffered—but enough
—may he, who in mercy dispenseth Anguish, be gracious
to me![571]

The military episode has some resemblance to the childhood one
following the attack on Frank: in difficulties, Coleridge yielded to
impulse, indulging himself in an exhibitionistic and yet 'desperate'
act. An undue passivity, an inability to fulfil the material requirements of the particular moment—what Thomas Poole called 'want
of thos inferiour abilities which are necessary to the rational discharge of the common duties'—was what so often got Coleridge
into trouble. To get out of it he frequently made reckless resolutions.
He was, as the letter to his brother shows, full of the fine repentance
of men who do indeed lack the 'inferiour abilities' to organize their
lives. But for the time being the self-sacrificial violence of his
gesture had got his debts paid for him. . . .

3

In June 1794 Coleridge went on a walking-tour to Wales with a
friend, Joseph Hucks. On the way he stopped at Oxford, where he
met Robert Southey of Balliol, the 'sturdy Republican', as Coleridge
described him in a letter written on 6 July.[572] Acquaintance with
Southey was to lead him into the most serious mistake of his life:
his marriage. Immediately on meeting him Coleridge felt his stolidity
and strength of character: he instinctively reached out for him, as
an 'anchor'; ignoring his essential mediocrity, he openly reverenced
his 'Health, Strength of Mind, and confirmed Habits of strict
Morality'.[573] In 1804, seeing the matter more clearly, he was to call
Southey 'not a man of warmth, or delicacy of feeling . . . a clear
handsome piece of Water in a Park, moved from without. . . .'[574]
Meanwhile, it was probably Southey's stern personal example that
caused him to give up whoring: he was maturing sexually, but

needed an excuse to do so—it was characteristic of him to choose this psychologically subservient sort of excuse.

By September 1794 he was enthusiastically writing to Southey about their joint 'Pantisocratic' project. The idea probably came from Southey, but the excitement and driving-force were Coleridge's. Pantisocracy was a 'pure' Utopian scheme by which twelve women, with twelve men, were to settle in North America, work co-operatively on communistic lines, and evolve an ideal society. Religious opinion would be free, minds would be properly cultivated, children would be properly educated. Coleridge gave his own brief account of what the scheme meant to him in introducing it to Charles Heath (who, far from ever residing on the shores of the Susquehannah, was twice mayor of Monmouth):

> Sir,
>   Your brother has introduced my name to you: I shall therefore offer no apology for this letter. A small but liberalized party have formed a scheme of emigration on the principles of an abolition of individual property. Of their political creed, and the arguments by which they support and elucidate it, they are preparing a few copies—not as meaning to publish them, but for private distribution. In this work they will have endeavoured to prove the exclusive justice of the system and its practicability; nor will they have omitted to sketch out the code of contracts necessary for the internal regulation of the society; all of which will of course be submitted to the improvements and approbation of each component member. As soon as the work is printed, one or more copies shall be transmitted to you. Of the characters of the individuals who compose the party, I find it embarrassing to speak; yet, vanity apart, I may assert with truth, that they have each a sufficient strength of head to make the virtues of the heart respectable; and that they are all highly charged with that enthusiasm which results from strong perceptions of moral rectitude, called into life and action by ardent feelings. With regard to pecuniary matters it is found necessary, if twelve men with their families emigrate on this system, that 2000£ should be the aggregate of their contributions; but infer not from hence that each man's quota is to be settled with the littleness of arithmetical accuracy. No; *all* will strain *every* nerve, and then I trust the surplus money of some will supply the deficiencies of others. The minutiae of topographical information we are daily endeavouring to acquire; at present our plan is, to settle at a distance, but at a convenient distance, from Cooper's Town on the

banks of the Susquehannah. This, however, will be the object of future investigation. For the time of emigration we have fixed on next March. In the course of the winter those of us whose bodies, from habits of sedentary study or academic indolence, have not acquired their full tone and strength, intend to learn the theory and practice of agriculture and carpentry, according as situation and circumstances make one or the other convenient.[575]

Coleridge, Southey and certain others were convinced that in April 1795 they would set out for America and proceed to found an ideal society. The details of the scheme were vague; but it was all very radical, republican, deistic (in Southey's case, atheistic), and thoroughly shocking to conventional opinion as represented by, for example the Rev. George Coleridge. On 1 September 1794 Coleridge wrote to Southey about the project in optimistic terms. He had been spending his evenings in The Salutation and Cat, in Newgate Street (where he used to drink with his schoolfellow Charles Lamb), and has here been meeting a most useful and well-informed young man, who is

> lately come from thence [America] as An Agent to sell Land. He was of our School—I had been kind to him— he remembers it—& comes regularly every Evening to 'benefit by conversation' he says—He says, two thousand Pound will do—that he doubts not, we can contract for our Passage under 400£.—that we shall buy the Land a great deal cheaper when we arrive at America—than we could do in England— or why (adds he) am I sent over here? That 12 men may *easily* clear *three hundred* Acres in 4 or 5 months–and that for 600 hundred Dollars a Thousand Acres may be cleared, and houses built upon them—He recommends the Susqusannah [*sic*] from it's excessive Beauty, & it's security from hostile Indians—Every possible assistance will be given us—We may get credit for the Land for 10 years or more as we settle upon it—That literary Characters make *money* there—that &c &c—He never saw a *Byson* in his Life—but has heard of them— They are quite backwards.—The Musquitos are not so bad as our Gnats—and after you have been there a little while, they don't trouble you much. He says, the Women's *teeth are* bad there—but not the men's—at least—not nearly so much—attributes it to neglect—to particular foods—is by no means convinced, it is the necessary Effect of Climate.—[576]

Through Southey, Coleridge met Sara Fricker, one of five sisters of Bath. Their father's business of exporting sugar-pans to Jamaica having failed, they supported themselves by sewing. Byron later maliciously referred to them as 'milliners'. Southey was by now engaged to Edith Fricker, but there is some evidence to suggest that in the first instance he may have addressed himself to, or at least shown interest in, Sara; this, if true, helps to explain the extremely strong moral pressure he put on Coleridge to marry her. But Southey, in spite of Coleridge's later accusation that he had been solely responsible, had nothing at all to do with Coleridge's initial proposal and engagement to Sara in mid-August 1794.

Coleridge seems to have been temporarily impressed with the rapt way in which Sara listened to his dissertations of the subject of Pantisocracy. No doubt her raptness had something to do with her ambitions to get herself a husband. But Coleridge's impulsive action still needs some explanation.

In July, while staying at Wrexham, he had coincidentally caught sight of Mary Evans and her sister Eliza: 'I turned sick, and all but fainted away!' he told Southey. 'The two Sisters . . . passed by the window anxiously, several times afterwards—but I had retired. . . .' He continued:

> My fortitude would not have supported me, had I recognised her—I mean, *appeared* to do it!—I neither eat, or slept yesterday—but Love is a local Anguish—I am 16 miles distant, and am not half so miserable.—I must endeavor to forget it amid the terrible Graces of the wildwood scenery that surrounds me—I never durst even in a whisper avow my passion, though I knew she loved me—Where were my Fortunes? And why should I make his miserable? Almighty God bless her—! her Image is in the sanctuary of my Heart, and never can it be torn away but with the strings that grapple it to Life.——Southey! There are few men of whose delicacy I think so highly as to have written all this—I am glad, I have so deemed of you—We are soothed by communication—[577]

Did he momentarily persuade himself, perhaps with the aid of a few discreet draughts of brandy, that he was in love with the rapt Sara Fricker in order to smother his disappointment over Mary Evans? Only a month later, on 18 September 1794, back at Jesus, he described his supposed passion for Sara in most unconvincing and embarrassingly stilted terms in a letter to Southey. They make an odd contrast with the terms in which he had described Mary Evans in the July letter to Southey:

> Well, my dear Southey! I am at last arrived at Jesus. My God! how tumultuous are the movements of my Heart— Since I quitted this room what and how important Events

have been evolved! America! Southey! Miss Fricker!—
Yes—Southey—you are right—Even Love is the creature
of strong Motive—I certainly love her. I think of her
incessantly & with unspeakable tenderness—with that
inward melting away of Soul that symptomatizes it.[578]

Coleridge seems to have been able to propose to Sara easily enough;
but to Mary, whom he loved more sincerely, he could not declare
himself. In this he again exhibited his passivity, his incapacity to
fulfil not only the duties—'demands' is perhaps a less offensive
word—but also the true emotional needs of the moment. He could
tell Southey, in a truly hideous phrase, that he had been 'pouring
forth the heart to Sara Fricker',[579] and that he felt himself to be her
'brother';[580] but it is evident that he was trying to persuade himself, that his emotional state was a false one. Smarting from Mary's
rejection of him—but had he ever offered himself?—he sought
refuge from his miseries in yet another recklessly impulsive action.

By mid-September Southey, with what Coleridge well called
his 'undeviating Simplicity of Rectitude',[581] was having to put
pressure on him to write to Sara; ultimately he was not strong
enough to resist. He was in the meantime indulging in a fairly
serious flirtation with a Miss Brunton.

Then, at the beginning of October, he received a letter from
Mary Evans. She had probably written to him at the instigation of
the Rev. George, that depressing representative of the norm, who
was horrified and alarmed at his brother's new and, to him, highly
subversive Pantisocratic plans. For three weeks Coleridge kept the
letter to himself; then, on 21 October 1794, he decided to throw
himself on Southey's mercy. It is revealing that at this crucial point
Coleridge should still have felt impelled to depend upon the view of
his 'sheet-anchor', Southey, rather than upon his own convictions;
yet now, and only now, did he begin to criticize Southey's proposal to
take a servant (Shad) with them to America. Only a month earlier
he had responded to the idea with 'SHAD GOES WITH US. HE IS MY
BROTHER!'[582] Now, however, zeal for Pantisocracy is associated with
marrying Miss Fricker, and he does not want to marry Miss Fricker;
so both Pantisocracy and Southey (who represents it) gradually
begin to come under attack.

But Coleridge lacked the resolution to state the true case to
Southey, just as he had lacked the resolution to declare himself to
Mary Evans (or at least to persist in his suit of her: what had actually
gone on between them is not clear). This is the first part of his long
letter to Southey, of 21 October 1794, in which he quotes Mary's
letter to him:

To *you alone*, Southey! I write the first part of this letter—
to yourself confine ir—

'Is this handwriting altogether erased from your Memory? To whom am I addressing myself? For whom am I now violating the Rules of female Delicacy? Is it for the same Coleridge, whom I once regarded as a Sister her best-beloved Brother? Or for one who will RIDICULE that advice from me, which he has *rejected* as offered by his family? I will hazard the attempt. I have no right—nor do I feel myself inclined, to reproach you for the Past. God forbid! You have already suffered too much from self-accusation. But I conjure you, Coleridge! earnestly and solemnly conjure you, to consider long and deeply, before you enter into any rash Schemes. There is an Eagerness in your Nature, which is ever hurrying you into the sad Extreme. I have heard that you mean to leave England: and on a Plan so absurd and extravagant, that were I for a moment to imagine it *true*, I should be obliged to listen with a more patient Ear to Suggestions, which I have rejected a thousand Times with scorn and anger—yes! whatever Pain I might suffer I should be forced to exclaim —"O what a noble Mind is here *o'erthrown*. Blasted with Exstacy"!—You have a Country. Does it demand nothing of You? You have doting Friends. Will you break their Hearts? There is a God—Coleridge! Though I have been told (*indeed* I do not believe it) that you doubt of his Existence and disbelieve a hereafter.—No! you have too much Sensibility to be an Infidel. You know I never was rigid in my opinions concerning Religion—and have always thought *Faith* to be only Reason applied to a particular Subject—In short, I am the same Being, as when you used to say—We thought in all things alike. I often reflect on the happy hours we spent together, and regret the Loss of your Society. I cannot easily forget those whom I once loved—nor can I easily form new Friendships. I find Women in general vain—all of the same Trifle: and therefore little and envious—and (I am afraid) without sincerity—: and of the other sex those, who are offered and held up to my esteem, are very prudent and very worldly.—If you value my peace of mind, you must *on no account* answer this Letter, or take the least Notice of it. I *would* not for the World *any part* of my Family should suspect, that I have written to you. My mind is sadly harassed by being perpetually obliged to resist the solicitations of those whom I love. I need not explain myself—Farewell—Coleridge—! I shall always feel that I have been your *Sister*.[']—

No name was signed;—it was from Mary Evans.— I received it about three weeks ago. I loved her, Southey!

almost to madness. Her Image was never absent from me for three Years—for *more* than three Years.—My Resolution has not faltered—but I want a Comforter.—I have done nothing—I have gone into Company—I was constantly at the Theatre here till they left us—I endeavored to be perpetually with Miss Brunton—I even hoped, that her Exquisite Beauty and uncommon Accomplishments might have cured one Passion by another. The latter I could easily have dissipated in her absence—and so have restored my affections to her, whom I do not love—but whom by every tie of Reason and Honour I ought to love. I am resolved—but wretched!—But Time shall do much—you will easily believe that with such feelings I should have found it no easy Task to write to [Sara]. I should have detested myself, if after my first Letter I had written coldly—how could I write *as warmly?*[583]

He proceeds to attack Southey for his plan to employ servants.

Now it is clear that Coleridge still hoped to escape his obligations towards Sara and to regain Mary; but he required this course to be approved of, even directed, by Southey, the symbol of moral authority. And if the symbol of moral authority was not prepared to endorse Coleridge's needs, then he would attack it for immorality in the Pantisocratic field. In a letter to Francis Wrangham of 24 October 1794 he speaks of having loved Mary 'for five years', 'almost to madness';[584] but despite this and the previous avowal of 'three years' to Southey, it seems unlikely that he had fallen in love with her before late 1793. However, there may have been an element of retrospection: on 4 November 1794 he told Southey that 'She [Mary] was VERY LOVELY. . . . We formed each other's minds—our ideas were blended . . .'. Further on he rightly describes himself as 'a child of frailty'.[585]

In early November he replied to Mary, unable to contain himself any longer:

Too long has my Heart been the torture house of Suspense. After infinite struggles of Irresolution I will at last dare to request of you, Mary! that you will communicate to me whether or no you are engaged to Mr ———. I conjure you not to consider this request as presumptuous Indelicacy. Upon mine Honor, I have made it with no other Design or Expectation than that of arming my fortitude by total hopelessness. Read this Letter with benevolence—and consign it to Oblivion.

For four years I have *endeavored* to smother a very ardent attachment—in what degree I have succeeded, you must know better than I can. With quick perceptions of moral Beauty it was impossible for me not to admire in you your sensibility regulated by Judgment, your Gaiety proceeding from a cheerful Heart acting on the stores of a strong Understanding. At first I voluntarily invited the recollection of these qualities into my mind—I made them the perpetual Object of my Reveries—yet I entertained no one Sentiment beyond that of the immediate Pleasure annexed to the thinking of You. At length it became an Habit. I awoke from the Delusion, and found that I had unwittingly harboured a Passion which I felt neither the power or the courage to subdue. My associations were irrevocably formed, and your Image was blended with every idea. I thought of you incessantly: yet that Spirit (if Spirit there be that condescends to record the lonely Beatings of my heart) that Spirit knows, that I thought of you with the purity of a Brother. Happy were I, had it been with no more than a Brother's ardor!

The man of dependent fortunes while he fosters an attachment commits an act of Suicide on his happiness. I possessed no Establishment—my views were very distant—I saw, that you regarded me merely with the kindness of a Sister——What expectations *could* I form? I formed no expectations—I was ever resolving to subdue the disquieting Passion: still some inexplicable Suggestion palsied my Efforts, and I clung with desperate fondness to this Phantom of Love, it's mysterious Attractions and hopeless Prospects. It was a faint and rayless Hope! Yet It soothed my Solitude with many a delightful day-dream. It was a faint and rayless Hope! Yet I nursed it in my Bosom with an Agony of Affection, even as a Mother her sickly Infant.——

But these are the poisoned Luxuries of a diseased Fancy! Indulge, Mary! this my first, my last request—and restore me to *Reality*, however gloomy. Sad and full of heaviness will the Intelligence be—my heart will die within me—I shall receive it however with steadier resignation from yourself, than were it announced to me (haply on your marriage Day!) by a Stranger! Indulge my request—I will not disturb your Peace by even a *Look* of Discontent—still less will I offend your Ear by the Whine of selfish Sensibility. In a few months I shall enter at the Temple—and there seek forgetful Calmness—where only it can be found —in incessant and useful Activity.

Were you not possessed of a Mind and of a Heart above the usual Lot of Women I should not have written you sentiments, that would be unintelligible to three fourths of your Sex. But our Feelings are congenial, though your [our?] attachment is doomed not to be reciprocal. You will not deem so meanly of me as to believe that I shall regard Mr —— with the jaundiced Eye of disappointed Passion. God forbid! He, whom you honor with your Affections, becomes sacred to me. I shall love him for *your* Sake—the time may perhaps come, when I shall be Philosopher enough—not to envy him for *his own*![586]

Mary was indeed engaged: to Fryer Todd, whom she married in October 1795. Her marriage, like Coleridge's, failed. When he met her in the street in 1808, and subsequently called on her and her husband, he saw in her 'a counterpart of the very worst parts of my own Fate, in an exaggerated form'.[587]

On 9 December 1794 he told the intractable Southey that he was not conscious of having injured Miss Fricker

otherwise, than by having mistaken the ebullience of *schematicism* for affection, which a moment's reflection might have told me, is not a plant of so mushroom a growth —had it ever not been counteracted by a prior attachment/ but my whole Life has been a Series of Blunders! God have mercy upon me—for I am a most miserable Dog.

It remained for him, however, to be 'externally Just', and he ended the letter with a message of love for Mrs. Southey, Edith Fricker 'and', pointedly, 'to whomever it is right or convenient'. Meanwhile, he remained 'a compleat Necessitarian', and even went beyond the materialistic philosopher Hartley, who had influenced him so strongly, in believing 'the corporeality of thought—namely, that it is motion—.'[588]

However, it should be emphasized that he was not—and never seems to have been, despite assertions to the contrary—an atheist. He said in December 1794 of Thomas Holcroft, who had just escaped trial for high treason, that he 'absolutely infests you with *Atheism*', and that his arguments were unconvincing.[589] True, his miseries and incertitudes did not yet drive him into a closer acceptance of orthodox Christianity: he remains critical of established religion, calling it 'that mongrel whelp that goes under [Christianity's] name', taught 'in some ague-fit of superstition'. But he is careful to respect the word 'Christianity' itself. Although he sometimes referred to himself in later years as having been in the past an 'infidel', he had in fact admitted to his brother George in a very early letter, of 30 March 1794, that he had 'too much tenderness of nature to be utterly an infidel'.[590]

On 24 December 1794 he wrote out a formal renunciation of Mary Evans, but admitted that 'To love you Habit has made unalterable'.[591] He repeated the phrase in a letter to Southey of a few days later:

I am calm, dear Southey! as an Autumnal Day, when the Sky is covered with grey moveless Clouds. To *love her* Habit has made unalterable: I had placed her in the sanctuary of my Heart, nor can she be torn from thence but with the Strings that grapple it to Life. This Passion however, divested as it now is of all Shadow of Hope, seems to lose it's disquieting Power. Far distant, and never more to behold or hear of her, I shall sojourn in the Vale of Men sad and in loneliness, yet not unhappy. He cannot be long wretched who dares be actively virtuous. I am well assured, that she loves me as a favorite Brother. When she was present, she was to me only as a very dear Sister: it was in absence, that I felt those gnawings of Suspense, and that Dreaminess of Mind, which evidence an affection more restless, yet scarcely less pure, that the fraternal. The Struggle has been well nigh too much for me—but, praised be the All-merciful! the feebleness of exhausted Feelings, has produced a Calm, and my Heart stagnates into Peace.

Southey! my ideal Standard of female Excellence rises not above that Woman. But all Things work together for Good. Had I been united to her, the Excess of my Affection would have effeminated my Intellect. I should have fed on her Looks as she entered into the Room—I should have gazed on her Footsteps when she went out from me.

To lose her!—I can rise above that selfish Pang. But to marry another—O Southey! bear with my weakness. Love makes all things pure and heavenly like itself:—but to marry a woman whom I do *not* love—to degrade her, whom I call my Wife, by making her the Instrument of low Desire—and on the removal of a desultory Appetite, to be perhaps not displeased with her Absence!—Enough! These Refinements are the wildering Fires, that lead me into Vice.[592]

On 4 October 1795 Coleridge and Sara Fricker were married.

The thought gave me a tinge of melancholy to the solemn Joy, which I felt—united to the woman, whom I love best of all created Beings.—We are settled—nay—quite domesticated at Clevedon—Our comfortable Cot!—!—

he told Poole on 7 October 1795.[593] Meanwhile, rather than disobey Southey, he had chosen to quarrel with him. The ostensible grounds were that Southey had considered taking orders, by which he might gain a sordid fortune, and had made judicious plans for himself that betrayed Pantisocracy.

Southey is not an attractive figure. He was, as Coleridge later charged, 'a man admirable for his abilities only, strict indeed in the lesser Honesties'.[594] There was nevertheless an element of hypocrisy in Coleridge's new attitude towards him:[595] he was simultaneously using him as a scapegoat for his own abandonment of Pantisocracy and revenging himself for his moral over-dependence upon him. Sara dutifully backed up her husband, who could now feel thoroughly virtuous. But it is most important, especially in considering the poems of 1797 and 1798, to realize that the suspiciously ecstatic phrasing of the letter written to Poole three days after his wedding was part of a new, and tragic process of self-delusion. He did not now love Sara as he had loved Mary Evans; rather, he was 'making her the Instrument of low Desire', and was therefore, for the time being, consciously satisfied. But when his 'desultory Appetite' was finally satisfied, he would be by no means 'displeased with her Absence'; guilt because of his error, and love for another, sexually inaccessible woman, were to undermine his happiness for the next twenty years of his life.

4

Coleridge undoubtedly made a determined effort to achieve harmony with his wife, and until 1799 all was superficially well. However, he must soon have seen that Sara was, as Dorothy Wordsworth later called her, 'a sad fiddle-faddler', a thoroughly conventional woman with little interest in literature, but—and this was hard—with no aptitude for household management either. She was notoriously ill-tempered, perhaps shrewish; and she was a wretched cook.[596] When Coleridge was planning his move to the cottage at Nether Stowey where he lived from January 1797 until 1800, he told Poole that he himself would '*instruct* the maid in *cooking*'.[597] The italics tell a sad story of mismanagement. Coleridge was undoubtedly unlucky from the beginning, in that his Fricker was not even efficient. Humphrey House's remark in his magnificent book on Coleridge, which marked a new epoch in Coleridge criticism, that she 'might have made many a man a good wife' is probably over-generous to her.[598] She was, or became, somewhat of a character, and she did not displease Southey; but she has not been, as an anonymous writer in the *TLS* recently claimed, subject 'to one of the cruellest bits of misrepresentation in literary history'.[599] After all, she could only really appreciate what sold. We do not need to forgive her for not being able to appreciate her husband's genius, and we can often sympathize with her in what she had to go through. But she had little warmth, and most defences of her are in fact apologies.

However, there are no complaints against her in Coleridge's

early letters; and although he was often away from home on various money-making schemes (unconsciously he probably preferred being absent), he continued to send her thoroughly affectionate letters right up until the time he met Sara Hutchinson, 'Asra', at Sockburn-on-Tees in November 1799. It was not until then that he lost all hope of realizing his dream of happiness with her. Such faults as there had been before then were certainly as much on Sara's side as on her husband's: against his eccentricities and rapidly forming, rapidly fading enthusiasms must be balanced her nagging and her mindless conventionalities. There is evidence, too, in a passage from a notebook of 1801[600] of sexual frigidity on Sara's part. This may have existed from the beginning of the marriage, but is more likely to have developed lated, after the meeting with Asra. There was jealousy of Coleridge's intimacy with the Wordsworths, and a growing scorn for all activity that did not produce money. During their years of comparative happiness, most of the effort came from Coleridge, who for all his faults was not only cleverer but more tender and more sensitive. To outsiders, the situation apparently seemed placid: Richard Reynell, who visited the household in 1797, described Sara as 'sensible, affable, and good-natured, thrifty and industrious, and always neatly and prettily dressed'. The affection between her and Coleridge was, he said, 'founded on . . . esteem'.[601] Perhaps Reynell was not an observant man and did not stay to lunch, but such evidence cannot be altogether ignored: while Coleridge still hoped both for prosperity and to turn his wife into a person who could understand him, the marriage held together, and probably did so because for the time being there was sexual compatibility.

Coleridge's relationship with the Wordsworths between 1795 and 1812 has been dealt with in some detail in the chapter on Wordsworth.[602] First, the worthy, intelligent and generous tanner, Thomas Poole—perhaps the truest and most stable of all Coleridge's friends—replaced Southey as his 'sheet-anchor'; then Wordsworth supplanted Poole when in 1800 the Coleridges moved to Greta Hall, in the Lake District, to be near the Wordsworths at Grasmere. From the point of view of Coleridge's well-being it was an unwise move, and he had some notion of this, for although Wordsworth was already pressing him in May 1799, in Germany, to come to the Lake District, he told Poole in a letter of 6 May 1799 that

> Finally, I told him plainly, that *you* had been the man in whom *first* and in whom alone, I had felt an *anchor*! With all my other Connections I felt a dim sense of insecurity & uncertainty, terribly uncomfortable / —W. was affected to tears, very much affected; but he deemed the vicinity of a Library absolutely *necessary* to his health, nay to his

existence. It is painful to me too to think of not living near him; for he is a *good* and *kind* man, & the only one whom in *all* things I feel my Superior—& you will believe me, when I say, that I have few feelings more pleasurable than to find myself in intellectual Faculties an Inferior / . But my Resolve is fixed, *not to leave you till you leave me*! I still think that Wordsworth will be disappointed in his expectations of relief from reading, without Society—& I think it highly probable, that where I live, there he will live, unless he should find in the North any person or persons, who can feel & understand him, can reciprocate & react on him.—My many weaknesses are of some advantage to me; they unite me more with the great mass of my fellow-beings—but dear Wordsworth appears to me to have hurtfully segregated & isolated his Being / Doubtless, his delights are more deep and sublime: / but he has likewise more hours, that prey on his flesh & blood.[603]

Coleridge's chief difficulty in 1795—and, indeed, for the rest of his life—was money. His magazine, *The Watchman* (1796), soon failed, despite an extensive trip in order to promote it. But, in compensation, his first son was born in September 1796, and was called David Hartley, 'in honor of the great Master of Christian [*sic*] Philosophy';[604] and he gained many friends and admirers: Joseph Cottle, who published his first volume of poems (1796), Dr. Beddoes, Bristol physician and father of the poet, the Unitarian John Prior Estlin, and others whom he had encountered on his *Watchman* trip. Meanwhile he engaged in lay preaching and desultory journalism, and toyed with various projects, including one of starting a school in Derby. He moved from his 'comfortable Cot' to Bristol in March 1796, and at the beginning of 1797 to Nether Stowey.

In 1797 Cottle published a new edition of his poems, to which were added poems by Lamb and a vicious, mentally unstable young epileptic, Charles Lloyd, whom Coleridge took into his home for a time. Money was short, as always, and Poole organized a fund for him. Finally, in January 1798 he was about to take up a post as Unitarian minister at Shrewsbury, had even arrived there, when Thomas and Josiah Wedgwood—sons of the potter—offered him an annuity of £150 a year for life.[605] He accepted, and returned to Nether Stowey. Soon after this—it was the period of his best work as a poet, the so-called *Annus Mirabilis*—he went on a trip to Germany with the Wordsworths[606] where he studied intensively in German philosophy—and for a book on Lessing that never got written. Three more children were born: Berkeley (1798), who died in the following year while Coleridge was in Germany, Derwent (1800) and Sara (1802).

From 1800 until 1804 Coleridge was living at Greta Hall, Keswick—from which he was frequently absent—torn between his love for the Wordsworths and his duties as a husband and father. This was the second crucial period of his life, which produced *Dejection*.

From 1804 until 1806 he was in Malta, where he was Acting Secretary to the Government, ostensibly for his by then atrociously bad health, but really to try to dissolve his feelings for Asra and yet at the same time get away from his wife. On his return he found himself unable to live with Sara, and eventually she agreed to a separation; she now had little affection for him, and the difficulties she made were due entirely to her fear of what might be 'said', a view that must invite our total contempt.

Coleridge's sojourn at Coleorton in 1806–7 was not a success,[607] and from then until he finally quarrelled with Wordsworth in 1810 their relations continued to worsen. *The Friend* (1808–10), a magazine whose object was 'to uphold those truths and those merits, which are founded in the nobler and more permanent parts of our nature, against the caprices of fashion', was a commercial failure, owing not only to bad luck and mismanagement but also to its intrinsic nature. It is only just beginning to be recognized that *The Friend* was a triumphant success of integrity; that the seriously ill, unhappy and harassed Coleridge—maligned by Chambers and others as incapable of regular effort—worked hard during the whole of its existence: the quality and volume of what he wrote, single-handed, in addition to the labours of printing and distribution have not been fully appreciated until now.[608]

From 1808 until the early 1820s Coleridge found a fluctuating source of income in lecturing. His performances varied from brilliant to appalling, depending on how ill he was, and on how much opium and/or alcohol he had taken. The lectures contain much of his best criticism.

Now without an 'anchor', he began to depend on John Morgan and his wife and sister-in-law. Morgan was an early acquaintance of Coleridge's and Southey's who began as a lawyer and ended as a 'gentleman tobacconist', a congenial but financially inauspicious transition. He was not, like Coleridge's other anchor-men, a stable or self-sufficient person. He had wasted 'a considerable patrimony', says Chambers, who, ever ready to criticize lack of business acumen in moral terms, twice calls him 'this unfortunate man'. In 1813 he may have been in prison for debt, and his cheese and tobacco businesses were in trouble. But he and the two women of his household were sympathetic to Coleridge, and did not moralize at him—an attitude that, in the light of modern medical opinion, has proved to be a correct one. For since about 1800 he had become, in addition to his other illnesses, increasingly dependent on opium. Coleridge made considerable personal and financial sacrifices in order to help Morgan, and proved himself a loyal and dependable friend.

His last anchor-man was Dr. James Gillman. In 1816 he consulted a Dr. Joseph Adams, who recommended his case to Gillman. Gillman fell under the spell of his personality, and Coleridge went into residence with him at Highgate, remaining there for the last eighteen years of his life. He was never able to give up opium; but he did at last find some happiness as mage and centre of the sympathetic attention of younger men. Of his old friends only Charles and Mary Lamb remained close, or gave him his proper due; but he made new ones. His last act, half an hour before going into a coma, in July 1834, was to write a note to 'beg, expect . . . fain hope' that a collection 'as may suffice for a handsome Legacy' might be made for his faithful servant and attendant of seven years, Harriet Macklin.[609] Its last words were: 'I never ask for myself'. The results of an autopsy suggested that he had been ill since his early life: his heart was grossly enlarged. Asra, who was herself to die within two years, laconically noted: 'the disease was at his heart'.

5

Conjecture about the effect drugs had on Coleridge was for a long time vitiated by ignorance about drugs themselves. The truth lies in Coleridge's own authoritative statements, most of them in letters, about his habit. The idea that drug-addiction necessarily involves self-indulgence, or lack of self-discipline, rather than a state of physical dependence, dies hard even today. The basis for understanding the nature of Coleridge's addiction is the recognition that he was, despite his hypochondria, a physically sick man. He suffered from a serious bout of 'rheumatic fever'[610] while still at school (for which he was almost certainly given laudanum), and this may have been what first affected his heart and stomach. He was subject to rheumatic, neuralgic and 'internal' pains, and swellings ('gout'), which sometimes made him scream, prostrate himself and 'writhe like a worm' (as Wordsworth put it) with pain. And while we may, if we wish, be critical of his lack of restraint, even of the perhaps partly self-induced abnormal lowness of his pain-threshold, we cannot deny the existence of the pain itself. He suffered from a 'nervous stomach': when upset, he would be afflicted with uncontrollable diarrhoea. His predisposition to attacks of dysentery possibly suggests some kind of chronic disorder of the stomach, perhaps a virus condition. He had plenty, in the way of physical pain and discomfort, to contend with. That he did not bear it with silent fortitude does not mean that he did not bear it.

Since opiates were then universally prescribed for just such illnesses as those from which Coleridge suffered, it is not surprising that he took to them.[611] In a letter of November 1791 to his brother George, who had been ill, he showed that he was already well acquainted with opium as a medicine. 'Opium,' he said ominously, 'never used to have any disagreeable effects on me—but it has upon many.'[612] On 22 February 1796 he tells Cottle, in a passage which should hang above the desk of every writer:

> ... I am forced to write for bread—write the high flights of poetic enthusiasm, when every minute I am hearing a groan of pain from my Wife—groans, and complaints & sickness!—The present hour, I am in a quickset hedge of embarrassments, and whichever way I turn, a thorn runs into me—. The Future is cloud & thick darkness—Poverty perhaps, and the thin faces of them that want bread looking up to me!—Nor is this all—my happiest moments for composition are broken in on by the reflection of—I *must* make haste—I am¹too late—I am already months behind! I have received my *pay* before hand!—O way-ward and desultory Spirit of Genius! ill canst thou brook a task-master! The tenderest touch from the hand of *Obligation* wounds thee, like a scourge of scorpions!—
> I have been composing in the fields this morning. . . .[613]

Clearly financial worry and some degree of suppressed domestic tension were forcing Coleridge to do his work out in the fields, and were undermining his resolve. On 12 March 1796 he complains to the Rev. John Edwards that he has been 'tottering on the edge of madness', and has therefore 'been obliged to take Laudanum almost every night'.[614] Within less than a year of his marriage, then, Coleridge had unwittingly become dependent upon narcotics to relieve his mental perturbations as well as his physical pain. On 5 November 1796 he told Poole that he was taking '25 drops of Laudanum every five hours'. This was to relieve 'an intolerable pain' running from his right temple to his right shoulder, which drove him 'nearly frantic' and caused him, perhaps to the consternation of his wife, to run 'about the House naked, endeavouring by every means to excite sensations in different parts of my body, and so to weaken the enemy by creating a division [*sic*: diversion?]'. But Coleridge admitted that the pain might have originated in 'excessive anxiety', and this was also the opinion of his doctor. The 'ease and *spirits* gained' by the laudanum had 'enabled' him to write Poole 'this flighty, but not exaggerated, account';[615] and the next letter to Poole, of 7 November 1796, begins by stating 'I wrote you on Saturday night under the immediate inspiration of Laudanum—

& wrote you a *flighty* letter, but yet one most accurately descriptive both of its facts & feelings'.[616]

The terms of these early references to opium are most important. Opium (of which laudanum is a tincture) was regarded by Coleridge as an analgesic; but it was also already being employed as an *inspiration*, which led to a *flighty accuracy*. We may associate this word, 'flighty', with another, 'streamy', which occurs in one of Coleridge's most famous notebook entries, of 29 December 1803:

> I will at least make the attempt to explain to myself the Origin of moral Evil from the *streamy* [note the italicization of this word, as of '*flighty*' in the quotation above] Nature of Association, which Thinking = Reason, curbs and rudders. . . . Do not the bad Passions in Dreams throw light and shew of proof upon this Hypothesis?—Explain these bad Passions: & I shall gain Light, I am sure. . . .[617]

Thus, it is clearly established that by 1796 Coleridge felt guilt about taking opium, not because he believed it would harm him, but because the 'flighty accuracy' he achieved by using it became associated in his mind with some kind of disturbance, probably that caused by 'bad Passions'. In a letter of 15 May 1814 he told Morgan that he had never taken opium to induce '*pleasurable* sensations', but 'by cowardice of pain, first of mental pain. . . .'[618]

By 1801 it had become not a practice but a habit: opium had established a hold on his physique. In a letter to Cottle of 26 April 1814, one of the many he wrote on the subject at this time, he traced his 'ignorant' acquirement of the 'ACCURSED Habit' back to an illness of 1801, when his knees swelled up.[619] From this time onwards, he suffered not only from both organic and psychosomatic illnesses, but also from the pains of withdrawal from the drug when he tried, as he often did, to give it up; withdrawal was only very vaguely understood by the doctors of his time, few of whom were aware of its physical basis. By 1802 he was openly admitting to his dependence. In a letter of 16 November 1802, written to his wife from Wales, he wrote:

> . . . & once in the 24 hours . . . I take half a grain of purified opium. . . . I am fully convinced . . . that to a person, with such a Stomach & Bowels as mine, if any stimulus is needful, Opium in the small quantities, I now take it, is incomparably better in every respect than Beer, Wines, Spirits, or any *fermented* liquor. . . .[620]

And he goes on to say, repeatedly, how 'pernicious' he thinks tea is, and instructs his wife to give Hartley and Derwent as little of it as possible. Sara was an avid tea-drinker, and Coleridge was no doubt able to relieve himself of a portion of his guilt by snidely reminding her of her own habit. He did not quite keep to his regimen of November 1802, which he said he would give 'a *fair, compleat* Trial of one month', because, although he kept on with the opium, he also had frequent recourse to spirits, mostly brandy.

In terms of health and happiness, 1803 was one of the worst years of Coleridge's life. He often spoke of dying, and took out a life policy for the benefit of Sara. His letters are full of unhappiness. He told Southey that 'In an evil day for me did I first pay attentions to Mrs. Coleridge; in an evil day for me did I marry her', and confessed that although brandy and laudanum made him 'well, during their first operation . . . the secondary Effects increase the cause of the Disease'.[621] In early 1803 he was planning a meeting with Tom Wedgwood, his benefactor and, as Mr. Yarlott rather unkindly puts it, 'fellow drug-addict'; in Wedgwood's company he evidently felt that he could relax his usual feelings of guilt, for in a letter to him of 17 February 1803 he seems to be planning an orgy as well as a meeting: 'We will have a fair Trial of *Bang*—Do bring down some of Hyoscyamine Pills—& I will give a fair Trial of opium, Hensbane, & Nepenthe'.[622] Coleridge had said, 'I was heavy with thought & with *want* of Sleep, tho' not with the desire of it. . . .'[623] He described his nocturnal difficulties in a memorable poem, *The Pains of Sleep*, which he did not publish until 1816, in the volume containing *Christabel* and *Kubla Khan*.[624]

Apart from one allusion, to having taken '30 drops of Laudanum' for a 'raging Fever' contracted within a few days of his landing at Valetta (on 18 May 1804), Coleridge ominously failed to mention opium in any of his surviving letters home. It was here, perhaps, as Griggs suggests, that the habit was finally and fatally confirmed. On 3 December 1808, writing to his old Uniterian friend John Prior Estlin (who six years later attacked him bitterly for abandoning his former theological position), he made it clear that he (and his doctors) believed opium could not be abandoned 'without Loss of Life'; but he had reduced his dose to 'one *sixth*' of what it was, and felt better:[625] he had surrendered to the inevitable.

The rest of the story may be shortly told. He struggled with himself, vainly consulting physician after physician, until he entered Gillman's house in 1816. Previous attempts to break the habit altogether, including the employment of an elderly 'guard' (whom, inevitably, he cheated), had been abandoned. Gillman cut down his intake (to what extent is not known, but probably drastically); but he still found it necessary to deceive him. Thus we find him requesting his publisher, John Murray, on 23 April 1816, soon after he had entered Gillman's household, to deliver some books he has procured for him, and

> At the same time I should feel *very much* obliged to you if
> you would immediately on the receipt of this dispatch a
> Porter [the address of a druggist in Fleet Street is given]
> with the inclosed note who is to wait for an answer—and
> that you will order your young man to pack up, whatever
> the Porter brings back, carefully with the Books.[626]

And a series of seven notes to a Mr. Dunn, a chemist of Highgate
and later of Tottenham Court Road, apologizing for not settling
outstanding bills and asking for 'Liquid Morphii' and 'Acetate of
Morphine', shows that he consistently went over and above Gillman's
prescriptions.[627] However, he certainly reduced his intake under
Gillman's benevolent régime; it is unlikely that taking opium in
itself shortened his life. But the conflict continued, marked by such
'illicit' doses as he could get from Dunn (and no doubt others) and
such temporary remorse as he shows in a letter of 22 March 1832
to Joseph Henry Green, an ardent disciple, telling him that he was
'quiet' by 'the mercy of God',

> and so far from any craving for the poison that has been
> the curse of my existence, my shame and my *negro-slave*
> inward humiliation and debasement, I feel an aversion or
> horror at the imagining, so that I doubt whether I could
> swallow a dose without a resiliency amounting almost to a
> convulsion.

But, significantly, he has no compensatory *'genial* feeling': his
temporary abstinence is induced by feelings of guilt. 'The grasp of
mortality seems too tight, too constant'.[628]

6

Considering his achievement, Coleridge was, as Humphry House
pointed out in 1953, almost absurdly modest about his poetry. Few
critics, however prejudiced against his personality, would put him
below the more prolific Wordsworth, to whose genius he so consistently deferred. Quite apart from the three poems for which he is
most famous, he wrote the 'conversation poems' (as he called
them), *Dejection*, *The Pains of Sleep*, the 'Asra poems' as collected
together by George Whalley[629]—many of which deserve to be
better known—and some unjustly neglected later poems such as
Limbo and *The Garden of Boccaccio*. Thus, he did not dry up
poetically as suddenly or as completely as Wordsworth. But he
did lose much of his power and sense of poetic direction, and was
acutely conscious of it.

    While possessed of full poetic power, in the early years of his marriage, Coleridge said little in letters about his own poetry. His need to abase himself before a stronger personality probably caused him to think more about Wordsworth's poetry than about his own. Sincere and justified regard for Wordsworth's genius, and generosity, made him 'feel . . . a *little man by his side*';[630] but this self-abasement gave him the immediate feelings of security that he craved for. He never mentioned *Kubla Khan*, either when he wrote it or when it was published (1816). His allusions to *The Ancient Mariner* and *Christabel* are merely casual. He did write two verse-letters, *Dejection* and *The Pains of Sleep*; but here he was writing, compulsively, in poetry, not about it. Few succeeding poets of comparable public stature have said so little in letters about their own poems, especially the best of their poems, for there is much more about the immature verse of his first volume (1796) than about the poems of the marvellous year of 1797/8. But even if Coleridge's silence on this subject is explained by his inability to face certain issues raised—as I believe it is—as well as by his natural modesty, he was remarkably consistent.

Sending his 1796 volume to his radical and atheistical friend John Thelwall (who had been acquitted on a treason charge in 1794) in late April 1796, he begged his acceptance of them, but freely admitted 'much effeminacy of sentiment, much faulty glitter of expression'.[631] Over twenty years later, in *Biographia Literaria*, he said that when he wrote these early poems he had even then seen and admitted 'an austerer and more natural style'. His lifelong acknowledgement of his shortcomings and his refusal to boast of his achievements are remarkable—perhaps, among poets, unique— qualities. But there were motives for this reticence.

Coleridge had, even before he discovered his enormous poetic powers, a reluctance to acknowledge the reasons of poetry in himself: besides being afraid of his truth-telling proclivities, he clearly understood the proditorious nature of poetry, knew that it fundamentally threatened not only society, organized on false principles, but also all kinds of conventional well-being. Answering Thelwall's long and intelligent letter of criticism[632] of his 1796 volume on 13 May 1796, he is airily complacent about the charge of introducing '*metaphysics*' into poetry, and argues that 'That poetry pleases which interests': *Religious Musings* (his own favourite of his early poems) 'interests the *religious*'. There should be no 'act of *Uniformity* against Poets': there is room for love verses and for political poems.[633]

This is a perfectly fair defence against Thelwall's criticisms; but what is most revealing here is the casualness of Coleridge's tone: most poets are violently upset by any criticisms of their poems, especially from friends—and Coleridge was deeply susceptible to upset. A Richard Poole, of Sherborne, had also told him that

Religious Musings was 'too *metaphysical for common readers*', and Coleridge admitted to Thomas Poole, on 5 May 1796, that this was 'good & acceptable advice'; but 'I answer—the Poem was not written for common readers'. True, there is 'vicious affecattion' in its phraseology, but it has more '*mind*' than another of his own poems which he favoured less. There is something perverse about his remarkably objective, but nevertheless confused attitude: Richard Poole's advice is 'good', but actually the poem is not meant for the common reader. The tone is nearly, if not quite, facetious. 'Oh damn this poetry!' he seems to be saying. And he is more serious about a scheme to start a school for '8 young men at 100 guineas each', where he would '*perfect*' them in studies of 'Man as Animal' and 'Man as a Religious Being'; he ends his letter to Poole by announcing a secondary plan: to become a 'Dissenting Parson & abjure Politics & carnal literature'.[634] The use of the word 'carnal' to describe literature is significant even if, in the context, a little silly.

Again, to Thelwall on 19 November 1796, grumbling about 'literary *Adventure*' being 'but bread and cheese *by chance!*', he says that although he is 'a library cormorant', '*deep* in all out of the way books', he nevertheless seldom reads 'except to amuse myself'; he '*will* be (please God) an Horticulturalist & a Farmer. I compose very little—& I absolutely hate composition'. None of this is absolutely serious; but Coleridge must nevertheless mean something by it. It is not the result of disappointment over the failure of *The Watchman*, but something much more fundamental: he says he does not 'like History. Metaphysics & Poetry, & "Facts of mind" (i.e. Accounts of all the strange phantasms that ever possessed your philosophy-dreamers . . .)'.[635] When one recollects the primeval and terrifying, as well as lovely, nature of some of the 'strange phantasms' of his poetry, one does not wonder that he did not '*like*' the intimations of them that must at this time have been stirring in his mind.

On 13 December 1796 he is still actively resisting the flood of poetic inspiration that was to engulph him within a few months: he tells Poole that his poems are Cottle's property, not his own; that

> Literature, tho' I shall never abandon it, will always be a secondary Object with me—My poetic Vanity & my political Furore have been exhaled; and I would rather be an expert, self-maintaining Gardener than a Milton, if I could not unite both'.[636]

This ideal of 'the *Whole man*', who could 'unite both', was to become a leading feature of his thought. But he never achieved his ideal, for he could never come to terms with his own sensuality. When he

used to say 'I have the brow of an angel, and the mouth of a beast',[637]
he was alluding to a familiar enough dichotomy, but one which
peculiarly disturbed and preoccupied him. In the 19 November
1796 letter to Thelwall, already quoted from, he described himself
as unable to breath through his nose, and therefore perpetually
open-mouthed, 'with sensual thick lips'.

7

Coleridge was happy with Sara for much of the first five years of
their marriage: he still had hope, and happiness feeds on hope.
Nothing bad enough happened to undermine his conscious hopes
for ultimate domestic bliss. However, Coleridge was never in love
with his wife as he had been in love with Mary Evans. Although he
wrote in his notebook, very early on in his marriage, 'Mem—not to
adulterize my time by absenting myself from my wife',[638] there is—
and surely this is suggestive—no entry in it that expresses spontaneous, involuntary love for her, of the type he had cherished for
Mary Evans. Indeed, since he was soon to be frequently away from
home (he was not there for the birth of Hartley), this particular
'Mem' had just such an air of resolution about it as do his references
to his 'love' for Sara in letters to Southey and to the grimly dutiful
'solemn joy' he told Poole he had felt on the occasion of his marriage.
Besides, would a man really in love need to admonish himself so
stiffly, and in writing?

Later Coleridge wrote in his notebook (1796) that 'Love
transforms the souls into a conformity with the object loved'.[639]
For him this was always a vital notion. Had he not told Southey
that his and Mary's 'ideas were blended'? Certainly this was one
of the cardinal reasons why she was so 'VERY LOVELY' to him. Sara
could never be 'lovely' to him in this way; he could never suggest
that she had any ideas to blend with. True, she had listened
admiringly to his Pantisocratic outpourings in the summer of 1794;
but it must very rapidly have become clear that she had nothing
intellectual to offer him. That he knew this intuitively even before
the marriage is proved by *The Eolian Harp* (August 1795), the
pattern of which is prophetic. The poem embodies a fundamental
contradiction which, however, it tries vainly to hide.

> My pensive Sara! thy soft cheek reclined
> Thus on mine arm, most soothing sweet it is
> To sit beside our Cot, our Cot o'ergrown
> With white-flower'd Jasmin, and the broad-leav'd Myrtle,
> (Meet emblems they of Innocence and Love!)
> And watch the clouds, that late were rich with light,

Slow saddening round, and mark the star of eve
Serenely brilliant (such should Wisdom be)
Shine opposite! How exquisite the scents
Snatch'd from yon bean-field! and the world *so* hush'd!
The stilly murmur of the distant Sea
Tells us of silence.

       And that simplest Lute,
Placed length-ways in the clasping casement, hark!

How by the desultory breeze caress'd,
Like some coy maid half yielding to her lover,
It pours such sweet upbraiding, as much needs
Tempt to repeat the wrong! And now, its strings
Boldlier swept, the long sequacious notes
Over delicious surges sink and rise,
Such a soft floating witchery of sound
As twilight Elfins make, when they at eve
Voyage on gentle gales from Fairy-Land,
Where Melodies round honey-dropping flowers,
Footless and wild, like birds of Paradise,
Nor pause, nor perch, hovering on untam'd wing!
O! the one Life within us and abroad,
Which meets all motion and becomes its soul,
A light in sound, a sound-like power in light,
Rhythm in all thought, and joyance every where—
Methinks, it should have been impossible
Not to love all things in a world so fill'd;
Where the breeze warbles, and the mute still air
Is Music slumbering on her instrument.

    And thus, my Love! as on the midway slope
Of yonder hill I stretch my limbs at noon,
Whilst through my half-clos'd eye-lids I behold
The sunbeams dance, like diamonds, on the main,
And tranquil muse upon tranquillity;
Full many a thought uncall'd and undetain'd,
And many idle flitting phantasies,
Traverse my indolent and passive brain,
As wild and various as the random gales
That swell and flutter on this subject Lute!

    And what if all of animated nature
Be but organic Harps diversely fram'd,
That tremble into thought, as o'er them sweeps
Plastic and vast, one intellectual breeze,
At once the Soul of each, and God of all?

But thy more serious eye a mild reproof
Darts, O belovéd Woman! nor such thoughts
Dim and unhallow'd dost thou not reject,
And biddest me walk humbly with my God.
Meek Daughter in the family of Christ!
Well hast thou said and holily disprais'd
These shapings of the unregenerate mind;
Bubbles that glitter as they rise and break
On vain Philosophy's aye-babbling spring.
For never guiltless may I speak of him,
The Incomprehensible! save when with awe
I praise him, and with Faith that inly *feels*;
Who with his saving mercies healéd me,
A sinful and most miserable man,
Wilder'd and dark, and gave me to possess
Peace, and this Cot, and thee, heart-honour'd Maid!

It is evident that this poem, of which I have here quoted Coleridge's
final version (lines 26–33 were added much later), is an attempt, as
his marriage was, to reconcile the practice of poetry with a harmon-
ious domestic life. It begins by describing a moment when the
young couple contentedly looked out from beside their cottage-to-be
at the happy scene; clearly it wishes to imply in their joint content-
ment a situation in which 'ideas were blended'. But that is as far as
it can go: as a whole it is simply Coleridge—with a tinge of sexual
anticipation—'doing his duty' just as he had promised Southey he
would. The theme of the poem, which has been admirably explained
by Humphry House,[640] is that of human oneness, harmony, with
Nature, a concept closely related to that of harmony between two
individuals. The first and longer part of the poem (lines 1–48) is
happy and affirming: a poet's flexing of his muscles in acknowledgement of his possession of vast poetic powers of response to creative
wind and the harmonies of Nature. But when we read this first part
carefully we note that Sara is really an intruder. He has her there,
but she is in fact a dummy, sitting there listening to him; only in
line 35 does he jerk himself into uttering a deferential 'my Love!'.
The poem is not, structurally or otherwise, a love poem. It would
like to be 'about' Sara, but she has no more part in it than she
really had in Coleridge's heart: she is in no way integrated into his
poetic response to Nature. This is surprising, because within six or
seven weeks Coleridge was going to marry her—to be, as we must
not forget he had told Southey only ten months earlier, 'externally
Just'. In *Lines Written At Shurton Bars* (September 1795), he had
certainly been anticipating the physical delights of the marriage-bed
in their role as compensation for lack of spiritual harmony. *Shurton
Bars* ends, prophetically:

And so shall flash my love-charged eye
When all the big heart's ecstasy
        Shoots rapid through the frame!

Southey, whose stern example had caused him to renounce the
delights of the Cambridge whores, was not going to have things all
his own way. . . . So Sara, the bride-to-be, does get worked into
The Eolian Harp, if only figuratively and in a way Coleridge did not
consciously desire: the harp itself reacts to the 'desultory breeze'
(how appropriate a description this is of Coleridge's mental passion
for Sara) like a 'coy maid half-yielding to her lover', and pouring
'such sweet upbraiding' as must tempt the lover 'to repeat the
wrong'. The use of the word 'wrong' is revealing: Coleridge was
rationalizing his instincts; but there can be no doubt that he was
preparing to use Sara 'as an instrument of low desire', to indulge his
'desultory'—the repetition of this adjective should be noted—
'Appetite', and that he knew it in his heart.

But Coleridge's poetic conscience, as he proceeds, cannot
bear the strain: so in a final paragraph he makes Sara 'reprove'
him, and in effect accepts a totally conventionalized, orthdox, mean-
ingless Christianity, consisting of clichés ('walk humbly with my
God'; 'unregenerate mind', and so on) that are far beneath his own
mental level; this attitude goes perfectly with the 'Cot', and peace,
and of course, the 'Maid' whom he is soon, guiltily but enjoyably,
to deflower. It is possible that when, after 4 October 1795, he was
able to make licit love to Sara he imagined she was Mary Evans,
with whose ideas his were, or were capable of being, blended (or so
he believed, which is what is important). And just as in the poem
he had had Sara, 'Meek Daughter in the family of Christ!' (one
would suspect irony if one did not know Coleridge and his problems),
tell him off—not really for his unexceptionable Platonizing, for she
was incapable of understanding more than that certain kinds of
thinking would not help Coleridge to 'get on', but generally, for
vain theorizing when there was practical, 'Christian', profit-making
labour to be attended to—so in his life he made a bid to resist the
'vanity' of his poetry, the mainsprings of which he saw were pagan
rather than Christian, and to become 'an Horticulturalist & Farmer'
instead.

He found he could not manage to give up writing poetry,
but did his best to discredit his reasons for doing so. *Reflections on
Having Left a Place of Retirement* (1795) he described in the *Monthly
Magazine*, where he published it, as 'A poem which affects not to be
Poetry'; *Religious Musings* was described as 'desultory'.

The end of *The Eolian Harp* may not make for good poetry—
it is an attempt at a deliberate abandonment of it—but it cannot
be called hypocritical or insincere, although it proved self-deluding,

in the context of Coleridge's life. The poem perfectly explains why, in 1796, he was telling Thelwall and Poole that he hated composition, would be a parson, and would treat literature as 'secondary'. He knew, as he said in *Biographia Literaria*, that 'we unconsciously imitate those whom we love'; now he was engaged in conscious imitation of one whom he did not love, in order to turn her into a beloved, whom he then might properly imitate.

To make a success of his marriage Coleridge needed to give up what poetry really entailed: not the mere writing of verse, but actually being and thinking poetically. For Sara did not like it, and it did not like her: the poet in Coleridge obstinately considered Mary Evans. But the man desperately wanted to make a success of his marriage. He might, in a conventional sense, have succeeded, even with Sara. But an irresistible poetic impulse to achieve a reconciliation between lust and love, to achieve what he meant at this time by 'sublimity', perpetually undermined and eventually destroyed all his efforts in this direction. In 1894 he had written of how he sought

> the cottag'd dell
> Where Virtue calm with careless step may stray,
> And dancing to the moonlight roundelay,
> The wizard Passions weave an holy spell.[641]

Even then, engaged to Miss Fricker, obsessed with Miss Evans, he was hopefully contemplating the unity of possibility of unifying virtue and magic, of making himself into a 'whole man'. Now he possessed the 'cottag'd dell', he had the sexual 'Passions' and even the sexual 'spell'. But the Passions were not 'wizard', the spell was not 'holy'.

8

T. S. Eliot spoke, sourly, of *Kubla Khan*'s 'exaggerated repute'; Livingstone Lowes's view of it was that it was essentially a piece of divine nonsense; more recently, Professor William Walsh has characterized it, somewhat cunningly, as 'non-sense'. George Watson, in a discussion of the poem that is acutely intelligent but vitiated by his wilful disregard of the poetic excitement it generates, startlingly asserts that it is essentially a piece of literary criticism.[642] But the poem's wild and undoubtedly magical remoteness from 'ordinary' experience is only apparent. Its extraordinary rhythmical authority, its sublime confidence as a statement, imply its high status as a document of mysterious exactness. Its meaning is so tragic, so accurate, so universal in its application to the human sexual condition, that few of us want to understand it: so we say it is a 'beautiful opium-image', non-sense, and so on. In 1816 Coleridge deliberately led himself, and hoped to lead us, into this error. Only recently has this impression of the poem been seen to be incorrect.

Here I deal mainly with *Kubla Khan* and the original *Dejection* (itself actually a letter), because these two poems stand, respectively, at the beginning and the very end of Coleridge's most intense poetic period. Furthermore, although *Kubla Khan* is never actually mentioned, there are perhaps more direct clues to its date and its meaning in letters than there are to *The Ancient Mariner* and *Christabel*.

Kubla Khan, as Werner W. Beyer has pointed out in his fascinating book tracing Coleridge's conscious and unconscious debt to Wieland's *Oberon*,[643] is 'intensely hopeful, vital and *pro*spective, rather than retrospective, resigned and tragic like *Dejection, an Ode* of 1802'.

It is likely to have preceded *The Ancient Mariner* and the first part of *Christabel*. Three dates have been suggested for its composition: October 1797, May 1798 and some time in 1799/1800. The last date, put forward by Miss Elizabeth Schneider, is not very persuasive, and is made less so by her odd view of the poem itself, which she regards as 'a fragment with a postscript'.[644] The first two, however, are plausible.

When in 1816 Coleridge published the poem, reluctantly but no doubt curiously, he felt constrained to apologize for it

> The following fragment is here published at the request of a poet and great and deserved celebrity [Byron], and, as far as the Author's own opinions are concerned, rather as a psychological curiosity, than on the ground of any supposed *poetic* merits.
>
> In the summer of the year 1797, the author, then in ill health, had retired to a lonely farm-house between Porlock and Linton, on the Exmoor confines of Somerset and Devonshire. In consequence of a slight indisposition, an anodyne had been prescribed, from the effects of which he fell asleep in his chair at the moment that he was reading the following sentence, or words of the same substance, in 'Purchas's Pilgrimage': 'Here the Khan Kubla commanded a palace to be built, and a stately garden thereunto. And thus ten miles of fertile ground were inclosed with a wall.' The Author continued for about three hours in a profound sleep at least of the external senses, during which time he has the most vivid confidence, that he could not have composed less than from two to three hundred lines; if that indeed can be called composition in which all the images rose up before him as *things*, with a parallel production of

the correspondent expressions, without any sensation or consciousness or effort. On awaking he appeared to himself to have a distinct recollection of the whole, and taking his pen, ink, and paper, instantly and eagerly wrote down the lines that are here preserved. At this moment he was unfortunately called out by a person on business from Porlock, and detained by him above an hour, and on his return to his room, found, to his no small surprise and mortification, that though he still retained some vague and dim recollection of the general purport of the vision, yet, with the exception of some eight or ten scattered lines and images, all the rest had passed away like the images on the surface of a stream into which a stone has been cast, but, alas! without the after restoration of the latter!

> Then all the charm
> Is broken—all that phantom-world so fair
> Vanishes, and a thousand circlets spread,
> And each mis-shape['s] the other. Stay awhile,
> Poor youth! who scarcely dar'st lift up thine eyes—
> The stream will soon renew its smoothness, soon
> The visions will return! And lo, he stays,
> And soon the fragments dim of lovely forms
> Come trembling back, unite, and now once more
> The pool becomes a mirror.

Yet from the still surviving recollections in his mind, the Author has frequently purposed to finish for himself what had been originally, as it were, given to him. Εαμερον αδιον ασω [Αὔριον ἄδιον ἄσω 1834]: but the to-morrow is yet to come.

As a contrast to this vision, I have annexed a fragment of a very different character, describing with equal fidelity the dream of pain and disease.[645]

The first paragraph alone should be enough to put us on our guard against taking this Preface at its face value; it shows Coleridge at his old, over-modest game of minimizing his '*poetic* merits'. For we know, and of course Coleridge knew too, that if the merits of *Kubla Khan* are not '*poetic*' then they do not exist. That he knew it is proved by his remark towards the end of the Preface, where he speaks of the poem as having been 'given to him'. He tries to make out that it was composed in an 'anodyne'-induced (i.e. opium-induced) dream, whereas it is now common knowledge that opium in itself is not hallucinogenic, and induces no such types of vision or dream. What he meant was that *Kubla Khan* had been composed without an effort, that it represented something vital to him—of which he was, however, deeply ashamed.

In 1816 he was at the height of his moral struggle against 'the ACCURSED habit', which he associated with poetry. His 1816 volume printed, for the first time, earlier poems that deeply disturbed him; therefore he presented the most disturbing material of all, *Kubla Khan*, with despairing irony, as 'a psychological curiosity' which had arisen from the prescription of an 'anodyne'. But all the opium actually did was to release his poetic potentialities. It did not in any sense at all create them, as Coleridge hoped the reader would think. Doubtless he relied on his contemporaries to accept the phrase 'a vision in a dream' literally, and on their treating it as a 'beautiful opium-image', which it was even in the eyes of Lowes. But it was his own 'bad most shocking *Dreams*' (my italics) that disturbed and horrified Coleridge. He felt that he could trace the 'origin of evil' from his study of them; and in them, when they were distempered, 'things & forms in themselves common & harmless' inflicted 'a terror of anguish';[646] his 'night-horrors in . . . sleep' were 'almost epileptic'.[647]

Many scholars, following E. H. Coleridge in his edition of the poems, have assumed that for 'the summer of 1797' Coleridge should have written 'the May of 1798'. This is on the strength of a MS. note, of 3 November 1810, in which Coleridge connected what E. H. Coleridge called 'the retirement between "Linton and Porlock" and a recourse to opium, with his quarrel with Charles Lloyd. . . . That quarrel was at its height in May 1798.'

E. H. Coleridge should more properly have written '*a* retirement': it is likely Coleridge went to this place on two or more occasions. There would be no reason to connect the visit of May 1798 with the composition of *Kubla Khan* except that Coleridge wrote, in the 1810 note, that 'at the retirement between Linton & Porlock was the first occasion of my having recourse to Opium': so those who saw *Kubla Khan* as an opium-dream were naturally the more tempted to associate its composition with this occasion. But for Coleridge there were many 'first occasions' of his having recourse to opium: he more often tended to link it (as we have seen from his letters) with his illness of 1801, when his knees swelled up.

According to Miss Kathleen Coburn, who should know better than anyone, Coleridge's memory for dates—apart from one or two consistent lapses, such as his notion that he was a year and a day older than he actually was—was not half as unreliable as Chambers, to whom such things seem to have been tantamount to moral slackness, pretended. When in 1934 the Crewe MS., an autograph copy of *Kubla Khan* (in the MS. it is 'Cubla', and there are one or two other trifling variants), turned up, Coleridge's own note repeated almost the same information he gave in 1816:

This fragment with a good deal more, not recoverable,

composed in a sort of Reverie brought on by two grains of
Opium, taken to check a dysentery, at a Farm House
between Porlock & Linton, a quarter of a mile from
Culbone Church, in the fall of the year,1797.

'The fall of the year, 1797' is perhaps an even closer approximation
to the date of the poem, as we shall see; and this note was probably
written well before 1816, since it is on the same paper as Coleridge
used for a letter of 1796. The holograph seems to have been sent to
Lord Crewe, for his collection, by either 'Mr.' or 'Mrs.' Southey—
surely it is likely that Coleridge gave it to Southey, perhaps up in
the Lake District some time before he left for Malta, when he was
still likely to have possessed a stock of the 1796 paper? The most
interesting difference between this note and the 1816 Preface is,
however, the phrase 'in a sort of Reverie': taken together with the
faint ambiguity of the 1816 phrase, 'sleep, at least of the external
senses', it suggests that the poem was written in a poetic trance, the
kind of trance that Coleridge had been trying to resist throughout
1796 and 1797, and which he distrusted and associated with opium
throughout his life.

Certain remarks in letters of 1796/8, besides clinching the
matter of the date, cast light on the meaning of the poem. We know
that by 1796 Coleridge was capable of using opium to relieve mental
distress and tension as well as physical pain (whatever he may have
claimed in the 1810 note): in great physical pain, he had managed
to write to Poole on 5 December 1796 *because of* the '25 drops of
Laudanum' he had taken, which gave him 'ease & spirits'. Before
taking the laudanum his imagination, with 'a gloomy wantonness',
had been 'coquetting with the hideous *Possibles* of Disappointment':
'my ever-shaping & distrustful mind still mingled gall-drops, till
out of the cup of Hope *I almost* poisoned myself with Despair!'[648]
Here, interestingly, he could already be pejorative, when in periods
of depression unrelieved by opium, about the 'ever-shaping' faculty
of his mind. His depression was not due merely to poor financial
prospects. . . . 'Hope', however he may subsequently have meta-
physicized it, was always a partly erotic notion for Coleridge. A notebook entry of January 1805, written in Malta, reads (decoded):

Important metaphysical Hint the influence of bodily vigor
and strong Grasp of Touch in facilitating the passion of
Hope: eunuchs—in all degrees even to the full ensheath-
ment and the both at once.[649]

In a continuation of this entry, again dealing with the importance
of touch, he asks himself if the nipple of a woman's breast ever
becomes 'the seat of a particular feeling, as one would guess by its
dormancy & sudden awakings', and considers the significance of the

feeling in his penis when he is making love (as he puts it in his code: 'mem. vi / Riley. injects of Es*sex*').[650] We can guess, then, at the nature of his chief 'Hope' in the early winter of 1796, an ambiguous and partly guilty hope: on the one hand, the innocent wish that love would transform the nature of his use of Sara as an 'Instrument of low Desire', which his intelligence told him was useless; on the other, the guilty retrospective desire for Mary Evans, the hope that someone might take her place (as, of course, Asra did in 1799).

On 17 July 1797 Coleridge sent Southey an early version of his newly written poem, *This Lime Tree Bower My Prison*. The Wordsworths and Lamb came to visit him at Stowey, and within a day 'dear Sara' 'Accidentally emptied a skillet of boiling milk' on his foot; so while his guests walked, Coleridge was confined to the 'arbour of T. Poole's garden', which adjoined his. Here he wrote the poem. In a very early version he gave, as his reason for being left behind, that he had been 'lam'd by the scathe of fire', a good description of Sara's feelings about the Wordsworths and her consequent milk-spilling propensities. The cancelled version of lines 6 and 7 reads

> [My friends] . . .
> Wand'ring well-pleased, look down on grange or dell
> Or deep fantastic [altered, in the MS., from 'deep gloomy']
> Rift, where many an Ash. . . .[651]

Afterwards this was altered to

> Wander delighted, and look down, perchance,
> On that same rifted Dell, where many an Ash. . . .

And in the version printed in the 1800 *Annual Anthology*, which does not differ materially from that of *Sibylline Leaves*, it was further corrected to:

> Wander in gladness, and wind down, perchance,
> To that still roaring dell, of which I told. . . .

Coleridge got progressively further from his original conception of simply looking down into the 'deep fantastic Rift' so suggestive of the 'deep romantic chasm' of *Kubla Khan*: finally the walkers actually 'wind down' into it. This was more appropriate in *This Lime-Tree Bower*; but what is interesting, if only in relation to *Kubla Khan*, is Coleridge's obsession with, and confusion about, the meaning of this dell or rift. Already, in July, one of the major themes of *Kubla Khan* was uppermost in his imagination. First it was a 'deep gloomy Rift'; then a 'deep fantastic' one; but then it became something quite different: a 'rifted Dell'. What has happened is that the strange, wild place has become transformed, in *This*

Lime-Tree Bower, into a dell; the one which, for Coleridge, was a false symbol of domestic bliss. In the final version all of this is rightly removed, as irrelevant to the poem: the place becomes simply a 'roaring dell, of which I told'. (Does this indicate that he had told the walkers, specifically the urban Lamb, about it? Or has he been thinking so hard about it that he forgets that he has 'told' the reader nothing about it?) Griggs says that the 'wild, romantic dell' at Alfoxden is the one described in the poem;[652] if this is so, then Coleridge should not have had quite so much trouble in describing it—unless, of course, the very idea of it had intensely powerful emotional connotations for him. So far as *Kubla Khan* is concerned, the other interesting aspect of *This Lime-Tree Bower* is the total absence of 'dear Sara' from a poem that is again about love for and harmony with Nature. A man in love with his wife, and of Coleridge's loving temperament, might, in such a poem, have been consoled for the loss of his friend's company by her presence. Coleridge, however, is consoled by his meditations and his love for the gentle Charles Lamb—Sara is conspicuously not one of the things in the bower that, in the printed 1800 version, 'sooth'd' him. So, because Sara is quite absent from it, the poem does not suffer from the confusions of *The Eolian Harp*; that absence alone, in lieu of opium, helped Coleridge to relax.

On 1 August 1797, writing to Josiah Wade, Coleridge spoke of a 'Journey to Paradise': he would defer this in order that Wade might spend a week at Stowey. He knew of 'nothing in the ordinary events of life' that would give him such pleasure, thus implying the existence of extraordinary things that would give more than pleasure.[653] Coleridge was aware of a great poetic excitement stirring within him: the contrast between a 'Journey to Paradise' and 'the ordinary events of life' implies something quite different from the conversation poems. Throughout August, however, he was distracted and made unwell by the affair of 'the government spy': Thelwall, already a marked man, had been in the area, and an absurd government snooper (who, however, ultimately had the wit to report that his quarries were literary men and not subversive agents) suspected Wordsworth, Coleridge and their radical friend of favouring a French invasion, and preparing for it. Not unnaturally, Coleridge was upset.

Then, on 14 October 1797, Coleridge wrote to Thelwall from Stowey:

> I have just received your letter—having been absent a day of two—& have already, before I write you, written to Dr Beddoes—I would to heaven, it were in my power to serve you—but alas! I have neither money or influence—& I suppose, that at last I must become a Unitarian minister

as a less evil than starvation—for I get nothing by literature —& Sara is in the way of repairing the ravages of war, as much as in her lies.——You have my wishes, & what is very liberal in me for such as atheist reprobate, my prayers. ——I can *at times* feel strongly the beauties, you describe, in themselves, & for themselves—but more frequently *all things* appear little—all the knowlege, that can be acquired, child's play—the universe itself—what but an immense heap of *little* things?—I can contemplate nothing but parts, & parts are all *little*—!—My mind feels as if it ached to behold & know something *great*—something *one* & *indivisible*—and it is only in the faith of this that rocks or waterfalls, mountains or caverns give me the sense of sublimity or majesty!—But in this faith *all things* counterfeit infinity!—'Struck with the deepest calm of Joy' I stand

Silent, with swimming sense; and gazing round
On the wide Landscape gaze till all doth seem
Less gross than bodily, a living Thing
Which acts upon the mind, & with such Hues
As cloath th' Almighty Spirit, when he makes
Spirits perceive his presence!——

It is but seldom that I raise & spiritualize my intellect to this height—& at other times I adopt the Brahman Creed, & say—It is better to sit than to stand, it is better to lie than to sit, it is better to sleep than to wake—but Death is the best of all!—I should much wish, like the Indian Vishna, [Vishnu] to float about along an infinite ocean cradled in the flower of the Lotos, & wake once in a million years for a few minutes—just to know that I was going to sleep a million years more. . . .[654]

As Griggs suggests, this tends to confirm Coleridge's own date of 'the fall of the year 1797' (a phrase he actually uses in the letter) for *Kubla Khan*. Distressed over the spy incident, it would have been natural for him to go to Ash Farm, or to Broomstreet Farm, near Culbone, which lies between Lynton and Porlock, to recuperate.[655] Here he wrote *Kubla Khan*. Certainly he then ignored it, because its implications profoundly disturbed him. It is surely significant that he neither published it in a newspaper or in *Lyrical Ballads*, nor ever mentioned it in a notebook or letter. But the writing of it was an experience in itself: he must have realized that it reflected tragic and challenging awarenesses that he had been trying to ignore. That the letter to Thelwall—with its descriptions of his feelings of wanting to 'know something *great*', its quotation from the

Lime-Tree poem, and its wish to emulate Vishnu—is related to the mood of *Kubla Khan* is obvious.

In November 1797 Coleridge published a series of poems in the *Monthly Magazine*, signed 'Nehemiah Higginbottom': they were 'mock sonnets in ridicule of my own, & Charles Lloyd's, & Lamb's, &c &c', as he put it to Cottle.[656] This started a quarrel with the neurotic and spiteful Lloyd, into which Lamb became drawn. Coleridge's satirical recklessness in tactlessly parodying not only his own earlier style but also the less talented Lamb's and Lloyd's styles (their poems had been added to his own in the 1797 volume) is surely explained by a new—if reluctantly acknowledged—feeling of poetic confidence and power. For in this November, the month following the composition of *Kubla Khan*, on walks with the Wordsworths, both *Christabel* and *The Ancient Mariner* were conceived. Contact with Wordsworth, then at the height of his own poetic powers, excited and stimulated Coleridge; but, true not only to his psychological need to abase himself, to seek a father-figure, but also to his equally pressing need to reject the impulses of poetry, he remained strangely modest about his achievements.

Then came the visit to Shrewsbury of January 1798, and the acceptance of the annuity of £150 from the Wedgwoods. Coleridge's near reluctance to accept it arose from his desire to avoid yielding to the poetic impulses that were raging in him as well as from delicacy. But by the middle of the year *The Ancient Mariner* and the first part of *Christabel* were finished.

Those who object to the October 1797 date for *Kubla Khan*, preferring May 1798, cite a letter Coleridge wrote to the Rev. George on about 10 March 1798. He had been recovering from an infected tooth-stump, and said

> Laudanum gave me repose, not sleep; but YOU, I believe, know how divine that repose is—what a spot of inchantment, a green spot of fountains, & flowers & trees, in the very heart of a waste of Sands.[657]

This, with its echo of *Kubla Khan*, has led commentators to believe that the letter is an anticipation of the poem, which they believe was written two months later. But as Chambers pointed out 'the "blessed unviolated spot of earth" and "enchanted spot" described in *Bartram's Travels*', which Lowes showed formed part of Coleridge's raw material for *Kubla Khan*, is already linked in this letter with laudanum: 'that link was first forged when *Kubla Khan* itself was written'.[658] For although the drug played no part in the actual composition of the poem, opium remained indissolubly associated with it, and all it stood for, in Coleridge's mind. The most salient statement in the letter to George is that opium gave him repose: peace, tranquillity, release from the tension created by 'the ordinary events of life', and consequent ability to concentrate uninhibitedly upon poetry, a 'Journey to Paradise'. It did *not*, he says specifically, give him sleep. The phrase of the Crewe MS., 'a sort of reverie', is vindicated.

9

I have given my view of the nature of Coleridge's sexual predicament at the time he wrote *Kubla Khan* in some detail: it figures in the poem. His financial situation is another pertinent factor. He was seriously thinking of becoming a Unitarian minister, of giving up literature in favour of 'a regular job'—and a moralizing one at that. After two years of marriage, he had failed to support his family by writing. His wife, fundamentally out of sympathy with poetry— but tolerant of successful verse such as the later Southey's—had had a miscarriage in late July and was probably ill and run down;[659] all this increased his anxieties. He had been further harassed by the 'spy' affair in August. It seems likely, then, that some time at the beginning of October, in 'the fall of the year', he sought solitary retirement between Linton and Porlock. He proceeded to take opium to relieve his nervously disturbed stomach, and this afforded him such relaxation that, in an unfamiliar solitude, he was able to give, for once, unequivocal expression to his profoundest feelings. All that opium did for *Kubla Khan* was to give its author the 'repose' he needed to write it.

Although few are immune to the spell the poem casts, there is surprisingly little agreement about its meaning or lack of meaning. For Lowes and many other readers it is, as we have seen, divine, non-symbolic nonsense. For G. Wilson Knight,[660] who is substantially followed by Marshall Suther,[661] Kubla is a symbol of God: the symbolic poem is not unfinished but a coherent whole. For Miss Schneider it is a confused fragment, unsusceptible to symbolic interpretation, and written in the spirit of *Dejection*. For J. B. Beer, a notable interpreter, it is 'a dialectic of a fallen world'. And so on. There are almost as many interpretations as critics. There is substantial agreement about perhaps only one detail: that the youth at the end, with his flashing eyes and floating hair, is an inspired poet-seer. We find him most familiarly in Plato's *Ion* and *Phaedrus*, but also before and after that. He is Shakespeare's poet with his eye in a fine frenzy rolling, inspired, in Socrates's words in the *Phaedrus*, by 'the madness of love', that kind of madness that proceeds not from 'human disease' but 'by an inspired departure from established usages'.

Five years later, after *Dejection*, Coleridge told Southey, in a letter of Christmas Day 1802, that 'Virtue and Genius' were 'analogous to the beautiful Diseases that colour and variegate certain Trees'—but then added it was his 'Faith' that 'Virtue & Genius' produced 'the Disease', 'not Disease the Virtue &c'.[662] The inspired poet-seer, the essential Pantisocrat, the perfect lover —the writer of *Kubla Khan*—had no foreseeable function in Coleridge's life by the end of 1802.

Thus, *Kubla Khan* is 'about' nothing less than being a poet. But its meaning is not therefore made inaccessible to those who do not write poetry: there is a poet in all men. Perhaps the single most useful definition of this function, of the poetic in those who do not write poetry, is that it preserves an intuitive awareness—whether effectually or not is beside the point here—of the difference between man as he is and man as he should or might be.

The critics (Beyer, Yarlott, Beer) who point out that Kubla's world is a fallen one, a false paradise, have grasped the essential basis of the poem; without this it cannot, I think, be fully understood. In the 1816 Preface, as I and others have suggested, Coleridge was taking evasive, misleading action; but on the kind of necessarily secret, ecstatic level at which *Kubla Khan* was written he remained true to himself. For although it is not a fragment, being as finished as any poem is ever finished, and although it was probably not actually composed in sleep and then recollected, *poetry*, its subject, is indeed unhappily fragmentary in terms of 'the events of ordinary life': all poetic 'journeys to paradise' are, in a tragic sense, visions in a dream.

The legendary cruelty, 'barbarity' and material omnipotence of the tyrannical Eastern potentate, Kubla, function most essentially in the poem as an ironic equivalent for the viciously bland confidence man has in his civilizing, reasoning faculty: the faculty which should and in some ways does elevate him, but which also, fatally, alienates him from his own innocent, instinctive animality. (One is reminded of the mariner's gratuitous sadism in killing the albatross, and of the similarly bland manner in which Coleridge deliberately leaves it unexplained in the ballad.) Here, absolutely himself, Coleridge recognizes that his 'cottag'd dell' cannot also be 'a romantic chasm', a confusion which had been implicit in the various early versions of *This Lime-Tree Bower*. His falsely idyllic dell becomes transformed, here, into what it truly is: the sexually luxurious Kubla's artificial paradise. The 'pleasure-dome', itself incidentally a breast-symbol (as Yarlott has pointed out, Coleridge's poetry continually and not very reticently reveals his particular if not peculiar erotic delight in breasts[663]) is 'decreed', tyrannically. Some lines from an Asra poem of about 1805, *Separation*, are apposite here:

> Is not true love of higher price
> Than outward Form, though fair to see,

Wealth's glittering fairy-dome of ice,
Or echo of proud ancestry?

The pleasure-dome, artificial and phallically sensual, the guarding, enclosing walls and towers, the cultivated spice trees, the irrigated gardens, stand in terrible contrast to the divine nature of the landscape: fertile, watered by a sacred river, whose name, 'Alph', gives rise to a large number of holy associations, the chief of which is 'sacred source of all things'—and the uncultivated, 'Gothic', forests, as old as the hills they grow on.

This first stanza presents no less than a picture of the human situation, of organization superimposed on natural beauty; but, by an ironic twist of Coleridge's imagination, the evil of civilized paradises is here revealed. The keys to the evil are seen as lust and power. But this is how all of us exist. Beer speaks of Coleridge's belief that civilization is 'an attempt to regain the lost paradise'; but what Coleridge implies here is that human 'order', civilization, itself represents precisely the demonic force that it pretends to exist in order to subdue. The evil is not in the landscape but in the Khan. His paradise abuses the landscape: unsatisfied with Nature, he has built a 'pleasure-dome' where it is hideously parodied. But the immense folly of that act is measure of his, of Coleridge's, of a universal failure to learn from Nature (whose instructive powers Coleridge made the theme of several poems, including *This Lime-Tree Bower*). This is exemplified by Coleridge's own situation: by his sexual use of a woman he did not love, his own attempts to construct a false, inorganic, rationalized paradise, the 'cottag'd dell'.

However, within this false paradise exists the true one, composed of the ancient forests, the hills, the sunny spots of greenery, the life-giving river of imagination falling through bottomless caverns into a sunless sea mysterious as death. And so in the second stanza the angle of vision shifts: whereas before we have had an aerial view, so to speak, of Kubla's domains, we now see a part—an important part—of them, in close-up. This is the 'deep romantic chasm', 'athwart a cedarn cover', which contains the violently eruptive source of the sacred river.

Crude sexual symbolism ('cedarn cover' = pubic hair, 'chasm' = vagina, etc.) has been brought to bear on this stanza,[664] but to little avail. Such a reading makes nonsense of the rest of the poem. The notion that the eruption of the fountain is a metaphor for orgasm is too grotesque, considering the dancing rocks, to be taken very seriously. It is not necessary to concede more than that a generally sexual feeling has been introduced into the stanza, in contrast to the preceding one. No kind of arbitrary symbolism can help in the approach to this poem, because it simplifies what cannot be simplified; the introduction into it of a vagina, pubic hair and an orgasm, when they are not capable of being in any way integrated into its structure, is pointless.

Like the earliest form of Greek drama, *Kubla Khan* is a monodrama in which the actor (Coleridge) takes on various different dramatic roles: we see him as Kubla (= himself-as-husband), as the invoked but absent demon-lover, as Kubla again, and as himself-as-poet. In the first stage of the poem we see the falsity of the 'domestic solution'. Now in the second stage (which ends at '. . . war!': the 1816 edition rightly printed the next six lines separately, and editors should but do not follow it) we are shown the place of poetic reality, the romantic chasm where, under a waning moon (which is, as Yarlott points out, 'a Coleridgean emblem for declining powers of imagination'), a woman wails for her demon-lover by a sacred fountain. But the poet, the lover, the organic antithesis to Kubla, is absent.

The imagery at this point becomes sinister: the chasm slants down the hill, is a savage place, haunted by a wailing woman. And the woman is undoubtedly the wild, undomesticated 'muse' whom Robert Graves has made familiar to modern readers: the pagan Goddess whom Coleridge, by his unwise sacrifice of himself to the genteel Sara and by his plans to become a Unitarian minister, had failed to serve—but whom he did, in that aspect of himself that he considered 'demon', violently love. This wailing woman is 'The Night-mare LIFE-IN-DEATH . . ./Who thicks man's blood with cold'. She wails for the demon-lover because he is redolent with poetic power—with which his obsession with her has inspired him—but he is not there. Where is he? He is, literally, absent in the person of the Khan, whose false pleasure-dome, 'rational' tyranny and mechanically sensual sexual indulgence are all expressions of his terror of confronting her at the one spot in his domain over which he has no control: the origin and source of the sacred river.

The river becomes calm after its violent emergence from the earth, but is again 'in tumult' as it sinks to the 'lifeless sea' it feeds. Kubla is afraid of the sacred fountain, of the violent anarchic potentialities of birth and the creative power of the imagination (he was afraid to respond to the wailing woman, to become the 'demon-lover'). He is equally afraid of the tumultuous mysteries of death, of the death of the imagination (the waning moon). An articulate, strongly developed side of Coleridge himself, as we have seen, desired the 'death' of poetic power in himself: he wanted to be safe, to devote himself to that notably unbestial paradigm of virtue, Wordsworth, to be happily married, not to suffer from a need for perfection. But his poetic resistance to his prosaic if understandable desire, that his sacred river of imagination should sink into a lifeless ocean of tame domesticity, made a 'tumult'. So Kubla's guilt at his anti-natural tyranny caused the voices of his primitive, natural ancestors—the voices within him—to prophesy 'war': the upset of his dominions, the smashing down of his walls and towers, the destruction of his pleasure-dome.

In the strange, short third stanza the scene shifts again, this time to the waves. Upon the river, or upon the ocean,[665] floats the shadow of the pleasure-dome, while the sounds of the fountain and the river's tumultuous final exit, the beginning and the end, mingle there. We find here, if the waves are those of the sea, an apparent contradiction, which cannot be ignored: a shadow can only be cast by the sun, but this sea was 'sunless'; and sounds could hardly be heard in a 'lifeless' ocean. Thus, Coleridge may be indicating that the nature of this sea has changed. Although the receptacle of the sacred river, the ultimate mystery, it was sunless and lifeless under the Khan's tyranny—just as creation seems purposeless to materialists, obsessed with lust and power; just as Coleridge himself tried to treat literature as 'secondary'. But now, with natural instincts asserting themselves, the dome of pleasure may legitimately be pictured as dissolved into a shadow floating amidst the elemental music of birth and death. It is a measure of the potentialities of poetry.

The phantom ('shadow') palace that now floats on the waves, whether of river or ocean, is a miracle in which extremes of heat and cold (with all that these imply) are reconciled. It is not now 'stately', but 'a miracle of rare device'. However, it is not yet real. It is a melting and transitory vision; such a dome can be built 'in air' only with the inspiration of love. So, in the fourth and last stanza the poet speaks of himself, directly, as poet—and finally as sacred and heroic figure. The Abyssinian Maid, whom Yarlott identifies with Mary Evans, is the wailing woman in another, more benign aspect: she is now inspiring her poet, who is at last present as he should be. The triumphant mood of this stanza reflects Coleridge's faith in poetry as against politics. Three months earlier, on 23 July 1797, he had written to Estlin '. . . I am wearied with politics, even to soreness.—I never knew a passion for politics exist a long time without swallowing up, or absolutely excluding, a passion for Religion.'[666] He was then trying to canalize his poetic instincts into an orthodox form of religion; but religion, when not fulfilling its specifically anti-poetry function, sometimes came to stand for poetry. So in these final lines the poet can actually create the sunny ice-dome; whereas, his heart haunted by ancestral voices, Kubla Khan—Coleridge-as-husband—can do no more than create a floating phantom of it, a theoretical solution of the problem. The triumphant poet can build a dome that is not an artefact because it is spontaneously created rather than 'decreed'. The contrast is between artificial pleasure and spontaneously achieved joy. Thus, when built 'in air', the dome is no longer a 'pleasure-dome': it functions to reconcile the opposites, heat and cold. Yet it remains an illusion, a possibility; and being unreal, it is in a sense 'measureless' and infinite. The caves of its necessarily 'measured' blocks of ice no longer parody the 'measureless' caverns. One is reminded of an 1802 notebook entry: 'Something inherently mean in action. Even the Creation of the Universe disturbs my Idea of the Almighty's greatness—Would do so, but that I conceive that thought with him creates'.[667] But although the poet is wholly triumphant (which he very rarely is in Coleridge), it should be noted that he is a terrifying figure. Unworshipped, he is dangerous. It was just this aspect of himself that Coleridge could neither accept not yet wholeheartedly reject.

10

When H. S. and D. T. Bliss, in an article on *Kubla Khan* already cited,[668] conclude that Coleridge 'gave up poetry' because he was horrified by its sexuality, they fly in the face of the facts and do scant justice to his intelligence. He probably wrote both *Christabel* (Part 1) and *The Ancient Mariner* after *Kubla Khan*; nor did he every quite give up poetry, even if he lost most of his poetic power. But the unsubtle, clumsy pronouncement does contain a hint of the truth. There really was a sort of *demon-adventurer*—profligate, drinker, gambler, drug-addict—locked up inside the high-minded Coleridge. He was afraid of this aspect of himself, but most particularly of his powerful sexuality. He had agreed to marry Sara out of stupidity and weakness; but he married her out of lust. When he realized this he was horrified. Just as his fear and shame had 'used' the example of the moral Southey in order to give up whoring, so— if only at one level—he used the official morality of religion as another kind of sheet-anchor, to protect himself from the violence of his sexual desires. Geoffrey Yarlott's view, that he 'discovered the impossibility of living up to the articles of his faith—that the true Poet must be a *good* man', and thus developed a 'psycho-neurosis' based on guilt because he wished his wife and children dead is true as far as it goes. But it does not do enough justice to Coleridge's intelligence. He did not possess the necessary strength to face up to the wildness and 'lawlessness' of his involuntary desires. He was therefore weak; but, in terms of one kind of morality, he was also a sort of hero. Having no trace of coarseness in his nature, he immediately shrank away from much of what his acute vision revealed to him. His great and good unhappiness—it still cries out to those who study him—is not so much 'neurotic' (except in the, alas, mostly philistine terms of the blindly optimistic social welfare

worker or marriage guidance counsellor) as simply human: he saw
in himself no more than is in us all, but he alone was almost too
sensitive to be able to bear it.

The theme of *The Ancient Mariner* parallels that of *Kubla
Khan* in at least one respect: the protagonist commits a crime
against love, and learns a way of redemption. Coleridge finished
both poems. But *Christabel* remained unfinished. He said that he
had Crashaw's lines on Saint Teresa's martyrdom 'ever present'
to his mind when writing the second part of the poem in 1800, 'if,
indeed', as House wrote, 'by some subtle process of the mind they
did not suggest the first thought of the whole poem'.[669] Now
Crashaw's poem is about what House calls 'the psychological
border land where matters of religion overlap with matters of
sex. . . . In the seventeenth century such double references could
be carried together in the mind without any intellectual unease and
without any moral shame or awkwardness. In 1800 that was not
so.' Furthermore, when writing the first part (1797/8) Coleridge
had not met Asra; in 1800 he had, and he sexually desired her.

The subject of *Christabel* is more sexual than religious. It is
a truly daemonic poem, whose real heroine is the vampire-werewolf
Geraldine, and not her victim Christabel. But Coleridge could not
accept this. His inability to finish the poem troubled him for the
rest of his life. When Hazlitt viciously but shrewdly pointed out
that there was something 'disgusting at the bottom of his subject',
he protested. He would have liked to find a way of ending it that
was not 'disgusting'. In the three differing accounts he gave of
how he proposed to end it, one can discern some uneasy rationalizations.[670] In one version Christabel becomes a Christian figure,
'vicariously' suffering for 'wrongs' committed by her lover abroad;
in another Geraldine turns into a false spectre of the lover, whom
Christabel, horrified, almost marries (until the real man arrives).

Despite the rather odd doubts of Griggs and Chambers,
Coleridge certainly wrote at least some of a third part, but was
evidently so disgusted by it that he suppressed it. The poem as we
know it comprises 677 lines. Writing to Humphry Davy, on 9
October 1800, he said, 'The Christobel [*sic*] was running up to
1300 lines'.[671] As late as 24 November 1807 he told Dorothy
Wordsworth that he had 'about doubled the length of Christabel—
2 thirds are finished'.[672] In a letter of 22 October 1815 he told
Byron, who had decided to take him up (he gave him £100), that
he had heard from Lady Beaumont before he went to Malta that
Scott had recited and admired the poem (he plagiarized it in *The
Lay of the Last Minstrel*), and that this had surprised and gratified
him; then,

What occurred after my return from Italy [i.e. from Malta

in 1806], and what the disgusts were (most certainly not originating in my own opinion or decision) that indisposed me to the completion of the Poem, I will not trouble your Lordship with—It is not yet a Whole: and as it will be 5 books, I mean to publish it by itself. . . .[673]

The sentence in parentheses is suspicious. On 10 November 1799 he had written to Southey:

In my last letter I said I would give you my reasons for thinking Christabel, *were* it finished & finished as spiritedly as it commences, yet still an improper opening Poem [in a collection]. My reason is—it cannot be expected to please all/Those who dislike it will deem it extravagant Ravings, & go on thro' the rest of the Collection with the feeling of Disgust—& it is not impossible that were it liked by any, it would still not harmonize with the *real-life* Poems that follow. . . . The first ought, me judice, to be a poem in couplets, didactic or satirical—such a one as the lovers of genuine poetry would call sensible and entertaining, such as the Ignoramuses & Pope-admirers would deem genuine Poetry. . . .[674]

A certain convoluted bitterness, about both himself and public taste, is apparent here; but so is his persistent association of *Christabel* with 'disgust' and impropriety. On 1 November 1800 he told Josiah Wedgwood that he had tried to finish the poem,

but the deep unutterable Disgust, which I had suffered in the translation of that accursed Wallenstein [by Schiller], seemed to have stricken me with barrenness—for I tried & tried, & nothing would come of it. I desisted with a deeper dejection than I am willing to remember. The wind from Skiddaw & Borrowdale was often as loud as wind need be —& many a walk in the clouds on the mountains did I take; but all would not do—till one day I . . . some how or other drank so much wine, that I found some effort & dexterity requisite to balance myself on the hither Edge of Sobriety. The next day, my verse-making faculties returned to me, and I proceeded successfully. . . .[675]

The 'deep unutterable Disgust' had little, we may fairly suspect, to do with *Wallenstein*. The poet in Coleridge felt a strong compulsion to finish *Christabel*; but its daemonic, totally anti-domestic implications horrified him: despite the inspiration offered by the wind, his old poetic ally, he needed the de-inhibiting experience of semi-drunkenness to relax, at least temporarily, the tension that had built up in him between moral revulsion and poetic elation. In saying the wind blew 'as loud as need be' he was acknowledging his capacity to write the poem. But the specifically un-Christian nature of its theme alarmed him. For terror and guilt drove Coleridge into progressively tamer kinds of Christianity, until he ended, unconvincingly, as a repentant Anglican. Ultimately he felt himself not to be in a position to challenge any kind of morality, however commonplace. *Christabel* was subversively pagan: he could not accept the public Coleridge as the author of it. Yet his conscience never allowed him to Christianize it, either; so it remained uncompleted. To recall Socrates's words in the *Phaedrus*, Coleridge was capable of 'inspired departures', but 'established usages' had, in the end, too strong a hold upon him.

I I

Yarlott calls the *modus vivendi* established between Coleridge and Sara on his return from Germany in 1799 'curiously amicable',[676] and evidently feels that it might have continued indefinitely had he not met Asra. He believes that Coleridge had come 'to accept their incompatibility', and to support this view quotes a phrase from a letter of 30 September 1799 to Southey, in which he described Sara as 'tired off her legs with servanting . . . I however, sunk in Spinoza, remain as undisturbed as a Toad in a Rock'. What Yarlott does not quote, however, is a notebook entry of 1796/7, probably referring to Charles Lloyd: 'I discovered unprovoked malice in his hard heart, like a huge Toad in the centre of a marble rock'.[677] Coleridge's use of the word 'undisturbed' in the letter is misleading, perhaps deliberately so: it is clear that he did not equate the idea of the toad in the rock with happiness (as Southey did, for he once contemplated writing a sonnet on the happiness of a toad in a rock), but with 'malice' and evil. Yarlott writes that in the autumn of 1799 'there was no thought in his mind . . . of parting with Sara'. He was nevertheless looking elsewhere, if only unconsciously. If it had not been Asra, then it would have been someone else. The intensely spiritual nature of his expressions (in poems and notebooks) of love for Asra is partially explained by the intensely physical nature of his feelings towards her, which on at least one occasion he left unconcealed in his notebooks.[678] As further evidence that Coleridge was prepared to accept his situation, Yarlott quotes his remark to Southey in a letter of 15 October 1799, eleven days before he met Asra: '. . . the wife of a man of Genius who sympathises effectively with her Husband in his habits & feelings is a rara avis with me. . . .' But in fact this suggests just the opposite: *rarae aves* were always precisely what Coleridge was interested in finding; he was looking for one now. Furthermore, Yarlott has not quoted the end of the sentence, which continues: 'tho' a vast majority of her own sex & too many of ours will scout her for a rara piscis'.[679] Nothing could be more indicative of the way in which Coleridge's mind was working.

He was not, as he told Southey in the letter of 30 September 1799, 'in a poetical mood', and was already planning his 'Great Work'; he was determined to publish nothing under his name until this was completed. This great work, whose scope gradually widened until in 1815 it received the title of *Logosophia*, haunted him until his death; it was never finished as such, although his life's work may well be said to amount to something better than it. The idea of completing it always acted as a metaphysical compensation for his failure to finish *Christabel* and perhaps (in his own estimation) *Kubla Khan*, or to write other poems on the level of *The Ancient Mariner*. It is significant that he first conceived the project of the great work before meeting Asra. The corrosive guilt-process had begun before this: although his attachment to her precipitated his unhappiness, she was a symptom rather than a cause.

Few details are known of Asra's side of this relationship.[680] Coleridge's side is known from his notebooks, which make it clear that he was obsessed with her for eleven years, from 1799 until his estrangement from the Wordsworths in 1810. It was at first light-hearted, but then passed into an agonizing relationship, probably for both parties. It is extremely unlikely that the affair was ever consummated, although the possibility cannot be entirely ruled out. Certainly there was hand-pressing, and doubtless rather more than this: those long walks that both Coleridge and all the Wordsworths and Hutchinsons were in the habit of taking provided plenty of opportunity. In the early years there was a high degree of physical intimacy between the group: it was nothing for Mary Hutchinson to lie with her head in Coleridge's lap. It is likely that Asra returned Coleridge's love in the early years.

Yarlott's book on Coleridge is excellent, but he seems to me to be unduly censorious about Coleridge's love-affair. He forgets, when he accuses Coleridge of changing his mind about some of his former 'high-minded principles', that we all have to learn not to be puritanical—if we learn at all—from our own experience; and he forgets that Coleridge discovered an intelligent interest in his poetry in Asra that poor Sara could not possess. Furthermore, a large proportion of Coleridge's suffering was incurred simply because he believed, or told himself that he believed, in the principle of the sanctity of marriage.

By the end of 1800 Coleridge was turning to metaphysics, the furtherance of Wordsworth's genius, religion and even to such 'Christian Hope' as that his and Thelwall's dead infants may have 'met and talk'd of their Fathers in a happier place'.[681] He had increasing need of such—for one of his mental calibre—vulgar (though not untouching) consolations. His strenuous efforts on behalf of the 1800 *Lyrical Ballads* were entirely in Wordsworth's interests. He told Thelwall on 17 December 1800 that his 'literary pursuits' were the northern languages, as an amusement, and 'as a serious object, a metaphysical Investigation of the Laws, by which our Feelings form affinities with each other, with Ideas, & with words'. The corruption of the poet was generating the critic. 'As to Poetry,' he continued, 'I have altogether abandoned it, being convinced that I never had the essentials of poetic Genius, & that I mistook a strong desire for original power.'[682] Writing to Francis Wrangham two days later, on 19 December 1800, he announced that Wordsworth was 'a great, a true Poet—I am only a kind of a Metaphysician'.[683]

In a letter of 11 January 1801 to Humphry Davy he describes a swelling in his left testicle, to which he had applied a potion

> to considerable purpose; but the smart was followed by such a frantic and intolerable *Itching* over the whole surface of the Scrotum, that I am convinced it is the identical Torment which the damned suffer in Hell, & that Jesus, the good-natured one of the Trinity, had it built of Brimstone,[684] in a pang of pity for the poor Devils.—In all the parts thro' which the Spermatic Chord passes, I have dull & obtuse pains. . . .[685]

If the illness itself was not psychosomatic, a symptom of sexual unease and guilt, the language he used to describe it, however jocular, is certainly interesting: the itching of his scrotum is identified with the tortures of the damned, and 'dull & obtuse pains' are located in 'the Spermatic Chord'. He feels, he says, like a 'Column of Sand informed & animated only by a Whirl-blast of the Desart'. The sustaining powers of his imagination were hardly accessible to him, not because they had vanished, but because he could not now regard the 'joyous circumstances' he associated with them as anything other than evil. As he said to William Collins nearly twenty years later, writing from Highgate on 6 December 1818

> Poetry is out of the question. The attempt would only harry me into that sphere of acute feelings, from which abstruse research, the mother of self-oblivion, presents an asylum. Yet sometimes, spite of myself, I cannot help bursting out into the affecting exclamation of our Spenser, (his 'nine' and 'ivy garland' interpreted as competence and joyous circumstances,)—
>
> Thou kenn'st not, Percy, how the rhyme should rage!
> Oh if my temples were bedewed with wine,

> And girt with garlands of wild ivy-twine,
> How I could rear the Muse on stately stage!
> And teach her tread aloft in buskin fine,
> With queen'd Bellona in her equipage—
>
> But ah, my courage cools ere it be warm!
>
> But God's will be done. To feel the full force of the
> Christian religion, it is perhaps necessary, for many tempers,
> that they should first be made to feel, experimentally, the
> hollowness of human friendship, the presumptuous empti-
> ness of human hopes.[686]

One can see from this into what sort of consolation, by 1818, he had
turned 'the Christian religion', which, however, may be misused
more compliantly than may a woman. But in the earliest years of the
century he was tragically aware that a more meaningful, but inaccessible power lay, for him, in his poetic imagination. In a retrospective letter to Wordsworth of 4 May 1812 he reminded his old
friend that in

> the natural activity of my Intellect God had given me a
> counteracting principle to the intensity of my feelings, & a
> means of escaping from a part of the Pressure. . . . But
> for this I had been driven mad. . . .[687]

His Christianity and his metaphysics did indeed keep him from
madness; but they did not keep him from despair. He knew that
he kept the needed notion of their efficacy alive in himself only by
constant intellectual effort. On 27 May 1814 he admitted to Cottle
that

> the consolations, at least the *sensible* sweetness, of Hope, I
> do *not* possess. On the contrary, the Temptation, which
> I have constantly to fight up against, is a fear that if
> Annihilation & the *possibility* of Heaven were offered to my
> choice, I should choose the former.[688]

This ia roundabout way of saying that he was not really a Christian,
although he knew that he had to be because it was the only medicine
suitable for his case.

Metaphysics was often blamed for Coleridge's 'downfall' as
a poet. But metaphysics was something produced by Coleridge himself in his struggle against poetry; in itself it 'did' nothing to him.
Nor, of course, was the struggle within him entirely one-sided,
especially in the earlier years. He early began to feel that his poetic
imagination was in some sense deficient. He told Godwin (25 March
1801):

> The Poet is dead in me—my imagination (or rather the

Somewhat that had been imaginative) lies, like a Cold Snuff on the circular Rim of a Brass Candlestick, without even a stink of Tallow to remind you that it was once cloathed & mitred with Flame. That is past by!—I was once a Volume of Gold Leaf, rising & riding on every breath of Fancy— but I have beaten myself back into weight & density, & now I sink in quicksilver, yea, remain squat and square on the earth amid the hurricane, that makes Oaks and Straws join in one Dance, fifty yards high in the Element.[689]

The comparison of metaphysics with quicksilver was often employed by Coleridge. There is a famous passage in the *Biographia Literaria* where he speaks of himself as 'delving in the unwholesome quick-silver mines of metaphysic depths', and of his 'mismanaged sensibility in abstruse researches'. During 1801 he was still fruitlessly trying to turn his 'abstruse researches' into a kind of poetry. He told Poole, in a feverishly ambitious letter of 16 March 1801, that he had succeeded in overthrowing 'the doctrine of Association . . . especially, the doctrine of Necessity', and that he would shortly be about 'to solve the process of Life & Consciousness'. Poole was to mention it to no one. . . . Wordsworth, he wrote in the same letter, had become worried about him, and had persuaded him to intermit his over-excited abstract studies—in consequence of which he announced his intention to interrupt them by getting *Christabel* 'ready for the press'.[690] However, the agonies of opium withdrawal, illness, frustrated desire for Asra and the unpleasantnesses of domestication with his wife prevented him from realizing either of these projects, even the more awe-inspiring one of solving 'the process of Life & Consciousness. He tells Southey that he has enjoyed his coinage of the term 'Metapothecaries' for metaphysicians, but at the same time hopefully (and surely erroneously) announced that there had been no '*deep* metaphysician who was not led by his speculations to an austere system of morals. . . . It is not *thinking* that will disturb a man's morals . . . it is *talking—talking—talking* —*that* is the curse & the poison'. Needing desperately to reconcile his then continuing 'animal enjoyment' of Mrs. Coleridge with his love for Asra, he said in the same letter to Southey 'That to be in love is simply to confine the feelings of animal enjoyment to one woman is a gross mistake—it is to associate a large proportion of all our obscure feelings with one form'.[691] He felt that his life was 'gangrened . . . in it's very vitals—domestic Tranquillity';[692] but he must at the same time have known that his attachment to Asra was part of the cause of this.

If he behaved without tact, Sara apparently behaved without restraint. That her sense of injury was based upon external notions of propriety rather than upon anything she felt or thought out for herself—as he so often pointed out—was not of much help to him; nor was his continued sexual use of her,[693] which may well have given rise to some sarcastic gibes, especially in view of her by now—understandably—frigid sexual make-up.

He eventually resolved his sufferings in the verse-letter, *Dejection*, to Asra of 4 April 1802. This earliest draft of the famous ode exists in a MS. at Dove Cottage, but was not known until de Selincourt published it in 1937;[694] it is still not as well known as it should be, and has not yet been included in any collected edition of Coleridge's poems. Despite its length, 340 lines, I therefore reprint it here.

It is possible to argue that the finished version, published by Coleridge in the *Morning Post* on 4 October 1802, his seventh wedding anniversary and Wordsworth's wedding day, had 'a unity lacking in its epistolary form', as Griggs believes. But in the published version Coleridge was forced to omit the personal passages, and at least partly to disguise his theme, so that it lacks the integrity of the original. In the light of the quotations from the letters of this period that I have given and discussed, this version will need little critical exegesis. The letter Coleridge had sent to Asra, which caused her so much unhappiness, is lost; it probably announced his intention of separating from Sara, and hopefully asked Asra for her opinion about this step.

APRIL 4, 1802—SUNDAY EVENING

Well! if the Bard was weatherwise, who made
The grand old Ballad of Sir Patrick Spence,
This Night, so tranquil now, will not go hence
Unrous'd by winds, that ply a busier trade
Than that, which moulds yon clouds in lazy flakes,
Or the dull sobbing Draft, that drones and rakes
Upon the Strongs of this Eolian Lute,
        Which better far were mute.
For, lo! the New Moon, winter-bright!
And overspread with phantom Light,
(With swimming phantom Light o'erspread
But rimm'd and circled with a silver Thread)
I see the Old Moon in her Lap, foretelling
The coming-on of Rain and squally Blast—
O! Sara! that the Gust ev'n now were swelling,
And the slant Night-shower driving loud and fast!

A Grief without a pang, void, dark, and drear,
A stifling, drowsy, unimpassion'd Grief
That finds no natural Outlet, no Relief
        In word, or sigh, or tear—

This, Sara! well thou know'st,
Is that sore Evil, which I dread the most,
And oft'nest suffer! In this heartless Mood,
To other thoughts by yonder Throstle woo'd,
That pipes within the Larch tree, not unseen,
(The Larch, which pushes out in tassels green
It's bundled Leaflets) woo'd to mild Delights
By all the tender Sounds and gentle Sights
Of this sweet Primrose-month—and *vainly* woo'd
O dearest Sara! in this heartless Mood
All this long Eve, so balmy and serene,
Have I been gazing on the western Sky
And it's peculiar Tint of Yellow Green—
And still I gaze—and with how blank an eye!
And those thin Clouds above, in flakes and bars,
That give away their Motion to the Stars;
Those Stars, that glide behind them, or between,
Now sparkling, now bedimm'd, but always seen;
Yon crescent Moon, as fix'd as if it grew
In it's own cloudless, starless Lake of Blue—
A boat becalm'd! dear William's Sky Canoe!
—I see them all, so excellently fair!
  I see, not feel, how beautiful they are.

      My genial Spirits fail—
      And what can these avail
To lift the smoth'ring Weight from off my Breast?
      It were a vain Endeavor,
      Tho' I should gaze for ever
On that Green Light which lingers in the West!
I may not hope from outward Forms to win
The Passion and the Life whose Fountains are within!
These lifeless Shapes, around, below, Above,
      O what can they impart?
When even the gentle Thought, that thou, my Love!
      Art gazing now, like me,
      And see'st the Heaven, I see—
Sweet Thought it is—yet feebly stirs my Heart!
      Feebly! O feebly!—Yet
      (I well remember it)
In my first Dawn of Youth that Fancy stole
With many secret Yearnings on my Soul.
At eve, sky-gazing in 'ecstatic fit'
(Alas! for cloister'd in a city School
The Sky was all, I knew, of Beautiful)
At the barr'd window often did I sit,

And oft upon the leaded School-roof lay,
    And to myself would say—
There does not live the Man so stripp'd of good affections
As not to love to see a Maiden's quiet Eyes
Uprais'd, and linking on sweet Dreams by dim Connections
To Moon, or Evening Star, or glorious western Skies—
While yet a Boy, this Thought would so pursue me
That often it became a kind of Vision to me!

    Sweet Thought! and dear of old
    To Hearts of finer Mould!
Ten thousand times by Friends and Lovers blest!
    I spake with rash Despair,
    And ere I was aware,
The Weight was somewhat lifted from my Breast!
O Sara! in the weather-fended Wood,
Thy lov'd haunt! where the Stock-doves coo at Noon,
    I guess, that thou hast stood
And watch'd yon Crescent, and it's ghost-like Moon.
And yet, far rather in my present Mood
I would, that thou'dst been sitting all this while
Upon the sod-built Seat of Camomile—
And tho' thy Robin may have ceas'd to sing,
Yet needs for *my* sake must thou love to hear
    The Bee-hive murmuring near,
That ever-busy and most quiet Thing
Which I have heard at Midnight murmuring.

    I feel my spirit moved—
    And wheresoe'er thou be,
    O Sister! O Beloved!
    Those dear mild Eyes, that see
    Even now the Heaven, *I* see—
There is a Prayer in them! It is for *me*—
And I, dear Sara—*I* am blessing *thee*!

It was as calm as this, that happy night
When Mary, thou, and I together were,
To low decaying Fire our only Light,
And listen'd to the Stillness of the Air!
O that affectionate and blameless Maid,
Dear Mary! on her Lap my head she lay'd—

    Her Hand was on my Brow,
    Even as my own is now;
And on my Cheek I felt thy eye-lash play.
Such joy I had, that I may truly say,

My Spirit was awe-stricken with the Excess
And trance-like Depth of it's brief Happiness.

Ah fair Remembrances, that so revive
The Heart, and fill it with a living Power,
Where were they, Sara?—or did I not strive
To win them to me?—on the fretting Hour
Then when I wrote thee that complaining Scroll
Which even to bodily Sickness bruis'd thy Soul!
And yet thou blam'st thyself alone! And yet
    Forbidd'st me all Regret!

And must I not regret, that I distress'd
Thee, best belov'd! who lovest me the best?
My better mind had fled, I know not whither,
For O! was this an absent Friend's Employ
To send from far both Pain and Sorrow thither
Where still his Blessings should have call'd down Joy!
I read thy guileless Letter o'er again—
I hear thee of thy blameless Self complain—
And only this I learn—and this, alas! I know—
That thou art weak and pale with Sickness, Grief, and Pain—
    And *I—I* made thee so!

O for my own sake I regret perforce
Whatever turns thee, Sara! from the Course
Of calm Well-being and a Heart at rest!
When thou, and with thee those, whom thou lov'st best,
Shall dwell together in one happy Home,
One House, the dear *abiding* Home of All,
I too will crown me with a Coronal—
Nor shall this Heart in idle Wishes roam
    Morbidly soft!
No! let me trust, that I shall wear away
In no inglorious Toils the manly Day,
And only now and then, and not too oft,
Some dear and memorable Eve will bless
Dreaming of all your Loves and Quietness.

Be happy, and I need thee not in sight.
Peace in thy Heart, and Quiet in thy Dwelling,
Health in thy Limbs, and in thine Eyes the Light
Of Love, and Hope, and honorable Feeling—
Where e'er I am, I shall be well content!
Nor near thee, haply shall be more content!
To all things I prefer the Permanent.
And better seems it for a heart, like mine,

Always to *know*, than sometimes to behold,
    Their Happiness and thine—
For Change doth trouble me with pangs untold!
To see thee, hear thee, feel thee—then to part
    Oh!—it weighs down the Heart!

To *visit* those, I love, as I love thee,
Mary, and William, and dear Dorothy,
It is but a temptation to repine—
The transientness is Poison in the Wine,
Eats out the pith of Joy, makes all Joy hollow,
All Pleasure a dim Dream of Pain to follow!
My own peculiar Lot, my house-hold Life
It is, and will remain, Indifference or Strife.
While *ye* are *well and happy*, 'twould but wrong you
If I should fondly yearn to be among you—
Wherefore, O wherefore! should I wish to be
A wither'd branch upon a blossoming Tree?

But (let me say it! for I vainly strive
To beat away the Thought) but if thou pin'd,
Whate'er the Cause, in body or in mind,
I were the miserablest Man alive
To know it and be absent! Thy Delights
Far off, or near, alike I may partake—
But O! to mourn for thee, and to forsake
All power, all hope of giving comfort to thee—
To know that thou art weak and worn with pain,
And not to hear thee, Sara! not to view thee—
    Not sit beside thy Bed,
    Not press thy aching Head,
    Not bring thee Health again—
    At least to hope, to try—
By this Voice, which thou lov'st, and by this earnest Eye—
Nay, wherefore did I let it haunt my Mind
    The dark distressful Dream!

I turn from it, and listen to the Wind
Which long has rav'd unnotic'd! What a Scream
Of agony by Torture lengthen'd out
That Lute sent forth! O thou wild Storm without!
Jagg'd Rock, or mountain Pond, or blasted Tree,
Or Pine-grove, whether Woodman never clomb,
Or lonely House, long held the Witches' Home,
Methinks were fitter Instruments for Thee,
Mad Lutanist! that in this month of Showers,
Of dark brown Gardens, and of peeping Flowers,

Mak'est Devil's Yule, with worse than wintry Song
The Blossoms, Buds, and timorous Leaves among!
Thou Actor, perfect in all tragic Sounds!
Thou mighty Poet, even to frenzy bold!
    What tell'st thou now about?
'Tis of the Rushing of an Host in Rout—
And many Groans from men with smarting Wounds—
At once they groan with smart, and shudder with the Cold!
'Tis hush'd! there is a Trance of deepest Silence,
Again! but all that Sound, as of a rushing Crowd,
And Groans and tremulous Shudderings, all are over—
And it has other Sounds, and all less deep, less loud!
    A Tale of less Affright,
    And temper'd with Delight,
As William's Self had made the tender Lay—
    'Tis of a little Child
    Upon a heathy Wild,
Not far from home—but it has lost it's way—
And now moans low in utter grief and fear—
And now screams loud, and hopes to make it's Mother hear!

'Tis Midnight! and small Thoughts have I of sleep—
Full seldom may my Friend such Vigils keep—
O breathe She softly in her gentle Sleep!
Cover her, gentle Sleep! with wings of Healing.
And be this Tempest but a Mountain Birth!
May all the Stars hand bright above her Dwelling,
Silent, as tho' they *watch'd* the sleeping Earth!
Healthful and light, my Darling! may'st thou rise
    With clear and cheerful Eyes—
And of the same good Tidings to me send!
    For, oh! beloved Friend!

I am not the buoyant Thing, I was of yore—
When I like an own Child, I to Joy belong'd;
For others mourning oft, myself oft sorely wrong'd,
Yet bearing all things then, as if I nothing bore!

    Yes, dearest Sara! yes!
There *was* a time when tho' my path was rough,
The Joy within me dallied with Distress;
And all Misfortunes were but as the Stuff
Whence Fancy made me Dreams of Happiness:
For Hope grew round me, like the climbing Vine,
And Leaves and Fruitage, not my own, seem'd mine!
But now Ill Tidings bow me down to earth
Nor care I, that they rob me of my Mirth

But oh! each Visitation
Suspends what Nature gave me at my Birth,
    My shaping Spirit of Imagination!

I speak not now of those habitual Ills
That wear out Life, when two unequal Minds
Meet in one House, and two discordant Wills—
    This leaves me, where it finds,
Past cure, and past Complaint—a fate austere
Too fix'd and hopeless to partake of Fear!

But thou, dear Sara! (dear indeed thou art,
My Comforter! A Heart within my Heart!)
Thou, and the Few, we love, tho' few ye be,
Make up a world of Hopes and Fears for me.
And if Affliction, or distemp'ring Pain,
Or wayward Chance befall you, I complain
Not that I mourn—O Friends, most dear! most true!
    Methinks to weep with you
Were better far than to rejoice alone—
But that my coarse domestic Life has known
No Habits of heart-nursing Sympathy,
No Griefs, but such as dull and deaden me,
No mutual mild Enjoyments of it's own,
No Hopes of it's own Vintage, None, O! none—
Whence when I mourn'd for you, my Heart might borrow
Fair forms and living Motions for it's Sorrow.
For not to think of what I needs must feel,
But to be still and patient all I can;
And haply by abstruse Research to steal
From my own Nature all the Natural Man—
This was my sole Resource, my wisest plan!
And that, which suits a part, infects the whole,
And now is almost grown the Temper of my Soul.

My little children are a Joy, a Love
    A good Gift from above!
But what is Bliss, that still calls up a Woe,
    And makes it doubly keen
Compelling me to *feel*, as well as KNOW,
What a most blessed Lot mine might have been.
Those little Angel Children (woe is me!)
There have been hours, when feeling how they bind
And pluck out the Wing-feathers of my Mind,
Turning my Error to Necessity,
I have half-wish'd, they never had been born!
That seldom! But sad Thoughts they always bring,

And like the Poet's Philomel I sing
My Love-song, with my breast against a Thorn.

With no unthankful Spirit I confess,
This clinging Grief too, in it's turn, awakes
That Love, and Father's Joy; but O! it makes
The Love the greater, and the Joy far less.
These Mountains, too, these Vales, these Woods, these Lakes,
Scene full of Beauty and of Loftiness
Where all my Life I fondly hop'd to live—
I were sunk low indeed, did they *no* solace give;
But oft I seem to feel, and evermore I fear,
They are not to me the Things, which once they were.

O Sara! we receive but what we give,
And in *our* Life alone does Nature live.
Our's is her Wedding Garment, our's her Shroud—
And would we aught behold of higher Worth
Than that inanimate cold World allow'd
To the poor loveless ever-anxious Crowd,
Ah! from the Soul itself must issue forth
A light, a Glory, and a luminous Cloud
        Enveloping the Earth!
And from the Soul itself must there be se[nt]
A sweet and potent Voice of it's own Bir[th,]
Of all sweet Sounds the Life and Element.

O pure of Heart! thou need'st not ask of me
What this strong music in the Soul may be,
        What, and wherein it doth exist,
This Light, this Glory, this fair luminous Mist,
This beautiful and beauty-making Power!
Joy, innocent Sara! Joy, that ne'er was given
Save to the Pure, and in their purest Hour,
Joy, Sara! is the Spirit and the Power,
That wedding Nature to us gives in Dower
        A new Earth and new Heaven
Undreamt of by the Sensual and the Proud!
Joy is that strong Voice, Joy that Luminous Cloud
        We, we ourselves rejoice!
And thence flows all that charms or ear or sight.
All melodies the Echoes of that Voice,
All Colors a Suffusion of that Light.

Sister and Friend of my devoutest Choice!
Thou being innocent and full of love
And nested with the Darlings of thy Love,
And feeling in thy Soul, Heart, Lips and Arms

Even what the conjugal and mother Dove
That borrows genial warmth from those, she warms,
Feels in her thrill'd wings, blessedly outspread—
Thou free'd awhile from Cares and human Dread
By the immenseness of the Good and Fair
    Which thou see'st every where—
Thus, thus should'st thou rejoice!
To thee would all Things live from Pole to Pole,
Their Life the Eddying of thy living Soul—
O dear! O Innocent! O full of Love!
A very Friend! A Sister of my Choice—
O dear, as Light and Impulse from above,
Thus may'st thou ever, evermore rejoice!

13

Just over a month after writing this poem, on 7 May 1802, Coleridge told Poole that he had been unwell and unhappy, but

> ... I can venture to promise you that by the end of the year I shall have disburthened myself of all my metaphysics, &c.—& that the next year I shall, if I am alive & in possession of my present faculties, devote to a long poem. ... I mean to write few, if any, small poems, hereafter. ...

The reference to his 'present faculties' is interesting: clearly he was pleased with the poetic success of *Dejection*, and was perhaps contemplating the writing of another, longer poem. But, as always, he was distressed by its implications. He ended the letter with the curious remark that he had, 'on the 4th of April last', written Poole 'a letter in verse', but thought it 'dull & doleful—& did not send it'.[695] This can hardly refer to anything other than *Dejection*. Does it mean that Coleridge, struggling to get the original into publishable form, had tried to turn it into a letter to Poole? His difficulties in this matter—difficulties involving the concealment of his real motives—should give food for new thought to those who prefer the *Ode* to the *Letter*. The fate of *Dejection* is, in one way, aptly symbolic of Coleridge's fate as a poet. It is a highly personal poem, and because of this he felt (reasonably enough in this case, since people were involved) that he could not publish it. But he also found the daemonic sexual horrors of *Christabel* 'personal'; and these he felt he could not disguise.

By June the tide of his poetic inspiration, his courage to look into himself, was again ebbing. Hearing that an acquaintance was going into Devon, he made him the bearer of a letter to George, who although only (as he said) his 'brother by midwifery', always acted as a convenient symbol, in times of deep depression, of

Christian Respectability. By 1 July 1802 he could write to him, 'My Faith is simply this—that there is an original corruption in our nature, from which . . . we may be redeemed by Christ'. It was not his faith 'simply', and Coleridge makes as much clear by his quali-fying remark about the redeeming 'effect' of the Crucifixion: '. . . this I believe—not because I *understand* it; but because I *feel*, that it is not only suitable to, but needful for, my nature and because I find it clearly revealed'.[696] The last six words were doubtless put in to please George: the admission, from Coleridge of all men, that he did not '*understand*' is all-revealing. No wonder orthodox Christian apologists, of whom his brother George serves as a splendid repre-sentative, have tended to treat Coleridge's eventual lapse into Anglicanism coldly and with suspicion. For his pathetic latter-day piety was the last refuge of a man defeated by the pagan brilliance of his imagination; the theological preoccupations were the last writhings of that imagination, made harmless within the drab structure of orthodox Victorian Christianity. The thirty-year-old Coleridge could not entirely keep irony out of his tone when writing to George, and so spoke of not censuring those 'who cling to the Church of England as they cling to their Wives'; the choice of metaphor, much as it must have discomforted George, is revealing.

In July the poet and dramatist William Sotheby, long known to Coleridge as the translator of Wieland's *Oberon*, a poem by which he was deeply influenced, visited him at Keswick. This seems to have refreshed his spirits, for he wrote him two long letters imme-diately on his departure. It is noteworthy that it was people from outside the Wordsworth circle who tended to refresh Coleridge at this time of his greatest intimacy with them. Poole, as well as Sara, felt that the closeness of his friendship with the Wordsworths was unhealthy and harmed him. In a way they were right: in Devon the relationship had inspired him, now, complicated as it was by his feelings for Asra, it depressed him. He was even able to tell Sotheby, on 19 July 1802, something that he could never have told Wordsworth: that he believed 'that by nature I have more of the Poet in me' than the metaphysician. He wanted, he said in shrewd passage of self-analysis, to force himself

out of metaphysical trains of Thought—which, when I trusted myself to my own Ideas, came upon me uncalled, —& when I wished to write a poem, beat up Game of far other kind—instead of a Covey of poetic Partridges . . . or wild Ducks *shaping* their rapid flight in forms always regular . . . up came a metaphysical Bustard, urging it's slow, heavy, laborious, earth-skimming Flight, over dreary and level Wastes. . . . Sickness & some other & worse afflictions, first forced me into *downright metaphysics.* . . .[697]

He then goes on to quote long parts of *Dejection*, much revised; this time he referred to it as a poem 'written to Wordsworth, & the greater part of a private nature'. He was able to say, under the relaxing influence of Sotheby's recent presence, and of working hard over *Dejection*, that 'my better mind has returned to me'. On 19 July 1800 he told Southey that although the 'stern Match-maker' had never, he supposed brought together 'two minds so utterly contrarient in their primary and organical constitution', yet Mrs. Coleridge had been made '*serious*' by the thought of separation, to which 'awful Step' he had some time previously made up his mind. Now there was 'more love & Concord in my House, than I have known for years before': Sara had 'promised to set about an alteration in her external manners & looks & language, & to fight against her inveterate habits of puny Thwarting & unintermitting Dyspathy—this immediately. . . .' But even in this very temporary flush of optimism he allowed himself to become prey to the false and hopeless wish that the newly achieved 'external Conformity' would 'gradually generate a greater inward Likeness of thoughts, & attachments'—the attachment he had most in mind, no doubt, was Asra.[698]

By November, when he was in Wales with Wedgwood, the domestic situation had once again deteriorated. He had been away for much of the time. On 13 November 1802 he impetuously told Sara that he disliked '*Gentility*', and that, in contrast to her, he was 'connected' with 'things without me by the pleasurable sense of their immediate Beauty . . . and not at all by my knowledge of their average value in the minds of people in general'.[699] Hard, if true words. On 22 November 1802 he told her, with 'no feeling of Pride', that 'in sex, acquirements, and in the quantity and quality of natural endowments whether of Feelings, or of Intellect' she was 'the Inferior'; he then pulled his aggressive tactlessness up short with the grotesquely inadequate, indeed ghastly remark: 'You know, Sally Pally! I must have a Joke—or it would not be me!' Inked out of the MS. of this letter is the statement that if she should read it with 'tenderness', she would 'contribute . . . to the turning of a Cat-hole into a Dove's nest'.[700]

By December 1802, however, he had received a reassuring letter from her, and was once more confident that their 'future Days will be Days of Peace, & affectionate Happiness'. He is with the Wedgwoods at Crescelly, benefitting from 'extreme Temperance', and sleeping placidly: 'no *difficulties* in my Dreams, no Pains, no Desires'.[701] Again, the last two words have been inked out; they suggest that part of the tension between husband and wife was generated by a combination of what she felt to be his excessive sexual appetite, and his resentment at her lack of erotic interest in him. The words occur in a reassuring context, and seem to imply:

'I recognise that I am sexually unreasonable; I am not being troubled by this hideous disease just at present'. Sara was nearly at the end of her pregnancy. Coleridge had been away for the birth of Hartley, and probably deliberately absented himself for the birth of Sara, doubtless because yet another child represented yet another bond. But he did suggest that Asra, rather than Dorothy or Mary Hutchinson, might come in, 'because you will hardly have another opportunity of having her by yourself & to yourself, & of learning to know her, such as she really is'.[702] In this Coleridge reached the nadir of selfishness, tactlessness and dishonesty. Was it unmitigated ill treatment, or was Sara's behaviour in the house really intolerable by any standards?

Coleridge returned to Keswick on Christmas Eve, just a day after Sara was born; on Christmas Day 1802 he wrote to Southey, 'We are all sick, all mad, all slaves!'[703] On 17 December 1802 he told Mary Robinson that poetic composition had become 'laborious & painful' to him.[704] He was off again by 5 January 1803, in the company of the Wordsworths, informing Sara that she must 'receive with love & a ready & docile mind any thing' he might say seriously to her; further, he hoped to arrive home the next evening, perhaps with Sara Hutchinson, for he had '*some few reasons* for wishing to be with you immediately'.[705] Was he, as Chambers suggests, expecting to be able to tell her that Asra would soon marry John Wordsworth, thus putting her jealousy to rest? It is likely that throughout the affair he insisted to her that his regard for Asra was platonic. But Sara, like most wives, would doubtless have preferred—had her respectability allowed her—the more straightforward kind of physical adultery. What survives of the January 5 letter, parts of which have unfortunately been cut away, ends with an outburst against tea: Derwent had been 'manifestly tea-poisoned', '. . . if I have twenty children, Tea. . . .' Back at home, he writes to Southey to praise him for his magnanimous behaviour towards their former Pantisocratic colleague George Burnet; he himself had 'no heart to spare for a Coxcomb mad with vanity & stupified with opium'.[706]

14

1803 was the worst year of his life: 'one painful Dream', he called it in October.[707] 'It seemed a Dream', he told Godwin on 10 June 1803, that he 'had ever *thought* on Poetry—or had ever written it'.[708] He was 'diseased in voluntary power'.[709] He was planning to leave England for a warm climate, ostensibly for his health but chiefly to cure himself of his love for Asra and at the same time to get away from his wife. He felt like

an herbaceous Plant, as large as a large Tree, with a Trunk
of the same Girth, & Branches as large & shadowing—but
with *pith within* the Trunk, not heart of Wood—that I had
power not *strength*—an involuntary Imposter—that I had
no real Genius, no real Depth. . . .[710]

He must have regarded this comparison as particularly appropriate,
for he repeated it in a letter of 25 March 1804 to Humphry Davy.[711]

Coleridge's symptoms of illness during 1803 present a complex picture; they have yet to be fully investigated by a medically
qualified writer. His own views of them, however, are noteworthy.
'I fully believe,' he told Southey 'that I have that which common
people mean, when they say/that an Eruption has been driven *in*,
or driven back into the Blood'; if he could pass a year in a hot
climate, he felt confident that he could recover his health, which he
would gladly purchase 'at the price of an Eruption, that would kill
all Love not purely spiritual'.[712] Since the years abroad was mainly
contemplated as a means of curing himself of his desire for Asra,
the sexual implication of this is not difficult to follow. It is reminiscent of a notebook entry of mid-1803: 'Were I Achilles, I would
have had my leg cut off to have got rid of my vulnerable Heel'.[713]

In 1803, towards the end of his long walking tour of Scotland,
which he made in the company of the Wordsworths, Coleridge wrote
The Pains of Sleep, which he informed Southey, on 10 September
1803, was addressed to him. There is probably something in this:
Coleridge continued to envy Southey's stability and reliability (while
rightly despising him for his meanness and mediocrity): his sympathy
was always worth gaining. At the time of writing the poem Coleridge
had just returned to Perth from Fort Augustus, where he had been
mistakenly arrested as a spy; this experience had further distressed
him. Nevertheless, he found time to begin his letter with a touching
and unforced condolence to Southey on the loss of his only child.
He had walked '263 miles in eight Days'; 'my spirits are dreadful,
owing entirely to the Horrors of every night—I truly dread to sleep/
it is no shadow with me but substantial Misery foot-thick, that
makes me sit by my bedside of a morning, & *cry*'. Then follows what
is the earliest draft of *The Pains of Sleep*, which was eventually
published in the *Kubla Khan* volume of 1816:

> When on my bed my limbs I lay,
> It hath not been my use to pray
> With moving Lips or bended Knees;
> But silently, by slow degrees,
> My spirit I to Love compose,
> In humble trust my eyelids close,
> With reverential Resignation,
> No Wish conceiv'd, no Thought exprest,

Only a *Sense* of Supplication,
A *Sense* o'er all my soul imprest
That I am weak, yet not unblest:
Since *round* me, *in* me, every where,
Eternal Strength & Goodness are!—

But yesternight I pray'd aloud
In Anguish & in Agony,
Awaking from the fiendish Crowd
Of Shapes & Thoughts that tortur'd me!
Desire with Loathing strangely mixt,
On wild or hateful Objects fixt:
Pangs of Revenge, the powerless Will,
Still baffled, & consuming still,
Sense of intolerable Wrong,
And men whom I despis'd made strong
Vain-glorious Threats, unmanly Vaunting,
Bad men my boasts & fury taunting
Rage, sensual Passion, mad'ning Brawl,
And Shame, and Terror over all!
Deeds to be hid that were not hid,
Which, all confus'd I might not know,
Whether I suffer'd or I did:
For all was Horror, Guilt & Woe,
My own or others, still the same,
Life-stifling Fear, Soul-stifling Shame!

Thus two nights pass'd: the Night's Dismay
Sadden'd and stunn'd the boding Day.
I fear'd to sleep: Sleep seem'd to be
Disease's worst malignity.
The third night when my own loud Scream
Had freed me from the fiendish Dream,
O'ercome by Sufferings dark & wild,
I wept as I had been a Child—
And having thus by Tears subdued
My Trouble to a milder mood—
Such Punishment[s], I thought, were due
To Natures, deepliest stain'd with Sin,
Still to be stirring up anew
The self-created Hell within;
The Horror of their Crimes to view,
To know & loathe, yet wish & do!
With such let Fiends make mockery—
But I—O wherefore this on *me*?
Frail is my Soul, yea, strengthless wholly,
Unequal, restless, melancholy;

> But free from Hate, & sensual Folly!
> To live belov'd is all I need,
> And whom I love, I love indeed—&c &c &c &c—
>
> I do not know how I came to scribble down these verses to
> you—my heart was aching, my head all confused—but they
> are, doggrels as they may be, a true portrait of my nights.—
> What to do, I am at a loss:—for it is hard thus to be withered,
> having the faculties & attainments, which I have. . . .[714]

Coleridge felt uneasy at revealing himself in this light; but he
could not disguise his satisfaction with the poem itself. He lied[715]
to Sir George and Lady Beaumont (at present comparative strangers
to his 'horrors', but genuine admirers), in a letter of 22 September
1803, pretending that he had written the poem in 1794:

> . . . while I am in possession of my will & my Reason, I
> can keep the Fiend at arm's length; but with the Night my
> Horrors commence—during the whole of my Journey three
> nights out of four I have fallen asleep struggling & resolving
> to lie awake, & awaking have blest the Scream which
> delivered me from the reluctant Sleep. Nine years ago I
> had three months' Visitation of this kind, and I was cured
> by a sudden throwing-off of a burning corrosive acid—
> these Dreams with all their mockery of Guilt, Rage, un-
> worthy Desires, Remorse, Shame & Terror formed at that
> time the subject of some Verses, which I had forgotten till
> the return of the Complaint, & which I will send you in my
> next as a curiosity.[716]

Coleridge's dread was of non-marital lust. The existence of desire
for Asra was not acceptable to his conscience; he therefore tended
to repress it so severely that it assailed him in nightmares and
'dreams', probably of a distressingly sado-erotic kind: there was a
strong element of sadism in his make-up. At least he could fairly
disclaim these afflictions as 'involuntary', even if such a disclaimer
also meant cutting himself off from 'involuntary powers'. . . .

Only six days before writing to Sir George and Lady
Beaumont, to whom he wished to appear as more respectable than
he was, he had criticized Hazlitt to Tom Wedgwood as 'addicted
to women, as objects of sexual Indulgence'.[717] He saw the same
kind of shortcoming in himself. His harmless lie about the date of
the poem, which pleased him so much that he could not resist
mentioning it to the Beaumonts, is a fantasy: such horrors *can* be
thrown off, 'as a burning corrosive acid'. Had he not thrown them
off in 1794, in the form of Mary Evans, who threatened his duty?
The choice of the year 1794 is no accident.

He told his brother George, ever the refuge of his more

pious hopes, that he had undertaken the Scottish tour in the hope that 'hard Exercise' might drive the 'Host of Horrors' that rushed in when he slept 'into the *Extremities*'. Now, on 10 October 1803, there were signs that disease was 'ripening' in his feet: 'No Bridegroom ever longed for rapture with more impatience than I do for Torture'.[718] Again his choice of metaphor, with its association of a bridegroom, 'rapture' and 'Torture', gives us a clue to a persistent feature of Coleridge's erotic fantasies and dreams. As he frequently did when pleased with a figure, he repeated it to Poole in a letter written soon afterwards.[719]

By 1814, when Coleridge was most earnestly seeking to cure himself of his drug habit, he tended, at times, to blame his miseries on to opium itself. The excerpt he quoted from *The Pains of Sleep* in a letter of 19 May 1814 to one of his doctors, Henry Daniel, is interestingly different from either the early or the published version, and it indicates that Coleridge worked hard at the poem, probably over a long period:

> Not for the Poetry, *believe* me! (though as the lines have both sense & logic, there *is* worse stuff going under the name of Poetry than *even* these) but as an exact and most faithful portraiture of the state of my mind under influences of incipient bodily derangement from the use of Opium, at the time that I yet remained ignorant of the cause, & still *mighty proud* of my supposed grand discovery of Laudanum, as the Remedy or Palliative of Evils, which itself had mainly produced, & at every dose was reproducing, the lines may not be without interest to you, both as a *thinking* medical man, & under God, I trust, as one about to be entitled to my life-long, affectionate gratitude for my emancipation from a Slavery more dreadful, than any man, who has not felt it's iron fetters eating into his very soul, can possibly imagine.
>
> God bless you
> S. T. C.

'Diseased Sleep', a fragment from a larger poem, composed 1808.

> Written as a letter & of course never intended to be published, and which, I trust, never will be.

O, if for such such sufferings be,
Yet why, O God, yet why for me?
From low desires my Heart hath fled,
On Beauty hath my Fancy fed;
To be beloved is all I need,
And whom I love, I love indeed.
My waking thoughts with scorn repell

Loveless Lust, Revenge[full] spell:—
O why should Sleep be made *my* Hell.

The above was part of a long letter in verse written to a
friend, while I yet remained ignorant that the direful
sufferings, I so complained of, were the mere effects of
Opium, which I even to that hour imagined a sort of
Guardian Genius to me! . . .[720]

It can be asserted that neurosis, or weakness of character, rather
than metaphysics, 'ruined' Coleridge. But, whatever the exact nature
of his 'Horrors', this would be no more true than that metaphysics
ruined him. He was an unhappy and remorseful man. In that sense,
perhaps, he was ruined. But he produced as much or nearly as much
major non-dramatic poetry as any other English poet; as the author
of this he understood the nature of his defeat. It was a massive
defeat, though resisted on multitudinous fronts and with the aid of
a uniquely formidable intellect. But is any human being victorious?
It is the very massiveness of Coleridge's defeat that gives it its
humanity.

Even *The Pains of Sleep*, not one of his supreme poems,
belongs to all readers: although its themes are Coleridge's own self-
pity, the horrors of his own sleep, its intensity and its desire to pene-
trate to the truth transcend the personal. It thus becomes a vivid
metaphor for a universal pain in living, is a primary document in
the history of what we now call 'dread', or 'angst'. When by 'sleep'
we understand both 'ignorance' and 'loss of innocence' we can read
into the poem a good deal more than Coleridge thought (at the
time he wrote it) he meant.

Despite the outwardly tame orthodoxy of Coleridge's Highgate years, we can learn through him that the way to truth must lie
through terror and spiritual death. He had earned his serenity, false
though this was, and it is appropriate that his last words—written,
it seems, when he knew he was dying—should have been concerned
not with pious abstractions but with the well-being of a fellow
human.

Coleridge's suffering, or much of it, stemmed from his
inability to bear his own physical existence—'something inherently
mean in action'. He was, in one sense, a hero. He had too much
modesty ever to know this. But we know it, and, for all the shabby
faults, not above a dozen human beings have lived who are as
worthy of our honour.

Notes

In the notes that follow page references are to the first edition cited, or as otherwise indicated. The following abbreviations are used:

v.   = volume(s)
rev. = revised
EL   = Everyman's Library, Dent, London
OUP = Oxford University Press, London
NY   = New York
CP   = Clarendon Press, Oxford
WC   = World's Classics, Oxford University Press, London
HUL = Home University Library, Oxford University Press, London
CUP = Cambridge University Press, London
TLS = Times Literary Supplement
MLR = Modern Language Review
RES = Review of English Studies
ML   = Muses Library, Routledge and Kegan Paul, London (this applies
           only to the new issues of ML)
PQ   = Philological Quarterly

The enclosure of an abbreviation of a book's title or author in square brackets immediately after it has been cited means that it will thereafter be referred to by means of this abbreviation.

I

1. K. G. Hornbeak, *The Complete Letter-Writer in English, 1568–1800*, Smith College Studies in Modern Languages, v, XV, Northampton, Mass, 1934, 3–4.
2. Wyatt's poems were not printed in his lifetime. When some of them did first appear, in Tottel's *Miscellany*, they had been 'improved'. Fortunately there are several manuscript collections, of which the most important is the Egerton MS. in the British Museum. See K. Muir (ed.), *Collected Poems of Thomas Wyatt*, ML, 1949; Harvard UP, Cambridge, Mass., 1950; and his *Thomas Wyatt and His Circle: Unpublished Poems*, English Reprint Series, Liverpool UP, Liverpool, 1961. Wyatt printed one book in his lifetime, a prose translation of Plutarch *Quyete of Mynde* (1528).
3. K. Muir, *The Life and Letters of Thomas Wyatt*, Liverpool UP, Liverpool, 1963 [Muir], 68.
4. Muir, 178–84.
5. Muir, 40–1.
6. Muir, 42.
7. Transcriptions of these letters are printed in the standard edition of

Kyd's works, F. S. Boas (ed.), *Works of Thomas Kyd*, CP; OUP, NY (1902), 1955. But slightly more correct versions appear in the appendices to Arthur Freeman, *Thomas Kyd; Facts and Problems*, OUP; OUP, NY, 1967 [Freeman], and I have quoted from these.

8. This patron, as Freeman suggests, 32–6, is most likely to have been Henry Radcliffe, fourth Earl of Sussex.

9. They are printed in v. II of E. Edwards, *The Life of Sir Walter Raleigh*, 2 v., Macmillan, London, 1868 [Edwards]. A new edition is badly needed. The most stimulating modern biography, though not a literary study, is W. M. Wallace, *Walter Raleigh*, Princeton UP, Princeton; OUP, 1959. The best study of the poems is W. F. Oakeshott, *The Queen and the Poet*, Faber, London; Barnes and Noble, NY, 1960 [Oakeshott]. The standard edition of the poems, which is indispensable, is A. Latham (ed.), *The Poems of Walter Raleigh*, ML; Harvard UP, Cambridge, Mass., 1951; her earlier edition, Constable, London, 1930, contains certain textual details not incorporated in the later.

10. J. B. Neale, *Queen Elizabeth*, Cape, London, 1934; St. Martin's Press, NY, 1959; I quote from the edition published by the Reprint Society, London, 1942 [Neale], 309. This book, regarded as standard, has been reprinted in *Pelican* and *Anchor* paperbacks.

11. Neale, 308. Probable Ralegh married in 1588, but was not found out until 1592.

12. Neale, 309.

13. Oakeshott, 48.

14. Edwards, 51–2.

15. Edwards, 50.

16. Edwards, 54.

17. 10 May 1593, to Cecil, Edwards, 80.

18. Edwards, 46.

19. Edwards, 39.

20. But by 1597 R may actually have been intriguing with Cecil and Essex against the Queen. More likely, the three of them had talked against her, probably not very seriously in practical terms. He tells Cecil in a letter of 6 July 1597 that Essex was 'also wonderfull merry att your consait of "Richard the Second" '. Edwards, 169.

21. They are printed in C. H. Herford and P. Simpson (eds.), *Complete Works of Ben Jonson*, 11 v., CP; OUP, NY, 1925–52, 1 [H & S].

22. Three similarly petitioning letters from Chapman refer to the same matter. These, with others by Chapman, were printed by B. Dobell in the *Athenaeum*, 1901: *Newly Discovered Documents of the Elizabethan and Jacobean Period*, 169, 403, 437.

23. H & S, 140.

24. B. N. de Luna, *Jonson's Romish Plot*, CP, 1967 [de Luna].

25. H & S, 196.

26. H & S, 200.

27. A pun: want = mole.

28. H & S, 240–1.

29. H & S, 213–14.

30. H & S, 203–4.

31. See M. Eccles, *Jonson and the Spies*, RES, xiii, 285 (October 1937).

32. H & S, 202.

33. H & S, 139.

34. H & S, 202.

35. de Luna, 135.

36. My quotations are from the Introduction, in v. 1, to the old Muses Library edition of Drummond's poems, W. C. Ward (ed.), *Poems of*

William Drummond, 2 v., Routledge, London, n.d. (1894) [W. C. Ward]. The standard edition of the poems is L. E. Kastner (ed.), *The Poetical Works of William Drummond*, Manchester UP, Manchester, 1913.
37. W. C. Ward, lj.
38. W. C. Ward, lxj.
39. The only satisfactory modern edition of Suckling's works is A. H. Thompson (ed.), *Works in Prose and Verse of Sir John Suckling*, Routledge, London, 1910; Russell, NY, 1964. My brief quotations are from *Works of Sir John Suckling*, London, 1719 [Works JS], Jacob Tonson's reprint of the edition of 1696.
40. A. C. Baugh (ed.), *A Literary History of England*, Routledge, London; Appleton (Meredith), NY, 1950 [Baugh], 659. This work has since been revised and reissued by Appleton Century Crofts, NY, 1967.
41. Works JS, 103.
42. Works JS, 153–4.
43. Works JS, 135–40.
44. Milton permitted publication of 31 letters, all in Latin, in *Johannis Miltonii Angli Familiarum Liber Unus*, 1674; ten more have been discovered. The 1674 letters were translated by E. M. W. Tillyard and P. B. Tillyard, *Milton: Private Correspondence*, CUP, 1932 [Tillyard]. I quote from this translation. Most now appear, together with newly discovered ones, in new translations by W. A. Turner and A. T. Turner in *The Complete Prose Works of John Milton*, Yale UP, New Haven, 1953: I, 307–43; II, 759–75; IV, pt. 2, 826–74 [M's Prose].
45. Tillyard, 37.
46. Tillyard, 13.
47. M's Prose, I, 319–31. W. A. and A. T. Turner publish here 'only what seems to us to have been Milton's final intention, putting in brackets the editorial additions'. I print their reconstruction here, with some omission of editorial detail.
48. The letters to Savile have been edited by J. H. Wilson, *The Rochester–Savile Letters 1671–80*, Ohio UP, Columbus, 1941. The only reliable edition of Rochester's poems is V. de S. Pinto (ed.), *Poems of John Wilmot*, ML; Harvard UP, Cambridge, Mass. (1953) 1964; the best biography is V. de S. Pinto, *Enthusiast in Wit*, Routledge (1935); Nebraska UP, Lincoln, Nebraska, 1962.
49. F. Bickley, *The Life of Matthew Prior*, Pitman, London, 1914; L. G. W. Legg, *Matthew Prior: A Study of his Public Career and Correspondence*, CUP, 1921 (this concentrates on P's diplomatic career); C. K. Eves, *Matthew Prior: Poet and Diplomatist*, Columbia UP, New York; OUP, 1939. The definitive text of the poems has been edited by M. B. Wright and M. K. Spears, *The Literary Works of Matthew Prior*, 2 v., CP; OUP, NY, 1959 [Works MP], which may be consulted for the provenance of MS. letters.
50. Works MP, II, 832–3.
51. Works MP, II, 899–900.
52. These have been edited by C. F. Burgess, *The Letters of John Gay*, CP, 1967 [Burgess]. This has an excellent introduction. The best edition of Gay's poems is G. C. Faber, *Poetical Works of JG*, OUP, 1926.
53. Burgess, 39–40.
54. Burgess, 40–1.
55. Burgess, 47.
56. Burgess, 45–6.

57. 15 February 1727/8, Burgess, 70.
58. Burgess, 75.
59. Burgess, 87.
60. Burgess, 132.
61. E. J. Morley (ed.), Manchester UP, Manchester, 1918; E. D. Jones (ed.), *English Critical Essays: Sixteenth to Eighteenth Centuries*, WC; OUP, NY, 1922. Young has been edited by J. Mitford, *Poetical Works of Edward Young*, 2 v., Pickering, London (1830–6) 1852, and by J. Doran, *Complete Works*, London, 1854. The only full length biography is H. C. Shelley, *Life and Letters of Edward Young*, Pitman, London, 1914, which contains some letters [Shelley]. 150 further letters, exchanged between Young and his friend Samuel Richardson, the novelist, were printed in the *Monthly Magazine*, December 1813–August 1818. These are unrewarding. See also H. T. Swedenberg, Jr., *Letters of EY to Mrs. Judith Reynolds*, Huntingdon Library Quarterly, 11, 1938.
62. See p. 209.
63. Shelley, 33–4.
64. Shelley, 144–5. The extract from *Night Thoughts* differs in several respects from the final text as printed in Mitford, I, 35–6.
65. The most easily available edition of their poems is in a single volume: R. A. Willmott (ed.), *The Poetical Works of Mark Akenside and John Dyer*, Routledge, 1875 [Willmott]. This contains lives, quotations from letters and some excellent notes; but it does not print the later 'irregular' version of *Grongar Hill*. Some letters of Dyer's to John Hughes are contained in v. III of W. Dunscombe (ed.), *Letters to Several Eminent Persons*, 3 v., London, 1773.
66. Willmott, xij.
67. Willmott, xxvj.
68. Willmott, 47–8. No date is given by Willmott for this letter, which is to 'Fordyce'—presumably the educationist and theologian David Fordyce.
69. Willmott, 125.
70. Shenstone's letters have been edited twice in modern times: M. Williams (ed.), *The Letters of William Shenstone*, Blackwell, Oxford, 1939; and D. Mallam, *The Letters of William Shenstone*, Minneapolis UP, Minneapolis; OUP, 1939. The latter contains 30 fewer letters than the former, but prints some not included in it. The most easily obtainable edition of the poems is G. Gilfilian (ed.), *Shenstone's Poetical Works*, Nicol, Edinburgh, 1854. There is no modern edition.
71. Fourteen of Thomson's letters are in a *A Collection of Letters to Aaron Hill, Esq.*, London, 1751; others are in W. Goodhugh (ed.), *The English Gentleman's Library Manual*, London, 1827; and in P. Cunningham (ed.), *Unpublished Letters from T to Mallet* [David Malloch], Philobiblion Society Miscellany, IV, 1854. See also A. D. McKillop (ed.), *James Thomson: Letters and Documents*, Kansas UP, Kansas, 1961. The standard edition of the poems is J. L. Robertson (ed.), *The Complete Poetical Works of James Thomson*, OUP; OUP, NY, 1908. Many letters are quoted in the still useful Memoir included in the Aldine edition, P. Cunningham (ed.), *The Poetical Works of James Thomson*, Bell and Daldy, London (1830), 1860 [Cunningham], rev. D. Tovey, 1897.
72. 11 December 1720, Cunningham, xiij.
73. 7 August 1735, Cunningham, lxiv.
74. 14 December 1747, Cunningham, cj.
75. Cunningham, cxlvij–cxlvix.

2

76. The only reliable edition of Sidney's poems is W. Ringler (ed.), *Poems of Sir Philip Sidney*, CP; OUP, NY, 1961. The letters are printed in A. Feurillerat (ed.), *Complete Works of Philip Sidney*, 4 v., CUP, London and NY, 1912–26, III [Feurillerat].

77. Geoffrey Shepherd (ed.), *An Apology for Poetry*, Nelson, London; Barnes and Noble, NY, 1965, 7. This is an admirable (though modernized) edition, with a most valuable introduction.

78. The only direct account of the quarrel is given by Fulke Greville in his life of Sidney, *The Life of the Renowned Sir Philip Sidney*, 1652 (N. Smith (ed.), CP, 1907). Mona Wilson, *Sir Philip Sidney*, Duckworth, London, 1930; Hart Davis, London, 1950, quotes it in full 97–9.

79. David Kalstone, *Sidney's Poetry*, Harvard UP, Cambridge, Mass.; OUP, 1965. This is the best and shrewdest study of Sidney's poetry.

80. Feurillerat, 137.

81. 28 March 1581, Feurillerat, 134.

82. 28 December 1581, Feurillerat, 140.

83. This was translated from the Latin, which is printed in Feurillerat, by S. A. Pears. Pears's translation is unsatisfactory, but as yet there is no other. I quote from *The Correspondence of Philip Sidney and Hubert Languet*, translated S. A. Pears, Pickering, London, 1845 [Pears].

84. Pears, 7.

85. Feuillerat, 119.

86. Pears, 8.

87. Pears, 28–9.

88. Pears, 88–9.

89. Pears, 143.

90. Pears, 50.

91. Feuillerat, 124.

92. Feuillerat, 124–5.

93. Feuillerat, 127.

94. Sir Henry Sidney had recalled Robert's favourite servant in a rage. Philip secured his return.

95. Effects = affects: feelings.

96. Feuillerat, 128.

97. Feuillerat, 129.

98. Feuillerat, 129.

99. John Buxton, *Sir Philip Sidney and the English Renaissance*, Macmillan, London (1954); St. Martin's Press, NY, 1964 [Buxton].

3

100. The Spenser-Harvey correspondence has been published in A. Grosart (ed.), *Complete Works of Edward Spenser in Verse and Prose*, 9 v., incomplete, printed for private circulation, London, 1902–4, v. IX, 261–78 [Grosart]; and in G. Gregory Smith (ed.), *Elizabethan Critical Essays*, 2 v., OUP, 1904, v. I, 87–126 [Gregory Smith]. Spenser's side of the correspondence, together with an extract from one of Harvey's replies, is also included in the many times reprinted Globe edition of Spenser's work, Macmillan, London, 1869, in Appendix II. The letter to Ralegh is reprinted in all editions of Spenser: the standard edition is now E. Greenlaw and others (eds.), *Works of Edward Spenser; A*

Variorum Edition, 9 v., John Hopkins UP, Baltimore, 1932–49; the most inexpensive reliable edition is that of J. C. Smith and E. de Selincourt, *Poetical Works of Edward Spenser*, OUP, London, 1912.

101. Grosart, 261–3.
102. Gregory Smith, 226–302.
103. *The Scolemaster*, 1570, Book II. Reprinted Gregory Smith, I, 1–45.
104. Reprinted Gregory Smith, I, 46–57.
105. S. J. Kunitz and H. Haycraft (eds.), *British Authors Before 1800*, H. W. Wilson, NY, 1952, 252.
106. W. Nelson, *The Poetry of Edward Spenser*, Columbia UP, NY and London, 1963 [Nelson].
107. Grosart, 264–71.
108. Gregory Smith, 94–7.
109. Grosart, 272–5.
110. Gregory Smith, 117.
111. C. S. Lewis, *English Literature in the Sixteenth Century*, CP; OUP, NY, 1954 [Lewis], 364–5.
112. Gregory Smith, 119.
113. K. Williams, *Spenser's Faerie Queene, The World of Glass*, Routledge, London, 1966.
114. This text of the letter to Ralegh is taken from the Globe edition.
115. J. W. Bennett, *The Evolution of the Faerie Queene*, CUP, 1942; Chicago UP, Chicago, 1943. Lewis, 379.
116. Nelson, 124–5.

4

117. *Letters to Several Persons of Honour*, London, 1651: this was reprinted, in a limited edition, edited by C. E. Merrill Jr., C. E. Merrill, NY, 1911. More letters by Donne were included in *A Collection of Letters, made by Sir Tobie Mathews*, London, 1660, which was prepared for the press by D's son, who had also edited *Letters to Several Persons of Honour*. In the absence of I. A. Shapiro's edition, promised as long ago as 1939 but not yet forthcoming, the disposition of Donne's letters is wide. E. Gosse collected many of them, including those in the two seventeenth century collections, in his *The Life and Letters of John Donne*, 2 v., Heinemann, London, 1899; Peter Smith, Gloucester, Mass., 1959 [Gosse], but in modernized texts. As a biography this was a pioneer study, but can no longer be regarded as reliable. The most recent selection of Donne's letters, an excellent one, appears in Evelyn Simpson (chosen by), Helen Gardner and Timothy Healy (eds.), *John Donne: Selected Prose*, OUP, London, 1967 [Gardner-Healy], 105–72. The editors have taken advantage of Mr. I. H. Shapiro's expertise in their dating, and whenever possible I have quoted both letters and prose from this edition. However, wherever appropriate, I have also given reference to the text of J. Hayward's *John Donne: Complete Poetry and Selected Prose*, Nonesuch Press, Bloomsbury, London (1929); 1962 [Nonesuch], which prints the fullest non-modernized selection from Donne's letters. Some other letters are in E. Simpson, *A Study of the Prose Works of John Donne*, CP; OUP, NY (1924), 1962 [Simpson]. A letter to Sir Nicholas Carey of 1626 was separately printed by T. Spenser, Harvard UP, Cambridge, Mass., 1930. The most attractive edition of Donne's poetry (with selected prose) is still the Nonesuch; but it is also necessary to consult the following editions: H. J. C. Grierson (ed.), *Poems*

of *John Donne*, CP; OUP, NY, 1912 [Grierson], upon which the Nonesuch is, broadly speaking, based; the same editor's one-volume edition, OUP, 1929, reprints this text, with some corrections; Helen Gardner (ed.), *The Divine Poems of John Donne*, CP; OUP, NY, 1952, *The Elegies and Songs and Sonnets*, CP, 1965 [Gardner S & S], and W. Millgate (ed.), *The Satires, Epigrams and Verse Letters*, CP, 1967, with their extensive notes and commentaries, at least valuably supplement Grierson, and in some respects certainly supersede his text. There is no satisfactory biography of Donne. The earliest is in Izaak Walton's, *Lives*, London, 1675 (G. Saintsbury (ed.), WC, 1927); Evelyn Hardy, *Donne: A Spirit in Conflict*, Constable, London, 1942, incorporated some original research, but is inaccurate and critically of no value. A useful summary of facts is Edward Le Comte's *Grace to a Witty Sinner*, Gollancz, London; Walker, NY, 1965 [Le Comte], which has an exceptionally full bibliography, but does not cite references. An important critical study of sources, if not of poetic meaning, is J. B. Leishmann, *The Monarch of Wit*, Hutchinson, London; Hillary House, NY (1952), rev. 1962 [Leishmann]; I have quoted from the first, 1952 edition.

118. Le Comte, 65.
119. Gardner-Healy, 107.
120. But see Leishmann, 27-8, who dissents.
121. Gardner-Healy report that I. H. Shapiro is doubtful; but they, 108-9, and Nonesuch, 439-40, print the letter. It was first printed, from the Burley MS. (which was destroyed by fire) by Simpson, 303-4, who admits of no doubt as to its authenticity.
122. *Skialetheia*, London, 1598.
123. Simpson, 307.
124. Gardner-Healy, 49-50.
125. Simpson, 310.
126. Gardner S & S, lviij, n 2. Millgate, whose edition arrived too late for me to consult, wholly rejects this view.
127. Gardner-Healy, 111-12; Nonesuch, 400-1. I. H. Shapiro agrees that this letter is 'undoubtedly Donne's', but states flatly that 'it cannot have been written to Wotton'. Gardner-Healy nevertheless think it 'probably . . . to Wotton'.
128. The Earl of Arundel was notorious as having been dominated by his wife. Donne could have seen *The Taming of the Shrew* at Newington Butts Theatre in June 1594, when he was still at Lincoln's Inn; it was not published until 1623, and no performance is recorded between 1594 and 1633.
129. The subtle sense of this seems to depend on a punning use of 'pert': 'a man beautiful enough to love, yet too clever to be believed'. According to NED, the former sense was already archaic.
130. Dante, *Inferno*, 3, 59-60. Pietro de Morrone (1215-95), Pope Celestine V, gave up the Papacy five months after being elected in 1294, having been persuaded, by Cardinal Gaetano, that it was against his soul's health. He was canonized in 1313. The majority of Dante commentators agree that the reference is to Morrone, since Dante derogates him elsewhere, and disliked the Pope in whose reign he became a saint. (It is hardly necessary to add that Cardinal Gaetano succeeded Celestine V.)
131. 'que trahunter ab effectibus': 'which are drawn from effects'. We should write 'quae'.
132. Gardner-Healy, 109-10; Nonesuch, 441-2.

133. Donne later went out of his way, in his Sermons, to attack the notion of Purgatory.
134. 'Dropsical.'
135. 'More glorious.'
136. Gardner-Healy, 112–14; Nonesuch, 443–5.
137. Gardner-Healy, 114–15; Nonesuch, 445–6.
138. Gosse, I, 106–7.
139. Gosse, I, 109–10.
140. Nonesuch, 448–9.
141. Gardner-Healy, 123; Nonesuch, 447.
142. Gosse, I, 298.
143. Gardner-Healy, 153.
144. It is Donne's dullest work. Nonesuch omits it altogether; Gardner-Healy, 43–55, give a brief selection, including the most important parts: the *Advertisement to the Reader* and the *Preface*.
145. Gosse, v. I, 156.
146. Gardner-Healy, 26–40, print an excellent selection from it; it was first published by Donne's son in 1646.
147. Gardner-Healy, 123–4.
148. Leishmann, 39.
149. He begins this letter by telling Goodyer that he is seriously ill and likely to die.
150. Published in 1633.
151. Gardner-Healy, 130–2; Nonesuch, 451–4.
152. Gosse, I, 168–9.
153. Gardner-Healy, 125–6.
154. Gosse, I, 173.
155. i.e. hysteria.
156. Gosse, I, 183–5. This is headed 'To Sir H. G.' in the 1651 letters.
157. To Sir Henry Goodyer, *c.* 1608, Nonesuch, 450–1.
158. Le Comte, 172, quotes from a Sermon of 30 May 1621.
159. Gardner-Healy, 127–8; Nonesuch, 455–6.
160. Gardner-Healy, 128–30; Nonesuch, 455–6.
161. Leishmann, 152–4.
162. Gardner S & S, 212.
163. Gosse, I, 178.
164. Grierson, II, 149, cites Paracelsus. Donne was still interested in 'Mummy' in 1626, when he mentioned it in a sermon, Gardner-Healy, 278.
165. Gardner S & S, 182.
166. Grierson, II, 36 [Gosse, II, 49].
167. 'Pot' may, possibly, in a secondary meaning of 'deep hole', refer back to 'loves Myne'; but its primary meaning here is certainly 'alchemist's retort'.
168. 'Day' here means the one day that each orgasm was supposed to subtract from the life-span: i.e. the brief sexual pleasure that we do manage to achieve; the 'winter-seeming summers night'.
169. There is, too, the likelihood that Donne is punning on 'Mummy' in the sense of 'mother'. 'Mummy' is early nineteenth century; but 'Mammy' goes back to at last a century before Donne's birth. This adds yet another, and certainly 'outrageous' dimension to the poem— one that is not considered by Grierson, Dr. Gardner or by Clay Hunt in his analysis of the poem in *Donne's Poetry*, Yale UP, New Haven; OUP, 1954, 32–41. The sense of 'women are but mothers when possessed' hardly needs glossing. D's own title for the poem is likely to

have been 'Mummy': only three MSS. and the 1633 edition of the poems entitle it *Love's Alchemie.*

170. Arnold Stein, *John Donne's Lyrics; the Eloquence of Action*, Minnesota UP, Minnesota; OUP, 1962, 173–4.
171. Grierson, II, 25.
172. Gardner S & S, 215.
173. Gardner S & S, 259–65.
174. Gardner-Healy, 134; Nonesuch, 460.
175. The story of Donne and the Drurys has been told in detail by R. C. Bald, *Donne and the Drurys*, CUP; CUP, NY, 1959. Sir Robert Drury genuinely admired Donne, and gave him use of an apartment, probably at a nominal rent, near his large Drury Lane house. He remained the tenant of the Drurys until 1621, six years after he had entered the Church.
176. Gardner-Healy, 142; Nonesuch, 463–4.
177. Gardner-Healy, 141; Nonesuch, 467. It has not been established that this letter is to Mathew or that it was written from Paris; but Gardner-Healy, Simpson and I. H. Shapiro all agree in thus assigning it.
178. Viscount Rochester, later Earl of Somerset. Not to be confused with his protégé and namesake, to whom Donne also wrote letters, and who became Earl of Ancrum.
179. Gosse, II, 22.
180. Gosse, II, 22–3.
181. Gosse, II, 46–7.
182. Gosse, II, 45–6.
183. The Countess of Bedford, to whom Goodyer himself was close. She helped Donne substantially, but disappointed him by paying him only £30 (in fact a fairly generous sum) for his elegy on her brother. Soon after Donne's ordination she came under the influence of a puritan, John Burges, and the association with Donne ceased altogether.
184. Robert Ker, Earl of Somerset.
185. At the end of the *Obsequies to the Lord Harington* Donne had written:

> Doe not, faire soule, this sacrifice refuse,
> That in thy grave I doe interre my Muse,
> Who, by my griefe, great as they worth, being cast
> Behind hand, yet hath spoke, and spoke her last.

186. Gardner-Healy, 144–5.
187. Gardner-Healy, 152; Nonesuch, 470.
188. Gardner-Healy, 145–6; Nonesuch, 465–6.
189. Gardner-Healy, 148–9; Nonesuch, 471–2.
190. Gardner-Healy, 147–8; Nonesuch, 469. I. H. Shapiro disagrees with the date of 1616 for this letter, and assigns it to 1613–14; but Gardner-Healy seem to me to be correct in placing it in 1616, particularly in view of the passage quoted.
191. Nonesuch, 479.
192. Gosse, II, 215.

5

193. H. E. Toliver, *Marvell's Ironic Vision*, Yale UP, New Haven and London, 1965, 154–62.
194. P. Legouis, *Andrew Marvell: Poet, Puritan, Patriot*, CP; OUP, NY, 1965 [Legouis]. This, a recension of an earlier book in French, of the same title, Didier, Paris, 1928; Russell, NY, 1965, is the standard biographical study.

195. *Milton's Prose*, IV, 838.
196. H. M. Margoliouth (ed.), *Marvell's Poems and Letters*, 2 v., CP (1927); OUP, NY, 1953 [Margoliouth]. This is the standard edition of the poems. H. Macdonald, *Poems of Andrew Marvell*, ML; Harvard UP, Cambridge, Mass. (1952), 1956, is a reprint of the 1681 folio with some useful notes.
197. Margoliouth, II, 7.
198. Legouis, 126. A. Birrell, *Andrew Marvell*, English Men of Letters Series, Macmillan, London, 1905, is still a useful book; Birrell had had political experience, and understood this aspect of M's life at least as well as any subsequent critic.
199. Legouis, 168.
200. G. F. de Lord (ed.), *Poems on Affairs of State, Augustan Satirical Verse, 1660–1714*, I, 1660–78, Yale UP, New Haven and London, 1963, 99. This provides a useful introduction to Marvell's political background.
201. Margoliouth, II, 291–2.
202. Margoliouth, II, 293.
203. Margoliouth, II, 302.
204. Margoliouth, II, 104–5.
205. Margoliouth, II, 304–5.
206. Margoliouth, II, 308–9.
207. Margoliouth, II, 309–11.
208. Margoliouth, II, 322–3.
209. Margoliouth, II, 324–5.
210. Legouis, 223.
211. This refers to the fact that Edmund, to the elegy on whose death this is a covering note, had died of the same disease, smallpox, only very shortly after his brother.
212. Margoliouth, II, 298.

6

213. The only edition is C. E. Ward (ed.), *The Letters of John Dryden*, Duke UP, Durham, North Carolina, 1946 [Ward]. The standard biography is C. E. Ward, *The Life of John Dryden*, North Carolina UP, Chapel Hill; OUP, 1961. A definitive edition of Dryden's works is in progress, and will amount to about 14 v.: E. N. Hooker and others (eds.), *The Works of John Dryden*, California UP, Berkeley; CUP, 1956–. The standard edition is J. Kinsley, *The Poems of John Dryden*, 4 v., CP; OUP, NY, 1958. V. 2 of the Old Mermaid edition of the plays, G. Saintsbury (ed.), *Plays of John Dryden*, 2 v., Benn, London (1904), 1949, was until recently available. The best prose selection is W. P. Ker (ed.), *Essays*, 2 v., CP, 1900; Russell, NY, 1961.
214. Ward, 7–11.
215. Ward, 11–12.
216. Published in 1680, it satirizes the practice of 'keeping' mistresses, a subject upon which the King was well informed.
217. Thomas Rymer (1641–1713) is most famous for his adverse criticism of *Othello*. Model of a bad literary critic, he was a painstaking historian of importance.
218. Ward, 13–14.
219. Ward, 71–2.
220. Ward, 59.

221. A boy was 'custos' at Westminster if he happened to be the last caught talking at dinner, or to be—as Dryden hints here—the temporary victim of the others' malice.
222. Ward, 18–20.
223. Ward, 33–6.
224. Ward, 71–2.
225. This circumstance was in one sense mitigated by the fact that Dryden's salary had for a long time been seriously in arrears: by 1685 he was owed a large sum of money by the Treasury, which he did not recover under James II.
226. Symbol of office, particularly of the Lord Treasurer.
227. Ward, 27.
228. L. I. Bredvold, *The Intellectual Milieu of John Dryden*, Michigan UP, Ann Arbor, 1934.
229. His *Aeneid*.
230. Ward, 85–6.
231. Ward, 123.
232. Ward, 93–4.

7

233. Denis Johnston, *In Search of Swift*, Hodges Figgis, Dublin; Macmillan, London, 1959. Johnston asserts that Jonathan senior was dead ten months before Jonathan's death.
234. B. Dobrée, *English Literature in the Early Eighteenth Century, 1700–1740*, CP; OUP, NY, 1959 [Dobrée], 61. This contains admirable sections on Swift.
235. Swift's letters were first properly edited by F. E. Ball, *Letters of Jonathan Swift*, 6 v., Bell, London, 1910–14, in a modernized edition that is still valuable for its notes. This has been superseded by H. Williams, *The Correspondence of Jonathan Swift*, 5 v., CP; OUP, NY, 1963–5 [Williams]. The *Journal to Stella*, which consists of letters to Esther Johnson, has also been edited by H. Williams, 2 v., CP; OUP, NY, 1948 [Williams S]. The definitive edition of the poems is H. Williams, *Poems of Jonathan Swift*, 3 v., CP, (1937); OUP, NY, 1958; the late Herbert Davis completed a convenient single volume edition, based on this, but with the poems in chronological order, just before his death, *Poems of Jonathan Swift*, OUP, 1967. The prose was edited by H. Davis: *Prose Works of Jonathan Swift*, 9 v., Blackwell, Oxford; Princeton UP, Princeton, 1939–63 [Davis]. A useful selection of prose and poetry is J. Hayward (ed.), *Gulliver's Travels and Selected Prose and Verse*, Nonesuch Press, Bloomsbury, London (1934), 1942 [Nonesuch S]. The standard biography, which will consist of 3 v., is I. Ehrenpreis, *Swift: The Man, his Works and the Age, I: Mr Swift and his Contemporaries*, Methuen, London, 1962; *II: Dr. Swift*, Methuen, London, 1967 [Ehrenpreis]. In readability this does not supersede H. Craik, *The Life of Swift*, Macmillan, London (1882), 2 v., 1894. The best introductions to Swift are R. Quintana, *Swift: An Introduction*, OUP, London (1955); OUP, NY, 1965 [Quintana] and J. M. Murry, *Swift: A Critical Biography*, Cape, London, 1954; British Book Centre, NY, 1967 [Murry], and an excellent collection of essays ranging over a wide period, A. N. Jeffares (ed.), *Fair Liberty Was All His Cry*, Macmillan, London, 1967 [Jeffares].
236. *Thoughts on Various Subjects*, Nonesuch S, 460.
237. Vincent Voiture (1598–1648), French letter-writer, poet and wit.

238. 12 February 1722/3, Williams, II, 449.
239. 14 June 1737, Williams, V, 45–6.
240. Murry, 45–8.
241. See D. Johnson, *A Literary Chestnut: Dryden's 'Cousin Swift'*, PMLA, LXVII, 1952.
242. 10 November 1718, Williams, II, 301–2.
243. Doubtless Swift took his revenge in his next poem, which survives in a transcript by Stella: *A Quiet Life, and a Good Name*, to which Faulkner, who first published it in 1735, gave the title *To a Friend, who Married a Shrew*. Stella wrote 'To &c.'
244. Williams, I, 5–6.
245. H. Read, *Selected Writings*, Faber, London; Horizon, NY, 1963 [Read Sel], 131.
246. *Thoughts on Various Subjects*, Nonesuch S, 459.
247. This poem has not survived; nor is the identity of the 'young lady in Ireland' known.
248. Williams, I, 8–10.
249. Williams, I, 14.
250. Ehrenpreis, I, 139.
251. To Bolingbroke and Pope, 5 April 1729, Williams, III, 329.
252. Williams, I, 109.
253. Williams, III, 330.
254. Williams, I, 18–23.
255. Ehrenpreis, 168.
256. Murry, 60.
257. Williams, I, 32–6.
258. 30 April 1713, Williams, I, 345–6.
259. Williams S, II, 586.
260. Williams III, 293.
261. 5 April 1733, Williams IV, 138.
262. Williams, III, 506.
263. Williams, V, 139–40.
264. Williams, IV, 153. Pope suppressed this passage when he came to print the letter.
265. See pp. 220–8.
266. Williams, IV, 320–2.
267. It is appropriate to mention here Herbert Davis's essay, *Swift's View of Poetry* (1931), repr. Jeffares, 62–97. This takes a categorically opposite view; but it seems to me to be psychologically obtuse in failing to account for Swift's anti-romantic vehemence.
268. Williams, IV, 50–4.
269. Williams, IV, 202.
270. It is printed in Nonesuch S., 421–41. My quotations are all from Davis, ix, 327–45. The latest objective evidence, based on computor-tests, is that it is by Swift.
271. J. M. Bullitt, *Jonathan Swift and the Anatomy of Satire*, Harvard UP, Cambridge, Mass.; OUP, 1953, 130.
272. Williams, IV, 406–8.
273. Williams, IV, 410–11.
274. Williams, III, 103.
275. Williams, III, 118.
276. Williams, I, 364.
277. Williams, III, 236.

8

278. There is still no satisfactory complete biography of Pope. G. Sherburn, *The Early Career of Alexander Pope*, CP, 1934; repr. Russell, NY, 1963 [Sherburn EC] was not followed up. The best complete life, which utilized new material, is still 'George Paston' [E. M. Symonds], *Mr. Pope: His Life and Times*, Hutchinson, London, 1909, but is now frowned upon because Miss Symonds, although generally objective, was critical of Pope; certainly, too, she did not have access to facts newly discovered. Nevertheless, the book is not as bad as it has sometimes been stated to be; E. Sitwell, *Alexander Pope*, Faber, London, 1930, is inferior to it, being hysterically overwritten and less informed, but conveys the author's enthusiasm. A. L. Williams is reported to be preparing a complete biography. Important modern critical studies include G. Tillotson, *Pope and Human Nature*, CP; OUP, NY, 1958 [Tillotson], and *On the Poetry of Pope*, CP (1938); OUP, NY, 1950; A. L. Williams, *Pope's Dunciad*, Methuen, London, 1955; N. Ault, *New Light on Pope*, Methuen, London; Shoe String, Hamden, Conn. 1949. His correspondence is superbly edited by G. Sherburn, *The Correspondence of Alexander Pope*, 5 v., CP; OUP, NY, 1956 [Sherburn]. The standard edition of the poems is J. Butt and others (eds.), *Poems of Alexander Pope*, 14 v., Methuen, London; Yale UP, new Haven, 1954–67. This was reduced to one handy volume, excluding translations, J. Butt (ed.), *Poems of Alexander Pope*, Methuen, London; Yale UP, New Haven, 1963. Another, equally good, single volume edition is H. Davis (ed.), *Pope: Poetical Works*, OUP, 1966.
279. The strictures of Robert Graves are unfortunately unaccompanied by any detail, although he repeats (without acknowledgement) Tennyson's criticism of Pope's handling of the letter *s*.
280. E. Pound, *Selected Poems*, Faber, London, (1928); New Directions, NY, 1951. Introduction by T. S. Eliot, 18.
281. H. Read, *Collected Essays in Literary Criticism*, Faber, London, 1938, 41–56.
282. Read Sel, Introduction by A. Tate, 11.
283. Sherburn, I, 154–6.
284. 25 April 1708, Sherburn, I, 46.
285. Sherburn, I, xi.
286. Sherburn, II, 404–5.
287. See p. 212.
288. Sherburn, V, 172.
289. Sherburn, II, 501.
290. Sherburn, II, 419.
291. Repr. Sherburn, I, xxxj.
292. The first law of literary copyright had been passed by Parliament in 1709. It protected works for fourteen years. Essentially it was a logical extension of an exception in the 1623 Statute against Monopolies.
293. Sherburn, I, xii. So much for Professor McCutcheon.
294. James M. Osborn (ed.), Joseph Spence, *Anecdotes and Characters of Books and Men*, 2 v., Southern Illinois UP, 1965; CP, 1966 [Spence]; I, sec. 349, 155.
295. Sherburn, III, 55–6.
296. This and many other details of the complex Pope-Curll relationship may be found in Sherburn EC, 149–85.
297. For a doubtless exaggerated but amusing account of this, see Pope's own pamphlet, *A Full and True Account of a Horrid and Barborous Revenge by Poison on the Body of Mr. Edmund Curll*, London, 1716.

This is repr. in N. Ault and others (eds.), *Pope's Prose Works*, v. I and II published only, Blackwell, Oxford, 1936.

298. Sherburn, III, 387–8.
299. Sherburn, III, 395–6.
300. Sherburn, III, 476 n.
301. 2 November 1732, Sherburn, III, 327.
302. Sherburn, III, 458–67.
303. To Oxford, 17 June 1735, Sherburn, III, 468.
304. To the Earl of Orrery, 12 June 1735, Sherburn, III, 470. One must admire the irony of the final sentence.
305. Sherburn, I, xiij.
306. Sherburn, III, 252.
307. The best text of the transcript is in Williams, IV, 383–5; Sherburn gives a version at V, 16–18; Pope's doctored text is in Sherburn, III, 491–3.
308. Williams, I, xiv.
309. Sherburn, IV, 58–60.
310. Sherburn, IV, 61–2.
311. 23 March 1736/7, Sherburn, IV, 62–4.
312. Sherburn, IV, 64–5.
313. Williams, V, 41–2.
314. Williams, V, 58.
315. Sherburn, IV, 241.
316. Sherburn, IV, 256–7.
317. Sherburn, IV, 264.
318. The gist of Pope's lie is that *he* had wanted them in order to burn them, but the vain Dead had selfishly retained them for publication.
319. Sherburn, IV, 309–12.
320. Sherburn, IV, 314-20.
321. Sherburn, IV, 321.
322. Dobrée, 204.
323. Sherburn, I, 191.
324. Sherburn, I, 236.
325. Sherburn, II, 228.
326. Sherburn, I, 110.
327. Sherburn, I, 18–19.
328. No. 143, Tuesday 30 July 1751.
329. Sherburn, I, 22–5.
330. Spence, I, sec. 73, 32.
331. Sherburn, I, 324.
332. Sherburn, II, 273–5.
333. Sherburn, III, 290–1.

9

334. Cowper's letters await a modern editor. T. Wright's editions are the most complete: *Correspondence of William Cowper*, 4 v., Hodder & Stoughton, London, 1904 and *Unpublished and Uncollected Letters of Cowper*, Farncombe, London, 1925. In 1950 it was announced that a new edition was being prepared by N. Campbell, but this has not yet appeared. There are several good selections, notably W. Hadley (ed.), *Selected Letters of William Cowper*, EL, 1926 and E. V. Lucas (ed.), *Letters of William Cowper*, WC (1908), 1911 [Lucas], from which I quote. The standard edition of the poems is H. Milford (ed.), *Poetical Works of William Cowper*, OUP (1905), 1950.

335. Lucas, 43.
336. To John Newton, 10 December 1785, Lucas, 227.
337. To William Unwin, 5 January 1782, Lucas, 99–100.
338. Lucas, 89.
339. Lucas, 362.
340. E. M. Forster (ed.), *The Life of George Crabbe by his Son*, WC, 1932 [Life]. This prints the 'Bunbury letter' as an appendix. A. M. Broadley and W. Jerrold, *The Romance of an Elderly Poet*, Stanley Paul, London, 1913 [Broadley]. The best complete edition of Crabbe's poems is still the original *Poetical Works of George Crabbe*, 5 v., London, 1823; see also A. W. Ward (ed.), *Poems of George Crabbe*, CUP, 1905–7 and R. M. Carlyle (ed.), *Poetical Works of George Crabbe*, OUP, 1908. The best modern edition, a selection with a perceptive introduction, is Howard Mills (ed.), *George Crabbe: Tales, 1812, and other Selected Poems*, CUP, 1967; all these are supplemented by A. Pollard (ed.), *New Poems by George Crabbe*, Liverpool UP, Liverpool, 1960.
341. Not to be confused with the socially much more elevated profession of physician.
342. Life, 86–8. No date is given for this letter.
343. Life, 307–15.
344. Life, 310.
345. Life, 275.
346. Life, 277.
347. Life, 245–6.
348. Broadley, 9.
349. Broadley, 46.
350. Broadley, 49.
351. Broadley, 120.
352. Broadley, 228.
353. Broadley, 242.
354. G. Keynes (ed.), *William Blake: Complete Writings*, OUP; OUP, NY, 1966 [Keynes]. Sir Geoffrey Keynes has edited a separate edition of the letters, *The Letters of William Blake*, Hart-Davis, 1956. The best biographies are Ruthven Todd's edition of A. Gilchrist, *Life of Blake (1863)*, EL, 1950 and M. Wilson, *The Life of William Blake*, Hart-Davis, London (Duckworth, London, 1927), rev. 1948. V. de S Pinto's essay introducing his valuable anthology of Blake's writings, *William Blake*, Batsford, London; Shocken, NY, 1965, is one of the most illuminating every written on the poet.
355. Keynes, 793.
356. Keynes, 799.
357. Keynes, 801.
358. Keynes, 802.
359. Keynes, 803.
360. Hayley. An unnecessary piece of false modesty.
361. Keynes, 804–6.
362. Keynes, 808.
363. Keynes, 809–10.
364. Keynes, 811–13.
365. Keynes, 825.
366. Keynes, 828–9.
367. Keynes, 878.
368. Keynes, 792.
369. Wordsworth to James Grey, January 1816, E. de Selincourt (ed.), *Letters of William and Dorothy Wordsworth; The Middle Years*, 2 v., CP; OUP, NY, 1937, 709.

370. As I correct the proofs of this book J. Kinsley's splendid edition has appeared, *The Poems and Songs of Robert Burns*, 3 v., OUP, 1968. The bawdy poems alone are available in S. G. Smith and J. Barke (eds.), *The Merry Muses of Caledonia*, (1959), Capricorn Books, NY, 1965. A still convenient edition of the polite poems is J. L. Robertson (ed.), *The Poetical Works of Robert Burns*, OUP, London (1906) 1910. Among the best biographies are F. B. Snyder, *Life of Robert Burns*, Macmillan, NY, 1932 and J. de L. Ferguson, *Pride and Passion*, OUP, NY, 1939. The best introduction is D. Daiches, *Robert Burns*, Deutsch, London (1952); British Book Centre, NY, 1966 [Daiches].

371. The letters were admirably edited by J. de L. Ferguson, *The Letters of Robert Burns*, 2 v., CP; OUP, NY, 1931 [Ferguson].

372. Actually it was in 1779, when he was in his twentieth year.

373. Robert Ferguson (1750–74) was a representative of the non-lyrical, 'evergreen' tradition which Burns in his own poetry united with the lyrical 'tea table miscellany' tradition. Burns was devoted to his memory.

374. Ferguson, I, 104–16.

375. Ferguson, I, 26–30.

376. Ferguson, I, 30–1.

377. Ferguson, I, 179.

378. Ferguson, I, 309.

379. Ferguson, I, 311.

380. Ferguson, II, 143–5.

381. Ferguson, II, 195.

382. To S. Clark, jun., Ferguson, II, 234.

383. Ferguson, II, 249–50.

384. Ferguson, II, 212–13. 1793 is only conjecturally the year in which this letter was written. Ferguson did not print the poem, but it is in Daiches, 276–7.

385. Ferguson, II, 283–4.

I O

386. There is an excellent selection from Gray's later letters from this point of view in E. D. H. Johnson, *The Poetry of Earth*, Gollancz, London; Athenaeum, NY, 1966, 45–60.

387. Lord D. Cecil, *Two Quiet Lives*, Constable, London, 1948. The other 'quiet life' dealt with in this book is that of Dorothy Osborne.

388. The standard edition of the correspondence is P. Toynbee and L. Whibley (eds.), *The Correspondence of Thomas Gray*, 3 v., CP; OUP, NY, 1935 [Toynbee]. J. Beresford (ed.), *Letters of Thomas Gray*, WC; OUP, NY, 1925, contains a useful introductory selection. The standard edition of the poems is H. W. Starr and J. R. Hendrickson (eds.), *The Complete Poems of Thomas Gray: English, Latin and Greek*, CP; OUP, NY, 1966.

389. R. W. Ketton-Cremer, *Thomas Gray*, CUP; CUP, NY, 1955 [Ketton-Cremer]. This is the standard biography.

390. Toynbee, I, 52–3.

391. Toynbee, I, 56.

392. Gray dated his letters from abroad according to the New Style, which was not adopted in England until 1752. The continental calendar was thus eleven days ahead of the English at this time. Gray's own dating is given here, as it is in Toynbee.

393. Walpole, because of his father's importance, was *persona grata* in the highest places.

394. Toynbee, I, 155–7.
395. Toynbee, I, 310.
396. The celebrated story of how undergraduates caused him to jump from a window into a tub of water by raising a false alarm of fire (about which he certainly had a phobia) is untrue; but it may well have been circulating in Cambridge during Gray's last years there.
397. Later, as a result of others' political manoeuvring, he was made to feel guilty about this. But at the time he took it up the post was a sinecure.
398. Quoted in Ketton-Cremer, 253.
399. George Sherburn, in Baugh (see n. 40), 1012.
400. 27 May 1742, Toynbee, I, 209. This letter as a whole is probably one of Mason's conflations, but this extract is clearly from a single letter.
401. Ketton-Cremer, 251.
402. Toynbee, III, 1112.
403. Toynbee, III, 1114.
404. Toynbee, III, 1115.
405. Toynbee, III, 1118–19.
406. Nicholls' letter to Gray is not extant, but G thanked him for his words on 14 April 1770, which he said he would transcribe and send on to Bonstetten.
407. Toynbee, III, 1127–8.
408. Toynbee, III, 1132.
409. Toynbee, III, 1133.
410. Toynbee, III, 1184–5.
411. 24 May 1771, Toynbee, III, 1189.
412. To Norton Nicholls, 20 May 1771, Toynbee, III, 1188.
413. See p. 278
414. 15 April 1700, Toynbee, III, 1124. This letter gave Warton Gray's own outline for a history of English poetry.
415. Four are easily accessible in J. Drinkwater and L. Gibbs (eds.), *Poems, Letters and Essays of Thomas Gray*, EL (1933) 1955. *The complete Works of Thomas Gray*, were woefully edited by E. Gosse, 4 v., Macmillan, London, 1884; AMS, NY, 1968.
416. 11 September 1746, Toynbee, I, 241.
417. *Facetiae Cantabrigiensis*, 1836. Ketton-Cremer, 86, disbelieves this story.
418. 4 April 1742, Toynbee, I, 190.
419. J. W. H. Atkins, *English Literary Criticism, 17th and 18th Centuries*, Methuen, London (1951); Barnes and Noble, NY, 1966, [Atkins], 198.
420. 13 January 1758, Toynbee, II, 521–3.
421. June 1758, Toynbee, II, 571.
422. Toynbee, II, 608.
423. 3 February 1746, Toynbee, I, 230.
424. Toynbee, III, 946.
425. Atkins, 199.
426. Toynbee, II, 583, n.
427. The poem, unpublished by Gray, begins 'With beauty, with pleasure surrounded, to languish', and has been given the title of *Amatory Lines*.
428. Toynbee, I, 335.
429. July 1752, Toynbee, 364.
430. The Latin dictionary giving circumlocutory equivalents for single words, used in schools to aid the composition of Latin verse.
431. Toynbee, I, 250.

432. All my quotations from Gray's poems are taken from his own letters. They often differ from the received versions.
433. Toynbee, I, 299–300.
434. To Wharton, 17 March 1747, Toynbee, I, 277–8.
435. Toynbee, I, 346–8.
436. Toynbee, I, 360. The complete letter, or letters, have been lost.
437. Toynbee, I, 336. The version from which I quote is printed in I, 337–40.
438. July 1752, Toynbee I, 364.
439. Ketton-Cremer, 131.
440. Toynbee, I, 421.
441. Toynbee, III, 1017–20.

I I

442. Wordsworth's and his sister's letters were edited by E. de Selincourt, *Letters of William and Dorothy Wordsworth* in six v., 1935–9. This edition is now being revised by C. L. Shaver, and so far *The Early Years, 1787–1805*, CP; OUP, NY, 1967 [EY], has appeared. For letters written before 1805 I give the references to this v. and to the first edition, *The Early Years, 1787–1805*, CP; OUP NY, 1935 [EY1]. All other letters are quoted from *The Middle Years* [MY], see n. 369, and *The Later Years*, 2 v., CP; OUP, NY, 1939 [LY]. The definitive edition of the poems is E. de Selincourt and H. Darbishire (eds.), *Poetical Works of William Wordsworth*, 5 v., OUP (1940–9); OUP, NY, 1952–4 [PW]. My quotations, unless otherwise indicated, are from the standard one-volume edition, T. Hutchinson (ed.), *Poetical Works of William Wordsworth*, OUP (1895); OUP, NY, rev. E. de Selincourt 1936 [Hutchinson]. For *The Prelude* I have quoted from E. de Selincourt's short edition of the 1805 text, OUP; OUP, NY, 1933 [Prelude].
443. EY, 399–401; EY1, 332–4.
444. To Sir Henry Bunbury, 30 July 1838, LY, 957.
445. To John Wilson ('Christopher North'), 5 June 1802, EY, 353; EY1, 293.
446. F. W. Bateson, *Wordsworth, A Reinterpretation*, Longmans, London; Barnes and Noble, NY (1954) 1962 [Bateson].
447. *c.* 23 February 1805, EY, 547; EY1, 451.
448. When it was first built, in 1805, for a Mr. ('a wretched creature') and Mrs. ('still more wretched') Crump, Wordsworth called it a 'temple of abomination' which would 'entirely destroy' the character of the vale: letter to Richard Sharp, *c.* 7 February 1805, EY, 534; EY1, 441.
449. E. Batho, *The Later Wordsworth*, CUP, 1933; Russell, NY, 1963. B. Groom, *The Unity of Wordsworth's Poetry*, Macmillan, London, 1967.
450. 6 and 16 September 1790, EY, 328; EY1, 30–37.
451. EY, 55–7; EY1, 56–9.
452. EY, 61–3; EY1, 60–1.
453. M. Moorman, *William Wordsworth*, 2 v., CP; OUP, NY, 1957–66 [Moorman]. This adds few new facts and is not critical except in an elementary sense; but it gives a most valuable and sympathetic summary, and is very readable. It does not supersede G. M. Harper, *William Wordsworth, His Life and Work*, 2 v., Murray, London, 1916; rev., 2 v., Russell, NY, 1929.
454. H. Read, *Wordsworth*, Faber (1930), rev. 1948; Hillary House, NY, 1949 [Read].

455. F. M. Todd, *Politics and the Poet*, Methuen, London; Hillary House, NY, 1957 [Todd], 42.
456. EY, 75–7; EY1, 77.
457. Todd, 41.
458. EY, 80–1; EY1, 77.
459. EY, 89; EY1, 83.
460. 17 February 1794, EY, 112; EY1, 109.
461. Dorothy to Jane Pollard, 10 and 12 July 1793, EY,101–2; EY1, 99.
462. 10 and 12 July 1794, EY, 100; EY1, 97.
463. This is reprinted in W. Knight (ed.), *The Prose Works of William Wordsworth*, Paterson, London, 1896; and in A. B. Grosart (ed.), *The Prose Works of William Wordsworth*, 3 v., London, 1876; AMS, NY, 1967.
464. Todd, 60–2.
465. EY, 111–13; EY1, 108–10.
466. EY, 118–19; EY1, 115–16.
467. 20 November 1795, EY, 156–9; EY1, 143–5.
468. See Bateson, 120–2.
469. *To the Daisy*, 1802.
470. EY, 134–6; EY1, 126–8.
471. 24 December 1794, EY, 136–9; EY1, 128–31.
472. EY, 156–9; EY1, 143–5.
473. EY, 172–8; EY1, 156–62.
474. EY, 199–212; EY1, 176–87.
475. EY, 210–12; EY1, 187–9.
476. EY, 215; EY1, 190.
477. 3 October 1798, EY, 231–2; EY1, 201–2.
478. EY, 267; EY1, 229.
479. EY, 267; EY1, 229.
480. EY, 235–43; EY1, 203–11.
481. To Coleridge, 27 February 1799, EY, 256; EY1, 222.
482. EY, 277; EY1, 237.
483. EY, 298; EY1, 250–1.
484. EY, 329–33; EY1, 272–6.
485. Letter to Mrs. Coleridge, 2 September 1803, E. L. Griggs, *Letters of Samuel Taylor Coleridge*, 4 v., CP; OUP, NY, 1956–ﾠﾠﾠ[Griggs], II, 978: '. . . for Wordsworth's Hypochondriacal Feelings keep him silent, & self-centred'.
486. EY, 406–7; EY1, 340–1.
487. EY, 453; EY1, 368.
488. Todd, 206.
489. LY, 577.
490. LY, 1094–5.
491. 31 August 1804, EY, 499; EY1, 409.
492. EY, 563; EY1, 463.
493. Moorman, 357–8.
494. T. Raysor (ed.), *Coleridge's Miscellaneous Criticism*, Constable, London, 1936, 155.
495. Griggs, II, 848–50.
496. LY, 910.
497. Hutchinson, 589.
498. Fragment of letter of September 1799 to Wordworth, Griggs, I, 527.
499. 1799–1800, Moorman, I, 446.
500. 6 March 1804, EY, 452; EY1, 368.
501. EY, 464; EY1, 379–80.
502. 16 January 1805, EY, 529; EY1, 437.

503. To Sir George Beaumont, 17 and 24 October 1705, EY, 628; EY1, 528.
504. MY, 63.
505. MY, 168.
506. The factual details of the quarrel are very well recorded in Moorman, II, 187–219. But this account, which favours Wordworth as far as it favours anyone, should be read in conjunction with Griggs's headnotes to Coleridge's many letters about the matter, Griggs, III, 297 ff.
507. See, for example, her letter to Catherine Clarkson of 12 May 1811, MY, 448–9.
508. MY, 498–9.
509. Griggs, IV, 564.
510. To Wordworth, 30 May 1815, Griggs, IV, 570–7.
511. MY, 669–70.
512. The standard edition of *Biographia Literaria* is edited by J. Shaw-cross, 2 v., CP; OUP, NY, 1907; another good edition is G. Watson (ed.), EL; Dutton, NY, 1956.
513. Griggs, IV, 579.
514. MY, 791.
515. E. J. Morley (ed.), *The Diary of Henry Crabb Robinson*, 3 v., Dent, 1938; AMS, NY, 1967. An accessible selection, which is admirable, and from which I quote, is D. Hudson (ed.), *The Diary of Henry Crabb Robinson*, OUP, 1967 [Robinson], 55.
516. Robinson, 56.
517. Robinson, 57.
518. 14 or 21 December 1798, EY, 236–8; EY1, 204–6.
519. Bateson, 30–5. The final version of both poems is in Hutchinson, 86.
520. Quoted in Bateson, 152.
521. EY, 241–2; EY1, 206–8.
522. *Intimations of Immortality* . . ., XI, 4.
523. Moorman, I, 302.
524. EY, 312–15; EY1, 259–65.
525. Todd, 109.
526. Todd, 109.
527. 30 July 1838, LY, 957.
528. Wilson later became a literary critic of repute and a neighbour and personal friend of the W's.
529. EY, 352–8; EY1, 292–8.
530. EY, 491; EY1, 402.
531. Griggs, II, 1013.
532. MY, 126–30.
533. To Sir George Beaumont, January or February 1808, MY, 170.
534. EY, 264; EY1, 226–7.
535. EY, 262–3; EY1, 225.
536. Moorman, I, 442.
537. EY, 329–33; EY1, 275–6.
538. 'A slumber did my spirit seal' was sent to Coleridge from Goslar in a now lost letter; 'Three years she grew' (1799) is the other; the sixth, 'Among all lovely things my love had been', was written in 1802.
539. See H. M. Margoliouth, *Wordsworth and Coleridge 1795–1834*, HUL, 1953, 52–7.
540. EY, 346–9; EY1, 286–9.
541. Bateson, 152 n.
542. To Thomas Poole, 6 April 1799, Griggs, I, 479–80.
543. EY, 361–8; EY1, 302–7.
544. See p. 318.

545. To Sir George Beaumont, 12 March 1805, EY, 556; EY1, 460.
546. EY, 566; EY1, 466.
547. *c.* 16 April 1805, EY, 585; EY1, 487.
548. MY, 50.
549. 11 February 1805, EY, 450; EY1, 446.
550. K. Coburn (ed.), *The Notebooks of Samuel Taylor Coleridge*, 2 v. (each volume in two separate parts: notebooks and editorial notes), Routledge and Kegan Paul, London; Pantheon Books, NY, 1957–62 [Coburn], I, 1606 and n.

12

551. For letters up to 1819 the definitive edition is Griggs, see n. 485. Until Griggs completes his edition which is announced by OUP for 1968, the letters written after 1819 (which are considerably less interesting than those which precede them) must be found in E. H. Coleridge (ed.), *Letters of Samuel Taylor Coleridge*, 2 v., Heinemann, 1895 [Letters], and E. L. Griggs (ed.), *Unpublished Letters of Samuel Taylor Coleridge*, 2 v., Constable, London, 1932 [Griggs UL].
552. The only completed serious modern biography, E. K. Chambers, *Coleridge*, CP; OUP, NY, 1938 [Chambers], is a sorry affair, all the more so because of the eminence of its author in other fields: critically inept, Victorian-minded in the worst sense, mean in its judgements, it presents a distorted as well as an unsympathetic portrait. But it is factually scrupulous. L. Hanson, *The Life of Samuel Taylor Coleridge: The Early Years*, Allen and Unwin, London, 1938; Russell, NY, 1962, is better, but only covers the early years. M. Carpenter, *The Indifferent Horseman*, Elek, 1951, is vulgar, and should have been written as fiction. There is considerable biographical detail in G. Whalley's *Coleridge and Sara Hutchinson*, Toronto UP, Toronto; Routledge and Kegan Paul, London, 1955 [Whalley], and some good interpretation in G. Yarlott, *Coleridge and the Abyssinian Maid*, Methuen, London, 1967 [Yarlott], which although it adds no new facts, and is primarily critical, is notably objective and penetrating.
553. The best criticism is in H. House, *Coleridge*, Hart-Davis, London; Dufour Editions, Chester Springs, Pa., 1953 [House], a pioneer study; other essential books on Coleridge include J. L. Lowes, *The Road to Xanadu*, Constable, London, 1927 (I quote from the rev. paperback edition, Vintage, NY, 1965); and J. B. Beer, *Coleridge the Visionary*, Chatto and Windus, London, 1959; Collier, NY, 1964.
554. See n. 550. These extend so far to 1808; other similar material relating to 1808–34 is to be found in E. H. Coleridge (ed.), *Anima Poetae*, Heinemann, London, 1895 [AP] and K. Coburn (ed.), *Inquiring Spirit*, Routledge and Kegan Paul, London, 1951.
555. See n. 553.
556. 6 February 1797, Griggs, I, 302–3.
557. 'Sunday', March 1797, Griggs, I, 310–12.
558. 9 October 1797, Griggs, I, 347–8.
559. Endorsed 16 October 1797, Griggs, I, 352–4.
560. Endorsed 19 February 1798, Griggs, I, 387–9.
561. Griggs, I, 734. This is confirmed by a Notebook entry, Coburn I, 1926; and by a passage in a letter to John Morgan, Griggs, III, 514–15. In 1796 Coleridge received a letter describing him as 'the *digito monstratus*' of Cambridge, Chambers, 20.
562. 22 February 1792, Griggs, I, 33.

563. Griggs, I, 28.
564. See n. 562.
565. Griggs, I, 35.
566. To George Coleridge, Griggs, I, 37.
567. To George Coleridge, Griggs, I, 46.
568. Griggs, I, 47–9.
569. Griggs, I, 49–52.
570. Griggs, I, 53–4.
571. Griggs, I, 67–8.
572. Griggs, I, 84.
573. To Southey, 13 July 1794, Griggs, I, 85.
574. Coburn, I, 1816.
575. 29 August 1794, Griggs, I, 96–7.
576. Griggs, I, 99.
577. 13 July 1794, Griggs, I, 87.
578. Griggs, I, 103.
579. 19 September 1794, Griggs, I, 105.
580. To Edith Fricker, 17 September 1794, Griggs, I, 102.
581. 22 September 1794, Griggs, I, 106.
582. 18 September 1794, Griggs, I, 103.
583. Griggs, I, 112–13.
584. Griggs, I, 115.
585. Begun 3 November 1794, Griggs, I, 123.
586. Griggs, I, 129–31.
587. To Daniel Stuart, Griggs, III, 91.
588. Griggs, I, 137.
589. To Southey, 17 December 1794, Griggs, I, 139.
590. Griggs, I, 78.
591. Griggs, I, 144.
592. Griggs, I, 145.
593. Griggs, I, 160.
594. To Southey, 13 November 1795, Griggs, I, 166.
595. See, however, his later masterly analysis of his own behaviour during this quarrel, in Coburn, I, 1605.
596. See Coburn, I, 173 n.
597. 28 November 1796, Griggs, I, 263.
598. House, 41.
599. TLS, 27 July 1967, 686.
600. Coburn, I, 979 and n.
601. Chambers, 84.
602. See pp. 321–8.
603. Griggs, I, 491.
604. To Benjamin Flower, 2 November 1796, Griggs, I, 247.
605. He lost half of it in 1812, when Josiah (Thomas died in 1805) told him that he was having to pay his share of it out of capital.
606. See p. 312.
607. See p. 323.
608. The rifacimento of 1812, added to in 1818 and reprinted as *The Friend*, Bell, London, 1904, does not properly represent the 27 issues as they were first printed. *The Friend* in its original form is scheduled as the first volume of the projected *Complete Coleridge*.
609. Griggs UL, II, 457.
610. Probably 'serious influenza with rheumatism', House, 38.
611. The best accounts of Coleridge's drug habits are in Griggs, III, xxx–xlj, and Elizabeth Schneider, *Coleridge, Opium and Kubla Kahn*, Chicago UP, Chicago, 1953 [Schneider].

612. Postmarked 28 November 1791, Griggs, I, 18.
613. Griggs, I, 185–6.
614. Griggs, I, 189.
615. Griggs, I, 249–51.
616. Griggs, I, 253.
617. Coburn, I, 1770.
618. Griggs, III, 491.
619. Griggs, III, 476. For an account of this illness given at the time he suffered it, see letter to Poole, 18 April 1801, Griggs, I, 721–2.
620. Griggs, II, 884.
621. 17 February 1803, Griggs, II, 929.
622. Griggs, II, 934.
623. See n. 611.
624. E. H. Coleridge (ed.), *Complete Poetical Works of Samuel Taylor Coleridge, Excluding the Dramas,* OUP; OUP, NY, 1910 [Poems], 389–91. There is no satisfactory edition of Coleridge's poems, although one is being prepared by G. Watson. The notes and biography in J. D. Campbell, *Poetical Works of Coleridge,* Macmillan, London, 1893 are still valuable. The nearest to a standard edition is E. H. Coleridge (ed.), *Complete Poetical Works of Samuel Taylor Coleridge,* 2 v., CP; OUP, NY, 1912. This is the basis of the one v. edition cited above.
625. Griggs, III, 128.
626. Griggs, III, 633.
627. These notes, six of which probably date from 1824, are printed in Griggs, UL, II, 328–30, 431, 439.
628. Griggs UL, II, 440.
629. Whalley, 151–80.
630. To Cottle, 8 June 1797, Griggs, I, 325.
631. Griggs, I, 205.
632. Thelwall's reply is printed in MLR, January, 1930, 85–90.
633. Griggs, I, 215.
634. Griggs, I, 207.
635. Griggs, I, 260.
636. Griggs, I, 275.
637. According to a likely enough Stowey tradition: Chambers, 66.
638. Coburn, I, 73.
639. Coburn, I, 189.
640. House, 74–8.
641. Included in a letter to Southey, 18 September 1794, Griggs, I, 104. Poems, 68–9. Yarlott, 80, mistakenly conflates this poem, entitled *Pantisocracy* in the 1796 v., with the *Song* from the play, *The Fall of Robspierre,* beginning 'Tell me on what holy ground/May Domestic Peace be found?'
642. G. Watson, *Coleridge the Poet,* Routledge and Kegan Paul, London, 1966, 117–30.
643. W. W. Beyer, *The Enchanted Forest,* Blackwell, Oxford; Barnes and Noble, NY, 1963, 140.
644. Schneider, 247.
645. Poems, 296.
646. Coburn, I, 205.
647. Coburn, II, 2398.
648. Griggs, I, 250.
649. Coburn, II, 2398.
650. Coburn, II, 2399.
651. Griggs, I, 334–5 and n.

652. Griggs, I, 335 n.
653. Griggs, I, 338.
654. Griggs, I, 349–50.
655. W. Sypher, PQ, October 1939, 353–66, identifies the place of com-position as Ash Farm. But Coleridge himself, in a recently recovered piece of table-talk, stated that he wrote the poem at Brimstone, which 'Morchard Bishop' identified as Broomstreet Farm, TLS, 10 May, O. Salter, 1957, 293.
656. *c.* 20 November 1797, Griggs, I, 357.
657. Griggs, I, 394.
658. Chambers, 102.
659. To Wade, 1 August 1797, Griggs, I, 339. If Berkeley, born 14 May 1798, was a nine-month baby, then she was pregnant again by the mid-August of 1797—not a fact remarkable in itself, but striking evidence of Coleridge's sexual eagerness.
660. J. W. Knight, *The Starlit Dome*, OUP, 1941, 83–178.
661. M. Suther, *Visions of Kanadu*, Columbia UP, NY and London, 1965.
662. Griggs, II, 902.
663. This is a small point, but there is no warrant for sneering at it, as a critic did in his review of Yarlott's book in TLS, see n. 599.
664. H. S. and D. T. Bliss, *Coleridge's Xubla Khan*, American Imago, VI, 4, 1949, 261–73.
665. One does not easily think of a meandering river as having waves, which in any case are associated more naturally with the sea. On the other hand, the sea is far away from the pleasure-dome, while the river does flow beside it—but does this kind of logic operate in a poem like *Kubla Khan*?
666. Griggs, I, 338.
667. Coburn, I, 1071.
668. See n. 654.
669. House, 128.
670. These are well summarized in A. H. Nethercot, *The Road to Tryer-maine*, Chicago UP, Chicago, 1939, a somewhat underrated study.
671. Griggs, I, 631.
672. Griggs, III, 39.
673. Griggs, IV, 708.
674. Griggs, I, 545.
675. Griggs, I, 643.
676. Yarlott, 128.
677. Coburn, I, 148 and n.
678. Coburn, I, 1718 and n.
679. Griggs, I, 540.
680. The best account is in Whalley, but see also T. M. Raysor, *Coleridge and Asra*, SP, XVII, 1929, 305–24.
681. 17 December 1800, Griggs, I, 656.
682. Griggs, I, 656.
683. Griggs, I, 658.
684. It is curious that Coleridge should have called Broomstreet Farm, where he wrote *Kubla Khan, Brimstone*—or is it?
685. Griggs, II, 663.
686. Griggs, IV, 893.
687. Griggs, III, 402.
688. Griggs, III, 498.
689. Griggs, II, 714.
690. Griggs, II, 706.
691. 21 October 1801, Griggs, II, 768.

692. To Southey, 31 December 1801, Griggs, II, 778.
693. At least until the late spring, when she became pregnant with Sara; but most probably after this: in a letter to Poole of 7 May 1802 he says icily: 'I have too much reason to suspect [Sara] is breeding again/an event which was to have been deprecated', Griggs, II, 799.
694. E. de Selincourt, *Coleridge's Dejection: an Ode*, Essays and Studies by Members of the English Association, XXII, Murray, London, 1937, 7–25. Since then it has been reprinted six times: House, 157–65; Whalley, 155–68; Griggs, II, 790–8; J. Reeves (ed.), *Selected Poems of Samuel Taylor Coleridge*, Heinemann, London, 1952; J. Reeves and M. Seymour-Smith (eds.), *A New Canon of English Poetry*, Heinemann, London, 1967; D. Wright (ed.), *The Penguin Book of English Romantic Verse*, Penguin, Harmondsworth, 1968. The shortened, received version is in Poems, 362–8.
695. Griggs, II, 799.
696. Griggs, II, 807.
697. Griggs, II, 814.
698. Griggs, II, 832.
699. Griggs, II, 881.
700. Griggs, II, 888.
701. Griggs, II, 889–90.
702. Griggs, II, 894.
703. Griggs, II, 902.
704. Griggs, II, 903.
705. Griggs, II, 908–9.
706. Griggs, II, 910.
707. Coburn, I, 1577.
708. Griggs, II, 950.
709. To Southey, 29 June 1803, Griggs, II, 953.
710. To Southey, 1 August 1803, Griggs, II, 959.
711. Griggs, II, 1102.
712. 13 January 1804, Griggs, II, 1102.
713. Coburn, I, 1374.
714. Griggs, II, 982–4.
715. This is proved by the letter to Henry Daniel of 19 May 1814 quoted on pp. 425–6.
716. Griggs, II, 993.
717. 16 September 1803, Griggs, II, 990.
718. Griggs, II, 1005.
719. 30 October 1803, Griggs, II, 1010.
720. Griggs, III, 495–6.

NOTE: A complete list of letters quoted in the text will be found at the end of the entries for the poets studied. Titles are indexed separately, unless special circumstance requires mention also under the author.